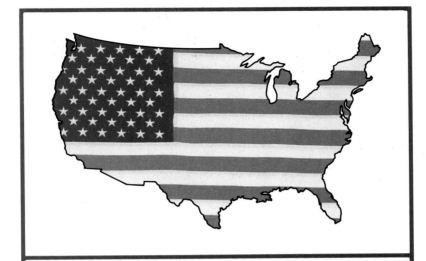

United States History

United States History

Jerome R. Reich

Edward L. Biller

HOLT, RINEHART AND WINSTON

AUSTIN NEW YORK SAN DIEGO CHICAGO TORONTO MONTREAL

REVIEWERS

The publisher wishes to thank the following reviewers of *United States History* for the valuable comments and direction given during the preparation of this textbook. They have provided specific assistance in the areas of organization, content, difficulty level, and assurance of historical accuracy. Their review has been invaluable for creating a textbook that will be very usable for the teacher and profitable for the student.

Henry Billings
Developer of Educational
  Social Studies Materials
Lebanon, NH

Dr. Jack Bridner
Social Studies Specialist
Howard County Public Schools
Ellicott City, MD

Larry L. Bybee
Secondary Social Studies
  Supervisor
Northside Independent School
  District
San Antonio, TX

Paul Horne, Jr.
Social Studies Educator
Richland School District #1
Columbia, SC

Robert Lyons
American Studies Specialist
Regina Dominican High School
Wilmette, IL

John Morris
Social Studies Chairperson
Arlington High School
Indianapolis, IN

Dr. Jack Nicholson
Social Studies Department Chairperson
Anderson High School
Anderson, IN

Editorial Development: Book Production Systems, Inc.
Design and Production: Book Production Systems, Inc.

Cover: Detail of painting shown on page 223. Edward Percy Moran, *By Dawn's Early Light*. Courtesy of The Peale Museum, Baltimore.

TO THE STUDENT

Learning about history is much like being a good detective. A good detective asks a lot of questions—What happened? Who did it? When? Where? How? Why? Someone who wants to know about the past must find the answers to these questions, too.

Good historians use the latest tools and methods to get information. For example, scientists have developed the carbon-14 test to tell the age of very old objects. Historians use this test on Indian artifacts to find out how long people have lived in North America.

United States History can be your tool as you study history. It is organized for easy use. The book has twelve units and thirty-eight chapters. Each chapter is divided into sections. Each section begins with a box which includes the main ideas of the section, some questions to think about as you read, and some key terms used in the section. This information gives you a guide to follow as you read. Each section then ends with questions so you can be sure you have understood the reading.

Special features of the book make it even more useful to you. Note, for example, all the art. More than five hundred images are included so you can ``see'' history. Information and questions forming the captions of the pictures help you respond fully. Two pictorial essays—one for the Revolutionary War and one for the Civil War—also use visuals and explanations to round out your knowledge about these important wars.

Three other features found in every chapter—the Map Workshop, Skills Focus, and History Maker pages—increase your skills and give you more information about people and events. Chapter and Unit Reviews give you a regular means of checking yourself on the highlights of history. Finally, a special atlas of maps, a glossary, and an index are included at the back of *United States History* to help you as you learn about the past.

Why bother with the past? While we cannot know everything that happened, each bit of information adds another clue to the story of human life on earth. As you read this book, think of yourself as a detective looking for answers to questions about our country's past. The answers you find will help you understand how we got where we are today. This knowledge will also help you make decisions about our future.

MAP WORKSHOPS

From Old Lands to New

UNIT 1
50,000 B.C.–
1732 A.D.

Chapter 1
50,000 B.C.–1500 A.D.
Earliest Americans,
Earliest Visitors

Chapter 2 • 1492–1650
European Colonies

Chapter 3 • 1585–1732
The Thirteen
English Colonies

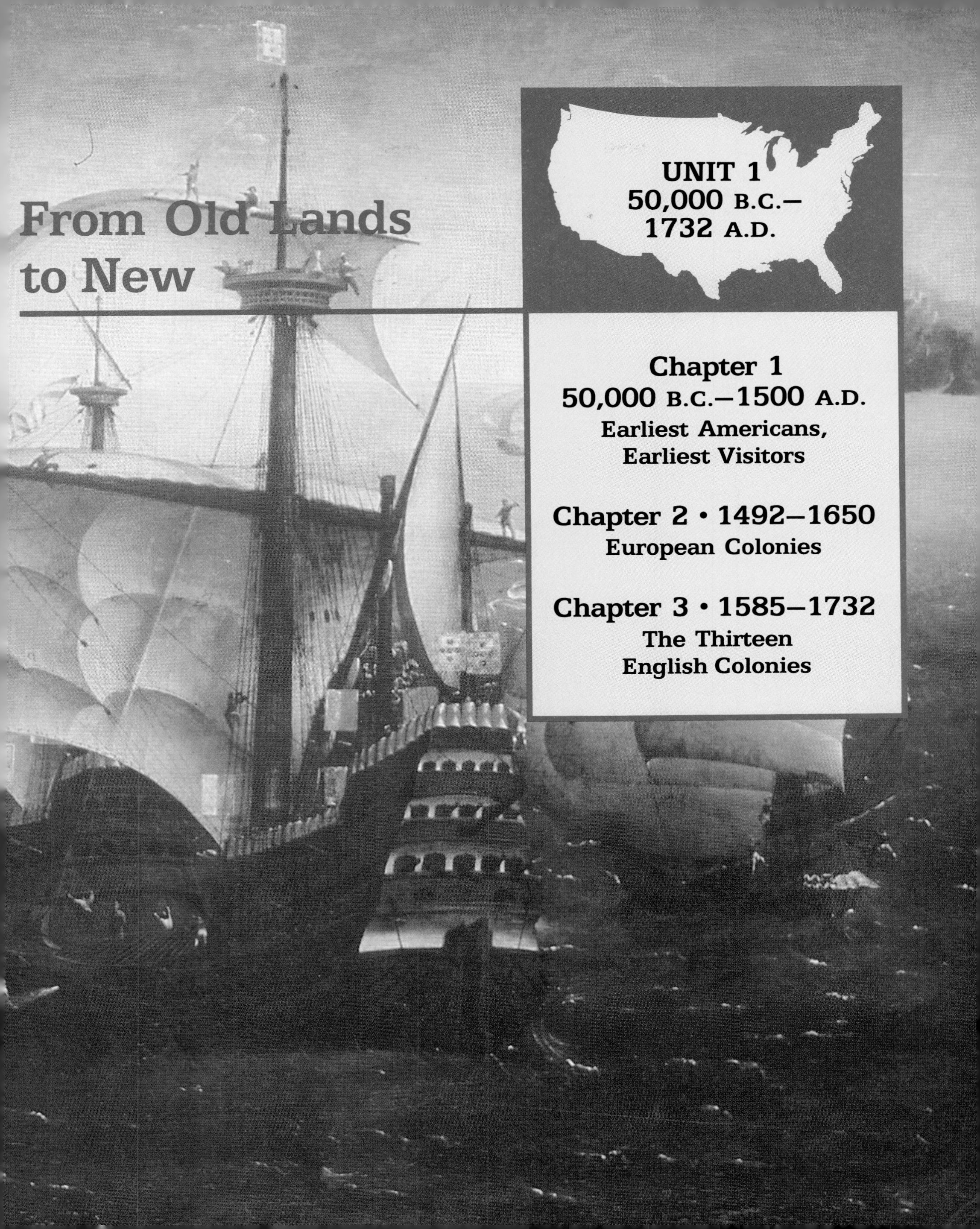

1
Earliest Americans, Earliest Visitors

Years 50,000 B.C.—1500 A.D.

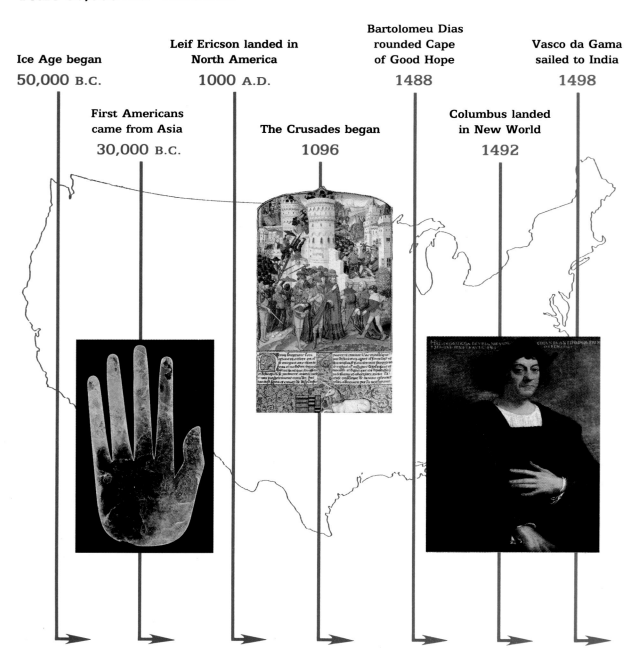

Ice Age began
50,000 B.C.

First Americans
came from Asia
30,000 B.C.

Leif Ericson landed in
North America
1000 A.D.

The Crusades began
1096

Bartolomeu Dias
rounded Cape
of Good Hope
1488

Columbus landed
in New World
1492

Vasco da Gama
sailed to India
1498

1. The First Americans

Learn these important terms:

Ice Age
Inca Indians
Maya Indians
Aztec Indians
Mound Builders
Northwestern Indians
terraces
Pueblo Indians
Eastern Woodland Indians
Plains Indians

Remember the main idea:

The first Americans were probably people who crossed a land bridge from Asia thousands of years ago. Slowly these people spread over North and South America. They developed great cultures.

Look for answers to these questions:

1. Who were the first Americans? How did they get to America?
2. What kinds of cultures, or ways of life, did Indians build in the Americas?
3. How did the Indians of South America differ from the Indians of North America?

Most of us think of Christopher Columbus as the discoverer of America. We also think of the European settlers who followed him as the first Americans. However, America was discovered long before Columbus was born. And people lived in America as long as thirty thousand years ago. These people are an important part of America's history.

You will learn about the earliest Americans as you read this chapter. You will learn about how they came to America and how they made a way of life. You will read about some great civilizations they built.

You will also learn about the first discovery of America. You will see what was happening in Europe at that time. And you will learn why the voyage of Columbus happened when and how it did.

As you read this chapter, think about how all the events tie together. Be a good historian as you read. Find out the answers to your questions.

How many times have you heard someone say, "It never used to get this hot," or, "We never had snow this time of year when I was young"? People often comment on changing local weather patterns. But weather patterns can change in larger ways—ways that cover the entire world and last thousands of years. These changes are known as global changes.

LAND BRIDGE FROM ASIA

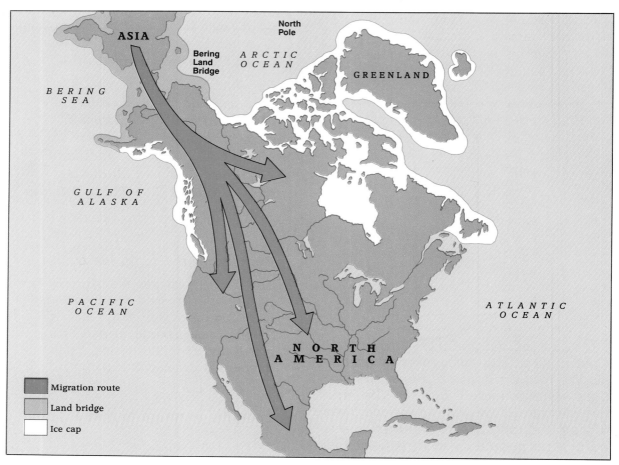

The Land Bridge

Global changes take place over long periods of time. The last global change, which began about 50,000 years ago, brought a harsh **Ice Age**. Temperatures dropped dramatically. The polar ice caps grew to cover much of the globe. As more water froze into ice, the level of the oceans dropped.

During the Ice Age, the lowered ocean level exposed a broad strip of land connecting Asia and North America. This bridge was in the area now called the Bering Strait. Scientists believe that the first North Americans were people who crossed this land bridge from Asia thousands of years ago.

Recent Discoveries

Recently, a University of Kentucky scientist, digging in Chile, found tools dating back thirteen thousand years. This was an exciting find, but not unique. However, digging deeper, he found other human traces from about thirty-three thousand years ago. These are the oldest discoveries yet made in the Americas.

The Ice Age ended more than ten thousand years ago. The waters of the ocean rose over the land bridge, closing it forever. Putting these pieces of the puzzle together, most scientists believe that the first Americans crossed over from Asia at least ten thousand years ago and possibly thirty-three thousand or more years ago.

Indians Settle Across the Americas

The Indians (as Columbus named them) who came to the Americas lived by hunting, fishing, and gathering whatever fruits and berries they could. Slowly, they moved southward. As they moved, they settled different parts of North and South America. Their movement across the continents lasted thousands of years.

Over time, the Indians gained skills other than hunting and gathering. They learned to plant seeds for food crops. As Indians became farmers, they could produce enough food to store for the future. This allowed their settlements to become larger and more permanent. The Indians no longer had to move around to find enough food. In time, groups of Indians developed great civilizations, with cities, governments, arts, and sciences. Three of these civilizations were especially advanced.

The Inca Indians

In the Andes Mountains of South America, the **Inca** civilization rose. Most scientists believe that the Incas were the first people in the Americas to practice agriculture. To do so, they built **terraces**, stairways of flat land up the steep mountainsides. They also built great roads to connect their large empire. Inca runners, working in relays, covered up to 150 miles a day carrying news to and from the powerful king.

Think: High in the Andes, the Incas built the spectacular city of Machu Picchu. The only way to get into the city was by following a narrow mountain road. The city was probably the Incas' last stronghold when the Spanish were conquering the Americas. Respond: **Why might the Incas have built Machu Picchu?**

The Maya Indians

Earlier and farther north, in what is now Guatemala and southern Mexico, the *Maya Indians* had established another great culture. A thousand years before Columbus reached America, the Mayas were building cities and huge pyramids. They also cleared land in the dense jungle to use for farming. The Mayas were very advanced. They developed a calendar that was better than the one Europeans used at that time. They also had the first system of writing in the Americas. The Mayas, however, also practiced human sacrifice as part of their religion. For some unknown reason, the Mayas died out about one thousand years ago. By the time the first Europeans arrived, only the overgrown ruins of their jungle cities were left.

The Aztec Indians

Farther north, in the area of what is now Mexico City, the *Aztec* civilization grew. The Aztecs were a warlike people. They took over the lands of an earlier people, the Toltecs, sometime before 1300. The Toltecs had farmed the fertile land, and the Aztecs learned about agriculture from them.

The Aztecs built a beautiful capital city on an island in the center of a lake. The city was easy to defend because it could be entered only by crossing drawbridges. These could be pulled up in time of war. From this strong capital city, the Aztecs controlled many other Indian peoples.

The Indians of North America

The Indians of North America were not as advanced as the Indians of Mexico and Central and South America. Many different, smaller groups with simpler ways of life lived in North America. However, the *Mound Builders* did develop a complex culture in the Ohio and Mississippi River valleys. Although these people died out about five hundred years ago, they left behind huge mounds of earth. Many of

SKILLS FOCUS: Previewing a Reading

When explorers arrived in North America, they first looked around, or made a survey, to get a general idea of the place where they had landed. Then they may have asked themselves these questions about the land: Who lives here? Where can we find water and food? How can we explore the land? The explorers' survey and questions gave them a purpose as they went on to learn about the new place.

You can use steps similar to the explorers' when you preview a section in this book. Follow the steps of previewing below for the section "The First Discovery of America."

Survey

Look at the headings. The title of the section tells that it is about the first discovery of America. The first heading tells that the Norse discovered America. Other headings tell about the land and times in which the Norse lived. The pictures and words under them are also useful in giving you a general idea of what the section will be about.

Question

After your survey, you can ask yourself questions about what you might learn in this section. Think of questions that begin with *who, what, when, where, why,* and *how.* One way to come up with questions is to turn some of the headings in the section into questions.

Read

After you survey and make up questions, you are ready to read the section in order to find the answers to your questions.

An important help for previewing in this book is the material at the beginning of each section. There you are asked to learn some important terms, remember a main idea, and look for answers to some questions. Paying attention to this material as well as previewing the section will give you a purpose for reading.

Now preview the next section, "Europe Discovers a New World."

1 *Survey*: What are the title and the headings? What pictures and maps appear?

2 *Question*: Who? What? When? Where? Why? How? Ask yourself questions that you thought of during your survey. Turn headings into questions.

3 *Read*: Read the material at the beginning of the section. Notice the important terms, the main idea, and the questions to keep in mind as you read the rest of the section.

What answers did you find to the questions you made up?

Think: Pueblo Indians occupied Cliff Palace, a 200-room apartment house, nearly 1000 years ago. Respond: Why do you think the Pueblos built their homes high in the cliffs?

these mounds are shaped like animals and are hundreds of feet long. The Mound Builders practiced agriculture and were great traders. It is believed that thousands of people lived in some of the Mound Builder cities.

Another North American Indian people who successfully practiced agriculture were the **Pueblo Indians** of the Southwest. They, too, developed a large and thriving culture hundreds of years ago.

The rest of the North American Indians did not rely on farming. Instead, they hunted and fished and gathered whatever food they could find. They lived in small groups or family units.

North American Indians built shelters from materials they found nearby. The **Eastern Woodland Indians** built houses of wooden poles and wood bark. The Pueblos built huge "apartment houses" of mud brick. The **Plains Indians**, who followed the herds of buffalo, built tepees of poles and hide. These could easily be moved from one place to another. The wealthy **Northwestern Indians** lived in large log houses. They used their great woodworking skills to carve colorful totem poles. These poles told stories about the people who carved them.

Everywhere the Indians lived, they made use of the things that nature provided. They survived because of their skill and knowledge. In the rest of this chapter, you will read about the first Europeans to discover America.

Section Review

1. Who were the first Americans?
2. What were the three great civilizations of Mexico and Central and South America?
3. What skill made it possible for people to live in larger, more permanent communities?
4. What were most of the Indians of North America like?

2. The First Discovery of America

Learn these important terms:

artifacts   *feudal system*
Norse   *barter*
Vikings   *the Crusades*
serfs   *vassals*

Remember the main idea:

America was first discovered by Norse, or Viking, sailors around the year 1000. At that time, Europe lived in isolation under the feudal system. Europe did not become interested in exploration until after the Crusades.

Look for the answers to these questions:

1. What is L'Anse aux Meadows?
2. Who were the first Europeans to discover America?
3. What kinds of changes took place in Europe between 1000 and 1300, and why did they occur?

In the early 1960s, at a site called L'Anse aux Meadows (lans o may-DOH) on the northern tip of Newfoundland (NOO-fuhn-luhnd), Canada, a Norwegian scientist and his wife made an extraordinary discovery. There, in a meadow near a shallow bay, they uncovered the remains of an ancient village. **Artifacts**, or objects made by humans, that they found were definitely Viking. And testing placed the settlement around the year 1000—almost five hundred years before Columbus reached America.

The Norse Discover America

The **Norse**, or **Vikings**, were a sailing people of northwestern Europe. Sailing west, they had first settled in the British Isles, then in Iceland, and later on in Greenland. Even before the find at L'Anse aux Meadows, scientists had believed that Vikings had been the first Europeans to reach the Americas. An ancient book called the *Greenland Saga* tells of the voyage of Leif Ericson to North America. Although other Norse sailors had sighted the land before, Leif seems to be the first to have set foot in North America. He called the new country Vinland.

No one knows for sure if L'Anse aux Meadows is the Vinland of the *Greenland Saga*. But the findings there do show that

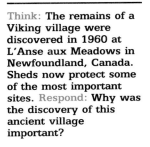

Think: The remains of a Viking village were discovered in 1960 at L'Anse aux Meadows in Newfoundland, Canada. Sheds now protect some of the most important sites. Respond: Why was the discovery of this ancient village important?

HISTORY MAKERS

——Leif Ericson——

Discoverer of a New World

The time was summer. The year was 1001. The men in the graceful ship stared across the water at the rocky shore. Gulls cried and waves pounded, but no one spoke. Leif Ericson, the ship's captain, signaled for the small boats to go ashore.

As he waited, Leif Ericson wondered what he and his men might find on this unknown shore. For hundreds of years, Norsemen like Ericson had roamed the seas. Some were explorers looking for new lands. Others were traders and settlers. Some were pirates, hunting and robbing for treasure. Others were soldiers, serving anyone for pay. Leif Ericson had sailed with his father, Eric the Red. Together they discovered a new land that Eric named Greenland. Now Leif looked at another coast beyond Greenland. What would he find here? Would he find gold or other treasures? Would he see cities, towns, and farms? Would there be people or monsters? Might this be the dropping off place—the end of the world?

The Norsemen made three landings on the new shore. They built large houses and spent the winter at a camp that Ericson named Vinland. There they explored the countryside but saw no signs of human life. In the spring, Leif Ericson and his crew sailed home. Without knowing it, they were the first Europeans to reach North America.

People told the story of the voyage of Leif Ericson for hundreds of years. In the thirteenth century, two versions of his adventures, called sagas, were written down. Until recently, those sagas were the only proof of the Norsemen's early arrival in North America. In the early 1960s, however, a Norwegian scientist discovered the ruins of several houses on the coast in Newfoundland, Canada. The houses are like others in which eleventh-century Norsemen lived. One saga's description of Leif's winter camp fits the site on the coast. Scientific tests date the ruins to around the year A.D. 1000.

Human curiosity, the search for adventure, and the desire to explore led Leif Ericson and his men to Vinland. Five hundred years before Columbus, Europeans had arrived in the New World.

Vikings were in North America at the time the book describes, and that they built settlements.

Yet another mystery exists about the Vikings in America. How long did they stay? According to the saga, the Vikings met Indians, whom they called Skraelings (SKRAY-lings). At first, relations were friendly. Later, one of the Vikings killed a Skraeling as he tried to take a weapon. In the end, the Vikings abandoned Vinland. Were there other settlements? Did the Vikings who came here ever learn of the Mound Builders, who were busy building their cities farther south? Did the Norse ever dream that this land extended thousands of miles to the west? There, even as the Norse built their first homes in the north, the mighty cliff cities of the Pueblos were at their peak.

Think: This wood carving was among the goods found in an ancient Viking burial ship. It was an honor to be buried at sea. Respond: Why was the sea important to the Vikings?

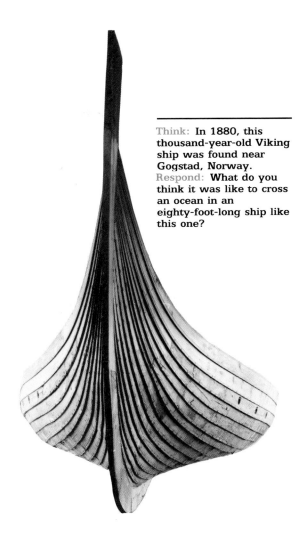

Think: In 1880, this thousand-year-old Viking ship was found near Gogstad, Norway. Respond: What do you think it was like to cross an ocean in an eighty-foot-long ship like this one?

Europe in the Year 1000

In the year 1000, Europe was not as advanced in many ways as some of the civilizations in the Americas. It was broken into small states ruled by powerful lords. The lords owned all the land. Usually some of a lord's lands were given to less important lords, or *vassals*. In return for land, the vassals pledged their loyalty to the lord.

Most of the people, however, were *serfs*, farmers who worked the lands of the lord. Each lord had great control over his serfs. When there was a war between lords for land or power, the serfs as well as the vassals were required to fight for their lord. This entire way of life was called the *feudal system*.

Under the feudal system, serfs had little freedom to move about. Trade between states was rare. As a rule, people **bartered**, or exchanged goods with other people nearby for things that they needed. Few people could read, and there were no printed books. Most people knew very little about the world outside their own small villages.

Nations as we know them did not exist. There were very few cities and towns.

The only thing that the hundreds of small states had in common was the Christian Church. Indirectly, it was the Church that brought an end to the feudal system.

The Crusades

The birthplace of Christianity was Palestine, where Israel is today. Located at the eastern end of the Mediterranean Sea, Palestine had long been the Holy Land for Christian people. It had been controlled for hundreds of years by local Muslims, people who follow the teachings of the prophet Muhammad. But around the year

Think: **Feudal laborers toiled throughout the year. Life was very hard for them, but easy for nobles.** Respond: **Why was this picture used to illustrate the work of September?**

Think: **Feudal lords and ladies are shown near Paris in this illustration from Froissart's chronicles.** Respond: **Compare these nobles with the laborers in the picture above.**

Think: **The Crusades meant that many people traveled far distances to new places.** Respond: **Why do you think the artist made this picture of the Crusades so colorful and crowded?**

1000, the Holy Land was taken over by Muslims from Turkey. They tried to keep Christians out.

In 1096, Pope Urban II sent out a call to all Christian people to capture the Holy Land from the Turks. The religious wars called *the Crusades* began. Over the next two hundred years, thousands and thousands of Europeans, including children, answered the call. They traveled great distances and put up with great difficulties. In the end, the Crusades did not win back the Holy Land. But they did have other far-reaching effects on the course of world history.

The Riches of Asia

Before the Crusades, most Europeans had had no contact with Asia. But Crusaders returning from Palestine told stories about the riches of the East. They brought back silks, carpets, gems, and spices such as pepper.

At that time in Europe, even the homes of the most powerful lords were not very comfortable. They were cold, drafty, and smelly. Food was not very tasty, either. Often meat would go bad, yet it was served at the table.

Carpets and wall hangings from the East could warm the rooms. Drapes could cut down on drafts. Spices could be used to improve the flavor of foods and make them last longer. It is no wonder that the people of Europe quickly grew fond of these things that made life more pleasant.

The demand for goods from Asia grew. Seaports developed as centers of trade, particularly along the Mediterranean coast. Merchant ships began regular voyages to and from the eastern end of the Mediterranean. On the eastward trip, they carried the cloth, leather goods, and metalwares that Europeans had learned to make. They returned filled with the riches of Asia.

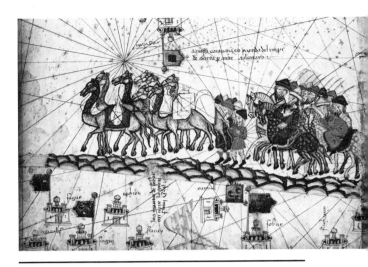

Think: Merchant caravans traveled from Europe to China. Expeditions such as this opened the door of trade with the East. Respond: What things from the East were needed in Europe?

Europe in the Year 1300

By the year 1300, Europe was very different from the way it had been in the year 1000. The feudal system was breaking up. Cities and towns were growing. Farmers were moving into these centers and becoming skilled craftspeople. Gold and silver coins were being used instead of barter. As trading with Asia developed and spread, new ideas came to Europe along with the goods from the East. In the rest of this chapter, you will read about how these changes led to the rediscovery of America.

Section Review

1. Who were the first Europeans to discover America, and when did they come?
2. What was Europe like around the year 1000?
3. What were the Crusades?
4. In what ways did the Crusades help change Europe?

---

3. Europe Discovers a New World

Learn these important terms:

trade routes　　*caravel*
astrolabe　　　*the Indies*
navigator

Remember the main idea:

Europeans rediscovered the New World while searching for new trade routes to the East.

Look for answers to these questions:

1. What led to the development of unified nations in Europe?
2. Why were trade routes to Asia so important?
3. How did Portugal take the lead in exploration?

The Viking ships that sailed from Greenland to North America were remarkably small. It is hard to believe they could survive the long trip across the open ocean. Imagine trying to sail a ship of that time three times as far. That's what southern Europeans had to do to reach America. Imagine some of the problems they faced. How could they stay at sea long enough to make the trip? How could they carry enough supplies to feed the sailors? How could they be sure they were on course when they were not even sure what the course should be?

From Leif Ericson's time, it took five hundred years and a number of important scientific advances before European sailors solved these problems. Then there was no stopping them.

The Growth of Strong Nations

The Crusades had broken forever the isolation of the small states of Europe. Trade with Asia was encouraging the growth of cities. As trade grew, so did travel and communication between the small states. But there were problems. Whenever merchants wanted to cross from one state to another, they had to pay taxes to the local lords. In each state, the tax was different, and so were the laws. The merchants wanted the states to be united into larger nations. They thought that a nation ruled by one king or queen following one rule of law would be better for them. Then, they would have to pay only one tax.

The merchants' ideas worked. Nations were set up as a result. The merchants, rich from the profits of trade, paid taxes to the most powerful ruler. He or she used the money to build a strong army. With a strong army, the ruler was able to control the warring lords of the country. The lords were forced to obey the ruler. By the end of the 1400s, Portugal, Spain, England, and France all were strong nations. Each had a single king or queen ruling it.

Control of Trade with Asia

Two of the most powerful areas in Europe during the 1400s were not part of a nation. They were city-states in what is now Italy. These two city-states, Genoa and Venice, were closer to Asia than the rest of Europe was. This location allowed the city-states to control the trade with Asia. Ships left Venice and Genoa and sailed across the Mediterranean to Asia. They returned with rich cargoes. Then the merchants in Genoa and Venice sold the goods to traders from other parts of Europe. They charged high prices and became quite wealthy. They also controlled who received what goods.

Think: Merchants in the city-state of Genoa controlled trade with Asia. The port of Genoa became very wealthy. Respond: How do you think life in Genoa compared to life on a manor?

The rulers of Spain, Portugal, France, and England saw how rich and powerful Venice and Genoa were because of their control of the *trade routes*, or paths followed by merchants. These rulers thought that they could get some of that wealth if they could establish their own trade routes to the East. Since land routes were long and full of danger, Europeans looked to the sea.

New Inventions Help the Search for New Trade Routes

In the years since 1000, many scientific advances had been made that affected sailing. The compass, used to find direction at sea, had been improved. A new tool, the *astrolabe*, which helps sailors determine the distance from the equator, was developed. And the *caravel*, a ship that was faster than other ships when sailing into the wind, was invented. The caravel, with a new type of sail, was larger than earlier ships. The caravel could carry more supplies at a higher speed. This greatly increased the distance the ship could go.

Portugal Takes the Lead

Many of these advances came about because of the efforts of one man—Prince Henry of Portugal. In the early 1400s, Henry began looking for a new trade route to Asia. He developed a school for *navigators*. A navigator sets the course of a ship and determines its position. Because of his school, Prince Henry became known as Henry the Navigator.

Portugal took an early lead in sea exploration. It was the first nation to develop its own trade route to Asia. In 1488, Bartholomeu Dias (bahr-THOL-uh-myoo DEE-uhs) sailed down the coast of Africa and rounded the southern tip, which he named the Cape of Good Hope. The hope was that this was a new route to the East. Ten years later, Vasco da Gama (VAS-koh duh GAH-muh) sailed around Africa and reached India. The Portuguese had found their route.

Prince Henry of Portugal (1394–1460) encouraged the scientific study of navigation. He also paid for many voyages. He died a poor man who had never traveled beyond North Africa.

IN SEARCH OF THE RICHES OF ASIA

Maps present a quick, clear picture of information. For example, one look at this map gives you a sense of the distance between the major cities of Europe and the major cities of Asia. Closer study of this map will help you to understand why Europeans were so eager to find sea routes to Asia.

Begin the map study by reading the title to find out what the map is about. Every map is a drawing of some part of the world. The lines of the drawing divide land from water and show boundaries. The names of important places are given. In addition, most maps have *symbols*, marks that stand for something else.

The symbols on a map may be of several kinds. Colors can be used as symbols to show differences. Some symbols, usually dots, give the locations of cities. Sometimes little lines called *hachures* (HAY-shurz) are used to show mountains. Find these symbols on the map.

Other kinds of symbols are usually explained in a small box called a *map key*. Look at the map key on this page. What does each symbol stand for?

Now use the symbols on the map to answer these questions.

1. A trader is returning from China to Venice. Through which cities will he pass if he travels by land only? Through which cities will he pass if he travels by sea without going around Africa?

2. What advantages do you think Da Gama's route had? What disadvantages did it have?

3. Columbus did not find Asia. Of what value were his voyages?

4. Looking at this map, why do you think Europeans wanted to find a direct sea route to Asia?

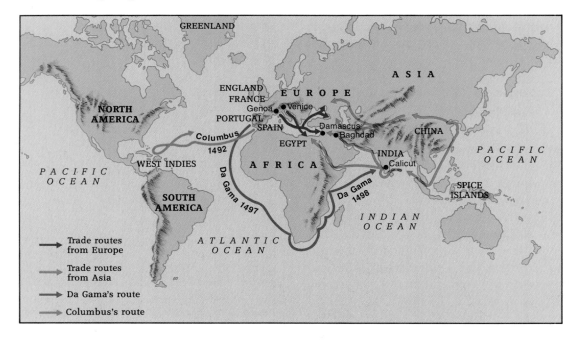

- → Trade routes from Europe
- → Trade routes from Asia
- → Da Gama's route
- → Columbus's route

Columbus's Search for a Western Route

Christopher Columbus, a sea captain from Genoa, was like many educated men of his time. He believed that the world was round. Therefore, he reasoned, Asia could be reached by sailing west. What he and others of his time did not know was how far west Asia was—so far that another huge continent lay in the path.

Columbus approached several European rulers with his idea. He needed ships and supplies in order to sail. At last, Queen Isabella of Spain decided to take a chance. She gave him three ships and the backing he needed.

Columbus's Discovery of America

In ships barely one hundred feet long, Columbus set sail. After ten weeks at sea, the crew was beginning to lose faith. If they didn't turn back soon, they asked, how would they have enough food to reach home? Then they sighted land. On October 12, 1492, Columbus and his ships reached an island in the Caribbean Sea. Columbus thought he had reached Asia, or *the Indies*, as it was also called. For this reason, he called the people he met on the island Indians.

Permanent settlements were later built on the islands Columbus explored. Columbus made three more trips across the Atlantic. Until his death years later in Spain, he claimed that he had reached the

Christopher Columbus (c. 1451–1506) made the discovery which began the exploration of the Americas. He also discovered better ways of using the wind and currents when sailing.

Indies. He never knew he had discovered the New World. In spite of this fact, he had opened the New World to permanent settlement. He also started what would be known as the Age of Exploration, which you will read about in the next chapter. It is for these reasons that Columbus is remembered.

Queen Isabella I (1451–1504) was queen of Castile, later known as Spain. She is remembered for lending her patronage to Columbus and for increasing her nation's military strength.

Section Review

1. What happened to the feudal system after the Crusades? What new forms of government replaced the feudal system?
2. Why were Genoa and Venice so rich and powerful?
3. What scientific advances helped the search for new trade routes?
4. Why is Christopher Columbus, not Leif Ericson, called the discoverer of America?

CHAPTER SUMMARY

Between 50,000 and 10,000 years ago, a land bridge linked Asia and North America. Scientists believe that the first Americans crossed this bridge from Asia sometime during this period. Over thousands of years, these people spread over North and South America. They developed many different cultures.

Before Columbus, there were at least three advanced civilizations in the Americas. These were the Inca, the Maya, and the Aztec. Other Indians of North America were less advanced.

Sometime around the year 1000, Norse explorers landed in North America. The Norse built houses, but they developed no permanent settlements.

Europeans at the time of Leif Ericson lived in isolation under the feudal system. But the Crusades caused great changes in Europe. The Crusades made Europeans aware of new ideas and new products, particularly those from Asia. Demand for Asian goods grew. Trade developed, and European nations became unified.

Scientific advances made it possible for ships to sail much farther than ever before. In 1488, a Portuguese captain sailed to the southern tip of Africa. Then, in 1492, Columbus discovered the New World and claimed it for Spain. His discovery led to permanent settlements and more exploration.

Key Words

Write a sentence to explain the meaning of each of these terms.

Aztec Indians	*Pueblo Indians*
Mound Builders	*feudal system*
barter	*the Indies*

Major Events

Choose the answer that best completes the statement.

1. The first people probably arrived in North America
   a) between 15,000 and 20,000 years ago.
   b) between 10,000 and 33,000 or more years ago.
   c) between 30,000 and 50,000 years ago.

2. Viking sailors probably reached North America
   a) around the year 1400.
   b) around the year 500.
   c) around the year 1000.

3. In 1096, Europeans set out to
   a) recapture the Holy Land.
   b) build new seaports.
   c) explore the coast of Africa.

4. The first nation to take the lead in exploration was
   a) England.
   b) Spain.
   c) Portugal.

5. Columbus discovered the New World while searching for
   a) proof the world was round.
   b) a western route to the Indies.
   c) a route around the tip of Africa.

Review

Important Facts

Answer each question with at least one complete sentence.

1. What were the three great civilizations that developed in the New World before Columbus?

2. Name two ways in which Indian groups of North America differed from one another.

3. What is the importance of L'Anse aux Meadows?

4. What was Vinland?

5. Under Europe's feudal system, what was a serf's life like?

6. What were the Crusades?

7. Why did merchants favor the growth of nations?

8. Which strong nations had appeared in Europe by the end of the 1400s?

9. What kinds of things did Europeans want to buy from the East?

10. Which European city-states controlled the trade routes with the East?

11. Why was Prince Henry of Portugal important in the history of exploration?

12. What did Vasco da Gama achieve?

13. How was Columbus's voyage different from other voyages of the time?

14. What did Columbus think he had discovered?

Skill Review

Study the map below, then answer the following questions.

1. What two kinds of symbols does this map use?

2. How did the most advanced groups make their living?

3. What did the Northwest Indians and the Eastern Woodlands Indians have in common?

□ Inca
○ Maya
△ Aztec
● Plains
■ Pueblo
▲ Northwestern
◢ Moundbuilders
■ Eastern Woodlands

☐ Intensive Farming
Farming, Hunting and Gathering
Hunting and Gathering, Fishing

Indian Civilizations

Critical Thinking

Write a paragraph to answer each question.

1. What factors led to Europe's isolation before the Crusades?

2. Describe the part that the Crusades played in awakening Europe's interest in trade and the East.

2
European Colonies

Years 1492–1650

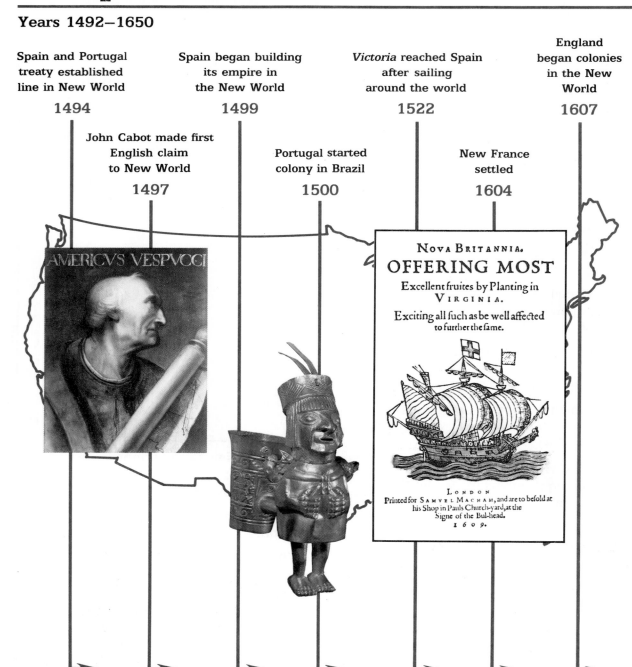

Spain and Portugal
treaty established
line in New World

1494

Spain began building
its empire in
the New World

1499

Victoria reached Spain
after sailing
around the world

1522

England
began colonies
in the New
World

1607

John Cabot made first
English claim
to New World

1497

Portugal started
colony in Brazil

1500

New France
settled

1604

AMERICVS VESPVCCI

NOVA BRITANNIA.
OFFERING MOST
Excellent fruites by Planting in
VIRGINIA.
Exciting all such as be well affected
to further the same.

LONDON
Printed for SAMVEL MACHAM, and are to be sold at
his Shop in Pauls Church-yard, at the
Signe of the Bul-head.
1609.

1. Spain in the New World

If you were to discover a new mountain peak in a distant part of the world today, you would get a very special honor. You would be able to name the peak. Would you name it after yourself, as many explorers did, or would you name it after someone or something else?

During the time of the New World explorations, the explorers sometimes did not know what lands they had found. They named the new areas what they thought they had discovered. When Columbus explored the islands in the Caribbean, he named them the Indies because he thought he had landed near India.

Around 1500, a navigator named Amerigo (called Americus) Vespucci (uh-MAYR-ih-kus ves-POO-chee) made several voyages and wrote of discovering a new continent. When a German mapmaker, Martin Waldsee-müller (VAHLT-zay-mool-uhr), published some of Vespucci's maps, he named the land after him: America. Waldseemüller believed Vespucci deserved this honor because he was the first person to discover the ''fourth part of the world.''

Today the land Vespucci mapped is known as South America. Vespucci really was not the discoverer of South America. He was, however, the first person to use the term *New World*. As you will see as you read this chapter, European nations eagerly set about exploring and settling the land that carries Vespucci's name.

Learn these important terms:

colonies
missions
conquistadors

Remember the main idea:

In the 1500s, Spain built a rich and powerful empire in the New World. It then sent people to settle the Americas. Spain spread its government and religion over North and South America.

Look for answers to these questions:

1. What were some important discoveries made by the Spanish explorers?
2. How did Spain go about ruling the New World?
3. What changes did the Spanish bring to the New World?

Columbus never found a great amount of gold in America. But after his second voyage, he brought back gold nuggets the size of birds' eggs for the king and queen of Spain. He hoped that this prize would win their continued support for his search. Columbus's plan worked. If greater riches were found, the rulers knew Spain would become very wealthy.

The Search for Gold Continues

Columbus's third and fourth voyages failed to find the great treasures he hoped for. But other explorers were waiting to take up the search. The first of these

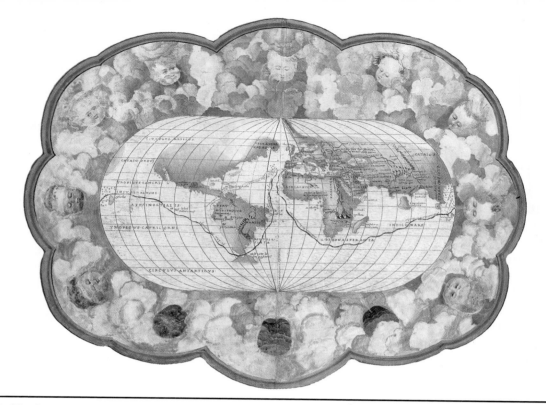

Think: The famous mapmaker, Battista Agnese, made this map around 1545. The gold-bordered map once belonged to Emperor Charles V of Spain. It traces the route followed by Magellan on his world voyage. Notice that parts of some of the continents are missing. Compare the shapes of the continents as shown on this map with the shapes of the continents on a modern map. **Respond:** Why is this map not as accurate as today's maps?

adventurers, Vasco de Balboa (duh bal-BO-uh), set sail in 1513. He explored Central America. Balboa was looking for gold and pearls but did not find them. Instead, he discovered the Pacific Ocean.

In the same year, 1513, Ponce de León (PON-suh day lee-OHN), the Spanish governor of Puerto Rico, sailed northward from there, looking for gold and "the Fountain of Youth." De León believed Indian stories of a fountain with waters that could make one young forever. De León, too, was disappointed in his search. However, he discovered a mainland to the north—Florida.

Magellan's Voyage

The discoveries of the Pacific Ocean and Florida expanded what Europeans knew of the New World. But as yet, no one had "the big picture" of the continents of North and South America. Nor did anyone know just where the continents were in relation to Asia.

In 1519, one of the most important voyages ever made was begun. Ferdinand Magellan (FUHR-dih-nand muh-JEL-uhn), a Portuguese captain sailing for Spain, again tried to reach Asia by sailing westward. With five ships, he crossed the Atlantic and followed the coast of South America southward and around to the Pacific Ocean.

No European had ever sailed across the Pacific Ocean, but Magellan set sail across it toward Asia. The trip was long and dangerous. Magellan himself was killed along the way, and only one of the five ships completed the voyage. That ship, the *Victoria*, finally reached Spain in 1522 after sailing around the world. This remarkable three-year voyage showed that two large continents, North and

Think: Magellan's ship *Victoria* is shown in this drawing made in the 1500s. Notice the detail with which the artist worked. He showed many of the men at work raising sails and in the look out. He included an officer standing on the bridge. The cannons show that the ship could protect itself. The *Victoria* was the first ship to travel around the world. It was the only one of Magellan's five ships to complete the voyage. Respond: **Why did the artist include sea monsters and a guardian angel in his work?**

South America, stood between Europe and Asia. It also proved beyond doubt that the world was round.

Riches of the Aztecs and Incas

In the same year that Magellan set sail, 1519, another explorer led a small Spanish army into Mexico. This leader, Hernando Cortés (er-NAN-doh kor-TEZ), had been in the West Indies, where he had heard tales of a rich Indian people on the mainland to the west. Cortés was a brave soldier and soon captured the island capital of the Aztec Indians. He then went on to conquer the rest of the large Aztec empire. The gold and silver Cortés captured soon helped make Spain the richest nation in Europe.

In 1532, another Spanish explorer, Francisco Pizarro (fran-SIS-koh pih-ZAHR-oh), led a large army into South

Hernando Cortés (1485–1547) began life as the unhealthy son of nobles. He was a gentleman farmer before gaining fame and fortune as a conquistador.

Little is known about the early years of Francisco Pizarro (c. 1475–1541). His fame began when he conquered the Incas, founded Lima, and extended the Spanish empire.

Think: Potosí Mountain in Bolivia held the richest silver deposit ever found. The Spanish mined the silver, sending it to their homeland in Spain. This 1584 drawing shows the mines, the processing plant, and pack llamas. Respond: Would you have done what the Spaniards did? Why, or why not?

America. There he conquered the empire of the Inca Indians. The treasure he captured was even richer than what Cortés had found. The wealth and power of Spain grew even greater, and more Spaniards went to the New World. They were called *conquistadors*—the Spanish word for conquerors.

Gold, God, and the Glory of Spain

Spain got its gold by destroying two native-American civilizations. However, no one in Spain felt that this was wrong. The Spanish thought that anything that added to the glory of Spain was right. Because Spain was a strongly Roman Catholic nation, the Spanish also felt it was their responsibility as Christians to convert the Indians to their religion.

Spain's Empire in the New World

During the mid-1500s, Spain continued to expand its empire in the New World. As the flood of gold and silver began to die down, Spain looked for other ways to profit from its holdings.

Spanish *colonies*, settlements which were controlled by the mother country, were established in South America, Central America, Mexico, the West Indies, Florida, California, and the southwestern part of the United States. Colonists ran mines or ranches. Much of the profits went to Spain.

Because few Spanish women traveled to the New World, men were encouraged to marry Indian women. Still, there were not enough settlers to work the mines and ranches. The Spanish first tried to force the Indians to work as slaves. Many of them died, however. Others could not adjust to the Spanish way of life and did not work well. In the end, Spain began to use black people from Africa as slaves. Thus, as early as the 1500s the slave trade in the Americas had begun.

Spain's Control of Its Colonies

The Spanish colonists had little say in their government. Instead, they were ruled from Spain. Spain split its empire in the New World into two parts. A governor from Spain ruled each part.

Land was granted to certain settlers and to the Catholic Church. The Church set up *missions*, or religious centers, to teach Indians the Spanish culture and the Catholic religion. Some Indians were willing to learn. Others were forced to. They were also forced to work for the Spanish.

ROUTES OF SPANISH EXPLORERS

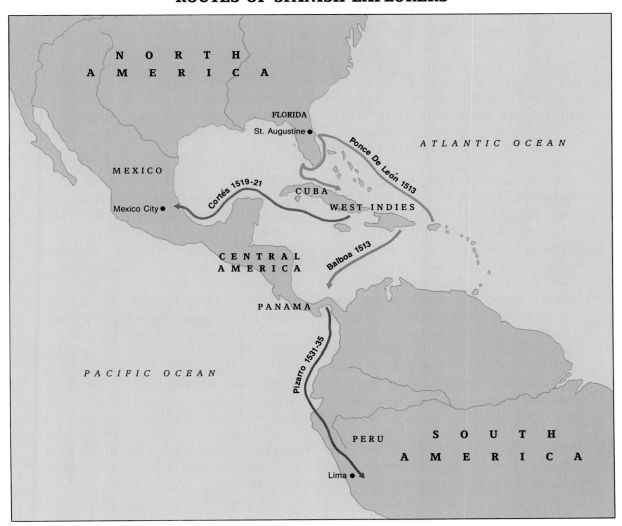

HISTORY MAKERS

Montezuma and Cortés

The Emperor and the Conqueror

Montezuma, emperor of the Aztecs, was worried. The omens were terrible. A comet raced across the sky, voices cried out at night warning of disaster, and strange creatures appeared in the east. The Aztecs were not sure if these creatures were men or gods. They were amazed by their pale skin, metal clothing, and huge beasts. Montezuma sent many precious gifts to the mysterious beings and requested that they leave Mexico. He wanted no challenges to his leadership of the Aztec empire.

Unfortunately, the gifts of jewels, gold, and silver made the strangers want to stay. The creatures, wearing armour and riding horses, were Spanish explorers. Their leader was the conquistador Hernando Cortés.

Cortés was delighted by Montezuma's gifts. He had come to Mexico hunting for gold and glory. The Spanish were dazzled by the Aztecs' beautiful cities, their art, their calendar, their libraries, law courts, and treasury. They were horrified by the Aztec religion and its use of human sacrifice. Cortés planned to gain glory as he conquered the Aztec empire, seized the gold, and converted the Indians to Christianity.

The conquistadors and thousands of Indian allies marched to the Aztec capital, Tenochtitlan (tay-nohch-TEE-tlahn). They were treated as guests until Cortés took Montezuma prisoner. Fighting broke out and the emperor was killed. The Spaniards retreated from the impressive city.

Months later, the conquistadors and their allies returned and attacked the capital. The Aztecs fought fiercely but were defeated. The beautiful city of Tenochtitlan was destroyed. The Aztecs became slaves. The Aztec civilization disappeared forever.

Cortés brought to Mexico a religion, a language, and many customs that are part of Mexican culture today. He built Mexico City, the capital, on the ruins of Tenochtitlan. There are no statues of Cortés in Mexico now, however. He is regarded as an invader who destroyed a civilization and enslaved a people. It is Montezuma, emperor of the long lost Aztecs, who is honored in modern Mexico.

Many priests spoke out against this mistreatment of the Indians, and at last the king promised them his protection.

Lasting Signs of Spain's Empire

The Spanish held their colonies in the New World for about three hundred years. During this time (from the 1500s to the 1800s), more than half the land that now makes up the United States belonged to Spain.

The Spanish settlers brought the first wheat, rice, oranges, cherries, olives, and figs to America. They also brought the first horses and sheep. In turn, they took back to Europe foods that they found in America, including corn, potatoes, tomatoes, and cocoa. Much of what Americans eat today is owed to the Spanish.

Spanish settlements were built in the classic style of Spain. Buildings were placed around the four sides of a central square. The buildings themselves had a particular Spanish style, too. Today, many of these buildings still stand in California and the Southwest.

Place names in parts of the United States once ruled by Spain often serve as reminders also. Sante Fe, Los Angeles, and San Antonio are all Spanish names. Spanish-speaking people in these parts of the United States keep alive a culture more than four hundred years old.

Section Review

1. Why was Magellan's voyage so important?
2. What two conquests in the New World made Spain the wealthiest nation in Europe?
3. How did Spain treat the Indians?
4. How big was Spain's empire in the New World, and how long did it last?

2. Other European Empires in the New World

Learn these important terms:

New France
trading company
Northwest Passage

Remember the main idea:

Portugal, France, Sweden, and the Netherlands all started colonies in the New World.

Look for answers to these questions:

1. Where was Portugal's colony in the New World?
2. Where was New France?
3. How were New France and New Spain similar? How were they different?
4. Where were the Swedish and Dutch colonies?

After Columbus's discovery of "the Indies," a race was on in Europe. The other nations wanted their share of the trade. Portugal was the first European nation after Spain to establish a colony in the New World. When this happened, it was mostly by accident.

Portugal's Claim in the New World

In 1500, Portuguese explorer Pedro Cabral (PAY-droh kuh-BRAHL) was sailing down the west coast of Africa when he was blown off course. He sailed farther and farther out into the Atlantic until he finally reached land—a small part of

South America that juts eastward. Under an agreement with Portugal signed in 1494, Spain held all claim to the lands west of a certain treaty line. However, Cabral landed to the east of that line. His ''accident'' resulted in a Portuguese colony in what is now Brazil.

New France

In 1524, France entered the race. The king of France sent Giovanni Verrazano (jee-oh-VAH-nee vair-uh-ZAH-noh) to look for the so-called **Northwest Passage**, or sea route to Asia. Ten years later, in 1534, Jacques Cartier (zhahk CAHR-tee-ay) continued the search on the behalf of France. Neither explorer found the Northwest Passage, but their efforts did give France a claim to North America.

The first French settlers in the New World did not arrive until 1604. Their settlements in Nova Scotia (NOH-vuh SKOH-shuh), Canada, and all along the Saint Lawrence River were called **New France**. Samuel de Champlain (duh sham-PLAYN) led the exploration of New France. He established a French settlement, Quebec (kuih-BEK), that became the most important town in New France.

Building the Empire

France began to extend its empire toward the southwest. First, French explorers claimed the Great Lakes. Then in 1682, Robert La Salle (luh SAHL) traveled all the way down the Mississippi River to the Gulf of Mexico. France claimed all the lands drained by that river.

Soon, small French settlements dotted different parts of New France. French people did not seem as eager as the Spanish to move to the New World. As a result, the French population of New France remained small.

In spite of having few settlers, New France was a very profitable colony because of its fur trade. French fur traders bought furs cheaply from the Indians and sold them for great profit in the countries of Europe.

How France Ruled Its Empire

The government of New France was similar to that of New Spain. The settlers had little say about what went on. The French king sent two representatives to govern for him. Only Catholics were allowed to settle there. As in New Spain,

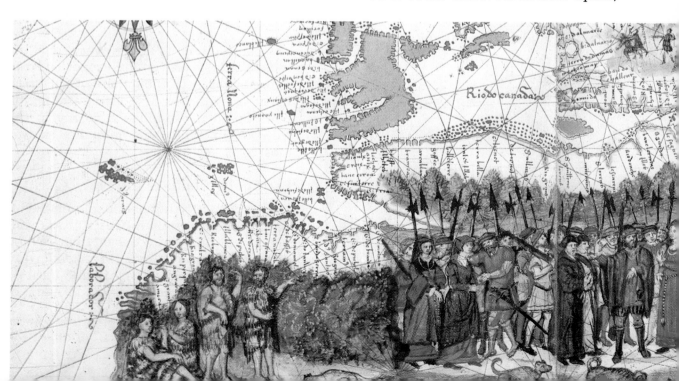

Think: **New France was rich in fish and wild animals. But few people from France moved to North America.**
Respond: **What were the benefits and hardships of settling in New France?**

Think: **In this detail of a 1542 map, an explorer and his expedition are shown at the mouth of the St. Lawrence River. Indians wearing fur are in the surrounding forests.** Respond: **What similarities and differences can you see between the French and the Indians as shown?**

the male settlers outnumbered the females. French men married Indian women, as the Spanish did.

However, there were many striking differences between the French and Spanish empires in the New World. For example, many of the French traders took on Indian ways instead of forcing the Indians to learn French ways. In addition, although French priests tried hard to convert the Indians in New France, they did not force the Indians to become Catholic, as the Spanish did.

Sweden's Colonies in the New World

In 1638, Sweden also started a colony in North America. Its settlements were located along the Delaware River in what are now the states of Delaware and Pennsylvania. The Swedish colonists farmed and traded with the Indians. They lived in log cabins, which later became the kind of homes built by most other American

S KILLS FOCUS: Using a Time Line

Every chapter of this book begins with a time line that shows when the major events of that chapter happened. The time line gives you a preview of the chapter and shows the order of events.

Look at the time line that appears at the beginning of this chapter, on page 20. It shows some events in the settlement of the New World. The time line begins in 1492 and ends in 1650. Between those dates are the years in which Spain, Portugal, France, England, Sweden, and the Netherlands began their colonies in the New World. You can see which countries started their colonies before other countries. You can also see the number of years between the founding of each colony.

The time line below shows important events in the exploration of the New World. It includes the names of some of the explorers who journeyed to the New World.

Use the time line to answer the questions.

1 How many years are shown on the time line?

2 Did Cabral or Pizarro reach South America first?

3 Which two explorers searched for the Northwest Passage?

4 The second of those explorers started his journey how many years after the first explorer?

5 What happened during the same year in which Balboa sailed to Central America?

6 Why isn't Champlain's 1604 exploration of Canada shown on this time line?

7 If there had been an important exploration of the New World in 1509, between which two explorers' names would it appear on this time line?

Explorers In The New World

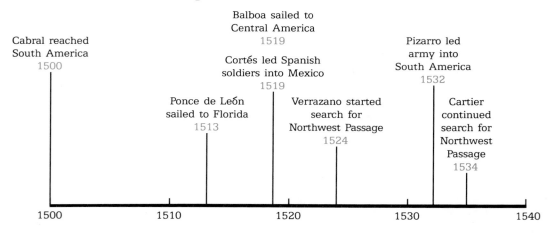

Cabral reached South America
1500

Balboa sailed to Central America
1519

Cortés led Spanish soldiers into Mexico
1519

Ponce de León sailed to Florida
1513

Verrazano started search for Northwest Passage
1524

Pizarro led army into South America
1532

Cartier continued search for Northwest Passage
1534

1500   1510   1520   1530   1540

settlers. Within a short time, however, the Swedish colonies were taken over by the Dutch colony of New Netherland.

The Dutch Colony of New Netherland

In 1624, a Dutch **trading company**, or group of merchants, formed the colony of New Netherland. The colony was located on land that Henry Hudson had earlier claimed for the Netherlands. The farmers and fur traders of New Netherland came from all over Europe. Because of this, there were many different customs and religions in the colony.

The colonists of New Netherland built settlements on the island of Manhattan and farther up the Hudson River, and the colony began to grow. But the colony did not last because the Dutch trading company was more interested in trade than in settlement. A few years after the Dutch took over Sweden's settlements, an English fleet sailed into the harbor of New Amsterdam. The colonists were overpowered by the English. New Netherland became an English colony. New Amsterdam was renamed New York, in honor of an English duke. In the next section, you will read more about the English presence in the New World.

Section Review

1. After Spain, what was the first European nation to establish a colony in the New World? Where was it?
2. What area did the colony of New France cover?
3. Where were Sweden's colonies in the New World? What happened to them?
4. How was New Netherland different from other colonies?

3. England in the New World

Learn these important terms:

Spanish Armada
balance of trade
Church of England
raw materials
market

Remember the main idea:

England explored the northeast coast of North America in 1497. But Spain's control of the Atlantic caused England to wait until the late 1500s to start colonies there. Then the colonies provided many benefits for England and for the English people.

Look for the answers to these questions:

1. What was the Spanish Armada? How did it affect England's policy in the New World?
2. Why did English people want to settle in the colonies?
3. What were the benefits England got from its colonies?

You probably know a certain sports team that seems unbeatable. It always controls the league. In the 1500s, Spain's naval fleet seemed like that team. Spain's ships controlled the Atlantic Ocean. They guarded the Spanish treasure ships that sailed between the New World and Spain. In this section, you will read how Spain's control of the Atlantic affected England's policy in the New World.

Many historians consider Queen Elizabeth I (1533–1603) the most important woman ruler in history. She helped create a stable England which held an important place in world affairs.

Sir Francis Drake (c. 1543–1596) rose from a childhood of poverty and persecution to become a wealthy hero. The first English captain to sail around the world, Drake symbolized the spirit of the professional seaman.

England's Claim to North America

In 1497, while Columbus was on his third voyage to the New World, England sent John Cabot to search for a water route to Asia. Cabot sailed westward from England until he reached North America. There he explored the northern part of the east coast of North America. He found no route to Asia, but his exploration did give England a claim to North America. It would take almost one hundred years for the English to follow up on that claim.

Spain's Armada

During the 1500s, Spain controlled the Atlantic Ocean completely. About 1560, however, the English navy began to grow stronger. English sea captains, such as John Hawkins and Francis Drake, attacked and captured many Spanish treasure ships. When Spain protested, Queen Elizabeth I ignored the outcry. She even made one of her "sea dogs," Francis Drake, a knight.

In 1588, the Spanish king sent his huge fleet, called the **Spanish Armada** (ahr-MAH-duh), to conquer England and stop

the sea dogs forever. In one of the greatest sea battles in history, the smaller English fleet defeated the Spanish Armada. England's victory ended Spain's control of the Atlantic Ocean. Now England and other nations were free at last to set up colonies in North America.

Opportunities in the New World

Both the English government and the English people had reasons for wanting to set up colonies in North America. In the 1500s, English landowners had discovered that they could make more money by raising sheep and selling wool than by farming. Raising sheep took fewer workers than farming. As a result, many English farmworkers lost their jobs.

Many of these jobless people became beggars. The English government did not know what to do. Sending these people to colonies in North America might give them a chance for a better life.

Many English landowners also faced hard times. In the 1500s, prices in England were very high. Many landowners found that it cost them more money to live than they earned from their lands. Therefore, some landowners sold their lands. With the money from their sales, these landowners hoped to buy land—and a new beginning—in America.

Religious Differences in England

Religious differences also made many English people think of settling in America. Until the 1530s, the English people were all members of the Roman Catholic Church. However, in 1534, King Henry VIII differed with the Catholic Church. He decided to form a new church, the **Church of England**. He had a law passed which said that every English citizen had to attend the new church.

The law made many English people unhappy. Many Catholics did not want to change their religion. Other English people were neither Catholic nor members of the Church of England. They wanted to follow their own religion. Nonetheless, Henry VIII and the rulers who followed him made life difficult for those who did not join the Church of England. Some people were fined. Others were jailed. Some were even put to death.

Finally, in 1558, Elizabeth I came to the throne. While she did not punish people outside the Church of England, she did not provide true religious freedom either. Neither did her successors. When England began to found colonies, they were very appealing to people outside the official church. They knew that they could practice their religion there.

Economic Benefits of the Colonies

The English government had many economic reasons for wanting to build colonies in the New World. One of these had to do with England's **balance of trade**. The balance of trade compares what a nation buys from other nations with what other nations buy from it. If other nations buy more from it than the nation buys from others, the balance of trade is good.

England did not have a good balance of trade. It needed many goods that it did not make or grow. The English weather was too cold to grow sugar cane, and England did not have enough trees to

Think: Trade became all important during the 1500s. Much wood was needed to build trading ships, but European forests were shrinking. Respond: How did England solve this problem?

MAP WORKSHOP MAP SCALE

EUROPEAN COLONIES IN THE NEW WORLD, 1638

All maps are much smaller than the places they show. How much smaller depends on the scale to which they are drawn. Find the *scale ruler* in the upper left corner of this map.

You can use the scale on a map to find distances on earth. For example, you might want to know how far it is from St. Augustine to Quebec. If you want to know the answer in miles, measure the distance on the map in inches. (If you want to know the answer in kilometers, measure in centimeters.) How many inches (or centimeters) is it between these two cities on the map? Check the map scale to see how far one inch (or one centimeter) stands for. Now multiply the number of inches (or centimeters) by the scale on the map.

Use a ruler and the map scale to answer these questions.

1. How many miles is Guadeloupe from Tobago?

2. How far would one have to travel over water to get from the southern tip of Florida to the

Mississippi River? Give your answer in kilometers.

3. How many miles would one have to travel to go from James Bay to New Sweden?

4. An English colonist in Plymouth was how many miles from Newfoundland?

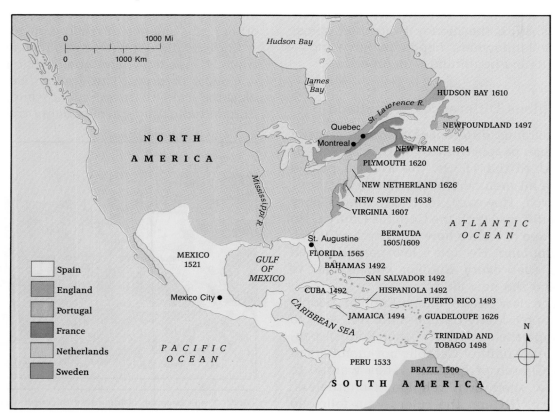

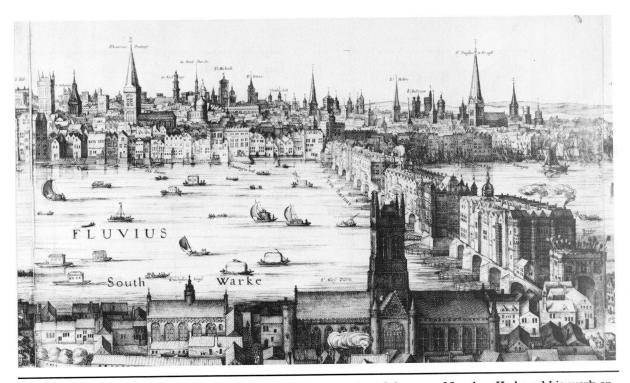

Think: In 1616, Visscher created *Londonium*, the above illustration of the port of London. He based his work on John Norden's *Description of the Moste Famous City of London*. Notice the number of churches in the work.
Respond: What things does the artwork show as being important to the English in the 1600s?

supply the wood needed to build ships. As a result, England had to buy goods such as sugar and wood from other nations. In turn, other nations bought wool and other products from England. If England had colonies in the New World, they could supply **raw materials** to England. These products from nature, such as wood, were necessary if England were to improve its balance of trade.

The colonies could also become a new **market**, or place to sell products, for English goods. The colonists would need many supplies, such as tools and cloth, and English merchants would provide them. This would create more business and more jobs in England.

In time, many English merchants grew rich from this trade with the colonies. The English government also grew rich by taxing the people who shipped the goods to the colonies.

A Stronger Claim

In addition to economic benefits to the nation, the colonies also strengthened England's claim to North America. The first permanent English settlement was at Jamestown, Virginia, in 1607. As more settlers moved to the English colonies, it became clear that the English were in the New World to stay.

Section Review

1. When did England first explore the New World? When did England first build colonies there?
2. What were some of the reasons English people wanted to settle in the colonies?
3. How did the English colonies benefit England?

CHAPTER SUMMARY

Many Spanish explorers followed Columbus into the New World. De Balboa explored Central America and discovered the Pacific Ocean. Ponce de León discovered Florida.

In 1519, Cortés conquered the Aztecs. In the 1530s, Pizarro conquered the Incas. The gold and silver they captured made Spain the richest nation in Europe. Spain spread its rule and its religion throughout the New World.

Other European nations planted colonies in the New World. Portugal built a colony in what is now Brazil. France built a large empire called New France. Sweden founded colonies along the Delaware River, but these were later taken over by the Dutch colony of New Netherland. New Netherland had been formed in 1624 by a Dutch trading company and was settled by people from all over Europe. Later, New Netherland was taken over by the English.

John Cabot had explored North America for England in 1497. But the English did not build colonies until after England's navy defeated the Spanish Armada in 1588. English settlers came to North America looking for religious freedom and better opportunities. The colonies offered many economic benefits for the English nation, too, including an improved balance of trade.

Key Words

Write a sentence to explain the meaning of each of these terms.

colonies

trading company

balance of
  trade

missions

Spanish Armada

Church of
  England

Major Events

Choose the answer that best completes the statement.

1. The first voyage around the world was begun in 1519 by
   a) Magellan.
   b) Columbus.
   c) de Balboa.

2. Spain's empire in the New World lasted for about
   a) 100 years.
   b) 300 years.
   c) 500 years.

3. In 1500, Portugal claimed land in the New World in
   a) Brazil.
   b) Peru.
   c) the Caribbean.

4. Between 1524 and 1534, France gained claims to the New World through the explorations of
   a) Cabot and La Salle.
   b) Champlain and La Salle.
   c) Verrazano and Cartier.

5. Settlements along the Delaware River were started in 1638 by
   a) the Netherlands.
   b) Sweden.
   c) England.

Review

Important Facts

Answer each question with at least one complete sentence.

1. What was de Balboa's great discovery?

2. What was de León looking for, and what did he find?

3. What did Cortés accomplish on behalf of Spain?

4. What did Pizarro accomplish on behalf of Spain?

5. Why did Spain feel that the conquest of the Indians was "for the glory of God"?

6. Why did Spain bring African slaves into its colonies?

7. What were some of the crops that the Spanish introduced into the New World?

8. What was the Northwest Passage?

9. What area was claimed by France in the New World?

10. How was the Dutch colony of New Netherland different from other colonies?

11. Which nation's colonies were taken over by other colonies or nations?

12. By the mid-1600s, which European nations still had colonies in the New World?

13. What benefits did England hope to get by establishing colonies?

14. What reasons did some English people have for wanting to settle in colonies far from home?

Skill Review

Study the time line, then answer the following questions.

1. Where would the discoveries of de Balboa and de León fall on this time line?

2. How many years passed between the discovery and the settlement of Puerto Rico?

3. Would a Spanish colonist be more likely to settle in Cuba or in Mexico in 1520? Why?

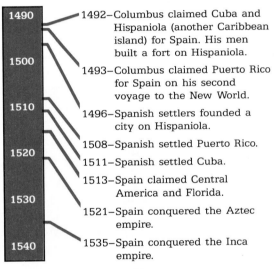

1490
1500
1510
1520
1530
1540

1492–Columbus claimed Cuba and Hispaniola (another Caribbean island) for Spain. His men built a fort on Hispaniola.

1493–Columbus claimed Puerto Rico for Spain on his second voyage to the New World.

1496–Spanish settlers founded a city on Hispaniola.

1508–Spanish settled Puerto Rico.

1511–Spanish settled Cuba.

1513–Spain claimed Central America and Florida.

1521–Spain conquered the Aztec empire.

1535–Spain conquered the Inca empire.

Growth of the Spanish Empire

Critical Thinking

Write a paragraph to answer each question.

1. Why was Magellan's voyage so important?

2. Why was England slower than some other European nations in establishing colonies in the New World?

3
The Thirteen English Colonies

Years 1585–1732

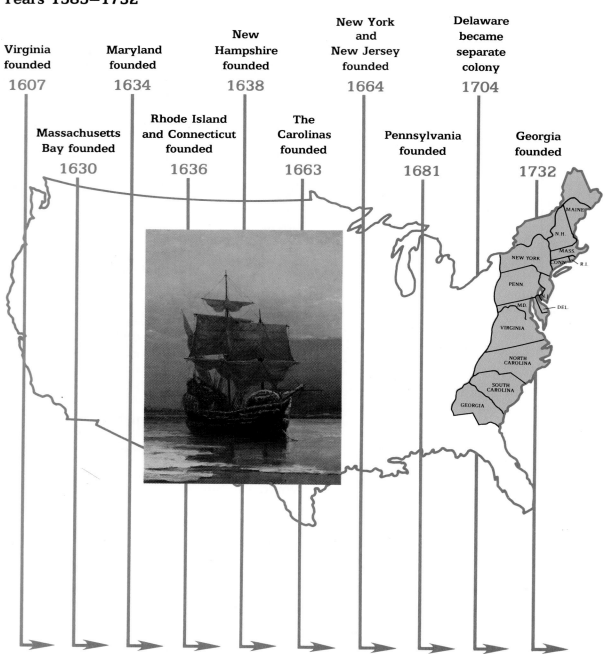

Virginia
founded
1607

Massachusetts
Bay founded
1630

Maryland
founded
1634

Rhode Island
and Connecticut
founded
1636

New
Hampshire
founded
1638

The
Carolinas
founded
1663

New York
and
New Jersey
founded
1664

Pennsylvania
founded
1681

Delaware
became
separate
colony
1704

Georgia
founded
1732

MAINE
N.H.
MASS
NEW YORK
CONN
R.I.
PENN.
N.J.
MD.
DEL.
VIRGINIA
NORTH
CAROLINA
SOUTH
CAROLINA
GEORGIA

1. The First English Colonies

Learn these important terms:

cash crop
plantations
headright system
House of Burgesses
legislature

Remember the main idea:

The first successful English colony in America was founded in 1607 at Jamestown, Virginia.

Look for answers to these questions:

1. What was the Lost Colony?
2. What were some of the problems faced by the Jamestown colony?
3. What two things helped the Jamestown colony survive?
4. How did the London Company attract settlers to the colony?

Right of ownership is something most of us understand. We can say: *That is my tennis shoe. That is her car.* These statements certainly seem simple enough. However, in the 1600s, the right of ownership to the New World was not clear at all.

At first, Spain claimed the New World west of the treaty line it had with Portugal. Portugal held the land that is now Brazil. But this simple division did not last long. As we have seen, France, Sweden, and the Netherlands were all staking claims. But were their claims lawful?

In the late 1500s, Queen Elizabeth I of England answered that question. She said that the right to land in the New World should depend on a country's ability to settle permanent colonies there. She called this *effectively occupying* the land. With this in mind, the English began building colonies in the New World. They set their sights on the Atlantic coast between the Spanish settlements to the south and the French to the north.

What would it take to start a colony? This was a question the English faced in the late 1500s. First, it would take colonists—people willing to leave their homes, friends, and families and make the hard voyage to America. It would take food to see them through until they could raise their own crops. And it would take supplies of things from England that they would be unable to find or make in the New World. The English would learn the hard way that without these things a colony could not survive.

The Lost Colony of Roanoke

England's first attempt to start a colony in North America was made in 1583 by

Sir Humphrey Gilbert. But Gilbert was lost at sea, and the colony was never started. Two years later, Gilbert's half brother, Sir Walter Raleigh (RAHL-ee) organized the building of a colony in the New World. He sent colonists to Roanoke (ROH-uh-nohk) Island, off the coast of what is now North Carolina. But after one year, short of supplies and other support, the discouraged colonists returned to England.

Raleigh sent a second group to settle Roanoke. But in 1590, when an English ship visited the colony, the colonists were gone. To this day, no one knows what happened to Roanoke—the Lost Colony.

Sir Walter Raleigh (c. 1552-1618), a favorite of Queen Elizabeth I, sponsored many settlements in the New World. He himself never saw the colonies in America.

Think: John White, a colonist, made detailed drawings of Roanoke Island and its surroundings. Notice how sandbanks protected the island from the ocean. The dotted areas show where the water was shallow. This engraving was based on White's drawings. Examine the map's details. Study the locations of the Indian settlements. Respond: Why do you think the artist included a sea monster and wrecked ships in his map?

HISTORY MAKERS

Virginia Dare

Child of the Lost Colony

''Nothing. Not a trace, not a clue,'' moaned John White, governor of Roanoke colony as he wandered the island. ''How could 118 people just disappear like this?''

''Look here, sir. The word 'Croatoan' is carved on a post. What does it mean?''

''So that's where they went! Croatoan is an island nearby. Before I left, I told the colonists to carve a message on a tree if they left Roanoke. We must sail to Croatoan at once to find them! I pray that they are still alive. What a joy it will be to see my little granddaughter and the rest of the colonists.''

Like all grandfathers, John White thought his grandchild was special. But this little girl was indeed special. She was the first English child born in North America.

Three years earlier, in 1587, John White had led a group of colonists to settle on Roanoke Island, off the coast of present-day North Carolina. He knew the area well, for he had explored it in 1585. His drawings of the plants and wildlife of Roanoke helped others learn about the area.

Interested people, including his daughter, joined him in settling the colony.

Soon after White's group arrived, his daughter, Eleanor Dare, gave birth to a baby girl. She named the child Virginia, in honor of England's virgin queen.

It was not long before the Roanoke colonists ran short of food and supplies. They sent White back to England for help. But a war between England and Spain delayed White's return for three years. When he finally reached Roanoke, no one was there.

Governor White explored Croatoan Island, but he never found Virginia Dare or any of the other colonists. To this day no one knows what happened to them. Were they killed by unfriendly Indians? Did they join the Croatoan Indians? Some Croatoans today are fair-haired and blue-eyed, and they have the same last names as the Roanoke settlers. Could they be descendants of Virginia Dare and the others? If you visit Roanoke Island, you will see this statue of Virginia Dare as an artist imagined she would have looked as a young woman.

Think: Captured by Indians, John Smith was sentenced to die. Pocahontas convinced her father to spare the captain's life. Respond: What does this tell you about Indian trials?

This detail from a portrait of Pocahontas (c. 1596-1617) shows her dressed as an Englishwoman. Her marriage to John Rolfe created hope that Indians and settlers could work together.

The Founding of Jamestown

The experiences at Roanoke taught the English a very important lesson. They learned that colonies needed good support in the early years in order to survive. One person could not start a colony alone. Instead, a group of people, a large amount of money, and careful planning were needed. As a result, in the 1600s, King James I gave a well-prepared group, the London Company, the right to start a colony in North America.

In the spring of 1607, more than one hundred colonists arrived in what is now Virginia. There, far up the James River, they formed the Jamestown settlement. They named both the river and the settlement after their king. But life was harder than the colonists expected, and Jamestown nearly became another lost colony.

Jamestown was swampy and unhealthy. Food was a problem, too. At first, the settlers spent their time looking for gold or searching for a water route to Asia. Few of them planted crops or hunted for food. Hunger and sickness took many lives. Indians attacked and killed many settlers, too.

The colonists had few skills to deal with the hard, unfamiliar life. Most were not farmers. Many were adventurers looking for quick riches and not intending to stay. To make matters worse, the leaders of the colony were weak, and people did not trust one another. In the end, all of these problems nearly destroyed the colony.

Strong Leadership and a Good Cash Crop

During those dark times, one leader arose to help the colonists through their first winter. He was Captain John Smith, a rough soldier, only twenty-seven years old. He made the colonists obey one important rule: Work or starve! Under Smith's leadership, the colonists planted crops and built homes and forts. Smith was also able to get food for the settlers from local Indians who were sometimes helpful and friendly.

Still, in order to succeed as a colony, Jamestown had to do more than just stay alive. It had to provide profits for the London Company and the king. What it needed was a **cash crop**, something that could be sold. John Rolfe found an answer in the tobacco trade.

Think: Examine this tobacco label used for advertising. Respond: What do the Indian, the English gentleman, and the symbols around them express?

London Company reasoned that more people would want to settle there if they could help make the laws of the colony. So the colonists were given the right to elect a **legislature**, or law-making group.

The Virginia legislature, called the **House of Burgesses**, met for the first time in 1619. It set an important example for all the English colonies. All future English colonies would give colonists the right to help make their own laws. Even when King James I decided to rule Virginia himself in 1624, the House of Burgesses continued to meet.

Think: The House of Burgesses gave colonists a voice in making their own laws. Respond: How might the United States be different today had that not been the case?

In the early 1600s, tobacco smoking was very popular in Europe. Rolfe had learned about tobacco in the West Indies. Rolfe used his experiences to produce tobacco in Jamestown. He proved tobacco could be grown successfully in the colony. Soon tobacco was being grown everywhere, even in the streets. The money from tobacco brought better times and more settlers to the colony.

How England Ruled the Colony

The London Company developed plans to try to get more people to settle in the colony. At first, a governor and his officials had run the Virginia Colony. But the

VIRGINIA COLONY AND JAMESTOWN SETTLEMENT

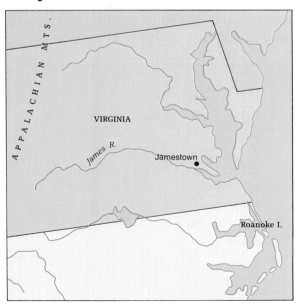

Think: Tobacco plantations were important to the success of the English colonies. Respond: Compare the roles played by the English and the blacks.

The Headright System

Also in 1619, the London Company came up with another plan to encourage settlers. The company made it easier to own land in Virginia. Any person able to pay his or her way to Virginia would receive fifty acres of land. A colonist could pay the way of his family or servants and receive an additional fifty acres per person, or per head. Thus, the plan was called the **headright system**.

The headright system was very successful in bringing more people to Virginia. It also helped some colonists become the wealthy owners of large farms, or **plantations**.

While Virginia was just beginning to benefit from the headright system and the tobacco crops, another English colony was being founded to the north. You will read about this in the next section.

Section Review

1. What was the first successful English colony in North America? When was it founded?
2. What were some of the problems the colonists faced?
3. How did Captain John Smith and John Rolfe help Jamestown to succeed?
4. Why was the House of Burgesses important?

2. Pilgrims, Puritans, and the New England Colonies

Learn these important terms:

Pilgrims	*Puritans*
Parliament	*frontier*
Mayflower	*constitution*
Compact	*charter*
town meetings	
royal colony	

Remember the main idea:

Pilgrims and Puritans came to America to find religious freedom. However, the Puritans who settled in Massachusetts Bay did not allow religious freedom for people who did not believe as they did. People who disagreed left and started other colonies nearby.

Look for answers to these questions:

1. Why did the first colonists come to New England?
2. Why did colonists leave the Massachusetts Bay Colony and found Rhode Island and Connecticut?
3. In what ways were the new colonies alike? In what ways were they different?

In September of 1620, a small ship, the *Mayflower*, set out from England for Virginia. On board were more than one hundred colonists, including about fifty **Pilgrims**. The Pilgrims were a religious group that differed with both the Catholic Church and the Church of England. Many Pilgrims had moved from England to

Holland to avoid being punished for their beliefs. However, they missed many things about England. When the chance for religious freedom in an English colony came, they were eager to take it.

Plymouth Colony

The passengers on the *Mayflower* carried an agreement with the Virginia Company for land in the northern part of the Virginia colony. However, during the journey, a storm forced the ship off course. When the colonists finally sighted land in late November, they knew they were not seeing Virginia. Instead, they were hundreds of miles north in what is now Massachusetts. The Virginia Company did not have authority over this land. The passengers wondered what they should do.

The Pilgrims were strong leaders. They drew up the **Mayflower Compact**, an agreement to make laws and obey them. It stated for the first time the colonists'

Think: William Halsall painted this view of the *Mayflower* in Plymouth Harbor. The ice-covered ship gave shelter to the Pilgrims while their houses were being built. Notice the bleak background and the small boat heading for shore. Respond: What feelings does Halsall's painting express?

PLYMOUTH AND MASSACHUSETTS BAY COLONIES

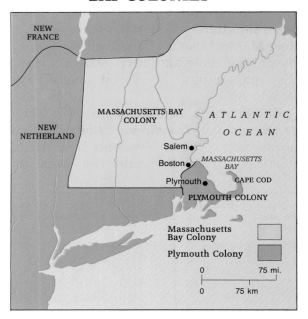

right to form their own government. They called their colony Plymouth.

By the time the colonists arrived, it was too cold to plant crops. Nearly half of the Plymouth Colony died that first winter. But under their leader, William Bradford, and with the help of friendly Indians, the others were able to survive. As soon as spring came, the colonists planted crops. A good harvest that first fall proved that the colony could succeed.

Massachusetts Bay Colony

The **Puritans** were another group of English people who were unhappy with the Church of England. They tried to change the church, but their ideas were not easily accepted. Like the Pilgrims, the Puritans were often punished for their beliefs. Many of them decided to found a colony of their own in Massachusetts. The Puritans were richer than the Pilgrims. With their own money, they were able to form the Massachusetts Bay Company to run the colony.

In 1630, the company sent about one thousand colonists to America. These colonists settled north of Plymouth Colony. The Puritans called their settlement the Massachusetts Bay Colony.

At first, members of the Massachusetts Bay Company ran the new colony. John Winthrop, the governor, and a few other men were the only members of the company. Gradually, the colonists demanded a greater part in the government. Puritan men were given the right to vote. They elected town officers who met and made decisions in **town meetings**. Later they won the right to elect the governor and to select representatives to make the laws of the colony.

The Puritans had come to America to find religious freedom. Yet they did not give freedom of religion to other people in the colony. Only Puritans were allowed to vote. Everyone had to attend the Puritan Church and to obey laws that told people how to behave in Puritan ways. For example, there were laws against smoking in public or wearing fancy clothes.

John Winthrop (1588-1649) came to America when his law career in England seemed doomed by prejudice toward Puritans. He strongly led the Massachusetts colonists for 20 years.

A few LINES on
Magnus Mode, Richard Hodges & J. Newington Clark.
Who are Sentenc'd to ſtand one Hour in the
Pillory at Charleſtown;
To have one of their EARS cut off, and to be Whipped 20 Stripes at the public Whipping-Poſt, for making and paſſing Counterfeit DOLLARS, &c.

Think: Criminals were punished in public gatherings in Massachusetts. People would watch curiously. This public notice was posted to announce the punishment of criminals. **Respond:** What lesson did the leaders of the colony want the colonists to learn?

Rhode Island

Roger Williams, a Puritan leader, spoke out against the harsh Puritan rule in Massachusetts. He argued that the government did not have the right to force people to attend the Puritan Church. He also believed that people had the right to worship as they wished. He thought the land in Massachusetts belonged to the Indians, not to the Massachusetts Bay Company.

In 1636, Williams fled from Massachusetts Bay. With a group of friends, he founded the town of Providence (PRAHV-uh-dunts). Within a few years, other people fleeing Massachusetts had settled three more towns nearby. These four towns thought about joining together for

protection. Finally, in 1644, *Parliament*, the English law-making body, allowed them to become a colony. So they united to become the colony of Rhode Island.

Roger Williams became the first governor. He established important freedoms for the colonists, including freedom of religion. He also said that the churches and the government should be separate. Thus began the important American idea of the separation of church and state.

Colonists in Rhode Island had more control over their government than other English colonists had. There was a general assembly made up of freemen with various religious beliefs. For this reason, Rhode Island attracted many types of settlers.

Connecticut

Roger Williams and his friends were not the only people who left Massachusetts because they were unhappy there. In 1636, a church leader named Thomas Hooker led his entire church group to the rich Connecticut (kuh-NET-ih-kut) River Valley. They were looking for greater freedom and for good farm land. They settled in towns along the Connecticut River. These towns soon joined together to form a colony.

The people of the Connecticut colony created the first written **constitution,** or plan of government, in America. This 1639 plan even allowed people who did not attend any church to vote.

The settlement of Connecticut was an early example of the movement of people to the **frontier**, or the land with no settlers. There they could find land and create their own way of life, free from laws they did not agree with. This pattern of westward movement would continue for two hundred years. And it would help settle most of the land that is now the United States of America.

This westward movement also had a tragic result. As the settlers moved west, they drove the Indians off their lands. The Indians fought back. In Connecticut, for example, a war between the settlers and the Indians broke out. As in most of these wars, the Indians lost, and many of them were killed.

Maine and New Hampshire

John Wheelwright was another church leader who disagreed with the Puritans in

Think: The famous landscape artist Frederick Church (1826–1900) lived and painted in Hartford, Connecticut. In his painting, *Thomas Hooker's Party Coming to Hartford,* Church has shown the grandeur of Hartford and this historic moment. Notice the way in which Church presented nature. Respond: What feelings about Hartford does the painting express?

Wadsworth Atheneum, Hartford

SKILLS FOCUS: Taking Notes

When the Pilgrims aboard the *Mayflower* decided to draw up the Mayflower Compact, they probably first talked about it and took notes on what they wanted to include. Their notes may have looked something like this:

> loyal to King James I
> want to preserve order
> need laws
> will meet regularly to make laws
> votes for adult males
> all colonists to obey laws

After the colonists had made notes on what was important to include in the Mayflower Compact, they could put their notes into sentence and paragraph form.

When you read this textbook, you may find it useful to take notes on the most important facts. These notes will help you remember what you read and will be handy at review time. Notes should be a short version of the most important facts you read. Probably each note will be just a few words long instead of a complete sentence. To save time, you might want to abbreviate words. For example, you might write *govt.* instead of *government*.

Here are the notes you might make on the material under the first heading in this section, "Plymouth Colony."

> Mayflower passengers headed for northern Virginia but landed far north.
> Had to decide own leadership.

> Made Mayflower Compact.
> Stated 1st time colonists' right to form govt.
> Bradford leader.
> ½ colony died 1st winter.
> Indians helped colony survive.
> Had good harvest 1st fall.

Read the paragraphs under the heading "Rhode Island." Think about what would be most important to remember about the material. Then decide which of the following notes would best help you remember and review the material.

1. Roger Williams believed in freedom of religion.
2. Williams helped by group of friends
3. Williams set up colony of Rhode Island 1636
4. Providence a town in Rhode Island
5. Within a few years, 3 more towns besides Providence settled
6. Colonists had more control of govt. of Rhode Island.
7. Parliament Eng. law-making body
8. Rhode Island became colony 1644
9. Williams first to say church and state separate

Now read the paragraphs under the heading "Connecticut." Think about what is important to remember, and take some notes.

Massachusetts. In 1638, he led his followers to New Hampshire, where several small settlements had already been started. There, Wheelwright and his followers set up their own church.

Other settlers from Massachusetts moved into Maine. However, the number of settlers in New Hampshire and Maine remained small. Both colonies had poor soil and cold weather. They were often attacked by the Indians and the French from nearby New France.

At first, both colonies were ruled by Massachusetts. However, in 1680, New Hampshire became a *royal colony*, ruled directly by the English king. Maine remained part of Massachusetts until 1820.

The Royal Colony of Massachusetts

As you have read, many colonists were unhappy with the way in which the Massachusetts Bay Colony was run. The king was unhappy, too. Massachusetts Bay had become more and more independent. A colony could not be allowed to throw off royal control. In 1684, its *charter*, or list of rights, was taken away. For several years the fate of the colony swung back and forth as the English throne changed hands. Finally, in 1691, Massachusetts was made a royal colony. That royal colony included the much smaller Plymouth Colony and Maine.

Section Review

1. What groups settled Plymouth and Massachusetts Bay?
2. In what ways was religious freedom lacking in the Massachusetts Bay Colony?
3. How was Rhode Island settled?
4. Why didn't New Hampshire or Maine grow to be very large?

---

3. The Other Colonies

Learn these important terms:

Toleration Act
Quakers
proprietary colony
indigo
proprietor

Remember the main idea:

By 1732, England had thirteen colonies along the Atlantic coast from Canada to Florida.

Look for answers to these questions:

1. How did each new colony attract settlers?
2. How much religious freedom did each colony allow?
3. How much self-government was there in each colony?

While new colonies were sprouting in New England, others were being started farther south. Many of these southern colonies were near the original, steadily growing colony of Virginia.

Maryland

In the 1630s, the King of England gave land just north of Virginia to his friend Lord Baltimore. The first settlers arrived in this new colony, called Maryland, in 1634. They made a success of growing tobacco, and soon were sending thousands of pounds of it back to England.

Lord Baltimore had the power to rule the colony. Wisely, he offered colonists cheap land and as much self-government as the colonists in Virginia had. This drew many colonists to Maryland.

Religious freedom also attracted colonists. Lord Baltimore was a Catholic. He wanted Catholics to settle in Maryland and go to church as they wished. But many Puritans settled in Maryland, too. Baltimore knew that the success of the colony would depend on how well the two groups could get along. For this reason, he set up the **Toleration Act** (tahl-uh-RAY-shun), which granted religious freedom. It was passed in 1649. The act was an important step toward religious freedom in the English colonies.

The Carolinas

In 1663, the King of England gave the lands which are now the states of North and South Carolina to eight of his friends. The northern part of the colony was settled mainly by farmers from neighboring Virginia. The eight **proprietors**, or owners, of the colony allowed these settlers to elect their own legislature.

The southern part of the colony had good soil, a warm climate, and a fine seaport which grew into the town of Charleston. Rather than tobacco, rice and **indigo**, a plant used to make a rich blue dye, were the cash crops here. The colonists in the south had less say in their government than those in the north. The two parts of the Carolina settlement were different in other ways, too. Finally, in 1729, the colony was split into North Carolina and South Carolina. Both became royal colonies, ruled directly by the king.

New York and New Jersey

As the English colonies were growing in size and number, they were pushing west. As they did so, they pushed many Indians west, too. But along the Hudson and Delaware Rivers there were European settlers as well as Indians. The Dutch colony of New Netherland stood in the way of English colonies.

New Netherland had never been very large. But it had a very successful fur trade that the English wanted. In 1664, an English fleet took control of the Dutch colony. The king gave the colony to his brother James, Duke of York. James kept the northern part, New York. But he gave the southern part, New Jersey, to two of his friends, John Berkeley and George Carteret. Both parts were *proprietary colonies*, owned and ruled by one or more people instead of by the king. Neither colony offered much self-government.

Large land grants brought settlers to the Hudson River Valley. Puritans and the *Quakers*, a religious group that believed all people were equal, moved into New Jersey. There, they had the religious freedom they sought.

When the Duke of York became King James II in 1685, both New York and New Jersey became royal colonies. They were now ruled by the king.

Pennsylvania and Delaware

In 1681, King Charles II gave the land between New York and Maryland to William Penn, a Quaker. The grant was to repay a debt. The land became Pennsylvania, named in honor of Penn's father.

Penn used the colony to protect the Quakers. Quakers refused to bow or to take off their hats to anyone. They were laughed at and feared in England. Many were put into prisons.

Penn also used Pennsylvania to test Quaker beliefs, especially the belief that all people were equal. Instead of pushing Indians off the land, he recognized their rights and offered them a fair price. He welcomed people of other religions. And Penn drew up a Frame of Government that let all who owned land elect their government. Pennsylvania grew quickly, especially since Penn also offered headrights of fifty acres and cheap rents on other lands. By the early 1700s, Pennsylvania had become the largest of the English colonies.

Think: **Painted in the late 1730s, this scene shows the east side of Charles Town, which later became Charleston, South Carolina. The Cooper River is seen in the foreground. Notice the great detail in the buildings and ships.** Respond: **What do the numerous ships shown on the river tell you about trade in Charles Town?**

BRITISH COLONIES IN THE NEW WORLD, 1660

In order to find a certain place on the map, you need to know how far north or south the place is and how far east or west. Mapmakers draw a grid of lines on a map to help you find this information. These lines show *latitude* and *longitude*, which help you locate a place.

Find the lines running east and west on this map. These lines are called *parallels of latitude*. They are measured in degrees, or parts of a circle, because the earth is round. The equator is 0 degrees, the North Pole is 90 degrees north latitude, and the South Pole is 90 degrees south latitude.

Now look at the lines running north and south. These lines are *meridians of longitude*. They are measured in degrees east or west of the prime meridian (0 degrees), which runs through Greenwich, England.

Use the grid and compass on your map to answer the following questions.

1. The English colonies in America were located between which longitudes? Which latitudes were they between?

2. Between which longitudes and latitudes do you find the colony of New York?

3. Which colonies reached north of the forty-fifth parallel of latitude? Which colony stretched west of the eightieth meridian of longitude?

4. Give the longitude and latitude of the city of Boston. Would this answer be true on any map that you were looking at?

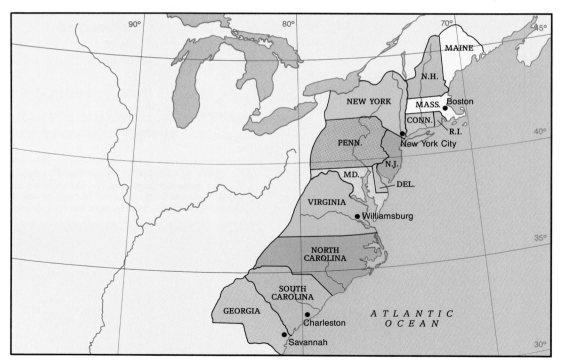

Think: Illustrations such as this engraving were created to attract colonists to Georgia. Examine the large amount of natural resources shown in the artwork. Notice the people working together and how perfect the scene appears. Respond: What image of Georgia does the engraving present, and why?

The southern coast of Penn's colony was different from the rest of the colony in many ways. Fewer Quakers lived there, for one thing. Also, the farmers there grew tobacco. In 1704, this area became a separate colony—Delaware.

Georgia

In the year 1732, King George II granted land for a new colony, Georgia. There were two purposes for the colony. First, it was to separate Spanish Florida and the English colony of South Carolina. Second, Georgia was to be a place where people from debtors' prisons could settle and make new lives.

The leader of the Georgia Colony was General James Oglethorpe (OH-gul-thawrp). He set strict rules for the colony. Slavery and the sale of liquor were not allowed. All farms had to be less than five hundred acres so that one person could not control too much land. But the dream failed. Few debtors came to Georgia. And eventually Georgia farmers used slaves on their indigo and tobacco plantations. In 1752, Georgia became a royal colony.

Georgia completed the English settlement of North America. By the 1730s, England had thirteen colonies in North America. In the next chapter, you will read about life in these thirteen colonies during the 1700s.

Section Review

1. Which colony was founded by a Catholic?
2. What is the difference between a proprietary colony and a royal colony?
3. How did Quaker beliefs influence the development of the colony of Pennsylvania?
4. Why was Georgia founded?

CHAPTER SUMMARY

The first permanent English colony in North America was Jamestown, Virginia. Its first years were very hard. To the north, Plymouth Colony, in present-day Massachusetts, was founded by the Pilgrims. It was run by rules that recognized the rights of colonists to govern themselves.

Another group, the Puritans, settled near the Pilgrims in Massachusetts Bay Colony. The Puritans forced their beliefs on everyone in the colony. As a result, groups of colonists left Massachusetts Bay to found colonies of their own. Rhode Island, Connecticut, New Hampshire, and Maine were all started by these settlers.

In the south, colonies were being started around Virginia, too. Maryland was begun as a Catholic colony. However, in 1649 it passed the Toleration Act, which allowed all Christians to worship as they wished.

The Carolinas were the next colonies to be founded. This settlement was eventually divided into North and South Carolina.

New York and New Jersey became English colonies when they were taken over from the Dutch.

Pennsylvania soon became the largest English colony. The southeast corner of Pennsylvania became the colony of Delaware.

Georgia was the last of the English colonies to be founded.

Key Words

Write a sentence to explain the meaning of each of these terms.

plantations House of
frontier Burgesses
indigo Parliament

Major Events

Choose the answer that best completes the statement.

1. In 1607, the first English colony was founded at
   a) Plymouth.
   b) Jamestown.
   c) Massachusetts Bay.

2. In 1620, Pilgrim settlers founded
   a) Plymouth.
   b) Jamestown.
   c) Massachusetts Bay.

3. In 1664, New Netherlands became the English colonies of
   a) Maine and New Hampshire.
   b) New York and New Jersey.
   c) Pennsylvania and Delaware.

4. In 1681, Quakers founded
   a) Maryland.
   b) Pennsylvania.
   c) Georgia.

5. In 1732, General James Oglethorpe founded the colony of
   a) South Carolina.
   b) Delaware.
   c) Georgia.

6. In 1649, Maryland passed the
   a) Holy Experiment.
   b) Toleration Act.
   c) Mayflower compact.

Review

Important Facts

Answer each question with at least one complete sentence.

1. What was Roanoke?

2. What were some of the problems the Jamestown colony had at the beginning?

3. What two things helped save Jamestown?

4. Why did the Pilgrims want to leave Europe to settle in the New World?

5. What was the importance of the Mayflower Compact?

6. How did Puritan beliefs affect the way the Massachusetts Bay Colony was run?

7. Name the colonies that were founded by colonists who left Massachusetts Bay.

8. What two colonies remained part of Massachusetts through the late 1600s?

9. What was the Toleration Act?

10. Why did the Carolinas split into two separate colonies?

11. Why was Pennsylvania so successful in attracting colonists?

12. What were some of the rules for colonists in Georgia that differed from rules in other colonies?

13. How was a proprietary colony different from a royal colony?

14. What were three of the important cash crops in the southern colonies?

Skill Review

This map shows five present-day states that began as colonies. Use the map grid to answer the following questions.

1. Between which degrees of latitude are these states located?

2. At approximately which meridian of longitude is the western border of Pennsylvania?

3. What are the latitude and longitude of Philadelphia?

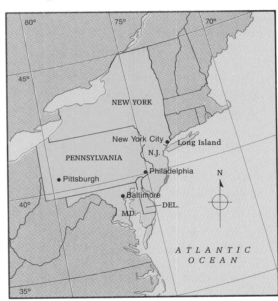

New Jersey and Surrounding States

Critical Thinking

Write a paragraph to answer each question.

1. What things were important to the success of a colony?

2. How did the level of religious freedom differ in the various English colonies?

Important People

Choose the answer that best completes the statement.

1. The Indian civilization that developed a calendar and the first system of writing in the Americas was the
   a) Inca.
   b) Maya.
   c) Aztec.

2. The first Europeans to discover the New World were
   a) the Vikings.
   b) the Spanish.
   c) the Portuguese.

3. The man who helped advance the science of sailing was
   a) Bartholomeu Dias.
   b) Vasco da Gama.
   c) Prince Henry.

4. France's claim to North America included land explored by
   a) Cartier and La Salle.
   b) Verrazano and Cabral.
   c) Champlain and Cabot.

5. The person responsible for the survival of Jamestown was
   a) Sir Walter Raleigh.
   b) King James I.
   c) Captain John Smith.

6. Roger Williams
   a) used his colony to test Quaker beliefs.
   b) left Massachusetts Bay to establish a colony where people could worship freely.
   c) set strict rules for his colony.

Main Ideas

Choose the answer that best completes the statement.

1. Scientists believe the first Americans
   a) came by boat from northwestern Europe.
   b) came across a land bridge from Asia.
   c) were brought by slave traders from Africa.

2. The Plains Indians
   a) were great traders.
   b) built huge "apartment houses" of mud brick.
   c) followed the herds of buffalo.

3. Europe did not become interested in exploration until
   a) the development of the astrolabe.
   b) after the Crusades.
   c) Columbus sailed to the New World.

4. Europe's early explorers were looking for a short sea route to
   a) Asia.
   b) Africa.
   c) Palestine.

5. Spain explored America and conquered Indians in search of
   a) the Northwest Passage.
   b) spices and fabrics.
   c) gold and silver.

6. French and Spanish settlers in the New World were not allowed
   a) to own land.
   b) a say in the government.
   c) to convert the Indians.

Review

7. England was free to set up colonies in North America after

   a) John Cabot explored the east coast.
   b) Henry VIII became King of England.
   c) the defeat of the Spanish Armada.

8. America attracted many English settlers because

   a) joblessness was a severe problem in England.
   b) it offered them religious freedom.
   c) Both of the reasons above are correct.

9. The first successful English colony in America was founded

   a) at Jamestown.
   b) at Plymouth.
   c) at Roanoke.

10. Rhode Island, Connecticut, Maine, and New Hampshire were

    a) royal colonies.
    b) proprietary colonies.
    c) settled by people who disagreed with Puritan rule.

11. Settlers in the south grew cash crops such as

    a) tobacco, corn, and beans.
    b) indigo, tobacco, and rice.
    c) corn, wheat, and tobacco.

12. By the 1730s, England

    a) was the wealthiest trading nation in the world.
    b) had thirteen colonies in North America.
    c) Both of the answers above are correct.

History Skills

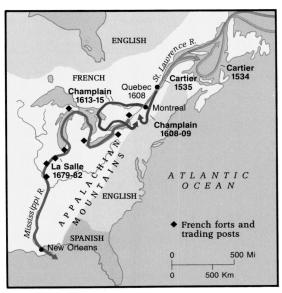

French Explorers in North America

Choose the answer that best completes the statement.

1. A good survey question about this map would be

   a) Where did French explorers go?
   b) Which explorer is missing?
   c) Why were forts built?

2. From Quebec to Montreal is

   a) exactly 500 miles.
   b) not quite 100 miles.
   c) about 200 miles.

3. The symbol that shows Champlain's first trip is a

   a) solid red line.
   b) dashed blue line.
   c) dashed red line.

4. Last on a time line would be

   a) La Salle.
   b) Champlain.
   c) Cartier.

Colonial Americans

4
Making a Living

Years 1607–1750

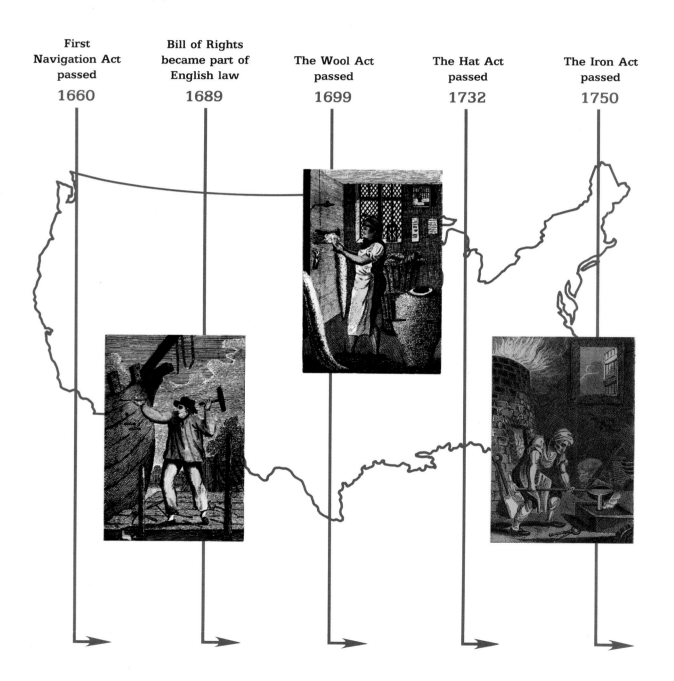

First
Navigation Act
passed
1660

Bill of Rights
became part of
English law
1689

The Wool Act
passed
1699

The Hat Act
passed
1732

The Iron Act
passed
1750

If you had left England for the colonies during the 1600s, you could have settled in New England, the middle colonies, or the southern colonies. Each region had its own type of land, soil, and climate. As a result, you would have seen different kinds of farming, trade, and manufacturing in each section. You would also have seen rapid growth in each section.

You would have left great unrest in England. During the colonial period, from 1607 to 1750, England had ten different leaders. Parliament struggled with kings for the power to govern the country. In 1689, a new king and queen had to accept Parliament's Bill of Rights in order to take the throne. The Bill of Rights assured representative government. It also ended the absolute power of the English kings. The Bill of Rights became very important to the colonies.

With so many changes of leaders, English policy toward the colonies changed many times. Sometimes the colonies were largely ignored. At other times, the ruler tried to tighten royal control. In this chapter, you will read about the ways colonists made a living. You will also see how England tried to limit the trade and industry developed by the colonists.

1. Farming in the Colonies

Learn these important terms:

girdling
subsistence farming
breadbasket colonies
coastal plain
indentured servants
commercial farming

Remember the main idea:

Farming was an important way of making a living in all three sections of colonial America. Because the soil, weather, and amount of good farm land varied, different kinds of farming developed in each section.

Look for answers to these questions:

1. What were the soil and climate like in each section of colonial America?
2. How and why did the size of farms differ from one section to another?
3. What were some of the things that farmers raised in each section of colonial America?

Owning land was very important in England and Europe during colonial times. But the Old World had been settled for a long time, and there was little land available. Land there was very expensive. So many people looked to America to buy their own land. Soon, like in the Old World, land became important as a measure of social standing in America. Often,

THE THREE REGIONS OF COLONIAL AMERICA

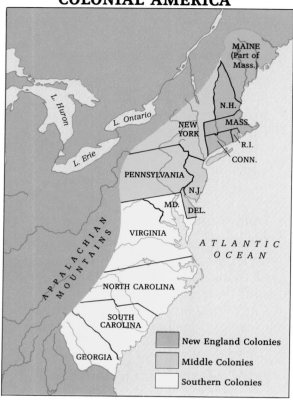

Legend:
- New England Colonies
- Middle Colonies
- Southern Colonies

a colonist had to own land in order to be able to vote. It is not surprising that most colonists owned land. After all, farming was the most important way of life in the colonies.

Learning to Farm in the Colonies

When the English settlers arrived in America, they tried to farm just as they had in England. Often, their old farming ways did not work. For example, wheat, the most important English crop, did not grow well in some parts of the colonies. The colonists had to find other crops and other methods of farming that were suitable to the new land.

The Indians were helpful in teaching the colonists new skills. They showed the settlers how to grow corn and other crops that do well in America. The Indians also taught the colonists an easy method of felling trees. The method was known as *girdling*. They stripped the bark off of the trees and waited for them to die. In time,

Think: An early New York farm is portrayed in this painting by a self-taught artist. The painting once hung in the farmhouse itself. The man and woman in front of the house were the farm owners. The unknown artist included many details about life on a farm in the early 1700s. Notice the variety of animals and types of workers. Many travelers pass by the farm. The Catskill Mountains are in the background. Respond: According to the painting, what was life like in early New York?

the trees fell, the land was cleared for fields or houses, and the wood was used for buildings or fences.

Farming in New England

The New England colonies were not well suited for farming. Glaciers had passed over the land thousands of years earlier, leaving only a thin, rocky layer of topsoil. The short, cool New England summers did not provide a growing season long enough for many crops. And much of New England is hilly. Only the *coastal plain*, a level area running along the Atlantic coast, is flat. Therefore, colonial New England farms were usually small. Most often, they were worked only by the farmer and his family.

Corn was the most important New England grain. But oats, barley, and rye were also grown. Most New England farmers grew fruits and vegetables and also raised useful animals such as oxen, horses, sheep, cattle, and hogs. Most New England farmers grew just enough to feed their families. They did not grow enough to sell their crops or livestock for money. This kind of farming is called *subsistence farming* (sub-SIS-tens).

Think: **These men are girdling trees. Indians taught early settlers to fell trees in this way.** Respond: **What does this tell you about how these Indians felt about the settlers?**

HISTORY MAKERS

Squanto

The Pilgrims' Teacher and Friend

The attack was planned for midnight. The men waited quietly as the night wore on. At the captain's signal, they burst into the Indian chief's house.

"Where is Squanto? Produce him at once, or every man here will die!" Captain Myles Standish looked around the room. There was no sign of Squanto. One of the captain's men climbed onto the roof and called Squanto's name. In a few minutes he appeared. He was unharmed.

Squanto, a Patuxet Indian (paw-TUHKS-et), was a valuable friend of the Pilgrims. When they learned that other Indians had taken him prisoner, they immediately sent an expedition to free him.

Squanto was so important to the Pilgrims because he spoke English. His life story was amazing. Years before the Pilgrims arrived in America, Squanto was kidnapped and sold into slavery. He was sent to England, where he learned English. In England he was kidnapped again and taken to Spain. He managed to return to the New World, only to find that his tribe had been killed by disease.

Imagine Squanto's surprise when he found English people in his native land. Imagine their delight upon finding him! It was Squanto who arranged the first treaty between the Plymouth Colony and the powerful Indian chief Massasoit (MAS-uh-SOYT).

Squanto aided the Pilgrims in many other ways. He told them the best places to plant their crops. He also may have told them to use fish as fertilizer for squash and corn. He helped with fishing and trapping, and he taught the Pilgrims to catch eels at low tide. He acted as a guide when they explored their new land.

Despite hard work and Squanto's good advice, the Plymouth Colony was often short of food. In November 1622, Squanto went with a group of Pilgrims to find corn. He became ill and died on the trip.

Squanto's knowledge helped the Pilgrims survive the first hard years in the New World. In his diary, Governor Bradford wrote that Squanto was "a special instrument sent of God for their good beyond their expectation."

Farming in the Middle Colonies

The middle colonies were better suited for farming than New England. They had rich soil and a mild climate. Farms in the middle colonies were larger than those in New England. Additional workers were needed to help on these large farms. Many of these workers were *indentured servants* (in-DEN-churd). Indentured servants were people who agreed to work for

Think: **Convicted of perjury, Elizabeth Canning was sentenced to one month in prison and seven years Transportation to the colonies.** Respond: **How do you think she felt about having to leave London to live in America?**

Think: **This poor oyster seller in London probably chose to become an indentured servant in America.** Respond: **Why might someone have chosen to be an indentured servant?**

Think: **This artwork shows Bethlehem, Pennsylvania, in 1757, when the town was only sixteen years old.** Respond: **How can you tell that the town's founders were hardworking?**

a person for a certain period of time, usually about seven years. In this way the servants paid off their passage to the colonies. When their time was up, indentured servants were given their freedom, and they were then able to set up their own farms.

The main food crops grown in the middle colonies were wheat, rye, barley, corn, vegetables, and fruit. The settlers also raised many cattle, sheep, and hogs for meat and hides. Much of the wheat and livestock raised in the middle colonies was sold to the other colonies or to other nations. In fact, the middle colonies grew and sold so much wheat that they became known as the *breadbasket colonies*.

Farming in the Southern Colonies

The southern colonies were best suited for farming because the southern soil was rich and the growing season was long. In addition, the coastal plain becomes wider at its southern end. This gave the southern colonies more flat land than New England or the middle colonies.

At first, the settlers in the south started small farms. But when tobacco, rice, and indigo became important and profitable crops, the southern farms increased in size. Through the headright system and other means, some colonists came to own thousands of acres of land. These huge farms became known as plantations.

Tobacco was the main crop grown in Virginia, Maryland, and North Carolina. Because tobacco requires a great deal of care while it is growing, southern tobacco plantations needed many workers. However, workers were hard to get in the colonies. At first, southern planters used indentured servants. Later, as you will read, the southern colonies brought in thousands of slaves to work the fields.

Think: Tobacco was an important cash crop in the South. Growing it required many workers. Respond: How did this cash crop make the southern colonies different from the rest?

In South Carolina and Georgia, the most important crops were rice and indigo, a plant used to make blue dye. Settlers in South Carolina began to grow rice in the 1690s. Within a few years, South Carolina was growing the best rice in the world. In the 1740s, the people of South Carolina started to grow indigo, which soon became South Carolina's second most important crop. Like tobacco, rice

Think: Indigo plantations became profitable in the 1750s. Like tobacco, the indigo plants required much care and many workers. Unfortunately, slaves were forced to do most of the work. Respond: Why would the indigo plantations have been far less profitable had they not used slaves?

and indigo both need much care while they are growing. South Carolina's rice and indigo farms used many slaves.

Cash Crops

The southern colonies also raised wheat, corn, fruits, vegetables, cattle, and hogs. But these crops and livestock were mainly for the farmer and his family. Southern farmers used most of their land to raise cash crops, which were grown to be sold. This type of farming is called *commercial farming* (kuh-MUR-shul).

Throughout Maryland, Virginia, and North Carolina the cash crop was tobacco. In South Carolina and Georgia, it was rice or indigo. Georgia took longer than the other southern colonies to find a suitable cash crop.

At first Georgia settlers thought their cash crop would be silk. Early colonists were required to plant mulberry trees as food for silkworms. The silkworms were to be brought into the colony by the proprietors. Unfortunately, no one had checked to see if silkworms could live in the Georgia climate. They could not, and so the experiment failed. At that point, Georgia farmers began to copy neighboring South Carolina farmers by planting rice and indigo, which did quite well in Georgia, too.

Section Review

1. What did the Indians teach the first English settlers about farming in America?
2. How did climate and soil vary among the New England colonies, the middle colonies, and the southern colonies?
3. What were the cash crops in each of the southern colonies?

Learn these important terms:

Navigation Acts *smuggling*
fishing banks *triangular trade*
naval stores *duty*

Remember the main idea:

Trade was very important to all the colonies. England passed laws to control colonial trade to make it more profitable for England. But the colonists found ways of getting around the laws.

Look for answers to these questions:

1. What were the Navigation Acts, and in what ways did they affect the colonies?
2. What kind of trade went on in the three regions of colonial America?
3. Why was there not enough money in the colonies?

Trade was extremely important in the English colonies. North America was isolated from most other parts of the world. Traders profited by moving goods to and from the colonies. They carried cash crops, foods, and other things produced in the colonies to the West Indies, England, Europe, and Africa. And they brought slaves, supplies, and goods from these regions back to the colonies. In the mid-1600s, Dutch traders were getting a large share of this business. English traders were unhappy about this, and the English

Elias Hasket Derby (1739-1799) was a famous colonial merchant who grew very wealthy from the shipping industry. His fine clothing and furniture display his wealth.

government moved to stop the Dutch traders. England also tried to control colonial trade in other ways that would benefit the English.

The Navigation Acts

Beginning in 1660, England passed a series of laws, called the **Navigation Acts**, to control the colonies' trade. The main points of the Navigation Acts were:

1. All goods shipped to or from the English colonies were to be carried in English ships. These ships were to be manned by English or colonial sailors.

2. Certain colonial products were to be sold only to England or to the other English colonies. These products included tobacco, rice, indigo, furs, cotton, tar, pitch, and turpentine.

3. All goods from foreign nations had to be brought to England before they could be shipped to the colonies. In England, a **duty**, or tax to be paid by the final buyer, was placed on the foreign goods.

The Navigation Acts had very deep effects on the colonies. Some of the effects were positive ones. For example, the colonial shipbuilding industry grew because of the acts. Ships had been built in the colonies from the earliest days. There was plenty of good lumber and a great need for ships. Colonial ships were known for their quality. The English bought many of their ships from the colonies. With the passage of the Navigation Acts, the demand for English ships went up sharply. Colonial shipbuilders became even busier.

However, in other ways, the Navigation Acts hurt trade in the colonies. The colonists had to sell many of their goods for lower prices in England than they could have gotten elsewhere. When there was too much of a certain product, such as tobacco, they might not be able to sell much of it. At the same time, colonists had to pay higher prices for non-English goods, such as French wines or Dutch fabrics, because of the duties placed on them in England.

For these reasons, most colonists disliked the Navigation Acts. They knew that these trade laws were passed to help English traders, not to help the colonists. Most colonial merchants and sea captains found ways to get around the Navigation Acts. **Smuggling**, or unlawful trade, became common. The English government was too far away to control it.

New England Trade

The lack of good farm land led many New Englanders to other ways of making a living. The colonists in New England wanted such goods as fancy cloth and weapons, which were made in Europe. In

MAP WORKSHOP TRADE MAPS

COLONIAL TRADE

A *trade map* shows you countries which trade with one another. This map shows the major colonial trade routes and the goods that were traded.

Follow the trade routes on the map. Notice that there are two trade routes. One of these trade routes forms a triangle. On one leg of the triangle, a ship would sail from the colonies to Africa. On the next leg of the triangle, it would start the journey home but stop off at the West Indies. The third and final leg of the triangle was from the West Indies to the colonies. On the way to Africa, the triangular trader carried rum, which New England distillers had made from West Indian sugar and molasses. What was carried on the second and third legs of the journey?

The other trade route was between the colonies and Great Britain.

Use your map to answer the following questions.

1. How did slaves help the colonies in their trade with Great Britain?

2. In what ways did the American forests aid colonial trade with Great Britain?

3. On which leg of the trade triangle were raw materials shipped? On which leg did ships carry a manufactured product? Human beings were shipped on which leg?

4. Judging from the goods they each traded, what was a major economic activity of Great Britain? Of the West Indies? Of the colonies?

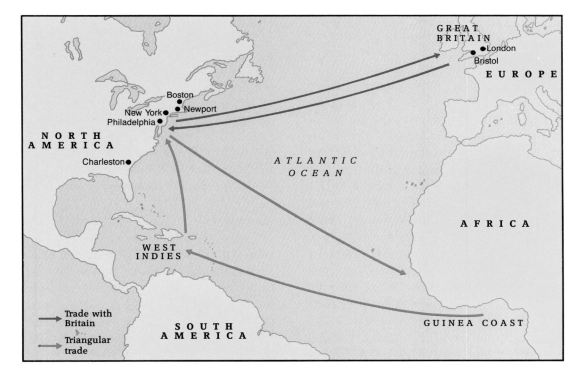

Think: In the 1700s, Philadelphia was one of the trading centers of the colonies. The New Englanders wanted many fine goods from England. In return, many raw materials, such as wood, were sent to England. Respond: Why did trade become so profitable in tne colonies?

order to get these goods, they needed products to trade for them. Since there were many trees in New England, the colonists used this raw material as the basis of trade. Much of the wood, or lumber, went to building ships. But much lumber was left to trade with other nations.

During the 1660s, most colonial trade passed through Boston, the main seaport in New England. Boston was the center of the important New England fishing industry, the basis of another major part of New England's trade. Some of the world's best **fishing banks**, places where large numbers of fish can be found, are located near New England. Many New England colonists turned to the sea for a living. These skilled fishermen caught tons of fish. Much of the catch was dried, salted, and sold in Europe and the West Indies.

Another important New England product was rum. This drink was very popular in every English colony and in many other nations. Molasses from the West Indies was shipped to New England to make rum. The rum was then sent to Africa,

Think: New England fishermen are shown catching, cleaning, and salting fish in this engraving. Respond: Why was fishing an important part of New England's system of trade?

where it was traded for slaves and gold. The slaves were taken to the West Indies and traded for sugar, molasses, and money. The molasses was used to make more rum. This important trade pattern became known as the **triangular trade.** With the money they earned from the trade, the New England colonists bought the goods they needed from England.

Trade in the Middle Colonies

The middle colonies had a lively trade in grain and livestock. They produced enough of these products to provide for themselves, other colonies, and the West Indies. Some was even shipped as far as Europe. By the 1670s, Philadelphia and New York, the two main ports in the middle colonies, were also the busiest ports in the colonies.

The middle colonies also traded in high quality lumber, which was in demand for making furniture throughout the colonies. And, as in the other regions of the colonies, the lumber industry produced *naval stores*, products to be used on ships. Some naval stores from the lumber industry included tar, pitch, resin, and turpentine. Furs, particularly from the frontier areas, were an important source of trade in the middle colonies, and to a lesser degree in the New England and southern colonies as well.

Trade in the Southern Colonies

Trade in the southern colonies was based mainly on the cash crops produced there. For example, tobacco from Maryland and Virginia was shipped to England

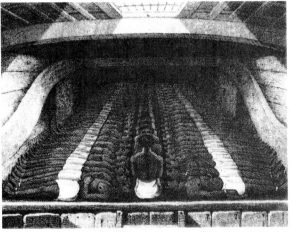

Think: **Slave ships were packed solid with people captured in Africa. Only greed influenced the slave traders.** Respond: **Describe how the captured Africans might have felt.**

to trade for iron goods, fabrics, and other things. These goods were then shipped to Africa, where they were traded for slaves. These slaves were then brought to the southern colonies to work on the steadily growing plantations.

Vast stands of yellow pine in the southern colonies also helped trade. They produced a large quantity of tar, pitch, and turpentine. These naval stores brought high prices in England.

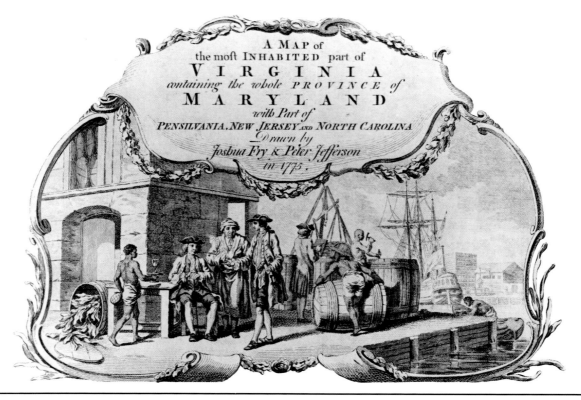

A MAP of
the moſt INHABITED part of
VIRGINIA
containing the whole PROVINCE of
MARYLAND
with Part of
PENSILVANIA, NEW JERSEY and NORTH CAROLINA
Drawn by
Joshua Fry & Peter Jefferson
in 1775.

Think: Bound for England and then Africa, a ship is shown being loaded with tobacco from Virginia. These three places formed the points of a triangle. On its route, the ship would drop off and receive goods at each point.
Respond: Why was this triangular trade important to the colonies?

Foreign Trade and Money Problems

The balance of trade between the colonies and England was heavily weighted in England's favor. The colonies bought much more from England than they sold to England, so they always owed money to English merchants. To make enough money to pay their English debts, colonial merchants had to rely on trade with the West Indies and Europe.

Even with their foreign trade, the colonies were always short of money—especially gold and silver coins. Indian wampum beads, tobacco, corn, sheep, cattle, rice, rum, and many other things were used as money at one time or another in the colonies. But these articles were difficult to carry around, and their value kept changing.

In 1652, Massachusetts minted a silver coin, the Pine Tree Shilling. The English did not recognize the right of the colony to make its own money, and the coin was removed some years later. During the 1700s, most of the colonies printed paper money. However, merchants in England and in the colonies often refused to accept the paper money. The control of money was another important way in which England maintained power over the American colonies. In the next section, you will read about several ways in which England controlled manufacturing in the colonies, too.

Section Review

1. What were some of the effects of the Navigation Acts on colonial trade?
2. What was the triangular trade?
3. Why was foreign trade important to the colonies?

3. Colonial Industry and Towns

Learn these important terms:

manufacturing
domestic industry
commercial industry
potash

Remember the main idea:

Manufacturing was important in all the colonies. Most manufacturing was carried on in the towns, which were the centers of colonial life. English laws to control manufacturing did not have much success.

Look for answers to these questions:

1. How did England try to control manufacturing in the colonies?
2. What kinds of manufacturing went on in the colonies?
3. Why did towns develop as they did in the colonies?

As you have read, England tried to rule the colonies in a way that was to its own best advantage. Control of trade through the Navigation Acts began in 1660. Later, the English government moved to control another important part of the colonies' livelihood—*manufacturing* (man-yoo-FAK-chur-ing). Manufacturing is the making of finished products such as cloth, pans, and tools from raw materials.

Control of Manufacturing

The English government wanted the colonists in America to buy their manufactured goods from England. For this reason, the English government passed several laws to stop the colonies from manufacturing certain goods. These three acts were the most important laws:

1. The Wool Act of 1699 allowed woolen goods to be sold only in the colony in which they were made.
2. The Hat Act of 1732 prevented the sale of beaver hats outside the colony in which they were made.
3. The Iron Act of 1750 allowed only certain types of iron products to be made in the colonies.

These laws were unpopular in the colonies. They were aimed at industries that were particularly successful and making a lot of money. To obey the laws would have greatly hurt the colonies' trade with Europe and elsewhere. So the laws were largely ignored.

Domestic Industry

The colonists needed manufactured products for use in their homes, on their farms, and in their shops. Many of these items were made in the colonies, since there was little money to buy English goods. Most colonial products were manufactured in the home. The colonial family usually produced its own food, drink, clothing, furniture, candles, soap, and certain tools. These products were for the family's use and were not sold. This type of manufacturing is called household industry, or *domestic industry*.

Commercial Industry

The colonists also manufactured goods for sale. This type of manufacturing is called *commercial industry* (kuh-MUR-shul). Lumbering was one of the commercial industries in the colonies. The wood from the trees was made into furniture, barrels, houses, and ships. American forests also provided other products that

Think: The whaling industry was important to New England. But the life of a whaler was harsh and often dangerous. Using only hand-thrown harpoons, ropes, and small boats, the whalers fought to take their massive prey. Many lives were lost. Respond: Why do you think these men chose to be whalers?

were needed in the colonies and in England. These included naval stores and **potash,** wood ashes needed in the colonies and used in England in the wool industry. As you know, many of these products were an important part of colonial trade.

Mining was another important commercial industry in America. Although the thirteen English colonies had no gold or silver, almost all of them had iron ore. The southern colonies mined iron ore. Then New England and the middle colonies turned the iron ore into finished iron products.

Iron was used in the manufacture of nails, pots and pans, tools, and weapons. Even a family that made most of its own goods had to buy these iron products. The Iron Act tried to force the colonists to buy many iron products from England rather than from the colonies. Still, the colonists manufactured many iron products. The trade of these products continued to be important to the colonies.

The fur trade was another important colonial industry. In New England and the middle colonies, the colonists trapped beavers. In the southern colonies, they caught deer. The skins of both these animals were sold for high prices in Europe. Also, beaver hats manufactured in the middle colonies had become very popular in England and Europe. This colonial hat-making industry did so well that the Hat Act was passed to protect the hat-making industry in England. The colonists got around this law, too.

The Need for Skilled Workers

Many other industries were carried on in the colonies. Glassmaking, brickmaking, papermaking, shoemaking, and flour milling were just a few. All this manufacturing required many skilled workers. However, such skilled workers were in short supply in the colonies.

Most people who came to the colonies wanted to own their own land. The only way to get skilled workers to come to the colonies was to offer high wages. Some colonies passed laws to keep wages low. Despite such laws, the wages of workers in the colonies were higher than wages in England.

Think: These engravings show some of the most common jobs in the colonies: the barrel maker, ship builder, and the wool comber. These workers learned their trades as teenagers. Eventually, they became masters and taught other young people. Respond: Why was the cycle of learning trades important in the colonies?

SKILLS FOCUS: Understanding Cause and Effect

The cartoon below shows a cause and an effect. You can see that the oversized beaver hat blocking the colonial gentleman's view is the cause. The effect is his landing on the ground, looking somewhat less dignified.

In the section you just read, a beaver skin hat was a cause for another effect. The beaver skin hats that colonists made sold so well that England passed the Hat Act to end the hat-making trade in the colonies. The section also told what happened and why in other areas of trade between England and America.

When you ask *why* something happened, you are looking for a cause. When you ask what happened when something else happened, you are looking for an effect. Here is one way to show this relationship:

cause ——→ effect

Copy the chart about the causes and effects of decisions about trade between England and America. To complete the chart, look at each effect and ask yourself, "Why did this happen?" Use your text for help.

Cause	Effect
Ships needed good harbors to carry traded goods between England and America.	Large towns grew up around harbors in America.
1	Colonists started making their own manufacturing goods.
2	Skilled workers left England for America.
3	England passed laws to keep American manufacturers from selling their goods outside their own colonies.

Think: Germantown was made up of a market square, one main street, several mills, and country estates. As did most colonial towns, it had a school, a church, and several shops. Respond: What needs of the people did the colonial towns meet?

Philadelphia Museum of Art, Collection of Edgar William and Bernice Chrysler Garbisch

The Growth of Cities and Towns

Most skilled workers settled in towns, where they were able to get plenty of work. The largest towns of the colonial period were located near good harbors. By the 1750s, Philadelphia, New York, Boston, Newport, and Charleston were the largest towns in the colonies.

Because of the large plantations in the south, there were fewer towns there. A plantation took care of most of its own needs. Often a plantation had its own dock so that crops could be loaded directly onto a ship, and incoming goods could be unloaded. Because of this, fewer large port cities developed.

The number of towns was probably largest in the New England colonies. Here, the early settlers had almost all been members of a particular church. As a result, each town was built around a church. As new groups split off, they moved away to establish their own towns, each centered around a church. Also, the smaller size of farms in this section of colonial America caused farmers to travel frequently to town centers. Here, they could purchase goods and services they could not provide for themselves.

Town Life in Colonial America

Towns in colonial America were full of activity. They were centers of business, trade, social life, education, and government. They were the centers of communication, as well. In taverns and coffee houses, news of the day was discussed. Towns were also the centers of colonial publishing. Colonists enjoyed reading histories and travel accounts. Newspapers also were published in the colonies beginning in the 1720s. However, these were not common even in England at that time, and there was no free press as we know it today.

There were problems in colonial towns, as well. Fire was always a danger because most houses were built of wood. Crime was hard to control since there were not enough police. The streets were dark and narrow, and often they were unpaved and filled with garbage. Still, the towns of colonial America were alive with people and possibilities unknown in England.

Section Review

1. What acts did England pass to try to control manufacturing in the colonies?
2. Why weren't there enough skilled workers in the colonies?
3. What were colonial towns like?

CHAPTER SUMMARY

Farming was the most important way of life in the colonies. New England farmers usually grew just enough for their own families. In the middle colonies, farms were larger and more productive. Indentured servants helped to raise extra crops and livestock for sale. In the southern colonies, cash crops such as tobacco, rice, and indigo were grown on plantations. Black slaves were brought to work in the fields.

Trade was vital to the colonies. The Navigation Acts tried to limit the colonies to trading only with England. Important trade items included ships, naval stores, fish, furs, and rum. In the triangular trade, rum was traded in Africa for gold and slaves. These were traded in the West Indies for molasses and money. In turn, these were shipped back to New England. Since money was scarce, trade with the West Indies and Europe was essential.

Industry was also important in colonial life. England passed laws to control the manufacture of certain goods. These laws were largely ignored. Skilled workers were in great demand and earned high wages. Manufacturing added to the growth of towns, which were the centers of colonial life. Philadelphia, New York, Boston, Newport, and Charleston became the largest cities in the colonies.

Key Words

Write a sentence to explain the meaning of each of these terms.

coastal plain
subsistence
  farming
naval stores

breadbasket
  colonies
smuggling
manufacturing

Major Events

Choose the answer that best completes the statement.

1. Beginning in 1660, England passed a series of laws

   a) to control the flow of settlers to the colonies.
   b) to control colonial trade.
   c) to protect slaves.

2. The Pine Tree Shilling of 1652 angered the English because

   a) it made trade difficult.
   b) it did not show their king.
   c) they had not given the colonies the right to coin money.

3. During the 1660s, most colonial trade passed through

   a) Boston.
   b) New York.
   c) Charleston.

4. In 1699, the Wool Act

   a) stopped all exports of wool.
   b) allowed woolen goods to be sold only in the colony in which they were made.
   c) controlled the sale of sheep.

5. The Iron Act was passed in

   a) 1699.
   b) 1732.
   c) 1750.

Review

Important Facts

Answer each question with at least one complete sentence.

1. What is girdling?

2. What did it mean to be an indentured servant? Why did people become indentured servants?

3. Where did most slaves work? Why weren't they used everywhere?

4. On what was Georgia's economy supposed to be based? Why did this not work out?

5. Which nation's ships carried the largest share of trade with the colonies in the mid-1600s?

6. What restrictions did the Navigation Acts place on foreign goods going to the colonies?

7. How did most colonists feel about the Navigation Acts, and why?

8. Name one industry that was helped by the Navigation Acts.

9. Why did many New Englanders turn to manufacturing or trade as a way of making a living?

10. Boston was the center of which important New England industry?

11. Name some products of the naval stores industry.

12. How were skilled workers attracted to the colonies? Why was this practice needed?

13. What were the three most important laws England passed to control colonial manufacturing? How well were they obeyed?

Skill Review

Study the bar graph, then answer the following questions.

1. On the average, did the colonies import or export more goods?

2. What caused the trade imbalance?

3. What effect did the trade imbalance have on the colonies?

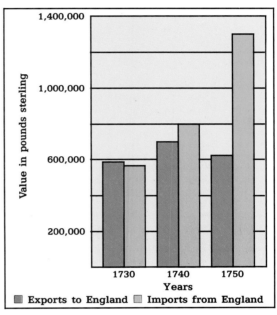

Colonial Trade with England

Critical Thinking

Write a paragraph to answer each question.

1. Compare farming in the three sections of colonial America. How did soil, climate, and weather differ? What kinds of crops and livestock were raised? How large were the farms in each section?

2. Why was the triangular trade important in the colonial economy?

5
Settlers from Many Lands

Years 1619–1760

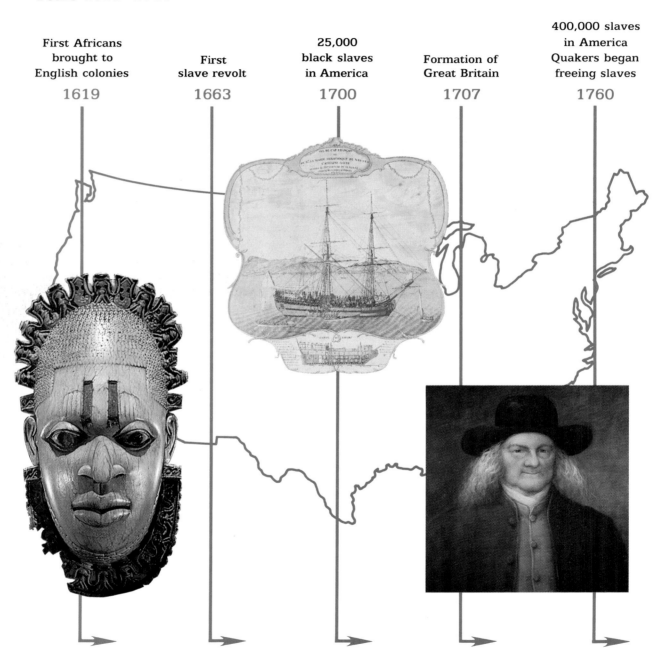

First Africans brought to English colonies
1619

First slave revolt
1663

25,000 black slaves in America
1700

Formation of Great Britain
1707

400,000 slaves in America Quakers began freeing slaves
1760

1. Newcomers to America

Learn these important terms:

immigrants
Scotch-Irish
Pennsylvania Dutch
Huguenots

Remember the main idea:

Immigrants came to America from many nations, and they came for different reasons. They brought new ideas and new ways of doing things.

Look for answers to these questions:

1. From which European nations did settlers come?
2. Why did these settlers come to America?
3. What is an immigrant? Where did immigrants settle?

From 1607 to about 1750, many influences were at work that shaped the growing colonies in America. People were arriving from all over Europe. They had different customs, languages, ideas, and ways of doing things. From Africa came other settlers—brought here against their will. These black slaves contributed to the growing life of the colonies, too.

Changes took place as the colonies absorbed these different people and what they brought with them. The colonies became less and less like the England that had been left behind. The land and weather were very different in places, of course. But the biggest differences had to do with the unique blend of people. Their customs and ideas were growing and changing the colonies.

For many people, the colonies offered opportunities which they never would have had in Europe. For others, the system of slavery brought an end to opportunity, freedom, and choice. This sharp contrast remained a part of America for a very long time.

During the 1600s, most of the settlers in the English colonies came from England. In general, those who were not English lived in the Dutch and Swedish colonies. These colonies were later taken over by the English. Thus, there were many Swedish settlers along the Delaware River and many Dutch settlers in New York.

Toward the end of the 1600s, settlers from all over Europe started coming to the English colonies. These settlers were called *immigrants* (IM-uh-gruhnts).

German Settlers

During the 1600s, Germany suffered from many wars. These wars destroyed

Johan Printz (1592-1663) is remembered as the first governor of Pennsylvania. He governed the area from 1643 to 1653, when it was known as New Sweden.

many farms and damaged trade and industry in Germany. At that time, Germany was not united under a single, powerful ruler. Instead, it was divided into hundreds of small states, each controlled by its own prince. Each German ruler taxed the people heavily. Often the ruler forced the people to attend the church he favored.

For these reasons many wanted to leave Germany. And because the colonies offered a chance for a better life, many Germans wanted to settle in America. However, most did not have the money to pay for their passage. Therefore, they agreed to let ship captains take them to America and then sell them as *indentured servants*. They had to work for a master or mistress for four to seven years. After serving their time, they were free to start their new lives in America.

In Germany and elsewhere in Europe, William Penn was advertising for settlers. Most German settlers were attracted by what Penn offered. They welcomed the opportunity to buy land cheaply and to worship as they wished. They settled in Pennsylvania in large numbers. Today descendants of these German settlers are still living in Pennsylvania and are known as *Pennsylvania Dutch*.

Other Germans settled along the western frontier of the middle and southern colonies, where land was cheapest. Wherever they settled, most German immigrants became farmers. They took great pride in their farms and were among the best farmers in the colonies. The German settlers lived close together and kept their own language and customs.

Think: These decorative letters from the *Ephrata ABC Book* are fine examples of Pennsylvania German folk art. Respond: How do they show the German settlers valued education?

Scotch-Irish Settlers

Another important group of immigrants who came to the English colonies were the *Scotch-Irish*. These settlers were descended from Scots who had moved to northern Ireland in the early 1600s. In Ireland, they had become farmers, cattle and sheep raisers, and woolen manufacturers.

The Scotch-Irish had many troubles in Ireland, though. The English government refused to let them sell their goods in England. Also, the Scotch-Irish were members of the Presbyterian (prez-buh-TEER-ee-un) Church and not members of the Church of England. For this reason, they were not allowed to serve in the English government or the English army. But, they were forced to pay taxes to support the Church of England.

These troubles led many Scotch-Irish people to immigrate to America during the 1700s. Like the Germans, many Scotch-Irish settlers came as indentured servants. They also settled first in Pennsylvania. Then some of them moved to the colonies in the South. Since few Scotch-Irish immigrants had money to buy land, however, most moved to unsettled land along the frontier.

Scots Immigrants

Another group of Scots, from the northern highlands of Scotland, also came to America. These Scots came because they did not like the English government.

In 1707, the government of England and the governments of Scotland and Wales were joined together. They formed the kingdom of Great Britain. Some Scots were against the joining of the countries. They refused to accept the English ruler as their king. Twice the Scots tried to throw off England's rule.

Think: England and Scotland became known as Great Britain in 1707. But many Highland Scots remained loyal to the Scottish throne. In 1745, the Highlanders revolted. Finally in 1746, the revolt ended when English troops won the decisive battle in Culloden Moor, shown here. Respond: How did this affect America?

Think: David and Phila Franks, shown here, were two of nine children in a Jewish family. Phila shocked her parents by marrying a Gentile. Respond: What family traditions would you find hard to change?

After a rebellion in 1745, the Scottish clans, or large family groups, were broken up. The English took their lands from them. Many Scots immigrated to America at this time. Some came on their own, but others were forced to leave Scotland by the English government. The largest number of them settled in North Carolina. Most of the Scots were farmers, but others were merchants or skilled workers.

French Settlers

A small but important group of European immigrants who came to the English

Think: Many people came to America to avoid religious persecution. These children were Huguenots, or French Protestants. Respond: What new ideas did these immigrants bring with them?

colonies were **Huguenots** (HYOO-guh-nahtz). The Huguenots were French Protestants, or non-Catholic Christians. In the late 1600s, the little religious freedom that they once had was taken away. They were no longer allowed to worship as they wished in France. Nor were they allowed to settle in the French colonies. Some Huguenots left France and settled in the larger towns of the English colonies along the Atlantic coast. Many Huguenots became rich and important citizens.

Immigrants Help the Colonies Grow

People from many other nations in Europe also settled in the English colonies. Jews fleeing religious persecution came to America. Other people from Ireland, Wales, and Switzerland came to make a better living or to worship as they wished. These European immigrants—like later immigrants—were very important to the growth of America. Immigrants brought new and better ways of farming, trading, and manufacturing with them. They helped develop the American idea that people from all European nations were free and equal in America.

Unfortunately, this freedom and equality did not extend to another group of people who came to America. Africans brought here against their will as slaves were not given freedom and equality. You will read about them in the next section.

Section Review

1. Why did many German settlers come to America during the late 1600s?

2. Who were the Scotch-Irish? Where did they settle?

3. What brought French Huguenots to America?

SKILLS FOCUS: Reading Line Graphs

If a colonial family wanted to record how much food they had stored for several winters, they might use a line graph similar to this one:

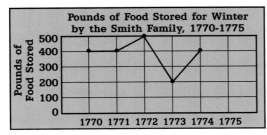

Pounds of Food Stored for Winter by the Smith Family, 1770-1775

The title of the graph tells what it is about. The numbers on the left of the graph stand for pounds of food. The numbers on the bottom of the graph tell the years. Sometimes these two locations for numbers on a graph are called the vertical axis and the horizontal axis.

You can see that the Smith family had 400 pounds of food stored for the winters of 1770 and 1771. In 1772, the Smiths had 500 pounds stored. The graph shows that 1774 might have been a difficult winter for the family since only 200 pounds of food were stored. By the following winter, food storage had doubled to reach 400 pounds again.

The line graph shows one way of recording information. It could help the Smith family compare their winter food storage year by year.

The line graph below shows how the population of the colonies grew between 1650 and 1770. Look at the graph and answer these questions.

1 What do the numbers on the left side of the graph stand for?

2 What do the numbers on the bottom of the graph stand for?

3 How many people were living in the colonies in 1650? In 1770? (Remember that the numbers are shown in thousands.)

4 How can you tell that the population of the colonies kept growing each year?

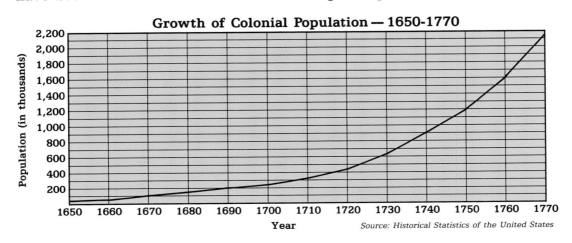

Growth of Colonial Population — 1650-1770

Population (in thousands)

Year

Source: Historical Statistics of the United States

2. Slavery in the Colonies

Learn these important terms:

middle passage
slavers

Remember the main idea:

Slavery began in the English colonies because of the need for workers. Thousands of Africans were brought to America against their will and used as slaves.

Look for answers to these questions:

1. What rights did the first blacks in America have?
2. How did the slave population grow in the English colonies?
3. What was it like for slaves being brought to the New World?

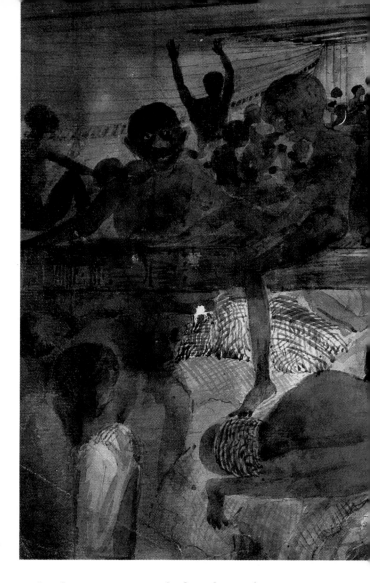

Sailors said that death hung around the *slaver* ships that carried African slaves to the New World. The conditions aboard these ships were cruel almost beyond belief. What led people to treat other human beings in this way? Profit is the answer. Slavery offered a cheap, constant source of workers and larger profits for plantation owners. Slavery grew with the plantation system.

The First Africans

In 1619, a Dutch ship arrived at Jamestown with twenty Africans. All twenty were sold to colonists as indentured servants. At first, the black indentured servants were treated much the same as white indentured servants. After a few years, they were given their freedom.

As the years passed, the plantation system grew. Southern planters found that indentured servants did not meet their need for workers. After serving their time, indentured servants were free to leave. Their masters or mistresses had to give them tools, clothes, and sometimes even land. In addition, indentured servants often ran away. They did not work to repay the debt for their passages.

For these reasons, southern planters began to look for other ways to get workers. They knew that Africans worked as slaves in the Spanish colonies. The planters thought that black Africans would be

ideal for many reasons. First, the Africans were used to a hot climate. Also, they would be easy to identify if they ran away. As a result of these thoughts, the status of blacks in America began to change.

First, laws were passed that forced black indentured servants to work for longer periods of time than white indentured servants. Before long, black indentured servants became servants for life. Their children also were made servants for life. By the 1660s, Virginia and Maryland had passed laws that made blacks slaves rather than indentured servants. And soon, all the other English colonies passed laws

Think: Some people who came to America did not do so by choice. Africans were captured from their homes and shipped to America. Respond: What might these people have been thinking?

that allowed slavery. Even so, at this time, many free blacks were still found in the English colonies.

Slaves were considered property. Plantation owners could keep their slaves for life. A slave's children and grandchildren also became the property of the owner. As a result, owners no longer had to train new workers to replace those gaining their freedom. Furthermore, new slaves

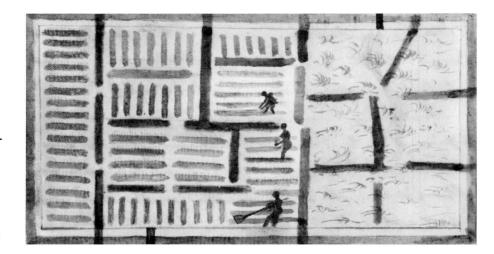

Think: **This drawing of sugar and rice fields (c. 1793) accompanied Samuel Gamble's description of farming techniques.** Respond: **Why weren't these crops profitable without slaves?**

no longer had to be bought since they were being born on the plantations. This system of slavery was very profitable for southern planters.

The Growth of Slavery in the Colonies

During the 1600s, not many slaves were brought to America. By the year 1700, about 25,000 black slaves lived in the English colonies. White indentured servants were still the largest group of workers in the colonies. But after 1700, thousands of slaves were brought to the southern colonies. By 1760, the number of slaves living in the English colonies increased to almost 400,000. This was about one-sixth of all the people in the colonies. Most of these slaves lived in the southern colonies and worked on the large tobacco, rice, and indigo plantations. In fact, two out of every three people in South Carolina were black.

The Africans who came to colonial America did so against their will. Many of them came from highly civilized black nations in western Africa. Most were farmers. That is one reason why they were in great demand as slaves in the colonies. However, many of the people of Africa had other skills as well. A number of them hunted, fished, or raised cattle. Many Africans were especially skilled as metalworkers, weavers, jewelers, artists, and woodcarvers.

The Roots of Slavery

Slavery was not a completely new idea to the people of Africa. For centuries,

Think: **When slaves were taken from present-day Benin, it was an advanced kingdom named Dahomey. There, beautiful pieces of art like these were made.** Respond: **What other art forms do these pieces tell about?**

HISTORY MAKERS

Olaudah Equiano

Victim of Slave Traders

"Five, four, three, two, one! Ready or not, here I come!"

The boy lifted his head and looked around, searching for his little sister's hiding place. He heard a rustling in the bushes and saw branches move. He tiptoed toward the sound. Suddenly, he was jerked off his feet! A hand over his mouth smothered his yell. He saw his sister struggling to free herself. He filled with fear. He and his sister had been captured by slave traders. Who knew what was in store?

Olaudah Equiano was eleven when he was kidnapped and sold to an English slave trader. He was terrified when he boarded the slave ship, sure that the English, ". . . these ugly men," were cannibals who were going to eat him. He had heard such stories, and worse. And where were they taking him?

On board the slave ship, some of the crew grabbed Olaudah and threw him back and forth like a rubber ball, ". . . to see if I were sound. . . ." Later food was brought, but he was so frightened and sick he couldn't swallow. Two sailors held Olaudah down and whipped him, forcing him to eat. Finally the ship's captain took on as many captives as he could, and the ship sailed west. A long voyage was ahead.

The Middle Passage, the trip from Africa to the West Indies, was the worst part of the voyage. It lasted six to ten weeks. The slaves were crammed below decks and chained so they couldn't move. There was very little air. The death rate on slave ships could be as high as 50 percent. Diseases spread quickly in the tight quarters, and starvation also claimed many victims.

When he reached America, Olaudah Equiano became a slave on a plantation in Virginia. Later he was sold to a sea captain. He learned to read and write, and he bought his freedom. As a free man, Olaudah Equiano became active in the anti-slavery movement. He published *The Interesting Narrative of the Life Of Olaudah Equiano or Gustavas Vassa, Written by Himself.* It is a powerful record of the horrors of slavery.

Think: Packed into transport ships, captured Africans were scarcely able to move and received little food and fresh air. Respond: Why did slave traders treat people this way?

Arab slave traders had captured and sold African slaves. Some African nations made slaves of other blacks whom they captured in wars. But only in the English colonies in America was the slave trade so large—or so cruel.

Captured slaves were often forced to march hundreds of miles to the coast of Africa. Many Africans died or were killed during this long march. Once they reached the coast, the slaves who lived through the march were branded. Then they were sold to a merchant or a sea captain. Thus they were ready to be taken to the New World.

The Middle Passage

Everything about slavery was terrible, but perhaps the worst part was called the *middle passage*. This was the long, inhuman voyage to the New World aboard the slaver ship. The slaves were chained together below the ship's decks. The captain tried to cram as many slaves as possible into this area. Each slave had a space about five feet long, sixteen inches wide, and three feet high. Slaves had to endure this crowding together, with no room to stand or stretch, for the entire voyage. A voyage could take two months or longer.

Many slaves did not live through the trip. Some slaves died from rotten food. Others died from sickness that spread quickly in the unsanitary holds of the ship. Sometimes the slaves tried to take over their ship, but these efforts almost always failed.

Arrival in the New World

During the colonial period, most slaves were first brought to the West Indies. There they were broken in by older slaves. The new slaves were separated from others of their own tribes. They were forced to speak English and to give up their African habits and customs.

During this time, the new slaves were taught their duties. They learned that they were no longer treated as human beings, but were considered property. They no longer had rights or freedom. This period lasted from one to three years. Only about half the slaves lived through these hard times. Those who did wondered what would happen to them in the land to which they were bound. In the next section, you will read what slave life was like in the English colonies.

Section Review

1. How did the legal rights of black Africans change during the colonial period?

2. About how large was the black population in the English colonies by the mid-1700s?

3. What was the middle passage? Why was it feared?

3. Slave Life

Most slaves got their first look at the English colonies from a slave auction block in Charleston, South Carolina. There, the slaves were bought by owners or their representatives. Although no slave had any rights or freedoms, the conditions under which slaves lived varied.

The Slave Codes

By law, slaves were considered property. The owners could treat the slaves as they wished. No matter how badly they were treated, the slaves had nowhere to turn for help. Nor were slaves allowed to own property.

Slave owners could sell or rent their slaves to other owners at any time. Since the children of slaves belonged to the owners, families were often broken up. Often owners would sell children or adult slaves without any regard for the families. Husbands, wives, and children were often separated, perhaps never to see one another again. These harsh practices made slavery in the English colonies the cruelest type of slavery in history.

All the English colonies in America passed *slave codes,* or laws to control the lives of slaves. These codes made it a crime for a slave to leave the plantation without the owner's permission. Some

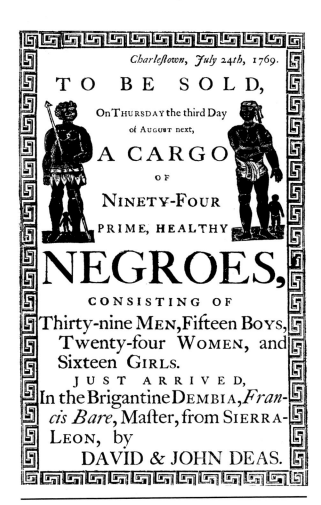

Think: **This 1769 advertisement informed people about the sale of newly arrived Africans.** Respond: **Today, what does this ad tell us about the rights of these immigrants?**

punishments for running away or for breaking any of the slave codes included whipping and branding.

As the slave population grew, the slave codes became harsher. Whites were always afraid that the slaves would rise up against their owners. In the South, where slaves often outnumbered whites, this fear was very strong.

The Search for Freedom

Many slaves who came to America tried to get their freedom. Some slaves ran away from their masters. Some tried to slow down the work on the plantation by breaking their tools or starting fires. Some slaves even killed their masters.

But what the southern planters feared most was a *slave revolt*, or uprising. As early as 1663, slaves in Virginia planned a revolt. This was the first of many slave revolts in the English colonies in America. During the colonial period, slave revolts broke out in New England and in New York, as well as in the South. Usually, many slaves who were fighting for their freedom, and even some who were not, were killed when these revolts were put

Think: Both men and women slaves labored hard in the fields, as shown in this painting by Benj. Henry Latrobe. Most field workers were unskilled. They were not valued as much as skilled slaves, nor treated as well as house slaves. Respond: If unskilled slaves ran away, could they support themselves? Explain.

Think: Very few slaves were lucky enough to be made house servants. Generally, house servants were treated better than the field hands. They also received better food and clothing. Respond: Why do you think the plantation owners treated the slaves who were around their families and guests better than the other slaves?

down. During the 1730s in South Carolina, the death rate of slaves may have been greater than the birth rate, largely because of the cruelty with which slave revolts were put down.

Freedom was hard to win for a slave in the English colonies, especially in the southern colonies. As the system of slavery became fixed, free blacks were considered a threat to the system. Virginia passed a law that all freed slaves had to leave the colony. Most owners never freed any of their slaves.

The one way that slaves could gain their freedom was to buy it. But since most slaves never were allowed to earn money, this did not happen often. When it did, it was usually because an owner hired out a slave to another plantation and let the slave keep part of the money the owner received for the slave's work.

This system was different from slavery in the Spanish colonies. There slaves were often given free time to earn money of their own. When a slave had saved enough money, he or she could buy freedom. Also, in the Spanish colonies, own-

ers often celebrated special family events such as births and marriages by freeing one or more slaves.

Daily Life for Slaves

Not all slaves were treated alike. How they were treated depended greatly on their jobs and owners or overseers. *House servants* were generally dressed and fed better than other slaves. They worked as cooks, maids, and coachmen in the master's house. House slaves were treated better than other slaves by the master and his family.

Certain slaves were taught such trades as tailoring, bricklaying, and carpentry. Since these skills were in demand, the slaves in these trades were generally treated well.

Most slaves were *field hands,* or the slaves who did the farm work on the plantation. Field hands were treated the worst of all slaves. They were worked the hardest, were cared for the least, and were punished the most cruelly.

Slave children did not attend school. Instead, as early as they were able, they

NATIONAL ORIGINS OF THE COLONISTS, 1770

Thematic maps give you information on a single topic. For example, a thematic map might show tobacco plantations in colonial times. From this information, you could see how important tobacco was to one region of the colonies. Look for the topic of a thematic map in its title. What kind of information will you get from the thematic map on this page?

A thematic map uses symbols to present its information. In this map, different colors are symbols for the different countries of origin of the colonists. Use the map key to find out what each color means. What does orange stand for? What color shows people of African origin?

Now use the key to read the map itself. In the key, find the color for settlers of Dutch origin. Then find this color on the map. Where did most people of Dutch origin settle? From your reading, why do you think they settled in this area?

Use the map and key to answer these questions.

1. Which group was most widespread throughout the colonies?

2. Where did people of Welsh origin settle?

3. Which group of people settled on the western frontier?

4. Where did most people of African background live? Why did they live there and not in other regions?

5. From a look at the map, can you tell which country had the greatest number of settlers in America?

6. Which group settled along the Hudson River?

7. Which group settled farthest north? Which group settled farthest south? How many miles separated the two settlements?

8. Which group had the smallest area of settlements?

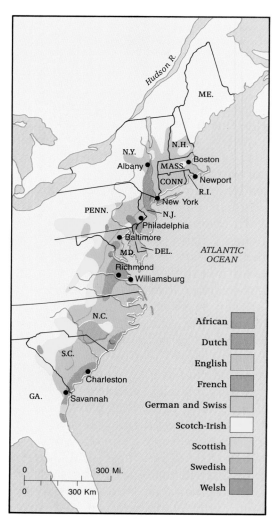

were expected to work. They led the oxen in the fields and did other chores.

Food, Clothing, and Shelter for Slaves

The food that a slave ate depended on the kind of work the slave did. House slaves often ate food that was left over from the master's table. Other slaves ate corn meal, salt pork, and bacon—the cheapest foods. A few masters let their slaves have small gardens.

House servants sometimes wore the old clothes of the master and his family. Other slaves wore clothes that they made out of the cheapest and longest wearing cloth. Most slaves wore shoes and jackets only during the winter.

Moses Brown, shown in this portrait attributed to Henry Kinney, heeded the message of fellow Quaker John Woolman. Brown became an abolitionist in the 1770s and set his slaves free.

House slaves often lived in small attic rooms in the master's house. Other slaves lived in houses or cabins that were poorly made. Usually these small huts had dirt floors, no windows, and few pieces of furniture. Few houses had beds in them. Often many slaves were crowded together in these huts. Too many people crowded together in these dirty places caused sickness and death among the slaves.

Indian Slaves

Although most slaves in the English colonies were black, there were also Indian slaves, especially in the Carolinas. Indian slaves were sold to traders in the West Indies, too. The English thought that it was not wrong to treat non-Christian, non-European people in this way. Moreover, they saw the advantage of having dark-skinned slaves. Runaways would be easy to spot. Any black or Indian was presumed to be a runaway slave unless he or she had papers to show otherwise.

Opposition to Slavery

Outside the southern colonies, there were people who spoke out against slavery. After 1760, many Quakers began freeing their slaves at the urging of John Woolman, a Quaker leader from New Jersey. And in New England, the Puritan influence had kept the number of slaves small. Only about one out of every fifty New Englanders was a slave.

Section Review

1. What were the slave codes?
2. Why was it hard for slaves to gain their freedom?
3. In what ways were house slaves treated differently than other types of slaves?

CHAPTER SUMMARY

During the colonial period, many new non-English settlers arrived in the colonies. Most of these new immigrants came as indentured servants.

In the late 1600s, large numbers of Germans came to America. First they settled in Pennsylvania, where they had been drawn by William Penn's advertisements. Later, Germans moved to land along the frontier.

Scotch-Irish immigrants came to America in large numbers, too. They came first to Pennsylvania. Then they, too, moved to unsettled lands along the frontier.

The Scots also came to the English colonies. They came following a war in which England took over Scotland and broke up many of the clans. Most Scots settled in North Carolina.

French Huguenots came to the New World in order to find religious freedom. Jews and settlers from many other nations in Europe also helped the colonies grow. Each group added its own customs and ideas.

By far the largest number of non-English people who came to the colonies were Africans. They were brought here against their will to provide cheap, constant labor for the plantations.

Slavery robbed the Africans of all their freedom. Slaves were considered possessions and had no rights of their own.

Key Words

Write a sentence to explain the meaning of each of these terms.

immigrants   *slave revolt*
middle passage   *field hands*
house servants

Major Events

Choose the answer that best completes the statement.

1. In 1745, a rebellion in that land brought many immigrants from
   a) Scotland.
   b) Ireland.
   c) France.

2. In 1619,
   a) the first Germans came to America.
   b) the first Africans were brought to America as servants.
   c) the first Huguenots came to America.

3. By the 1660s, laws making blacks slaves had been passed by
   a) Georgia and the Carolinas.
   b) Virginia and Maryland.
   c) Virginia and the Carolinas.

4. By 1760, slaves in the English colonies numbered about
   a) 400,000.
   b) 500,000.
   c) 750,000.

5. In 1707, Great Britain was formed by joining the governments of
   a) England and France.
   b) Scotland and Wales.
   c) England, Scotland, and Wales.

Review

Important Facts

Answer each question with at least one complete sentence.

1. From what nation did most early settlers of America come?

2. Why did many Swedes settle along the Delaware River?

3. When did many settlers from all over Europe begin to come to America?

4. Why did many immigrants settle first in Pennsylvania?

5. When was the big wave of Scotch-Irish immigration? Why did so many Scotch-Irish people come to the colonies?

6. Who were the Huguenots? Where did they settle in the colonies?

7. Which immigrant groups settled along the western frontier? Why did they go there?

8. What was a slaver?

9. Describe the conditions under which Africans were brought to the New World.

10. What factors determined how a slave was treated?

11. What were slave codes?

12. How did white colonists react to slave revolts?

13. Why was it hard for slaves in the English colonies to gain their freedom?

14. In which sections of the colonies was the number of slaves the lowest, and why?

Skill Review

Study the line graph, then answer the following questions.

1. In 1650, there were 1,600 blacks in the colonies. How many years later were there about ten times as many?

2. What was the black population of the colonies in 1730?

3. During which decade did the black population of the colonies increase the most? How much was this increase?

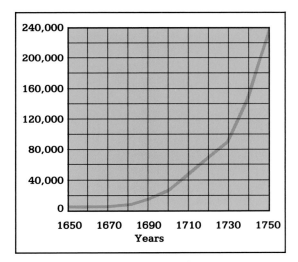

Black Population

Critical Thinking

Write a paragraph to answer each question.

1. What are some of the reasons for coming to America that were shared by various immigrant groups?

2. What factors contributed to the growth of the system of slavery?

CHAPTER

6

Life in the Colonies

Years 1640–1775

Massachusetts required all parents to teach their children to read

1642

Massachusetts required all towns to have schools

1647

Bacon's Rebellion

1676

Frontier about 100 miles from coast

1700

Boston News-Letter founded

1704

Frontier at the Appalachian Mountains

1775

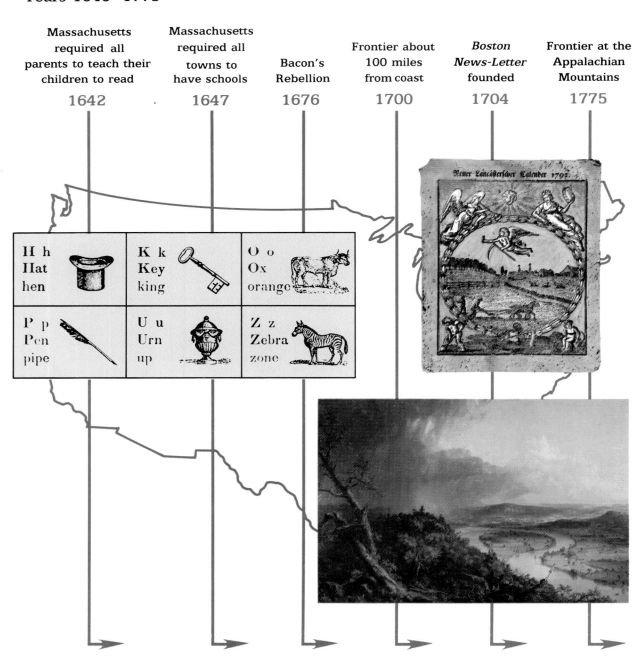

1. Daily Life in the Colonies

Learn these important terms:

social classes
work ethic
upward mobility

Remember the main idea:

Colonists belonged to social classes, but it was easy to change one's social class. For the most part, colonists had good homes, plenty of food, and enough leisure time to enjoy themselves.

Look for the answers to these questions:

1. In what ways were the lives of colonists better than those of people in England or Europe?
2. In what ways did colonists have fewer choices than Americans have today?
3. How did the English colonists spend their time?

Young people growing up in the countries of Europe during the 1600s and 1700s knew what their lives would be like. They knew they would live as their parents and grandparents had lived. Manners and traditions set the tone for their lives, and there was little chance for change.

On the other side of the Atlantic, life in the English colonies was full of change. With many opportunities for cheap land and high-paying work, people did not have to follow in the footsteps of their parents. Former servants could own their own land. Skilled craftspeople could go into business for themselves. Manners and traditions were adapted to fit new situations in the New World.

In this chapter, you will read how new land, new jobs, and new customs influenced the colonists' daily lives. You will see how big a part change played in the lives of the colonists. Styles, ideas about religion and education, even the size of the colonies—these things changed constantly. The colonies truly were a New World.

Imagine living in the English colonies 250 years ago. Where would you live? What would you eat? What kinds of clothes would you wear? And how would you spend your days? Would you have much free time? Life in the colonies was very different from life in America today. In many respects, people had fewer choices about their lives. But on the other hand, the colonists had more choices and better lives than most people in other places had at the time. The colonists could take advantage of change.

Think: *The James McCormick Family* was painted by the famous black artist Joshua Johnston in 1805. Cameras were not in use at that time. Having an artist paint your portrait took time. However, it was the only way to reproduce your likeness. Respond: Why was having your portrait painted a status symbol?

Social Classes

In the English colonies in America, people belonged to groups, or *social classes*, according to their position in society. One class of people—the slaves—were set apart from the rest of society. Other colonists belonged to one of three classes— the upper class, the middle class, and the lower class.

The upper class was made up of large landowners, rich merchants, church leaders, lawyers, and doctors. In the middle class were farmers, small businesspeople, and skilled workers. The lower class included unskilled city workers and farm laborers.

Although these class divisions were similar to those in England, they were different in one important way. In America, it was fairly easy for a person from a lower social class to climb to a higher one. Even people who came to the colonies as indentured servants were able to become members of the upper class. This easy movement from a lower class to a higher class, called **upward mobility**, helped make America a land of opportunity for people from Europe. Slaves were the only people who were not able to improve their lives. And most free blacks were not allowed to become a part of any of the three social classes.

The Value of Work

In the English colonies in America, labor was valued very highly. The colonists' religion taught that it was immoral not to work, unless you were unable. Also, because there was a shortage of workers, wages were higher in the colonies than in England or Europe. As a result, workers had a higher sense of their own worth. They were more respected in the colonies than in the Old World. Finally, work was seen as a way of rising to a higher social class. If you could learn a skill and become very good at it, you might "better" yourself in society. So a strong *work ethic*, or emphasis on the value and benefit of labor, developed.

Marriage and Family Life

Marriage in colonial days was different from what it is today. Rich families decided whom their sons or daughters would marry. They did this because marriage was a way to join together two large farms or two large fortunes. In all colonial families, children had to receive their parents' permission to marry. Once a couple was married, it was almost impossible for them to separate.

Family life was very important in the colonies. Most colonists married younger than people in Europe. Men usually married by the age of twenty-five, while women married at about age twenty-one. Large families with ten to fifteen children were common. This was the custom in Europe as well. It insured that, even if many children died, the family would still survive. However, fewer children died young in the colonies than in Europe. Therefore, the size of colonial families was slightly larger.

Family size was important to the success of a colonial family. Most families lived on farms where they grew their own food and made their own clothes, soap,

Think: **Women did not have as many choices in colonial times as they have now.** Respond: **In what ways does this tapestry picturing a wedding symbolize ways in which women were limited?**

candles, and almost all of the other things they used. A large family was needed for a farm to do well. Without many children, there simply were not enough hands to do all the work.

Even if the family owned a business instead of a farm, many helpers were needed. Children did all kinds of chores, and boys were taught the trade. Women often helped by working in the family-owned shop.

Think: **These poor colonial children sold fruit to earn money.** Respond: **In what ways were things different for America's lower class than for Europe's lower class?**

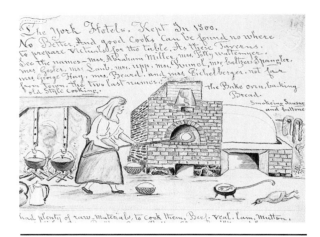

Think: **The kitchen of a York, Pennsylvania, inn is shown in this scene by Miller, a local artist. Notice the variety of foods cooking.** Respond: **How does this kitchen compare to today's?**

Food and Beverages

Colonial Americans had plenty of wheat, fish, meat, fruits, corn, and other vegetables to eat. In this way, they were better off than many Europeans at the time. Americans ate and drank a lot. Beer, apple cider, and rum were the favorite drinks. Rich colonists often drank wine and brandy from Europe.

Keeping food from spoiling was an important problem because people in colonial days did not have refrigerators. Vegetables such as potatoes and turnips were stored in cool cellars. Some foods, such as pork, were salted. Others were dried or pickled to keep them from spoiling. Meat and fish were kept from spoiling by smoking them over large fires. Smoking also gave foods a good flavor.

Ice was a luxury in colonial times. Each winter, colonists sawed off huge pieces of ice from frozen lakes and ponds. These blocks of ice were stored deep in the ground, covered with straw. In this way, ice would last through most of the year if it were used very sparingly. Those parts of the colonies where water did not freeze in winter paid generously for ice shipped there from other places.

Clothing

Wealthy people in the colonies followed the fashions in England and Europe. Most settlers, however, wore simple, home-made clothes made of strong materials. The men who lived on the frontier usually wore leather clothing and fur caps. Children wore clothes that were handed down from child to child until the clothes were completely worn out. Because cloth was expensive to buy and time-consuming to make, most colonists had few clothes.

Think: **For the most part, clothes were homemade from homegrown materials.** Respond: **Why was the ability to spin yarn and own a spinning wheel important in colonial times?**

SKILLS FOCUS: Learning from Pictures

In the section you just read, daily life in the colonies was described. For example, you learned about marriage and family life, food and beverages, and the clothing worn by colonists. Although the words gave you good descriptions of these things, you also learned a great deal from the pictures in the section. Often pictures can give you information in a clearer way than words.

Study the picture below to learn more about the colonists' daily lives. Imagine what it would be like to be in the room. Then answer the questions.

1 What is the woman at the right side of the picture doing?

2 The girl at the fireplace is stirring something in an iron cooking pot. Where is the kitchen in this colonial house? Why?

3 Why do you think much of the daily life of a colonial home took place around the fireplace?

4 What is the woman at the left side of the picture doing?

5 Why do you suppose none of the people in the picture are just sitting and doing nothing?

Think: Beginning with the settlement in Jamestown, sturdy wooden huts served as homes for many colonists. Respond: Why were these huts small and made with few windows?

Housing

The first houses built in the colonies were very much like huts. In time, however, the colonists started to build wooden houses that were one or one-and-a-half stories high. Because these houses were heated by fireplaces, the ceilings were low and the windows were small to keep in the heat.

In the 1700s, colonists in the upper class started to build houses in the Georgian style. This style was popular in England. Georgian homes were often built of brick and were large and airy. Most people, however, lived in small, one-story wooden houses. Many settlers along the frontier built log cabins. This style of building had been brought to the colonies by Swedish settlers.

Entertainment

The people in the colonies found many ways to have a good time, even when there was work to be done. Get-togethers such as plowing parties, quilting bees, house-raisings, and cornhuskings were common. Colonists would share stories and news while tackling jobs that were easier when many people helped. Hunting and fishing were popular, and so were such sports as wrestling, foot racing, swimming, and shooting. Wealthy people took part in horse racing, outdoor bowling, and billiards.

Think: This detail from a mantle cloth shows wealthy New Jersey landowners fox hunting. The hunters and their dogs would rid the area of foxes. Respond: Why was this sport practical?

Section Review

1. How were social classes in the colonies similar to those in England? How were they different?
2. Why were large families important in the colonies?
3. What did colonial Americans do for entertainment?

2. Colonial Thought

Learn these important terms:

tutors	*academies*
literacy	*almanacs*
Great Awakening	*blue laws*

Remember the main idea:

Most colonists knew how to read and were interested in books, newspapers, and education. Religion was also important to the colonists.

Look for answers to these questions:

1. What kind of education did colonial children receive?
2. What were some of the earliest colleges built in the colonies?
3. What was the role of religion in the lives of the colonists?

People coming to the colonies from England or Europe traveled on crowded ships. There was only enough space for passengers to bring things that would be useful in their new lives. The immigrants had to make tough choices. Yet, many colonists brought books with them to the new land. From the very beginning, education and books were highly valued in the colonies. People wanted their children to know how to read and write.

Education in the Colonies

American colonists were better educated than most Europeans of their day. In England at that time, only children of the upper class went to school. They attended private schools or church schools. For a time, this same idea was followed in the English colonies in America. Only upper-class children went to school. Many of them also went to private schools or church schools. Others had *tutors*, or private teachers, who taught them at home. Often, they were sent to English colleges to finish their education.

At first, most colonial children who were not upper class did not go to school. Sometimes they were taught to read and write at the same time they were taught a trade. Girls seldom went to school. Instead, they stayed at home and were taught by their mothers to cook, sew, and care for children.

Think: **Lydia Church, age 13, made this sampler while studying the art of embroidery in 1791. Notice the variety of stitches.** Respond: **How did a girl's education compare to that of a boy?**

Think: **As shown in this painting of a classroom in Pennsylvania, colonial schools were far different from schools of today. For example, students of all ages and abilities were often in the same class.** Respond: **What other differences can you identify?**

Most boys went only to elementary school. The few who did attend high school studied Latin and Greek, which were required to get into college. Later, high schools called *academies* were started. They began to teach more useful subjects, such as mathematics, science, geography, and bookkeeping.

Public Schools

An important step in colonial education took place in the New England colonies. There, the idea that all children should go to school began. The Puritans believed that everyone had to learn to read the Bible. They also believed that people who had an education made better citizens and better workers. For these reasons, the Massachusetts legislature passed a law in 1642 that required all parents to see that their children learned to read.

Five years later, in 1647, Massachusetts passed a law that required each small town to set up an elementary school. Large towns had to set up both

Think: **Early textbooks, called primers, were quite different from today's texts. Study the picture for each letter on the primer page above.** Respond: **Which pictures are now outdated? Why?**

elementary schools and high schools. All the children in the towns had to attend these schools. Although these schools were supported by taxes, parents still had to pay small amounts of money for their children to attend.

In the South, where there were few towns, public schools were uncommon. Usually children were educated at home, on the plantation. Once in a while, black children were taught to read and write along with the children of the owner. But this was unusual, and in many places it was against the law to teach slaves to read and write.

Colleges in the Colonies

Colleges were started in the colonies. At first they were set up to train ministers. Harvard, in Massachusetts, was the first. It was founded in 1636. Next came William and Mary, in Virginia, and Yale, in Connecticut. Later, six other colleges were started in the colonies. These new colleges began to offer courses in science, mathematics, and history. The colleges in the colonies were attended by many young men who later became colonial leaders. During this period, women could not attend colleges or universities.

Literacy, Books, and Newspapers

Literacy, or the ability to read, was fairly widespread in the colonies, compared with England or Europe. Many colonists could read—and the most widely read book was the Bible. *Almanacs* (ALL-muh-naks) were the most popular books in the colonies. Almanacs are books that contain stories, jokes, calendars, and helpful ideas for farmers. They are somewhat like today's magazines.

The first successful American newspaper, founded in 1704, was the *Boston News-Letter*. Many other newspapers soon appeared. Most of these colonial newspapers were printed once a week. They contained colonial news, European news, and advertisements.

Reading material was always highly prized and in short supply in the colonies. Therefore, many towns opened public libraries where colonists were able to borrow books at little or no cost.

Although most books came to the colonies from England, some books were written by colonists. American colonial writers wrote about religion, the history of the colonies, travels, and adventures with the Indians.

Religious Life

As you remember, religion had played an important part in founding many of the colonies. Colonial governments passed laws extending the influence of religion into people's lives. All the New England colonies except Rhode Island, and all the

Phillis Wheatley (c. 1753-1784), a slave whose owners educated her, was America's first black woman poet. She won praise for her work, including a poem she wrote to George Washington.

From the collections of Henry Ford Museum & Greenfield Village

Think: **This quilt shows worshipers attending church in a colonial town.** Respond: **What role did religion play in the early days of America?**

southern colonies had an official church. Everyone was supposed to attend this church. Most colonies also passed *blue laws*. These laws forbade dancing, drinking, playing games or sports, and taking part in other amusements on Sunday.

While colonial people followed these laws, their intense personal interest in religion seemed to drop off by the early 1700s. Those who moved westward were farther away from the established church. Many of the newcomers did not belong to the established church, either. Church leaders like Jonathan Edwards often commented that religion no longer guided young people's behavior.

But in the 1730s and 1740s, a new religious movement began. It was called the *Great Awakening*. This movement appealed to people's consciences and sparked a revival of interest in religion. Thousands of colonists began to go to church again. Many new religious groups were formed. As a result, there was greater freedom of religion.

The Great Awakening also helped education. New colleges were set up to train ministers and teachers. Greater activity in church affairs led many colonists to become more involved in government, too.

Arts and Sciences

Many colonial college graduates became ministers, but others became doctors and lawyers. A few Americans became scientists. The most famous of them was Benjamin Franklin of Philadelphia. Franklin developed a stove, reading glasses, and the famous lightning rod, in addition to publishing his almanac.

The American colonies also had some famous painters. Painters usually learned their art from other artists. Most early American artists painted portraits for a living. The two most famous colonial artists were John Singleton Copley and Benjamin West, both of whom painted portraits of wealthy colonists in eastern cities. Portraits of colonists who lived along the frontier would have looked quite different. There, life was much harder. In the next section, you will read about colonial life along the frontier.

Section Review

1. How did public education begin in America?
2. What things did people in the colonies read most often?
3. What was the Great Awakening?

HISTORY MAKERS

Benjamin Franklin

A Man of Many Talents

A group of men strolled along the bank of the stream, laughing and chatting. "How is your scientific work coming, Mr. Franklin?" asked one of the men, seriously.

"Ah, sir," replied his friend, "I have made an amazing discovery! As a result of some of my experiments, I have developed rare powers. For example, I can calm rough water simply by waving my cane over it."

"Indeed, sir! Show us! The wind has whipped up the brook water. Tame the waves!"

Benjamin Franklin stood at the edge of the brook and swung his cane back and forth. The water became smooth and calm.

His friends were amazed until Franklin showed them that his cane was hollow and filled with oil. When he waved the cane, the oil coated the water and smoothed it. Franklin learned the trick when experimenting with ways to help ships caught in stormy seas.

Benjamin Franklin was a man of enormous talents. He was a scientist whose inventions include the lightening rod, the Franklin stove, and the bifocal lens. He helped to establish a college, a medical school, fire brigades, and the United States post office.

Franklin was a printer, newspaper publisher, and writer. As a statesman, he represented the colonies in England and in France, helped to write the Declaration of Independence and the Constitution, and negotiated the treaty that finally brought an end to the American Revolution.

Franklin had a lively sense of humor. In *Poor Richard's Almanac*, his annual book of advice, astrology, information, proverbs, and weather predictions, Franklin wrote witty sayings. Examples include "Three can keep a secret if two are dead" and "Fish and visitors smell after three days."

Franklin's first concern was to help people better their lives. He was especially concerned about slaves. At eighty-two, Franklin was elected president of the Pennsylvania anti-slavery society. In 1790, he urged the first Congress to abolish slavery. And his last publication, *On the Slave-Trade*, made fun of arguments that defended slavery.

3. The Frontier

Learn these important terms:

pioneers   *Appalachian*
Bacon's   *Mountains*
  Rebellion   *Paxton Boys*
Regulators   *surplus*

Remember the main idea:

The American frontier was settled by pioneer farmers who developed new ideas about freedom and equality. They often disagreed with the eastern colonists.

Look for answers to these questions:

1. Who were the first people to settle the frontier?
2. What needs did the pioneers have that were not shared by the eastern colonists?
3. How did the frontier settlers win some of the things they wanted?

The first settlers in the New World were pioneers, in a sense. They left the world they knew to forge new lives. They braved dangers both known and unknown. But when we speak of *pioneers*, we are usually referring to people who settled the American frontier. These people left the relative comfort of the cities and towns of the East. They moved to the back country, far away from other people, from supplies, from safety. They had to cope with loneliness, hostile Indians, and their own lack of knowledge about the land. In many ways, these pioneers were different from colonists in the East.

Settling the Frontier

In the 1600s, most of the Atlantic coast was covered with forests. At that time, this area was the frontier, or unsettled land, in the colonies. By the early 1700s, the frontier was only about 100 miles inland. But by 1775, the frontier was as far west as the **Appalachian Mountains** (AP-uh-LAY-chun). By this time, about 250,000 people lived on the frontier.

At first, hunters and fur traders moved to the frontier. Later, they were followed by the colonists who settled the frontier lands—the pioneer farmers. Most pioneer farmers were European immigrants who settled in the western parts of the middle and southern colonies. They cut clearings in the forests and set up farms there. At first, they raised just enough food for themselves and their families. In time, however, pioneer farmers were able to grow more crops. Then they sold the **surplus**, or what they did not need, in the eastern part of the colonies.

The Pioneer Life

Most settlers on the frontier lived a different kind of life from colonists in the older settlements in the East. Frontier homes were smaller. Clothing and food were plainer, since pioneers had little chance to buy goods.

Life was hard on the frontier. As a result, the settlers had to make their own rules for getting along from day to day. Scotch-Irish, Germans, and Scots worked together, and they began to feel equal to one another. However, they were not as wealthy as people in the East and did not feel that they were being treated equally by them.

Differences Between Western and Eastern Colonists

Distance made any communication between the frontier and the East difficult.

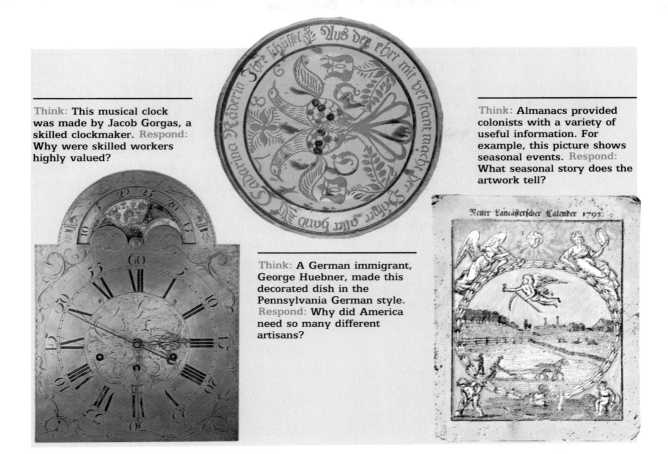

Think: **This musical clock was made by Jacob Gorgas, a skilled clockmaker.** Respond: **Why were skilled workers highly valued?**

Think: **Almanacs provided colonists with a variety of useful information. For example, this picture shows seasonal events.** Respond: **What seasonal story does the artwork tell?**

Think: **A German immigrant, George Huebner, made this decorated dish in the Pennsylvania German style.** Respond: **Why did America need so many different artisans?**

Different points of view developed, and distance prevented people from talking over differences and working them out. Bad feelings developed between the western settlers in each colony and the colonial governments. Frontier colonists felt that they were not allowed to elect enough members to the legislatures. They believed that the eastern colonists controlled the colonial governments.

The western settlers also felt that the eastern colonists did not do enough to help protect them from Indian attacks. And western settlers were angry because the legislatures refused to build roads to the frontier lands. Without roads, the western farmers were not able to send their crops to the East, or to buy the goods they needed.

The frontier settlers who lived in the southern colonies had another gripe. They did not like to pay taxes to support the official church in the eastern part of the colonies. Many of them did not belong to this church.

For all these reasons, hard feelings grew between the western settlers and the eastern colonists. These feelings would result in violence.

Think: **Many heated debates took place during town meetings. Argument was a part of growth in the colonies.** Respond: **How could meetings like this one be seen as the roots of American government?**

FRONTIER OF THE COLONIES

Historical maps tell you about trends and events in history. They can tell you what happened, where it happened, and when it happened. The title of the map will tell you the subject or event treated in the map.

Look at this map. What is the subject of the map? Is it a trend or an event? Look at the map key. What does each color stand for? Notice the map scale. What can this scale tell you about the frontier of the colonies?

Look now at the map itself. What symbols are on the map? What do these symbols stand for?

Use the map key, map scale, and symbols to answer the following questions.

1. What did the mountains mean to the frontier in 1700? What had changed by 1775?

2. How far westward from Jamestown did the frontier move between 1700 and 1775?

3. In which colonies were new settlements made between 1700 and 1775?

4. Which cities were settled between 1700 and 1775? Were any cities settled in the mountains?

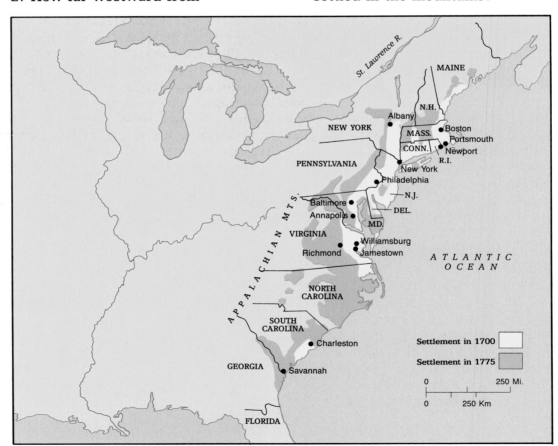

Bacon's Rebellion

In 1676, disagreement between Virginia colonists and frontier settlers erupted into a fight. **Bacon's Rebellion**, as the uprising was called, was caused by the western settlers' unhappiness with the Virginia government. They were angry because many pioneer settlers had been killed by Indians and the governor refused to send soldiers to protect them. The pioneers also felt that they did not have enough members in the Virginia legislature. In addition, they were unhappy with the high taxes and the low prices they received for tobacco.

Nathanial Bacon, a young Virginia settler, led the rebellion. First, he defeated the Indians. Then, he took control of Jamestown. However, Bacon died suddenly, and the rebellion failed. But the pioneers got what they wanted. The Indians were defeated, and western settlers were allowed to elect more members to the legislature.

Trouble in Pennsylvania and North Carolina

Trouble between eastern and frontier settlers took place in other colonies, too, over the same issues. In Pennsylvania, a group of western farmers called **Paxton Boys** (named for a town in western Pennsylvania) marched on Philadelphia to force the legislature to treat them more fairly. Benjamin Franklin met them and was able to talk them into going back home. In return, they were promised more members in the legislature.

In North Carolina, the trouble between the western settlers and the eastern colonists was not settled as easily. There, the frontierspeople were unhappy about the same issues—lack of protection from Indian attacks, too few members in the legislature, and high taxes. These farmers formed a group called the **Regulators**.

Think: Highly educated and well respected by his followers, Nathaniel Bacon fought for the rights of frontier settlers. Respond: What changes did he help bring about?

The governor of North Carolina raised an army that fought and defeated the Regulators. Many of them then left the colony.

Government was at the center of many of the differences between frontier settlers and eastern colonists. You have read how frontierspeople fought for representation in colonial governments. In the next chapter, you will read about how those governments were organized.

Section Review

1. Where was the frontier in the early 1700s? Where was it by 1775?
2. Which issues divided eastern colonists and the pioneers on the frontier?
3. What was Bacon's Rebellion?

CHAPTER SUMMARY

Three classes developed in colonial society according to wealth and occupation. A colonist could move to a higher class through skill and hard work. Slaves were outside the social classes.

The family was very important in colonial life. Large families were more successful because they had more people to do the work.

In general, the colonists were better fed, clothed, and housed than people in Europe at the time. Often, colonists grew their own food and made their own clothing and other things that they used. Colonists worked hard, but they also had leisure time.

Colonists were better educated than their European counterparts. Massachusetts set up public schools, and nine colleges were built in the colonies before Independence. However, girls were taught at home.

Religion played an important role in colonial life. In the 1730s, the Great Awakening brought increased involvement in churches.

The frontier moved westward. In 1700, it was about 100 miles from the Atlantic coast. It had shifted to the Appalachian Mountains by 1775. Important differences arose between western pioneers and eastern colonists. Problems occurred in Virginia, Pennsylvania, and North Carolina. Several times fights broke out.

Key Words

Write a sentence to explain the meaning of each of these terms.

social classes　　*work ethic*
literacy　　　　　*almanacs*
pioneers　　　　　*Appalachian*
blue laws　　　　　*Mountains*

Major Events

Choose the answer that best completes the statement.

1. Massachusetts passed a law that required towns to set up public schools in

   a) 1647.
   b) 1657.
   c) 1667.

2. The first college to be built in the colonies was

   a) William and Mary.
   b) Yale.
   c) Harvard.

3. The first successful newspaper in the colonies was founded in Boston

   a) in 1700.
   b) in 1724.
   c) in 1704.

4. The religious movement that swept the colonies in the 1730s was called

   a) the New Day.
   b) the Great Awakening.
   c) the Great Revival.

5. By 1775, the colonial frontier was

   a) 100 miles inland.
   b) the Appalachian Mountains.
   c) the Mississippi River.

Review

Important Facts

Answer each question with at least one complete sentence.

1. Into what three groups was colonial society divided? How did the groups differ from one another?

2. Where did slaves stand in relation to the three groups above? Why?

3. What is upward mobility? Was it different in the colonies than in Europe? Why, or why not?

4. What is the work ethic? What factors made it an important part of colonial life?

5. At what ages did colonial men and women marry? How did colonial marriages differ from modern marriages?

6. What were the early colonists' houses like? How did frontier homes differ from others?

7. What were some common colonial entertainments?

8. What subjects were taught in colonial academies?

9. How did colonial girls' education differ from boys'?

10. What caused Bacon's Rebellion? What outcome did it have?

11. Who were the Paxton Boys? What did they want? How did they achieve their goals?

12. Who were the Regulators? How were they like people in Pennsylvania and North Carolina? How were they different?

Skill Review

Look at the picture carefully, then answer the following questions.

1. To which social class or classes do these people belong?

2. Which details reveal social class in this picture?

Critical Thinking

Write a paragraph to answer each question.

1. Why was the family unit so important in colonial America? What effect did this have on colonial life?

2. Imagine that you are a frontier settler in Virginia, and that you are speaking before the House of Burgesses. State your concerns and how you want them resolved.

Important People

Choose the answer that best completes the statement.

1. The colonists learned many farming skills from

   a) the Indians.
   b) indentured servants.
   c) black slaves.

2. The settlers who came to the English colonies from all over Europe were called

   a) Huguenots.
   b) indentured servants.
   c) immigrants.

3. The Germans who settled in America were

   a) non-Catholic Christians.
   b) the best farmers in the colonies.
   c) merchants and skilled workers.

4. By the mid-1700s, the largest population group in South Carolina was

   a) Scottish.
   b) French.
   c) black.

5. The most famous American scientist of colonial times was

   a) Benjamin Franklin.
   b) John Singleton Copley.
   c) Benjamin West.

6. The leader of a pioneer rebellion in Virginia was

   a) Benjamin West.
   b) Nathanial Bacon.
   c) Paul Paxton.

Main Ideas

Choose the answer that best completes the statement.

1. Rocky soil and a short growing season meant that most New England farmers were

   a) commercial farmers.
   b) subsistence farmers.
   c) coastal farmers.

2. The middle colonies were known as the

   a) trading colonies.
   b) cash crop colonies.
   c) breadbasket colonies.

3. The Navigation Acts were passed

   a) to control colonial trade and to benefit England.
   b) to boost the colonial shipbuilding industry.
   c) to protect colonial industries from foreign competition.

4. Commercial industries in the colonies included

   a) mining and soap.
   b) lumber and mining.
   c) candles and lumber.

5. People came to the colonies from many parts of Europe

   a) to escape religious persecution and heavy taxes.
   b) to make a better living and to become landowners.
   c) Both of the above are correct.

6. The English colonies began to practice slavery because

   a) of the need for workers.
   b) indentured servants would not work as hard as slaves.

Review

c) the number of people coming to the colonies began to decline.

7. The long, inhuman voyage to the New World aboard a slave ship was called

   a) seasoning.
   b) the nightmare.
   c) the middle passage.

8. All slaves

   a) were poorly dressed and undernourished.
   b) were considered property.
   c) worked in the fields.

9. In America

   a) people found it easier to change their social class than in England.
   b) the upper class was larger than England's upper class.
   c) married couples tended to have more children than married couples in England.

10. Most colonists

    a) were free to choose a marriage partner.
    b) lived in log cabins.
    c) valued education and books highly.

11. Western settlers complained that eastern settlers

    a) did not involve themselves in the government of each colony.
    b) did not help protect them from Indian attacks.
    c) did not pay their fair share of taxes.

History Skills

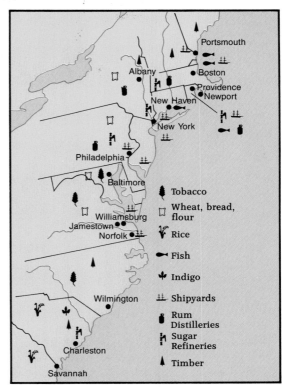

Colonial Products 1750

Choose the answer that best completes the statement.

1. A thematic map shows

   a) only one topic.
   b) events and trends.
   c) trade routes and products.

2. The state most heavily involved in the triangular trade was

   a) New Jersey.
   b) South Carolina.
   c) Rhode Island.

3. Georgia's main product was

   a) silk.
   b) rice.
   c) indigo.

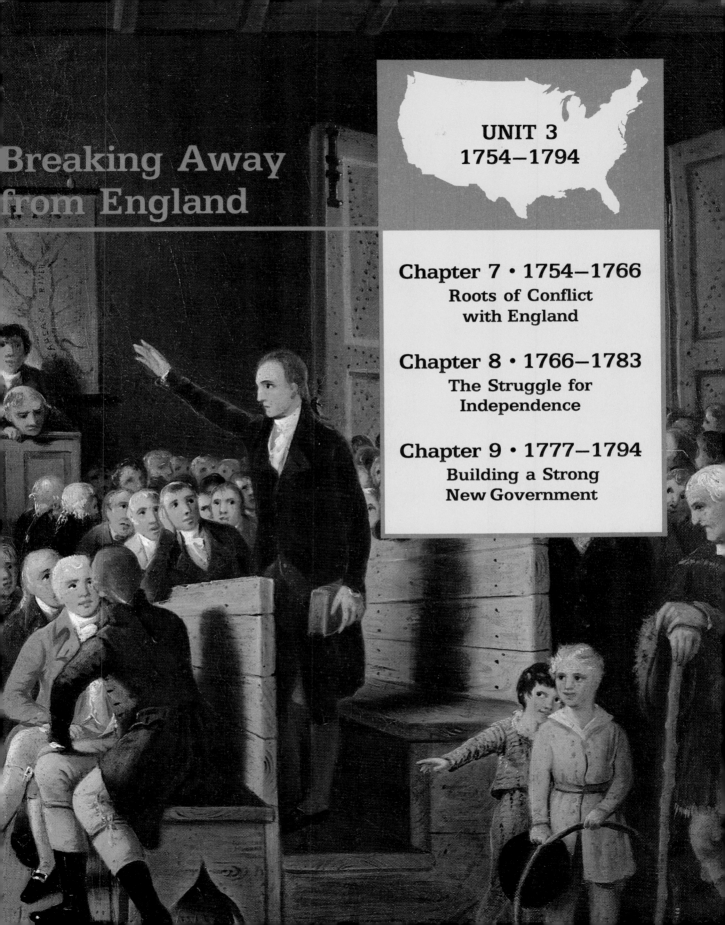

Breaking Away from England

Chapter

7
Roots of Conflict with England

Years 1754–1766

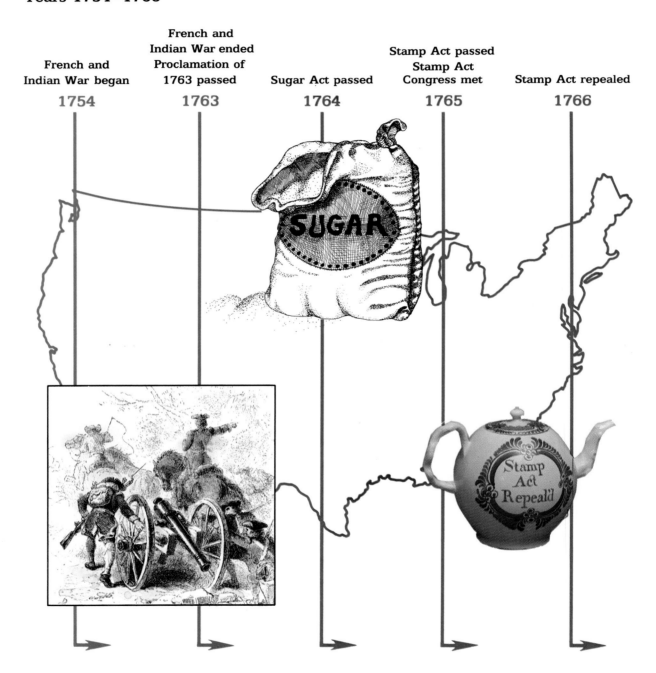

French and
Indian War began

1754

French and
Indian War ended
Proclamation of
1763 passed

1763

Sugar Act passed

1764

Stamp Act passed
Stamp Act
Congress met

1765

Stamp Act repealed

1766

SUGAR

Stamp
Act
Repeal'd

1. Colonists and Their Government

Have you ever moved to a new place? At first you probably still thought of yourself as being from your old neighborhood or town. Then you gradually began to see yourself as part of your new community.

Settlers in the English colonies went through the same process. At first, they thought of themselves only as English citizens. But after a while in the New World, they felt different from the English. While they still recognized their English heritage, they knew that life in the colonies had changed them. Some of their needs were different from those of people in England. They began to think of themselves as Americans. Yet, they were still English citizens.

This double identity led to problems in government. On the one hand, the colonists expected to have all the rights of other English citizens. As you will see in this chapter, colonial governments had their foundation in English tradition. On the other hand, the king treated the colonists differently than English citizens at home.

A dilemma was growing for the colonists. How could they be loyal to the king and protect their own interests at the same time? In this chapter, you will see how the relationship between England and the colonial governments changed after a war against France.

Learn these important terms:

Parliament
House of Lords
governor's council
disallow
veto
House of Commons
assembly
Board of Trade

Remember the main idea:

The English colonists played an important part in their government through their elected lawmaking assemblies.

Look for answers to these questions:

1. Who headed the government of an English colony?
2. How were colonial laws made?
3. What was the Board of Trade? Why was it important?

The government of the English colonies resembled the government of England in some ways. At the head of the English government was the king. He ruled with the help of his advisors, the Privy Council. However, the king's power was limited by *Parliament*, the English lawmaking body. Parliament had the right to pass laws, set taxes, and control the military forces of England. The king could not *veto*, or turn down, a law passed by Parliament.

Parliament had (and still has) two parts, or houses. Members of the upper house, the *House of Lords*, were nobles

Think: The House of Lords is the upper house of the British Parliament. It is made up of powerful nobles. When the Bill of Rights was passed in 1689, most of the power of the House of Lords was taken away. The grand Chamber of the House of Lords is shown here. Respond: In what ways were the House of Lords and the governor's council alike?

who inherited their positions. Members of the lower house, the **House of Commons**, were elected by landowners. The House of Commons gradually became the more powerful branch of Parliament.

Colonial Governors

At the head of each colonial government was a governor. In the self-governing colonies of Rhode Island and Connecticut, voters elected the governor. In the proprietary colonies of Maryland, Pennsylvania, and Delaware, the owners of the colony chose the governor. The remaining eight colonies were owned by the king, who appointed the governor.

In all thirteen English colonies, the duties and powers of a governor were about the same. The governor of a colony called for meetings of the legislature. He had to approve all laws before they were passed. If he disagreed with a law, he could veto that law. Each governor appointed judges and other colonial officials. He also commanded the armed forces. In addition, a governor had great control over the trade of his colony and over Indian matters.

The **governor's council**, like the king's Privy Council, helped to rule. Each council was made up of a small number of men. They usually were the richest and most important people in the colony. The governor's council often served as the highest court in the colony. In most of the colonies, members of the council were appointed, not elected.

Colonial Legislatures

Like Parliament, colonial legislatures had two houses. The governor's council was the upper house of the legislature. Its job was to approve all laws before they were passed.

More powerful, however, was the lower house of the legislature, called the *assembly*. In all the English colonies, the members of an assembly were elected by the voters.

Colonial assemblies had many of the same rights as the House of Commons. Each assembly won the right to make laws for its colony and to discuss freely all matters of importance to the colony. A colonial assembly also had the right to help its governor set up courts and to decide how it wanted to carry on business

Think: **The Chamber of the House of Commons is shown here. The House of Commons became the more powerful of the two houses of Parliament in 1689. All of its members are elected by the voters. Because of this, the House of Commons represents the people.** Respond: **In what ways were the House of Commons and the colonial assembly alike?**

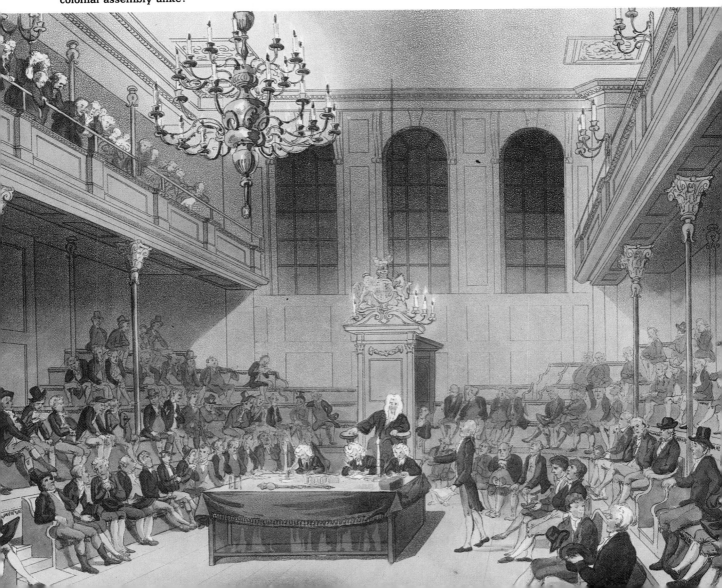

HISTORY MAKERS

Alexander Spotswood

The Knight of the Golden Horseshoe

A group of well-dressed men stood at the docks in Williamsburg, Virginia. As they spoke, they looked down the river for the ship bringing the new Deputy-Governor of Virginia.

"Well, gentlemen, after five years of long-distance rule from London, our colony will have a resident governor again," said one man. "I've heard good things about this new man!"

"Pray sir, share your information!"

"Alexander Spotswood is a military man, gentlemen, new to politics. He was appointed deputy-governor by Queen Anne, since our governor, The Earl of Orkney, will not live in the colonies. Spotswood and Orkney will share the governor's salary. Spotswood is said to be interested and concerned about the problems and the future of Virginia and, indeed, about all our British colonies in this land."

Alexander Spotswood was one of the best governors the colony of Virginia had. Spotswood worked hard to encourage trade, education, and treaties with the Indian tribes. He developed the mining and smelting of iron as a Virginia industry.

Spotswood also worried about the increasing number of French settlements in North America. He encouraged British settlement on the Virginia frontiers, and he led an expedition to explore the western boundaries of the Virginia colony. Spotswood gave each member of his expedition a small golden pin shaped like a horseshoe and set with jewels. The members of his expedition were known as Knights of the Golden Horseshoe.

In 1718, Spotswood, using his own money, sent ships to capture "dead or alive" the pirate Black Beard. He and his crew had been plundering ships along the mid-Atlantic coast. Governor Spotswood wanted to make the seas safe for trade. The Virginians defeated the pirates and killed Black Beard.

Although Spotswood worked hard for the Virginia colony, he was forced out of office after disagreements with the Governor's Council and the Virginia House of Burgesses.

While deputy-governor, Spotswood complained about the independent attitudes of Virginians, but he chose to stay in Virginia after his governorship. It was the land he had grown to love.

in the assembly. Most important, only the colonial assemblies had the right to raise money by passing tax laws.

An assembly's control over money and taxes in a colony made each assembly very powerful. If an assembly did not like what a governor did, it refused to pass tax laws to pay his salary. Most governors tried to get along with their assemblies.

Colonial Voters and Their Rights

Because their governments were similar to that of the Mother Country, English colonists believed they shared the rights of English people. The right to trial by jury was one of these rights. Perhaps most important was the right of landowners to vote for representatives to Parliament. Through their elected spokespeople, voters could help set tax laws and control government policy.

Not all colonists had the right to vote for members of their colonial assembly. Only free white men, usually twenty-one years of age or older, could vote. By the 1700s, colonists also had to own a certain amount of land or have a certain income to vote. Many colonies refused to give the right to vote to Catholics, Quakers, and Jews. None of the colonies gave Indians, slaves, free black men, or women the right to vote.

Think: Benjamin Franklin influenced the way people thought in Europe as well as in the colonies. Franklin is shown here addressing the Lords of the Privy Council in London. He was a publisher, civic leader, scientist, inventor, and statesman. Jefferson described him as "the greatest man . . . of the age and country in which he lived." Respond: Tell why you agree or disagree with Jefferson's statement.

English Control of the Colonies

Although they were thousands of miles away from England, the colonies were not independent of English control. The English king thought of the colonists as English subjects. He appointed members of his Privy Council to help him control the colonies. This group, known as the **Board of Trade**, kept a close watch on all colonial matters.

The Board of Trade paid special attention to business and government in the colonies. It checked over all colonial laws. If it did not like a colonial law, it suggested that the king **disallow**, or overturn, the law. The king did not disallow many colonial laws. When he did, the law usually disagreed with an English law or hurt English business interests.

The colonists became very angry whenever the king turned down a colonial law. While they accepted their responsibilities as English subjects, they expected to have the same rights as people in England. There the king could not veto an act of the legislature.

As you read the rest of this chapter, you will see how the tug of war between England and her colonies continued. You will read how the colonies helped England win a war, then resisted British taxes to pay for that war.

Section Review

1. What was the governor's council? What did it do?
2. Which branch of a colonial legislature was more powerful? Why?
3. Who could vote in colonial elections? Who could not vote?
4. How was the government of the colonies like the government of England? How was it different?

---

2. The French and Indian War

Learn these important terms:

Albany Congress
Proclamation of 1763
Albany Plan of Union
peace treaty

Remember the main idea:

The British gained a large part of North America by winning the French and Indian War. The colonists were unhappy because the British refused to allow them to settle in the Ohio Valley.

Look for answers to these questions:

1. Why did the French and the British go to war in 1754?
2. What was the outcome of the French and Indian War?
3. How did the war affect the English colonies?

In the 1700s the British and the French were rivals. Each wanted to be stronger and richer than the other. They fought several wars in Europe without ending the rivalry. Each country wanted to expand its colonies in the New World to strengthen its position. When England, or Great Britain as it became after 1707, and France claimed the same territories in the 1750s, war broke out again. This time, however, many of the battles were fought in North America.

Causes of the War

Both Great Britain and France wanted to own Nova Scotia because of the rich fishing waters along its coast. The fishing industry was a profitable one. Both nations also wanted the Ohio Valley, located west of the Appalachian Mountains. France needed the Ohio Valley to connect the French settlements in Canada and Louisiana. France also wanted to protect its valuable fur trade in the Ohio Valley. However, Great Britain wanted its colonists to settle there and control the profitable fur trade.

The French government sent soldiers to the Ohio Valley to build forts. In 1754, the governor of Virginia wanted the French soldiers to leave the Ohio Valley. He sent a young Virginia colonist named George Washington to deliver the orders. But the French refused to leave. So, Washington and his soldiers fought several small battles with the French. These battles began the French and Indian War.

In this war, Indians were the allies of the French. The Indians had fought several wars to stop British settlement and had lost. They joined the French in hopes of holding onto their land. Unlike the British, the French let the Indians continue their way of life. The French built trading posts and forts, but they did not force the Indians to move away.

The Albany Congress

After the war began, the British government called for a meeting of the colonies at Albany, New York. The British had two goals for this meeting, known as the *Albany Congress*. They wanted to win the support of the Iroquois Indians in the war. They wanted to organize the colonies to help fight the war.

The Iroquois were more willing than the colonies and promised to help the

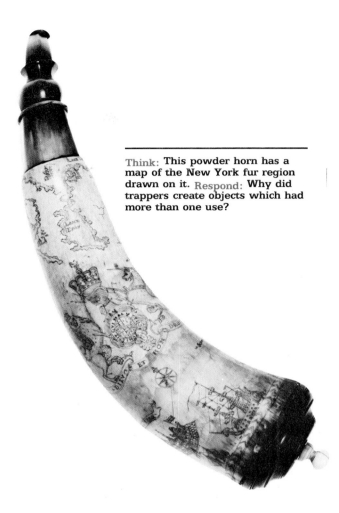

Think: This powder horn has a map of the New York fur region drawn on it. Respond: Why did trappers create objects which had more than one use?

British. The colonies, on the other hand, rejected Benjamin Franklin's plan to join together to fight the war. This plan was known as the *Albany Plan of Union.* It was unpopular because none of the colonies wanted to give up power to a central government. Nor did the colonies want to pay taxes for joint defense.

British Victory

The French and Indian War began badly for Great Britain. In 1755, General Edward Braddock, the British commander-in-chief, and more than one thousand soldiers marched into the Ohio Valley to fight the French. But they were no match for the smaller force of Frenchmen and Indians. The British were attacked by surprise from behind rocks and trees. Braddock lost the battle and was killed. Other British generals also did poorly.

Then in 1756 William Pitt became the leader of Parliament. Pitt picked younger generals who fought in ways better suited to the American forests. Pitt also sent more men and supplies to North America, and he won more colonial help.

Pitt's ideas worked, and soon the British won battle after battle. The most important battle of the war was fought near Quebec. The city of Quebec was built on cliffs overlooking the St. Lawrence Riv-er. The British army, led by General James Wolfe, planned a night attack. Secretly, they climbed a steep footpath up the cliffs of the city and attacked the French. Taken by surprise, the French army was defeated. The British army captured Quebec. Sadly, both General Wolfe and the French leader, General Montcalm, were killed. Later, the British also took Montreal.

Spain entered the war in 1762 to help France, but it was too late. In 1763 the French gave up, and the war ended in victory for Great Britain.

Think: General Braddock's troops were caught in a flurry of gunfire as the French and Indians attacked from within the forest. The British were expecting far different tactics during a battle. They were used to facing their enemies on an open field. The French had adopted Indian tactics. Respond: **Why was it important for the British to learn new ways of fighting wars?**

Think: **Led by General Wolfe, British troops are shown attacking the French fort above the city of Quebec. Notice the path up the cliff by which the British entered the fort. Although the painting shows the battle taking place in daylight, the attack actually took place at night. After the fort fell, the city was easily captured.** Respond: **Why was capturing Quebec important to the British?**

British Gains in North America

In 1763 Great Britain signed a *peace treaty*, or an agreement ending the war, with France and Spain. This treaty gave the British all the French land east of the Mississippi River, except for the city of New Orleans. Canada, a French colony, and Florida, a Spanish colony, also became British colonies. (See the Map Workshop on page 132.) The colonists in North America no longer had to worry about attacks from the French in Canada. They could move into the Ohio Valley.

The Indians knew that the colonists planned to move onto their lands in the Ohio Valley. As a result, the Indians, led by the great chief Pontiac, attacked in 1763. They captured all the British forts

MAP WORKSHOP COMPARING MAPS

CHANGES IN NORTH AMERICA, 1754–1763

Sometimes maps can show information more clearly and quickly than words. Read the text section "British Gains in North America." Then look at these two maps carefully. Both the text and the maps tell how much land Great Britain gained after the French and Indian War. Comparing the maps will help you understand how greatly the British empire in North America changed in just nine years. Begin by looking for things that stay the same in the two maps. Then look for differences. In this way you will increase your understanding of the information in the text.

Study the map titled "North America in 1754." Then answer these questions.

1. Which European countries claimed land?

2. Where did each country claim land?

3. What part of the continent was unexplored?

Now look at the other map, "North

America in 1763." Compare each colored area with the area of the same color on the first map.

4. What has happened to the amount of land claimed by Great Britain?

5. How has the area of French territory changed?

6. Do the changes suggest a shift in power in North America? Why, or why not?

NORTH AMERICA IN 1754

NORTH AMERICA IN 1763

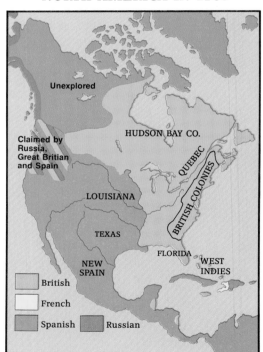

on the frontier except Detroit. Finally, after three years, Pontiac was forced to make peace.

No Settlement in the Ohio Valley

After the French and Indian War, Great Britain decided to keep settlers out of the Ohio Valley. The British government had three reasons for this decision. First of all, the British wanted to stop Indian attacks on the frontier. Second, the government wanted British fur traders to keep control of the fur trade in the Ohio Valley. Finally, the British government wanted to keep the colonists near the Atlantic coast. They needed the colonists along the coast to trade with Great Britain. They also wanted to force colonists to obey the Navigation Acts and the laws against manufacturing. If the colonists moved inland, British control would be lost.

For these reasons, the British government passed a law, the *Proclamation of 1763*. This proclamation outlawed settlement west of the Appalachian Mountains. Needless to say, the Proclamation of 1763 was very unpopular among the colonists. In the rest of this chapter you will read about other British actions which angered the colonists.

Section Review

1. Where are Nova Scotia and the Ohio Valley? Why were they important in 1754?
2. What was the Albany Plan of Union? Why did it fail?
3. What territory did Great Britain gain after winning the French and Indian War?
4. Why did the British issue the Proclamation of 1763? Why did the colonists dislike it?

3. Tighter English Control of Colonies

Learn these important terms:

admiralty courts
Sugar Act
Sons of Liberty
repeal
writs of assistance
Stamp Act
Stamp Act Congress

Remember the main idea:

Great Britain enforced the Navigation Acts and taxed the colonists to pay its war debt and defense costs. The colonists opposed the new tax laws because the colonies were not represented in Parliament.

Look for answers to these questions:

1. Why did Great Britain expect the colonists to help pay for the French and Indian War?
2. In what ways did Great Britain try to raise more money from the colonies?
3. What did the Sons of Liberty do?

Winning the French and Indian War gave Great Britain a great deal more land. But, it also created great problems. How would Great Britain pay off its large war debt? Moreover, how would it defend its newly expanded colonies?

Great Britain expected the colonies to help pay for the war because the colonies had profited from the British victory. Their western frontier was now safe from

Think: On trial, James Otis made the statement, "Taxation without representation is tyranny."
Respond: Why do you think the colonists felt so strongly about protecting their rights?

French and Indian attacks. Moreover, colonists had made much money selling food, ships, and supplies to the British during the war. It was clear to the leaders of Great Britain that they needed to raise money from the colonies. It was equally clear that to do so they needed to have greater control over them. These two needs led to serious disagreements between Great Britain and the colonies.

Strict Enforcement of the Navigation Acts

One way to get more money from the colonies was to enforce the Navigation Acts. These acts controlled colonial imports. Before the French and Indian War, the Navigation Acts had not been well enforced. Smuggling was common. After the war, British officials gave large rewards for information about smuggled goods. People accused of breaking the trade laws were now tried in *admiralty courts*. These were British, not colonial, courts and had no juries.

The British government also used *writs of assistance*, or search warrants, to enforce the Navigation Acts. The writs of assistance gave British officials the right to search a person's property. Houses, ships, and warehouses were searched for smuggled goods. The colonists believed the writs of assistance and the admiralty courts endangered their rights as free citizens. They were angered by them.

New Taxes

In addition to its war debt, the British government also had to pay for its army. Part of this army was still protecting the American frontier. To raise money, Parliament passed the *Sugar Act* in 1764. This law taxed sugar, molasses, and other products brought into the colonies from foreign countries. Businesses in New England and the Middle Colonies were hit hard by this tax. Sugar and molasses were an important part of their triangular trade. Many colonists talked of refusing to pay the tax. Others just continued their smuggling activities.

When the Sugar Act did not raise enough money, Parliament passed another tax law. This law, the *Stamp Act* of 1765, put a tax on many items. All newspapers, books, business and legal documents, calendars, and playing cards sold in the colonies were taxed. All these things had to be stamped to show that the tax had been paid.

Both the Sugar Act and the Stamp Act were unpopular in the colonies. In the

Think: In England the king could not veto, or turn down, a law passed by Parliament. When the king tried to veto colonial laws, colonists such as Patrick Henry, shown here, argued against this practice. Respond: Do you think the king should have been able to veto laws in the colonies and not in England? Explain.

past, Parliament had used taxes to control colonial trade. But the purpose of the Sugar Act was to raise money. In the past, only colonial legislatures had levied taxes on the colonists. Now Parliament, which had no colonial members, was taxing the colonists directly.

Resistance to the Stamp Act

The Stamp Act affected nearly everyone in the colonies, and no one liked it. Lawyers, newspaper and business people, and ministers were especially hit by the stamp tax. These were some of the most important people in the colonies. They helped to stir up many colonists. Before long, no one in the colonies was willing to pay the stamp tax. Some colonists formed the **Sons of Liberty**, a group of people against the tax. The Sons of Liberty often used force to make sure that no tax stamps were sold.

In October 1765, a group of leaders from nine colonies met in New York City. This meeting was called the **Stamp Act Congress**. The Stamp Act Congress asked

Think: Stamps, such as the two on the left, were marked on many items to show that the taxes on the items had been paid. Imagine having to pay taxes on every newspaper, magazine, poster, and book you bought. These taxes were sent to England, not used for the good of the colonies. The headline expresses the opinion of most colonists and some people in England who were against the Stamp Act. But British officials thought the tax was fair. Respond: Tell whose opinion you agree with and why.

SKILLS FOCUS: Understanding Two Sides of a Conflict

In this chapter you have read about several British actions which made the colonists angry. To understand why these disagreements grew into a conflict, it is helpful to look at the reasons each side gave for its position.

Begin with the issue of disallowing colonial laws. Reread the part of Section 1 under the heading "English Control of the Colonies." Now imagine that you are the king. You have just read a Massachusetts law that would mean lower profits for British businesses. You plan to disallow this law because colonies are supposed to help the mother country make money, not lose it. Furthermore, Massachusetts is a royal colony. You own it, and its people are your subjects. They must obey your rule.

Then think of yourself as a member of the Massachusetts assembly. You do not think the king has the right to disallow the law. The people of your colony have the same rights as people in England. There people elect representatives to Parliament, and the king cannot overturn a law passed by Parliament. Although colonists do not elect representatives to Parliament, they have their own elected legislatures. You believe that the king should not be able to overturn a law passed by a colonial legislature.

Copy the chart below on a separate piece of paper. The first issue has been done for you. Find and list reasons for each side on the second and third issues.

British Action	British Reasons for Action	Colonial Reasons Against Action
Disallowing a colonial law	Colonies are supposed to increase British profits, not colonies'. Colonists must obey king because they are his subjects; king owns colony.	Colonists are British citizens, with rights to representative government without royal veto over legislation.
Closing Ohio Valley to settlement	1	2
Using admiralty courts to try smugglers	3	4

OR THE FUNERAL OF MISS AME·STAMP

Think: "The Repeal or the Funeral of Miss Ame Stamp" is a political cartoon that was published in 1766, shortly after the repeal of the Stamp Act. The cartoon shows the buildings of several English ports. Notice the signs on the buildings and on the boxes, as well as the items carried by the English officials. Respond: What symbols can you find in the cartoon, and why is its name appropriate?

Parliament to *repeal*, or end, the Stamp Act. These colonial leaders said that Parliament had no right to tax the colonies because the colonists did not elect members to Parliament. Only the colonial legislatures had the right to tax the American colonies.

The Stamp Act Congress also asked colonists not to buy British goods as long as the Stamp Act was in force. Soon British merchants, manufacturers, and ship owners were losing a great deal of money without their colonial trade. They asked Parliament to repeal the tax, and in 1766 Parliament ended the Stamp Act.

Without the Stamp Act, Parliament needed other ways to tax and control the colonies. In the next chapter you will read about the actions of the British government which finally led the colonists to fight for their freedom.

Section Review

1. What were writs of assistance? How were they used?
2. What effect did the Sugar Act have on colonial businesses?
3. What was the purpose of the Stamp Act?
4. What did the Sons of Liberty do?
5. Why did Parliament repeal the Stamp Act?

CHAPTER SUMMARY

Colonial government was a delicate balance of power. The governor had the right to call the legislature into session. He could also veto any law. On the other hand, the assembly could refuse to pay the governor's salary. Only the assembly had the right to raise money by passing tax laws. Members of the assembly were elected by the voters.

English colonists believed they had the rights and responsibilities of English citizens. They supported England in a war against France to gain control of Nova Scotia and the Ohio Valley. However, colonial governments refused to join together under Benjamin Franklin's Albany Plan of Union. This plan proposed a central government which would collect money from the colonies.

England defeated France in 1763 and gained the disputed territory. The colonists were disappointed, however, when the English Proclamation of 1763 outlawed settlement of the Ohio Valley. They were further upset when England made changes in the way the colonies were governed after the war. To pay its debts, the English government began enforcing the Navigation Acts. In addition, Parliament passed the Sugar Act and the Stamp Act to tax the colonists. The colonies disliked these laws because they endangered their rights as Englishmen.

Key Words

Write a sentence to explain the meaning of each of these terms.

Parliament   *veto*
assembly   *Albany Plan*
admiralty courts   *of Union*
repeal

Major Events

Choose the answer that best completes the statement.

1. In the French and Indian War,
   a) the French fought against the Indians.
   b) the British fought against the colonists.
   c) the British fought against the French and their Indian allies.

2. To get support for the war, the British government
   a) called the Albany Congress.
   b) disallowed colonial laws.
   c) passed new Navigation Acts.

3. Under the peace treaty of 1763,
   a) Britain gained New Orleans.
   b) Canada became English.
   c) Indians were kept out of the Ohio Valley.

4. The Proclamation of 1763 stopped
   a) the French and Indian War.
   b) the colonial fur trade.
   c) settlement west of the Appalachian Mountains.

5. In October 1765, the Stamp Act
   a) was passed.
   b) was opposed by colonists.
   c) was repealed.

Review

Important Facts

Answer each question with at least one complete sentence.

1. What part did the colonists play in colonial government?

2. What powers did a colonial governor have?

3. What powers did colonial legislatures have?

4. Why were colonists angry when the King of England disallowed a colonial law?

5. Name two causes of the French and Indian War.

6. Why did colonial leaders oppose the Albany Plan of Union?

7. What were the results of the French and Indian War for Britain? For the colonies?

8. How did Chief Pontiac and his followers react to the outcome of the French and Indian War?

9. Name three reasons why the British government issued the Proclamation of 1763.

10. What problems did victory bring to the British?

11. How did the British attempt to solve these problems?

12. What were writs of assistance? Why did colonists oppose them?

13. How were the Stamp Act and the Sugar Act different from earlier laws passed by Parliament?

14. What methods did the colonists use to get Parliament to repeal the Stamp Act?

Skill Review

Complete the chart as you remember the two sides of the issues. Then answer the following questions.

1. Why did the British want strict enforcement of the Navigation Acts?

2. Why did Americans object to strict enforcement of the Navigation Acts?

3. How did each side feel about the Sugar Act?

	British View	American View
Strict enforcement of the Navigation Acts		
Sugar Act		

Critical Thinking

Write a paragraph to answer each question.

1. Why were the colonists unhappy with the Proclamation of 1763?

2. What reasons did Parliament have for passing the Stamp Act? What reasons did the colonists have for refusing to obey it?

8

The Struggle for Independence

Years 1766–1783

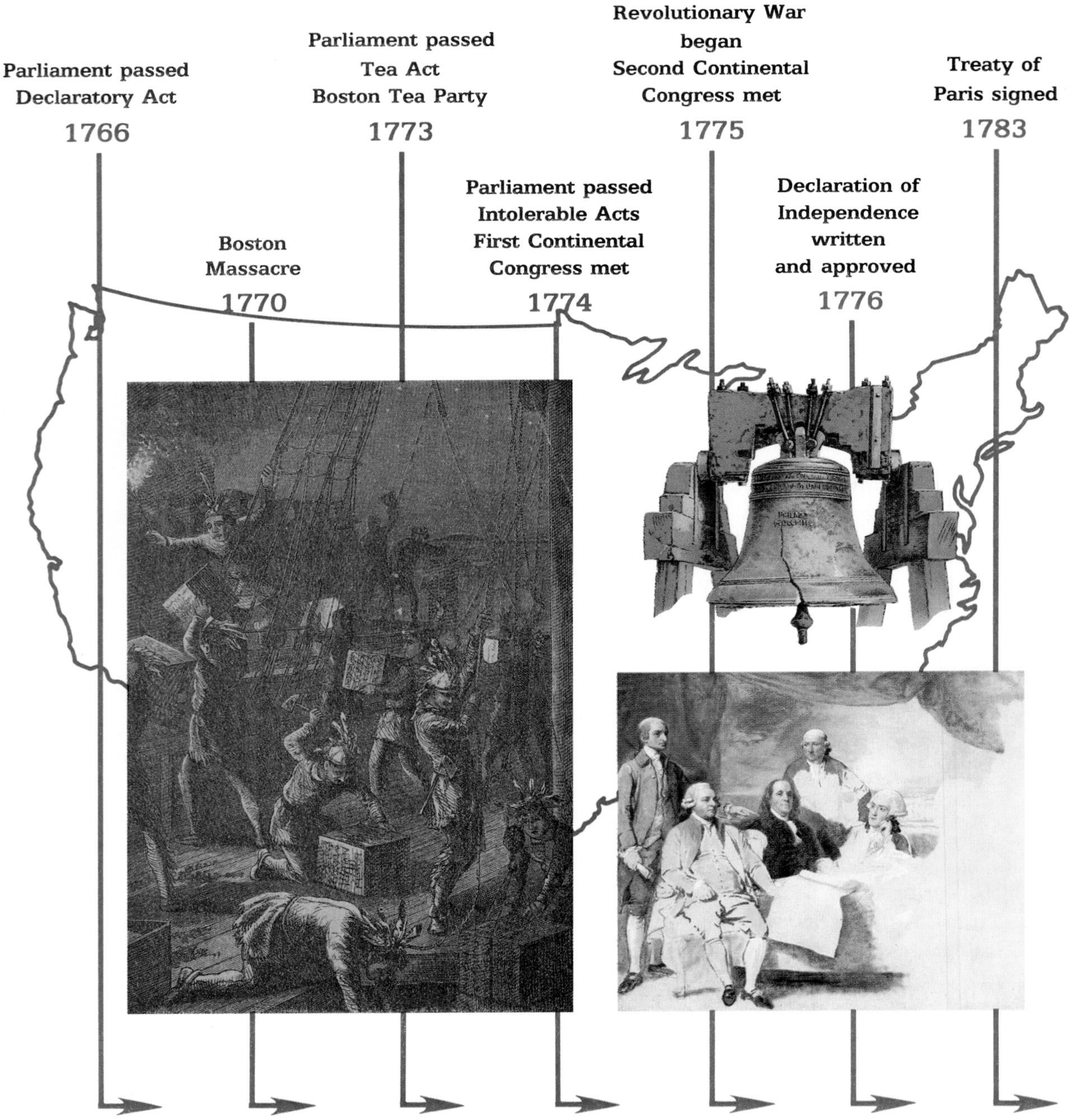

Parliament passed
Declaratory Act
1766

Parliament passed
Tea Act
Boston Tea Party
1773

Revolutionary War
began
Second Continental
Congress met
1775

Treaty of
Paris signed
1783

Boston
Massacre
1770

Parliament passed
Intolerable Acts
First Continental
Congress met
1774

Declaration of
Independence
written
and approved
1776

1. The Beginning of the Revolutionary War

Learn these important terms:

Declaratory Act
boycott
Tea Act
First Continental Congress
Boston Tea Party
Revolutionary War
Townshend Acts
Boston Massacre
Intolerable Acts
Minutemen
Committees of Correspondence

Remember the main idea:

The American colonies were unable to settle their differences with Great Britain peacefully. War broke out in 1775.

Look for answers to these questions:

1. What were some of the differences between the colonies and Great Britain?
2. How did the Boston Tea Party lead to the First Continental Congress?
3. Where and when did the Revolutionary War begin?

"Everyone complains about taxes, but nobody does anything" is an old saying. During America's struggle for independence from Great Britain, taxes became the key issue. But the colonists did indeed do something about taxes. "No taxation without representation" became their motto.

As you read this chapter, however, you will see that taxes were not the only problem. The colonists were angry about many things. More and more, the British were forcing themselves upon the colonists. British troops remained in the colonies. The colonists resented this visible presence. And the British made their presence felt in other ways, too. Their laws and restrictions angered the colonists. As you will see, their anger soon turned into violence. With that violence came war. And with war came independence for the colonies.

In this chapter, then, you will read about more than war. You will read about what the colonists gained. You will learn exactly what independence meant to the colonies.

Tensions between Great Britain and the colonies were high. When the Stamp Act was removed, the Americans felt they had won an important victory. But it soon became clear that the struggle for control of taxes and laws in the colonies was not yet over.

The Declaratory Act

On the same day that Parliament removed the Stamp Act, it passed the **Declaratory Act** (dih-KLAR-uh-tor-ee). This act said that Parliament had the right to pass any law it wished to make for the colonies. This was a very important act, but the colonists were distracted by the end of the Stamp Act. They failed to react to the new British law.

In 1767, however, Parliament passed new laws called the **Townshend Acts** (TOWN-zend). One of the Townshend Acts required colonists to provide housing for British troops. Other Townshend Acts put taxes on all glass, lead, paper, paint, and tea brought into the colonies. Part of the money gained from the taxes was to be used to support the British army in the colonies. The rest was to be used to pay the salaries of colonial governors.

The Townshend Acts were very unpopular with the colonists, who wanted control of the governors' salaries. Governors were appointed by the king. Controlling their pay was the only way to get them to pay attention to the colonists' needs. Colonists also resented the lodging of British troops in their villages and towns—especially at the colonists' expense.

To fight the Townshend Acts, the Sons of Liberty organized colonial merchants to **boycott**, or refuse to buy, British goods until the Acts were removed. The boycott was very effective. In 1770, all the Townshend Acts were repealed except the tax on tea.

The Boston Massacre

The presence of British troops in colonial towns often annoyed the colonists. The troops sometimes got out of line. Trouble was always a possibility. On March 5, 1770, that trouble broke out in Boston. A crowd of citizens started jeering and throwing snowballs at British troops. The situation got out of hand, and the British fired on the crowd. Five men were killed, including Crispus Attucks, a black seaman. He is sometimes considered the first victim of the Revolutionary War. But in fact, that war did not start for six years.

The **Boston Massacre**, as the fight was called, quickly became a rallying point for the Sons of Liberty. The leader of the Sons of Liberty was Samuel Adams. He was one of the earliest people to argue for independence from Great Britain. He published booklets about the British soldiers' killing of civilians.

Samuel Adams also helped to form **Committees of Correspondence** in Massachusetts, and soon the idea spread to other colonies. The Committees exchanged letters telling what was happening in the other colonies and in Great Britain. The Boston Massacre and the news brought by letters from the Committees convinced many colonists to turn against the British.

Samuel Adams (1722-1803) stirred up the patriots with his strong speeches and essays. When he signed the Declaration of Independence, Adams was happy to guarantee Americans their liberties.

The BLOODY MASSACRE perpetrated in King — Street BOSTON on March 5th 1770 by a party of the 29th REGt.

Engrav'd Printed & Sold by PAUL REVERE BOSTON

Unhappy Boston! see thy Sons deplore,
Thy hallow'd Walks besmear'd with guiltless Gore:
While faithless P—n and his savage Bands,
With murd'rous Rancour stretch their bloody Hands;
Like fierce Barbarians grinning o'er their Prey,
Approve the Carnage, and enjoy the Day.

If scalding drops from Rage from Anguish Wrung,
If speechless Sorrows lab'ring for a Tongue,
Or if a weeping World can ought appease
The plaintive Ghosts of Victims such as these;
The Patriot's copious Tears for each are shed,
A glorious Tribute which embalms the Dead.

But know, Fate summons to that awful Goal,
Where Justice strips the Murd'rer of his Soul:
Should venal C—ts the scandal of the Land,
Snatch the relentless Villain from her Hand,
Keen Execrations on this Plate inscrib'd,
Shall reach a Judge who never can be brib'd.

The unhappy Sufferers were Messrs. Saml. Gray, Saml. Maverick, Jams. Caldwell, Crispus Attucks & Patk. Carr
Killed. Six wounded; two of them (Christr. Monk & John Clark) Mortally

---

Think: Paul Revere's engraving of the Boston Massacre, featured on this poster, was meant to be informative. However, the poster only concentrates on the colonists' deaths. It does not show the mob's weapons, nor how riotous the crowd was. **Respond:** What were Revere's motives, and how did he want people to react?

Americans throwing the Cargoes of the Tea Ships into the River at Boston

Think: **On December 16, 1773, 150 patriots boarded English ships and dumped 342 chests of tea into Boston harbor. This and countless other Tea Parties throughout the colonies united the British public against the colonies.** Respond: **Do you think the patriots' actions were reckless or responsible? Why?**

The Tea Act

In 1773, Parliament passed a law called the *Tea Act*. It was intended to help the British East India Company, which was losing too much money. The Tea Act allowed the East India Company to sell its tea directly to the colonies without paying a tax to the British government. This meant that the company could sell its tea at a low price in the colonies. This would increase the amount of tea sold.

Colonial merchants were angry. They had been smuggling Dutch tea into the colonies to avoid having to buy the formerly high-priced India tea. The Tea Act meant that they could not sell their tea as cheaply as the East India Company could. Colonists were angry. They still had to pay a tax on tea, and the British were still forcing laws on the colonies without their consent. Throughout the colonies, Ameri-cans took action. The most famous response was the *Boston Tea Party*. Dressed as Indians, colonists boarded the East India Company's ship on the night of December 16, 1773. They dumped the entire cargo of tea into the harbor.

The Intolerable Acts

The British government, in turn, was angry. To punish the colonies, particularly Massachusetts, they passed new laws in May 1774. These became known as the *Intolerable Acts*. The port of Boston was to be closed until the colonists agreed to pay for the tea they had dumped. The powers of the Massachusetts legislature were cut, and town meetings were controlled by the governor. General Thomas Gage, the leader of the British army in North America, was made governor of Massachusetts and given much power.

Many historians blame George III (1738-1820) for the loss of the American colonies. However, his British subjects supported him in his actions.

The First Continental Congress

In September 1774, Americans from all of the colonies except Georgia met at Philadelphia to talk about their problems with Great Britain. This meeting was called the *First Continental Congress* (KAHN-tuh-NEN-tul). Most of the leaders at the meeting wanted to settle the colonies' problems with Great Britain peacefully. But they felt that Parliament must first stop punishing Massachusetts and taxing the colonies. The Congress called for another boycott of British goods in order to back up these demands.

Some British leaders wanted to give in to the colonists. But King George III and most members of Parliament refused. Finally, Parliament promised not to tax the colonies if the colonies agreed to tax themselves. The colonies refused.

The Coming of War

The First Continental Congress ended in late October 1774, and the colonial leaders went home. Those returning to Massachusetts found that the situation was coming to a head. The port of Boston was closed, the governor had been replaced by the head of the British army, and the people were being forced to house British soldiers. Other rights had been taken away. Many Americans began to prepare for war.

Outside Boston, Samuel Adams and John Hancock were gathering guns and training colonists to fight "at a minute's notice." For this reason, these colonists were called *Minutemen*. General Gage, the British commander, learned that many guns were stored in the town of Concord. In April 1775, General Gage

LEXINGTON AND CONCORD, 1775

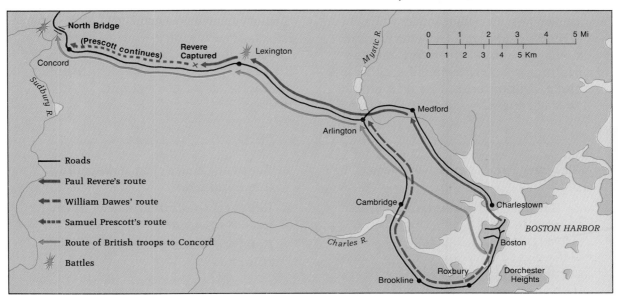

A point of view could be a place, such as the top of a hill, where a person stands to see something. A personal point of view is similar. It is a position from which a person views or judges something. A person's point of view can be formed by place of birth, age, experiences, and ideas about what is important in life.

In colonial America in 1776, nearly everyone was reading a short book called *Common Sense*, which argued for America's independence from England. No author's name appeared on the book. However, many people were able to figure out who wrote it by examining the point of view expressed in it.

Read the quotations from *Common Sense* and the phrases describing the point of view of the author, Thomas Paine. Match them.

___ 1 "I have never met a man, either in England or America, who has not confessed his opinion that a separation between the countries would take place one time or another."

___ 2 "I have heard it asserted . . . that as America has flourished under her . . . connection with Great Britain that [it] will always have the same effect. We may as well assert that because a child has thrived upon milk, . . . it is never to have meat."

___ 3 "I draw my idea of the form of government from a principle in nature, . . . that the more simple any thing is, the less liable it is to be disordered, and the easier repaired when disordered."

___ 4 "For all men being originally equals, no one by birth could have a right to set up his own family in . . . preference to all others forever. . . ."

___ 5 "The state of a king shuts him off from the world, yet the business of a king requires him to know it thoroughly; . . . the different parts . . . prove the whole character to be absurd and useless."

Thomas Paine's point of view:

a. Believed in the equality of all people.

b. Lived in both England and America.

c. Believed in keeping government uncomplicated.

d. Believed that change was often necessary in life.

e. Believed kings could not be good rulers.

Courtesy of Chicago Historical Society.

Think: **On April 19, 1775, the first shots of the Revolution were fired at Lexington; no one knows by which side. When English redcoats marched on the town, the Minutemen defended it. Amos Doolittle illustrated the battle.**
Respond: **Why had the British marched on the towns of Lexington and Concord?**

sent British soldiers from Boston to capture these guns. But in Boston, Paul Revere and William Dawes found out about Gage's plan. With Samuel Prescott, they rode out to warn the Minutemen, and Adams and Hancock escaped.

When the British soldiers reached the town of Lexington on April 19, the Minutemen were ready for them. The British told them to leave, and there was a moment's pause. Then a shot rang out. It is not clear which side fired first. But at the end of the battle, eight Minutemen were dead.

The British and colonists fought a second battle that day. That battle was at Concord. And all along the route back to Boston, colonists fired on the British troops. By the time the British reached the safety of Boston, 247 "redcoats," as they were called, were dead. Ninety-three Minutemen had lost their lives. From that point on, there was no turning back. The day's battles would later be called "the shot heard 'round the world," for the **Revolutionary War** had begun. In the next section, you will learn more about why the colonies decided to fight for their independence.

Section Review

1. What were some of the acts that angered the Americans?
2. What was the First Continental Congress?
3. What are the details of the first battle of the Revolutionary War?

2. The Declaration of Independence

Learn these important terms:

Second Continental Congress
Patriots
Loyalists
Battle of Bunker Hill
Common Sense
Declaration of Independence
Green Mountain Boys

Remember the main idea:

When the American colonists were unable to resolve their differences with Great Britain regarding taxes, they declared their independence from Great Britain.

Look for answers to these questions:

1. What were the major differences between Great Britain and the American colonies?

2. Why was the victory at Fort Ticonderoga so important?

3. How did the colonists drive the British army out of Boston?

After the opening battles of the Revolutionary War at Lexington and Concord, public opinion was divided. The people who favored independence from Great Britain were known as **Patriots**. But in Great Britain, they were known as traitors—and treason was punished by death. Clearly, the step toward declaring independence was a serious one. The Americans who took that step had to consider carefully what they were doing.

There were still many people in the colonies who wanted to repair relations with Great Britain. These people were called **Loyalists**, since they were loyal to the king. It is not known how many colonists were Loyalists and how many were Patriots. But even after the first battles of the War, another effort was made by the Americans to settle the problems with Great Britain.

The Second Continental Congress

In May of 1775, Americans from the various colonies met again at Philadelphia. Most of the leaders at this **Second Continental Congress** still hoped to settle the colonies' differences with Great Britain peacefully.

The recent battles at Lexington and Concord, however, made the leaders of the Second Continental Congress aware that they needed to be ready for war. Therefore, they voted to raise money and train men for an army and navy. George Washington, the Virginian who had led troops so successfully during the French and Indian War, was made the Commander in Chief.

Fort Ticonderoga

On the same day in May that the Second Continental Congress met, a Patriot band attacked a fort in northern New York. The group of volunteers was known as the **Green Mountain Boys**. Led by Ethan Allen, they captured the British-held Fort Ticonderoga (TY-kon-duh-ROH-guh). Allen's victory was important for two reasons. The Patriots gained much-needed weapons. And this victory opened the way for an attack on Canada later in the year.

The Battle of Bunker Hill

Ever since the fighting at Lexington and Concord, American troops had surrounded General Gage's troops in Boston. They could not take the city, but they had Gage's troops pinned down. In June 1775, the Americans began massing troops and supplies on a hill near Boston. The British army attacked. During the first two attacks, they were forced to pull back because of heavy losses. Finally, the British took the hill on their third try when the Americans ran out of ammunition. This battle is mistakenly known as the **Battle of Bunker Hill**. Actually, it took place on nearby Breed's hill.

Think: In *The Battle of Bunker Hill*, Trumbull shows the death of Dr. Warren (foreground) and the wounded Major Pitcairn. Respond: Why are such colorful records of events important?

King George's Anger

In early July 1775, the Second Continental Congress offered to make peace with Britain. They wrote to King George III to ask for his help in resolving their differences with Great Britain. They blamed Parliament, not the king, for these problems. However, the king was anything but pleased. The Battle of Bunker Hill had made him angry. The American attack on Canada in November would make him even angrier.

The American colonies resented Canada, mostly because the British had given that colony rights to land in the Ohio River Valley. This action cut off westward expansion of the American colonies. So, the American army attacked Canada and captured Montreal. However, Quebec held out against the American attack, and the French population remained loyal to Great Britain.

King George was outraged. In December 1775, he announced the colonies would be closed to all trade beginning March 1, 1776. He declared that the colonies were fighting against Great Britain and that the colonists were rebels. Great Britain began to capture American ships and the ships of other nations that tried to trade with the colonies. Great Britain also hired German troops to fight the war against the colonists.

Changing Minds

After the Battle of Bunker Hill, George Washington had taken command of the American army in Boston. In March 1776, American troops captured Dorchester Heights, overlooking Boston Harbor. The British were no longer able to hold the city, and the army fled from Boston by ship to Canada.

By this time, many American colonists believed that they must fight for their independence. Great Britain's actions after the Battle of Bunker Hill, in response to the offer of peace, had angered the Americans. They were outraged that King George had cut off trade.

Also, in January 1776, Thomas Paine had written a short book called **Common Sense**. Within two months, 150,000 copies were in the hands of colonists. This book convinced many Americans of the need for freedom from Great Britain. Paine wrote that Americans had everything to gain by becoming independent.

COMMON SENSE;

ADDRESSED TO THE

INHABITANTS

OF

AMERICA,

On the following interesting

SUBJECTS.

I. Of the Origin and Design of Government in general, with concise Remarks on the English Constitution.

II. Of Monarchy and Hereditary Succession.

III. Thoughts on the present State of American Affairs.

IV. Of the present Ability of America, with some miscellaneous Reflections.

Man knows no Master save creating HEAVEN.
Or those whom choice and common good ordain.
THOMSON.

PHILADELPHIA;
Printed, and Sold, by R. BELL, in Third-Street.
MDCCLXXVI.

Think: In 1776, Thomas Paine wrote *Common Sense,* in which he demanded independence from England. Shown is the pamphlet's title page. Respond: What effect did Paine's words have?

HISTORY MAKERS

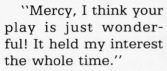

Mercy Otis Warren

Political Activist and Historian

"Mercy, I think your play is just wonderful! It held my interest the whole time."

"Thank you, Abigail. Did you recognize some of the characters in my kingdom of Upper Servia?"

"Of course, Mercy! The ruler is Governor Hutchinson, and General Gage is the military commander. I also recognize our two husbands, of course."

"I just hope the British get my message, Abigail. They should be careful. We *will* go to war if they don't recognize our rights."

"And we'll win, too—just like in your play, Mercy!"

Mercy Otis Warren and her good friend Abigail Adams often talked about politics. This was unusual at the time. Women were supposed to spend their lives caring for their families and homes, not participating in politics. However, Mercy and Abigail believed women should develop political ideas since home life was affected by politics.

Mercy Otis Warren went beyond talking about politics. She was a very busy woman. She published poetry, plays, patriotic pamphlets, and a history of the American Revolution. She raised four children and ran a large house in Plymouth, Massachusetts. She was a talented woman, but she worked hard. Women of her time were not easily accepted in many roles.

Like most girls growing up in the colonies, Mercy Otis Warren never went to school. She listened to her brother James's lessons with his tutor. After James went to college, Mercy continued to study at home. She educated herself.

The Warren household was a center for political discussions and plans for the Revolution. Mercy, her husband, James, and her brother, James Otis, were all committed to independence for the colonies.

Mercy Otis Warren made valuable contributions to the American Revolution. She helped to plan it and wrote in support of it. In addition, she was one of its first historians. Her three-volume account of the Revolution is an important firsthand view of people and events.

Think: The writers of the Declaration of Independence knew that the document would explain to the world America's reasons for wanting independence. This John Trumbull painting shows the writers giving the Declaration to the Congress. **Respond:** Why was it important for the Americans to explain their actions?

The Declaration of Independence

The leaders at the Second Continental Congress also began to favor American independence. In June 1776, Richard Henry Lee of Virginia demanded that the colonies declare their independence. The Congress named a committee, including Thomas Jefferson, John Adams, and Benjamin Franklin, to write a *Declaration of Independence*. They felt it was important to explain to the world why the American colonies were forming a new nation.

On July 2, 1776, the Second Continental Congress voted to declare the colonies independent of Great Britain. On July 4, 1776, the Congress approved the Declaration of Independence. The Americans had formed a new, independent nation—the United States of America.

Section Review

1. What were some of the actions taken by the Second Continental Congress?

2. What helped convince the colonists they needed independence from Great Britain?

3. Why did the colonists think it was necessary to write the Declaration of Independence?

The Declaration of Independence

IN CONGRESS, JULY 4, 1776

The Unanimous Declaration of the Thirteen United States of America

When in the Course of human events, it becomes necessary for one people to dissolve the political bands which have connected them with another, and to assume among the powers of the earth, the separate and equal station to which the Laws of Nature and of Nature's God entitle them, a decent respect to the opinions of mankind requires that they should declare the causes which impel them to the separation.

We hold these truths to be self-evident, that all men are created equal, that they are endowed by their Creator with certain unalienable Rights, that among these are Life, Liberty and the pursuit of Happiness.

That to secure these rights, Governments are instituted among Men, deriving their just powers from the consent of the governed.

That whenever any Form of Government becomes destructive of these ends, it is the Right of the People to alter or to abolish it, and to institute new Government, laying its foundation on such principles and organizing its powers in such form, as to them shall seem most likely to effect their Safety and Happiness. Prudence, indeed, will dictate that Governments long established should not be changed for light and transient causes; and accordingly all experience hath shewn, that mankind are more disposed to suffer, while evils are sufferable, than to right themselves by abolishing the forms to which they are accustomed. But when a long train of abuses and usurpations, pursuing invariably the same Object evinces a design to reduce them under absolute Despotism, it is their right, it is their duty, to throw off such Government, and to provide new Guards for their future security.

Such has been the patient sufferance of these Colonies; and such is now the necessity which constrains them to alter their former Systems of Government. The history of the present King of Great Britain is a history of repeated injuries and usurpations, all having in direct object the establishment of an absolute Tyranny over these States. To prove this, let Facts be submitted to a candid world.

He has refused his Assent to Laws, the most wholesome and necessary for the public good.

He has forbidden his Governors to pass Laws of immediate and pressing importance, unless suspended in their operation till his Assent should be obtained; and when so suspended, he has utterly neglected to attend to them.

He has refused to pass other Laws for the accommodation of large districts of people, unless those people would relinquish the right of Representation in the Legislature, a right inestimable to them and formidable to tyrants only.

He has called together legislative bodies at places unusual, uncomfortable, and distant from the depository of their public Records, for the sole purpose of fatiguing them into compliance with his measures.

Think: After the Congress approved the Declaration, the document was read to the people, as shown here. Respond: Compare the above presentation with today's press conferences.

He has dissolved Representative Houses repeatedly, for opposing with manly firmness his invasions on the rights of the people.

He has refused for a long time, after such dissolutions, to cause others to be elected; whereby the Legislative powers, incapable of Annihilation, have returned to the People at large for their exercise; the State remaining in the meantime exposed to all the dangers of invasion from without, and convulsions within.

He has endeavoured to prevent the population of these States; for that purpose obstructing the Laws for Naturalization of Foreigners; refusing to pass others to encourage their migrations hither, and raising the conditions of new Appropriations of Lands.

He has obstructed the Administration of Justice, by refusing his Assent to Laws for establishing Judiciary powers.

He has made Judges dependent on his Will alone, for the tenure of their offices, and the amount and payment of their salaries.

He has erected a multitude of New Offices, and sent hither swarms of Officers to harass our people, and eat out their substance. He has kept among us, in times of peace, Standing Armies without the Consent of our legislatures.

He has affected to render the Military independent of and superior to the Civil power.

He has combined with others to subject us to a jurisdiction foreign to our constitution, and unacknowledged by our laws; giving his Assent to their Acts of pretended Legislation:

For quartering large bodies of armed troops among us:

For protecting them, by a mock Trial, from punishment for any Murders which they should commit on the Inhabitants of these States:

For cutting off our Trade with all parts of the world:

For imposing Taxes on us without our Consent:

For depriving us in many cases, of the benefits of Trial by Jury:

For transporting us beyond Seas to be tried for pretended offences:

For abolishing the free System of English Laws in a neighbouring Province, establishing therein an Arbitrary government, and enlarging its Boundaries so as to render it at once an example and fit instrument for introducing the same absolute rule into these Colonies:

For taking away our Charters, abolishing our most valuable Laws and altering fundamentally the Forms of our Governments:

For suspending our own Legislatures, and declaring themselves invested with power to legislate for us in all cases whatsoever.

He has abdicated Government here, by declaring us out of his Protection and waging War against us.

He has plundered our seas, ravaged our Coasts, burnt our towns, and destroyed the lives of our people.

He is at this time transporting large Armies of foreign Mercenaries to compleat the works of death, desolation and tyranny, already begun with circumstances of Cruelty & perfidy scarcely paralleled in the most bar-

Think: This engraving by Edward Savage shows the members of Congress voting for independence. On July 4, 1776, the final draft of the Declaration of Independence was approved, two days after the document was presented to the Congress by its writers. **Respond:** Why were the members able to agree so quickly?

barous ages, and totally unworthy the Head of a civilized nation.

He has constrained our fellow Citizens taken Captive on the high Seas to bear Arms against their Country, to become the executioners of their friends and Brethren, or to fall themselves by their Hands.

He has excited domestic insurrections amongst us, and has endeavoured to bring on the inhabitants of our frontiers, the merciless Indian Savages, whose known rule of warfare, is an undistinguished destruction of all ages, sexes and conditions. In every stage of these Oppressions We have Petitioned for Redress in the most humble terms: Our repeated Petitions have been answered only by repeated injury. A Prince, whose character is thus marked by every act which may define a Tyrant, is unfit to be the ruler of a free people. Nor have We been wanting in attentions to our British brethren. We have warned them from time to time of attempts by their legislature to extend an unwarrantable jurisdiction over us. We have reminded them of the circumstances of our emigration and settlement here. We have appealed to their native justice and magnanimity, and we have conjured them by the ties of our common kindred to disavow these usurpations, which would inevitably interrupt our connections and correspondence. They too have been deaf to the voice of justice and of consanguinity. We must, therefore, acquiesce in the necessity, which denounces our Separation, and hold them, as we hold the rest of mankind, Enemies in War, in Peace Friends.

We, therefore, the Representatives of the United States of America, in General Congress, Assembled, appealing to the Supreme Judge of the world for the rectitude of our

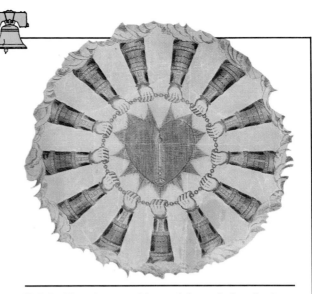

Think: **The above etching celebrated the signing of the Declaration of Independence. Notice the candle that represents enlightenment.** Respond: **What do the hands symbolize?**

intentions, do, in the Name, and by Authority of the good People of these Colonies, solemnly publish and declare, That these United Colonies are, and of Right ought to be free and independent states; that they are Absolved from all Allegiance to the British Crown, and that all political connection between them and the State of Great Britain, is and ought to be totally dissolved; and that as Free and Independent States, they have full Power to levy War, conclude Peace, contract Alliances, establish Commerce, and to do all other Acts and Things which Independent States may of right do.

And for the support of this Declaration, with a firm reliance on the protection of divine Providence, we mutually pledge to each other our Lives, our Fortunes and our sacred Honor.

3. Winning the Revolutionary War

Learn these important terms:

Treaty of Paris
Battle of Saratoga

Remember the main idea:

After many years of hard fighting, the new American nation won its independence from Great Britain.

Look for answers to these questions:

1. What were the strengths of each side in the war?
2. Why was the Battle of Saratoga so important?
3. How did the French help the United States win the war?

Although the American colonies had declared their independence, they would have to fight a long war in order to win that independence. Great Britain had a strong army and navy. And the British army expected help from the Indians and the Loyalists. During the war, however, the Americans learned that the British strength was not all it appeared. They also learned that the new nation had some strengths of its own.

British Against Americans

The British army depended on hired German soldiers to do much of the fighting in America. But the Germans did not want to die for Great Britain, so they did not fight with as much determination as expected. Nor did the British navy do as well as the Americans had feared. It was never able to cut off trade between Europe and America. And the British never got much help from the Indians or from the Loyalists.

On the other hand, the Americans discovered certain advantages they had.

Think: In 1779, John Paul Jones took command of the *Bonhomme Richard* (Poor Richard), which he named in honor of Benjamin Franklin's almanac. On September 23, 1779, the *Bonhomme Richard* attacked the British ship *Serapis,* which was larger and better equipped than Jones's ship. At times during this North Sea battle, the two ships were so close together that their riggings became entangled. When the British commander asked him to surrender, Jones shouted back, "I have not yet begun to fight!" The Americans went on to victory. Respond: Why was the unexpected American victory important?

Think: Trumbull's *The Surrender of Burgoyne at Saratoga* shows Burgoyne offering his sword to Gates, who returned it. Also in the painting is Daniel Morgan, in white. He, with Benedict Arnold (not shown), contributed to the victory. **Respond:** Why was the British surrender at Saratoga a turning point?

First, the country was far away from Great Britain. Therefore, Great Britain had problems getting supplies to its army. Second, America was very large. The British were never able to capture the southern, middle, and New England states (called colonies before) all at the same time. In general, Great Britain found it difficult to fight a war three thousand miles from home on unfamiliar ground. And American generals took advantage of their own knowledge of the land to trap and defeat the British.

America also won the support of France, Spain, and other European nations against the British. These nations supplied money, war supplies, men, and military advisors to the United States. All of this aid, combined with the outstanding leadership of George Washington, helped to win the war.

Victories on Both Sides

Each side in the Revolutionary War fought hard to gain ground. At first, it looked as if the British might be able to hold onto America. After the British army was forced to leave Boston in 1776, General Howe led a British attack on New York City. General Washington was unable to stop the British from taking the city in September 1776. The following September, a British army also took over the city of Philadelphia. However, the British did not follow up these victories.

Another British army, led by General John Burgoyne, marched south from Canada. Burgoyne planned to cut New England off from the other American states. However, an American army surrounded Burgoyne's army and trapped them at Saratoga, New York. Burgoyne had to surrender his whole army.

THE REVOLUTIONARY WAR
A Picture Essay

By the time the colonists' differences with England were heating up, America had become segmented. People had come to America over a span of 150 years. Many different reasons spurred their immigration. Colonies were of three types: royal, proprietary, and corporate. And the colonies were spread from present-day Canada in the north to Georgia in the south to the Appalachian Mountains in the west. Climate and geography created three distinct sections. Each of these three colonial sections—southern, middle, and northeastern—was characterized by its own way of life. Yet, as the colonists realized more and more their separateness from England, the sections became unified. This unity was important to the future independence of the colonies, as Thomas Paine realized when he wrote this passage:

> The Sun never shined on a cause of greater worth. 'Tis not the affair of a City, a County, a Province, or a Kingdom; but of a Continent—of at least one eighth part of the habitable globe.
>
> -from *Common Sense*

When the Revolutionary War began, the colonists who favored independence joined together to fight. And the fighting occurred throughout the colonies. Every section had its battles, and important victories in each helped the Americans achieve independence. Ways of fighting may have differed among sections, but unity of ideas was apparent.

Think: In the fall of October 1777, Germantown, near Philadelphia, was the stronghold of the British forces. More than 9,000 troops were stationed there. In a daring move, General Washington decided to take Germantown. He drew up a plan of attack. Two columns, one led by John Sullivan and the other by Nathanael Greene, marched separately through the early hours of October 4, 1777. They met on the road leading into Germantown. This painting by Xavier Della Gatta shows the arrival of the American troops. Notice the Redcoats entering the house. This house was actually like a castle. Its thick walls protected the soldiers. Although the British were losing the battle at the beginning, the Chew house gave them a place to reorganize. They were able to force the Americans to retreat. **Respond:** This painting was based on a description given by a British soldier who was there. Why would he have described the house as so small?

Think: As the Americans entered Princeton on January 3, 1777, George Washington, leading his troops on horseback, yelled, "It's a fine fox chase, my boys!" Washington had tricked the British by moving his forces in the night. The British, marching to attack Washington's forces at Trenton, left few soldiers behind in Princeton. **Respond:** Hugh Mercer, an important general for the Americans, was killed in the battle. His son painted the scene. Why do you think he wanted to make a lasting record of the battle?

Think: The uniform of this German soldier tells us he marched at the head of the right lines. Respond: What weapons did he use?

Think: As his yellow and blue uniform shows, this soldier belonged to the Royal Deux-Ponts, the largest French regiment. Respond: Why did Europeans wear such beautiful uniforms?

Think: This royal British officer spent up to three hours a day getting dressed and ready for battle. Respond: Why was a uniform like this impractical?

Think: In Sycamore Shoals, Tennessee, the "over-mountain men" gathered on September 25, 1780. These hardy pioneers from the Wautauga River basin intended to seek out and attack the British who planned to invade their area. On October 7, they won the battle of King's Mountain. Respond: What drove these Americans to fight?

The unity of the colonists who entered the war was best displayed by their soldiers. Although untrained and often dressed in ragged, unmatched clothing, the soldiers had courage and loyalty. They also had strong leaders. General George Washington in particular gained the respect of his men. He consistently held them together in the worst situations, and he made many brilliant military decisions. Still, it was the brave soldiers themselves who won the battles they volunteered to fight.

In contrast, the British soldiers—highly trained and beautifully groomed—were much less loyal. They seemed to care little about the cause behind the war. They even turned down offers of assistance from the colonists who remained loyalists. And the German troops who fought with the British certainly were disinterested. They were nothing more than paid professionals. Many were forced by their greedy king to fight.

When the Americans won the war, they won their freedom. But they also gave permanence to their unity as they formed the United States of America.

Think: American riflemen wore fringed uniforms of practical coarse cotton. Often they went barefoot. **Respond:** Why did the word ``Congress'' appear on their leather hats?

Feature Review

1. Why did America become segmented as it developed?

2. How did Thomas Paine feel about the fight for independence?

3. How did the colonial soldiers differ from those fighting for Britain?

4. In which colonial section did each battle pictured on these four pages occur?

Think: *Washington Reviewing the Troops at Valley Forge* by William Trego shows the harsh conditions of the winter of 1777 and 1778. The soldiers had little food and many didn't have shoes. They lived in crude huts. Three thousand died from the cold or from smallpox. But Washington held on. In the spring, with the help of Baron von Steuben and the support of France, Washington and his army marched successfully against the British. Respond: How did the winter at Valley Forge test the American troops' loyalty?

The ***Battle of Saratoga***, fought in October 1777, was the turning point of the Revolutionary War. It was the greatest victory won by either side up to that time. As a result of the Battle of Saratoga, the government of France decided to help the United States. This turned the tide.

Until French help came, however, the Patriot army was in bad shape. It spent the winter in Valley Forge, Pennsylvania. There, desperately short of food and supplies, Washington waited. The new nation did not have enough money to feed and clothe its soldiers or to pay them. Washington knew that he needed more than patriotism and bravery to win the war. Support from France was essential. By the time French help arrived, the American army had suffered badly from extreme cold and near starvation.

Britain's Offer of Peace

Almost from the beginning of the Revolutionary War, the British government hoped to make peace with the Americans as soon as possible. For this reason, General Howe did not follow up his victories at New York and Philadelphia. When the British government heard that France was going to help the United States, it decided to act quickly.

In 1778, the British government offered the United States freedom from taxation, the repeal of all the British laws passed since 1763, and pardons for all the leaders of the Revolution. However, the British offer came too late. With France backing them, the Americans demanded complete independence. The British government refused to agree to this.

Carolina and Virginia. Cornwallis settled at Yorktown, Virginia, and set up a base there. George Washington responded by moving his troops from New York to Yorktown. There the American army surrounded the British army.

The British tried to escape from Yorktown by sea. However, a French fleet met the British fleet off the coast of Virginia. The French defeated the British soundly and prevented Cornwallis from escaping from Yorktown. Cornwallis was trapped. In October 1781, he surrendered his army to General Washington.

The Treaty of Paris

After the American victory at Yorktown, Great Britain knew it could not win the war. By 1782, the British government and the British people decided that they must end the war and make peace with the United States. Great Britain still

Important American Victories in the West

Most of the important fighting in 1778 took place along the western frontier. During the war, the British encouraged the Indians to attack American frontier settlements north of the Ohio River. The state of Virginia sent George Rogers Clark, a frontier leader, to end these attacks. Clark captured several British forts in what are today Indiana and Illinois. Clark's victories stopped the Indian attacks. They also gave the United States a strong claim to this western frontier land after the war ended.

The War in the South

In 1778, the British decided that their best chance to win the war was to take over the southern states. By the end of that year, they captured Georgia. In 1780, they captured South Carolina. And in 1781, the British army, led by General Charles Cornwallis, marched into North

Think: George Rogers Clark and his men attacked Fort Sackville at Vincennes, Indiana, and two other British supply bases. Respond: What effects did Clark's victories have?

REVOLUTIONARY WAR BATTLES

Some maps give you a glimpse of history. From the map below, for example, you can trace the main course of the Revolutionary War. Look at the map. Notice that it gives you the location of some of the battles of the war and also the date on which each battle took place. Now look at the map key. What other information does it give you about each battle?

To see how the war progressed, list American victories in time order in one column. In another column list British victories in time order. Give the location of each battle and the date—month, day, and year.

Using the text of this chapter, the map, and your list of battles, answer the following questions.

1. Would you say that the war was going in favor of the British or the Americans at the end of the year 1775? Or was the war about even? At the end of 1776, which side seemed to be ahead? Which side was winning at the end of 1780?

2. This map shows many, but not all, of the important battles of the American Revolution. Which side won the most battles on this map? How many did the Americans win? How many did the British win?

3. How many battles shown on this map were fought along water? Why might each side have wanted to control the water routes? Which side won most of these battles?

4. Which side held the upper hand at each of the following dates?
   May 1775
   June 1775
   September 1776
   October 1777
   August 1780
   October 1781

5. Why do you think the Americans won the war?

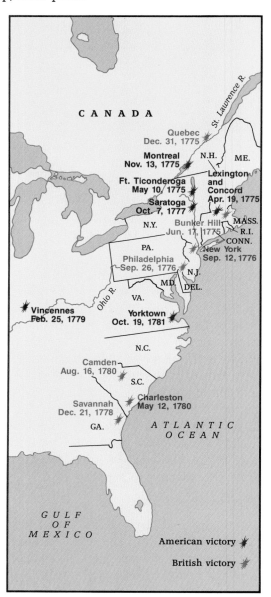

Think: The peace treaty was signed on September 3, 1783. Later, when Benjamin West began painting the event, only the Americans agreed to pose. They were John Jay, John Adams, Benjamin Franklin, Henry Laurens, and their secretary. Respond: Why did the American victory threaten the European colonial system?

hoped that America might remain part of the British empire. However, it was willing to agree to America's independence.

Benjamin Franklin, John Adams, and John Jay went to Great Britain to work on a peace treaty to end the war. In 1783, the *Treaty of Paris* was signed. This treaty, which ended the Revolutionary War, included these terms:

1. The United States became an independent nation.

2. The Mississippi River became the western boundary of the United States.

3. Americans were allowed to fish off the coast of Newfoundland.

4. Great Britain gave Florida back to the Spanish.

After years of hard fighting, the new American nation had won its independence. The next task was to build a government for the new nation.

Section Review

1. What were some difficulties the British had in fighting the war?

2. What was the turning point of the Revolutionary War? Why?

3. What treaty ended the Revolutionary War? When was it signed? What points did it include?

CHAPTER SUMMARY

The issue of taxation continued to divide the colonies and Great Britain. The presence of British troops in colonial towns also angered the colonists. In 1773, Parliament passed the Tea Act. Colonists reacted with anger and the Boston Tea Party.

The British government punished the colonies, and particularly Massachusetts, by passing the Intolerable Acts. In 1774, the First Continental Congress met to decide what to do about the acts.

Americans began planning for war. In April 1775, British troops met Patriot soldiers in the town of Lexington, in the first battle of the Revolutionary War.

A Second Continental Congress was called. It again tried for a peaceful settlement of the tax question. But the Congress also prepared for war.

Support for independence grew after the Battle of Bunker Hill. On July 4, 1776, the Second Continental Congress approved the Declaration of Independence.

The turning point of the war was the Battle of Saratoga, in October 1777. It was a great victory for the American army. After the battle, the French decided to help the United States. The French naval victory over the British fleet at Yorktown brought the Revolutionary War to an end. The Treaty of Paris in 1783 set the terms of the United States' victory.

Key Words

Write a sentence to explain the meaning of each of these terms.

boycott　　　　Minutemen
Patriots　　　　Loyalists
Common Sense

Major Events

Choose the answer that best completes the statement.

1. In 1767, Parliament passed new tax laws called
   a) the Townshend Acts.
   b) the Declaratory Acts.
   c) the Intolerable Acts.

2. In 1773, the passage of the Tea Act sparked
   a) the Boston Massacre.
   b) the Boston Tea Party.
   c) the Boston Boycott.

3. The Intolerable Acts
   a) made a British general governor of Massachusetts.
   b) punished Boston for the Tea Party.
   c) both a and b.

4. The first battle of the Revolutionary War was fought at the town of Lexington, Massachusetts, in
   a) April 1774.
   b) April 1775.
   c) April 1776.

5. The turning point of the war was
   a) the Battle of Bunker Hill.
   b) the Battle of Yorktown.
   c) the Battle of Saratoga.

Review

Important Facts

Answer each question with at least one complete sentence.

1. What was the Declaratory Act?

2. Why were the Townshend Acts repealed?

3. What were the Committees of Correspondence?

4. When did the First Continental Congress meet? What did it accomplish?

5. When did the Second Continental Congress meet? What did it do?

6. Why was the Patriot victory at Fort Ticonderoga so important?

7. How did the American army drive the British out of Boston? Where did the British army go from there?

8. Why did the Patriot leaders think it was necessary to have the Declaration of Independence? When was it approved?

9. Where and when was General Burgoyne's army captured? What was the long-term importance of this battle?

10. Where did the American army trap Cornwallis? Why didn't the British escape, as they had from Boston?

11. Which European nation most helped the Americans defeat the British? What forms of help did this nation give?

12. What was the Treaty of Paris, and what were its four points?

Skill Review

Study this map, then answer the following questions.

1. Which battles did the British win before Yorktown?

2. Which battles did the Americans win before Yorktown?

3. Which side won the battle before Yorktown? Where was it?

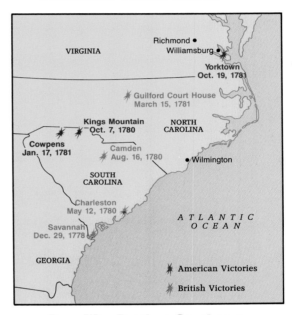

Rev. War Battles: Southeast

Critical Thinking

Write a paragraph to answer each question.

1. Why did the Second Continental Congress offer to make peace with Britain? What was King George's response, and why?

2. Compare the strengths and weaknesses of the British and American armies at the beginning of the war.

9

Building a Strong New Government

Years 1777–1794

Articles of Confederation
passed by
Continental Congress
1777

Shays's Rebellion
1786

Constitution approved
by states
1788

All states
approved Articles
1781

Northwest Ordinance
passed
Constitutional Convention
1787

Washington sworn in
as president
Judiciary Act passed
Bill of Rights proposed
1789

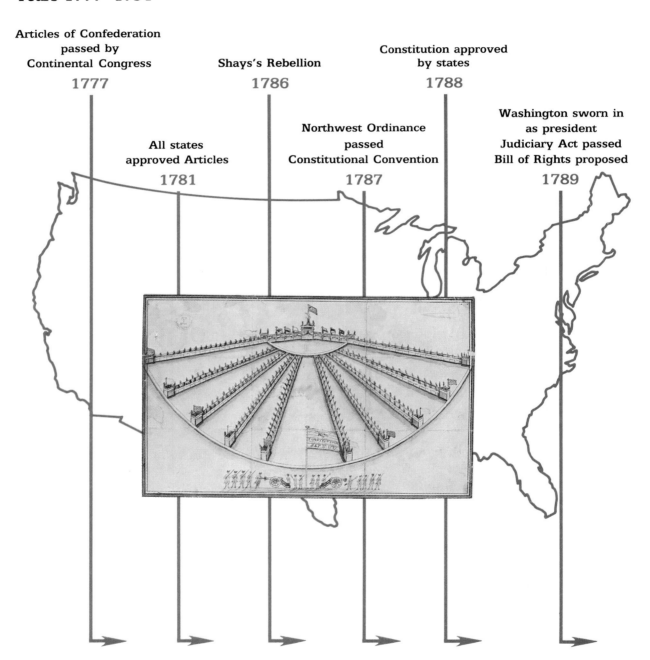

1. The Confederation Government

Learn these important terms:

bill of rights
Articles of Confederation
Northwest Ordinance
Shays's Rebellion

Remember the main idea:

Many important changes took place in America after the Revolution. But the first national government was too weak to rule the nation.

Look for answers to these questions:

1. Why did some people want a strong central government? Why did others oppose the idea?

2. What important land law helped the United States settle its western territories?

3. What event finally made many people realize that the country needed a stronger government?

Now that the states had won their independence, how would they govern themselves? This question was on the minds of many people after the Revolutionary War. The new nation was born, but it was not very strong. There were even some people who did not think the United States would survive. But great leaders like George Washington and Alexander Hamilton were willing to tackle the difficult problems facing the United States.

In this chapter, you will read about the first system of government in the United States. You will find out that this system of government was not strong enough to solve the nation's problems. You will see how the American leaders came together to create a new system of government. You will read about their differences and how they were solved. You will understand why the United States government is set up as it is. And you will also learn about the Constitution.

As you read, notice the thoughts and events that shaped America's government. Try to imagine how the Founding Fathers felt. Understand the difficult decisions they faced.

The American Revolution brought about many important changes. The new states were now free from British rule. They could no longer be taxed against their wishes. They could control their own trade and open their own schools. Laws were also changed so that prisoners were treated more fairly. In addition, most states no longer had official churches. Soon, most of the northern and middle states had also passed laws to end slavery. For a while, it seemed that the southern states might end slavery. However,

Think: After the Revolutionary War, the states had to decide whether to unite or remain separate. Although many people feared a strong central government, the states finally united. This coat of arms symbolizes that union. Respond: **What problems might arise for a nation with a weak central government?**

the rich southern planters believed that they needed slaves. These planters made sure that their states did not pass laws against slavery.

During the Revolutionary War, all the states except Connecticut and Rhode Island wrote new constitutions, or plans of government. Most of the state constitutions set up two-house legislatures. All of them gave their governors less power. Almost all of these constitutions also included a list of freedoms called a **bill of rights**. Because of these bills, people won the right to worship as they wished. They could speak and write freely, and they could meet together to discuss important matters. Everyone won the right to have a fair trial.

One of the most important things about the state constitutions was that they were written down. In England, most of the powers of the government were not written down. American leaders made sure that their government would be controlled by laws that anyone could read, rather than by the whim of one person.

A Government for All the States

In 1777, the new Continental Congress passed the *Articles of Confederation* (kun-FED-uh-RAY-shun). The Articles created a union of the states. This union was very important since the states needed to help each other during the war. The Articles of Confederation gave Congress the right to wage war and make peace. They also gave Congress the power to borrow money from foreign governments.

However, many people still opposed the idea of a national government. They were afraid that a national government might be like the one they had under the king, when they could not control their own trade or taxes. They believed that the states were fighting for their independence from such governments. It was not until 1781 that all the states approved the Articles of Confederation.

The government created by the Articles of Confederation lasted for eight years, but it did not have very much power. Even though it could raise an army, Congress could not pass tax laws to pay for it. Congress had the power to make treaties with other countries, but it did not have the power to make the states obey those treaties. It had a one-house legislature and no single leader such as a president to head the government. Nine of the thirteen states had to agree before Congress could pass an important law. All thirteen states had to agree before any of the Articles could be changed. The Congress could not pass laws to control trade among the states. There was not even a central system of money. Each state minted and issued its own coins.

The Articles of Confederation protected the independence of the states, but the Congress was too weak to solve many of the nation's problems. After the war, the country was deeply in debt. Merchants could no longer rely on the system of trade they had under British rule. There were often conflicts among the states over trading rights. Many people thought that only a strong central government could solve these problems. Other people were still afraid that a strong government would take away their independence. They thought that having a weak government protected their rights.

New Laws for New Lands

In 1787, the Congress of the Confederation passed an important land law. This law, called the *Northwest Ordinance* (OR-duh-nuns), was a plan for settling and governing the Northwest Territory. This was the land north of the Ohio River that the British had won in the French and Indian War. The Americans controlled this land after the Revolutionary War.

The Northwest Ordinance stated that when five thousand people lived in an area of the Northwest Territory, that area became a separate territory. The people there could set up their own legislature and send a delegate to the Congress in Philadelphia. When sixty thousand settlers lived in a territory, they had the right to ask Congress to allow their territory to become a state. The Northwest Ordinance also promised that the new state would be fully equal to the original thirteen states. The Northwest Territory eventually became five states—Ohio, Indiana, Illinois, Wisconsin, and Michigan.

THE NORTHWEST TERRITORY

Asking questions is a good way to get more out of reading your textbook. You can learn a lot more from a map by asking questions, too. Asking questions about the map on this page will help you learn more about how the young United States grew.

On the map locate the Northwest Territory in several ways.

1. What were its natural boundaries?

2. On which states did it border?

3. What was its location in latitude and longitude?

Now use the map to find out about the size of the Northwest Territory.

4. About how big was it from east to west? How big was it from north to south?

5. What problems might arise in settling so vast an area?

Look at the inset map, which shows the Northwest Survey System.

6. This system divided the land into squares, called townships, which were six miles on a side. Half the townships were divided into thirty-six sections, each one mile square. Both townships and squares were auctioned off to the public. Why do you think Congress set up this system of dividing and selling land?

7. What might have happened without this system?

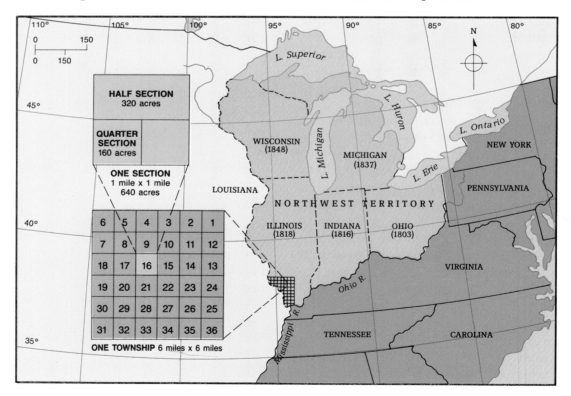

The Weakness of the Confederation

Congress passed a good land law, but it lacked the power to settle many problems. Conflicts between the states continued, and the nation's debt problem grew worse. After the war, the Confederation could not afford to raise an army. Because of this, Britain and Spain were able to create conflicts between Indians and settlers along the western frontier.

In 1786, something happened that proved to many people how important it was to have a strong national government. Farmers in western Massachusetts thought that they paid too many taxes. They had to borrow more money to pay these taxes. When the farmers could not pay back the loans, the bankers took their land. Led by Daniel Shays, who had been a captain during the Revolutionary War, the farmers rebelled.

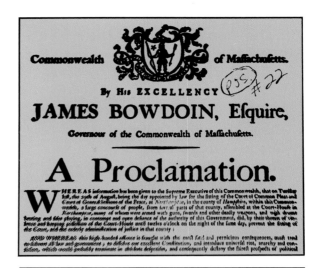

Think: **Soon after Shays's Rebellion, this proclamation called for the prevention of such rebellions.** Respond: **Why were rebellions dangerous to the new nation?**

The Congress of the Confederation had no troops to put down *Shays's Rebellion*. Congress had to ask the government of Massachusetts for help. It raised an army that soon defeated Shays and his followers. The rebellion showed many people that the country could not survive unless a stronger central government was formed. As you read the rest of the chapter, you will learn how the new American government was created.

Think: **During Shays's Rebellion, angry farmers hoped to stop the courts from taking away their farms.** Respond: **Tell if you agree with the farmers or not.**

Section Review

1. Why did some Americans want a weak central government?

2. In what ways was the central Confederation government weak?

3. Why did some people want a strong central government?

4. In 1786, why were farmers in western Massachusetts angry? What did they do?

2. The Constitution of the United States

Learn these important terms:

Constitutional Convention
Great Compromise
Three-Fifths Compromise
legislative branch
executive branch
judicial branch
separation of powers
Senate
House of Representatives

Remember the main idea:

When American leaders met in 1787 to strengthen the nation's government, they wrote a new Constitution.

Look for answers to these questions:

1. What problems did the Founding Fathers have to overcome in writing the Constitution?

2. How were the powers of the new government divided?

3. What powers were given to the president?

In September 1786, delegates of five states met at Annapolis, Maryland, to discuss trade problems. These men knew that they could do nothing about their problems unless more states became involved. Alexander Hamilton of New York said the group should call another meeting. He believed that delegates from all the states should gather to discuss revising the Articles of Confederation.

The Congress of the Confederation approved Hamilton's plan. In May 1787, fifty-five important American leaders met in Philadelphia, Pennsylvania. George Washington, James Madison, Alexander Hamilton, and Benjamin Franklin were among the people who attended these meetings. Many of the delegates had served in Congress, and seven had been state governors. Not everyone was in favor of the meetings, however. Leaders such as Patrick Henry of Virginia and Samuel Adams of Massachusetts thought that making the government more powerful would harm the freedoms won in the Revolutionary War. The state of Rhode Island even refused to send any delegates at all to the meeting.

At first, the delegates planned only to improve the Articles of Confederation. Soon, however, they decided that they must write a new constitution that gave more power to the central government. The men who met in Philadelphia are called the Founding Fathers of this new government, and their meeting became known as the *Constitutional Convention*.

Great Compromises

The Founding Fathers had many problems to overcome. They had to decide if the new Congress would have one house or two houses, like the British Parliament. They had to decide how to elect members to Congress. They also had to decide what powers to give to the different parts of the new government.

It was not easy for them to decide on these matters. The Founding Fathers came from different states, and they had

Think: **The Constitutional Convention was but one event that took place in the Philadelphia Statehouse.**
Respond: **Why do you think the Statehouse was later named Independence Hall?**

At the Constitutional Convention, many words were written, and many more were spoken. Perhaps all those words made things so confusing at times that the Founding Fathers drew diagrams. A diagram shows how the parts of something are organized and relate to one another.

The diagram on this page shows how the Founding Founders organized the three branches of government. The arrows that go from one box to another tell how the three branches relate to one another in a system called "checks and balances." These arrows show that each branch has some powers over the other two branches.

Use the diagram to answer these questions.

1 What powers does the executive branch have over the judicial branch? Over the legislative branch?

2 What powers does the judicial branch have over the executive branch? Over the legislative branch?

3 What powers does the legislative branch have over the executive branch? Over the judicial branch?

**Constitutional Separation of Powers
(Checks and Balances)**

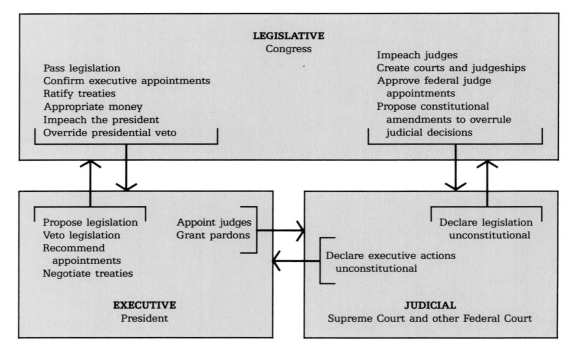

LEGISLATIVE
Congress

Pass legislation
Confirm executive appointments
Ratify treaties
Appropriate money
Impeach the president
Override presidential veto

Impeach judges
Create courts and judgeships
Approve federal judge
   appointments
Propose constitutional
   amendments to overrule
   judicial decisions

Propose legislation
Veto legislation
Recommend
   appointments
Negotiate treaties

Appoint judges
Grant pardons

Declare legislation
unconstitutional

Declare executive actions
  unconstitutional

EXECUTIVE
President

JUDICIAL
Supreme Court and other Federal Court

many different concerns. Northern states disagreed with southern states, and big states disagreed with small states. Just as the states had been in conflict, so the men at the Convention were often in conflict.

When they wrote the Constitution, the Founding Fathers settled their problems by making compromises (KAHM-pruh-miz-es), or agreements in which both sides got only part of what they wanted. For example, the large states wanted to have more members in Congress. The smaller states were worried that this would give the large states more power. They wanted each state to have the same number of members in Congress.

The Constitutional Convention decided on a compromise. Congress would be made up of two houses—the **Senate** and the **House of Representatives** (REP-rih-ZENT-uh-tivz). Each state would elect two members to the Senate. Each state would also elect members to the House of Representatives. However, the number of representatives would depend upon the number of people in the state. Both houses would have to agree before Congress could pass any law. This plan was called the **Great Compromise**. It pleased both the large and the small states.

Other important compromises were made over the issue of slavery. Many people at the Convention wanted the new Constitution to end slavery. The southern states wanted to keep slavery. If the Constitution had ended slavery, these states would never have approved it. The United States would not have come into being. So the Founding Fathers compromised. They stated that no law forbidding slavery in the United States could be passed until after the year 1808.

There was another important compromise about slavery. The new government would have the power to tax the people. The more people who lived in a state, the more taxes that state would have to pay. Since the southern states had so many slaves, they did not want the slaves counted for taxation. On the other hand, if the slaves were counted in their states, the southern states would have more members in the House of Representatives.

To compromise, the Founding Fathers decided that for every five slaves in a state, three would be counted for taxation and representation. This solution was the **Three-Fifths Compromise**.

Separation of Powers

In the new Constitution, the Founding Fathers created a strong federal government, or a government of all the states. They also made sure that the states kept the most important freedoms they had won during the Revolutionary War. The powers of government were divided fairly between the national government and the state governments. For example, the national government had the power to declare war and to coin money. The states had the power to make laws about such matters as marriage and divorce.

The national government was divided into three separate branches, or parts. The *legislative branch* was made up of the two houses of Congress. Its job was to make the laws. The *executive branch* was headed by the president. Its duty was to see that the laws passed by Congress were carried out. The executive branch also communicated with foreign governments. The *judicial branch* was made up of the federal courts. Their duty was to make sure that the government did not act unjustly and to help enforce laws by deciding criminal penalties.

Most Americans liked this *separation of powers* between the federal and the state governments, and among the three branches of the federal government. The new Constitution made a government that was strong enough to rule the country well. Yet, the separation of powers meant that no part of government had too much power. The freedoms won by Americans during the American Revolution would be protected. In the last part of the chapter, you will find out about the early years of the new government.

Section Review

1. What is the story behind the Great Compromise?

2. What compromises did the Founding Fathers make about the issue of slavery?

3. What is meant by the separation of powers?

3. The Nation's New Government

Learn these important terms:

Federalists
Cabinet
Bill of Rights
secretary of
   war
secretary of
   the treasury
amendments

Anti-
   Federalists
Judiciary Act
secretary of
   state
attorney
   general

Remember the main idea:

The Constitution was approved by the states, and under President Washington's leadership the new government got off to a good start.

Look for answers to these questions:

1. Why were some people opposed to the Constitution?

2. What jobs were given to the men who helped Washington lead the government?

4. What did Alexander Hamilton suggest the nation do to settle its money problems?

3. What problem did President Washington face in the Northwest Territory?

The Founding Fathers finished writing the Constitution in September 1787. At least nine states had to approve it before it went into operation. Many people opposed the Constitution, however. Some people believed the Constitution gave the president too much power. Others, like Thomas Jefferson and Sam Adams, did

Think: **Washington was well-loved for his victories during the Revolution. He was elected in 1789.**
Respond: **What symbols are in this work, which celebrates Washington?**

not think the Constitution protected the rights of individual citizens.

People who supported the Constitution were known as *Federalists*. Those who opposed it were *Anti-Federalists*. The Federalists were well organized, and they worked very hard to get the Constitution approved. They promised to add a bill of rights that would help protect people's freedom. By the summer of 1788, most states had approved the Constitution. It became the new plan of the new government of the United States.

After the Constitution was approved, the states elected representatives to the new Congress. There was also an election for the president. No one was surprised that George Washington was elected the first president of the United States. The American people trusted Washington. He was "first in war, first in peace, and first in the hearts of his countrymen." Washington was sworn in as president in New York City on April 16, 1789. John Adams became the nation's first vice president.

Think: **After many months of writing, arguing, compromising, and rewriting, the Founding Fathers were finally finished. Thirty-nine Founding Fathers signed the Constitution on September 17, 1787.** Respond: **Choose three Founding Fathers from the painting and tell what they might have been thinking and feeling.**

Think: **Washington met with Henry Knox, Alexander Hamilton, Thomas Jefferson, and Edmund Randolph.**
Respond: **Why is it important for a president to have advisors?**

To help the president, Congress created several new jobs. There would be a **secretary of war** to advise the president about the nation's defense. There would be a **secretary of the treasury** to help the president control the nation's economy. There would be a **secretary of state** who would advise the president on dealings with foreign nations. The secretary of state would also advise the president about problems in the United States that were not handled by the other secretaries. Together, these secretaries formed the president's **Cabinet**.

Washington named some outstanding leaders to his Cabinet. General Henry Knox became secretary of war. Alexander Hamilton was named secretary of the treasury. Thomas Jefferson became secretary of state. Washington also named Edmund Randolph as **attorney general** (uh-TUR-nee), to advise him on the nation's legal affairs.

The New Government Takes Office

One of the first laws Congress passed was the **Judiciary Act** (joo-DISH-e-er-ee) of 1789. This act set up a system of federal courts. The federal courts tried cases involving laws passed by Congress. There were three levels of federal courts. First were thirteen district courts, one for each state. Next were three circuit courts to hear appeals of district court decisions. Finally, there was the Supreme Court, the highest court in the land.

At this time, Congress took another important action. It added ten **amendments** (uh-MEND-munts), or changes, to the Constitution. These first ten amendments were called the **Bill of Rights**, and they protected the freedoms that people had been given by the state constitutions. The Bill of Rights stated that the federal government could not pass laws taking away people's rights to worship and speak freely, or their right to a fair trial. The Bill of Rights also protected the various powers of the states.

Think: **Federal Hall, in New York City, was the nation's first capitol under the Constitution. Shown here is the chamber of the House of Representatives. It is where the Bill of Rights was presented in 1789. The Bill of Rights protect the rights and freedoms of the people.**
Respond: **What does the magnificence of this building tell you about the hopes of the nation's founders?**

HISTORY MAKERS

Haym Salomon
A Generous Patriot

Courtesy of Borden Publishing Co.

"We are in agreement, then?"

"Yes, we are. I will back the treasury with my money and my name. In addition, Mr. Morris, I will continue to guarantee government loans. I hope this will be helpful in establishing our country's credit."

"Helpful? It will be invaluable, Mr. Salomon! You are doing our country a great service, sir, just as you did during the war."

"I love this nation, Mr. Morris. And I love freedom. As a Polish Jew, I know what it is to live without freedom. I will do whatever I can, sir, to support the country and to keep America free!"

Haym Salomon, a prominent Philadelphia banker, and Robert Morris, superintendent of finance to the new American republic, shook hands. Haym Salomon had once again promised financial support to the young government.

Haym Salomon left Poland and worked in business in France before he came to the colonies. His financial ability and knowledge of many languages were valuable assets to his new country. Haym Salomon helped finance the American Revolution and the new nation's government.

The Continental Congress and the army both needed money. Each colony had to pay its soldiers and Congressional delegates. Since the colonies had a hard time collecting taxes, soldiers and delegates were often unpaid. Haym Salomon made private interest-free loans to many army officers and delegates to Congress.

Haym Salomon used his connections in France to help arrange loans to the young government. He guaranteed many government loans, agreeing to repay the money if the government could not. Often those loans, and the private loans to army officers and to Congressional delegates, were not paid back. As a result, Haym Salomon was nearly penniless when he died.

Haym Salomon was devoted to the cause of freedom. He used his personal wealth to finance the American Revolution and the struggling new government. Americans owe him much more than money.

A Bank for the Nation

One of the big problems facing the new government was money. During the Revolutionary War, the government had borrowed money from France and Spain, and also from some Americans. Now it had to begin paying back this money. Most states also owed money they had borrowed while fighting the war. Alexander Hamilton, the secretary of the treasury, developed a plan to pay these debts. He wanted the federal government to pay off the national debt and the states' debts.

The southern states were opposed to the idea of having the federal government pay the states' debts. They had already paid off most of their debts. They did not want to be taxed to help pay the debts of other states. However, another compromise was made. Thomas Jefferson, who was from Virginia, helped Hamilton get his plan through Congress. In return, the capital of the United States would be moved to a place in the South. The new capital was first called Federal Town, but it later became known as Washington, D.C., in honor of George Washington.

Hamilton also wanted to set up a national bank. This bank would be owned by both the government and private citizens. It would hold the federal government's tax collections. It would print paper money for the nation. The bank would also earn money from interest on loans to states and businesses.

Some Americans did not want a national bank. They thought it favored the rich merchants and businesses of the North. Thomas Jefferson did not believe that the

Think: **Alexander Hamilton (right) worked to establish the Bank of the United States. The First Bank of the United States (1791–1811) had nine branches. The bank issued notes, or money, collected payments, and paid public officials.**
Respond: **What problems might arise with a government-owned bank?**

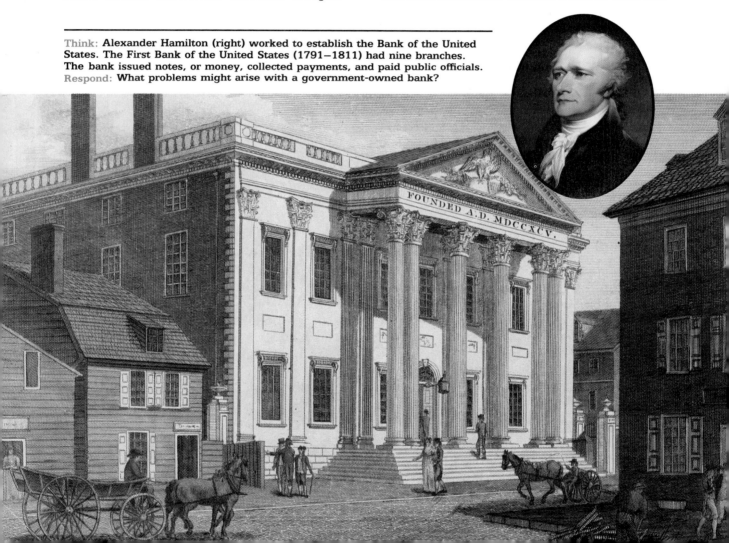

Think: **The victorious General Anthony Wayne is shown here during the Battle of Fallen Timbers. The Indians Wayne fought against felt the surrounding land was theirs. American settlers believed the land belonged to the United States.** Respond: **What reasons might both the Indians and the American settlers give?**

Constitution gave Congress the power to open a bank. Hamilton argued that the Constitution gave Congress the power to make laws that were "necessary and proper" to carry out the government's work. President Washington and the members of Congress agreed with Hamilton. The Bank of the United States opened in 1791.

The West Settles Down

While the new government was working out its problems, thousands of Americans were moving westward. Most of these people were farmers who wanted to own land in the Northwest Territory. The Indians in the Northwest Territory were not happy about all the people moving there. They believed that they owned this land. They attacked frontier settlements and defeated the armies that President

Washington sent against them. In 1794, Anthony Wayne, a famous Revolutionary War general, defeated the Indians at the battle of Fallen Timbers in Ohio. Wayne's victory made the Northwest Territory safe for American settlers for many years.

Section Review

1. Who were the Federalists? Who were the Anti-Federalists?
2. What jobs were created to help the president run the country?
3. What important changes were made in the Constitution?
4. As secretary of the treasury, what did Alexander Hamilton suggest to improve the nation's economy?

The Constitution
of the United States of America

PREAMBLE

We the people of the United States, in order to form a more perfect Union, establish justice, insure domestic tranquility, provide for the common defense, promote the general welfare, and secure the blessings of liberty to ourselves and our posterity, do ordain and establish this Constitution for the United States of America.

The Preamble lists the reasons for writing the Constitution

ARTICLE 1. LEGISLATIVE BRANCH

SECTION 1. CONGRESS

All legislative powers herein granted shall be vested in a Congress of the United States, which shall consist of a Senate and House of Representatives.

The power to make laws is given to a Congress of two houses.

SECTION 2. HOUSE OF REPRESENTATIVES

1. *Election and Term of Members.* The House of Representatives shall be composed of members chosen every second year by the people of the several States, and the electors in each State shall have the qualifications requisite for electors of the most numerous branch of the State Legislature.

Members of the House of Representatives are chosen every two years. They are elected by the voters who are qualified to vote for members of the state legislatures.

2. *Qualifications.* No person shall be a representative who shall not have attained to the age of twenty-five years, and been seven years a citizen of the United States, and who shall not, when elected, be an inhabitant of that State in which he shall be chosen.

A member of the House of Representatives must be at least 25 years old, a United States citizen for 7 years, and living in the state that he or she represents.

3. *Apportionment of Representatives and Direct Taxes.* Representatives and direct taxes shall be apportioned among the several States which may be included within this Union, according to their respective numbers, which shall be determined by adding to the whole number of free persons, including those bound to service for a term of years, and excluding Indians not taxed, three-fifths of all other persons. The actual enumeration shall be made within three years after the first meeting of the Congress of the United States, and within every subsequent term of ten years, in such manner as they shall by law direct. The number of representatives shall not exceed one for every thirty thousand, but each State shall have at least one representative; and until such enumeration shall be made, the State of New Hampshire shall be entitled to choose three, Massachusetts eight, Rhode Island and Providence Plantations one, Connecticut five, New York six, New Jersey four, Pennsylvania eight, Delaware one, Maryland six, Virginia ten, North Carolina five, South Carolina five, and Georgia three.

The number of Representatives for each state is based on the state's population.
A national census, or an official count of the population, must be taken every ten years.

4. *Vacancies.* When vacancies happen in the representation from any State, the Executive authority thereof shall issue writs of election to fill such vacancies.

Empty seats in the House of Representatives must be filled by special elections.

5. *Officers and Impeachment.* The House of Representatives shall choose their Speaker and other officers; and shall have the sole power of impeachment.

The House of Representatives has the power of impeachment, or the power to accuse a federal official of wrongdoing in office.

SECTION 3. SENATE

1. *Term and Number of Members.* The Senate of the United States shall be composed of two senators from each State, chosen by the legislature thereof, for six years; and each senator shall have one vote.

In the Senate, each state is represented equally by two senators. [The way of electing senators was changed by Amendment 17.]

2. *Three Classes of Senators.* Immediately after they shall be assembled in consequence of the first election, they shall be divided as equally as may be into three classes. The seats of the senators of the first class shall be vacated at the expiration of the second year, of the second class at the expiration of the fourth year, and of the third class at the expiration of the sixth year, so that one-third may be chosen every second year; and if vacancies happen by resignation, or otherwise, during the recess of the legislature of any State, the executive thereof may make temporary appointments until the next meeting of the legislature, which shall then fill such vacancies.

One-third of the senators are elected every two years. Each senator serves a six-year term. [This way of filling empty seats in the Senate was changed by Amendment 17.]

3. *Qualifications.* No person shall be a senator who shall not have attained to the age of thirty years, and been nine years a citizen of the United States, and who shall not, when elected, be an inhabitant of that State for which he shall be chosen.

A senator must be at least 30 years old, a United States citizen for 9 years, and living in the state that he or she represents.

4. *Vice President's Role.* The Vice President of the United States shall be President of the Senate, but shall have no vote, unless they be equally divided.

The Vice President is the officer in charge of the Senate, but he or she may vote only in the case of a tie.

5. *Other Officers.* The Senate shall choose their other officers, and also a President pro tempore, in the absence of the Vice President, or when he shall exercise the office of President of the United States.

The Senate elects a temporary officer in charge from among its members to serve when the Vice President is absent or when he or she becomes President.

6. *Trial of Impeachments.* The Senate shall have the sole power to try all impeachments. When sitting for that purpose, they shall be on oath or affirmation. When the President of the United States is tried, the Chief Justice shall preside; and no person shall be convicted without the concurrence of two-thirds of the members.

The Senate has power to hold a trial in cases of impeachment. A two-thirds vote declares an impeached official guilty.

7. *Penalty for Conviction.* Judgment in cases of impeachment shall not extend further than to removal from office, and disqualification to hold and enjoy any office or honor, trust or profit under the United States; but the party convicted shall nevertheless be liable and subject to indictment, trial, judgment and punishment, according to law.

The Senate can remove from office officials found guilty on impeachment charges. These officials also may have a court trial if they have broken any laws.

SECTION 4. MEETINGS AND ELECTIONS

1. *Holding Elections.* The times, places and manner of holding elections for senators and representatives, shall be prescribed in each State by the legislature thereof; but the Congress may at any time by law make or alter such regulations, except as to the places of choosing senators.

Election rules are set by the states. But Congress may pass laws that set new election rules.

2. *Meetings.* The Congress shall assemble at least once in every year, and such meeting shall be on the first Monday in December, unless they shall by law appoint a different day.

[The meeting time of Congress was changed by Amendment 20. Congress now meets January 3.]

SECTION 5. RULES OF PROCEDURE

1. *Quorum and Membership.* Each house shall be the judge of the elections, returns and qualifications of its own members, and a majority of each shall constitute a quorum to do business; but a smaller number may adjourn from day to day, and may be authorized to compel the attendance of absent members, in such manner, and under such penalties as each house may provide.

Each house of Congress decides whether its members are qualified and were elected fairly. A majority (more than half) of the members, or a quorum, must be present before each house may carry on its work.

Members of either house of Congress may be required to attend meetings in order that Congress can carry on its activities.

2. *Discipline.* Each house may determine the rules of its proceedings, punish its members for disorderly behavior, and, with the concurrence of two-thirds, expel a member.

3. *Journal.* Each house shall keep a journal of its proceedings, and from time to time publish the same, excepting such parts as may in their judgment require secrecy; and the yeas and the nays of the members of either house on any question shall, at the desire of one-fifth of those present, be entered on the journal.

Each house of Congress must print an official record of its activities.

4. *Adjournment.* Neither house, during the session of Congress, shall, without the consent of the other, adjourn for more than three days, nor to any other place than that in which the two houses shall be sitting.

Neither house of Congress may adjourn, or put off meeting, for more than three days unless the other house agrees to it.

SECTION 6. PRIVILEGES AND RESTRICTIONS

1. *Compensation and Privileges.* The senators and representatives shall receive a compensation for their services, to be ascertained by law, and paid out of the Treasury of the United States. They shall in all cases, except treason, felony and breach of the peace, be privileged from arrest during their attendance at the session of their respective houses, and in going to and returning from the same; and for any speech or debate in either house, they shall not be questioned in any other place.

Members of Congress are paid salaries and receive extra sums of money for certain things they must do.
Members of Congress cannot be arrested for anything they say in Congress. But they can be arrested for serious crimes while Congress is meeting.

2. Restrictions. No senator or representative shall, during the time for which he was elected, be appointed to any civil office under the authority of the United States, which shall have been created, or the emoluments whereof shall have been increased during such time; and no person holding any office under the United States, shall be a member of either house during his continuance in office.

A member of Congress cannot hold any other federal office while he or she serves in Congress.

SECTION 7. HOW BILLS BECOME LAWS

1. Money Bills. All bills for raising revenue shall originate in the House of Representatives; but the Senate may propose or concur with amendments as on other bills.

All tax bills must be started in the House of Representatives, but the Senate can suggest changes.

2. President's Veto Power. Every bill which shall have passed the House of Representatives and the Senate, shall, before it become a law, be presented to the President of the United States; if he approves he shall sign it, but if not he shall return it, with his objections to that house in which it shall have originated, who shall enter the objections at large on their journal, and proceed to reconsider it. If after such reconsideration two thirds of that House shall agree to pass the bill, it shall be sent, together with the objections, to the other House, by which it shall likewise be reconsidered, and if approved by two thirds of the House, it shall become a law. But in all such cases the votes of both Houses shall be determined by yeas and nays, and the names of the persons voting for and against the bill shall be entered on the journal of each House respectively. If any bill shall not be returned by the President within ten days (Sundays excepted) after it shall have been presented to him, the same shall be a law, in like manner as if he had signed it,

unless the Congress by their adjournment prevent its return, in which case it shall not be a law.

A bill passed by Congress must be sent to the president. If the president signs the bill, it becomes a law. If the president vetoes, or refuses to sign, the bill, it returns to the house where it was started.

The president's veto may be overcome by a two-thirds vote of each house of Congress.

The president can let a bill become a law without signing it. But a bill sent to the president during the last 10 days when Congress is meeting does not become law if the president does not sign it.

3. Actions Other Than Bills. Every order, resolution, or vote to which the concurrence of the Senate and House of Representatives may be necessary (except on a question of adjournment) shall be presented to the President of the United States; and before the same shall take effect, shall be approved by him, or being disapproved by him, shall be repassed by two thirds of the Senate and House of Representatives, according to the rules and limitations prescribed in the case of a bill.

The president must either sign or veto everything passed by Congress, except when Congress votes to put off meeting.

SECTION 8. POWERS DELEGATED TO CONGRESS

1. Taxes. The Congress shall have power to lay and collect taxes, duties, imposts and excises, to pay the debts and provide for the common defense and general welfare of the United States; but all duties, imposts and excises shall be uniform throughout the United States.

2. Borrowing. To borrow money on the credit of the United States;

3. Commerce. To regulate commerce with foreign nations, and among the several States, and with the Indian tribes;

4. Naturalization and Bankruptcy. To establish a uniform rule of naturalization, and uniform laws on the subject of bankruptcies throughout the United States;

5. Coins and Standards. To coin money, regulate the value thereof, and of foreign coin, and fix the standard of weights and measures;

6. Punishment of Counterfeiting. To provide for the punishment of counterfeiting the securities and current coin of the United States;

7. Post Offices and Roads. To establish post offices and post roads;

8. Patents and Copyrights. To promote the progress of science and useful arts, by securing for limited times to authors and inventors the exclusive right to their respective writings and discoveries;

9. Lower Courts. To constitute tribunals inferior to the Supreme Court:

10. Punishment of Piracy. To define and punish piracies and felonies committed on the high seas, and offenses against the law of nations;

11. War. To declare war, grant letters of marque and reprisal, and make rules concerning captures on land and water;

12. Army. To raise and support armies, but no appropriation of money to that use shall be for a longer term than two years;

13. Navy. To provide and maintain a Navy;

14. Regulation of Armed Forces. To make rules for the government and regulation of the land and naval forces;

15. Militia. To provide for calling forth the militia to execute the laws of the Union, suppress insurrections and repel invasions;

16. Organizing the Militia. To provide for organizing, arming, and disciplining the militia, and for governing such part of them as may be employed in the service of the United States, reserving to the States respectively, the appointment of the officers, and the authority of training the militia according to the discipline prescribed by Congress:

17. District of Columbia. To exercise exclusive legislation in all cases whatsoever, over such district (not exceeding ten miles square) as may, by cession of particular States, and the acceptance of Congress, become the seat of the Government of the United States, and to exercise like authority over all places purchased by the consent of the legislature of the State in which the same shall be, for the erection of forts, magazines, arsenals, dockyards, and other needful buildings;

18. Elastic Clause. And to make all laws which shall be necessary and proper for carrying into execution the foregoing powers, and all other powers vested by this Constitution in the Government of the United States, or in any department or officer thereof.

The powers given to Congress are:

1. to vote for and collect equal taxes, to pay debts, and to provide for the defense and general welfare of the nation

2. to borrow money

3. to make rules for trade between the states and with other nations

4. to set up rules on how foreign-born persons become citizens, and rules about failure to pay debts

5. to coin money and to decide what weights and measures shall be used

6. to fix rules for punishing any person who makes false money

7. to establish post offices and roads for carrying mail

8. to prevent the works of writers and inventors from being copied by others unlawfully

9. to set up federal courts

10. to punish piracy, or robbery at sea

11. to declare war

12. to raise and support armies

13. to support a navy

14. to make rules for the armed forces

15. to provide for calling out the militia (the National Guard)

16. to help states support their militia

17. to set up and govern the District of Columbia (Washington, D.C.), and to govern other federal property

18. to make all "necessary and proper" laws. Number 18 is called the "elastic clause," because it allows Congress to stretch its powers and to take many actions not named in the Constitution.

SECTION 9. POWERS DENIED TO THE FEDERAL GOVERNMENT

1. Slave Trade. The migration or importation of such persons as any of the States now existing shall think proper to admit, shall not be prohibited by the Congress prior to the year one thousand eight hundred and eight, but a tax or duty may be imposed on such importation, not exceeding ten dollars for each person.

2. Habeas Corpus. The privilege of the writ of habeas corpus shall not be suspended, unless when in cases of rebellion or invasion the public safety may require it.

3. Special Bills. No bill of attainder or ex post facto law shall be passed.

4. Direct Tax. No capitation, or other direct, tax shall be laid, unless in proportion to the census or enumeration herein before directed to be taken.

5. Export Duties. No tax or duty shall be laid on articles exported from any State.

6. Interstate Commerce. No preference shall be given by any regulation of commerce or revenue to the ports of one State over those of another; nor shall vessels bound to, or from, one State, be obliged to enter, clear, or pay duties in another.

7. Treasury Withdrawals. No money shall be drawn from the Treasury, but in consequence of appropriations made by law; and a regular statement and account of the receipts and expenditures of all public money shall be published from time to time.

8. Titles of Nobility. No title of nobility shall be granted by the United States, and no person holding any office of profit or trust under them, shall, without the consent of the Congress, accept of any present, emolument, office, or title, of any kind whatever, from any King, Prince, or foreign State.

The powers forbidden to Congress are:
[1. to try to stop the slave trade before the year 1808]
2. to refuse to allow a prisoner to hear the charges against him or her, except when the nation is in danger
3. to take away a guilty person's property, or to punish a person for doing something that was not yet against the law when he or she did it
4. to vote for direct taxes, except taxes based on a state's population. [This was changed by Amendment 16, the Income Tax Amendment.]
5. to tax goods sent out of a state
6. to pass a law that favors the trade of one state over another state
7. to spend money without voting for it in both houses
8. to give or accept any title of nobility (favored high position)

SECTION 10. POWERS DENIED TO THE STATES

1. Treaties, Coinage. No State shall enter into any treaty, alliance, or confederation; grant letters of marque and reprisal; coin money; emit bills of credit; make any thing but gold and silver coin a tender in payment of debts; pass any bill of attainder, ex post facto law, or law impairing the obligation of contracts, or grant any title of nobility.

2. Duties and Imposts. No State shall, without the consent of the Congress, lay any imposts or duties on imports or exports, except what may be absolutely necessary for executing its inspection laws; and the net produce of all duties and imposts, laid by any State on imports or exports, shall be for the use of the Treasury of the United States; and all such laws shall be subject to the revision and control of the Congress.

3. War. No State shall, without the consent of Congress, lay any duty of tonnage, keep troops, or ships of war in time of peace, enter into any agreement or compact with another State, or with a foreign power, or engage in war, unless actually invaded, or in such imminent danger as will not admit of delay.

The powers forbidden to the states are:
1. to make treaties, to coin money, and to do certain things also forbidden to the federal government
2. to vote for taxes on goods sent in or out of a state, unless Congress agrees
3. to keep troops or warships in peacetime or to deal with another state or a foreign nation, unless Congress agrees

ARTICLE 2. EXECUTIVE BRANCH

SECTION 1. PRESIDENT AND VICE PRESIDENT.

1. Four-Year Term. The executive power shall be vested in a President of the United States of America. He shall hold his office during the term of four years, and, together with the Vice President, chosen for the same term, be elected, as follows:

Executive power, or the power to carry out laws, is given to the president. The president serves in office for a four-year term.

2. Electors from Each State. Each State, shall appoint, in such manner as the legislature thereof may direct, a number of electors, equal to the whole number of senators and representatives to which the State may be entitled in the Congress; but no senator or representative, or person holding an office of trust or profit under the United States, shall be appointed an elector.

The president is elected by electors, or representatives, chosen by the people.

3. Former System of Election. The electors shall meet in their respective States, and vote by ballot for two persons, of whom one at least shall not be an inhabitant of the same State with themselves. And they shall make a list of all the persons voted for, and of the number of votes for each; which list they shall sign and certify, and transmit sealed to the seat of the Government of the United States, directed to the President of the Senate. The President of the Senate shall, in the presence of the Senate and House of Repre-

sentatives, open all the certificates, and the votes shall then be counted. The person having the greatest number of votes shall be the President, if such number be a majority of the whole number of electors appointed; and if there be more than one who have such majority; and have an equal number of votes, then the House of Representatives shall immediately choose by ballot one of them for President, and if no person have a majority, then from the five highest on the list the said House shall in like manner choose the President. But in choosing the President, the votes shall be taken by States, the representation from each State having one vote, a quorum for this purpose shall consist of a member or members from two thirds of the States, and a majority of all the States shall be necessary to a choice. In every case, after the choice of the President, the person having the greatest number of votes of the electors shall be the Vice President. But if there should remain two or more who have equal votes, the Senate shall choose from them by ballot the Vice President.

[This way of electing the president and vice president was changed by Amendment 12.]

4. Time of Elections. The Congress may determine the time of choosing the electors, and the day on which they shall give their votes; which day shall be the same throughout the United States.

Today, presidential elections are held on the first Tuesday after the first Monday in November. Electoral votes are cast on the first Monday after the second Wednesday in December.

5. Qualifications for President. No person except a natural born citizen, or a citizen of the United States at the time of the adoption of this Constitution, shall be eligible to the office of President; neither shall any person be eligible to that office who shall not have attained to the age of thirty-five years, and been fourteen years a resident within the United States.

The president must be a citizen born in the United States, at least 35 years old, and living in the United States for at least 14 years.

6. Succession of the Vice President. In case of the removal of the President from office, or of his death, resignation, or inability to discharge the powers and duties of the said office, the same shall devolve on the Vice President, and the Congress may by law provide for the case of removal, death, resignation, or inability, both of the President and Vice President, declaring what officer shall then act as President, and such officer shall act accordingly, until the disability be removed, or a President shall be elected.

If the president dies, or for any reason cannot carry out his or her duties, the vice president will act as president. If the vice president also is unable to serve, Congress has voted that the Speaker of the House, and, after him or her, the temporary president of the Senate, will serve as president.

7. President's Salary. The President shall, at stated times, receive for his services, a compensation, which shall neither be increased nor diminished during the period for which he shall have been elected, and he shall not receive within that period any other emolument from the United States, or any of them.

The president must be paid a salary, and the amount he or she is paid cannot be changed during his or her term in office.

8. President's Oath of Office. Before he enter on the execution of his office, he shall take the following oath or affirmation: ''I do solemnly swear (or affirm) that I will faithfully execute the office of President of the United States, and will to the best of my ability, preserve, protect and defend the Constitution of the United States.''

The president takes an oath of office, or is ''sworn in,'' before he or she begins the duties of office.

SECTION 2. POWERS OF THE PRESIDENT

1. Commander in Chief. The President shall be Commander in Chief of the Army and Navy of the United States, and of the militia of the several States, when called into the actual service of the United States; he may require the opinion, in writing, of the principal officer in each of the Executive Departments, upon any subject relating to the duties of their respective offices, and he shall have power to grant reprieves and pardons for offenses against the United States, except in cases of impeachment.

2. Treaties and Appointments. He shall have power, by and with the advice and consent of the Senate, to make treaties, provided two thirds of the Senators present concur; and he shall nominate, and by and with the advice and consent of the Senate, shall appoint ambassadors, other public ministers and consuls, Judges of the Supreme Court, and all other officers of the United States, whose appointments are not herein otherwise provided for, and which shall be established by law; but the Congress may by law vest the appointment of such inferior officers, as they think proper, in the President alone, in the courts of law, or in the heads of departments.

3. Vacancies. The President shall have power to fill up all vacancies that may happen during the recess of the Senate, by granting commissions which shall expire at the end of their next session.

The powers of the president are:
1. to act as commander in chief of the armed forces. The president may ask for help from the heads of each federal government department, who make up the president's Cabinet.

The President may give pardons to, or set free, persons who acted against the United States, except in cases of impeachment.
2. to make treaties and to appoint federal officials, with the agreement of the Senate.
3. to appoint temporary officials to fill empty federal offices, without the agreement of the Senate when Congress is not meeting

SECTION 3. DUTIES OF THE PRESIDENT

He shall from time to time give to the Congress information of the state of the Union, and recommend to their consideration such measures as he shall judge necessary and expedient; he may, on extraordinary occasions, convene both houses, or either of them, and in case of disagreement between them, with respect to the time of adjournment, he may adjourn them to such time as he shall think proper; he shall receive ambassadors and other public ministers; he shall take care that the laws be faithfully executed, and shall commission all the officers of the United States.

The president must send or read a report on the ''state of the Union''—the condition of the nation—at each opening meeting of Congress. He or she also may send special messages to Congress.

The president may call special meetings of Congress.

The president must meet with foreign ambassadors, carry out the laws of the nation, and sign orders appointing new officers in the armed forces.

SECTION 4. IMPEACHMENT AND REMOVAL FROM OFFICE

The President, Vice President and all civil officers of the United States, shall be removed from office on impeachment for, and conviction of, treason, bribery, or other high crimes and misdemeanors.

The president and other federal officials may be removed from office if they are found guilty in cases of impeachment

ARTICLE 3. JUDICIAL BRANCH

SECTION 1. FEDERAL COURTS

The judicial power of the United States shall be vested in one Supreme Court, and in such inferior courts as the Congress may from time to time ordain and establish. The judges, both of the supreme and inferior courts, shall hold their offices during good behaviour, and shall, at stated times, receive for their services, a compensation, which shall not be diminished during their continuance in office.

Judicial power, or the power to judge the law, is given to a Supreme Court and to lower federal courts set up by Congress.

Federal judges serve in office for life, but they may be removed in cases of impeachment.

SECTION 2. JURISDICTION OF FEDERAL COURTS

1. *Cases Under Federal Jurisdiction.* The judicial power shall extend to all cases, in law and equity, arising under this Constitution, the laws of the United States, and treaties made, or which shall be made, under their authority; to all cases affecting ambassadors, other public ministers and consuls; to all cases of admiralty and maritime jurisdiction; to controversies to which the United States shall be a party; to controversies between two or more States; between a State and citizens of another State, between citizens of different States, between citizens of the same State claiming lands under grants of different States, and between a State, or the citizens thereof, and foreign States, citizens or subjects.

Federal courts judge cases that concern the meaning of the Constitution, federal laws, and treaties. They also judge cases that concern the United States, a state, citizens of different states, and citizens of foreign nations.

2. *Cases for the Supreme Court.* In all cases affecting ambassadors, other public ministers and consuls, and those in which a State shall be a party, the Supreme Court shall have original jurisdiction. In all the other cases before mentioned, the Supreme Court shall have appellate jurisdiction, both as to law and fact, with such exceptions, and under such regulations as the Congress shall make.

Cases that concern ambassadors or other officials of foreign nations, and cases that concern states, are judged by the Supreme Court. Other cases begin in lower courts, but they may sometimes be judged again in the Supreme Court.

3. *Conduct of Trials.* The trial of all crimes, except in cases of impeachment, shall be by jury; and such trial shall be held in the State where the said crimes shall have been committed; but when not committed within any State, the trial shall be at such place or places as the Congress may by law have directed.

All federal crimes, except cases of impeachment, are to be judged in trials in the states where the crimes took place.

SECTION 3. CASES OF TREASON

1. *Treason Defined.* Treason against the United States shall consist only in levying war against them, or in adhering to their enemies, giving them aid and comfort. No person shall be convicted of treason unless on the testimony of two witnesses to the same overt act, or on confession in open court.

Treason is carefully explained as making war against the United States or helping its enemies.

2. *Punishment.* The Congress shall have power to declare the punishment of treason, but no attainder of treason shall work corruption of blood, or forfeiture except during the life of the person attainted.

The family of a person found guilty of treason cannot also be punished.

ARTICLE 4. RELATIONS AMONG THE STATES

SECTION 1. TREATMENT OF OFFICIAL ACTS

Full faith and credit shall be given in each State to the public acts, records, and judicial proceedings of every other State. And the Congress may by general laws prescribe the manner in which such acts, records and proceedings shall be proved, and the effect thereof.

All states must respect one another's laws, records, and lawful decisions.

SECTION 2. TREATMENT OF CITIZENS

1. *Privileges.* The citizens of each State shall be entitled to all privileges and immunities of citizens in the several States.

Each state must treat citizens of other states as it treats its own citizens.

2. *Extradition.* A person charged in any State with treason, felony, or other crime, who shall flee from justice, and be found in another State, shall on demand of the executive authority of the State from which he fled, be delivered up, to be removed to the State having jurisdiction of the crime.

A person accused of a crime who runs away to another state must be returned to the state where the crime took place.

3. *Fugitive Slaves.* No person held to service or labour in one State, under the laws thereof, escaping into another, shall, in consequence of any law or regulation therein, be discharged from such service or labour, but shall be delivered up on claim of the party to whom such service or labour may be due.

[This rule about runaway slaves was not used after Amendment 13 ended slavery in 1865.]

SECTION 3. ADMITTING NEW STATES

1. *Process for Admitting States.* New states may be admitted by the Congress into this Union; but no new State shall be formed or erected within the jurisdiction of any other State; nor any State be formed by the junction of two or more States, or parts of States, without the consent of the legislatures of the States concerned as well as of the Congress.

New states cannot be formed by dividing or joining present states, unless the state legislatures and Congress agree. New states may be admitted into the Union by Congress.

2. *Public Lands.* The Congress shall have power to dispose of and make all needful rules and regulations respecting the Territory or other property belonging to the United States; and nothing in this Constitution shall be so construed as to prejudice any claims of the United States, or of any particular State.

Congress has power to make laws for the territories and for federal property.

SECTION 4. GUARANTEES TO STATES

The United States shall guarantee to every State in this Union a republican form of Government, and shall protect each of them against invasion; and on application of the legislature, or of the executive (when the legislature cannot be convened) against domestic violence.

Each state is promised a republican form of government, or a government in which the people elect their representatives. The federal government must protect states against foreign attack or trouble within the state.

ARTICLE 5. METHODS OF AMENDMENT

The Congress, whenever two thirds of both Houses shall deem it necessary, shall propose amendments to this Constitution, or on the application of the legislatures of two thirds of the several States, shall call a convention for proposing amendments, which, in either case, shall be valid to all intents and purposes, as part of this Constitution, when ratified by the legislatures of three fourths of the several States, or by conventions in three fourths thereof, as the one or the other mode of ratification may be proposed by the Congress; provided that no amendment which may be made prior to the year one thousand

eight hundred and eight shall in any manner affect the first and fourth clauses in the Ninth Section of the First Article; and that no State, without its consent, shall be deprived of its equal suffrage in the Senate.

Amendments may be suggested by a two-thirds vote of each house of Congress or at the request of two-thirds of the states. Amendments must be ratified, or approved, by the legislatures of three-fourths of the states or by the voters in three-fourths of the states.

No amendment may take away from a state, against its wishes, its right to an equal vote in the Senate.

ARTICLE 6. NATIONAL SUPREMACY

1. *Existing Obligations.* All debts contracted and engagements entered into, before the adoption of this Constitution, shall be as valid against the United States under this Constitution, as under the Confederation.

The federal government must respect all debts and agreements of the United States that were made before the adoption of the Constitution.

2. *Supreme Law.* This Constitution, and the laws of the United States which shall be made in pursuance thereof; and all treaties made, or which shall be made, under the authority of the United States, shall be the supreme law of the land; and the judges in every State shall be bound thereby, anything in the Constitution or laws of any State to the contrary notwithstanding.

The Constitution, laws, and treaties of the United States are the highest law of the nation. No state or local laws may disagree with them.

3. *Oath of Office.* The senators and representatives before mentioned, and the members of the several State legislatures, and all executive and judicial officers, both of the United States and of the several States, shall be bound by oath or affirmation, to support this Constitution; but no religious test shall ever be required as a qualification to any office or public trust under the United States.

All federal and state officials must promise to support the Constitution.

Religion is not important in deciding if a person is qualified to serve in a federal office.

ARTICLE 7. RATIFICATION

The ratification of the conventions of nine States shall be sufficient for the establishment of this Constitution between the States so ratifying the same.

Done in convention by the unanimous consent of the States present the seventeenth day of September in the year of our Lord one thousand seven hundred and eighty seven and of the Independence of the United States of America the twelfth. In witness whereof we have hereunto subscribed our names.

George Washington—President and deputy from Virginia
Attest: William Jackson, Secretary

New Hampshire
John Langdon
Nicholas Gilman

Massachusetts
Nathaniel Gorham
Rufus King

Connecticut
William Samuel Johnson
Roger Sherman

New York
Alexander Hamilton

New Jersey
William Livingston
David Brearley
William Paterson
Jonathan Dayton

Pennsylvania
Benjamin Franklin
Thomas Mifflin
Robert Morris
George Clymer
Thomas FitzSimons
Jared Ingersoll
James Wilson
Gouverneur Morris

Delaware
George Read
Gunning Bedford, Jr.
John Dickinson
Richard Bassett
Jacob Broom

Maryland
James McHenry
Daniel of St. Thomas Jenifer
Daniel Carroll

Virginia
John Blair
James Madison, Jr.

North Carolina
William Blount
Richard Dobbs Spaight
Hugh Williamson

South Carolina
John Rutledge
Charles Cotesworth Pinckney
Charles Pinckney
Pierce Butler

Georgia
William Few
Abraham Baldwin

The Constitution was to become the law of the nation when it was ratified, or approved, by nine states.

AMENDMENTS

AMENDMENT 1. RELIGIOUS AND POLITICAL FREEDOM (1791)

Congress shall make no law respecting an establishment of religion, or prohibiting the free exercise thereof; or abridging the freedom of speech, or of the press; or the right of the people peaceably to assemble, and to petition the Government for a redress of grievances.

Congress may not set up an official church or pass laws that limit freedom of religion, speech, the press, assembly (public meeting), and petition (asking the government to do certain things).

AMENDMENT 2. RIGHT TO BEAR ARMS (1791)

A well regulated militia, being necessary to the security of a free State, the right of the people to keep and bear arms, shall not be infringed.

Citizens have the right to keep weapons.

AMENDMENT 3. QUARTERING OF SOLDIERS (1791)

No soldier shall, in time of peace be quartered in any house, without the consent of the owner, nor in time of war, but in a manner to be prescribed by law.

Military troops may not take over private houses in peace time.

AMENDMENT 4. SEARCH AND SEIZURE (1791)

The right of the people to be secure in their persons, houses, papers, and effects, against unreasonable searches and seizures, shall not be violated, and no warrants shall issue, but upon probable cause, supported by oath or affirmation, and particularly describing the place to be searched, and the persons or things to be seized.

The government is limited in its right to search or take persons and property.

AMENDMENT 5. CRIMINAL PROCESS; DUE PROCESS (1791)

No person shall be held to answer for a capital, or otherwise infamous crime, unless on a presentment or indictment of a Grand Jury, except in cases arising in the land or naval forces, or in the militia, when in actual service in time of war or public danger; nor shall any person be subject for the same offense to be twice put in jeopardy of life or limb; nor shall be compelled in any criminal case to be a witness against himself, nor be deprived of life, liberty, or property, without due process of law; nor shall private property be taken for public use, without just compensation.

A person cannot be put on trial for a serious crime unless he or she is accused by a grand jury. He or she cannot be tried for the same crime twice. He or she cannot be forced to give evidence against himself. No person's right to life, liberty, or property can be taken away except by lawful means.

AMENDMENT 6. RIGHT TO JURY TRIAL (1791)

In all criminal prosecutions, the accused shall enjoy the right to a speedy and public trial, by an impartial jury of the State and district wherein the crime shall have been committed, which district shall have been previously ascertained by law, and to be informed of the nature and cause of the accusation; to be confronted with the witnesses against him; to have compulsory process for obtaining witnesses in his favor, and to have the assistance of counsel for his defense.

A person accused of a crime has the right to a fair, public trial by a jury in the state where the crime took place. He or she must be told the charges against him or her. He or she has the right to have a lawyer defend him or her, to question people who speak against him or her, and to call people to speak in his or her favor.

AMENDMENT 7. CIVIL TRIALS (1791)

In suits at common law, where the value in controversy shall exceed twenty dollars, the right of trial by jury shall be preserved, and no fact tried by a jury, shall be otherwise reexamined in any court of the United States, than according to the rules of the common law.

A person has a right to a jury trial in most cases that concern him or her.

AMENDMENT 8. PUNISHMENT FOR CRIMES (1791)

Excessive bail shall not be required, nor excessive fines imposed, nor cruel and unusual punishments inflicted.

Prison bails, fines, and punishments must be fair.

AMENDMENT 9. OTHER RIGHTS (1791)

The enumeration in the Constitution, of certain rights, shall not be construed to deny or disparage others retained by the people.

The promise of certain rights in the Constitution does not mean that these rights are the only rights the people have. The people have other rights that may not be taken away or limited by the government.

AMENDMENT 10. POWERS RESERVED TO THE STATES (1791)

The powers not delegated to the United States by the Constitution, nor prohibited by it to the States, are reserved to the States respectively, or to the people.

All powers not given to the federal government are left to the states and to the people.

AMENDMENT 11. SUITS AGAINST STATES (1798)

The judicial power of the United States shall not be construed to extend to any suit in law or equity, commenced or prosecuted against one of the United States by citizens of another State, or by citizens or subjects of any foreign State.

No state may have a law case brought against it by a citizen of another state or of a foreign nation.

AMENDMENT 12. ELECTING PRESIDENT AND VICE PRESIDENT (1804)

The electors shall meet in their respective States, and vote by ballot for President and Vice President, one of whom, at least, shall not be an inhabitant of the same State with themselves; they shall name in their ballots the person voted for as President, and in distinct ballots the person voted for as Vice President, and they shall make distinct lists of all persons voted for as President, and of all persons voted for as Vice President, and of the number of votes for each, which lists they shall sign and certify, and transmit sealed to the seat of the government of the United States, directed to the President of the Senate; The President of the Senate shall, in the presence of the Senate and House of Representatives, open all the certificates and the votes shall then be counted; The person having the greatest number of votes for President, shall be the President, if such number be a majority of the whole number of electors appointed; and if no person have such majority, then from the persons having the highest numbers not exceeding three on the list of those voted for as President, the House of Representatives shall choose immediately, by ballot, the President. But in choosing the President, the votes shall be taken by States, the representation from each State having one vote; a quorum for this purpose shall consist of a member or members from two-thirds of the States, and a majority of all the States shall be necessary to a choice. And if the House of Representatives shall not choose a President whenever the right of choice shall devolve upon them, before the fourth day of March next following, then the Vice President shall act as President, as in the case of the death or other constitutional disability of the President. The person having the greatest number of votes as Vice President, shall be the Vice President, if such number be a majority of the whole number of electors appointed, and if no person have a majority, then from the two highest numbers on the list, the Senate shall choose the Vice President; a quorum for the purpose shall consist of two-thirds of the whole number of Senators, and a majority of the whole number shall be necessary to a choice. But no person constitutionally ineligible to the office of President shall be eligible to that of Vice President of the United States.

Electors (members of the Electoral College) shall vote separately for president and vice president.

AMENDMENT 13. ABOLITION OF SLAVERY (1865)

Section 1. Neither slavery nor involuntary servitude, except as a punishment for crime whereof the party shall have been duly convicted, shall exist within the United States, or any place subject to their jurisdiction.

Section 2. Congress shall have power to enforce this article by appropriate legislation.

Slavery is ended. Congress is given power to enforce the ending of slavery.

AMENDMENT 14. RIGHTS OF CITIZENS (1868)

Section 1. All persons born or naturalized in the United States, and subject to the jurisdiction thereof, are citizens of the United States and of the State wherein they reside. No State shall make or enforce any law which shall abridge the privileges or immunities of citizens of the United States; nor shall any State deprive any person of life, liberty, or property, without due process of law; nor deny to any person within its jurisdiction the equal protection of the laws.

The states cannot pass laws that take away the rights and protections promised to all United States citizens by the Constitution.

Section 2. Representatives shall be apportioned among the several States according to their respective numbers, counting the whole number of persons in each State, excluding Indians not taxed. But when the right to vote at any election for the choice of electors for President and Vice President of the United States, Representatives in Congress, the executive and judicial officers of a State, or the members of the legislature thereof, is denied to any of the male inhabitants of such State, being twenty-one years of age, and citizens of the United States, or in any way abridged, except for participation in rebellion, or other crime, the basis of representation therein shall be reduced in the proportion which the number of such male citizens shall bear to the whole number of male citizens twenty-one years of age in such State.

A state's representation in Congress may be made less if the state refuses the right to vote to any citizen who is qualified.

Section 3. No person shall be a Senator or Representative in Congress, or elector of President and Vice President, or hold any office, civil or military, under the United States, or under any State, who, having previously taken an oath, as a member of Congress, or as an officer of the United States, or as a member of any State legislature, or as an executive or judicial officer of any State, to support the Constitution of the United States, shall have engaged in insurrection or rebellion against the same, or given aid or comfort to the enemies thereof. But Congress may by a vote of two-thirds of each house, remove such disability.

Any United States government official who later became an officer of the Confederate States of America may not hold federal or state office.

Section 4. The validity of the public debt of the United States, authorized by law, including debts incurred for payment of pensions and bounties for services in suppressing insurrection or rebellion, shall not be questioned. But neither the United States nor any State shall assume or pay any debt or obligation incurred in aid of insurrection or rebellion against the United States, or any claim for the loss of emancipation of any slave; but all such debts, obligations and claims shall be held illegal and void.

All debts of the federal government connected with the Civil War must be paid. All debts of the Confederate states are unlawful and will not be paid by the federal government.

Section 5. The Congress shall have power to enforce, by appropriate legislation, the provisions of this article.

AMENDMENT 15. RIGHT OF SUFFRAGE (1870)

Section 1. The right of citizens of the United States to vote shall not be denied or abridged by the United States or by any State on account of race, color, or previous condition of servitude.

No citizen can be refused the right to vote because of race or color, or because he or she was once a slave.

Section 2. The Congress shall have power to enforce this article by appropriate legislation.

AMENDMENT 16. INCOME TAX (1913)

The Congress shall have power to lay and collect taxes on incomes, from whatever source derived, without apportionment among the several States, and without regard to any census or enumeration.

Congress is given the power to pass a law to tax incomes (the money people earn).

AMENDMENT 17. DIRECT ELECTION OF SENATORS (1913)

Section 1. The Senate of the United States shall be composed of two senators from each State, elected by the people thereof, for six years; and each senator shall have one vote. The electors in each State shall have the qualifications requisite for electors of the most numerous branch of the State legislatures.

Senators are to be elected by the voters of each state.

Section 2. When vacancies happen in the representation of any State in the Senate, the executive authority of such State shall issue writs of election to fill such vacancies: **Provided**, that the legislature of any State may empower the executive thereof to make temporary appointments until the people fill the vacancies by election as the legislature may direct.

An empty seat in the Senate may be filled by a special election. Or, the legislature of a state may ask the governor to appoint someone to fill the seat until the next election.

Section 3. This amendment shall not be so construed as to affect the election or term of any senator chosen before it becomes valid as part of the Constitution.

AMENDMENT 18. NATIONAL PROHIBITION (1919)

Section 1. After one year from the ratification of this article the manufacture, sale, or transportation of intoxicating liquors within, the importation thereof into, or the exportation thereof from the United States and all territory subject to the jurisdiction thereof for beverage purposes is hereby prohibited.

Section 2. The Congress and the several States shall have concurrent power to enforce this article by appropriate legislation.

Section 3. This article shall be inoperative unless it shall have been ratified as an amendment to the Constitution by the legislatures of the several States, as provided in the Constitution, within seven years from the date of the submission hereof to the States by the Congress.

The making, sale, and carrying of alcoholic drinks in the United States are prohibited, or outlawed. [This amendment was ended by Amendment 21.]

AMENDMENT 19. WOMEN'S SUFFRAGE (1920)

Section 1. The right of citizens of the United States to vote shall not be denied or abridged by the United States or by any State on account of sex.

Section 2. Congress shall have power to enforce this article by appropriate legislation.

The right to vote is given to women. Congress is given the power to enforce this right.

AMENDMENT 20. "LAME DUCK" AMENDMENT (1933)

Section 1. The terms of the President and Vice President shall end at noon on the 20th day of January, and the terms of Senators and Representatives at noon on the third day of January, of the years in which such terms would have ended if this article had not been ratified; and the terms of their successors shall then begin.

The president and vice president are to take office on January 20. Members of Congress are to take office on January 3.

Section 2. The Congress shall assemble at least once in every year, and such meeting shall begin at noon on the third day of January, unless they shall by law appoint a different day.

Congress is to meet at least once every year.

Section 3. If, at the time fixed for the beginning of the term of the President, the President elect shall have died, the Vice President elect shall become President. If a President shall not have been chosen before the time fixed for the beginning of his term, or if the President elect shall have failed to qualify, then the Vice President elect shall act as President until a President shall have qualified; and the Congress may by law provide for the case wherein neither a President elect nor a Vice President elect shall have qualified, declaring who shall then act as President, or the manner in which one who is to act shall be selected, and such person shall act accordingly until a President or Vice President shall have qualified.

If the newly-elected president dies before January 20 or fails to qualify for office, the office of President is to be filled in the order given here.

Section 4. The Congress may by law provide for the case of the death of any of the persons from whom the House of Representatives may choose a President whenever the right of choice shall have devolved upon them, and for the case of the death of any of the persons from whom the Senate may choose a Vice President whenever the right of choice shall have devolved upon them.

Section 5. Sections 1 and 2 shall take effect on the 15th day of October following the ratification of this article.

Section 6. This article shall be inoperative unless it shall have been ratified as an amendment to the Constitution by the legislatures of three-fourths of the several States within seven years from the date of its submission.

AMENDMENT 21. REPEAL OF PROHIBITION (1933)

Section 1. The eighteenth article of amendment to the Constitution of the United States is hereby repealed.

Amendment 18 is repealed, or ended.

Section 2. The transportation or importation into any State, Territory, or possession of the United States for delivery or use therein of intoxicating liquors, in violation of the laws thereof, is hereby prohibited.

The states have the right to outlaw the sale of alcoholic drinks.

Section 3. This article shall be inoperative unless it shall have been ratified as an amendment to the Constitution by conventions in the several States, as provided in the Constitution, within seven years from the date of the submission hereof to the States by the Congress.

AMENDMENT 22. TWO-TERM LIMIT FOR PRESIDENTS (1951)

Section 1. No person shall be elected to the office of the President more than twice, and no person who has held the office of President, or acted as President, for more than two years of a term to which some other person was elected President shall be elected to the office of the President more than once. But this Article shall not apply to any person holding the office of President when this Article was proposed by the Congress, and shall not prevent any person who may be holding the office of President, or acting as President, during the term within which this Article becomes operative from holding the office of President or acting as President during the remainder of such term.

A president may only serve two full terms in office. If a vice president has already served more than two years as president, he or she may be elected president only once.

Section 2. This Article shall be inoperative unless it shall have been ratified as an amendment to the Constitution by the legislatures of three-fourths of the several States within 7 years from the date of its submission to the States by the Congress.

AMENDMENT 23. VOTING IN THE DISTRICT OF COLUMBIA (1961)

Section 1. The District constituting the seat of Government of the United States shall appoint in such manner as the Congress may direct: A number of electors of President and Vice President equal to the whole number of Senators and Representatives in Congress to which the District would be entitled if it were a State, but in no event more than the least populous State; they shall be in addition to those appointed by the States, but they shall be considered, for the purposes of the election of President and Vice President, to be electors appointed by a State; and they shall meet in the District and perform such duties as provided by the twelfth article of amendment.

People who live in the District of Columbia (Washington, D.C.) are given the right to vote for president and vice president. The District of Columbia is given three electoral votes.

Section 2. The Congress shall have power to enforce this article by appropriate legislation.

AMENDMENT 24. ABOLITION OF POLL TAXES (1964)

Section 1. The right of citizens of the United States to vote in any primary or other election for President or Vice President, for electors for President or Vice President, or for Senator or Representative in Congress, shall not be denied or abridged by the United States or any State by reason of failure to pay any poll tax or other tax.

A poll tax, or a tax on voters, cannot be required in elections for federal officials.

Section 2. The Congress shall have power to enforce this article by appropriate legislation.

AMENDMENT 25. PRESIDENTIAL DISABILITY AND SUCCESSION (1967)

Section 1. In case of the removal of the President from office or of his death or resignation, the Vice President shall become President.

If a president dies or resigns from office, the vice president becomes president.

Section 2. Whenever there is a vacancy in the office of the vice president, the president shall nominate a vice president who shall take office upon confirmation by a majority vote of both Houses of Congress.

If the office of vice president becomes empty, the president may appoint someone to fill this office, with the agreement of Congress.

Section 3. Whenever the President transmits to the President pro tempore of the Senate and the Speaker of the House of Representatives his written declaration that he is unable to discharge the powers and duties of his office, and until he transmits to them a written declaration to the contrary, such powers and duties shall be discharged by the Vice President as Acting President.

If the president feels unable to carry out the duties of office, he or she shall tell Congress so in a written message. The vice president shall act as president until the president declares that he or she is again able to carry out the duties of office.

Section 4. Whenever the Vice President and a majority of either the principal officers of the executive departments or of such other body as Congress may by law provide, transmit to the President pro tempore of the Senate and the Speaker of the House of Representatives their written declaration that the President is unable to discharge the powers and duties of his office, the Vice President shall immediately assume the powers and duties of the office as Acting President.

Thereafter, when the President transmits to the President pro tempore of the Senate and the Speaker of the House of Representatives his written declaration that no inability exists, he shall resume the powers and duties of his office unless the Vice President and a majority of either the principal officers of the executive department or of such other body as Congress may by law provide, transmit within four days to the President pro tempore of the Senate and the Speaker of the House of

Representatives their written declaration that the President is unable to discharge the powers and duties of his office. Thereupon Congress shall decide the issue, assembling within forty-eight hours for that purpose if not in session.

If the Congress, within twenty-one days after receipt of the latter written declaration, or, if Congress is not in session, within twenty-one days after Congress is required to assemble, determines by two-thirds vote of both Houses that the President is unable to discharge the powers and duties of his office, the Vice President shall continue to discharge the same as Acting President; otherwise, the President shall resume the powers and duties of his office.

If the vice president and a majority of the Cabinet members feel that the president is unable to carry out the duties of office, they shall tell Congress so in a written message. The vice president shall act as president. When the president feels ready to carry out the duties again he or she shall declare so to Congress. But if the vice president and a majority of the Cabinet members do not agree with him or her, then Congress must decide by a two-thirds vote within 21 days who is president.

AMENDMENT 26. VOTING AGE LOWERED TO 18 (1971)

Section 1. The right of citizens of the United States, who are 18 years of age or older, to vote shall not be denied or abridged by the United States or by any State on account of age.

No person 18 years of age or older may be denied the right to vote in either a federal or a state election.

Section 2. The Congress shall have power to enforce this article by appropriate legislation.

CHAPTER SUMMARY

During the Revolutionary War, new state constitutions were written and slavery was ended in many states. The Articles of Confederation set up the first national government. After the war, the Confederation passed an important land law, the Northwest Ordinance. However, the Confederation could not raise money through taxes, or settle important conflicts between the states. Many people thought that the government was too weak to solve the nation's problems. And Shays's Rebellion proved that the United States needed a stronger form of central government.

In 1787, the Founding Fathers wrote a Constitution that gave the nation a strong government. They had to make compromises to satisfy different needs. The Constitution divided the powers of government between the states and the federal government. The federal government was made up of the legislative, executive, and judicial branches.

Americans disagreed about the Constitution, but it was approved by the states. George Washington was elected the first president and formed a Cabinet to help him lead the nation. The Bill of Rights was added to the Constitution. Alexander Hamilton made plans to solve the nation's money problems. People began to settle in the frontier territories to the west.

Key Words

Write a sentence to explain the meaning of each of these terms.

Articles of Confederation
Northwest Ordinance
Constitutional Convention
Judiciary Act
Bill of Rights
Cabinet

Major Events

Choose the answer that best completes the statement.

1. The Northwest Ordinance controlled land north of the

   a) Great Lakes.
   b) Canadian border.
   c) Ohio River.

2. In 1787, Congress asked for help from Massachusetts to

   a) stop Shays's Rebellion.
   b) raise taxes.
   c) pay the Founding Fathers.

3. The dispute over how slaves would be counted for taxation was settled by the

   a) Great Compromise.
   b) Three-Fifths Compromise.
   c) first ten amendments.

4. The new Constitution was opposed

   a) by the Federalists.
   b) by the Anti-Federalists.
   c) by the Congress.

5. In 1794, Anthony Wayne

   a) won the Battle of Fallen Timbers.
   b) was elected senator from Ohio.
   c) started a bank.

Review

Important Facts

Answer each question with at least one complete sentence.

1. What freedoms were included in the bills of rights of most state constitutions?

2. Under the Articles of Confederation, what powers did Congress have?

3. How did the United States gain the Northwest Territory?

4. What plan for the Northwest Territory was outlined in the Northwest Ordinance?

5. What did Shays's Rebellion prove about the national government?

6. Name three of the Founding Fathers.

7. What was the Great Compromise?

8. What are the three branches of government? What does each branch do?

9. Why did some Americans oppose the new Constitution?

10. What are some of the rights and freedoms protected by the Bill of Rights?

11. What financial problems did the young United States face? How did Alexander Hamilton want to solve them?

12. Why did Alexander Hamilton want a national bank? Why did some people oppose this idea?

13. Why were the Indians in the Northwest Territory unhappy about the new settlers there?

Skill Review

Study this diagram, then answer the following questions.

1. How many branches did the Confederation government have?

2. Which state had the most power under the Confederation?

3. What kind of federal court system did the Confederation have?

| **13 States** |
| Each state has only 1 vote. |

Congress of the Confederation

Legislature can wage war, make peace, borrow money; cannot pass taxes, print money, control trade between states.

| Committee of States runs government when Congress is not in session. | Congress acts as a court to settle disputes between states. |

Critical Thinking

Write a paragraph to answer each question.

1. Compare the United States government under the Articles of Confederation to the government under the Constitution.

2. Why did the Founding Fathers have to make compromises in writing the Constitution?

Important People

Choose the answer that best completes the statement.

1. Each of the English colonies was headed by

   a) an assembly.
   b) the king.
   c) a governor.

2. The British began to win the French and Indian War when

   a) Braddock marched into the Ohio Valley.
   b) Pitt became the leader of Parliament.
   c) Wolfe captured Quebec.

3. Samuel Adams was

   a) the first victim of the Revolutionary War.
   b) the leader of the Sons of Liberty and an early supporter of independence.
   c) a Loyalist.

4. The commander of the American army during the war was

   a) George Washington.
   b) Ethan Allen.
   c) George Rogers Clark.

5. The leader of a farmers' rebellion against taxes was

   a) Patrick Henry.
   b) Alexander Hamilton.
   c) Daniel Shays.

6. The people selected to advise the president are called

   a) senators.
   b) the Cabinet.
   c) Federalists.

Main Ideas

Choose the answer that best completes the statement.

1. Like Parliament, colonial legislatures

   a) had two houses.
   b) could have their decisions vetoed by the king.
   c) met in London.

2. The French and Indian War was the result of rivalry between

   a) France and the Iroquois.
   b) France and the colonies.
   c) France and Great Britain.

3. The Proclamation of 1763

   a) finally ended the French and Indian War.
   b) outlawed settlement west of the Appalachian Mountains.
   c) opened up the fur trade in the Ohio Valley to everyone.

4. The Stamp Act Congress called for the repeal of the Stamp Act because

   a) the colonists were broke after the war.
   b) the colonists already had their own postal system.
   c) it was taxation without representation.

5. The colonists protested against unfair British laws

   a) by boycotting British goods.
   b) by trading with the French.
   c) in every colony except Georgia.

R e v i e w

6. The Declaration of Independence

   a) was written before any fighting had broken out.
   b) explained why the colonies were forming a new nation.
   c) created a constitutional government.

7. The British decided to end the war and make peace with the United States after

   a) the Battle of Yorktown.
   b) the Battle of Saratoga.
   c) the Battle of Bunker Hill.

8. The Articles of Confederation

   a) created a strong central government.
   b) created a good system for paying the country's debts.
   c) were replaced by the Constitution.

9. The Great Compromise

   a) settled the slavery issue.
   b) created a two-house Congress.
   c) gave Congress the power to make laws.

10. The executive branch

    a) sees that the laws passed by Congress are carried out.
    b) makes sure the government does not act unjustly.
    c) has more power than the other branches of government.

11. During Washington's presidency

    a) the Supreme Court set up a system of federal courts.
    b) a national bank was set up and began operating.
    c) Cabinet leaders ruled the nation.

History Skills

> **A** "The British Parliament has no right to tax the Americans. . .Taxation and representation are inseparably united."
>
> **Thomas Pratt**, Earl of Camden

> **B** "Which is better, to be ruled by a tyrant three thousand miles away or by three thousand tyrants not a mile away?"
>
> **Mather Byles**, Loyalist

> **C** "The fact is, that the. . .colonies are represented in Parliament. . .for every Member of Parliament sits in the House, not as representative of his own [voters], but as one of that august Assembly by which all the commons of Great Britain are represented."
>
> **Thomas Whately**, Member of Parliament

Choose the answer that best completes the statement.

1. Speaker B preferred the

   a) Sons of Liberty.
   b) King of England.
   c) Minutemen.

2. On the issue of the Stamp Act, it is likely that Speaker A sided with

   a) the colonists.
   b) the House of Lords.
   c) the tax collectors.

3. Two speakers who had opposite views on colonial representation in Parliament were

   a) A and C
   b) B and C
   c) A and B

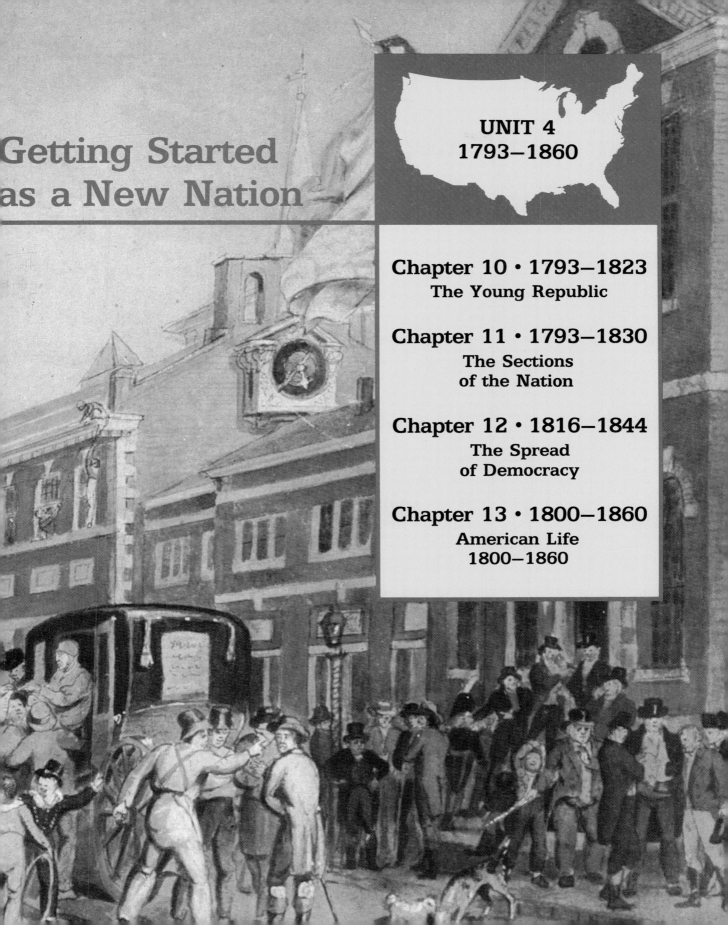

Getting Started as a New Nation

CHAPTER
10
The Young Republic

Years 1793–1823

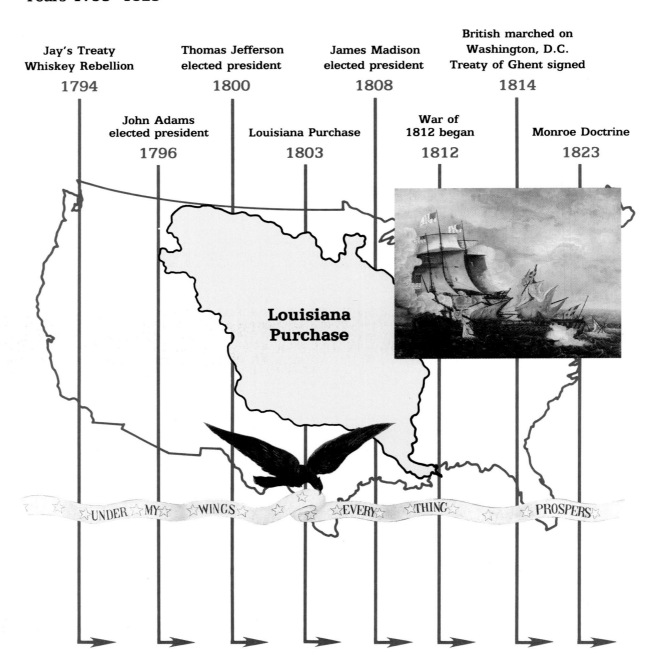

Jay's Treaty
Whiskey Rebellion
1794

John Adams
elected president
1796

Thomas Jefferson
elected president
1800

Louisiana Purchase
1803

James Madison
elected president
1808

War of
1812 began
1812

British marched on
Washington, D.C.
Treaty of Ghent signed
1814

Monroe Doctrine
1823

**Louisiana
Purchase**

☆ UNDER ☆ MY ☆ ☆ WINGS ☆ ☆ ☆ ☆ EVERY ☆ ☆ THING ☆ ☆ ☆ PROSPERS ☆

The Founding Fathers created a good government for the United States. The Constitution was working, and Congress was passing important laws. George Washington, a great leader, helped to guide the country through its early years. The nation was growing in size and strength.

Life for Americans had improved in many ways, but serious problems still faced the young nation. Many of these problems were based on America's dealings with foreign governments. In this chapter, you will see how a war in Europe created problems for Americans. You will also see how conflicts with Great Britain led to war.

As you read, you will learn about three new presidents. You will learn how they fit into the new political scene. Americans with different ideas had joined together to form two groups. You will read about what each group believed. You will see how the beliefs of each group affected American government. You will also see how the government handled the battles and wars of the early 1800s. Would there be a lasting peace?

1. Washington's Second Term

Learn these important terms:

Republican Party
political parties
Federalist Party
neutral
Farewell Address
Whiskey Rebellion

Remember the main idea:

During Washington's second term as president, the United States was able to stay out of war. Two political parties were formed. Americans elected John Adams as the second president.

Look for answers to these questions:

1. How did Washington prevent war with Great Britain?
2. Why did a rebellion take place in the West?
3. What were the two political parties? How were they different from each other?

At the end of his first term as president, George Washington did not want to run for a second term. Most Americans, however, wanted him to remain president. They believed that his leadership had improved life in the country. Washington finally agreed to run again. He was reelected in 1792.

Although life within the United States had improved, the nation had problems with foreign governments. Sometimes

George Washington (1732–1799) commanded the Continental Army during the Revolution. Later, he became the first president of the United States. Gilbert Stuart painted this famous unfinished portrait of Washington.

France had helped Americans during the Revolutionary War. Now France expected help from the United States. Many Americans, including Thomas Jefferson, wanted the French to win the war. Others, like Alexander Hamilton, favored the British. Washington wanted the United States to stay out of the European war. He thought that the young country needed peace to grow strong. For this reason, he announced that the United States was **neutral** (NOO-trul), or not taking sides in the war.

The United States soon found that it was not easy to stay neutral. One French diplomat, or representative, tried to convince Americans to attack Canada and capture British ships. Washington made France stop such pressure. At the same time, relations with Great Britain grew worse. British ships sometimes captured American ships that traded with France. The British also supplied guns to the Indians in the Northwest Territory. War between Great Britain and the United States seemed likely. To prevent this war, Washington sent John Jay to Great Britain in 1794 to settle the differences between the two nations.

John Jay worked out a treaty with the British. Great Britain promised to give up the forts in the Northwest Territory. However, the British refused to stop capturing American ships that traded with France. Most Americans did not like Jay's Treaty. The Senate barely approved it. Although Washington did not like the treaty either, he knew peace was important. He finally signed Jay's Treaty.

A Rebellion in the West

Washington faced problems within the United States as well. One important problem occurred in western Pennsylvania. In the 1790s, only rough mountain roads connected the West with the cities

Great Britain treated the United States unfairly. Many British people still hoped to win back their American lands. After the Revolutionary War, the British had promised to remove their forts from the Northwest Territory. Now they refused to remove them.

In addition, events in France created problems in Europe and in the United States. In 1789, during Washington's first term, a revolution had begun in France. The king and many nobles were killed. Great Britain was worried about the changes in France. The British thought that revolutionary ideas might spread to Great Britain. In 1793, at the beginning of Washington's second term, Great Britain declared war against France.

along the Atlantic coast. Farmers in western Pennsylvania could not always carry their grain to the market towns over these roads. To make money, the farmers sometimes used their grain to make whiskey. Whiskey was easier to transport, and it brought a good profit.

In 1791, the federal government placed a tax on whiskey. The farmers thought that this tax was unfair, and they refused to pay it. Tax collectors were often attacked. One of them was tarred and feathered. Since the local sheriffs could not stop the attacks, the government could not collect the tax.

Washington remembered the trouble that Shays's Rebellion had caused. This time he wanted the federal government to take a strong stand against rebellions. In 1794, Washington led fifteen thousand soldiers into western Pennsylvania. With him rode Alexander Hamilton.

When the army marched into the area, all the rebels ran away. No blood was shed, but a few farmers were arrested and given trials. The **Whiskey Rebellion** showed the nation that the government was able to enforce its laws.

Think: Many Americans opposed the treaty Jay made with the British. Here, people are shown burning an effigy, or doll, of Jay. Respond: Why were feelings about the treaty so strong?

Think: Organizing his troops at Fort Cumberland, Washington prepared to end the Whiskey Rebellion in Pennsylvania. Other problems at home and abroad forced Washington to take a strong stand on several issues.
Respond: Why was it important for the young nation to have a strong president?

Federalists and Republicans

Although few disagreements caused as much trouble as the Whiskey Rebellion, Americans often disagreed about what their government should do. At first they disagreed about approving the Constitution. They also disagreed about slavery and about the war in Europe. As their differences grew, Americans began forming *political parties*, or groups of people who share certain ideas about government.

President Washington did not want political parties in the United States. He was afraid that they might divide the nation. For him, unity was very important. During his second term, however, two political parties were formed. One was the *Federalist Party*. The other was the *Republican Party*.

The leader of the Federalist Party was Alexander Hamilton. The Federalists favored a strong president and a strong central government. They wanted bankers, landowners, and rich merchants to run the country. They also wanted Great Britain to win the war in Europe. The Federalist Party was popular in the New England states.

The Republican Party leaders were Thomas Jefferson and James Madison. The Republicans did not want a strong central government. They wanted the states to have more power. They favored planters, small farmers, and workers in the cities. They wanted France to win the war in Europe. The Republican Party was strong in the southern states, in Pennsylvania, and in New York.

Farewell to a President

Washington refused to run for president in 1796. The Federalists chose John Adams, the vice president, to run for president. The Republican Party chose Thomas Jefferson. The election was very close. Adams won, and Jefferson became vice president.

John Adams (1735–1826), as second president of the United States, worked to avoid war with France. Earlier in his life, he helped adopt the Declaration of Independence.

Before George Washington left office, he gave a speech known as a *Farewell Address*. In this speech, Washington told Americans to be careful of disagreements between political parties. He said that unity was very important for the country. He also said that the United States should be careful in dealing with foreign countries. It was good to remain friendly with foreign countries, Washington reasoned. However, the United States should not become deeply involved in the problems of other countries.

When John Adams took office as president, the conflicts with Great Britain and France were not yet settled. In the rest of this chapter, you will read how those problems grew much worse before they were finally solved.

Section Review

1. What treaty kept the United States out of war with Great Britain? Why did some Americans dislike this treaty?

2. How did Washington put an end to the Whiskey Rebellion?

3. What two political parties were formed in the 1790s? In what ways did they differ?

4. What points did Washington make in his Farewell Address?

Abigail Adams

Abigail Adams, the wife of President John Adams, wrote hundreds of letters in her seventy-four years. Many of them have survived and give us an idea of the daily lives of people of that time. Her letters are a *primary source* of information. Primary sources are first-hand reports of events or opinions. They are an important tool for historians.

In 1796, as the time approached for her to become First Lady, Abigail Adams had worries about living in the White House. She wrote to her husband:

> My dearest friend,
> I should say that I have been so used to a freedom . . . that I know not how to place so many guards about me . . . to look at every word before I utter it, and to impose a silence . . . when I long to talk.

This letter, a primary source, tells you about the role Abigail Adams thought she should play as the president's wife. But Abigail Adams did not stop speaking her mind on matters outside of the White House. In 1797, she enrolled a black child in school. When someone objected, she replied:

> My dear sir,
> The boy is a freeman as much as any of the young men, and merely because his face is black, is he to be denied instruction? How is he to be qualified to procure a livelihood? . . . I have not thought it any disgrace to myself to take him into my parlor and teach him both to read and write.

Abigail Adams's earlier letters also talked about individual rights. In 1776, she wrote to her husband about the setting up of the new government of the United States:

> . . . Remember the ladies and be more generous to them than your ancestors. Do not put such unlimited power in the hands of husbands. If particular care and attention is not paid to the ladies, we are determined to foment rebellion, and will not be bound by any laws in which we have no voice or representation.

Answer the following questions about the letters.

1 What does Abigail Adams's second letter tell you about how blacks were often treated?

2 What does her third letter tell you about most men's attitude toward rights for women at that time? Does Abigail agree?

2. Adams and Jefferson

Learn these important terms:

Alien Acts
Louisiana
  Purchase
expedition

Embargo Act
Sedition Act
impressed
aliens

Remember the main idea:

Adams prevented war with France. Jefferson purchased Louisiana and tried to keep America out of war with Great Britain.

Look for answers to these questions:

1. What unpopular laws were passed under President Adams?
2. How did Jefferson double the size of the United States?
3. What unpopular act did Congress pass under President Jefferson?

During the early years of the nation, American presidents had many difficulties dealing with Great Britain and France. Washington kept the United States out of war with Great Britain. When Adams became president, trouble broke out between the United States and France. The French navy began to capture American ships that traded with Great Britain. President Adams sent three men to France to try to settle this trouble.

The Americans wanted to see a French leader named Talleyrand (TAH-lay-rahn). He refused to see them unless they gave him a large sum of money. In addition, he wanted the United States to lend France ten million dollars. Without this money,

France would continue its attacks on American ships.

The French threat angered President Adams and the American people. Instead of paying the money, they started to prepare for war. The American army grew from thirty-five hundred to ten thousand men. The American navy added many ships. They chased French ships away from the Atlantic coast.

Some Americans wanted a war in order to gain more land. Alexander Hamilton wanted the United States to fight France and its ally Spain. Hamilton thought the United States could take away Spain's territories, Florida and Louisiana. Adams did not agree to this plan. He continued to work for peace until a new treaty was signed. By 1801, the United States and France were on friendly terms again.

The Alien and Sedition Acts

In 1798, while the nation was preparing for war, the Federalists in Congress passed some unpopular laws. Three of these laws dealt with *aliens* (AY-lee-unz), people who had come from foreign lands but were not yet American citizens. These *Alien Acts* were aimed mainly at people from France. One of the acts made it harder to become an American citizen. Another act gave the president the power to force aliens to leave the country if he thought they were dangerous. The third act said the president would put aliens in prison during wartime.

The law that caused the most trouble was the *Sedition Act* (seh-DISH-un). This law made it a crime to write or say anything against the government or the president. The Federalists used the Sedition Act to silence Republican newspapers that disagreed with them. The Republicans thought that this law went against the Constitution, which promised freedom of speech and of the press.

Thomas Jefferson (1743–1826) wrote the Declaration of Independence. Later, he became the third president of the United States. He was an inventor and a supporter of education.

The Third President of the United States

Thomas Jefferson, elected president in 1800, soon repealed, or stopped, many Federalist laws. He lowered taxes. He got rid of the tax that had started the Whiskey Rebellion. When the Alien and Sedition Acts expired, or ended, he did not renew them. He released all the people who had been jailed under the Sedition Act.

During Jefferson's first term, thousands of farmers moved west to the lands between the Appalachian Mountains and the Mississippi River. They sent their crops down the river to New Orleans to be sold. At that time, New Orleans was part of the Spanish territory. This territory stretched from the Mississippi River to the Rocky Mountains, and from the Gulf of Mexico to Canada. It was known as Louisiana.

In 1801, Jefferson learned that Spain was going to give this land back to France. He knew that the French leader Napoleon wanted to make Louisiana into a French empire. Jefferson feared that the French would not let Americans use the port of New Orleans anymore. After the French closed New Orleans to Americans in 1802, he told Robert Livingston and James Monroe to try to buy New Orleans from France.

Meanwhile, Napoleon had given up his hopes of an empire in Louisiana. Instead, he turned his attention to a plan to conquer Europe. When Monroe and Livingston offered him ten million dollars for New Orleans, Napoleon offered to sell all of Louisiana for fifteen million dollars. This sale gave him money for his armies and removed the threat to France from British Canada.

THE LOUISIANA PURCHASE

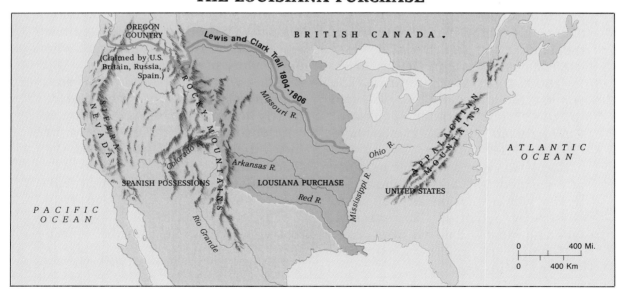

HISTORY MAKERS

Sacajawea

Guide to the American Northwest

"Captain Lewis must be crazy! He's bringing along a woman and a two-month-old baby? What could he be thinking?"

"He's not crazy. I heard him explaining it to Captain Clark. She's a Shoshone Indian (shoh-SHOH-nee). Lewis hopes she can buy horses from the Shoshone to carry supplies between the Missouri and Columbia Rivers. Without horses, we can't take enough supplies."

The men paddled on, up the Missouri River. They were part of the Lewis and Clark expedition. Its newest members were a fur trader hired as guide and interpreter, his wife, Sacajawea (sa-ka-juh-WAY-uh), and their infant son Baptiste.

Sacajawea was born about 1786. In 1800, she was captured by the Hidatsa Indians. Later she was sold to the French trader Toussaint Charbonneau (TOO-sant shar-bon-OH), and they married.

Sacajawea was a valuable member of the expedition. She was important to the whole mission as well as to day-to-day activities. For example, when her husband nearly overturned a boatload of important supplies, Sacajawea rescued many items swept overboard.

As the expedition moved westward, Sacajawea began to recognize landmarks from her childhood. In August, the expedition met a band of Shoshones. As Sacajawea began to interpret, she turned to the Shoshone chief. She stared for a moment, and then threw her arms around him and wept with joy. After many years and many miles, Sacajawea was reunited with her brother and her tribe.

Sacajawea and her family went on to the Pacific with Lewis and Clark. She helped guide the expedition through territory she knew, and her presence reassured Indians who were wary of the white men.

Clark was fond of Sacajawea's son, and he paid for the boy's education, partly in thanks to Sacajawea. He felt she deserved "a greater reward for her attention and service than we had in our power to give her . . ."

Sacajawea was an important member of an important expedition. With her help, Lewis and Clark explored, mapped, and opened up the American Northwest.

☆UNDER ☆MY☆ ☆WINGS☆ ☆EVERY☆ ☆THING☆ ☆PROSPERS☆

Think: Boqueto de Woieseri painted this view of New Orleans in 1803, the year of the Louisiana Purchase. Examine the great detail of the work. Notice the many forms of transportation included in the work. **Respond:** Why was New Orleans important to American transportation?

Monroe and Livingston were not sure if the Constitution gave them or Jefferson the right to make this purchase. However, they knew that the French offer was a great opportunity. They decided to buy Louisiana. The *Louisiana Purchase* doubled the size of the United States.

After the United States purchased Louisiana, Jefferson chose Meriwether Lewis and William Clark to lead an *expedition* (ex-puh-DISH-un), or journey, into the new territory. Lewis and Clark spent two years exploring and mapping northern Louisiana. They traveled from St. Louis all the way to the Pacific coast and back again. They learned much about the lands and Indian tribes of this vast new area of the United States.

Jefferson's Second Term

During his second term, Jefferson had many problems with foreign governments. Great Britain and France were at war again. They tried to stop each other's trade with foreign countries. France captured American ships trading with Great Britain. Great Britain captured American ships trading with France.

Great Britain not only captured American ships. It also *impressed* American sailors, or forced them to serve on British ships. This angered the American people. Many Americans wanted the United States to go to war. Jefferson thought it would be better to stop trade with Great Britain. Congress agreed with Jefferson's plan. In 1807, Congress passed the *Embargo Act*, which stopped foreign ships from carrying goods to or from the United States. The Embargo Act also stopped American ships from trading in foreign ports.

Unfortunately, the Embargo Act hurt the United States more than it hurt Great Britain. Great Britain was still able to trade with Canada and South America, but American trade was completely cut off. American sailors and shipbuilders lost their jobs. American farmers and businesspeople could no longer trade with foreign merchants. Finally, Jefferson agreed that the Embargo Act had failed.

James Madison (1751–1836) helped build a strong federal government during the Constitutional Convention. Later, he became the fourth president of the United States.

In 1809, three days before he left office, he repealed the Embargo Act.

The Embargo Act turned many Americans against Jefferson's party, the Republicans. In the election of 1808, more Federalists were elected to Congress. However, James Madison, a Republican, was elected president. He had been Jefferson's secretary of state. As president, Madison continued many of Jefferson's ideas. In the rest of this chapter, you will see that these ideas did not solve the problems with Great Britain. War soon began between the two nations.

Think: This artwork stirred up emotions. Sailors, like this young boy, were forced to work on British ships. Some were killed.

Respond: How is this artwork like today's TV news?

THE IMPRESSMENT OF AN

American Sailor Boy

Section Review

1. How did Talleyrand anger President Adams and the American people?

2. What were the Alien and Sedition Acts? Why did many Americans dislike them?

3. How did Jefferson, Monroe, and Livingston double the size of the United States?

4. How did President Jefferson try to stop Great Britain from capturing American ships? What were the results of his plan?

3. The War of 1812

Learn these important terms:

Treaty of Ghent
Monroe Doctrine
privateers
War Hawks

Remember the main idea:

The United States defeated Great Britain in the War of 1812. After the war, American trade with foreign countries improved.

Look for answers to these questions:

1. What were the causes of the War of 1812?
2. What was the British plan of attack in the war? How did it fail?
3. What changes took place after the War of 1812?

Even without the Embargo Act, the United States continued to have problems with foreign trade. Great Britain and France still attacked American ships. When France finally agreed to stop capturing American ships, British attacks continued. The British also continued to impress American sailors. The American government could not find a peaceful way to stop these attacks.

In addition, there were problems along the western frontier. The Indians who lived there believed that American settlers were taking Indian land. Under the great Indian leader Tecumseh (tuh-KUM-suh), many Indian tribes joined together to protect their lands. In 1811, William Henry Harrison, the governor of the Indiana Territory, defeated the Indians at the Battle of Tippecanoe. This battle led to an Indian war in the West.

Many westerners believed that British leaders in Canada were helping the Indians. These settlers wanted the United States to go to war against Great Britain. They also wanted to conquer Canada. Congressmen from the West who wanted war became known as **War Hawks**. In

Think: Tecumseh, the Shawnee chief, is shown in this detail from a painting by Catherine Reynolds. The great chief had hoped to form a single Indian nation made up of all the American tribes. He was killed while fighting for the British in the War of 1812. Respond: Do you agree with Tecumseh's idea of a single Indian nation? Why, or why not?

1812, the War Hawks led Congress to declare war against Great Britain.

Defeats and Victories

The United States was not prepared to fight the War of 1812. The nation lacked money and supplies. At first, Congress refused to vote for taxes to raise money for the army and navy. The United States also had trouble getting men to join the armed forces.

Despite these problems, the Americans thought they would have an easy victory in Canada. Most British soldiers were in Europe, fighting Napoleon's army. When the Americans attacked Canada, howev-er, they did badly. Instead of conquering Canada, the United States lost much of the land around the Great Lakes to the British forces. Later, American armies were able to win back this territory.

The first American victories were not on land but at sea. This was surprising because most people believed that Great Britain had the best navy in the world. However, the American navy defeated British ships again and again. The most famous American ship, the *Constitution,* won so many battles that it came to be known as "Old Ironsides." When the British blocked American ports, American ships called **privateers**, which were not part of the navy, captured many British ships. Captain Oliver Hazard Perry built a whole fleet of ships and defeated a British fleet on Lake Erie in the famous Battle of Put-In Bay.

Think: The *USS Constitution* was appropriately nicknamed "Old Ironsides." The ship is shown here defeating the British *Guerriére*. Respond: Why were the American sea victories unexpected?

Think: During the War of 1812, Francis Scott Key boarded a British ship to ask for the release of his fellow American, William Beane. The British ship then began to attack Fort McHenry. Key, being held prisoner, looked on in horror. Through the night the ship bombarded the fort. In the morning, Key anxiously looked for signs telling who had won the battle. Then through the smoke and fog, he could see the fifty-foot American flag that inspired him. Quickly he wrote most of the words to what would become our national anthem, "The Star-Spangled Banner."

Respond: When have you been inspired by an event or a symbol?

In 1814, the British defeated Napoleon, and the war in Europe ended. Great Britain was now able to send more troops to fight in America. Because the British army was large and well trained, the British generals thought it would be easy to win the war. They decided to attack the United States in three different ways. They planned to send an army from Canada into New England and New York. They would also raid important cities along the Atlantic coast. Finally, they would attack New Orleans by sea.

The first part of the British plan failed. The British were stopped by a small American fleet on Lake Champlain. The second part of the British plan started better. In August 1814, British soldiers landed near Washington, D.C. They defeated a large American army and marched into the nation's capital. The British burned many government buildings.

The British army then went on to attack Baltimore. This time the Americans held them back. British ships attacked Fort McHenry for a day and a night. In the morning, the American flag was still flying over the fort. The British attack had failed. Francis Scott Key wrote a poem about this battle. His famous poem, "The Star-Spangled Banner," was later set to music. It is now our national anthem.

The Final Battle

The British still had one more plan of attack. During the fall of 1814, they sent thousands of soldiers to attack New Orleans. The British army landed just a few miles from the city. Andrew Jackson, the American general, quickly attacked the British. The battle was a draw, but it made the British delay their next attack for several days. When the British finally marched on the city of New Orleans, the Americans were ready.

Jackson's army was made up of farmers, frontiersmen, black citizens of New Orleans, and pirates. The British thought they would have an easy victory. They

marched straight toward the city. When they were two hundred yards away from Jackson's army, the Americans opened fire. In a short time, two thousand British soldiers were killed or injured. Only about seventy Americans were killed or injured. The last battle of the war was over. The Americans had won.

Think: The American victory at the Battle of New Orleans was overshadowed by tragedy. It was fought after a peace treaty between the Americans and the British had been agreed to. The wasteful loss of thousands of lives took place because the delivery of messages took so long. Respond: **Why would this kind of tragedy be less likely to occur today?**

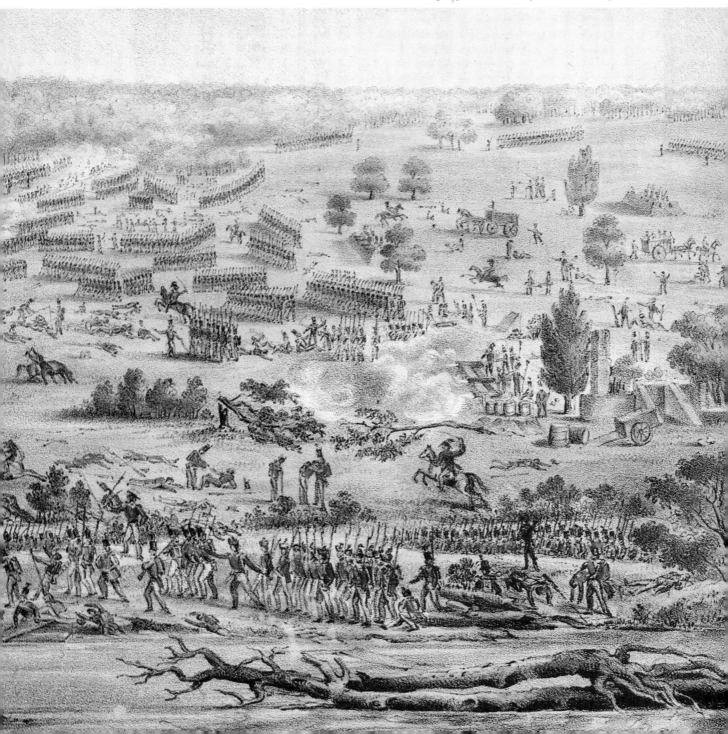

WAR OF 1812

Maps can give you information about time as well as about space. Maps can tell you *when* an event occurred as well as *where* it occurred. Both kinds of information increase your understanding of an event.

Putting events into *chronological*, or time, order can help you to understand the course of the War of 1812. Make a list of all the battles shown on this map, in chronological order. First put the full date. Then beside each date show with an *A* or *B* whether it was an American or British victory.

Using your text and the list that you have just made, answer the following questions.

1. How long was it between the first battle and the last?

2. How long was it between the first battle and the first American victory?

3. In what year did most of the fighting occur?

4. What battle on your list took place on land and at sea?

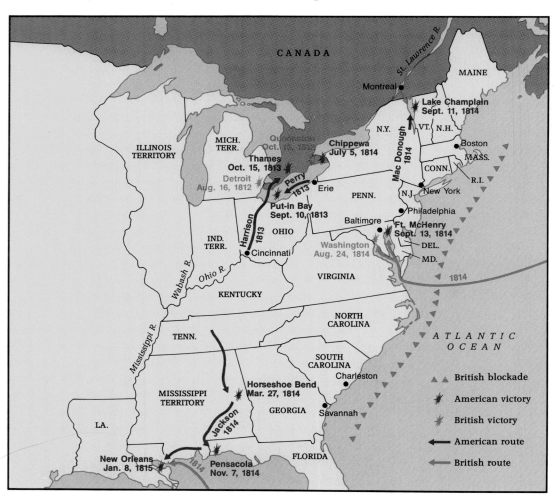

Peace and Great Changes

The Battle of New Orleans was a great victory for the United States, but it was also tragic. The two armies did not know that the United States and Great Britain had already signed the **Treaty of Ghent**, which ended the war. News of the treaty had not reached New Orleans in time to stop the battle.

After the War of 1812, Great Britain realized that the United States was a strong nation. It could not be defeated. The British stopped attacking American ships. Both nations agreed to keep their warships off the Great Lakes. The two nations agreed on most of the border, or boundary line, between the United States and Canada.

The war caused other changes as well. During the war, the United States could not bring most of its goods in from foreign countries. People in the northern states began to produce the goods that were needed. By the end of the war, New England was a center of manufacturing.

Settlers in the West were also helped by the war of 1812. Indian forces centered around the Great Lakes and south of the Ohio River were defeated by American armies during the war. The western frontier became much safer for American settlers.

In the years that followed, other important changes also took place. Spain's power over its territories was growing weaker. In 1819, the United States was able to purchase Florida from Spain for five million dollars. During the 1820s, many South American countries won their independence from Spain. In 1823, President James Monroe gave an important speech known as the **Monroe Doctrine**. He told the nations of Europe to stay out of the affairs of the United States and South America. In return, the United States promised to stay out of European affairs.

Think: **This painting by Forestier shows the signing of the Treaty of Ghent. Notice the men's expressions.** Respond: **How might they change after hearing news from New Orleans?**

The Monroe Doctrine was important because it declared that all American nations were free of European control. It also said that the United States would protect countries in South America.

Before the War of 1812, the United States had many problems with foreign countries, especially Great Britain and France. After the war, the United States became more successful in dealing with foreign governments. In the next chapter, you will read about changes within the United States after 1815.

Section Review

1. How successful were American forces as the war began?
2. Who was Tecumseh? What happened to his forces at the Battle of Tippecanoe?
3. Why was the Battle of New Orleans a great victory? Why was it also tragic?
4. How did America's relations with foreign governments improve after the War of 1812?

CHAPTER SUMMARY

During Washington's second term, problems with Great Britain continued. Jay's Treaty kept the Americans out of war, but it did not end British attacks on American ships. The government stopped the Whiskey Rebellion. The Federalist Party and the Republican Party were formed. John Adams was elected the second president. In his Farewell Address, Washington warned the young nation to be careful in dealing with foreign governments.

Adams kept the United States out of war with France. However, he made some unpopular laws. Jefferson was elected president in 1800. The United States purchased Louisiana from France. Conflicts with Great Britain grew worse. Jefferson passed the Embargo Act to stop attacks on American ships, but it hurt American trade. When Madison became president, he could not improve relations with Great Britain. War against the Indians broke out.

In 1812, the United States declared war on Great Britain as a result of British attacks on American ships. The American forces had difficulties at first, but eventually they defeated the British. After the war, the United States bought Florida from Spain. President Monroe declared that nations in the western hemisphere should be free of European control.

Key Words

Write a sentence to explain the meaning of each of these terms.

political parties   **Alien Acts**
neutral   **Sedition Act**
Treaty of   **Embargo Act**
  Ghent

Major Events

Choose the answer that best completes the statement.

1. After the French Revolution, Great Britain
   a) sent aid to the French.
   b) declared war on France.
   c) had its own revolution.

2. In 1794, Washington sent John Jay to Great Britain to
   a) buy arms.
   b) plan a war against France.
   c) work out a treaty.

3. Washington and Hamilton led troops into Pennsylvania to
   a) fight the Indians.
   b) stop Shays's Rebellion.
   c) stop the Whiskey Rebellion.

4. After the British forces burned Washington, they
   a) burned Baltimore.
   b) were unable to capture Baltimore.
   c) captured Fort McHenry.

5. The Battle of New Orleans took place
   a) in the middle of the War of 1812.
   b) toward the end of the war.
   c) after a peace treaty was signed.

Review

Important Facts

Answer each question with at least one complete sentence.

1. After the Revolutionary War, what happened to British forts in the Northwest Territory?

2. What side did the United States take in the war between Great Britain and France?

3. How did the government stop the Whiskey Rebellion?

4. Who was the leader of the Federalist Party? Who led the Republican Party?

5. How did the Federalists differ from the Republicans?

6. How did the Alien and Sedition Acts affect the election of 1800?

7. In 1803, what was one way that Napoleon raised money for his armies?

8. Whom did Jefferson send to explore the new western territories?

9. What did Great Britain do to American sailors when it captured their ships?

10. What effects did the Embargo Act have?

11. What was the name given to the Congressmen who wanted war with Great Britain?

12. What happened to the American plan to conquer Canada?

13. What was the final battle of the War of 1812? What was the outcome of this battle?

Skill Review

Read this primary source, then answer the following questions.

> On July 1, 1812, President James Madison said to Congress: Our commerce has been plundered in every sea, the great staples of our country have been cut off from their legitimate [rightful] markets, and a destructive blow aimed at our agriculture and maritime [seagoing] interests . . . Not content with . . . laying waste to our neutral trade, the cabinet of Britain resorted at length to the sweeping systems of blockades.

1. In your own words, what has Britain done to American trade?

2. What is Madison's opinion about British actions?

3. What action does Madison see as the "last straw"?

4. Which words show Madison's strong feelings about the British actions he describes?

5. Which words does Madison use to defend the American position?

Critical Thinking

Write a paragraph to answer each question.

1. Why did Americans form political parties? Why did Washington oppose political parties?

2. What was the Monroe Doctrine? Why was it important?

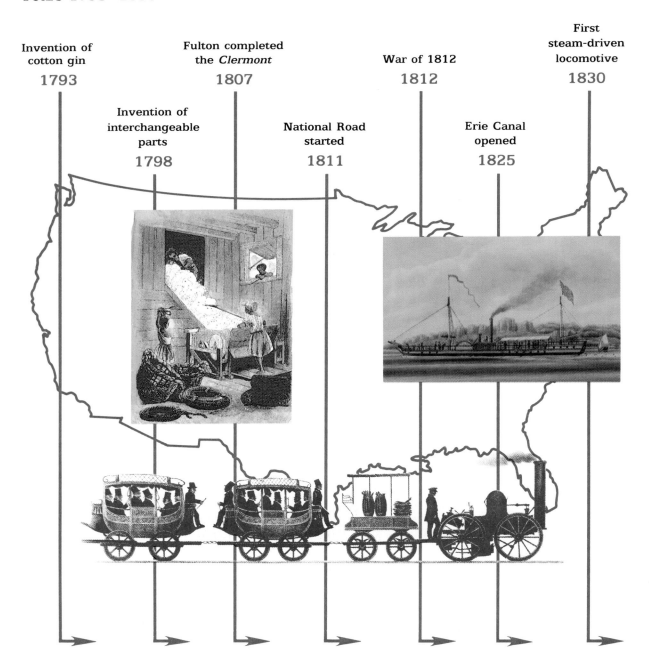

Invention of
cotton gin
1793

Invention of
interchangeable
parts
1798

Fulton completed
the *Clermont*
1807

National Road
started
1811

War of 1812
1812

Erie Canal
opened
1825

First
steam-driven
locomotive
1830

The Revolutionary War and the War of 1812 proved that Americans could work together. However, there were still many differences among Americans. The nation was very large. Bankers in Boston had different interests than farmers in Georgia had. Fur traders on the western frontier had different needs than schoolteachers in Philadelphia had.

Early citizens of the United States did not think of themselves only as Americans. Often they thought of themselves as Georgians, or New Yorkers, or Vermonters. They also thought of themselves as people from one of three large sections, or areas: the Northeast, the South, and the West. The Northeast was made up of New England and the middle states— New York, New Jersey, Pennsylvania, and Delaware. The South was made up of the southern states and some lands west of the Mississippi River, including Louisiana, Arkansas, and Texas. The West included land around the Great Lakes and the other lands west of the Mississippi River.

In this chapter, you will read about how the different sections of the nation grew. You will find out about some inventions that changed life in America. You will see how improvements in transportation helped the sections work together. What was it like to live in the different sections of the United States?

1. The Northeast

Learn these important terms:

Industrial Revolution
textile mills
interchange-able parts
mass produced
unions
immigrants
artisans

Remember the main idea:

In the 1800s, the Northeast became the leading trading, banking, and manufacturing section of the nation.

Look for answers to these questions:

1. What important inventions changed life in the Northeast?
2. Who worked in the factories?
3. Why was life in the cities hard for many people?

For a long time, the United States was largely a rural nation. The majority of the American people were farmers. Thomas Jefferson thought that the United States should remain a nation of farmers. He believed that the democracy would be stronger if most people owned their own land.

Unlike Jefferson, Alexander Hamilton thought that the strength of the United States lay in its cities. He believed that bankers and merchants would make America strong. He also believed that many American businesspeople should turn to manufacturing.

At the time of the Revolutionary War, only about five percent of the American

SECTIONS OF THE UNITED STATES IN 1840

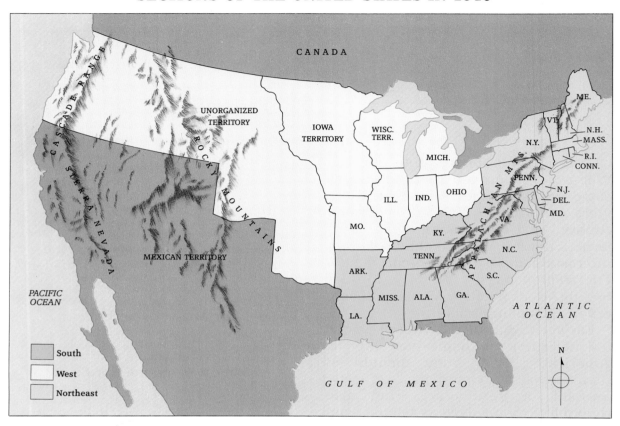

people lived in cities. Most American cities had only a few thousand people. Generally, people came to cities for short periods to trade and ship goods, or to do banking. Then they went back to their farms. Cities were centers of commerce, but there was little industry.

Jefferson's vision of a rural America held true for a long time. As late as the 1900s, most Americans still lived in rural areas. However, in the early 1800s this situation was changing. Many factories opened. Cities were growing. The Northeast was becoming a center of industry as well as commerce. Inventions made these changes possible.

A Revolution of Machines

In the late 1700s, an important change was taking place in Great Britain. Before this time, most people in the world got all their clothing, tools, and other goods in two ways. They either made these goods by themselves, or they bought them from **artisans**, people who make goods by hand. During the 1700s, however, people began inventing new machines. These machines could do the work much faster than artisans could.

These inventions started an **Industrial Revolution** (in-DUHS-tree-uhl) in Great Britain. More and more factories began to appear in British cities. Thousands of poor farmers moved to the cities to find work in factories. Great Britain soon became famous for its **textile mills**, or factories where cloth is made. The British began shipping their manufactured goods all over the world. Most factory owners grew very wealthy.

The British did not want other nations to learn how to build these factories. The British government passed a law against taking a textile machine out of the country. Textile workers were not allowed to leave Great Britain, either.

However, some people who worked in the mills did leave Great Britain. One of them, Samuel Slater, came to the United States in 1789. He had memorized the plans for a spinning factory. In Rhode Island, he met a wealthy merchant named Moses Brown. Together they built the first American textile mill. Other people who knew how to make textile machines moved to the United States. More factories appeared. The Industrial Revolution had come to America.

Home-Made Machines

Americans did not rely on the British for all their machines. Americans built many machines of their own. Some of the greatest inventors were Americans. One American inventor, Eli Whitney, not only invented a new machine. He invented a whole new way of manufacturing.

Whitney had a plan for making muskets, or rifles. Before, artisans had made guns one at a time. If one part of a gun were broken, an artisan had to make a

Think: The new technology of the power loom did little to change attitudes toward women. Respond: Why were women hired to run these looms?

special part to fit that gun. Whitney had a better idea. He wanted to make guns with **interchangeable parts**, or parts that could be used in all the muskets made in the factory he planned to build.

In 1800, Whitney took some of his muskets to Washington, D.C. He met with President Adams, Vice President Jefferson, and the Cabinet. He took the muskets apart and mixed up the parts. Then he put the muskets back together. Each of the new muskets was made up of pieces from the muskets he had taken apart.

The President and his Cabinet knew that Whitney had a good idea. They gave

Think: William Giles Munson painted *The Eli Whitney Gun Factory* in the 1860s. Notice that the factory is located near its source of power, water. Respond: How is this factory scene different from those of today?

HISTORY MAKERS

Lucy Larcom

The Factory Girl

"I have only one job open for a child, Mrs. Larcom. I need a bobbin girl. It's simple work. Your daughter will change the bobbins as they fill with thread. It takes about fifteen minutes, and must be done once an hour. When she is not changing bobbins, Lucy can sew or read, play quietly in the mill yard, or even go home to help you. Since you are one of our boardinghouse keepers, you know what her hours will be. Work begins at five o'clock in the morning and ends at seven o'clock at night. Workers go to their boardinghouses for breakfast from seven o'clock to half-past seven, and for lunch from half-past twelve to one. Since Lucy is eleven, she will have three months each year to attend school, until she is fifteen. If you like, she can begin tomorrow."

Lucy Larcom began work as a bobbin girl in the spinning room of the Lawrence mill in Lowell, Massachusetts. Many women came from New England farms and villages to work in the textile factories. These new jobs gave women a chance to earn money and be independent. Before the mills opened, women's jobs were limited to domestic work or farm work.

The new factory workers had to obey many company rules. These included living in houses owned by the textile companies, attending church regularly, getting home no later than ten o'clock at night, and behaving properly at all times.

The mill girls worked long hours, but in the evenings and on holidays they were often busy reading, going to lectures and evening schools, and joining in groups called self-improvement circles. From the improvement circles came literary magazines written by mill girls. For example, Lucy Larcom's early writing was published in *The Operatives' Magazine* and *The Lowell Offering.*

Lucy Larcom worked in the textile mills for ten years. Later she taught in Illinois and Massachusetts, but her first love was writing. She became a popular author, and her books about mill life are a valuable record of New England textile mills as they were before the Civil War. Thus did a mill girl help preserve history.

him money for his factory. In this factory, the parts were not only interchangeable. They were also **mass produced**, or made in large quantities. In Whitney's factory, each worker ran a machine that made one part for many guns. Other parts were made on other machines. Later, workers put the parts together. In this way, more guns could be made in less time than it took artisans. Many industries soon used Whitney's system of manufacturing.

In the early 1800s, as a result of inventions such as these, factories were started in many parts of New England. New England banks supported the factories. New England merchants carried the goods in their shops. In addition, New England's swift-flowing rivers provided water power to run the machines.

The War of 1812 also helped speed up the growth of industry. During the war, the United States could not always import goods. As a result, more American merchants began manufacturing goods. By the end of the war, the Northeast was a center of industry.

Working

When Slater and Brown started their mill, only the thread was made in the factory. The thread was then ''put out'' to people outside the factory. These people would weave the thread into cloth on looms in their own homes.

Francis Cabot Lowell thought of another way to use workers. He wanted all the work to be done in his factory. However, he did not want to copy the conditions of British factories. Life for British workers was hard, for the factories were dirty and dangerous. Workers had to live in bad housing. Much of the work was done by children. Often, men had to leave their farms to find work in factories.

Lowell wanted his factory to be a better place for workers. When he opened his

Think: Examine this title page from a publication written by owners of a Lowell factory. Respond: What kind of feeling about working in a Lowell mill does the title page give?

Think: *Mill Girl Winding Bobbins*, by Winslow Homer, illustrated a poem by William Cullen Bryant. Respond: What does it tell you about the life of a mill worker?

Think: Richmond, Virginia's capital, was influenced by Jefferson's idea of the perfect American lifestyle. Respond: What ideals are portrayed in this painting of Richmond?

Think: In 1834, New York was bustling with people and shops. Hamilton believed America's strength lay in cities such as this. Respond: What things in the drawing support this view?

factory in Massachusetts, he hired young, unmarried women from nearby farms. Lowell gave his workers clean, safe housing near the factory. He helped them save money for their families. After they worked for a few years, he wanted them to return to their farms and start their own families.

Life for the "Lowell girls" was hard. But conditions in many other factories were worse. Work hours were long, and the wages were very low. Factories were often unsafe.

Some workers tried to improve these conditions. The workers joined together into **unions**, or groups of workers who help each other. Sometimes these unions went on strike, or stopped work, to force factory owners to improve working conditions. The early unions were weak, however. Their strikes were usually unsuccessful. Conditions in most factories remained poor.

As people moved to cities to work, they could not always find good places to live. **Immigrants**, or people from foreign countries, were also arriving in the cities. The cities grew so quickly that many problems arose in them. Working people often had to live in crowded slums. There were not enough police or firefighters. Streets and water were not always clean.

Because of the Industrial Revolution, life in the Northeast changed in many ways. In the South and the West, however, the Industrial Revolution did not take hold. As you will read in the rest of this chapter, life in those sections changed in different ways.

Section Review

1. What did Jefferson and Hamilton say about the way Americans should live and work? Whose vision turned out to be true?

2. Where and how did the Industrial Revolution begin? How did it reach the United States?

3. What important contributions did Eli Whitney make to American industry?

4. What was Lowell's plan for factory workers? What were working and living conditions like for most American factory workers?

2. The South

Learn these important terms:

Old South
Old Southwest
cotton gin

Remember the main idea:

In the 1800s, cotton became the main crop of the South. As cotton farming grew in importance, the number of slaves increased.

Look for answers to these questions:

1. Why did many Southerners want to stop slavery after the Revolutionary War?
2. How did the cotton gin make slavery more popular in the South?
3. Why were laws passed to control free blacks?

The South had three parts. The states of the **Old South** had once been colonies. These states were Maryland, Virginia, Georgia, North Carolina, and South Carolina. States of the **Old Southwest** lay south of the Ohio River. These states were Kentucky, Tennessee, Alabama, and Mississippi. The third part of the South contained lands west of the Mississippi River—Louisiana, Arkansas, and Texas (after 1845).

Most of the people in the South were farmers. Some of them lived on plantations. Before the Revolutionary War, most planters grew tobacco, rice, and indigo. However, after the Revolutionary War, the price of tobacco went down. Rice and indigo growers also had trouble finding good markets for their crops. Hard times began for the South. Many southern planters could no longer afford to grow their old crops. Some planters tried to grow new crops, such as wheat. Other planters continued trying to sell their tobacco and indigo.

A large tobacco or indigo plantation used many slaves. When the market for tobacco and indigo became bad, however, southern farmers could not afford as many slaves as they once had. Southerners began to think there was no reason to keep their slaves.

After the Revolutionary War, many Southerners also began to realize that slavery was wrong. People began talking about ending slavery. Some planters freed their slaves right away. Other planters arranged to have their slaves freed after they died. A few Southerners even helped freed slaves return to Africa.

A Great Change

In 1793, Eli Whitney invented something very important—the **cotton gin**. This simple machine removed seeds from cotton plants fifty times faster than a worker could remove them by hand. Several southern states had soil that was ideal for growing cotton. And the new textile mills of Great Britain and the Northeast created a great demand for cotton. Suddenly, cotton was a very profitable crop.

The cotton gin changed life in the South. Hard times ended. The economy of the South rapidly improved. People who owned large plantations in the Old South grew rich. Other planters moved west to start new plantations. The populations of Alabama and Mississippi soared.

With a greater demand for cotton came a greater demand for slaves. Southern planters believed that many slaves were

Think: **Prior to the mechanical cotton gin, growing cotton was not profitable.** Respond: **What changes for slaves and landowners did the invention of the cotton gin bring?**

needed for growing and picking cotton. According to the Constitution, no laws forbidding slavery could be made until 1808. So Southerners continued to bring slaves into the United States.

Even after 1808, the number of slaves in the United States grew. In 1800, there were one million slaves. In 1860, there were over four million slaves. Most of these slaves were born in the United States. Prices for slaves also went up during this period. In 1800, a field worker in Virginia sold for about three hundred dollars. By 1860, a field worker in Virginia could cost over one thousand dollars. Slaves cost even more in the western states of the South. In 1860, a field worker in New Orleans could cost as much as two thousand dollars.

As more cotton farms appeared in the western states of the South, the slave trade there became a big business. Western slave traders bought most of their slaves in Virginia, Maryland, Tennessee, and Kentucky. Then they took the slaves to New Orleans. From New Orleans, the slaves were sold to planters in Louisiana, Mississippi, Arkansas, and Texas.

Some Southerners owned huge plantations with hundreds of slaves. However, most southern planters had much smaller farms. Even in 1860, only about ten thousand families in the South owned more than fifty slaves. Three-fourths of the white families in the South owned no slaves at all.

Why, then, did so many Southerners support slavery in the South? The planters believed that slaves were needed for growing and harvesting cotton. Slavery was profitable. A planter got a lot more out of his slaves than they cost him. The more slaves he owned, the more important he was.

The farmer with one or two slaves also supported slavery. He wanted to become a rich planter, too. Slaves were a sign of wealth. The small farmer hoped to buy more slaves and become more important. Even the poor white farmer with no slaves often dreamed of becoming a rich planter with many slaves.

Think: **Slaves bore the burden that brought profit to the white landowners.** Respond: **Had cotton not been so profitable, how might the lives of southern blacks have been different?**

Think: **Free blacks in the North and the South were hardworking. But white Southerners felt free blacks posed a threat.** Respond: **How did white Southerners control free blacks, and why?**

Free Blacks

Not all blacks living in the South were slaves. In the 1800s, thousands of blacks in the South were free. Some blacks were given their freedom by their owners. Others worked hard and saved money until they were able to buy their freedom. A few free blacks in the South became very rich. Most of these rich blacks lived in Louisiana. However, most of the free blacks were small farmers. Others worked in cities.

Some Southerners believed that free blacks living in the South were dangerous to the system of slavery. Slave owners thought that free blacks might start slave revolts. The owners were also afraid that free blacks might help black slaves to escape from plantations.

Because of these fears, Southerners passed laws to control free blacks. Free blacks in the South had to carry special papers to prove they were free. They could not vote. They could not work in the government or in certain other jobs. In most states, they could not testify against white people in court. Other laws kept free blacks from moving from place to place in the South. And free blacks could not own guns.

Industry Does Not Take Hold in the South

Some southern planters did not like sending their cotton to the factories in the Northeast. They thought that the best place for cotton mills was in the South, near the plantations. The Southerners wanted to make the same profits from textile mills that northern manufacturers were making.

However, only a few mills were built in the South. Most southern bankers were unwilling to support such a change. Since cotton growing was so profitable, getting money to start other businesses was hard. Unlike farmers in the Northeast, most Southerners were not willing to leave their farms to work in factories. The South also had few rivers strong enough to power the machines.

Factories changed the Northeast. In the southern states, however, it was cotton that changed many aspects of life. The desire to make money by growing cotton led many Southerners to settle new land. It also made slavery a fixed part of southern life. During this period, many changes were also taking place in the West. In the rest of the chapter, you will read about life in the West.

Section Review

1. What problems did southern planters have after the Revolutionary War? How did one invention solve those problems?

2. Why did many Southerners want to end slavery after the Revolutionary War? Why did they change their minds?

3. Why were laws passed to control free blacks in the South? What were some of these laws?

SKILLS FOCUS: Comparing and Contrasting

COTTON CLEANING BEFORE THE INVENTION OF THE COTTON GIN.

EAGLE COTTON GIN, AT THE CRYSTAL PALACE, NEW YORK.

Compare the two pictures above. They are the same in one way. Both show a way of removing seeds from cotton. However, the ways are also different and can be contrasted. One way requires only a person, while the other requires a person and a machine called a cotton gin. Another way in which the two methods contrast is the speed of the work. A person using a cotton gin can remove cotton seeds much faster than a person doing it by hand.

The sections of the country can also be compared and contrasted. In the years 1800—1850, the sections of the United States were alike in some ways and different in others. Although all sections were governed by the same national government, in many ways the sections were also becoming increasingly different from one another.

For example, the Northeast and the South were alike in the fact that farming was important to both sec-

tions. The crops grown in each section were different, however. In the South, cotton was the most important crop. In the Northeast, other crops, such as wheat, were the most important.

One way to contrast the Northeast and the South is to make a list of the ways in which the two sections were different. Copy the list of contrasts below and finish it. If you need help, look back at Sections 1 and 2 of this chapter.

Contrast of the Northeast and the South

	North	South
Most important farm product	wheat	cotton
Most important occupations	_____	_____
Factories	_____	_____
Attitude toward slavery	_____	_____
Cities	_____	_____

3. The West

Learn these important terms:

speculators   *squatters*
turnpikes   *National Road*
Erie Canal   *steamboat*
flatboat   *canal*

Remember the main idea:

In the 1800s, the West became the largest and fastest growing section of the nation.

Look for answers to these questions:

1. Why was travel to and from the West difficult?
2. What inventions and improvements made travel to the West easier?

When early Americans talked about "the West," they could not always be sure about the meaning of the word. As the nation grew, the West kept moving westward. During the colonial years, the West was the unsettled land inland from the Atlantic coast. After the Revolutionary War, the West included lands between the Appalachian Mountains and the Mississippi River. Later, after the Louisiana Purchase, the West included lands west of the Mississippi River.

In the 1800s, the West became the largest and fastest growing section of the nation. In 1820, one-fourth of all Americans lived in the West. By 1840, one-third of the people living in the United States were Westerners.

Settlers and the Land

Americans usually moved to the West to find land. The states north of the Ohio River had good soil for farming. Farmers came from the eastern states and from Europe to settle there. Most of these settlers grew wheat and corn. Much of the wheat was sold in the Northeast. The farmers used the corn to feed their hogs and cattle. When the animals were fat, the farmers sold them in the Northeast.

At first, the federal government owned most of the land in the West. The government sold some of this land to settlers. Sometimes the price was higher than poor settlers could afford. In 1785, for example, the government sold land for $1 an acre. However, settlers had to buy 640 acres. Many settlers could not afford $640 for land.

However, *speculators* (SPEK-yoo-lay-turs), or people who buy land to resell it for a profit, could afford to buy the land. A speculator would buy a large piece of land for a dollar an acre. He or she would divide the land into small sections, then sell the sections to poor farmers for two or three dollars an acre.

Think: *Leaving the Old Homestead*, by James Wilkins, shows a family pulling up its roots and moving to the West. Respond: **Why do you think this family decided to head west?**

Think: With all the westward movement, many people built toll roads. At first the roads were barely cleared paths. But eventually some of the roads were covered with gravel. Many had beautiful bridges. **Respond:** Why were people willing to pay tolls to use the roads?

The government did not want speculators to control all the land. For this reason, Congress made it easier for poor people to buy land. After 1820, a settler could buy eighty acres of land for just one hundred dollars. However, some people still could not afford to buy land. Poor people often settled on government land without paying for it. These settlers were called *squatters* (SKWAH-turs). In 1841, Congress passed a law that gave squatters the chance to buy the land they had settled on.

Roads to the West

After the Louisiana Purchase was final, the United States became one of the largest nations in the world. Travel between the sections was slow and difficult. There were few roads and most of them were bad. In some places, people built roads across their own land and charged travelers a fee to use their roads. The roads were usually blocked by a pole, or a pike. When the traveler paid, the pike was raised or turned. These roads became known as *turnpikes*.

Think: **Waiting for the water levels in the locks to equalize, passengers relax.** Respond: **What opportunities did the opening of the Erie Canal bring to travelers and businesses?**

For a long while, the federal government and the states did not build their own roads. As the West grew, however, farmers needed better roads in order to send their crops to eastern markets. Factory owners in the Northeast also wanted good roads in order to send their products to the West.

To meet the need for a good road connecting the East to the West, the federal government built the ***National Road***. Construction on the road began in 1811. When the National Road was finished, it ran from Cumberland, Maryland, to southern Illinois. Many states also built roads from the East to the West.

Highways of Water

In the early years of the nation, farmers in the West often sent their goods to the East on boats. Large rafts, called **flatboats**, floated down the Mississippi River. At New Orleans, the farmers' goods were loaded on ships. The ships sailed around Florida to cities on the Atlantic coast. This voyage was long and expensive. Also, it was hard to ship goods northward on the Mississippi River against the current.

Another way to move goods on water was to build **canals**, or waterways made by people. In 1817, there were only a few miles of canals in the United States. Then the state of New York began to build the **Erie Canal**. When this canal was finished, it ran 364 miles across New York State. The Erie Canal connected the Great Lakes with the Hudson River. Soon, other states began to build canals. By 1837 there were more than 3,000 miles of canals in the United States.

A new kind of boat made travel on rivers much easier. In 1807, Robert Fulton, an inventor, sailed the *Clermont* up the Hudson River. It was the first successful **steamboat**, a vessel powered by a steam engine. By the 1830s, hundreds of steamboats carried passengers and goods up and down western rivers.

As people moved westward, towns grew up along large rivers, lakes, and canals. Some of these towns became centers of trade and industry. Cincinnati, on the Ohio River, and Chicago, on Lake Michigan, became important trading centers. The location of St. Louis made it very important, also. The Mississippi River, the Missouri River, and the Illinois River all meet there. Boats from many parts of the West passed through St. Louis. Settlers leaving for lands beyond the Mississippi could get supplies there. Lewis and Clark began their expedition in St. Louis.

Think: Built by Fulton, the *Clermont* (inset) was the first successful commercial steamboat. But few people could see a future in the steamboat. However, the steamboat soon became a common sight on American rivers, such as the Hudson. Respond: Why was the steamboat important to industry and trade?

AGRICULTURE AND INDUSTRY IN 1840

A *thematic map* gives you ideas in addition to information. Look at this map. Read its title. What is the map about? What kinds of symbols are used? These symbols give you two kinds of information. They tell you *what* products were grown or produced in 1840, and *where*. From these facts you get ideas.

For example, study the map, first for facts, then for ideas. Look at the symbols in the key that show agricultural activity, including forestry. Find the symbols that indicate industrial activity. Look at the map to see where both of these activities take place. From these facts, do you get the idea that more people were working in agriculture or in industry? You must conclude that America in 1840 was still an agricultural nation.

Use the map to answer the following questions. First find the facts. Then think about the ideas they contain.

1. Is agriculture the principal economic activity in the North or in the South? From this fact, what do you conclude about the use of slaves?

2. In which section of the country do you find the most textile mills? Are most of the iron resources and iron mills in the North or in the South? What differences between North and South might result?

3. This was a period in which some important inventions were made. How would the invention of the cotton gin, which speeded up the sorting of cotton, affect the South? How would it affect the North?

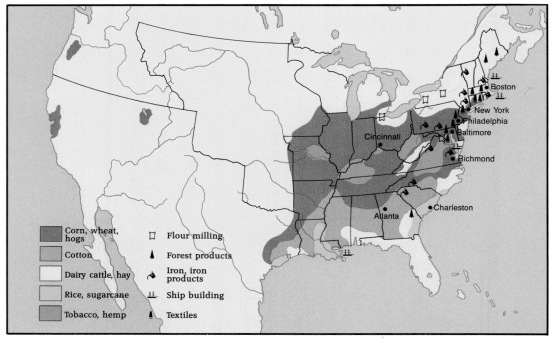

Key:
- Corn, wheat, hogs
- Cotton
- Dairy cattle, hay
- Rice, sugarcane
- Tobacco, hemp
- Flour milling
- Forest products
- Iron, iron products
- Ship building
- Textiles

Think: This detail of a painting by Edward Lamson Henry shows the first train ride on the Mohawk and Hudson Railroad. The artist carefully researched the subject before painting the picture. **Respond:** How have railroad cars changed since this first version of the train?

The Iron Road

In 1830, an invention appeared that was even more important than the steamboat: the first steam-driven locomotive. Shipping goods by railroad was a good option. Railroads were easier to build than canals, and they did not freeze over in winter. Railroads could go places that canals could not go. Trains were also faster than steamboats were.

By 1840, thousands of miles of railroads covered the Northeast. Soon, the railroads began to head west. They carried new settlers and goods to western towns. They carried farm goods and cattle to eastern cities. In 1869, railroads would connect the Atlantic and Pacific coasts.

Roads, canals, steamboats, and railroads helped change the West. New towns grew up. Older towns grew into cities. New businesses were started. New markets were opened for goods produced in the Northeast. The West became an important part of the nation.

Each section of the nation grew in different ways. For this reason, new problems were created as the nation grew. Sometimes there were conflicts among the three sections. In the next chapter, you will read how the United States faced these problems.

Section Review

1. Why was it difficult for some setklers to buy land in the West? How did the government help these settlers?

2. What important inventions and improvements helped change life in the West?

3. Where did towns and cities grow up in the West?

CHAPTER SUMMARY

The early United States was made up of three sections: the Northeast, the South, and the West. As the nation grew, different types of changes occurred in the sections.

Most people in the Northeast were farmers. However, the Industrial Revolution changed life there. Many new factories were built. Eli Whitney invented interchangeable parts and mass production. More people moved to cities to work in the factories. Often, the workers' lives were very hard.

After the Revolutionary War, the markets for southern crops such as tobacco, indigo, and rice became bad. Southerners talked about ending slavery because it looked like slaves might no longer be needed. Then Eli Whitney invented the cotton gin. Cotton became the main crop in the South, and some planters grew rich. More slaves were brought in to work on the cotton plantations. Laws were passed to control free black people. Plans to build textile mills in the South failed.

The West was the largest section. Many settlers moved there. New forms of transportation helped to settle the West. Roads were improved. Some states built canals into the West. Fulton invented the steamboat, which improved travel on rivers. Railroads also began to appear.

Key Words

Write a sentence to explain the meaning of each of these terms.

Industrial Revolution
interchangeable parts
mass produced
cotton gin
turnpikes
National Road

Major Events

Choose the answer that best completes the statement.

1. Samuel Slater and Moses Brown built the nation's first
   a) rifle factory.
   b) steamboat.
   c) textile mill.

2. Eli Whitney took his muskets to Washington, D.C., to
   a) sell them in a store.
   b) show them to the nation's leaders.
   c) build a new factory there.

3. After the Revolutionary War, southern planters
   a) thought about ending slavery.
   b) imported more slaves.
   c) made great profits.

4. People who bought land in the West and sold it for a profit were called
   a) squatters.
   b) speculators.
   c) developers.

5. In 1817, New York began
   a) building the National Road.
   b) Fulton's Folly.
   c) building the Erie Canal.

Review

Important Facts

Answer each question with at least one complete sentence.

1. What did Jefferson think was the best way for the nation to remain a strong democracy? How did Hamilton's ideas differ?

2. How did Great Britain try to protect its textile mills?

3. What was Eli Whitney's plan for making rifles?

4. How did the War of 1812 help American industry?

5. What were conditions like in British factories? How did Lowell try to make conditions in his factory better?

6. How did workers try to improve conditions in factories?

7. What invention changed life in the South? Why was it important?

8. What did white Southerners do to control free blacks?

9. What happened to the plan for factories in the South?

10. How did the government try to help poor people buy land in the West?

11. How did the government improve travel to and from the West?

12. What invention helped to improve travel by water? Who invented it?

13. In what ways were railroads better than other forms of travel in America?

Skill Review

Study the map, then answer the following questions.

1. Compare and contrast farming in Indiana and New Jersey. How are they alike? How do they differ?

2. Compare and contrast industry in Indiana and New Jersey.

3. What differences do you see between the Northeast and the West?

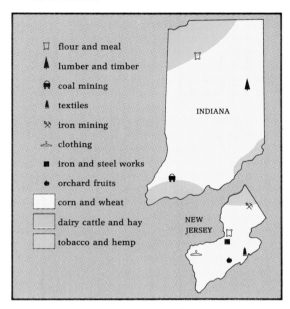

Key:
- flour and meal
- lumber and timber
- coal mining
- textiles
- iron mining
- clothing
- iron and steel works
- orchard fruits
- corn and wheat
- dairy cattle and hay
- tobacco and hemp

INDIANA

NEW JERSEY

Farming and Industry

Critical Thinking

Write a paragraph to answer each question.

1. In what ways did the Industrial Revolution change American life?

2. Why did slavery almost end in the South after the Revolutionary War? Why did it grow again in the 1800s?

CHAPTER

12
The Spread of Democracy

Years 1816–1844

James Monroe
elected president

1816

John Quincy Adams
elected president

1824

Martin Van Buren
elected president

1836

William Harrison
elected president

1840

Missouri
Compromise
approved

1820

Tariff of 1828
Andrew Jackson
elected president

1828

Trail
of Tears

1838

John Tyler
became president

1841

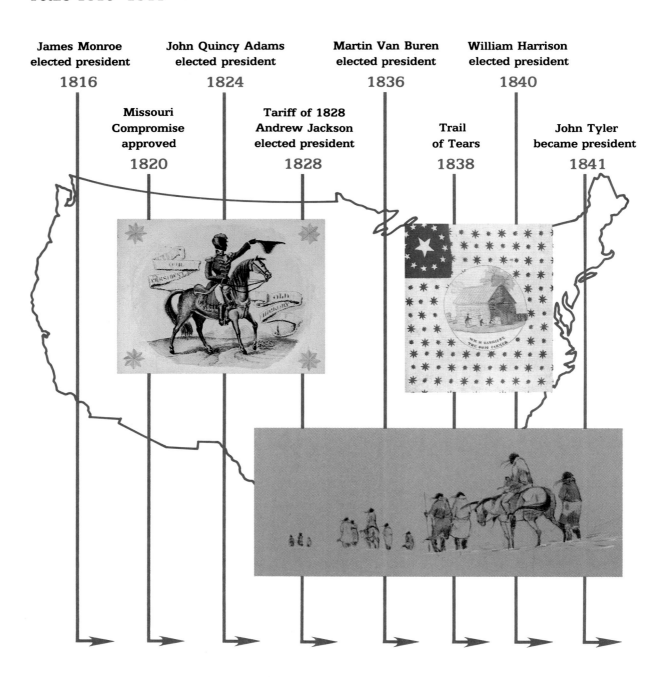

1. The Era of Good Feelings

Learn these important terms:

American System
tariffs
Tariff Act of 1816
protective tariff
McCulloch v. Maryland
judicial review
Missouri Compromise

Remember the main idea:

The period between 1816 and 1824 was a time when the American nation and its government became stronger. Americans settled the problem of slavery for awhile.

Look for answers to these questions:

1. Why was the period between 1816 and 1824 known as the "Era of Good Feelings"?

2. What were protective tariffs? Why did some Americans want them? Why were others opposed to them?

3. What problem arose over the territory of Missouri? How was this problem settled?

After the War of 1812, the sections of the nation grew rapidly. Northeastern industry and southern cotton made many people wealthy. More and more settlers moved west. However, the sections of the nation had different interests and needs. They did not always work together. Often, conflicts arose among them.

In this chapter, you will read about how the United States government tried to help the sections of the nation work together. You will see how some of the plans worked, while others failed to settle differences among the three sections.

In this chapter, you will also read about six presidents. One of these presidents was especially strong. You will learn about the many changes he made in the nation. The other presidents are remembered for their own reasons, too.

As you read, watch for signs of compromise. The nation continued to grow and change. Fortunately, the people still compromised with one another.

Many people in Great Britain had hoped that the War of 1812 would put an end to the United States. The American victory proved to Great Britain and the world that the United States would not disappear. The victory made the American people feel great pride in their nation and its leaders.

James Monroe (1758–1831) served the United States as a diplomat, Cabinet member, and the fifth president. He worked to expand the United States and free it from Euorpean interference.

In the years after the war, there was also a new feeling of national unity. This was partly due to the end of the Federalist Party. James Monroe, a Republican, ran for president in 1816 and 1820, and he was elected with ease. The unity of the people was evident. With unity came pride. These feelings of national pride and unity made people think of the period between 1816 and 1824 as "the era of good feelings."

The American System

After the War of 1812, Congress planned ways to help the sections of the nation work together. Henry Clay, a Republican congressman from Kentucky, called this plan the **American System**. It had three parts. The first part, which included the National Road, aimed to improve transportation between regions. The National Road brought western farm goods to eastern cities, and products from northeastern factories to the West.

The second part of the American System called for a national bank to handle the government's money. Since 1811 the country had been without such a bank. Congressional Republicans had refused to renew the charter of the Bank of the United States in that year. By 1816, they realized their mistake and approved the Second Bank of the United States. This Bank, like the first one, held the government's tax collections, loaned money to the states, and printed paper money.

The third part of the American System was a policy of high *tariffs* (TAIR-iffs). A tariff is a tax on goods coming into one nation from another. The **Tariff Act of 1816** marked the beginning of the American System plan.

The purpose of the Tariff of 1816 was to keep foreign manufactured goods out of the United States. The tariff raised the costs of foreign goods. Therefore, goods from American factories cost less than foreign goods. Americans would buy American goods because they were cheaper. The tariff protected American factories and gave them a chance to grow. For this reason, the Tariff of 1816 was called a **protective tariff**.

Many people thought that the tariff would also help the western farmers. The

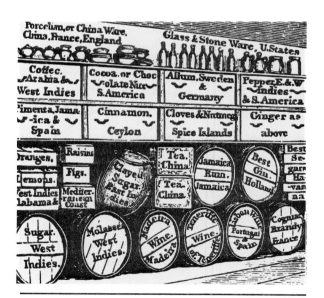

Think: This 1816 woodcut shows a general store packed with foreign goods. Respond: How could people in favor of a high tariff on foreign goods use pictures such as this one to convince others?

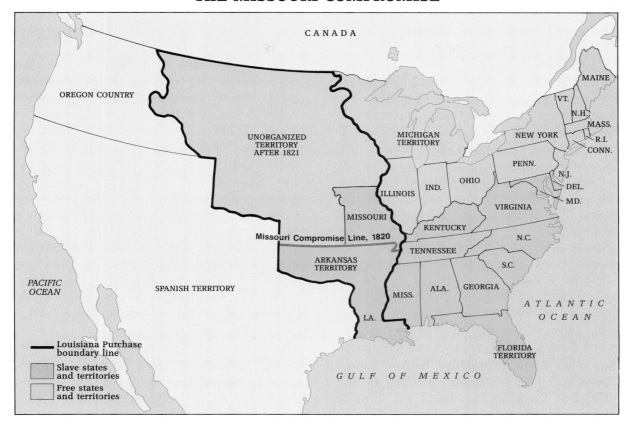

CANADA

OREGON COUNTRY

UNORGANIZED
TERRITORY
AFTER 1821

MICHIGAN
TERRITORY

MAINE

VT.

N.H.

MASS.

NEW YORK

R.I.

CONN.

PENN.

N.J.

ILLINOIS

IND.

OHIO

DEL.

MD.

VIRGINIA

MISSOURI

KENTUCKY

Missouri Compromise Line, 1820

N.C.

TENNESSEE

ARKANSAS
TERRITORY

S.C.

PACIFIC
OCEAN

SPANISH TERRITORY

MISS.

ALA.

GEORGIA

ATLANTIC
OCEAN

LA.

Louisiana Purchase
boundary line

Slave states
and territories

Free states
and territories

FLORIDA
TERRITORY

GULF OF MEXICO

tariff would make eastern cities richer. Richer cities would provide better markets for farm products.

The South Reacts

The period between 1816 and 1824 was generally an era of good feelings. There were also some conflicts among the sections, however. Southerners did not like the American System because it did not help them. They did not want to pay taxes to build the National Road from the East to the West. Also, the tariff raised the cost of imported manufactured goods that Southerners needed. They did not want to pay to help the industries in the Northeast.

Southerners did not like the Bank of the United States, either. Southern banks lost some of their business to the Bank. As a result, some states tried to place a tax on the Bank. Americans who supported the Bank said that it was unconstitutional for a state to tax the Bank.

In 1819, Supreme Court Chief Justice John Marshall said that the states could not tax the Bank of the United States. This case, known as **McCulloch v. Maryland**, was very important. It established that the Bank was constitutional.

This decision also extended the power of the Supreme Court. Marshall proved that the Court had power to declare a state law unconstitutional. Marshall had already shown that the Supreme Court had the power to declare federal laws unconstitutional in an earlier case, *Marbury v. Madison*. The Supreme Court's power to decide whether laws are constitutional is known as **judicial review**.

A Troubled Compromise

Another important problem developed in 1819. The territory of Missouri asked to be admitted to the Union as a slave state. At that time, the United States had eleven slave states and eleven free states. The free states did not want Missouri to become a slave state. They did not want the slave states to have more votes in the Senate than they had.

One congressman suggested that slavery be ended in Missouri over a period of years. The slave states refused to accept this suggestion. Then Henry Clay suggested the **Missouri Compromise**. This compromise said that Missouri would become a slave state. However, Maine would enter the union at the same time as a free state.

In 1820, Congress approved the Missouri Compromise. Congress also drew a line across the map of the United States. Slavery would be allowed south of this line, but no slavery would be allowed north of it. Many Americans thought that the Missouri Compromise was a good way to settle the problem of slavery. Others thought that the Missouri Compromise only put off a problem that was bound to get worse.

A Strange Election

In the election of 1824, each section tried to elect its own candidate for president. The Northeast backed John Quincy Adams, son of the second president. The South backed William H. Crawford of Georgia. The West backed two candidates. One was Henry Clay of Kentucky, the "Great Compromiser." The other candidate was Andrew Jackson, a senator from Tennessee and the hero of the Battle of New Orleans.

Andrew Jackson received the largest number of votes. However, Jackson did not have a majority of the electoral votes. If no candidate has a majority of the votes in an election, the House of Representatives must elect the president.

When the election went to the House, Henry Clay decided to support Adams. Clay reasoned that both he and Adams favored the American System and a high tariff. Jackson, the leading candidate, opposed the tariff. As a result of Clay's support, Adams won the election in the House of Representatives.

Think: **This political cartoon illustrates the election of 1824. Both ships are heading toward a dock to the left (not shown). Although out in front, Jackson's ship blows under the pressure. Adams's ship pulls ahead to victory.**
Respond: **What might be pictured in a cartoon of Jackson's 1828 victory over Adams?**

HISTORY MAKERS

John Marshall
The Great Chief Justice

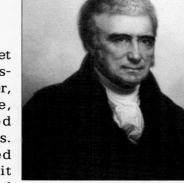

The farmer's market was crowded with customers buying butter, eggs, cider, cheese, and freshly picked fruits and vegetables. One stall displayed meat pies and fruit tarts. Another had plump rabbits, chickens, and turkeys for sale. As the farmer's wife completed a sale, her well-dressed customer called to a roughly dressed man standing nearby.

"You, fellow! I need someone to carry this turkey for me," he said. "You look as though you could use a little money. If you'll deliver this to my home, I'll pay you well. Will you do it?"

The tall man grinned and nodded his head.

"Good man. Pick up the turkey and follow me! It's not far, but we must move quickly."

Once home, the customer paid the delivery man well, not knowing that his turkey had been delivered by the Chief Justice of the United States Supreme Court, John Marshall.

John Marshall was a man of simple tastes. His greatness was not in his outward appearance, but in his leadership of the Supreme Court. During his twenty-two years as Chief Justice, Marshall developed the idea of judicial review. The practice of judicial review allows the Supreme Court to decide if laws follow the Constitution. If the Court decides that a law clashes with the Constitution, the Court declares the law unconstitutional. This is true for local, state, and national laws. Under Chief Justice Marshall's leadership, the Court thus became the interpreter of the Constitution.

Judicial review firmly established a balance among the three branches of the federal government. As proposed in the Constitution, the executive branch, the Supreme Court, and the Congress check one another.

As Chief Justice, Marshall made clear the power of the Constitution and the federal government over individual states. He set high standards for the Supreme Court and led the Court in shaping the laws of the land. For these reasons, he is known as the Great Chief Justice.

Historians have called John Quincy Adams (1767–1848) the greatest American secretary of state. He was also the only son of a president to become president—the nation's sixth.

Adams respected Henry Clay. After the election, he named Clay to be his secretary of state. This angered Jackson's supporters. They thought that Clay had made a secret deal with Adams. At that time, the secretary of state usually became the president in the next election. Jackson's supporters thought Clay had supported Adams just to become president.

It is very unlikely that Adams and Clay made such a deal. However, Jackson's supporters accused Adams and Clay of a "corrupt bargain." They began to work to elect Jackson in the 1828 election. In the next section, you will read how Jackson came back from his defeat to become the president of the United States. You will also read about the many changes he made as president.

Section Review

1. Why was the period between 1816 and 1824 known as the "Era of Good Feelings"?
2. What did the American System include? Who gave it its name?
3. Why were the southern states opposed to the tariff of 1816?
4. Why were some Americans angry about the election of 1824?

2. The Jackson Era

Learn these important terms:

Tariff of 1828
Democratic Party
spoils system
nullify
secede
Removal Act
Trail of Tears

Remember the main idea:

Jackson was a strong president with new ideas for the nation. He believed that all the states had to follow the laws of the federal government.

Look for answers to these questions:

1. Why was the election of 1828 different from earlier presidential elections?
2. What happened as a result of the Tariff of 1828?
3. What happened to the Indians east of the Mississippi River?

John Quincy Adams was not a popular president. The rumor of a deal with Clay turned many Americans against him. Some people thought that his ideas were old-fashioned, left over from the Federalist era. Other people thought he only cared about the Northeast.

The most important law passed during Adams's term was the *Tariff of 1828*. It was the highest tariff ever passed by Congress. Southerners called it the "Tariff of Abominations" (uh-bahm-ih-NAY-shuns) because they found it grossly unfair and therefore disliked it.

In the election of 1828, Adams and Jackson opposed each other. This election was different from earlier ones in several ways. In the first place, there was once again a strong two-party system. During Adams's term, Jackson had formed a new party, the **Democratic Party**. The Democrats spent the years between 1824 and 1828 working to get Jackson elected.

In the second place, the campaign was noisy. Earlier campaigns had been very quiet. In 1828, however, supporters of the two candidates fought bitterly. Each party misrepresented the other party's candidate. Also, much was made of the fact that Jackson was a war hero, but little was said about important issues.

In the third place, more voters could vote than ever before. During the 1820s, most states gave all white male voters the right to vote. Some of these new voting laws were already in place for the 1828 election. This meant that many poor and working people as well as landowners could vote.

Jackson was very popular with these new voters. Although he was the richest man in Tennessee, he was not from a rich

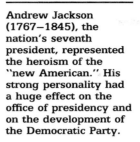

Andrew Jackson (1767–1845), the nation's seventh president, represented the heroism of the "new American." His strong personality had a huge effect on the office of presidency and on the development of the Democratic Party.

family. People said that Jackson was a "common man." He had educated himself and worked hard to succeed. He was also a war hero. The majority of Americans wanted such a man to be their president. Thus, Jackson defeated Adams with ease and became the seventh president of the United States.

A New Kind of President

Jackson was sworn into office on March 4, 1829. After the ceremony, a party was held at the White House. In the past, such parties had been quiet affairs for government officials. Jackson, however, stated that everyone was welcome.

The party was unlike any other ever held at the White House. A huge mob came to see the new president. They overturned furniture, knocked down waiters, broke glasses, and spilled food and drinks on the rug. For a while, it looked as if the White House would be ruined. Then someone said that punch was being served on the lawn. This news cleared the crowd from the White House. As for the new president, he had already escaped through a window. He spent his first night as president in a hotel.

The party gave people a clue that Jackson would be a new kind of president. Before this, no one had ever thrown open the doors of the White House to so many ordinary people.

Think: This 1830 watercolor with silhouette celebrates Jackson, who had been nicknamed Old Hickory during the War of 1812. Respond: How did Jackson use his military fame?

Think: Jackson invited everyone to the White House to celebrate his inauguration. A mob descended on the president's house. Respond: How did Jackson's invitation reflect his political beliefs?

After Jackson took office, he proved he was different from earlier presidents in more important ways. For example, Jackson believed that the president had just as much right as Congress or the Supreme Court to decide what laws were good for the nation. He was the first president to veto a law because he did not like it. Earlier presidents vetoed laws only if they believed that these laws were unconstitutional. Only nine laws had been vetoed by the first six presidents. Jackson himself vetoed twelve laws during his eight years as president.

Jackson also believed that the president must be the leader of his political party. He thought that party members should be rewarded for helping the party. These rewards would make the party stronger. As president, Jackson had the power to give people jobs in the federal government. He removed about nine hundred jobholders and replaced them with loyal Democrats. The system of giving government jobs to party members became known as the *spoils system*.

There were other reasons why Jackson gave government jobs to new people. He believed that replacing government workers every few years was a good way to get more people involved in government. Unlike many earlier presidents, Jackson also believed that ordinary people should have the right to work in the government. He wanted to give these people a chance to help their country.

Problems of Jackson's Presidency

Although Jackson was a very popular president, he had many problems during his term in office. There were still conflicts among the sections of the nation. The Northeast wanted a high tariff to protect its factories. It wanted the government to pay for "internal improvements," such as roads and canals. It also wanted high land prices in the West so that workers would not leave their jobs in factories and move west.

The South did not want a high tariff. It did not want to pay taxes for building roads and canals. The South wanted to protect its slaves and its cotton markets. However, the South did want high land prices in the West. This would make it harder for Westerners to grow cotton.

The West wanted to protect its farming. It wanted low land prices and a high tariff. It also wanted the government to pay for roads and canals.

Jackson tried to please as many people as possible. He agreed to the building of roads when he felt they served the needs of the whole nation. However, when he thought that an improvement would only help one of the sections, he refused to support it.

Jackson's plan slowed down the building of roads and canals. For this reason, some Westerners did not like the plan. Jackson kept their support by favoring low prices for western land.

The Fight over the Tariff

The Tariff of 1828 caused many problems. The South was opposed to protective tariffs. The vice president, John C. Calhoun of South Carolina, spoke for the South. He declared that a state had the right to *nullify* (NUHL-uh-fy), or refuse to obey, a federal law that it thought was unconstitutional. Some Southerners went even further than Calhoun. They believed that a state had the right to *secede* (suh-SEED), or leave the United States, if the state felt a federal law was unfair.

In 1832, Congress passed a lower tariff, but South Carolina nullified it. South Carolina then said it would secede if the United States forced it to obey the tariff.

John Caldwell Calhoun (1782–1850) served in various offices of the federal government for forty years. A loyal Southerner, he nevertheless always worked for solutions to hold the nation together. *(Detail from a portrait)*

Calhoun even gave up his job as vice president in order to actively fight the tariff in Congress.

Jackson disliked the tariff, too. However, he thought every state should obey the laws passed by Congress. To make sure South Carolina obeyed the tariff, Jackson sent warships there. He also said he would lead an army into South Carolina to enforce the law. Many Americans were afraid that a civil war would begin. Calhoun and Henry Clay quickly worked out a compromise. Congress lowered the tariff, and South Carolina accepted it.

The Removal of the Tribes

In the early 1800s, many Indian tribes lived peacefully among the white people. In the eastern part of the nation, these peaceful tribes often learned how to farm and practiced many white customs. However, the Indian tribes kept their own governments. This made the federal government uneasy. The government wanted to be able to rule the Indians. In addition, many white settlers wanted to take over Indian lands.

Jackson respected the Indians, but he thought the states should have the Indian lands. For this reason, he asked Congress to approve the *Removal Act*, which said that the Indians had to move to lands west of the Mississippi River. In 1830, Congress passed this law. Almost one hundred tribes moved west during the years Jackson was president.

Some tribes accepted this law without struggle. Others fought for their land. Two wars broke out with Indian tribes. In Illinois, Chief Black Hawk led Sauk and Fox Indians in a war with United States troops. The Indians soon lost Black Hawk's War. In Florida, however, the Seminole Indians (SEM-uh-nohl) fought for years before their lands were taken away. The Seminoles were helped by runaway slaves.

INDIAN REMOVAL

Thematic maps give you information on a single theme or subject. This thematic map shows you the major tribes involved in President Jackson's policy of relocating Indians west of the Mississippi. It shows the Indians' old lands, their new reservations, and the routes they traveled.

Study the map and the map key.

1. Does it appear that there is more yellow or more orange territory on this map?

Find the tribe names in the yellow areas. Then look at the names of the surrounding states and territories.

2. How many tribes does this map show? Were these the only tribes which were removed?

3. In which states and territories were these tribes settled before removal?

Now follow the red arrows from yellow areas to orange areas.

4. The relocation lands are part of which states today?

5. Which two tribes traveled by means other than foot or horseback?

6. Which tribes traveled the shortest distance? About how many miles was the trip? Which tribes had to travel the farthest? About how many miles did they go?

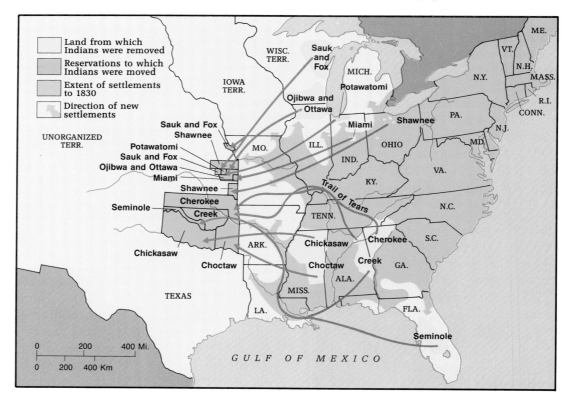

Think: *The Endless Trail* by Jerome Tiger shows the Cherokee's march to Oklahoma on the Trail of Tears. Consider the fairness of their being forced to leave their homes and land. Respond: **What do you think the Cherokees were thinking and feeling?**

One tribe, the Cherokees of Georgia, went to court to protect their lands. The Supreme Court decided that the state of Georgia had no power over the Cherokee nation. However, the state of Georgia still took the Indians' lands.

Jackson agreed with the Georgia legislature. In 1835, he ordered the removal of the Cherokees to Oklahoma. Some Cherokees moved, but others refused. In 1838, federal troops moved the rest of the Cherokees. Thousands of them died on the march west. The Cherokees called their tragic journey the *Trail of Tears*.

Andrew Jackson was a strong and popular president. When he ran for president again in 1832, he easily defeated Henry Clay. In the rest of the chapter, you will read about events during Jackson's second term as president. You will also read about the three presidents who followed him.

Section Review

1. Why was the election of 1828 different from earlier elections?

2. How did Jackson reward members of the Democratic Party?

3. Why did the South oppose the Tariff of 1828? How did South Carolina try to stop the tariff? What happened as a result of South Carolina's actions?

4. Why did some white Americans want the Indians to move west of the Mississippi? How did different tribes react to the Removal Act?

3. Four Presidents

Learn these important terms:

Jacksonian Democracy
state banks
Whigs
depression
treasuries

Remember the main idea:

Jacksonian Democracy gave the people a larger part in their government. However, in the years between 1837 and 1844, the nation suffered hard times.

Look for answers to these questions:

1. What changes did Jacksonian Democracy make in America?

2. What action did President Jackson take toward the Bank of the United States? How did his action create problems after he left office?

3. What did the Whigs plan to do if they won the election of 1840? Were they able to carry out any of their plans?

The ideas of Jackson and his followers are often called *Jacksonian Democracy*. Jackson disagreed with the people who thought that only landowners, merchants, and bankers should have power in government. He believed that workers and small farmers should have political power as well.

Jacksonian Democracy made important changes in the state governments. New state constitutions were written. These constitutions gave most white male citizens the right to vote and hold office. However, women and blacks still did not have these rights.

Under the old state constitutions, governors were chosen by the state legislatures. Under the new constitutions, the governors were elected by the people. The powers of the governors were also increased. The voters elected judges and other state officials as well.

Although Jackson was a rich Westerner, many of his followers were workers in the Northeast. They joined the Democratic Party because it promised to improve conditions in factories and cities. The Democratic Party got some states to pass laws that made the workday shorter and factories safer. The Democratic Party also worked for laws to start free public schools throughout America.

Think: George Catlin painted this picture in 1829, showing the delegates who rewrote the Virginia Constitution. Although most new state constitutions gave all white men the right to vote, Virginia still required voters to own land. Respond: Do you agree or disagree with Virginia's decision?

Think: **Many people were tired of Jackson's battles with the Bank of the United States. This cartoon illustrates their views.** Respond: **What nightmarish symbols is Jackson fighting in the cartoon?**

The Fate of the Second Bank

The Second Bank of the United States had a charter to last for twenty years. Unless Congress passed a new law, the Second Bank would close in 1836. Many congressmen thought the Bank was doing a good job. They wanted it to stay open.

Think: **The Second Bank of the United States closed in 1836 after years of controversy.** Respond: **Name good reasons for closing the bank and good reasons for leaving it open.**

However, Jackson was opposed to the Bank. He believed that it was unconstitutional and had too much power. He thought that the Bank helped business-people in the Northeast, but that it did not help the whole nation.

In 1832, Congress passed a law allowing the Bank to remain open. Jackson quickly vetoed this law. In the next four years, the Bank of the United States grew weaker. It closed in 1836.

The end of the Bank created many problems. For example, the Bank controlled *state banks* by controlling the amount of money it lent them. This made the Bank very powerful. Jackson took federal money out of the Bank of the United States and gave it directly to the state banks. This policy had two effects. It weakened the Bank, and it made the state banks harder to control.

The state banks printed paper money and lent it to farmers and businesspeople. When Jackson put federal money into state banks, they lent even more paper money. The paper money was supposed to stand for gold and silver in the banks. However, some banks printed too much paper money. They could not back it up with gold and silver.

Jackson did not like this practice. He ordered that government land in the West would only be sold for gold and silver. However, his actions created serious problems. When Westerners tried to cash in their paper money for gold and silver, the banks could not pay all of them. Many banks had to close. This meant many people lost their savings.

Van Buren and Hard Times

In 1835, Jackson decided not to run for a third term as president. The Democratic Party chose Jackson's vice president, Martin Van Buren, as their candidate in the 1836 election. The people who disliked Jackson and his ideas formed a new political party called the *Whigs*.

The Whigs took their name from a political party in England that had opposed King George III. The Whigs called Jackson "King Andrew I" because they

Think: When banks closed in 1837, money was not available to pay bills. People needing loans could not get them. Others who had put their money in banks could not get it back. Respond: How did this affect the economy?

thought he had too much power. They supported three men for president. Each was from a different section of the nation. As a result, the Whigs were not united in the election, and Van Buren won.

Soon after Van Buren became president, a *depression*, or period of hard times, hit the United States. This depression was largely the result of the banking problems that arose during Jackson's second term in office. Many banks had closed. Without banks to borrow money from, many factories and businesses also had to close down. Thousands of workers lost their jobs. Farmers were hard hit because many people did not have the money to buy farm products. Also, the value of their land went down.

Americans at this time did not know how to end a depression. The government did nothing to help city workers, farmers, or businesspeople. President Van Buren only took the federal government's money out of the state banks. He had Congress pass an act that set up *treasuries*, or places to store the government's money. The government treasuries kept the money safe, but they did not help to end the depression.

Martin Van Buren (1782–1862), Jackson's most trusted advisor, was America's eighth president. He vowed to continue Jackson's policies, but was forced to turn his full attention to America's economic troubles.

Tippecanoe and Tyler, Too

The depression hurt the Democratic Party. Because many Americans blamed Van Buren for the hard times, the Whigs thought they had a good chance to win the election of 1840. To gain western votes, the Whigs chose William Henry Harrison of Ohio as their candidate. Harrison was famous for defeating the Indians in the Battle of Tippecanoe in 1811. To win southern votes, the Whigs chose John Tyler of Virginia to run as Harrison's vice president.

In the election of 1840, the Whigs focused on the image of the candidates, rather than on important issues. They told voters that Van Buren ate off gold dishes and wasted the people's money. The Whigs talked about how Harrison was a war hero. One of their slogans, "Tippecanoe and Tyler, Too," became famous. The Whigs said that Harrison was a poor farmer who lived in a log cabin. In fact, Harrison was a rich man from an old Virginia family. The Whig plan worked. William Henry Harrison defeated Van Buren in the election of 1840.

Think: During his campaign, Harrison tried to present himself as a common man. Although Harrison lived in a twenty-two room mansion, the log cabin became his symbol. Respond: How did this symbol help him win the presidential election?

WM. H. HARRISON. THE OHIO FARMER.

The first to vigorously campaign for the presidency, William Henry Harrison (1773–1841) had no time to enjoy his victory. The country's ninth president, he was the first to die in office.

President Andrew Jackson was a popular president, but like all presidents, he had enemies as well as friends. His enemies were quick to attack him in the daily newspapers. Not all this criticism was in words, however. *Political cartoons* often appeared in the newspapers. A political cartoon shows a particular opinion about a political event. It uses art and humor to get across its point and to catch the reader's interest.

The cartoon below appeared in newspapers in 1832, when Jackson was running for his second term as president. It pictures Andrew Jackson's government as a garbage wagon pulled by a broken-down horse with the face of Jackson. Martin Van Buren, a close advisor of President Jackson, leads the wagon. The figure driving the wagon is made up of kitchen tools of the day. It represents Jackson's informal group of advisors, called his Kitchen Cabinet. The rats on the roof probably represent Jackson's first group of advisors. They are shown scurrying away from a failing government, as rats are thought to do from a sinking ship.

Look at the 1834 political cartoon below and answer the questions about it.

1 Whom is the cartoon about? The cartoon title and the face of the figure give you hints.

2 What role is he pictured to be playing?

3 What do the torn documents under his feet say about "King Andrew's" possible opinion of the Constitution?

4 Do you think the cartoon shows a good or bad opinion of "King Andrew"?

KING ANDREW THE FIRST.

Think: The artwork on the right celebrates Harrison's inauguration. Many think the chill he caught on this day caused his death soon after. His plans were never put into action. Respond: How did Harrison's plans differ from Tyler's?

Under Harrison, the Whigs planned to open a new Bank of the United States and pass a higher tariff. They also wanted to give the money from the sale of western lands to the states. However, their plans were upset when Harrison died only one month after he took office.

After Harrison's death, Vice President John Tyler became president. Tyler did not have the same ideas most of the Whigs had. He agreed with the Democrats rather than with the Whigs on many issues. He was against a new bank and a higher tariff. Although the tariff was raised a little while Tyler was president, he vetoed other parts of the Whig plan.

Gradually, economic conditions in the United States began to improve. Farmers began to make more money. Businesses got back to normal. Once again, workers were able to find jobs.

In this chapter, you have read about many developments in American government in the first half of the nineteenth century. Many other changes were taking place in American life at this time as well. Writers and thinkers introduced new ideas about how Americans should live. Women began working for more rights. Many people tried to help the slaves. In the next chapter, you will read about these and other changes.

The first vice president to succeed a president, John Tyler (1790–1862) had to fight to be accepted. His use of the veto showed his strong stance on certain issues.

Section Review

1. What changes did Jacksonian Democracy make?

2. Why did Jackson want the Bank of the United States to end? What happened after it ended?

3. What happened to the nation during Van Buren's term?

4. What changes did the Whigs want to make if they won the election of 1840? What happened to their plans?

CHAPTER SUMMARY

After the War of 1812, Americans enjoyed an "Era of Good Feelings." The American System helped the sections work together. Under this system, Congress approved the National Road, the Second Bank of the United States, and a protective tariff. However, the South opposed the tariff. To maintain a balance in Congress, the Missouri Compromise made Missouri a slave state and Maine a free state. John Quincy Adams was elected president in 1824.

Andrew Jackson defeated Adams in 1828. Jackson was seen as a "man of the people" and a very strong president. He vetoed many laws and slowed down internal improvements. Jackson forced South Carolina to obey the tariff. During his term, the government also moved many Indian tribes to land in the West.

Under Jacksonian Democracy, more people got the right to vote. Jacksonian Democracy helped workers and started free public schools. Jackson ended the Bank of the United States. As a result, many state banks closed down. After Jackson's successor, Martin Van Buren, became president, the nation suffered a depression. The Whigs blamed the depression on Van Buren.

William Henry Harrison became president in 1840. When Harrison died after one month in office, John Tyler became president.

Key Words

Write a sentence to explain the meaning of each of these terms.

American System
McCulloch v. Maryland
Missouri Compromise

spoils system
Removal Act
Jacksonian Democracy

Major Events

Choose the answer that best completes the statement.

1. The Tariff Act of 1816 raised the cost of foreign goods to
   a) help foreign manufacturers.
   b) keep foreign goods out of the United States.
   c) raise money for an army.

2. In the election of 1824,
   a) Adams supported Clay.
   b) Jackson was elected president.
   c) the House of Representatives chose the president.

3. In the 1820s, Andrew Jackson formed the
   a) Republican Party.
   b) Whig Party.
   c) Democratic Party.

4. John C. Calhoun said that a state had the right to
   a) end slavery.
   b) nullify federal laws.
   c) raise the tariff.

5. The depression of the 1830s was in part caused by
   a) high tariffs.
   b) the Whigs.
   c) the collapse of state banks.

Review

Important Facts

Answer each question with at least one complete sentence.

1. What was the Tariff of 1816?

2. How did the South react to the Tariff of 1816?

3. What is judicial review? Why is it important?

4. What opinions did Americans have about the Missouri Compromise?

5. What was the most important law passed during Adams's term? Why was it important?

6. How was the presidential campaign of 1828 different from earlier campaigns?

7. In what ways was Jackson a new kind of president?

8. What was the "Trail of Tears"?

9. During Jackson's term, what changes were made in state constitutions?

10. How did the Bank of the United States control the state banks? How did Jackson try to break that control?

11. How did Van Buren try to stop the depression? How well did his plan work?

12. What effect did the depression have on the election of 1840?

13. What was the meaning of the campaign slogan, "Tippencanoe and Tyler, Too"?

14. What problems arose between Tyler and the Whigs?

Skill Review

Study this political cartoon, then answer the following questions.

1. What is Andrew Jackson riding?

2. What does the slogan at the base of the statue mean?

3. What is the cartoonist's opinion of the spoils system?

4. What political party do you think the cartoonist supports?

Critical Thinking

Write a paragraph to answer each question.

1. Why did the government want to remove the Indian tribes? How did the Indians try to stop the government?

2. Why did Jackson oppose the Bank of the United States? How did his actions cause a depression?

CHAPTER
13
American Life 1800-1860

Years 1800—1860

Gabriel Prosser led
slave revolt
1800

Denmark Vesey
tried to
start slave revolt
1822

Women's rights
convention,
Seneca Falls
1848

Gallaudet
started school
for the deaf
1817

Nat Turner's
revolt
1831

Segregation
ended in
Massachusetts
schools
1855

'Oh, woman! am not I thy sister?'

1. Changes in American Life

Learn these important terms:

revival meetings
reaper

Remember the main idea:

In the years between 1800 and 1860, there were many changes in American education, literature, and religion.

Look for answers to these questions:

1. What inventions improved life on farms and in the cities?
2. Why did many Americans want free public schools?
3. Who were the great American writers of the early 1800s? What ideas did they share? In what ways did they differ?
4. What new religious movements began in the United States?

In the early 1800s, the United States was becoming a great nation, full of new opportunities for people. Americans like Andrew Jackson could start in life with few advantages and become rich and powerful. After all, the Constitution promised that all Americans should have an equal chance to become successful. However, many people did not really have the same opportunities as others. Some were trapped in poverty. Others had physical disabilities. Women and black Americans did not have many important rights.

In this chapter, you will read about some of the ways Americans in the 1800s tried to help themselves and other people. You will read about important social improvements. You will read about Americans' attempts to find the ideal in America. Some turned to religion, others to forming new communities. But always Americans worked together. They worked to improve the American way of life.

As you will see, one of the biggest efforts during this time was toward helping blacks. Many Americans in the North and the South cared about this issue. Unfortunately, the practice of slavery still continued.

In the early years of the 1800s, most farm families lived very much like farm families of the colonial period had. They still made most of the things they needed. They did not sell many of the crops they grew on their farms.

After the War of 1812, life changed for the American farmer. Industry in the Northeast grew rapidly. Travel and shipping between the sections improved. Farmers shipped more of their crops to cities in the East. With the money they earned from their crops, farmers bought things they needed from merchants selling factory goods.

Think: Americans were taking great strides in the movement westward and in the use of the reaper. The original caption for this poster art read: "WESTWARD THE COURSE OF EMPIRE TAKES ITS WAY WITH McCORMICK REAPERS IN THE VAN." Respond: Why were the westward movement and the reaper important to America?

In the 1850s, new farm machines made some of the farmers' work easier. The steel plow helped farmers plant larger crops in less time. One of the most important new inventions was the **reaper**, invented by Cyrus McCormick. The McCormick reaper helped the farmer harvest crops more quickly.

Americans in cities were also able to buy more things they needed. Improvements in travel brought more farm goods to the cities. Factory goods, such as clothing and household items, could also be bought more easily. In the 1820s, Americans learned how to pack food in cans. Canning prevented food spoilage. Thanks to canned goods, it was easier to feed the growing population of the cities.

Think: The demand for McCormick's reaper was so great that his factory, shown above, stayed in production day and night. Respond: Why was the demand for the reaper so great?

Improvements in Schools

Some of the most important improvements were in education. Until about 1830, the United States had few public schools. Rich people sent their children to private schools. A few workers' children were able to go to schools run for free by churches. However, there were too few schools to educate most poor children.

Horace Mann of Massachusetts led the movement for free public schools. He knew that people needed a good education to help them improve their lives. Mann started colleges to train teachers, and he also improved teachers' pay. He worked to build better school buildings and to make classes more interesting.

With Mann's help, Massachusetts built many new public schools. Other states soon adopted Mann's ideas. By the 1850s, the states of the Northeast and some western states had free public elementary schools. These schools were supported by taxes. Most high schools, however, remained private.

American Writers

Americans not only wanted their own schools. They also wanted their own books to read in the schools. After the Revolutionary War, Americans stopped using British textbooks in their schools. They started using American books such as Noah Webster's famous *Spelling Book* and his dictionary of American words.

American adults also wanted to read books by American writers on American life and history. The first American writers to become famous were Washington Irving and James Fenimore Cooper. Cooper wrote adventure stories, such as *The Deerslayer,* about life in the American

---

Think: **The opening of free public schools was a turning point for American children. By becoming educated, they were given the chance to make choices about their futures. Winslow Homer painted this picture in 1871.**
Respond: **What might school have been like in the days when this picture was painted?**

The psychologically probing stories of Nathaniel Hawthorne (1804-1864) often used places and events from his life.

Washington Irving (1783-1859) was America's first successful professional writer. He wrote biographies in addition to humorous fiction.

Today Herman Melville (1819-1891) is a highly regarded author. In his lifetime, he received little acclaim. *(Detail from a portrait)*

wilderness. Irving wrote humorous stories, such as "Rip Van Winkle," about life in old New York.

Some of the greatest American writers of the 1800s came from New England. Ralph Waldo Emerson wrote that people should love nature. He also believed that people should follow their own consciences, or moral ideals. Another writer, Henry David Thoreau (thor-OH), put some of Emerson's ideas into practice. He built a cabin in the woods and wrote about life in nature. Once, he went to jail for refusing to pay his taxes. He believed it was wrong to pay taxes as long as the government supported slavery.

Emerson and Thoreau believed people were basically good. Another great New England writer, Nathaniel Hawthorne (nuh-THAN-ee-uhl HAW-thorn), did not share many of their ideas. He wrote about how people can sometimes be cruel and unfair. His most famous novel, *The Scarlet Letter,* tells of the cruelty of people living in an early Puritan town.

The New Yorker Herman Melville was also concerned with the problem of evil. Melville often based his novels on his own experiences as a sailor. *Moby Dick* is a novel about a hunt for a huge white whale. But it is also about the struggle between good and evil.

Another great writer from New York was Walt Whitman. Whitman broke away from the old forms of poetry and began to

Walt Whitman (1819-1892) was a truly American poet. He created new forms and new words to fit the ideas of his time. His poems are best appreciated when read aloud.

Think: This vivid and dramatic scene from Washington Irving's ''Rip Van Winkle'' was painted by John Quidor. He captured Irving's sense of humor and imagination. In the story, published in 1820, Rip Van Winkle fell asleep for 20 years, only to return to a changed world. Respond: What changes might he have seen in 1840?

write what is now called free verse. Whitman was a poet of the common people. His book *Leaves of Grass* reflects Americans' pride in their nation.

The most famous writer from the South was Edgar Allan Poe. Poe wrote poems and short stories full of mysterious and frightening events. Many people today think of him as the father of the modern detective story.

Religion in American Life

Writers like Emerson, Thoreau, and Melville were deeply concerned about the human spirit. Many Americans shared this concern. In the early 1800s, religion became a more important part of American life. New religious movements began. Some of these movements differed from the stern groups of the past, like the Puritans. The new movements sometimes included elements from the democratic way of American life. For example, the Universalists believed that all people received God's grace. Another group, the Unitarians, believed that human beings were essentially good. Emerson was a Unitarian minister for many years.

Groups like the Universalists and the Unitarians built many new churches in the Northeast. In the West, churches were not so common. Most towns were very small, and people often lived on farms spread over the countryside. Once a year,

CHANGES IN POPULATION, 1820–1840

Cities are centers of population. Look at the map below. It shows you where the major centers of population were in the United States at two dates in the 1800s, before the Civil War. Look at the map key. Notice that the red dots stand for the nation's major cities in 1820. The blue dots stand for new major cities, those that sprang up or grew between the years 1820 and 1840.

Cities usually grow where there is transportation. A city will spring up where there is a good harbor, for example. Bodies of water—oceans, rivers, and lakes—were important to transportation before the development of railroads, automobiles, and airplanes. Look at the map. What bodies of water seem to have led to the development of the red cities?

Between 1820 and 1840, the invention of the flat-bottomed, steam-driven river boat and the development of canals greatly aided transportation of freight between sections of the country. Which blue cites benefited from each of these developments?

Using this chapter and the map and the key, answer the following questions.

1. In 1840, what forms of water transportation served the following cities?
    Albany
    Buffalo
    Cleveland
    New Orleans

2. Why was the Erie Canal built from east to west across the state of New York?

3. What inventions would put the Erie Canal out of business?

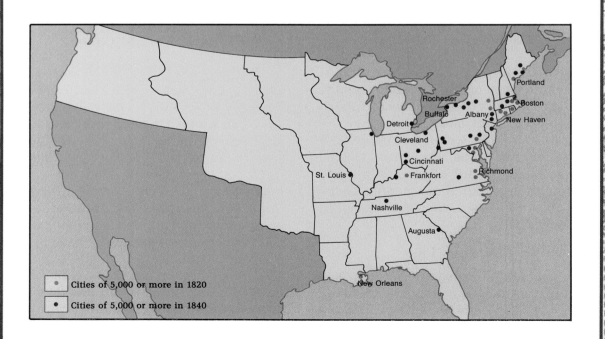

Cities of 5,000 or more in 1820
Cities of 5,000 or more in 1840

Think: Life on the frontier must have been lonely and often boring. People looked forward to the revival meetings that came to many parts of the frontier. During these week-long camp meetings, people listened to sermons and sang hymns. **Respond:** What needs did the revival meetings serve?

many westerners would leave their farms and travel to *revival meetings* (ree-VYE-vuhl). There, frontier people could gather and listen to religious sermons.

Thousands of people went to revival meetings. They traveled from miles around to meet in open meadows, sleep in tents, and attend religious meetings that often lasted for several days. The preachers urged people to lead better lives, lives free from sin. Revival meetings did more than help people with their religious beliefs. The meetings also brought people living on the frontier closer together.

Americans saw their nation as a land of great opportunity. They learned to help themselves and improve their own lives. In the next section of this chapter, you will read about some of the ways that Americans helped themselves. You will

also read about how some brave and generous Americans tried to help less fortunate people.

Section Review

1. How did farming become easier in the 1850s?

2. Who was Horace Mann? What changes did he want to make?

3. What ideas did Emerson and Thoreau share? In what ways did Hawthorne and Melville differ from them?

4. What was a revival meeting? Why were revivals important to people in the West?

2. Reform Movements

Learn these important terms:

utopian communities
reform
temperance movement
abolition movement
gradual abolition
immediate abolition

Remember the main idea:

In the years between 1820 and 1860, many reform movements tried to improve life in the United States. The effort to end slavery became the most important reform movement.

Look for answers to these questions:

1. Why did some Americans want to start separate communities in the United States?
2. What did prison reformers want to do?
3. Why did many women join together in the 1840s to work for women's rights?
4. What was the goal of the abolition movement?

Dorothea Dix (1802-1887) founded over thirty mental hospitals. This portrait, from a painting by Thomas Waterman Wood, shows her about the time of her appointment as Union Superintendent of Nurses.

People came to America looking for a better way of life. For some Americans, making life better meant starting a farm on the frontier. Others wanted to start businesses in the cities. There were some Americans, however, who did not want to make life better just for themselves and their families. They believed that America was a perfect place to build a *utopian community* (yoo-TO-pee-uhn), where an ideal way of life could be established.

Utopian communities were often begun by religious groups like the Shakers. Other utopian communities, like the Oneida community (oh-NYE-duh) and the Brook Farm, were not religious. Utopian communities were made up of groups of people who tried to live according to ideals they shared. For example, many utopians believed that if there were no private property, people would cooperate rather than compete with one another. Utopians believed that if everyone followed ideals like this, society would be perfect.

Utopian communities often separated themselves from the rest of American society. They did not want to be part of a society that did not live up to their ideals. Utopian communities often were set up in rural areas. People in the communities farmed the land, and sometimes they also became involved in crafts or manufacturing. Most utopian communities failed after a few years. However, their example inspired many other people to improve society.

Social Reforms

Only a few people left society to try to build utopian communities. Most people who wanted to improve life worked within society. In the years between 1820 and 1860, many Americans tried to *reform*, or make things better, for the people of the United States.

One reform movement tried to improve the treatment of prisoners. In the 1800s, prisons were cold, dirty, horrible places. Prison reformers tried to make prisons safer and cleaner. They also tried to give prisoners useful work to prepare them to lead better lives.

One of the women active in prison reform was Dorothea Dix. She was shocked to discover that mentally ill peo-

ple were also locked up in prisons. Dix felt that it was wrong to treat sick people like criminals. She worked to set up hospitals where mentally ill people could have better care.

Other reformers began a movement against the use of alcoholic drink. They thought that drinking alcohol caused people to lose their jobs and turn to crime. Members of this ***temperance movement*** forced some states to pass laws against the use of alcoholic drinks.

There were many other reforms as well. In 1817, Thomas Gallaudet (gal-uh-DET) started a free school for the deaf. In the 1830s, Samuel Gridley Howe started a school to help blind people learn to live useful lives. He also developed a way to print books with raised type. Blind people could read the words by touching them with their fingers. In the 1850s, Charles Loring Brace started a society to help homeless children in New York. Other reformers worked to improve the conditions of workers in the cities.

Think: **A portion of the Oneida Community is shown here with its bearded founder, John Noyes. The photograph was taken ten years after the community was begun. Oneida ranks among the most successful utopian societies begun in America.** Respond: **What is your idea of a perfect society?**

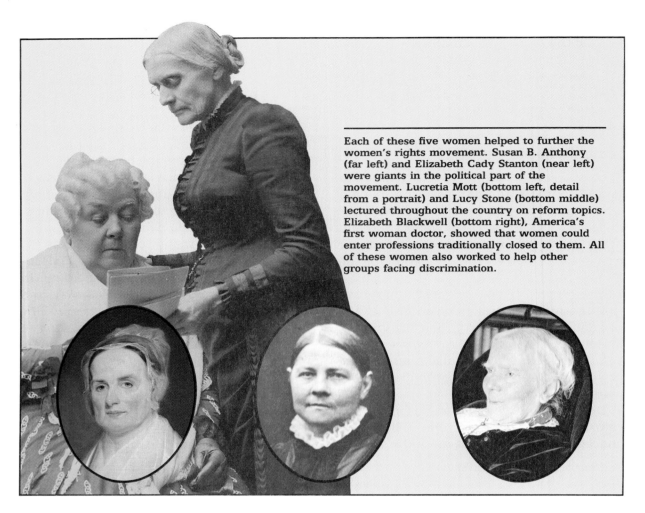

Each of these five women helped to further the women's rights movement. Susan B. Anthony (far left) and Elizabeth Cady Stanton (near left) were giants in the political part of the movement. Lucretia Mott (bottom left, detail from a portrait) and Lucy Stone (bottom middle) lectured throughout the country on reform topics. Elizabeth Blackwell (bottom right), America's first woman doctor, showed that women could enter professions traditionally closed to them. All of these women also worked to help other groups facing discrimination.

Women's Rights

The struggle for women's rights in America has a long history. As early as colonial times, women asked for equal rights. However, in the 1800s, women still could not vote, hold office, or work at many other kinds of jobs.

In the 1830s and 1840s, women joined the movement to end slavery. Most men did not welcome them in this movement. Many women thought these men were being unfair. Why should men support slaves' rights but not women's rights? As a result, many women decided to work to improve their own position. Elizabeth Cady Stanton, Emma Willard, Lucy Stone, and Lucretia Mott were some of the leaders of the women's rights movement.

In 1848, a Women's Rights Convention met in Seneca Falls, New York. Elizabeth Cady Stanton wrote a "declaration of independence" for women. This declaration, modeled on the one written in 1776, made twelve demands. One of these demands stated that women should be allowed to vote.

As a result of the women's movement, women won more rights. For example, Susan B. Anthony, just before the Civil War, got several states to give married women the right to own their own property. Women also entered careers that had once been held only by men. Elizabeth Blackwell became the first woman to go to medical school and become a physician in the United States.

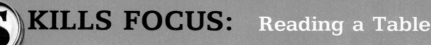

Changes in American Education in the 1800s

Subject	Goal	Leader
elementary schools	free elementary schools	Horace Mann
textbooks	textbooks written in U.S.	Noah Webster

A table organizes information so that it is easier to understand and remember. Above is part of a table on changes in American education.

The table has columns and rows. The columns run down the page and have these headings: *Subject, Goal,* and *Leader.* The rows go across. Each row gives information about one subject. This table contains in short form some of the most impor-tant information found in Chapter 13 of your textbook under the headings ''Improvements in Schools'' and ''American Writers.''

The incomplete table below has information about some of the reform movements. Look through Section 2 in your textbook to find information to complete the table.

Reform Movements in the United States in the 1800s

Subject	Goal	Leader
prisoners	safer and cleaner prisons	Dorothea Dix
mentally ill people	hospitalization	Dorothea Dix
deaf people	free schools	1
blind people	2	3
women	rights	4
		5
		6
7	abolition	Frederick Douglass
		8
		9

'Oh, woman! am not I thy sister?'

Think: **An abolitionist society chose this as its official symbol. The picture was spread throughout the nation.** Respond: **What effect did the abolitionists hope this image would have?**

The Fight Against Slavery

In the 1800s, the most important reform groups were those that worked to end slavery. The Quakers were among the first Americans to speak out against slavery. In the early 1800s, other religious groups in the North also began to teach that slavery was wrong. Soon, many Americans who were members of other reform groups joined the effort to end slavery. This effort became known as the **abolition movement**.

Before 1830, most leaders of the abolition movement believed that slavery should be ended slowly. This was called **gradual abolition**. These abolitionists also believed that planters should be paid for their slaves. This was a plan with which even some Southerners agreed. Other abolitionists believed slavery was so evil that it must end at once. They believed in **immediate abolition**. They did not agree that slave owners should be paid for their slaves.

Many people in the abolition movement had known slavery firsthand. Frederick Douglass was a slave who escaped to the North. He became a famous speaker and writer against slavery. Sojourner Truth was a slave who became free in 1827. Later, she traveled through the Northeast and West telling Americans the truth about slavery. There were even a few abolitionists, like the Grimké sisters, who were former slave owners.

Think: **The Liberator** was an antislavery newspaper that spoke mainly to whites, but was financed mostly by blacks. Despite southern attempts to get rid of it, this influential paper remained in circulation until slavery was abolished. Respond: **What stories does the paper's heading tell?**

Think: Sojourner Truth (right) spoke out against slavery and for women's rights. A former northern slave, she knew first hand the sufferings of the slaves.
Respond: Why is her chosen name appropriate?

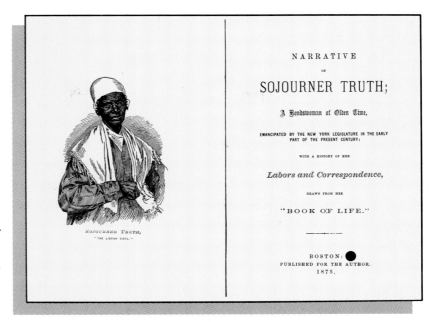

NARRATIVE

OF

SOJOURNER TRUTH;

A Bondswoman of Olden Time,

EMANCIPATED BY THE NEW YORK LEGISLATURE IN THE EARLY
PART OF THE PRESENT CENTURY;

WITH A HISTORY OF HER

Labors and Correspondence,

DRAWN FROM HER

"BOOK OF LIFE."

BOSTON:
PUBLISHED FOR THE AUTHOR.
1875.

SOJOURNER TRUTH,
"THE LIBYAN SIBYL."

Think: Below, a mob destroyed a printing press that had been used to print an antislavery newspaper. Its owner was later killed.
Respond: How and why was this picture used by an antislavery almanac?

At first, many Northerners disagreed with the abolitionists. Slaves were seen as property. Northern property owners did not like the idea of taking property away from people. Northern businessmen were afraid that the abolition movement might hurt their trade with the South. Northern workers were worried that freed slaves might come north and take their jobs.

Some Northerners tried to stop the abolition movement. They used force to break up abolitionists' meetings. Mobs smashed presses that printed abolitionist papers. William Lloyd Garrison, who printed an abolitionist newspaper, once had to be put in prison to protect him from an angry mob. Elijah Lovejoy, a famous Illinois abolitionist, was killed by a mob. However, the abolition movement continued.

Abolitionists believed that slavery was wrong. They wanted to help blacks improve their lives. In the next section, you will read about the lives of slaves in the South. You will also read about how blacks in the North lived.

Section Review

1. What is a utopian community?

2. What were some important reforms made by Americans in the years between 1820 and 1860?

3. What happened at Seneca Falls, New York, in 1848?

4. What was the most important reform movement in the years between 1820 and 1860? Why did people in that movement disagree with one another? How did some Northerners react to the movement?

3. Black Americans

Learn these important terms:

slave codes
Underground Railroad
segregated
poll tax
boycotted
benefit societies
black conventions

Remember the main idea:

Black Americans never accepted slavery. Slaves often tried to gain their freedom. Free blacks in the North struggled to gain equal rights and to end slavery.

Look for answers to these questions:

1. What was life like for slaves?
2. How did some slaves escape from the South?
3. How did blacks in the North try to improve their lives?

Many people became abolitionists when they learned how hard the life of a slave was. Slaves usually lived in tiny shacks with little heat. They worked long hours all year round. They had very few rights and could not improve their conditions. With the growth of the cotton industry, slavery conditions grew even worse. *Slave codes*, or the rules controlling slaves, became more strict. Slaves were often beaten, and fewer slaves were freed by their owners.

As cotton growing spread westward, many slaves were also forced to move to the West. At such times, families were often separated. If a slave owner bought a field worker but not his wife or children, the slave had to leave his family. Since slaves were not allowed to learn to read or write, the slave could not even write letters to his family.

Many Southerners tried to convince people that slavery was good for blacks. Slave owners said they took good care of their slaves. Southerners claimed that free blacks could not get along well in American society. Slave owners wanted people to believe that the blacks they owned liked being slaves.

In fact, slaves hated slavery. The proof is that thousands of slaves tried to escape. Escaping was not easy. Slaves often had

Think: Growing cotton required large numbers of workers. The work was hard and couldn't pay well because the profits were not great in comparison to the amount of work. Thus, slaves were used. Respond: How did the growth of the cotton business cause slavery conditions to worsen?

HAULING THE WHOLE WEEKS PICKING

Think: At auction, a good field hand sold for $1,800. Fathers, mothers, sons, and daughters were often separated. Respond: Compare what the buyers and sellers might be thinking with what the slaves might be thinking.

Courtesy of Chicago Historical Society.

RAFFLE

Mr. Joseph Jennings respectfully informs his friends and the public that, at the request of many acquaintances, he has been induced to purchase from Mr. Osborne, of Missouri, the celebrated

DARK BAY HORSE, "STAR,"

Aged five years, square trotter and warranted sound; with a new light Trotting Buggy and Harness; also, the dark, stout

MULATTO GIRL, "SARAH,"

Aged about twenty years, general house servant, valued at *nine hundred dollars*, and guaranteed, and

Will be Raffled for

At 4 o'clock P. M., February first, at the selection hotel of the subscribers. The above is as represented, and those persons who may wish to engage in the usual practice of raffling, will, I assure them, be perfectly satisfied with their destiny in this affair.

The whole is valued at its just worth, fifteen hundred dollars; fifteen hundred

CHANCES AT ONE DOLLAR EACH.

The Raffle will be conducted by gentlemen selected by the interested subscribers present. Five nights will be allowed to complete the Raffle. BOTH OF THE ABOVE DESCRIBED CAN BE SEEN AT MY STORE, No. 78 Common St., second door from Camp, at from 9 o'clock A. M. to 2 P. M.

Highest throw to take the first choice; the lowest throw the remaining prize, and the fortunate winners will pay twenty dollars each for the refreshments furnished on the occasion.

N. B. No chances recognized unless paid for previous to the commencement.

JOSEPH JENNINGS.

Think: This advertisement lists a girl for sale along with a horse, as if she were a piece of property and not a person. Respond: Upon what might slave sellers have based their selling prices?

to travel hundreds of miles without supplies. If a runaway slave was caught, he or she often was cruelly whipped. Despite these dangers, many slaves were willing to take the risk. Between 1830 and 1860, more than sixty thousand slaves escaped to the North. Thousands of others were caught before they reached freedom.

Some runaway slaves were helped by the **Underground Railroad**, which was not a real railroad but a group of people who helped slaves to escape. The Underground Railroad had "conductors," or persons who led slaves out of the South. Every few miles, slaves ate and rested at

THE UNDERGROUND RAILROAD

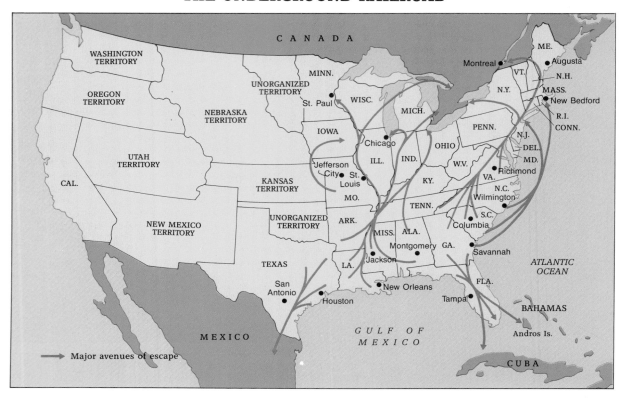

Major avenues of escape

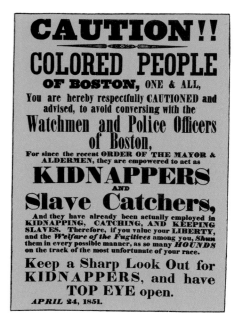

"stations," which were houses or farms. When the slaves reached the North, people helped them get a new start in life.

Although many white people helped, most conductors on the Underground Railroad were blacks. The most famous conductor was Harriet Tubman, an escaped slave who helped more than three hundred slaves reach freedom. At one time, southern plantation owners offered forty thousand dollars for her capture, dead or alive. Again and again she avoided being captured.

Revolts

A few slaves took more violent action. During the 1800s, slave revolts in the South became a serious problem. In 1800, a slave named Gabriel Prosser led a thousand slaves in a revolt near Richmond, Virginia. Denmark Vesey (VEE-zee) tried

Harriet Tubman (c. 1821-1913), born a slave named Araminta, had a hard early life. She was forced to work the fields and to marry against her will. She spent her life helping other slaves escape.

to start a revolt around the area of Charleston, South Carolina, in 1822. Both of these revolts failed, and their leaders were hanged.

The most famous slave revolt took place in Virginia in 1831. A slave named Nat Turner believed that the Bible told slaves to revolt. Turner and a small band of men killed nearly sixty white Southerners. Armed troops put down Nat Turner's revolt. Turner and many of his followers were hanged.

Slave revolts such as these frightened white Southerners. They blamed northern abolitionists for putting ideas into the slaves' minds. After Nat Turner's revolt, southern post offices refused to deliver abolitionist writings. For many years, southern congressmen also stopped Congress from talking about ending slavery.

White Southerners also made the slave codes stricter. Slaves were not allowed to meet together unless a white person was present, and they could not meet with free blacks at all. Armed patrols made

Think: Nat Turner was a well-educated slave. In 1831, he led a slave rebellion in Virginia in which sixty whites were killed. Respond: Why did this both surprise and frighten whites?

HISTORY MAKERS

──Frederick Douglass──

Educated Slave, Outspoken Free Man

''Mrs. Auld! What are you doing there with that boy?''

''Gracious, you startled me!''

''I'll ask you again, Ma'am. What are you doing with that boy?''

''I'm teaching him to read, Mr. Auld. He learned his alphabet very quickly, and now he's learning how to spell.''

''Frederick isn't here to learn, Mrs. Auld! He's here to wait on you and Tommy. It's against the law to teach a slave to read and write! If he learns the Bible, it will make him unfit to be a slave. He should know nothing but the will of his master, and he must learn to obey it!''

But Frederick Douglass wanted to learn. And he never lost sight of his goal. He felt learning to read and write would help him someday become free.

Born into slavery on a plantation in 1817, Frederick Douglass never knew his father and saw his mother only a few times as a young child. When Frederick was eight, his master sent him to Baltimore as a house servant to the Auld family. When he was sixteen, he returned to his master's plantation. After he began teaching Sunday school, he was hired out to a slave-breaker. When the slave-breaker tried to whip him, Frederick Douglass fought him off for two hours. The fight renewed his determination to become a free man, no matter what.

Four years later, in 1838, he escaped from Baltimore and slavery. Douglass went to Massachusetts, where he became active in the anti-slavery movement. He first served as a lecturer, then as the publisher of a weekly newspaper, *The North Star.* During the Civil War, Frederick Douglass urged Abraham Lincoln to free the slaves, enlist blacks in the army, and provide fair treatment for black soldiers.

After the war, Frederick Douglass was appointed to political offices in the District of Columbia. He was also named U.S. Minister to Haiti. He continued to work for civil rights for blacks and women. His autobiography is an important record of the slave system. The book also shows the courage and strength of this determined man.

sure that these rules were carried out. The patrols dealt harshly with any slave who left his or her plantation without a pass.

Life in the North

When Southerners argued that slavery was good for blacks, they often said that free blacks in the North led harder lives than slaves did. While it is not true that slavery was good, free blacks in the North did have very hard lives. Free blacks had few rights. They were not allowed to vote or to sit on juries. Skilled black workers often had to work in unskilled jobs. Worst of all, blacks were *segregated*, or separated, from whites in schools, churches, hospitals, restaurants, streetcars, and railroads. They even had to live in separate neighborhoods, often far away from whites.

In spite of all these problems, a few blacks did well. They became tailors, restaurant owners, and hotel keepers. James Forten of Philadelphia made a fortune as a manufacturer of ship sails. Other blacks owned grocery stores, barber shops, and stables. A few became professionals, such as lawyers, doctors, ministers, and schoolteachers.

The Struggle for Rights

Black Americans in the North worked hard to win their rights. Some blacks refused to pay the state *poll tax,* or voting tax, unless they were actually allowed to vote. Others refused to pay school taxes as long as the schools were segregated. One man sued the Boston school board for making him send his daughter to a segregated school. He lost his case in court, but in 1855, a state law was passed which ended segregation in Massachusetts schools. Some northern blacks also *boycotted*, or refused to use, segregated streetcars.

To fight for equal rights and freedom, black Americans often worked together in groups. Even before 1800, free blacks of the Northeast formed self-help groups known as *benefit societies*. Blacks also started their own churches. Benefit societies and black churches tried to help their members get good educations and better jobs. Also, black abolitionist groups were formed long before any white abolitionist groups.

In the 1830s and 1840s, several *black conventions* were held. In these conventions, groups of black leaders met and asked Congress to end slavery and give blacks equal rights. These conventions made the public more aware of the conditions under which black Americans lived and worked.

Blacks in both the North and South did not accept slavery. Slaves often escaped and sometimes revolted. In the North, black Americans struggled for their rights and tried to help end slavery. However, their efforts did not bring an end to slavery. As you read the next chapter, you will see how the continued growth of the United States made the slavery problem even worse.

Section Review

1. What was life like for slaves in the South? How did conditions become worse after the cotton industry began to grow?

2. What was the Underground Railroad? Who was its most famous conductor?

3. How did Southerners react to the slave revolts?

4. In what ways did blacks in the North try to improve their rights as citizens?

CHAPTER SUMMARY

After 1800, American life improved in many ways. New inventions made farming easier. Horace Mann helped improve schools in Massachussetts. Writers such as Cooper and Irving wrote about American life. Emerson, Thoreau, Hawthorne, Melville, Whitman, and Poe became important writers. Many Americans became involved in religious movements. New churches were started in the Northeast, and revival meetings became popular in the West.

Americans started many reform movements. Prisons were improved. Mentally ill people were given better care. Schools were opened for deaf and blind people. Reformers helped homeless children and factory workers. Some Americans tried to stop the drinking of alcohol. Women fought for and won many rights, but they did not win the right to vote. The most important reform movement was the abolition movement. It included many free blacks and former slaves, as well as former slave owners and other whites.

The life of slaves was hard and cruel. Thousands of slaves tried to escape. A few slaves started revolts, but they failed. In the North, blacks lived in segregated communities. Northern blacks became active in the abolition movement. They started benefit societies to help one another, and they worked for equal rights.

Key Words

Write a sentence to explain the meaning of each of these terms.

reaper

reform

abolition
  movement

poll tax

Underground
  Railroad

black
  conventions

Major Events

Choose the answer that best completes the statement.

1. Under the leadership of Horace Mann, Massachusetts built many

   a) churches.
   b) factories.
   c) schools.

2. Many people today think that the detective story was invented by

   a) James Fenimore Cooper.
   b) Edgar Allan Poe.
   c) Moby Dick.

3. In 1817, Samuel Gallaudet started a free school for

   a) the deaf.
   b) homeless crippled children.
   c) the blind.

4. In 1801, 1822, and 1831, blacks in the South started

   a) reform movements.
   b) schools for slaves.
   c) slave revolts.

5. In 1855, Massachussetts passed a state law which ended

   a) slavery.
   b) segregation.
   c) the use of alcohol.

Review

Important Facts

Answer each question with at least one complete sentence.

1. In the 1850s, what inventions made farming easier?

2. How did Thoreau put Emerson's ideas into practice?

3. Who were the Unitarians? What did they believe?

4. What religious gatherings brought people together in the West?

5. What name was given to the people who believed in ideal communities?

6. What did Dorothea Dix try to accomplish?

7. What movement tried to end the use of alcoholic drink?

8. In what ways did Samuel Gridley Howe help blind people?

9. What did the Women's Rights Convention of 1848 accomplish? What problems still remained to be solved?

10. What differences of opinion existed within the abolition movement?

11. How did some Northerners try to stop the abolition movement? Why did they do this?

12. Who was Nat Turner? What did he do?

13. How did blacks in the North help one another?

14. What effect did slave revolts have on white Southerners?

Skill Review

Study this table, then answer the following questions.

	1790	1850
Boston, Mass.	18,320	136,881
Buffalo, N.Y.	—	42,261
Cincinnati, Oh.	—	115,435
Louisville, Ky.	200	43,194
New Orleans, La.	—	116,375
New York, N.Y.	49,401	696,115
Philadelphia, Pa.	28,522	121,376
Richmond, Va.	3,761	27,570
St. Louis, Mo.	—	77,860
Washington, D.C.	—	40,001

Population

1. Which were the three largest cities in 1790?

2. Which cities in 1850 did not exist in 1790?

3. Which city grew the most between 1790 and 1850? By how much did it grow?

4. Which city grew the most as a result of westward settlement?

Critical Thinking

Write a paragraph to answer each question.

1. Why do you think many Americans became involved in reform movements?

2. Why do you think blacks in the North fought against slavery?

Important People

Choose the answer that best completes the statement.

1. In the European war, President Washington wanted the United States

   a) to help France.
   b) to help Great Britain.
   c) to stay neutral.

2. The Federalist Party was led by

   a) Thomas Jefferson.
   b) John Jay.
   c) Alexander Hamilton.

3. The inventor of the idea of interchangeable parts was

   a) Cyrus McCormick.
   b) Eli Whitney.
   c) Thomas Jefferson.

4. Henry Cabot Lowell was

   a) an inventor.
   b) the owner of a textile mill.
   c) a leader in the abolition movement.

5. The spoils system was first used

   a) by John Quincy Adams.
   b) by James Monroe.
   c) by Andrew Jackson.

6. *The Scarlet Letter* was written by

   a) Herman Melville.
   b) Walt Whitman.
   c) Nathaniel Hawthorne.

7. Elizabeth Cady Stanton, a reformer, was best known for her role in

   a) the women's rights movement.
   b) the abolition movement.
   c) the temperance movement.

Main Ideas

Choose the answer that best completes the statement.

1. The Whiskey Rebellion showed Americans that

   a) the federal government could enforce its laws.
   b) citizens could refuse to pay unpopular taxes.
   c) the temperance movement was weak in the West.

2. The size of the United States was doubled through

   a) the Missouri Compromise.
   b) the Louisiana Purchase.
   c) the Lewis and Clark Expedition.

3. As a result of the War of 1812,

   a) Great Britain saw that the United States was strong.
   b) the South became an industrial center.
   c) the United States gained Canada.

4. The Industrial Revolution began

   a) in France.
   b) in Great Britain.
   c) in the United States.

5. Most Southerners

   a) lived on large plantations.
   b) owned small farms.
   c) worked in factories.

6. In the 1800s the fastest growing section of the nation was

   a) the Northeast.
   b) the South.
   c) the West.

Review

7. The American System, proposed by Henry Clay, called for

   a) low tariffs.
   b) high tariffs.
   c) taxes on factory goods.

8. The presidential election of 1824 was decided by

   a) the popular vote.
   b) the electoral vote.
   c) a vote in the House of Representatives.

9. Under Jacksonian Democracy

   a) rich bankers and landowners were given power.
   b) ordinary people had increased opportunities in all areas of government.
   c) free blacks gained the vote.

10. The depression under President Van Buren was largely caused by

    a) problems with the banks.
    b) bad conditions for workers in factories.
    c) high land prices.

11. The movement against the use of alcoholic drinks was called

    a) the abolition movement.
    b) the temperance movement.
    c) the utopian movement.

12. Before 1830, most abolition leaders believed that

    a) planters should be paid for their slaves.
    b) slavery should end at once with no payment to owners for slaves.
    c) slaves should be sent back to Africa.

History Skills

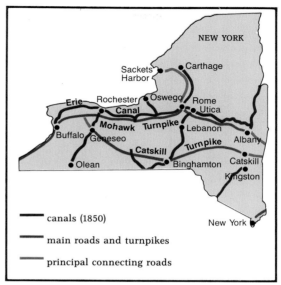

Canals and Highways 1820-50

Choose the answer that best completes the statement.

1. Major transportation routes in New York connected

   a) Lake Erie and Lake Ontario.
   b) the Great Lakes and the Hudson River.
   c) Albany and New York City.

2. You would expect Rome to be a bigger city than Carthage because it was

   a) on the Erie Canal.
   b) at the junction of the Erie Canal and two major roads.
   c) in the center of the state.

3. Buffalo grew to be a much larger city than Binghamton because it

   a) had highways and the canal.
   b) bordered on Canada.
   c) also handled Great Lakes shipping.

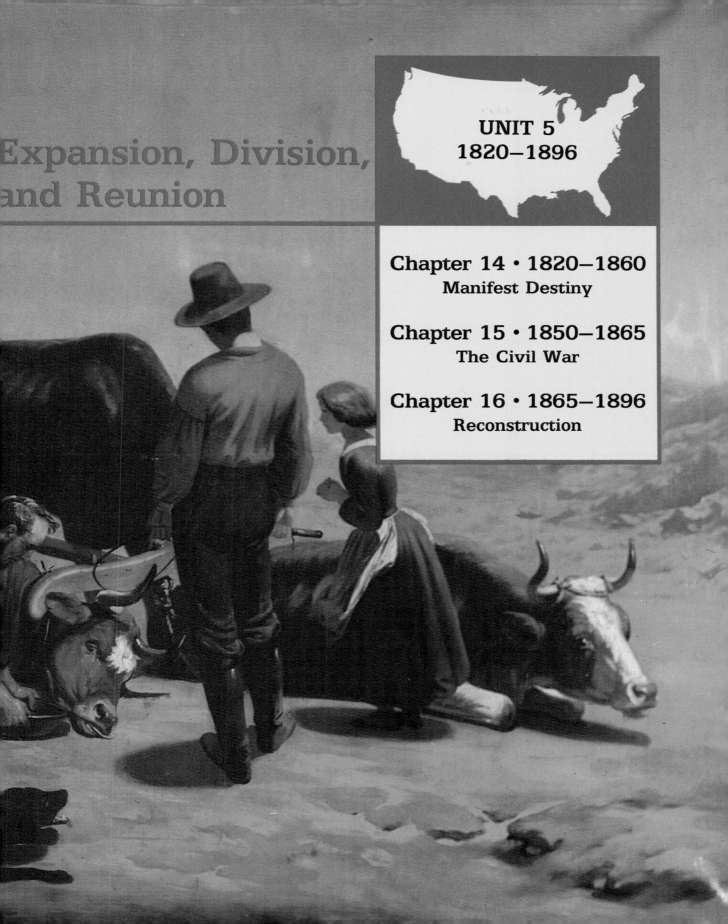

Expansion, Division, and Reunion

UNIT 5
1820–1896

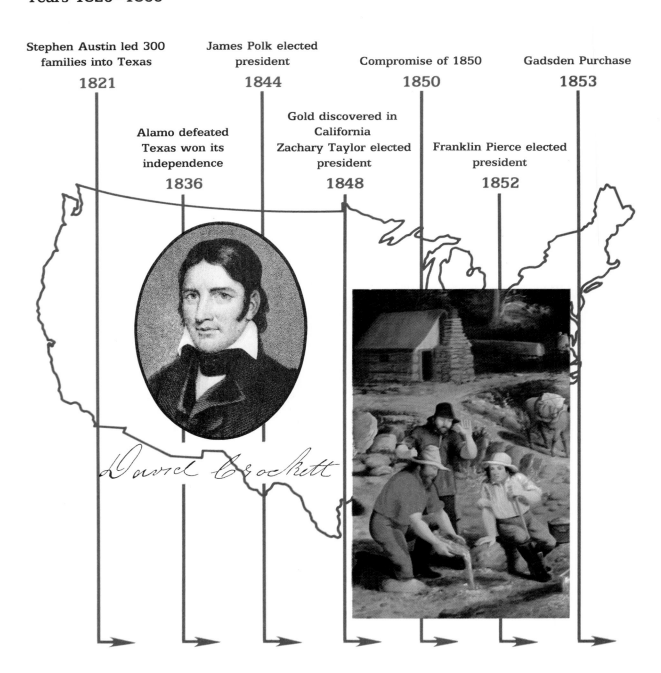

Stephen Austin led 300
families into Texas
1821

James Polk elected
president
1844

Compromise of 1850
1850

Gadsden Purchase
1853

Alamo defeated
Texas won its
independence
1836

Gold discovered in
California
Zachary Taylor elected
president
1848

Franklin Pierce elected
president
1852

David Crockett

Learn these important terms:

Lone Star Republic
Oregon Trail
Mormon Trail
missionaries
Mormons
annex

Remember the main idea:

Most Americans wanted the United States to reach the Pacific Ocean. Americans settled in Texas, Utah, Oregon, and California.

Look for answers to these questions:

1. How did Texas win its independence from Mexico?
2. Who settled in Oregon, Utah, and California?
3. Why did some Americans want to keep Texas out of the United States?

To Americans in the 1840s, the West meant new lands and new opportunities. At that time, however, the western boundary of the United States was in the Great Plains. This was east of the Rocky Mountains. Much of the western part of the continent still belonged to Mexico.

Many Americans wanted this land to belong to the United States. Settlers in the 1840s wanted the vast farm land that the West offered. Traders wanted to use the harbors along the Pacific coast for their ships going to and from China and Japan.

In the 1840s, Americans believed that the western part of the continent should belong to the United States. One writer said it was the *Manifest Destiny* (MAN-uh-fest DES-tuh-nee), or fate, of the United States to take over all the land between the Atlantic and Pacific Oceans.

In this chapter you will read about how the United States grew until it reached the Pacific coast. You will read about brave people in Texas who fought for their independence from Mexico. You will also read about another war. This war was between Mexico and the United States.

You will learn what the growth of the United States did to the conflict over slavery. Would the territories in the West become slave states? Could the nation's leaders help the United States grow without making the slavery problem worse?

In the first half of the 1800s, the United States expanded into the far west. Texas and then Oregon became states. But prior to statehood, each had its conflicts.

The New Texans

In the early years of the 1800s, few people lived in the Mexican territory of Texas. Around 1820, however, an American named Moses Austin learned that the land in Texas was good for growing cotton and raising cattle. He asked Mexico to let him bring American settlers into that region. Moses Austin died in 1821. But Mexico agreed to let his son, Stephen

The leadership of Stephen Austin (1793–1836) enabled Americans to settle in Texas and grow strong enough to separate themselves from Mexico.

Austin, lead three hundred families into eastern Texas.

By 1830, twenty thousand Americans had settled in Texas. The Mexican government considered these new settlers Mexicans. Most of the settlers, however, still thought of themselves as Americans, or simply as Texans. They did not even learn to speak Spanish. When Mexico passed a law against slavery, the Texans simply ignored it. Texas was far away from the Mexican government, so Texas planters felt safe in keeping slaves.

Mexico did not like the way the Texans were acting. In 1830, it passed another law against slavery. It also said that no more settlers could come into Texas from the United States. This law upset the Texans. Stephen Austin went to Mexico City to talk about the problem, but he was thrown into prison.

In 1835, the Texans revolted. A small army of Texans took over the Alamo, a Mexican fort near San Antonio. General Santa Anna, the Mexican leader, attacked the Alamo with thousands of troops. The Texans were outnumbered and short of supplies, but they refused to surrender. They knew that Sam Houston (HYOO-stun), the Texan general, was trying to gather an army to the east. By keeping Santa Anna busy, the Texans in the Alamo hoped to give Houston time to build his army.

The Mexicans attacked the Alamo many times, but they could not defeat the Texans. Then, on March 6, 1836, three thousand Mexicans made their final attack. The two hundred Texans in the

REPUBLIC OF TEXAS, 1836

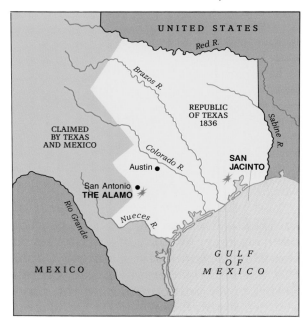

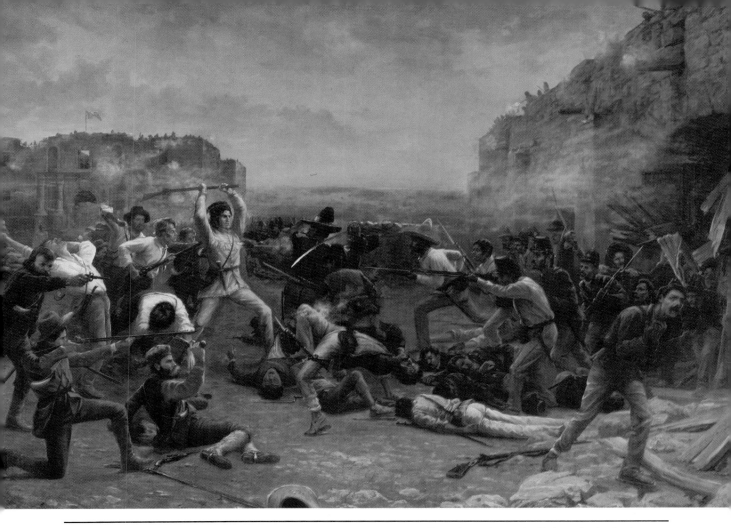

Think: **Davy Crockett fights off his attackers with his empty gun in** *Fall of the Alamo* **by Robert Onderdonk. Crockett, Jim Bowie, and nearly 200 others died defending the abandoned mission they had made into a fort.**
Respond: **What did the Mexicans learn from the strong stand the Texans took at the Alamo?**

Alamo fought until the last man was dead. Among those who died in the battle were the famous frontiersmen Davy Crockett and Jim Bowie.

News of the battle of the Alamo brought new volunteers to Houston's army. When the Texans met Santa Anna's army at the Battle of San Jacinto (SAN juh-SIN-toh), "Remember the Alamo" was their battle cry. The Texans won the battle and captured Santa Anna. He agreed to give Texas its independence. Texas became an independent nation known as the ***Lone Star Republic***. Sam Houston was elected its first president.

Davy Crockett (1786–1836) became a living American folk hero because of his humorous speeches and his talent as a frontiersman.

Think: **Albert Bierstadt made the Oregon Trail look like paradise in his painting. However, life on the trail was harsh and dangerous. Many died trying to reach Oregon. Bierstadt painted *The Oregon Trail* after taking part in an expedition to map the trail.** Respond: **Why would he choose to show the trail like this?**

Houston and most other Texans wanted Texas to join the United States. Most Southerners and Westerners agreed with the Texans. However, the people of the Northeast did not want Texas to become part of the United States. They knew that the Southerners wanted to divide Texas into several slave states. Northerners did not want more slave states. They did not want the South to have more votes in Congress. Some Americans were also worried that if Texas joined the United States, war might break out with Mexico. Neither President Jackson nor President Van Buren wanted to stir up trouble. For the time being, Texas remained an independent nation.

The Far West

Texas was not the only western territory that interested American settlers. In the 1830s, a few traders, settlers, and *missionaries* (MIH-shun-air-eez), or religious workers, moved into the Oregon region. The Oregon region included what are now Oregon, Washington, Idaho, and parts of western Canada. This land was claimed by both the United States and Great Britain.

The early settlers sent news of Oregon to the eastern states. The settlers told of land that was good for farming. Soon, many new settlers were arriving in Oregon. Some traveled by ship all the way around South America. Most, however, traveled by land in covered wagons over the famous *Oregon Trail*. By 1845, over five thousand Americans had settled in Oregon. Like the Texans, the American settlers in Oregon wanted their territory to become part of the United States. In 1843, these settlers went to Congress with this request.

HISTORY MAKERS

Sam Houston
The Texas Raven

"My son," said the chief, "your Cherokee name will be Raven. The raven is a friend to the Cherokee. When the Great Spirit made fire, he put it in a hollow tree. Men wanted fire, so Raven flew into the tree and tried to snatch a burning coal. You too, are a friend, so we give you Raven's name."

Sam Houston lived with the Cherokee chief and his family for about three years. He liked Indian life much more than going to school, working on his mother's farm, or tending the general store.

Sam Houston was nineteen when the War of 1812 began. He joined the militia and fought under General Andrew Jackson. Jackson was impressed with Houston's courage in battle. When Houston was badly wounded, however, his injuries kept him from fighting. He was appointed Indian agent to the Cherokees. He persuaded the tribe to leave their lands in Tennessee and move west to government land.

After the war, Sam Houston became a lawyer. His friendship with General Jackson helped him enter Tennessee politics. He was elected to Congress twice, and in 1827 he became governor of Tennessee. Two years later he was running for reelection when his young wife suddenly left him. He resigned the governor's office, and returned to his friends, the Cherokees.

Sam Houston lived with the Indians for several more years. In 1832, encouraged by President Jackson, Houston went to Texas. He quickly became involved in Texas politics. As a result, he helped draft the Texas Declaration of Independence and Constitution. In addition, Houston led the Texas army that defeated Santa Anna and made Texas independent of Mexico. He was then made president of the Lone Star Republic. After Texas became a state, he served as governor and as a senator. Sam Houston worked long and hard to bring Texas into the United States. He opposed secession, and he left office when Texas seceded from the Union in the Civil War. Sam Houston remained loyal to those he supported—his Indian friends and the United States of America.

OREGON TERRITORY BOUNDARY SETTLEMENT, 1846

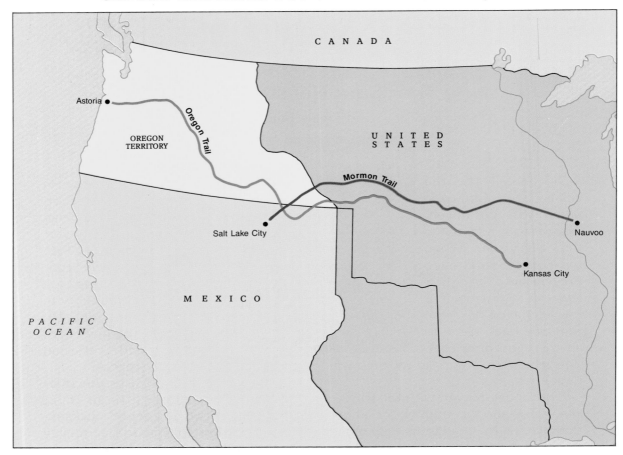

Another group of Americans who settled in the West was the **Mormons** (MORE-muns), a religious group begun in the 1820s. When the Mormons were forced to leave Illinois in 1846, they settled near the Great Salt Lake in Utah. The Mormons' route to Utah, known as the **Mormon Trail**, was later followed by many other settlers.

Americans were also interested in California. In the 1840s, California was part of Mexico. California offered great land for farming. It also had good ports, such as San Francisco, which were useful in trading with China and Japan. The American settlers in California wanted it, too, to become part of the United States.

The Election of 1844

During the presidential campaign of 1844, the debate over making Texas a state was very important. President Tyler wanted Texas to be a slave state. But Tyler did not get along with his party, the Whigs. They chose Henry Clay for their candidate. Clay did not want to make northern voters angry. He decided not to talk about Texas.

The Democrats had trouble even choosing a candidate. Many northern Democrats wanted Martin Van Buren, but the southern Democrats opposed him. They did not think he wanted Texas to become a slave state. The Democrats tried many times to choose a candidate but they could not agree.

Finally, they made a compromise. They chose James K. Polk, who had not even been in the running before. Polk believed in Manifest Destiny. He told the voters that he wanted both Texas and Oregon to become states. This pleased the American people, because Texas would become a slave state and Oregon would become a free state. The balance of slave states and free states would continue. Polk defeated Clay and became the new president of the United States.

James Knox Polk (1795–1849), America's eleventh president, worked extremely hard in office and accomplished most of his goals. Few presidents have shared his success rate.

Think: James Polk is shown here with his running mate, George Dallas. The two won the election of 1844. Respond: What symbols were used in this work celebrating the men?

As it turned out, Polk never had to act on the Texas question. At the very end of Tyler's term, Congress made Texas the twenty-eighth state.

After Polk became president, he tried to *annex* (an-NEKS) Oregon, or make it part of the United States. Many Americans were willing to go to war with Great Britain over the Oregon region. "54° 40' or Fight!" became a famous slogan, because 54° 40' was the latitude of the Oregon region's northern border.

For a while, it seemed that war over Oregon was likely. However, in 1846, the United States and Great Britain agreed to divide Oregon. The northern part of Oregon became part of Canada. The southern part became a territory of the United States. In 1859, Oregon became a free state. It was the thirty-third state.

In the 1840s, the United States won new territories that connected the Atlantic and the Pacific coasts. However, the trouble with Mexico was not yet over. In the next section you will see how conflict with Mexico led to war.

Section Review

1. Why did American settlers in Texas disagree with the Mexican government? What was the outcome of this disagreement?

2. Why did some Americans want Texas to become a state? Why did other Americans oppose annexing Texas?

3. Who won the election of 1844? Why did Americans give him their support?

4. What two nations claimed the Oregon region? How did Oregon become a territory of the United States?

2. The Mexican War and Its Results

Learn these important terms:

Rio Grande
Bear Flag Revolt
Mexican Cession
Free-Soilers
Mexican War
Treaty of Guadalupe Hidalgo
Wilmot Proviso

Remember the main idea:

The United States won a war against Mexico and gained new lands. The question of slavery in this new territory soon became a problem.

Look for answers to these questions:

1. What were the causes of the Mexican War? How did the outcome of the war solve these problems?
2. What leaders became heroes because of the Mexican War? Which of these heroes became president?
3. How did the new lands won in the Mexican War make the conflict over slavery worse?

In the 1840s, ill feeling grew between Mexico and the United States. Mexico was angry at the United States for annexing Texas. Mexico was also angry because the United States wanted settlers in California to break away from Mexico. The United States wanted New Mexico, the land between Texas and California, to become an American territory, too. Finally, the United States and Mexico disagreed about the southern boundary of Texas. The United States claimed the boundary was the *Rio Grande* (REE-oh GRAND), the 1,885-mile-long river. The Mexicans claimed that the Nueces River (noo-AY-sus), located further north, was the boundary of Texas.

The Mexican War

In 1845, President Polk sent John Slidell (sly-DELL) to talk to the Mexican government about these problems. Slidell was to offer Mexico thirty million dollars for California, New Mexico, and the area between the Nueces River and the Rio Grande. However, Mexican leaders refused to see Slidell.

When Polk learned that the Mexicans would not talk with Slidell, he took action. Polk ordered General Zachary Taylor to move his troops across the Nueces River. Although the Americans did not attack the Mexican army, the Mexicans saw this move as an invasion. They crossed the Rio Grande and attacked the Americans. Polk then asked Congress to declare war on Mexico. On May 13, 1846, Congress did so. The *Mexican War* had begun.

Mexico expected to win the war quickly. Its army was large and well trained and was fighting on its own land. In addition, the Mexican government thought Great Britain and France would help Mexico fight the war.

Furthermore, the Mexicans thought that the American army was very weak. When the war started, the American army had only eight thousand troops. These soldiers had to march hundreds of miles over rough country to fight the Mexicans. In Mexico, the Americans were far from their sources of supply. Moreover, Congress was slow in voting money for the war. Many northern Congressmen did not support war with Mexico.

Think: Richard Woodville's *War News from Mexico* shows the reactions of a variety of American stereotypes. Poor and wealthy alike gather on the porch of an American hotel and post office to get the latest news.
Respond: What do you think each person in the painting is thinking?

The Mexicans did not win the war, however. The help they expected from Great Britain and France did not come. As a result, the Mexican army ran short of supplies. Worst of all, it had poor leadership. The battles against the Texans had proved that Santa Anna was not a good general.

To the surprise of the Mexicans, the American army won three quick victories in northern Mexico. Then, early in 1847, General Taylor's army defeated the last important Mexican force in northern Mexico. His victory at the Battle of Buena Vista (BWEN-uh VEE-stuh) made Taylor a national hero. People called him "Old Rough and Ready."

Another small army, led by General Stephen Kearny (KAHR-nee), captured New Mexico before marching into California. When Kearny arrived, he discovered that the Americans and some Mexicans living there had already captured the fort at Sonoma. The Americans claimed that California was now an independent republic, like Texas. This revolt became known as the **Bear Flag Revolt.** Within a few months, General Kearny and John C. Fremont (FREE-mahnt) won control of all California.

The most important battles of the Mexican War were won by General Winfield Scott. In March of 1847, Scott's army landed on the east coast of Mexico. They captured the city of Veracruz (ver-uh-KROOZ). From Veracruz, Scott's men fought their way inland. They defeated Santa Anna's army and captured Mexico City. The Mexican leaders realized that they could not win. The war soon ended.

Courtesy of Chicago Historical Society.

Think: This lithograph shows General Scott (on the brown horse) marching into Mexico City's main square. Scott's forces had braved the treacherous route from Veracruz to Mexico City before taking Mexico's capital.
Respond: What can you learn about the Mexican people by looking at this image?

THE UNITED STATES IN 1848

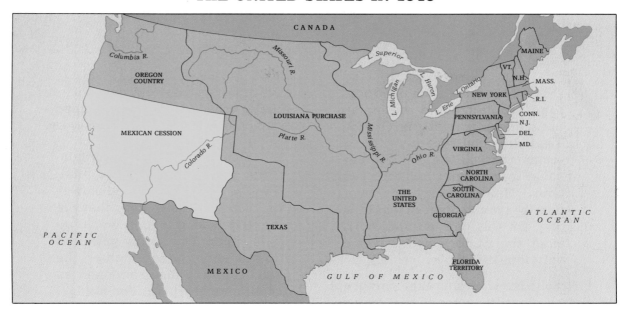

New Land and New Problems

Mexico agreed to peace by signing the **Treaty of Guadalupe Hidalgo** (GWAH-dah-LOO-pay ee-DAL-goh) in 1848. In this treaty, Mexico lost almost one-third of its land. New Mexico and California became territories of the United States. Also, the southern boundary of Texas became the Rio Grande. In return, the Mexican government received about fifteen million dollars—half of what Polk had once been willing to pay.

The land won by the United States in the Mexican War was called the **Mexican Cession** (SEH-shun). The United States now stretched from the Atlantic coast to the Pacific coast. It reached all the way north to Canada and south to the winding Rio Grande.

With this new land came new problems, however. The United States soon had to decide if slavery would be allowed in the Mexican Cession. Even before the war ended, the House of Representatives passed the **Wilmot Proviso** (WIL-maht pruh-VYE-zoh). This law said that slavery would not be allowed in any new land

won in the war. Southerners in the Senate refused to agree to this law. President Polk then suggested that the old Missouri Compromise Line of 1820 be extended to the Pacific coast. Slavery would be allowed south of the line, but not north of it.

Very few Americans liked Polk's plan. Many Northerners did not want slavery in any new territory of the United States. Many Southerners wanted Congress to allow slavery in all new territories. A third group of Americans thought that each territory should decide for itself about slavery.

The slavery question was important in the election of 1848. President Polk refused to run again. The Democrats picked Lewis Cass, a senator from Michigan, to become their candidate. The Whigs chose General Zachary Taylor, ''Old Rough and Ready.''

Neither candidate said clearly whether he was for or against the spread of slavery. Cass, the Democratic candidate, did say that he thought each territory should decide for itself about slavery. Since Cass did not oppose slavery, many Northerners

In 1843, more than one thousand people crossed the mountains and plains of the Oregon Trail. In good weather the ox teams that pulled the wagons could travel about two miles an hour. Thus, they could cover nearly twenty-five miles in a day. On this day in June, however, the wagons had traveled only four miles by nightfall.

You learn from the paragraph above that the wagons that traveled the Oregon Trail were pulled by ox teams. The paragraph states this information directly. You can also figure out that the weather on that particular day in June probably was not good. Although the paragraph does not directly give information about the weather that day, you can infer it, or figure it out. The paragraph has clues that help you make this inference. For example, the paragraph states that only four miles instead of twenty-five had been covered that day. The paragraph also states that good weather could result in many miles being covered. Therefore, you can guess that bad weather could result in few miles being covered. Inferring information in this way is sometimes called "reading between the lines." It requires you to do more than just read the stated information.

Read the following paragraph about travel on the Oregon Trail, and answer the questions. Some of the answers are stated directly. To answer other questions, you need to infer, or figure out, the answers.

The oxen struggled to pull the wagon through axle-deep mud. Progress was slower and slower until it was finally clear that the heavily loaded wagon would go no farther. The family gathered to talk about how to lighten the load. Sarah's face saddened as she heard the plan. For the last time she touched the heavy oak dresser that had been her mother's. She pulled her tiny, one-week-old baby closer. The baby's soft warmth comforted Sarah as she thought about the entry she would make in her journal that night. Its pages had nearly been filled during the two months since the family had left their home in Iowa.

1 Why was it difficult for the oxen to pull the wagons? Is the answer stated in the paragraph, or did you need to infer it?

2 How did the family make the load on the wagon lighter? Is the answer stated in the paragraph, or did you infer it?

3 From what place had the family started the trip? Is the answer stated, or did you infer it?

4 Where had the baby been born? Is the answer stated, or did you need to infer it?

Zachary Taylor (1784–1850) dressed simply, as a frontier farmer, even while president. He was a true patriot who worked to keep the nation united.

would not support the Democrats. Instead, they supported a new political party called the *Free-Soilers*. Free-Soilers were against the spread of slavery into any new territories. Their candidate was Martin Van Buren.

The conflict over the slavery question divided the Democratic Party. As a result, Zachary Taylor, the Whig candidate, won the election.

The United States now stretched from coast to coast. Those who believed in Manifest Destiny were very happy. However, the problem of slavery in the territories was still not settled. In the next section, you will see how Senator Henry Clay tried to settle the issue with one more important compromise.

Section Review

1. What conflicts arose between the United States and Mexico after Texas won its independence?
2. Which army was stronger at the beginning of the Mexican War? What American generals won important victories?
3. What was the Mexican Cession?
4. What problems arose over the new territories in the election of 1848? Who won the election?

---

3. Between Two Wars

Learn these important terms:

Forty-Niners
Compromise of 1850
Gadsden Purchase
Fugitive Slave Act
Know-Nothings

Remember the main idea:

The Compromise of 1850 settled the slavery question for awhile. A large number of new immigrants helped the nation grow and change.

Look for answers to these questions:

1. How did the discovery of gold change the history of California?
2. What did the Compromise of 1850 state?
3. In what ways did the United States change during the 1850s?

During the 1840s and 1850s, the issue of slavery continued to cause problems. Northerners wanted new states and territories to be free. Southerners wanted them to allow slavery. The issue of immigration also received much attention. As the United States continued to grow, these problems became bigger. As you will see, growth came about in several different ways.

Gold!

In 1839, the Mexican government allowed John A. Sutter to build a trading post in northern California. Sutter's Fort

Think: **Sutter's Mill (above) was a sawmill on the banks of the American River near what is now Sacramento.** Respond: **How did what happened here change California?**

became an important place for Americans traveling to California. When people began to settle around his fort, Sutter wanted to supply them with lumber. He sent workers to build a sawmill on a river a few miles away. One day in 1848, a worker found some bright yellow nuggets in the river bed. When he had these stones tested, he found that he had discovered gold.

News of his discovery spread like wildfire. Hundreds of people left San Francisco to search for gold. From San Francisco, the news quickly reached the rest of the nation. All over the country, people left their farms, shops, and factories to head for the gold fields. People even came from Europe, South America, and China. Within a year, eighty thousand people had come to California. They all hoped to strike it rich.

Only a few **Forty-Niners**, or people who came to California around 1849 looking

for gold, actually became rich. However, the Gold Rush changed California almost overnight. Thousands of new businesses were started to serve the miners. Many of the people who came to find gold took jobs and settled down. Mining camps grew into new towns, and San Francisco became a great city. By late 1849, about 100,000 people lived in California.

President Taylor wanted California to become a state without first becoming a territory. The people of California agreed. California was admitted as a free state in 1850. About the same time, New Mexico and Utah asked Congress to organize their areas into territories in which slavery was forbidden.

Conflict and Compromise

Southerners were very angry when they learned about California and the new territories. The Southerners were against California's becoming a free state, because free states would outnumber the slave states. The free states would then have more members in the Senate. Southerners talked about having their states secede, or withdraw from the United States. Most Northerners, on the other hand, were happy that California and the new territories did not want slavery.

Think: **A variety of ways to uncover gold are shown in this painting about the California Gold Rush.**
Respond: **How many different ways of mining can you find?**

Senator Henry Clay tried to settle the problem peacefully. Clay drew up a plan which became known as the *Compromise of 1850*. This Compromise contained five main points:

1. California would indeed become a free state.

2. Utah and New Mexico would become territories. The people of those territories would decide for themselves if they wanted slavery.

3. The slave trade (but not slavery) would be ended in Washington, D.C., the nation's capital.

4. Congress would pass a strong law called the *Fugitive Slave Act*. This law would force the northern states to return runaway slaves to their owners.

5. Congress would also pay the debts that Texas had developed when it was an independent republic.

There was bitter debate in Congress over Clay's plan. Both southern slave owners and northern abolitionists opposed it. Even President Taylor was against the plan. He did not like the idea of paying Texas's debts. And he saw no reason to argue about annexing California. However, during the debate over Clay's plan, President Taylor grew ill and died. His vice president, Millard Fillmore, became president. Fillmore was in favor of the compromise. Clay's supporters now worked even harder to get the compromise through Congress. They finally succeeded. With Fillmore's signature, the compromise became law.

Most Americans were happy that the Compromise of 1850 had passed. They knew how dangerous the debate had been. The South had come close to seceding. However, many Southerners were still unhappy about losing their majority in Congress. Also, the compromise angered abolitionists. They did not want to return runaway slaves. Because of the Fugitive Slave Act, many runaway slaves had to go to Canada to find freedom.

Millard Fillmore (1800–1874) rose through the political ranks in New York. When he became president upon Taylor's death, he pushed through the Compromise of 1850.

THE U.S. AFTER THE COMPROMISE OF 1850

Drawing an inference is like making a good, careful guess. Your guess must be based on facts, however—in this case the information given you directly on the map. The title of the map tells you that there was a compromise. From this alone, you can infer that there was some difference of opinion that had to be settled by each side giving in to some degree.

Look at the map key.

1. What does each of the three colors stand for? From this direct information, what do you infer the quarrel and compromise are about?

2. How many light green states or territories are there on the map? How many red states? What can you infer from this division?

3. What can you infer about the problem from the position of the compromise line?

4. What difference was there between the Missouri Compromise of 1820 and the Compromise of 1850? What can you infer from the fact that this new compromise was needed?

5. Can the three territories (peach) affect the balance between North and South mathematically?

6. Based on what you see, would you think that the Compromise of 1850 could solve the slavery question? Explain your answer.

7. If there were to be a war over slavery between the North and the South, which side would you guess Missouri, Kentucky, and Virginia would take? Why?

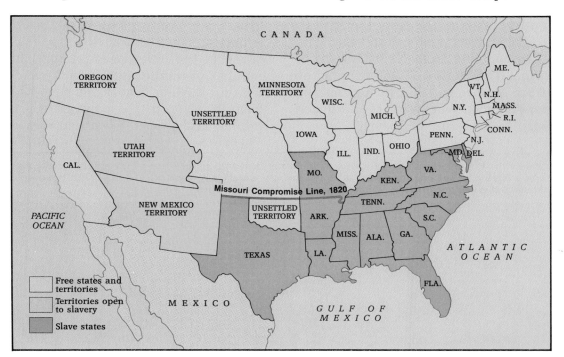

Free states and territories

Territories open to slavery

Slave states

When Franklin Pierce (1804–1869) was elected, he was dashing—the nation's youngest president. National conflicts during his term demanded his concentration, but Pierce's performance was marred by his grief over his son's death.

A New Purchase

In the election of 1852, the Democrats chose Franklin Pierce as their candidate. Pierce was a Northerner, but he was not an abolitionist. The Whigs chose General Winfield Scott, the Mexican War hero. Many southern Whigs left their party because they were angry at the northern, anti-slavery Whigs. As a result, the Whig party grew very weak. Pierce won the election with ease.

During Pierce's term in office, the United States gained a small strip of land in the southern part of the New Mexico territory. The government wanted this land for a railroad line from New Orleans to California. The United States bought the land from Mexico in 1853 for ten million dollars. This deal was called the *Gadsden Purchase* (GADZ-dun).

New Americans

Winning new lands was not the only way in which the nation grew. In the 1840s and 1850s, many new immigrants came to the United States. Some came from England, Sweden, Norway, and Denmark. A great famine in Ireland in 1846 brought thousands of Irish people to the United States. There was also a large number of German immigrants. In 1854 alone, over 400,000 immigrants arrived in the United States.

Most of these immigrants settled in the North. Very few went to the South. The Irish stayed mainly in the cities of the Northeast. The Germans often moved to farms or cities in midwestern states, such as Wisconsin and Missouri.

The new immigrants helped the United States grow in many ways. However, not all Americans welcomed them. Immigrants often stayed in their own groups and did not speak or dress like other Americans. Some Americans were upset by these differences. They blamed immigrants for the growth of slums. Some Americans also said that there was more crime in the cities because of the large number of immigrants.

In the 1850s, Americans such as these formed a group that opposed the immigrants. The groups' members were called

Think: Below, Irish immigrants touch American soil for the first time as they leave their ship. Extremely poor because of a famine in Ireland, many Irish accepted the low wages they were offered. Respond: How are all workers affected when one group is willing to work for very low wages?

Think: **Know-Nothings formed a secret society against immigrants. They formed a political party, which backed Millard Fillmore in an unsuccessful 1856 campaign. Above, a mob of Know-Nothings tears through the streets of Boston.** Respond: **Why were the Know-Nothings afraid of immigrants?**

Know-Nothings because they wanted their group to be secret. When anyone asked a member about the group, the member would answer, "I know nothing." The Know-Nothings tried to end immigration and to keep immigrants from becoming citizens and voting. They formed a political party and were strong for a few years, but their party soon died out.

The growth of the nation in the 1840s and 1850s made the United States one of the largest nations in the world. This growth also caused the slavery problem to worsen. Leaders such as Henry Clay worked hard to hold the nation together. But the compromises of these leaders could not solve the slavery problem once and for all. Within a few years, the conflict between the North and the South led to war. In the next chapter, you will read about this terrible war.

Section Review

1. What great discovery changed the history of California? How did this discovery make the conflict between the North and the South worse?

2. What was the Compromise of 1850? Who supported it? Who opposed it?

3. What deal did the United States make with Mexico in 1853? Why did the United States want to make this deal?

4. Why did some people oppose the coming of new immigrants to the United States? What was the name of one of these groups?

CHAPTER SUMMARY

Americans settled in Texas in the 1820s. In 1835, Texas revolted against Mexico and became an independent state. Texas wanted to join the United States as a slave state, but some people opposed this plan. Americans also settled in Oregon, Utah, and California. James Polk was elected president in 1844. Soon after, Texas became a slave state, and Oregon became a free territory.

By making Texas a state, the United States caused problems with Mexico. These problems led to war in 1846. After Mexico lost the war, the United States claimed California and New Mexico. Northerners and Southerners disagreed about allowing slavery there.

The Whig candidate, Zachary Taylor, became president in 1848. That same year, gold was discovered in California. In 1849, California asked to become a free state. Utah and New Mexico wanted to be free territories. Southerners were angry that slavery would not be allowed in these territories. To calm them, Henry Clay proposed a compromise. California became a free state, but Congress passed a stronger law against runaway slaves.

In 1852, Franklin Pierce became president. During his term, The Gadsden Purchase added land to the Southwest. New immigrants came to the United States.

Key Words

Write a sentence to explain the meaning of each of these terms.

Manifest Destiny

annex

Mexican Cession

Wilmot Proviso

Fugitive Slave Act

Know-Nothings

Major Events

Choose the answer that best completes the statement.

1. In 1835, a small band of Texans
   a) took over the Alamo.
   b) seceded from the United States.
   c) discovered gold.

2. In 1844, the Democrats compromised on a candidate for president and chose
   a) Henry Clay.
   b) Martin Van Buren.
   c) James Polk.

3. The Mexican War began when
   a) the Alamo was destroyed.
   b) California became a state.
   c) Mexican soldiers crossed the Rio Grande.

4. The final battle of the Mexican War was fought at
   a) Vera Cruz.
   b) San Antonio.
   c) Mexico City.

5. In 1853, the United States bought land from Mexico in order to build
   a) an army base.
   b) a railroad line.
   c) a shipping port.

Review

Important Facts

Answer each question with at least one complete sentence.

1. Who was Stephen Austin? What did he accomplish?

2. What is the Alamo? For what is it remembered?

3. What was the Lone Star Republic? What happened to it?

4. Why were some people opposed to Texas becoming a state?

5. What was the Oregon Trail? Why was it important?

6. Who were the Mormons? Where did they settle?

7. Why did the United States and Great Britain almost go to war in the 1840s?

8. What were the causes of the Mexican War?

9. What were the terms of the Treaty of Guadalupe-Hidalgo?

10. What was the Bear Flag Revolt?

11. Who were the Free-Soilers?

12. What event changed California almost overnight? How was it changed?

13. What was the Compromise of 1850?

14. What was the Gadsden Purchase?

15. From what countries did the new immigrants come? Where did they settle?

16. Name the areas which joined the United States as territories or states between 1840 and 1850.

Skill Review

Study this map, then answer the following questions.

1. The Mormons left Nauvoo in February 1846. What can you infer about the weather at that time?

2. Between April and July 1847, an advance party traveled about one thousand miles from Winter Quarters to Salt Lake. About how many miles did they go a day?

3. What can you infer about land and climate problems on this trip?

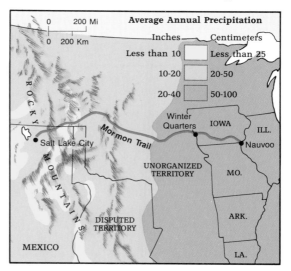

The Mormon Trail

Critical Thinking

Write a paragraph to answer each question.

1. In what ways was the "Manifest Destiny" of the United States fulfilled during the 1840s?

2. How did the conflict over slavery affect the nation in the 1840s and 1850s?

15
The Civil War

Years 1850–1865

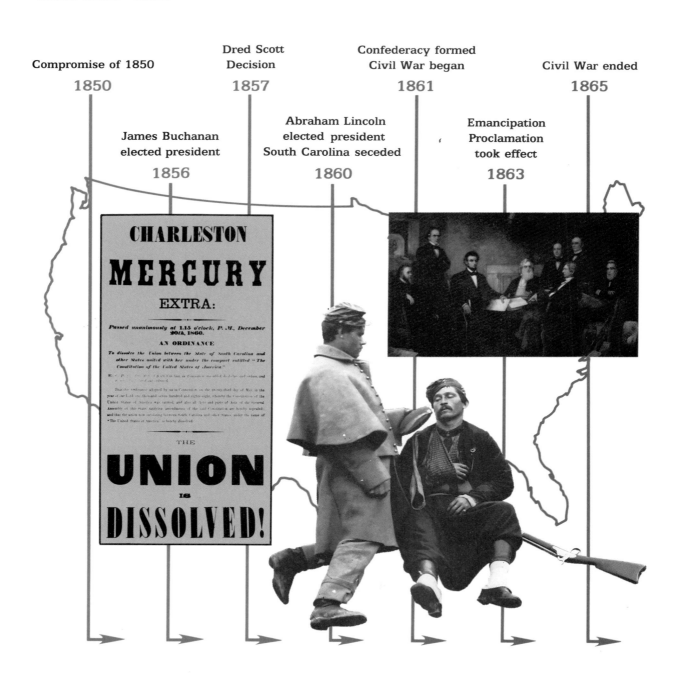

Compromise of 1850
1850

Dred Scott
Decision
1857

Confederacy formed
Civil War began
1861

Civil War ended
1865

James Buchanan
elected president
1856

Abraham Lincoln
elected president
South Carolina seceded
1860

Emancipation
Proclamation
took effect
1863

CHARLESTON

MERCURY

EXTRA:

Passed unanimously at 1.15 o'clock, P. M., December 20th, 1860.

AN ORDINANCE

To dissolve the Union between the State of South Carolina and other States united with her under the compact entitled "The Constitution of the United States of America."

THE

UNION

IS

DISSOLVED!

1. A Nation Divided by Slavery

Learn these important terms:

personal liberty laws
Republican Party
Kansas–Nebraska Act
Dred Scott Decision

Remember the main idea:

The slavery question divided the North and the South. Many more Northerners turned against slavery. Fighting over slavery broke out in the territory of Kansas.

Look for answers to these questions:

1. What book turned many Northerners against slavery?
2. Why did fighting break out in the Kansas territory?
3. How did the different sections of the nation feel about the Dred Scott Decision?

From the very beginning of the United States, the problem of slavery caused conflicts among the sections of the nation. As the nation grew, these conflicts grew worse. Southerners wanted slavery in the western territories, but Northerners wanted these territories to be free. In the 1840s and 1850s, many Northerners also became active in the abolition movement. Abolitionists not only wanted to keep slavery out of the West; they wanted all blacks to be free. As a result, Southerners fought harder to protect the slave system. They opposed the abolitionists and passed harsh new laws to control the slaves.

The nation's leaders tried many times to settle these conflicts peacefully. The Compromise of 1850 was the last great attempt to settle the question of slavery in the western territories. However, this compromise did not solve the slavery problem. In some ways, it made the problem even worse than it had been.

In this chapter you will read how the Compromise of 1850 and the events that followed it drove the North and the South further apart. You will see how the conflict between the North and the South finally led to a terrible war.

The Fugitive Slave Act, which was part of the Compromise of 1850, forced Northerners to return runaway slaves to the South. Many Northerners were angered by this law. Northerners were also angry because some free blacks were accused of being runaway slaves. Even worse, they were not given jury trials or allowed to speak in their own defense.

The unfairness of this law made more Northerners join the abolition movement. Some Northerners helped runaway slaves escape to Canada. Other Northerners

Harriet Beecher Stowe (1811–1896) lost a child to the disease cholera in 1849. She decided on that day to help slaves. She knew how it felt to be separated from a child.

attacked slave catchers and freed the slaves. In addition, several northern states passed **personal liberty laws** which stopped the arrest of free blacks as runaway slaves. Personal liberty laws also protected the right of free blacks to a jury trial. These laws made it difficult to enforce the Fugitive Slave Act.

Uncle Tom's Cabin, a novel by a northern abolitionist named Harriet Beecher Stowe, also turned many people against slavery. Stowe showed slavery at its worst. In one part of the book, a slave is beaten so badly that he dies. In another part, dogs are used to chase a family of escaped slaves.

When *Uncle Tom's Cabin* came out in 1852, it caused a huge sensation. Three hundred thousand copies were sold within one year. Thousands of people also saw *Uncle Tom's Cabin* as a stage play. After reading the book or seeing the play, many Northerners became abolitionists. Southerners were angry because so many Northerners believed all slaves were treated as badly as those in the book.

The Struggle for Kansas

Another conflict arose between the North and the South over the question of the railroad. After California became a state, more and more people became interested in building a railroad line to connect the Atlantic and Pacific coasts. At first it seemed that the railroad would follow a southern route, from New Orleans to California through the Gadsden Purchase. However, many powerful Northerners wanted the railroad to begin at Chicago or St. Louis.

Senator Stephen A. Douglas of Illinois was in favor of the northern route, which ran through lands that had not yet been settled. Douglas knew that the northern route was possible only if this land was organized into a territory. Therefore, he asked Congress to create the Nebraska Territory.

Douglas knew that southern congressmen would oppose his route, so he found a way to win their votes. He said that the people of Nebraska should be allowed to decide for themselves whether they wanted slavery. Southern congressmen liked this idea. They also wanted the people of Kansas to decide whether they wanted slavery.

The problem with this plan was that both Kansas and Nebraska were north of the Missouri Compromise line, where slavery was forbidden. To solve this problem, Congress repealed the Missouri Compromise and passed the **Kansas-Nebraska Act** in 1854. Kansas and Nebraska became territories where the settlers could decide the slavery question for themselves.

THE KANSAS-NEBRASKA ACT OF 1854

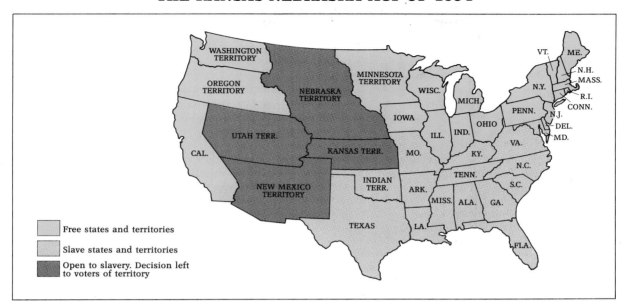

Free states and territories

Slave states and territories

Open to slavery. Decision left to voters of territory

Everyone knew that the settlers in Nebraska would choose to make their territory free, but Kansas was another matter. Southerners saw the new law as a chance to spread slavery into Kansas. Before the election that would decide the slavery question, people from Missouri who favored slavery rushed into Kansas by the thousands. "Free-Soilers" who wanted to keep slavery out of Kansas also rushed into the territory. Each side hoped to have enough voters in Kansas to win the election.

When the election was held, a pro-slavery government was elected. Instead of accepting the results of the election,

Northerners in Kansas set up their own government, which outlawed slavery. Kansas became divided.

Divided Kansas soon became "Bleeding Kansas." Southern settlers attacked and burned the town of Lawrence, where many Free-Soilers lived. Then an abolitionist named John Brown led an attack against some southern settlers. Soon, fighting broke out all over the territory. Federal troops had to be brought in to end the fighting. Congress did not settle the problem of slavery in Kansas until January 1861, when it made the territory a free state.

Think: **After proslavery groups in Missouri crossed the border to vote illegally in Kansas elections, a proslavery legislature was set up. After the Sack of Lawrence, Free-Soilers attacked back. "Bleeding Kansas" was in turmoil. Respond: Why didn't Douglas's plan to let each state decide the slavery issue work?**

Even his 40 years of political experience could not prepare James Buchanan (1791–1868) for the turmoil of pre-Civil War America. He put all his efforts into his "Save the Union" slogan.

The Election of 1856

The Kansas-Nebraska Act created other problems as well. New conflicts broke out in the political parties. Senator Douglas was a Democrat, and his party had supported the Kansas-Nebraska Act. But thousands of northern Democrats who opposed slavery left the Democratic Party. Those staying fought against southern Democrats for control of the party.

The Whig Party was also divided between Northerners and Southerners. This division weakened the party. In 1854, Free-Soilers and Whigs from the North and the West started a new party, the **Republican Party**. Their main goal was to stop the spread of slavery into the western territories.

In the election of 1856, the Republicans chose their first candidate for president, John C. Fremont. He was a hero of the Mexican War. The Democrats chose James Buchanan (byoo-KAN-un), a former congressman and senator from Pennsylvania. The Democrats said that the people of a territory had the right to decide if they wanted slavery.

The election showed how divided the nation was over the question of slavery. Fremont won in most of the northern states, and Buchanan won in most of the South. Buchanan won the presidential election only by winning close victories in a few northern states.

The Dred Scott Case

In 1857, before Buchanan took office, a black man named Dred Scott brought his struggle for freedom to the Supreme Court. Scott was a slave whose owner took him from Missouri, a slave state, into Illinois, a free state. Then the owner and Scott moved to Wisconsin, a free territory. After a few years, Scott was taken back to Missouri. Scott claimed that he was a free man because slavery was illegal in Illinois and Wisconsin, and he had lived there for four years.

Chief Justice Roger B. Taney spoke for the Court. He said that living in a free territory did not give Scott his freedom. Slaves were property, and the Constitution protected people's right to their property. The Missouri Compromise ignored this right by saying where people could and could not own slaves. Therefore, the Missouri Compromise was unconstitutional. No matter where Dred Scott lived, he was still a slave.

In the courts, Dred Scott failed to win his freedom or the rights of citizenship. His freedom only came upon the death of his owner. Scott died 16 months later.

SKILLS FOCUS: Analyzing Statistics

In the 1850s and 1860s, the differences between the North and South were growing greater each day. Some of these differences, such as the different attitudes people in the North and the South had toward slavery, can best be stated in words. Other differences can best be shown in numbers. These numerical facts are called *statistics*. Statistics can be collected and studied.

The bar graph on this page compares some statistics about the North and the South. It contains information on some resources that were important in the Civil War. Note that each bar represents 100% of the nation's resource at the outbreak of the war. The shaded portion of each bar shows the Union's share of that resource. The white portion shows the Confederate's share.

Use the graph to answer the questions that follow.

1 Which side had more people? How could this resource be useful in wartime?

2 Which side had more factories? How could this resource be useful in wartime?

3 Which side had more farmland? How could this resource be useful in wartime?

4 Which side had more miles of railroad? How could this resource be useful in wartime?

5 What percentage of all manufactured goods were made in the North? In the South? How would a lack of manufacturing hurt a country in wartime?

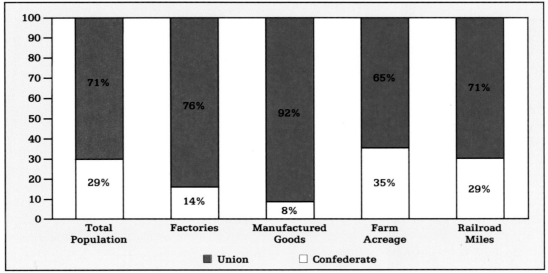

Resources of the Union and Confederacy, 1861

	Total Population	Factories	Manufactured Goods	Farm Acreage	Railroad Miles
Union	71%	76%	92%	65%	71%
Confederate	29%	14%	8%	35%	29%

■ Union   □ Confederate

On March 6, 1857, Chief Justice Roger B. Taney spoke for the Supreme Court regarding the Dred Scott decision. However, each of the nine justices wrote an individual decision.

The **Dred Scott Decision** made slavery lawful anywhere in the United States. Southerners were happy about this decision, but Northerners—especially the new Republicans—were very upset. It seemed that the conflict over slavery was growing worse by the day. In the next section you will read about how this conflict finally led to war.

Section Review

1. In what ways did Northerners oppose the Fugitive Slave Act?

2. Why did Senator Douglas want the people of Kansas and Nebraska to decide for themselves if they would allow slavery?

3. What were the results of the Kansas-Nebraska Act?

4. What new political party grew out of the conflict over slavery in the western territories? What was the main goal of this party?

2. The War Begins

Learn these important terms:

Constitutional Union Party
Confederate States of America
Confederacy
Union
border states
Crittenden Compromise
Civil War
Copperheads

Remember the main idea:

The North and South were unable to settle their differences, and war broke out in 1861. The war was fought to decide whether the United States would stay together or be divided into two nations.

Look for answers to these questions:

1. Why did some southern states decide to secede?

2. Which state was the first to secede? What six states seceded soon afterward?

3. What event caused the Civil War to begin?

In 1859, John Brown, an abolitionist who had fought in Kansas, appeared again, this time in Virginia. He planned to start a slave revolt. To get arms for this revolt, Brown and his followers captured a government arsenal, or storehouse of weapons, at Harpers Ferry, Virginia. Then Brown waited there for the slaves to join him.

No slaves came. They had never heard of Brown's raid. While he waited, federal troops headed by Robert E. Lee surrounded the arsenal. After a short battle, Brown and his followers were captured. Brown was tried for murder and treason, found guilty, and hanged.

Although John Brown's plan for a revolt failed, he became a hero to the abolitionists. The attack on Harpers Ferry also frightened the South. More and more, Southerners came to believe that the North would use force to end slavery.

Think: John Brown and his followers defended themselves at Harpers Ferry in the brick engine house at the left. The buildings to the right held guns. Respond: What had Brown hoped for?

A New President

The belief that the North wanted to end slavery in the South was important in the election of 1860. The Democratic Party was not able to agree on a candidate, and it split into two groups. Northern Democrats chose Stephen A. Douglas as their candidate. Southerners chose John C. Breckinridge (BREK-un-rij) of Kentucky. A new party, the **Constitutional Union Party**, chose John Bell of Tennessee.

The Republicans chose Abraham Lincoln of Illinois. In the 1840s, Lincoln had served in Congress. In 1858, he ran for senator of Illinois against Douglas. During their campaign, Lincoln and Douglas argued the important questions of the day

The term of Abraham Lincoln (1809–1865) offered more challenges, as he said, than that of George Washington. He met the challenges with dedication and humanity.

in public debates all over Illinois. Douglas won the election, but the debates made Lincoln a well-known figure nationally.

The spread of slavery into the new territories was the main issue in the 1860 election. Douglas repeated his position that settlers in a territory should decide if they wanted slavery. Breckinridge, the southern Democrat, said that slavery must be protected everywhere in the United States. Bell tried to stay away from the question of slavery altogether. Lincoln and the Republican Party said that slavery should not be allowed in any western territory.

It is important to remember that Lincoln did not plan to end slavery in the South. He believed that slavery was wrong, but he was not an abolitionist. He was afraid that the nation would become divided if the South was forced to give up the slaves. His position was only that the new territories should be free. However, many Southerners believed that Lincoln wanted to end slavery. They said that if Lincoln became president, their states would secede from the United States.

Lincoln did become president. The Republicans won most of the northern and western states. The division of the Democratic Party made it very weak. Southern votes were split between Breckinridge and Bell, and Douglas got only a few electoral votes.

A Nation in the South

Almost as soon as the election was over, South Carolina carried out its threat and seceded from the United States. Early in 1861, six more southern states—Georgia, Florida, Alabama, Mississippi, Louisiana, and Texas—also seceded. These states formed their own nation, called the **Confederate States of America**, or the **Confederacy**.

The Confederacy quickly wrote a new constitution. This constitution was like the one written by the Founding Fathers, except that it promised to protect slavery. After its constitution was finished, the Confederacy chose Jefferson Davis of Mississippi as its president.

When the Confederacy was formed, early in 1861, President Buchanan was still in office. He did not believe that the southern states had the right to secede. However, he also did not believe the federal government had the right to force these states to return to the **Union**, or the United States. Therefore, Buchanan did almost nothing to stop the southern states from seceding.

Some Northerners believed that the United States was better off without these slave states. Most Americans, however, thought that the division of the nation was a terrible thing. Before Lincoln took office, leaders of the **border states**, or the southern states which had not seceded, tried to get the South to return to the Union.

Senator John Crittenden (KRIT-un-dun) of Kentucky said that Congress should pass an amendment to the Constitution, protecting slavery in the South. He also wanted Congress to extend the old

THE UNION AND THE CONFEDERACY

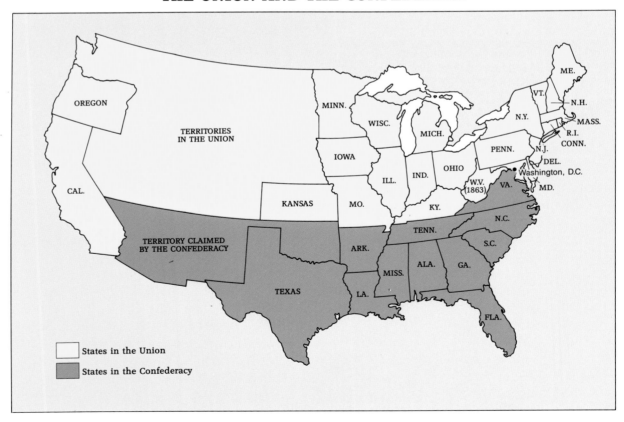

States in the Union

States in the Confederacy

Think: Jefferson Davis (left) ordered the attack on Fort Sumter (above), marking the beginning of the Civil War. Respond: What events lead to the Confederate president's decision?

Missouri Compromise line all the way to California. Slavery would be outlawed north of the line and allowed south of it. This plan was known as the *Crittenden Compromise*.

Crittenden's plan was not accepted. The Confederate states did not want to return to the Union, and the Republicans refused to allow slavery in the western territories.

War Breaks Out

When Lincoln took office in March of 1861, he made it clear that he planned to keep the Union together. However, he did not want to use force to make the Confederacy return to the Union.

Events soon changed his plans. After the Confederacy was formed, a few United States forts remained in the South. One of these was Fort Sumter, on an island off the South Carolina coast. Fort Sumter was cut off from its supply lines.

Lincoln told the governor of South Carolina that he planned to send food, but not weapons, to the fort.

Jefferson Davis said that this was an invasion of the Confederacy. He decided to attack the fort. On April 12, 1861, Confederate troops fired on Fort Sumter. Two days later, the fort surrendered. The *Civil War* had begun.

Preparing for Battle

After war broke out, the southern states that had not seceded had to decide which side they were on. Arkansas, Tennessee, and North Carolina became Confederate states. Virginia also joined the Confederacy, but the fifty counties that opposed slavery formed a new, free state, West Virginia. The border states—Maryland, Delaware, Missouri, and Kentucky—stayed in the Union.

Northerners believed they would win the war easily. There were twice as many

HISTORY MAKERS

Clara Barton

Angel of the Battlefield

''Tell me some things your men need, Major.''

''All our luggage was lost when we were attacked by the mob in Baltimore, Miss Barton. Truth to tell, in this hot Washington weather, we're miserable in our woolen clothes!''

The next day Clara Barton appeared at the army camp in Washington, D.C. With her were five men carrying heavy boxes filled with food and clothing for the men of the Sixth Massachusetts Regiment. It was the beginning of the Civil War and the beginning of Clara Barton's career as nurse and organizer of relief for wounded soldiers.

Clara Barton spent the Civil War years caring for the wounded. She was often on the battlefields before the fighting ended. At Antietam she was lifting a wounded soldier to give him a drink of water when he was shot and killed. In addition to serving as a nurse to the wounded, Clara Barton brought supplies of bandages, medicine, food, and clothing to the front lines. She organized kitchens and fed the wounded.

After the Civil War, Clara Barton used some of her own money to search for soldiers who were prisoners of war or who were missing in action. She established the National Cemetery at the Andersonville prison camp in Georgia.

In 1869, Clara Barton went to Europe. There she worked with the European Red Cross, helping victims of war, no matter what side they were on. She hoped to bring the Red Cross to the United States, but her plan was rejected. There no longer seemed to be a need for a wartime nursing organization. Clara Barton suggested that Red Cross work need not be limited to battlefields. To prove it, she organized Red Cross units in New York. Those units sent help to Michigan after a terrible forest fire there. The following year President Arthur signed the Geneva Convention treaty and made the American Red Cross official.

Today, Red Cross volunteers collect blood donations, teach first aid and water safety classes, and organize disaster relief. Clara Barton expanded a wartime nursing organization into an important part of American life.

Robert Edward Lee (1807–1870) was truly gifted as a military leader. He seemed able to guess his opponents' movements. He was also bold in his decisions and well-loved by his men.

Thomas Jonathan "Stonewall" Jackson (1824–1863) was a good partner for Robert E. Lee. He was bold and independent. When Jackson died, many believed the South's chances went with him.

Northerners as Southerners. The North had more factories and railroads and a strong navy. However, the North also had problems. At first, the Union army did not have good generals. Also, some Northerners opposed the war. A few, who were called *Copperheads*, even tried to help the South.

Southerners expected to win the war because they were defending their own land. They reasoned that it was easier to protect land than to capture it. They had trained troops and great generals, such as Robert E. Lee and Thomas Jackson. However, the Confederacy was also weak in many ways. There were few factories in the South to produce needed supplies. There were not enough railroads for transporting supplies and troops. In addition, there were fewer men who could fight the war. Many rich Southerners did not have to fight, and black men could not join the Confederate army.

In July of 1861, the Union army marched into the South. The Confederate army marched to stop them. Both sides expected an easy battle and a quick victory. They soon discovered that they were wrong. The Civil War lasted four years, and it was one of the bloodiest wars in history. In the next section, you will read about this war.

Section Review

1. Why did John Brown attack Harpers Ferry? What was the outcome of his raid?
2. Why did some southern states secede after the election of 1860? Which states seceded?
3. Did Lincoln plan to end slavery? What was his position at the time he took office?
4. What advantages and disadvantages did each side have at the beginning of the Civil War?

THE CIVIL WAR
On Land and Sea

Land battles of the Civil War differed little from those of a hundred years earlier. Soldiers still faced one another in hand-to-hand combat. They used the same weapons that their ancestors had used. Only the horror of a nation divided made this war on land seem different.

Civil War battles at sea, however, were much different than ever before. Two differences in particular marked the change: steam power replaced sail power, and ironclad ships replaced those of wood.

Both the Union and the Confederacy were inventive in trying to update their navies to keep up with these changes. The Union came out ahead only because it had the resources and heavy industry needed to support a large navy.

The South produced the first ironclad, the *Merrimac,* from a sunken Union ship which it salvaged. The North responded by building the *Monitor.* The Union set up effective blockades, but the South responded with fast and silent blockade-runners. And so modern naval vessels came into being—through invention born of necessity.

Think: In an attempt to prevent Admiral Porter's fleet of ironclads from penetrating the Vicksburg blockade, the Confederates set afloat burning rafts. One Union vessel did catch fire and sink, but the North still broke through.
Respond: **Why did the South have to be inventive in its defense?**

Think: The *Hunley,* built by Southerner Horace L. Hunley, was the first submarine to sink a ship. However, the submarine itself also went down, with nine aboard. Previously, twenty men had died in trial runs. Respond: Why did the South keep trying to make it work?

Think: New York's Novelty Iron Works, pictured in this lithograph, was used to its maximum during the Civil War. It supplied parts for the Union ironclads. Respond: How important were the North's industries and supplies of raw materials to its war effort?

Think: Both photographers and painters concentrated on catching the expressions of the young soldiers who fought in the Civil War. The photograph on the left shows Confederates. Winslow Homer's oil sketch shows a Union soldier. Notice the similarities in their expressions. Respond: What might these soldiers be feeling?

Think: In the colorful painting below, by James Hope, General McClellan is shown leading his troops through the Union camp at Cumberland Landing. The black-and-white photograph shows the same scene. Look for similarities and differences between the two pictures. **Respond:** What feeling do you get from each picture, and why?

The Civil War was shown to people in a new way: through picture journalism. Throughout Union and Confederate camps and battle sites, artists of all kinds could be found. They recorded what they saw in pictures. Some used sketching pencils to quickly preserve scenes. Later, these sketches were turned into paintings or engravings. Photographers were also found in the war zone, dragging their heavy, bulky photography equipment with them. They photographed, for the first time, a major war. Photography was still a long and involved process. But the camera artists stuck with it. Their portraits and scenes give us a haunting reminder of the war.

Truly, the ''noble army of artists'' who gave us a real and lasting record of the war had courage and vision. Their contribution to history will not be forgotten.

Courtesy, Museum of Fine Arts, Boston.

Feature Review

1. How were land battles of the Civil War similar to those of previous wars?
2. What two changes in naval battles came about during the Civil War?
3. Why was the North's navy more successful than the South's?
4. What is picture journalism?

3. The War Between the States

Learn these important terms:

blockade
Emancipation Proclamation
Battle of Gettysburg

Remember the main idea:

The Civil War lasted four years and was one of the most terrible wars in history. The North finally won the war and brought the Union back together.

Look for answers to these questions:

1. What was the Union's plan for winning the war?
2. What was the turning point of the war?
3. How did the North finally end the war?

The Union plan for the war had three parts. First, the Union planned to capture the Mississippi River and divide the Confederacy. Second, the Union planned to *blockade* the Confederacy by placing ships around all Southern ports. This would keep the Confederacy from trading with Europe. Third, the Union would capture Richmond, the Confederate capital, and other important Southern cities.

The plan to capture Richmond and quickly end the war failed. McDowell, the Union general, led thirty thousand troops into Virginia, but they were met by a strong Confederate force at Bull Run. The Union troops were unable to break through the Confederate lines, led by General "Stonewall" Jackson. When fresh Confederate troops arrived, the Union army retreated. Many Union soldiers threw down their guns and fled.

After the Battle of Bull Run, President Lincoln replaced General McDowell with George B. McClellan, who rebuilt the army and marched back into Virginia. He tried many times to capture Richmond. But in battle after battle, the Confederate army drove the Union soldiers back. These battles ended with huge losses on

Think: In two separate battles at Bull Run, the South won major victories. The first victory put to rest the belief that the North would quickly end the war. In the second Battle of Bull Run, the South regained most of Virginia.
Respond: How did the first weak leaders in the Union army affect the war?

© Wadsworth Atheneum, Hartford

Think: Standing in the rigging of the *Hartford*, Admiral Farragut watches his men battle the South's *Tennessee*. Farragut's victory tightened the North's blockade. *An August Morning with Farragut, The Battle of Mobile Bay* by William Overend records the event. Respond: **What did the blockade of Southern ports achieve?**

both sides, but the Confederacy succeeded in defending its lands.

When the Union invasion of Virginia failed, Robert E. Lee, the Confederate commander, decided to invade the North. Luckily for the North, a Union soldier found a copy of Lee's battle plans. The Union army marched to meet Lee's troops. At the Battle of Antietam (an-TEET-um) in Maryland, Lee was forced to retreat back to the South.

Lincoln was glad that the Confederate invasion had failed, but he was angry that McClellan had not chased and destroyed the Confederate army. He replaced McClellan with General Ambrose E. Burnside. Burnside quickly led his troops back into Virginia and met the Confederate army at Fredericksburg. Burnside's men charged six times, but each time Lee's artillery pushed them back. The Union suffered heavy losses.

Lincoln again chose a new commander, this time General Joseph E. Hooker. Hooker's Union army had twice as many men as the Confederate army did. However, Lee ordered his men to attack the Union troops. Lee was a great general, and at the Battle of Chancellorsville (CHANS-uh-lurs-vil) in Virginia, the Confederacy once more drove back the army of the North.

The War at Sea and in the West

The attack on Virginia failed many times, but the other parts of the Union plan went better. At first, the Union navy was too small to carry out a successful blockade of Southern ports. However, as the war went on, Northern shipyards built more ships, and the blockade became tighter. As a result, the Confederacy suffered from a shortage of supplies.

In the West, the Union did much better than it had in Virginia. In 1862, General Ulysses S. Grant led a Union army down the Cumberland and Tennessee Rivers into Tennessee. At the same time, a Union naval force under David Farragut (FAR-uh-guht) captured New Orleans. By the summer of 1862, the Union controlled most of the Mississippi River.

The Emancipation Proclamation

From the beginning of the war, many Northerners wanted Lincoln to free the slaves. At first, Lincoln wanted to free the slaves only after paying slave owners for their loss. In April 1862, Congress passed a law which freed the slaves in Washington, D.C., and allowed their owners to be paid. In June, Congress ended slavery in all the western territories.

In September of 1862, Lincoln wrote the *Emancipation Proclamation* (ih-MAN-suh-PAY-shun PRAHK-luh-MAY-shun). This Proclamation said that all slaves in Confederate states would be set free on January 1, 1863, unless the South surrendered before then.

The Emancipation Proclamation did not in fact end slavery. The border states that had stayed in the Union still had slavery. Lincoln's purpose in writing the Proclamation was to tell the Confederate states

that if they returned to the Union, they could keep their slaves. Lincoln hated slavery, but bringing the United States back together was his main goal.

Even though the Confederacy ignored it, the Emancipation Proclamation had important effects. It pleased many abolitionists, who believed the Civil War had become a fight to end slavery. Also, the Union army now began to accept black soldiers. Over 180,000 black soldiers served in the Union army. Many of these soldiers escaped from Southern plantations to fight against slavery. About one-fourth of all Union sailors were black.

The Turning Point

Before 1863, most of the war in the East was fought in northern Virginia. The Confederacy only invaded the Northern states once, in the Battle of Antietam. In July of 1863, however, Lee brought his army all the way into Pennsylvania. He wanted to try to win the war, rather than just defending the Confederacy. At the town of Gettysburg (GET-eez-burg), he was met by the Union army under a new commander, General George Meade.

Many historians consider the *Battle of Gettysburg* the turning point of the Civil War. The battle lasted three days, and both sides fought bravely. However,

Think: **One of the bloodiest in history, the Battle of Gettysburg was a turning point of the war. The victorious North lost 17,500 men. With the loss of 22,500 men, General Lee was never again able to launch a major offensive.** Respond: **Why should Northern troops have followed the retreating forces?**

the Union army had more men and a stronger position than Lee's army did. The Confederate army lost more than twenty thousand men in the Battle of Gettysburg and had to retreat to Virginia.

At the same time, in the West, General Grant won an important battle at Vicksburg, Mississippi. With this victory, the Union controlled all of the Mississippi River. Texas, Louisiana, and Arkansas were cut off from the rest of the Confederacy. Then Grant defeated a Confederate army under General Bragg at the Battle of Chattanooga (CHAT-uh-NOO-guh) in Tennessee.

After his great success as a general, William Tecumseh Sherman (1820–1891) was a popular speaker. Many wanted him to run for president, but he refused.

Think: From June 1864 to April 1865, Grant led a siege against Lee. From a base in Petersburg, Virginia, Grant's troops picked away at the Confederates. Respond: When is this type of warfare effective?

After the Battle of Chattanooga, Lincoln made Grant the commander of all the Union armies. Grant knew that the Confederacy had been weakened by the long war. Lee was running low on men and supplies. As a result, Grant decided to attack the Confederacy from two directions. He would lead an army south into Virginia. General William Tecumseh Sherman would attack the Confederacy from the west.

Sherman fought his way from Chattanooga to Atlanta, Georgia. He captured that city and burned it to the ground. Then he spread out his army and marched from Atlanta to the Atlantic coast. Sherman's army destroyed everything in its path. His plan was not only to capture territory but to destroy food, supplies, and railroads that might help the Confederacy continue the war. In December, Sherman's army reached Savannah. The Confederacy had been cut in half.

MAP WORKSHOP APPLYING GEOGRAPHY TO HISTORY

TOPOGRAPHY AND THE CIVIL WAR, 1861–1865

Topography, the part of geography that deals with the surface of the earth, is important to warfare. Mountains and rivers may be difficult for invaders to cross. On the other hand, mountains can protect defenders. And in the Civil War, rivers helped the northern generals to win the war.

Look at the topography shown on this map. Note the Appalachian Mountains especially.

1. During most of the war, Confederate General Robert E. Lee used his forces to defend Richmond, Virginia, and prevent an invasion of the South. In this situation, did Lee find the Appalachian Mountains an ally or an enemy? If the mountains had not been on the western side of Lee's army, what might the Northern armies have done?

2. What is to prevent the Northern armies from moving into the South on the western side of the Appalachians? Just how long did the Appalachians protect the South?

Now look at the Mississippi River and at the Ohio River.

3. Think of these rivers as the only way midwestern states had of shipping their farm products to foreign markets. What states were dependent on these rivers? Was it important to both the North and the South to control the Mississippi River? Why?

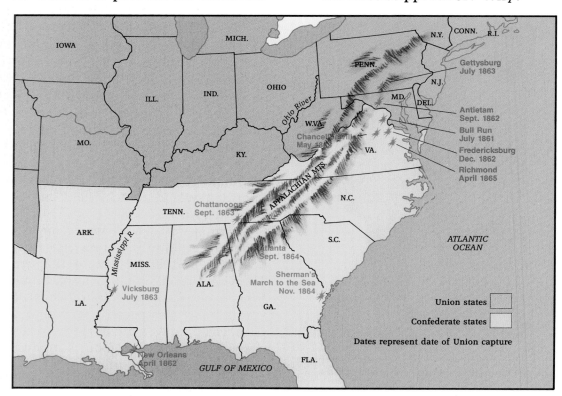

Think: **The dramatic meeting of Grant and Lee at Appomattox Court House was recorded by Louis Guillaume. Grant wore a simple private's uniform; Lee was in full regalia, complete with sword. The terms offered Lee were generous.** Respond: **What did General Grant's dress and actions symbolize?**

At the same time, Grant's army marched into the Confederacy. In several bloody battles, he drove Lee's tired armies back. Unlike the earlier Union commanders, Grant did not stop after battles, even when he lost thousands of men. He believed the war would only be won if he pushed all the way to Richmond, whatever the cost. In April of 1865, he finally captured the Confederate capital.

Lee's army was trapped southwest of the city. The Confederacy was out of men and money and could not keep up the fight. On April 9, 1865, General Lee surrendered to General Grant at the McLean House in the town of Appomattox Court House, Virginia.

The Civil War was over. The United States was back together, but at a terrible cost. About 360,000 Northerners and 258,000 Southerners died on the battle-

fields of the Civil War. The South was in ruins. In the next chapter, you will read about the effort to rebuild the South and heal the wounds of war.

Section Review

1. What were the three parts of the Union plan to win the Civil War? Which parts of the Union plan went well? Which part went badly, and why?

2. What was the Emancipation Proclamation? What effects did it have on the war?

3. What was the turning point of the war?

4. How did the Civil War come to an end?

CHAPTER SUMMARY

During the 1850s, conflicts over slavery grew worse. Nebraska became a free state, but Kansas voted to allow slavery. As a result, fighting broke out in Kansas.

Conflicts over slavery also divided the political parties. A new party, the Republicans, opposed slavery in the West. Although the 1856 presidential election was a close race between Republicans and Democrats, the Democratic candidate, James Buchanan, was elected. And in 1857, the Supreme Court ruled that slavery was legal anywhere in the United States.

In 1859, John Brown's revolt made many Southerners think that the North would use force to end slavery. The Republicans won the election of 1860, and Abraham Lincoln became president. Seven southern states seceded and formed the Confederate States of America. In 1861, war between the North and the South began.

The Civil War was long and bloody. By 1862, Union troops took control of the Mississippi River. Also in 1862, Lincoln's Emancipation Proclamation said that slavery would be ended in the South.

At the town of Gettysburg, in 1863, the turning point of the war occurred. After this battle, the Union forces gained strength under Grant's command. The Confederate forces surrendered in 1865. The Civil War was over.

Key Words

Write a sentence to explain the meaning of each of these terms.

Kansas-Nebraska Act

Dred Scott Decision

border states

Copperheads

blockade

Emancipation Proclamation

Major Events

Choose the answer that best completes the statement.

1. Personal liberty laws stopped the arrest of
   a) runaway slaves.
   b) free blacks.
   c) abolitionists.

2. When Kansas voted on slavery, the election was won by
   a) pro-slavery forces.
   b) anti-slavery forces.
   c) Free-Soilers.

3. After the Kansas-Nebraska Act, Whigs and Free-Soilers
   a) joined the Democrats.
   b) formed the Republican Party.
   c) moved to Nebraska.

4. When Lincoln tried to send supplies to Fort Sumter
   a) the supplies were taxed.
   b) Davis did not resist.
   c) Confederate troops attacked the fort.

5. At the Battle of Gettysburg, the Union army
   a) was badly defeated.
   b) controlled the Mississippi.
   c) won a decisive victory.

Review

Important Facts

Answer each question with at least one complete sentence.

1. How did Northerners react to the Fugitive Slave Act?

2. What was *Uncle Tom's Cabin*? Why was it important?

3. Why did Senator Douglas want Nebraska to become a territory?

4. What did John Brown do in Kansas? What did he do in Virginia?

5. What was the main issue in the 1860 election? Who won the election?

6. What was Lincoln's position on the slavery question?

7. What was the Crittenden Compromise? What was its outcome?

8. Why did Northerners think they would win the Civil War easily? What advantages did the South have?

9. What happened when the Union army tried to capture Richmond in 1861?

10. What accident helped the Union stop Lee's invasion of the North? Where did this battle take place?

11. Which battle marked the turning point of the war? Why was this battle so important?

12. What important victories did Grant win in the West? Why were they important?

13. What did Sherman's forces do?

Skill Review

Study the graph, then answer the following questions.

1. What percentage of all iron production was in the Union? What percentage was in the Confederacy?

2. How might the production of iron affect the outcome of the war?

3. What percentage of all merchant ships were Union? What percentage were Confederate?

4. How could merchant ships (not navy) influence the war?

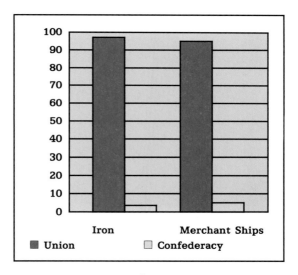

Critical Thinking

Write a paragraph to answer each question.

1. Why did the South finally secede from the Union?

2. What was the Union strategy in the Civil War? How was it carried out?

CHAPTER
16
Reconstruction

Years 1865–1896

Civil War ended
Lincoln assassinated
Andrew Johnson
became president

Congress passed
plan for
Reconstruction

Segregation
ruled illegal

Segregation
ruled lawful

1865

1867

1875

1896

Civil Rights
Act passed

Johnson impeached
Ulysses S. Grant
elected president

Rutherford B. Hayes
elected president

1866

1868

1876

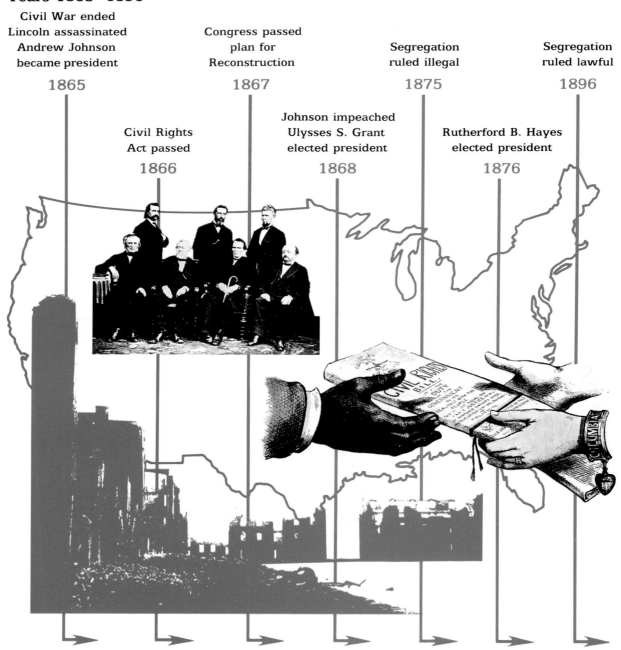

1. Reconstruction of the Nation

Learn these important terms:

Reconstruction
black codes
Reconstruction Act of 1867
impeach
Radical Republicans
Freedmen's Bureau

Remember the main idea:

After President Lincoln's death, Radical Republicans in Congress stopped his plan to bring the North and South together. The Republicans set up their own Reconstruction plan for the nation.

Look for answers to these questions:

1. What was Lincoln's plan for Reconstruction?
2. What group was set up to help former slaves?
3. Why did Congress bring President Johnson to trial?

The Civil War was one of the worst wars in history. Both the North and the South suffered terrible losses. Hundreds of thousands of soldiers lost their lives, and many thousands more were seriously wounded.

In other ways, however, the North did not suffer as badly as the South did. Only a few battles were fought in the North. As a result, very little damage was done to northern cities and farms. In fact, at the end of the war, the North was enjoying good times. Factories that had supplied soldiers with war goods were now working at top speed. Factory workers were earning good wages. In addition, farmers were able to sell their crops at high prices.

In the South, however, conditions were far different. Most of the fighting in the war had taken place on southern land. As a result, the South suffered terrible damage. Farms and plantations were destroyed. Railroad lines were torn up. Banks, businesses, and factories were closed. Cities such as Atlanta and Richmond were in ruins.

How would the nation's leaders bring the United States back together after the Civil War? In this chapter, you will read about President Lincoln's plan to rebuild the nation. You will see how Congress defeated that plan. You will also see how conditions changed for black Americans in the years after the war.

In 1863, President Lincoln explained his plan for rebuilding the nation after the war. In this plan, called *Reconstruction*, Lincoln made it clear he wanted it to be easy for the Southern states to return to the Union. At least one-tenth of the voters in each Southern state had to agree to support the United States Constitution. Then that state could write a new state constitution and elect new officials. When this was done, the state could return to the Union.

Think: This print, *The Funeral of President Lincoln*, was made in 1865 by Currier and Ives. For fifty years, the firm created works reflecting American life. This particular print records a tragic moment in American history.
Respond: What plan for Reconstruction did Lincoln have?

Lincoln was reelected in 1864. But before he could put his Reconstruction plan to work, a terrible tragedy occurred. On April 14, 1865, Lincoln and his wife went to see a play at Ford's Theater in Washington. Suddenly, a man appeared behind them and fired a gun at the president. The gunman, John Wilkes Booth, was an actor who had favored the Confederacy. Lincoln died the next day, just six days after the war ended.

Congress Against the President

After Lincoln's death, the vice president, Andrew Johnson of Tennessee, became president. At the beginning of the Civil War, Johnson was the only Southern senator who did not leave Congress when his state seceded. Now it was his job to bring the South back into the Union.

Johnson followed most of Lincoln's plan for Reconstruction. By the end of 1865, almost all the Southern states had set up new state governments. They had also elected new state officials. In addition, the Southern states had approved the Thirteenth Amendment to the Constitution, which ended slavery. Having met the requirements of Reconstruction, the states were asking to be allowed back into the Union.

The presidency of Andrew Johnson (1808-1875) has been called tragic, for it resulted in his impeachment and was characterized by bitterness among the nation's sections.

In Congress, however, many people were against this plan. They wanted Congress, not the president, to make Reconstruction plans for the South. These Congressional leaders were known as **Radical Republicans**. They stopped Congress from allowing the Southern states to return to the Union.

Congress's Plan

The Radical Republicans had several reasons for opposing the president's Reconstruction plan. First, they thought it was too easy on the South. They blamed the South for starting the Civil War and wanted to punish the Southern states. Second, the Radical Republicans were upset about the new leaders that voters in the South were choosing. Many of these leaders were the same people who had led the Confederacy. The Republicans thought that these people might cause more trouble for the nation.

Third, many congressmen were angry because the Southern states were not treating the former slaves fairly. The new state legislatures passed **black codes** to control blacks living in the South. Some states kept blacks from working anywhere except on farms or as household servants. Blacks living in the South could not vote, serve on juries, or carry guns. They could not move freely from place to place. The black codes kept many Southern blacks living like slaves even after slavery had ended.

For these reasons, Congress began to draw up its own plan for Reconstruction. First, Congress tried to extend the life of the **Freedmen's Bureau**, which was due to end in 1866. The Freedmen's Bureau had been started during the war to help blacks. It helped them get food, clothing, jobs, and medical treatment. The bureau also set up thousands of schools to help educate black Americans.

After President Johnson vetoed the Freedmen's Bureau bill, Congress passed the Civil Rights Act of 1866. This law gave black Americans the same rights that other American citizens had. Then Congress drew up the Fourteenth Amendment, which made black citizenship part of the Constitution. The Fourteenth Amendment also said that many former Confederate leaders could not hold government office.

President Johnson opposed the Republican plan for Reconstruction. He was angry because Congress was trying to take control of Reconstruction. He also thought that the South should choose its own leaders, even if they had served in the Confederacy.

Johnson vetoed the Civil Rights Act of 1866. However, Congress was able to override, or defeat, his veto. Then Johnson traveled around the nation speaking against the Fourteenth Amendment. Many people were angry with him

Think: The black codes fined people for not having jobs. When the man on the left could not pay his fine, his services were auctioned off. Respond: Do you believe this practice was fair? Explain.

because it seemed that he opposed fair treatment for blacks.

In the Congressional election of 1866, the Radical Republicans won more seats in Congress. They now had enough votes to pass any Reconstruction laws they wished. As a result, Congress took over the Reconstruction of the South.

The leaders of the Radical Republicans were Thaddeus Stevens of Pennsylvania and Charles Sumner of Massachusetts. Together Stevens and Sumner drew up the **Reconstruction Act of 1867**. In this plan, the South was divided into five districts. Each district would be governed by a Northern general and Northern troops. Also, the Southern states had to write new constitutions. Plus, each state had to approve the Fourteenth Amendment and give blacks the right to vote.

A Trial in Congress

Johnson's opposition to this Reconstruction plan almost cost him the presidency. Early in 1868, the Radical Republicans decided to *impeach* him. They charged him with breaking the rules of his office. When a president is impeached, he or she must stand trial, and the Senate acts as the jury. If the president is found guilty, he or she is removed from office. In Johnson's trial, Congress failed to remove him by only one vote.

After the trial, Johnson was still president, but not for long. Later that year, the Republicans chose General Ulysses S. Grant, instead of Johnson, to run for president. In the election, Grant defeated the Democratic candidate, Horatio Seymour (SEE-mor).

Think: In 1868, the Senate sat as a jury in the impeachment trial of President Johnson. The managers of the trial are shown here. (Stevens is seated second from left.) Respond: If the Radical Republicans had succeeded in removing Johnson from office, would the power of all future presidents have been weakened? Explain.

HISTORY MAKERS

Blanche Kelso Bruce

The Senator from Mississippi

The Senate chamber was hushed. Congressmen and visitors listened carefully as the senator from the state of Mississippi addressed his peers in the United States Senate.

"Mr. President . . . The close of the war found four millions of freedmen, without homes or property, charged with the duty of self-support and with the oversight of their personal freedom, yet without civil and political rights! That problem . . . was one of the gravest ever submitted to the American people. Shall these liberated millions of a separate race, while retaining personal liberty, be deprived of political rights?"

Peace and order in the South, continued the senator, could only be established when the rights of all citizens were respected. He reminded the Senate that since their emancipation, black citizens had produced almost forty million bales of cotton worth nearly two billion dollars— almost as much as the national debt! These citizens, he said, were vital to the nation's economy. They deserved not only the responsibilities, but the rights of citizenship, especially the basic right to vote.

Blanche K. Bruce, black Republican senator from Mississippi, was an outspoken champion of civil rights. During his one term in office, he worked for civil rights for blacks, American Indians, and Asians; the integration of the U.S. Army; and the return of Confederate leaders into the political process. He supported federal aid to education. He also worked for flood control and navigation improvements on the Mississippi River.

Blanche Kelso Bruce was born into slavery in 1841, but he learned to read and write. When he escaped from his master before the Civil War, he went to college and eventually taught school. He was elected to the United States Senate and served there from 1875–1881. The only black senator to serve a full term during Reconstruction, Blanche K. Bruce was interested in many things—from railroads to civil rights. He worked to make the United States a better country for all.

Ulysses S. Grant (1822-1885) was a brilliant military strategist—the Union's best—but an inexperienced politician unprepared for the presidency.

Grant won the 1868 election in part because black voters in the South voted for the Republicans. Republicans realized that if blacks were able to vote, most of them would vote for the Republicans. Therefore, in 1869, Republicans in Congress proposed the Fifteenth Amendment. This gave all adult male citizens the right to vote.

Congress's plan for Reconstruction was now at work. This plan was fairer to blacks but harder on white Southerners than Johnson's plan. In the next section, you will see how the South opposed Congress's plan, and how Reconstruction came to an end.

Section Review

1. What was Lincoln's plan for Reconstruction? Why was he unable to see it through?
2. Who were the Radical Republicans? Why did they oppose the Reconstruction plan?
3. What were the black codes? How did Congress respond to them?
4. What was Congress's plan for Reconstruction?

2. The End of Reconstruction

Learn these important terms:

scalawags
Ku Klux Klan
carpetbaggers
Amnesty Act

Remember the main idea:

During Reconstruction, new state governments were set up in the South. Many white Southerners were against these governments. In time, these Southerners regained control of the state governments.

Look for answers to these questions:

1. Why did most Southerners dislike the carpetbaggers?
2. How did the new state governments improve life in the South?
3. When did Reconstruction end?

Congress's Reconstruction plan sent twenty thousand federal soldiers into the South. The army held control of the Southern states until they wrote new constitutions setting up new governments. By the end of 1870, all the Southern states had written new constitutions. As a result, they were finally able to return to the Union.

New State Governments

The new state constitutions were improvements in several ways. They allowed more people to vote and hold office. The new laws made city and town governments better and taxes fairer. Under

Think: **The Freedmen's Bureau set up schools for black students. Still, many educational barriers existed for most blacks.** Respond: **Why is getting a good education important?**

these constitutions, farms, cities, and railroads were rebuilt. Free public schools were set up for the first time in most Southern states.

The Fourteenth Amendment kept previous Southern leaders from holding office in the new state governments. Many of these Southerners were angry about being kept out of the government. They said that the new leaders were enemies of the South. They called those leaders *scalawags* (SKAL-uh-wagz).

During Reconstruction, many Northerners also moved to the South. These Northerners were called *carpetbaggers*, because many of them carried cheap suitcases made of carpet cloth. Southerners were angry because carpetbaggers often held important positions in Southern state governments. The Southerners thought the carpetbaggers wanted to "get rich quick" and hurt the South. Many of the carpetbaggers, however, were honest people wanting to stay in the South and help build it up.

Black Leaders

The black citizens of the South played an important role during Reconstruction. Since the former leaders could no longer hold office, many positions were opened. Also, blacks could now exercise political power by voting for people to represent them. As a result, black Republicans were elected for the first time to many government positions.

Think: **In 1867, there were 703,000 black voters and 627,000 white voters. For the first time, black Americans had political power.** Respond: **What was the result?**

Think: During Reconstruction, several blacks were elected to Congress. Their voices helped pass the Civil Rights Act. Shown from left to right are Senator Revels and Representatives Turner, De Large, Walls, Long, Rainey, and Elliott. Respond: Why was the election of black legislators a turning point?

Black Americans served in state legislatures and other government offices. The state of Mississippi elected two black men, Hiram Revels and Blanche K. Bruce, to the United States Senate. Fifteen other blacks served in the House of Representatives during Reconstruction.

Most of these black leaders were either former slaves or came from the North. Many were teachers and ministers, and several were college graduates. These leaders worked hard to improve the condition of blacks. They also worked to help the whole South.

Southerners Against Reconstruction

Most white Southerners refused to accept the Reconstruction governments.

These Southerners had lost a war and, with it, a way of life. Northern soldiers had destroyed their cities and farms. After the war, Union troops took control of their governments. Many Southerners were forced to accept laws they did not like. In addition, they were not allowed to elect their old leaders to government positions. They felt they were being ruled by soldiers, carpetbaggers, scalawags, and former slaves and other blacks.

As a result, white Southerners often spoke out against the new state governments. They said that these governments were run by blacks and that they were dishonest. However, only once, and only for a brief period, did any Southern state legislature have a majority of black representatives in it.

Think: Robert Elliot is shown addressing the House of Representatives in 1874. The power of the black vote was being felt throughout the South. From 1867 to 1900, nineteen blacks served in Congress. Many others served in state and local governments. Respond: Why is the black vote a symbol of American freedom and democracy?

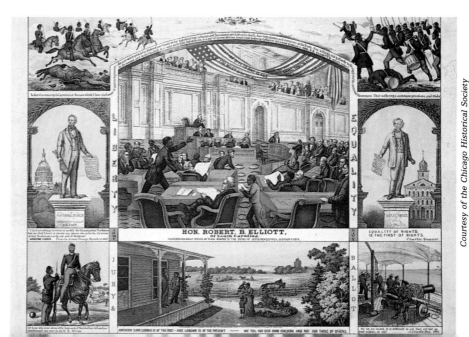

HON. ROBERT. B. ELLIOTT,
of South Carolina.

Courtesy of the Chicago Historical Society

Think: The Ku Klux Klan often used violence to oppose Reconstruction. In this engraving, the Klan is seen attacking a black family at home. Respond: Why did the Klan members choose to hide behind cloaks?

Also, the new state governments were not dishonest. At times, money raised by Southern state governments was wasted or spent foolishly. In a few cases, some Southern leaders spent state money for themselves. However, most Reconstruction governments were far more honest than the governments set up in the South after Reconstruction ended.

Many white Southerners wanted to get rid of the Reconstruction governments. Most of these people worked peacefully for change, but some were willing to use force. They formed secret groups to stop Reconstruction.

The best known of these groups was the *Ku Klux Klan*. Klan members wanted to keep blacks, carpetbaggers, and scalawags from running the South. They also wanted to stop blacks from voting. At first, the Ku Klux Klan only tried to frighten people. Klan members dressed in white sheets and hoods. They rode through the countryside at night, burning crosses on land belonging to their enemies. Later, the Klan began to threaten and even kill people who supported the Reconstruction government.

The Ku Klux Klan and groups like it were very successful in the South. They created a feeling of fear that made it hard for the Reconstruction governments to operate. Finally, in 1870 and 1871, Congress passed strong laws against the Klan. In addition, President Grant sent soldiers into the South to break up the Klan by arresting its members.

Reconstruction Comes to an End

In the early 1870s, Northerners began to lose interest in Reconstruction. The deaths of Thaddeus Stevens in 1868 and Charles Sumner in 1874 weakened the Radical Republicans' power in Congress. In 1872, Congress passed the *Amnesty Act*. This act gave the right to vote and hold office to most Southerners who had supported the Confederacy. Within four years, Southern Democrats controlled all the Southern state governments except in Louisiana, Florida, and South Carolina. In these states, federal troops kept the Reconstruction governments in power.

In the presidential election of 1876, Samuel J. Tilden, a Democrat, ran against Rutherford B. Hayes. At first it seemed that Tilden had won the election. However, Republican electors in Florida, Louisiana, and South Carolina changed their votes. Originally they promised to vote for Tilden, but they changed their votes so that Hayes would win. The Democrats

Mary Boykin Chestnut said that she had the luck ''always to stumble in on the *real show*.'' Her time and place in history made her a southern witness to the events of the Civil War. Mary Chestnut recorded in a journal what went on around her. Her entries include both factual accounts of events and her feelings about those events. Her journal is a primary source and gives a picture of what it was like to be a Southerner in the period after the Civil War.

Here is part of her journal entry for May 16, 1865:

> Such a hue and cry—whose fault? Everybody blamed by somebody else. Only the dead heroes left stiff and stark on the battlefield escape.
>
> "Blame every man who stayed at home and did not fight. I will not stop to hear excuses. Not one word against those who stood out until the bitter end and stacked muskets at Appomattox."
>
> Yesterday John Whitaker and Dr. Charles Shannon said they would be found ready enough to take up arms when the time came!
>
> Rip Van Winkle was a light sleeper to these two—the nap has lasted four years.

You can see how bitter Mary Chestnut is about the outcome of the war. She says that Southerners looked around for someone to blame for their defeat. But she points an accusing finger at two men she knew who avoided joining the fight. Like others around them, she states, they must have been asleep if they could not see the situation of the South was desperate. She compares them to Rip Van Winkle, who in legend fell asleep for twenty years.

A few weeks later, Mary Chestnut wrote this in her journal:

> Sunday afternoon I went to hear Mr. Trapier. . . . I felt sad and tremulous enough—but when he prayed we might be enabled to bear our bitter disappointment—ruined homes, desolated country, loss of freedom—and then a prayer for him who <u>was</u> our ruler. . . .
>
> I see he is put into a dungeon without lights. Two men watch him inside his den by day and by night. His parting with his wife and children sneered at. . . .
>
> Andy Johnson is bloody <u>minded</u>—his proclamation allows nobody over the rank of colonel to take the amnesty oath—and nobody who has assisted Confederates who owns over twenty thousand dollars . . . so JC [her husband] may look for his arrest any day—and he calmly prepares . . .

1 What three things does Mary feel the Southerners have lost?

2 What does Mary think about President Johnson's plan for Reconstruction?

3 What does she think will happen to her husband? Why?

President Rutherford B. Hayes (1822-1893) worked to heal the war-torn nation. His policies regarding minorities, economics, and public offices were backed by his "gentleman's principles."

were furious. Congress had to set up a special group of officials to decide the election. Eventually, the two political parties worked out a compromise. Hayes would become the new president, but federal troops would leave Florida, Louisiana, and South Carolina.

When these troops left the South in 1877, Reconstruction came to an end. White Southerners were once more in control of their state governments. These Southerners could now run the South as they wished. Conditions that had improved for black Americans during Reconstruction now changed for the worse. In the next section you will read about these and other changes in the South after Reconstruction.

Section Review

1. Who were the scalawags and carpetbaggers?
2. Why did some Southerners resent their state governments during Reconstruction?
3. What was the Ku Klux Klan? How did it oppose the Reconstruction governments?
4. Why was the election of 1876 unusual? How was the conflict over the election settled?

3. The New South

Learn these important terms:

New South
sharecroppers
literacy test
poll tax
tenant farmers
Plessy v. Ferguson

Remember the main idea:

After Reconstruction, the South set up new governments. Manufacturing grew, but farming remained the most important business. Blacks in the South lost many of their newly gained rights.

Look for answers to these questions:

1. How did southern industry grow after the Civil War?
2. How did farming change in the South after the war?
3. In what case did the Supreme Court rule that segregation was lawful?

After Reconstruction ended in 1877, white Southerners took control of their state governments. The new leaders included some of the plantation owners who had ruled before the war. But in addition, many merchants, factory owners, and bankers became leaders.

These leaders saw how wealthy the North had become through industry and commerce. They wanted to build a **New South** in which manufacturing and trade would become more important than farming. However, after the Civil War, the

Think: Birmingham had the raw materials needed to make steel: coal, iron ore, and limestone. Above, coal is baked at high temperatures in airtight ovens to make coke. Coke is a slow burning fuel needed to heat iron ore to its melting point. Respond: Why were steelmaking and other new industries important to the South?

South was very poor. Since Southerners lacked money to set up new factories, they asked Northerners to put money into southern businesses.

With the help of northern money, the leaders of the New South succeeded in improving southern industry. Iron and steel mills were built. By the 1890s, Birmingham, Alabama, was one of the leading centers for making iron and steel in the United States. Texas became a center of the oil industry. Tobacco products were manufactured in North Carolina. Other southern factories made furniture, paper, and wood products. New railroad lines connected southern cities.

The most important southern industry was the manufacturing of cotton cloth. Before the war, the South shipped its cotton to textile mills in the Northeast and

Great Britain. After the war, many new textile mills were built in the South. By 1900, half of all the textile mills in the United States were in the South.

However, even with all its new factories, the South was not able to catch up with northern manufacturing. In fact, by 1900, southern manufacturing was even further behind the North than it had been in 1860. There are many reasons for this. For example, some southern factories were owned by Northerners who only made part of their products in the South. The goods were finished in northern factories. Also, since southern factories were far away from the large markets of the Northeast, it cost more to ship the products. As a result, Southerners had to charge more for their products than northern factory owners did.

Farming in the South

Because of problems such as these, farming remained more important than manufacturing in the South. However, the old plantation system was no longer possible. After the Civil War there were no more slaves. Moreover, few plantation owners could afford to pay workers' wages. Many farmers could not afford seed and tools, either.

Southern farmers tried different ways to rebuild their farms. Some farmers borrowed money from bankers or from rich people. Sometimes the farmers were not able to pay back these loans. As a result, they had to give their crops to the lenders.

Large landowners often had to sell off part of their land to get money to work the remaining land. Some planters sold their entire plantations to rich carpetbaggers.

For a while, it even looked as though the government would take away the plantations. Thaddeus Stevens wanted to punish plantation owners for supporting slavery and the Confederacy. He said that the plantations should be broken up into small farms and given to former slaves. Every former slave should have ''forty acres and a mule.'' Congress did not approve this plan.

Many large landowners rented out sections of their land to **tenant farmers**. The

Think: **Many blacks hoped that freedom would also mean free land. But only land that was not suitable for farming was made available. Most blacks were forced to become sharecroppers. They worked someone else's land, paying their rent with a portion of the crops.** Respond: **Compare sharecropping with slavery.**

MAP WORKSHOP COMPARING MAPS

THE WEALTH OF THE NATION, 1860 and 1880

By comparing these two maps, you can see how the wealth of the United States shifted geographically between 1860 and 1880. The term *per capita wealth* is the total wealth of the state divided by the number of people living in it. Another way to say this is the average wealth per person. Remember that in 1860 slaves were counted as wealth.

Look at the map showing wealth in the United States in 1860.

1. On a separate sheet of paper, list the ten most wealthy states. How many of these states are southern? Which part of the nation was wealthier in 1860, the North or the South, would you say?

2. Was the South most successful in farming or in industry at this time? What role did slaves play in this economy?

3. Which southern state was poorest in 1860? How might you account for this?

Now look at the map of wealth in the United States in 1880.

4. Beside your first list, now list the ten most wealthy states in 1880. How many of these are southern?

5. How many southern states are in the lowest ranking of wealth? Which states changed the most in ranking after the Civil War?

6. Northern factories produced supplies for the Union forces during the war. How might this fact have affected the wealth of northern states after the war?

7. How can you explain the loss of wealth suffered by southern states? What effect did battles and the destruction of cities and farm land have? What effect did the freeing of the slaves have?

Compare the wealth of the states west of the Mississippi River in 1860 and in 1880.

8. The western states became more populated during these years. What effect do you think this had on the wealth of the states?

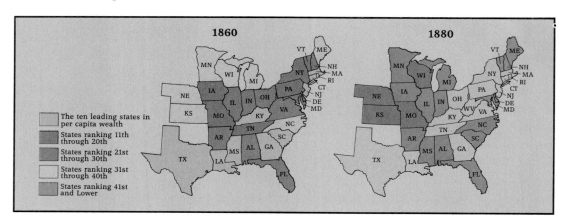

poorest tenant farmers paid their rent by giving the landowner part of their crops. Thus, these poor tenant farmers were called *sharecroppers*.

Sharecroppers paid from one-third to one-half of their crops as rent. They usually bought their food and supplies from the landowner on credit. For this reason, their debt for supplies grew during the year. Often, at harvest time, sharecroppers had to give the landowner most of their crops to pay their debts. A few landowners even cheated sharecroppers by adding on more debts than they really owed. The system was bad for both white and black sharecroppers.

The Loss of Rights

For many black sharecroppers, the new system was only a little better than slavery. They often worked the same land they had worked as slaves, and they never saw the profits of their work. Still, blacks in the South treasured their new freedom. Their lives were difficult, but at least their civil rights were protected.

However, after Reconstruction ended in 1877, black Americans in the South began to lose many of these rights. By the early 1900s, the southern states passed laws which took the right to vote away from black citizens.

Even before these laws were passed, Southerners found ways to keep black Americans from voting. One way was the *poll tax*, a tax that had to be paid for voting. Many poor southern blacks could not afford to pay this tax. Another way to stop black voters was the *literacy test*. This test required the voter to be able to read. Black voters were often given very difficult tests, while white voters were given easy ones.

In the 1890s, the southern states also began to segregate, or separate, black

Americans and white Americans. By 1900, black Americans were not allowed to use the same hospitals, restaurants, or streetcar seats as white people. Separate schools were also set up for black students and white students.

In 1875, Congress passed a Civil Rights Act which said that segregation in the South was illegal. In 1896, however, in the case of *Plessy v. Ferguson*, the Supreme Court ruled that segregation was lawful. The Court said that schools, for example, could be "separate but equal." In practice, segregation usually meant separation without equality. Schools for black children were rarely as good as schools for white children.

The Civil War and Reconstruction changed the South in many ways. The Old South of plantations and slaves gave way to the New South of smaller farms and segregation. The New South was also a place where industry took hold. After the Civil War, the rest of the nation also changed in many ways. Settlers and railroads tamed the West, and the growth of industry changed life in the North. In the next chapter, you will read about some of these changes.

Section Review

1. What changes did some leaders want to make in the South after the Civil War? In what ways were they successful? In what ways were they unsuccessful?

2. Why was the old plantation system impossible after the Civil War? How did farming change?

3. What is a tenant farmer? What is a sharecropper?

4. How did Southerners try to stop blacks from voting?

CHAPTER SUMMARY

Lincoln wanted to make it easy for the South to return to the United States after the Civil War, but he was killed before he could put his plan to work. President Johnson followed most of Lincoln's ideas, but Radical Republicans in Congress opposed him. They did not want Confederate leaders to have power, and they did not like the black codes. Congress tried to impeach Johnson, but the attempt failed. Ulysses S. Grant was elected president in 1868.

Congress made its own plan for Reconstruction. Union troops occupied the South. Southern states wrote new constitutions and returned to the Union. Confederate leaders were not allowed to serve in government. New leaders appeared, including many Northerners. Blacks held important government jobs. Many white Southerners opposed Reconstruction. In the presidential election of 1876, there was a dispute over the winner. The parties compromised, and Hayes, the Republican candidate, became president. In return, Union troops left the South.

Reconstruction ended in 1877. White Southerners took control of their state governments. New factories were built in the South, but farming remained important. Many landowners had to borrow money or sell their land. Others sold or rented parts of their land. Blacks lost many of their rights.

Key Words

Write a sentence to explain the meaning of each of these terms.

Reconstruction	*scalawags*
black codes	*carpetbaggers*
Radical Republicans	*sharecroppers*

Major Events

Choose the answer that best completes the statement.

1. On April 14, 1865, at Ford's Theater, Lincoln was
   a) honored by former slaves.
   b) criticized by Southerners.
   c) shot and killed.

2. After the Civil War, southern states had to write
   a) new constitutions.
   b) constitutional amendments.
   c) letters freeing the slaves.

3. Under the Reconstruction Act of 1867, the South was
   a) fined for fighting the war.
   b) governed by northern troops.
   c) kept out of Congress.

4. In the 1876 election, many Republicans
   a) changed their votes.
   b) voted for Samuel J. Tilden.
   c) voted for Ulysses S. Grant.

5. In the case of *Plessy v. Ferguson*, the Supreme Court ruled that
   a) slavery was illegal.
   b) segregation was legal.
   c) Dred Scott should have been freed.

Review

Important Facts

Answer each question with at least one complete sentence.

1. How did southern states treat former slaves after the war?

2. What was the Freedmen's Bureau? Why was it important?

3. Why did President Johnson oppose the Republican plan for Reconstruction?

4. Who were the leaders of the Radical Republicans? What did they want to do?

5. In 1868, what did Congress do to President Johnson? Why?

6. Why did the Fourteenth Amendment anger many former Confederate leaders?

7. What effect did the Fifteenth Amendment have on southern government during Reconstruction?

8. What role did black leaders play in Reconstruction?

9. What did white Southerners say about Reconstruction governments?

10. What was the Ku Klux Klan? What happened to it?

11. After 1877, who took control of state governments in the South?

12. What happened to the plantation system after the Civil War?

13. In what ways did white Southerners try to keep blacks from voting?

14. Why was the *Plessy v. Ferguson* case important?

Skill Review

Read this primary source, then answer the following questions.

A northern newspaper reporter wrote from Charleston on September 4, 1865:

A city of ruins, of desolation, of vacant houses, of widowed women, of rotting wharves, of deserted warehouses, of weed-wild gardens, of miles of grass-grown streets, of acres of pitiful and voiceful barrenness,—that is Charleston, wherein Rebellion loftily reared its head five years ago, on whose beautiful promenade the fairest of cultured women gathered with passionate hearts to applaud the assault of ten thousand upon the little garrison of Fort Sumter!...

Mothers yet teach their children hate of the North, I judge; for when I asked a bright-eyed girl of half a dozen years...whose girl she was, she promptly answered, "a Rebel mother's girl." Patience, good people who love liberty, patience; this petty woman's spite will bite itself to death in time...

1. What was the economy of Charleston based on before the war? What was it like at the time of the article?

2. How had the women of Charleston changed in five years?

3. Did the reporter think that the North and the South would be reunified easily?

Critical Thinking

Write a paragraph to answer each question.

1. Compare Lincoln's plan for Reconstruction to the Radical Republican plan.

2. In what ways did the South change during and after Reconstruction?

Important People

Choose the answer that best completes the statement.

1. Sam Houston

   a) died at the Alamo.
   b) helped defeat Santa Anna.
   c) led settlers into Texas.

2. Zachary Taylor won honors in

   a) the Mexican War.
   b) the Bear Flag Revolt.
   c) the Texas war for independence.

3. Henry Clay drew up

   a) the Wilmot Proviso.
   b) the Compromise of 1850.
   c) the Kansas-Nebraska Act.

4. Stephen A. Douglas

   a) was a famous abolitionist.
   b) opposed statehood for Nebraska.
   c) unsuccessfully ran for president in 1860.

5. In 1861, Jefferson Davis

   a) ordered the attack on Fort Sumter.
   b) invaded Virginia.
   c) became the top Confederate general.

6. General U.S. Grant

   a) destroyed Georgia's resources.
   b) captured Richmond.
   c) won the battle of Gettysburg.

7. President Andrew Johnson

   a) supported the Republicans' Reconstruction plan.
   b) was removed from office.
   c) opposed the 14th Amendment.

Main Ideas

Choose the answer that best completes the statement.

1. After the defeat of Santa Anna. Texas became

   a) the twenty-eighth state.
   b) an annexed territory.
   c) an independent nation.

2. In 1846, the United States avoided war with Britain by

   a) buying part of Texas.
   b) dividing Oregon.
   c) buying part of Oregon.

3. After the Mexican War, the U.S. boundary extended to

   a) the Pacific Ocean.
   b) the Nueces River.
   c) the latitude 54'40".

4. California gained statehood when

   a) the Compromise of 1850 became law.
   b) Pierce became president.
   c) Texas entered the Union.

5. The main purpose of the Compromise of 1850 was to

   a) end the slave trade.
   b) pay Texas's debts.
   c) keep the Union whole.

6. Personal liberty laws aided

   a) runaway slaves.
   b) free blacks.
   c) slavery in free states.

7. Free-Soilers rushed to Kansas

   a) to join John Brown's army.
   b) to get free land grants.
   c) to vote against slavery.

Review

8. Lincoln's hope in 1860 was to

   a) end slavery everywhere.
   b) keep slavery out of the western territories.
   c) free all southern slaves.

9. The Union war plan included

   a) blocking Southern ports.
   b) getting aid from Europe.
   c) having former slaves fight.

10. Lee surrendered because

    a) New Orleans had fallen.
    b) Grant was a better general.
    c) he was low on men and supplies.

11. Radical Republicans wanted to

    a) punish the Confederates.
    b) pass black codes.
    c) impeach Grant.

12. Grant won the 1868 election partly because

    a) Southerners could not vote.
    b) he ran against Johnson.
    c) many blacks voted for him.

13. One group of Southerners who hated Reconstruction were

    a) the scalawags.
    b) the Ku Klux Klan.
    c) the carpetbaggers.

14. Due to the Amnesty Act, blacks

    a) lost political power.
    b) gained their civil rights.
    c) voted in greater numbers.

15. In the New South, many plantations were

    a) broken up and sold.
    b) given to ex-slaves.
    c) turned into factories.

History Skills

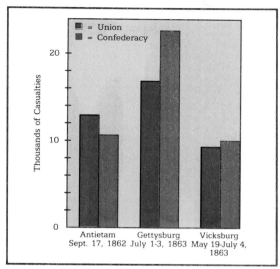

**Civil War Casualties
Three Battles**

Choose the answer that best completes the statement.

1. The heaviest casualties were suffered at

   a) Antietam.
   b) Gettysburg.
   c) Vicksburg.

2. The most casualties during a single day of combat were suffered

   a) on July 2, 1863.
   b) on May 31, 1863.
   c) on September 17, 1862.

3. You can infer that

   a) Vicksburg had the lowest casualty rate per day.
   b) Confederate forces lost more men when they were defending their own land.
   c) Union forces won more battles even though they lost more soldiers.

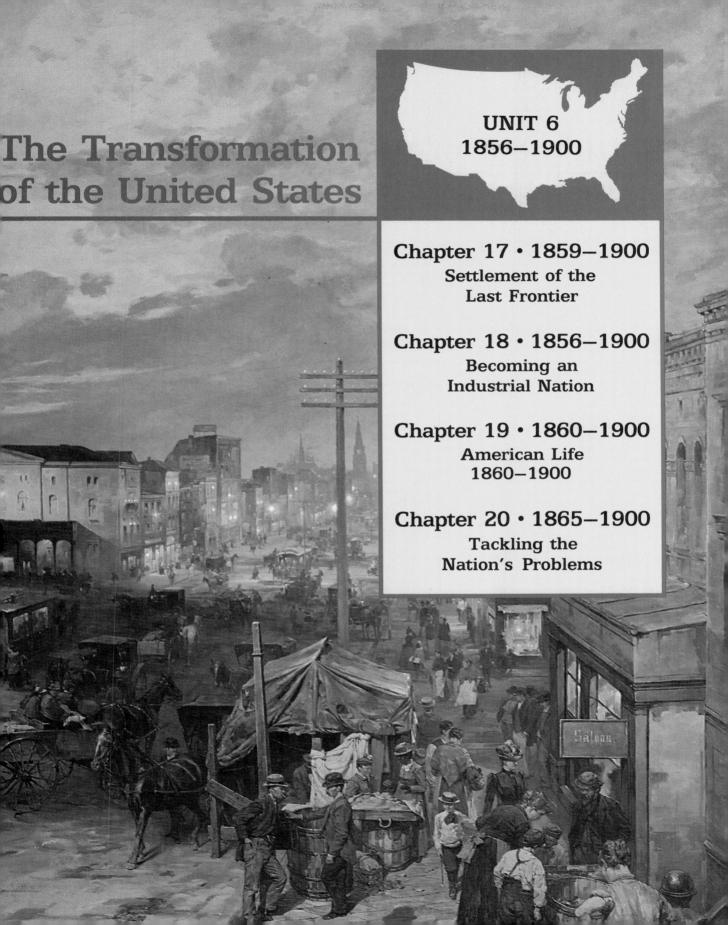

The Transformation of the United States

UNIT 6
1856–1900

17
Settlement of the Last Frontier

Years 1859–1900

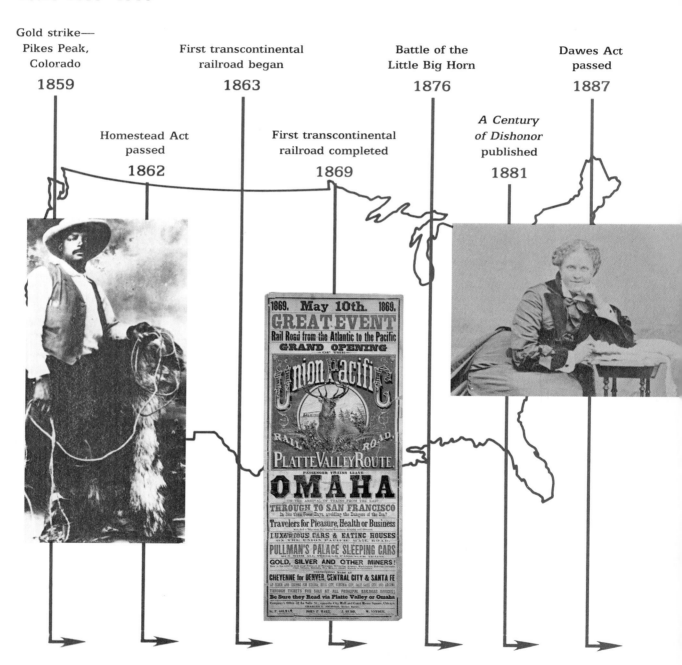

Gold strike—
Pikes Peak,
Colorado
1859

First transcontinental
railroad began
1863

Battle of the
Little Big Horn
1876

Dawes Act
passed
1887

Homestead Act
passed
1862

First transcontinental
railroad completed
1869

*A Century
of Dishonor*
published
1881

1. Opening the West

Learn these important terms:

boom town
vigilantes
transcontinental railroad
Comstock Lode

Remember the main idea:

Miners seeking gold helped open the unsettled lands west of the Mississippi River. A transcontinental railroad was built in 1869 that brought many new settlers to fill the frontier.

Look for answers to these questions:

1. How did miners help open up the unsettled lands of the West?
2. What is a boom town?
3. How was the first transcontinental railroad built?

At the time of the Civil War, the large area of land west of the Mississippi River was still unsettled. We call this region the Great Plains. To the settlers who passed through this dry land, it was known as the Great American Desert. It was known as home, however, to many different tribes of Plains Indians. They roamed the grasslands following great herds of buffalo as they moved from one part of the plains to another.

Many changes took place as this last frontier was settled. Mining towns were established, only to quickly become ghost towns. Ranchers and farmers replaced the miners. Railroads crisscrossed the once barren land. The millions of buffalo that grazed on the grasslands were replaced by cattle and wheat fields.

With these changes came hardships for many groups. Miners were disappointed. Farmers and ranchers struggled to make it. The Plains Indians and their way of life all but disappeared. Nevertheless, by 1890, almost five million people had settled on the Great Plains. In this chapter, you will read how they did it.

The first pioneers going west in the 1840s passed right through the flat, treeless land of the Great Plains. This dry land seemed unsuitable for farming, so the settlers pushed on over the Rocky Mountains. They traveled through the hot western deserts and settled in Utah, Oregon, and California.

During the 1850s, more people began to move into the vast areas of unsettled land west of the Mississippi River. One of the first groups to open this "last frontier" was the miners. They were looking for gold and silver.

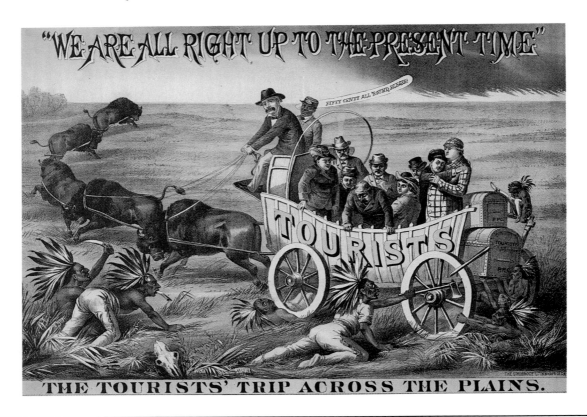

"WE ARE ALL RIGHT UP TO THE PRESENT TIME"

THE TOURISTS' TRIP ACROSS THE PLAINS.

Think: Fanciful stories about the West were told far and wide. Advertisements such as this one were created to attract the curious and adventuresome. Notice the real symbols of the West and the fanciful symbols as well. Respond: What fanciful story about the West does this advertisement tell?

The first gold rush was in California in 1849. Ten years later, miners heard of a gold strike near Pikes Peak in the Colorado Territory. Within a year, 100,000 people rushed into Colorado to search for gold. However, not many of the miners found any gold. Although many miners went back home, others stayed to become farmers or ranchers. By 1876, Colorado had grown large enough to become the thirty-eighth state.

The Comstock Lode

Nevada was the next site of gold and silver strikes. Thousands hurried to Nevada hoping to get rich. Two Irish miners, Pete O'Reilly and Pat McLaughlin, made the biggest find, the *Comstock Lode*. The discovery was named after Henry Comstock. Comstock was a fast-talking drifter who persuaded O'Reilly and McLaughlin to share their discovery with him.

Unfortunately, the three men did not know the value of their find. O'Reilly and McLaughlin sold their shares of the mine for several thousand dollars. Comstock received eleven thousand dollars for his share. The Comstock Lode would later become the richest mine in Nevada. The Comstock Lode produced about 300 million dollars worth of gold and silver over a twenty-year period.

Many mines, such as the Comstock, required expensive drilling machines to dig out the gold and silver. Most miners did not have enough money to work their claims. They were forced to sell to large companies. Big mining companies soon replaced individual miners. By the 1870s, mining was a big business in the West.

Boom Towns

With so many miners seeking riches, mining camps sprang up quickly. Many of these camps mushroomed into **boom towns**, communities that seemed to grow almost overnight. Owners of small businesses followed the miners into town. They built shops along the main streets and sold food, clothing, and mining tools to the miners. Hotels, banks, and gambling houses were quickly built. The streets were crowded with people, horses, and wagons.

Virginia City, Nevada, grew up around the Comstock mine. It was the most famous of the boom towns. Mark Twain, a famous American writer, described Virginia City in this way: "Money was as plenty as dust. . . . There were . . . fire companies, brass bands, banks, hotels, theaters, . . . wide open gambling palaces, . . . street fights, murders. . . ."

Think: Food was expensive in the boom town of San Francisco in the 1850s. This detail of a painting by Wilhelm Hahn of the Sansome Street Market shows the conditions in which many people lived. Respond: What does this street scene tell you about the life of the miners and others in San Francisco?

Think: **Chinese workers building the Central Pacific Railroad used the simplest of tools. Notice the handcarts used to carry dirt to fill in a gap between two mountains. The stronger dirt bridge will replace the wooden one.**
Respond: **How do these working conditions compare to those of today?**

Mining camps were wild, lawless places. Stealing and murder were common. There was no government or police force. Even in the towns, miners often had to control crime themselves. When things got out of hand, the citizens of the town formed committees to restore law and order. Members of the committees were called *vigilantes*. The vigilantes captured criminals, gave them quick trials, and punished them. The punishment was usually death by hanging.

Booms towns went up fast, but many did not survive long. When the mines gave out, boom towns often turned into ghost towns. Only towns along major transportation routes continued to thrive. The 1880s brought an end to gold fever. Although few miners got rich, many stayed to settle land in Colorado, Nevada, Idaho, Wyoming, Montana, and South Dakota.

The Transcontinental Railroad

Miners and other groups of settlers helped open the West. But it was the railroad that filled the frontier with people. President Abraham Lincoln believed that America needed railroads. He wanted to build a railroad that would connect the East with the West, all the way from the Atlantic Ocean to the Pacific Ocean. In 1862, Congress approved plans to build a *transcontinental railroad*.

Two railroad companies were chosen to build this railroad. In 1863, the Union Pacific Railroad began building westward from Omaha, Nebraska. The Central Pacific Railroad built eastward from Sacramento, California.

The Union Pacific employed thousands of Irish immigrants. Ten thousand Chinese immigrants worked for the Central Pacific. Laying track was difficult work

WESTERN MINING CENTERS AND RAILROADS, 1860-1890

In Chapter 14 you learned to draw inferences from your reading by looking for clues and making intelligent guesses. You can draw inferences from maps in the same way. From this map, you can figure out patterns of settlement.

First look at the railroads.

1. Which railroads were built by 1870? Which railroads were built between 1870 and 1890? What can you infer about the railroad industry during those years?

2. Where did railroad lines to the West begin? Where did they end? What reason can you infer for beginning and ending railroad lines in these places?

Now find the mining centers.

3. In which states are there mining centers?

4. Does each mining center have a city nearby? Why, or why not?

Look at the pattern of railroads, mining centers, and cities.

5. Does each mining center have a railroad nearby? What can you infer about the future growth of a mining center that was not near a railroad?

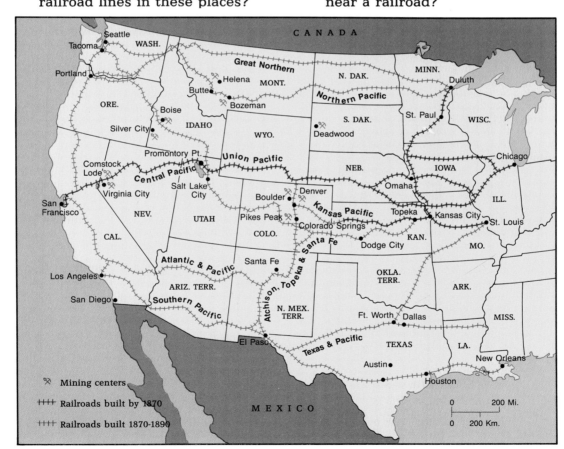

Think: A crowd watched as a golden spike joined the Union Pacific and Central Pacific. Posters announced the first ride on the new line. Respond: What changes would a transcontinental railroad bring?

In 1869, the two railroads joined at Promontory, Utah. The two railroad crews came together for a great celebration. Railroad officials drove in the spike connecting the two rails. The spike was made of gold, and the hammer was of silver. The first east-to-west railroad across the United States was finally completed. Thousands of people, eager to be miners, ranchers, and farmers, quickly poured into the West.

for both railroad crews. The Irish workers faced Indian raids, summer heat, and the cold winters of the plains. The Chinese workers had to lay track through the Sierra Nevada Mountains. In freezing temperatures, they dug railroad tunnels through the mountains. Snowstorms left snow drifts up to fifty feet high. Many workers lost their lives when snowslides struck. In spite of these hardships, the Chinese were able to work quickly. They set a world record by laying ten miles of track in one day!

Section Review

1. What was the Comstock Lode?
2. Name two states that were settled by miners looking for gold.
3. Why was life often violent in the mining camps of the West?
4. Who built the first transcontinental railroad? How did the railroad help settle the West?

2. Ranchers and Farmers Settle on the Great Plains

Learn these important terms:

sod houses   stampede
long drive   dry farming
cowboy   vaquero
longhorns   Homestead Act
droughts   cattle kingdom
Chisholm Trail

Remember the main idea:

Thousands of ranchers, farmers, and sheepherders settled on the Great Plains between the years of 1865 and 1900.

Look for answers to these questions:

1. Why was cattle ranching a big business from 1865 to 1885?
2. What brought an end to the cattle kingdom?
3. How did farmers turn the Great Plains into a successful farming region?

Cattle were brought to Mexico by Spanish explorers in the 1500s. By 1860, enormous herds had spread northward from Mexico to Texas. Millions of cattle grazed freely on the grasslands of the Great Plains.

These *longhorns*, as the cattle were called, were raised for beef by Texas ranchers. Before the Civil War, most Texas cattle were sold in the South. However, the biggest market for beef was in the eastern cities. The problem was how to get the cattle to market.

The answer to the problem was the railroad. Ranchers decided to drive the herds northward to the railroad towns of Abilene and Dodge City in Kansas. On a *long drive*, the cattle were herded one thousand miles or more across the Great Plains. The most famous of the cattle routes was the *Chisholm Trail* (CHIZ-uhm). At the railroad towns, the longhorns were loaded into railroad cars and sent to Chicago, Illinois. This city soon became the meat-packing center of the whole nation.

From 1865 to about 1885, the Great Plains was known as the *cattle kingdom*. Cattle ranching was a booming business. The ranchers could graze their herds across thousands of miles of open land. There was a good market for beef in the eastern cities and a good way to get the beef to market.

The Cowboy in the Cattle Kingdom

The hero of the cattle kingdom was the *cowboy*. The American cowboy learned how to herd cattle from the Mexican *vaquero* (vah-CARE-oh), or cowboy. The cowboy's outfit was Mexican in style, too. The wide-brimmed hat protected his eyes from the sun or the rain. The cowboy's high-heeled boots and spurs were suited for life on horseback. Lassos and the leather leggings called chaps also came from Mexico.

The cowboy's life was hard. The wages were low and the hours were long. Cowboys on the long drive often spent eighteen hours a day on horseback. The long drives lasted from three to four months, and the work was tiring and dangerous. The cowboy's worst fear was a *stampede*. A river crossing or an Indian raid could cause the cattle to run wildly in all directions. Thunderstorms or any loud noise could frighten the cattle and begin a stampede. Many cattle were lost in stampedes. Sometimes the life of a cowboy was lost as well.

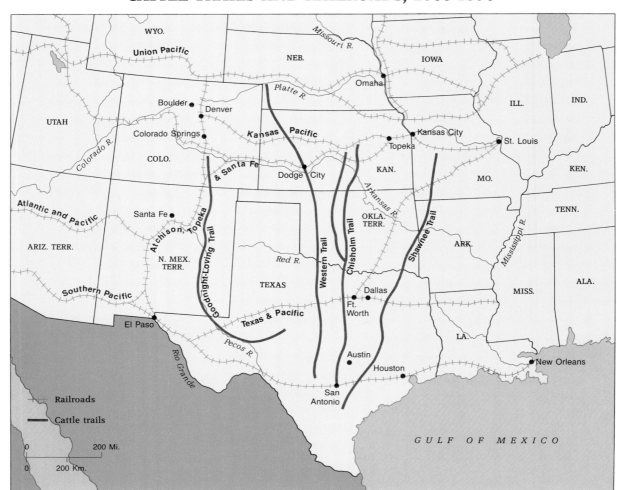

CATTLE TRAILS AND RAILROADS, 1860-1890

Many of the early cowboys were Mexicans and blacks. A black cowboy named Bill Pickett invented "bulldogging," or steer wrestling. This skill is still popular at western rodeos.

The End of the Cattle Kingdom

By the 1880s, more than six million cattle had been driven north from Texas. Many ranchers had made fortunes in the cattle business. However, the days of the long drive were soon over.

Sheepherders and farmers began to settle on the plains. Sheep ate the grass needed by the cattle. Ranchers and sheepherders each wanted the best grazing land for their animals. Wars broke out between the two groups. Farmers also wanted land. They fenced their property with barbed wire to keep the longhorns out. This made it hard for the cowboys to drive the cattle to market.

Falling beef prices made matters worse for the rancher. Too much beef on the market caused prices to drop. Finally, two bitterly cold winters brought an end to the cattle kingdom. Freezing temperatures and blizzards wiped out most of the herds. As some of the ranchers moved westward, more and more farmers took their places on the land.

Farmers on the Great Plains

In 1862, Congress passed the ***Homestead Act*** to encourage people to settle on the Great Plains. The Homestead Act offered free land to anyone willing to farm the land for five years. Many settlers rushed to accept this offer of free western land. Other settlers bought land from the railroad companies. These settlers followed the miners and ranchers onto the Great Plains.

Many settlers were not prepared for the hardships they faced on the plains. Farming was very difficult. Winters were bitterly cold and summers were hot and dry. There were dry years, or ***droughts***, when there was little or no rainfall. Farmers also faced dust storms, blizzards, and grasshoppers.

There was no wood on the plains to build houses or fences. Instead, farmers built their houses out of sod, bricklike

---

Think: Sheepherders and cattle ranchers competed for the best grazing lands. Unlike cattle, sheep ate the grass down to its roots, causing it to die. This angered farmers, who began to fence the land. Respond: What reasons did each group have for fighting?

Think: Plains farmers had to face many hardships. They had to dig their own wells. They had no wood to build houses or fences. In addition, grasshoppers sometimes swarmed, eating entire crops. Respond: In what ways are sod houses symbols of Americans' willingness to succeed, no matter what gets in their way?

chunks of earth and grass roots. These *sod houses* provided warm shelter, but they were dark and damp.

Plains farmers had to dig deep wells to get water for themselves and their crops. They used windmills to pump the water out of the wells up to ground level. The strong, steady winds of the plains turned the blades of the windmill. As the blades of the windmill turned, powerful pumps drew up the water.

Every drop of ground water and rainfall was precious. Farmers used **dry farming** to keep as much water as possible in the soil. Using steel-tipped plows, they dug deep into the soil, breaking it into small pieces. In this way, water could be absorbed into the soil. Less water was lost through evaporation.

In spite of these problems, the farmers stayed on the plains. Hard-working and determined, they planted and harvested crops. More settlers came and started farms. New farm machines helped increase farm production. Threshers beat the grains from their husks, and twine binders gathered bundles of wheat and bound them with twine. However, farm

machinery was expensive. Some farmers found ways to make enough money to buy farm machines. Others could not, falling deeper and deeper into debt.

The most successful farms were developed by large corporations. These huge farms, using all of the latest machinery, produced great quantities of crops. By the 1890s, the land west of the Mississippi was no longer a land of vast grasslands. It had completely changed. Almost five million people had settled on the Great Plains. The farms on the Great Plains produced more wheat than any other region in the world.

Section Review

1. What was the "long drive"? Why was it dangerous work?
2. Why did fighting break out between the ranchers and the sheepherders?
3. What was the Homestead Act?
4. What problems did the farmers of the Great Plains overcome?

To read a picture or bar graph, first read the title to see what is being compared. Then look at the graph key to see what the symbols in the graph mean.

The graph below is called a *picture graph* because it uses a certain picture to stand for what is being shown. On this graph, small barns are used to show the number of farms in the United States in the years between 1880 and 1980. The numbers down the left side of the graph tell the years for which information is presented. When you read the graph, you can compare what happened over time.

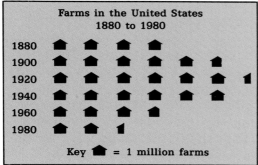

Farms in the United States 1880 to 1980

Key 🏠 = 1 million farms

From "Historical Statistics" and "Agricultural Statistics"

Use the picture graph to answer the following questions.

1 Look at the title. What does this picture graph show?

2 Look at the graph key. What does the symbol stand for?

3 About how many farms were added between 1880 and 1900?

4 For which year does the graph show the most farms?

5 What do you think will happen to the number of farms by the year 2000?

The other kind of graph on this page is a *bar graph*. It uses bars of different shades to make comparisons. The numbers on the left side of this graph tell the years. The numbers along the bottom show the number of acres.

Use the bar graph to answer these questions.

6 Look at the graph title. What two things does this bar graph compare?

7 Look at the graph key. What does each bar stand for?

8 In 1880, about how much land was used for raising crops? How much was used for grazing farm animals?

9 Between 1880 and 1900, what happened to the amount of crop land? What happened to the amount of grazing land?

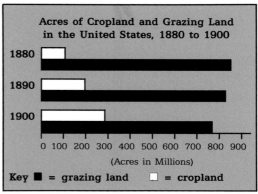

Acres of Cropland and Grazing Land in the United States, 1880 to 1900

(Acres in Millions)

Key ■ = grazing land □ = cropland

From "Historical Statistics"

Think: George Catlin painted this picture of Indians hunting. Indians killed only enough buffalo to meet their needs. Respond: How did their foresight guarantee enough buffalo for all?

3. The Plains Indians

Learn these important terms:

Dawes Act
Helen Hunt Jackson
reservation
Sarah Winnemucca

Remember the main idea:

The settlement of the Great Plains brought an end to the lifestyle of the Plains Indians. By the 1880s, the government had moved all Indians to reservations.

Look for answers to these questions:

1. What caused conflicts among Plains Indians and settlers?
2. How did the disappearance of the buffalo bring about the defeat of the Plains Indians?
3. What was the Dawes Act?

After the Civil War, about 200,000 Indians lived on the Great Plains. The Plains Indians were hunters. On horseback, they followed the great buffalo herds across the grasslands. Their lives depended on these animals. The buffalo provided food, clothing, and shelter. The strong buffalo skin made an excellent cover for the tepee. Buffalo hides made warm blankets. Even the buffalo hooves were boiled to make glue. With the glue, the Indians could make the buffalo hide hard and stiff for their war shields.

The thirty-one tribes of the Great Plains spoke many different languages. However, they could communicate with one another through a common and complex sign language. Although Plains Indians fought with one another, warriors were not often killed. The Indians fought one another to show their bravery in battle or to steal horses.

Conflicts Between Indians and Settlers

As settlers began to demand more and more land, fighting broke out between the Plains Indians and the white settlers. The United States government tried to settle the conflicts by making treaties with the tribes. The tribes were asked to give up some of their territory. In exchange, the government offered to give them land on a *reservation*, special land set aside only for Indians. The government promised this land "forever." The government also promised to keep settlers away.

As settlers demanded more land, the treaties were often broken. When the Indians saw their hunting grounds disappear, they grew angry. They began to fight back. The United States government sent soldiers to fight the Indians. Between 1869 and 1874, more than two hundred battles were fought between Indians and the United States cavalry.

The Battle of the Little Big Horn (or Custer's Last Stand)

One of the most famous battles between the Plains Indians and the United States Army was the Battle of the Little Big Horn in June 1876. The Black Hills reservation of the Sioux (SOO) Indians had been invaded by miners looking for gold. Chiefs Sitting Bull and Crazy Horse were determined to drive the miners out of their land. War broke out. The Cheyenne (shy-ANNE) joined the Sioux at a camp near the Little Big Horn River in Montana.

Colonel George Custer led his troops to the Sioux camp. Colonel Custer was looking for a quick victory. He was confident that he could put an end to the "Indian problem." However, Custer failed to find out how many Sioux were camped near the Little Big Horn. He split his small force into three groups. Without waiting for the other troops, Custer and his force of 264 men rode toward the camp. They were immediately attacked by several thousand Sioux and Cheyenne on a hill overlooking the Little Big Horn River. Not one soldier escaped.

Think: Little Big Horn was the site of the last important Indian victory. A Sioux artist drew this scene of the battle. It shows Crazy Horse riding majestically and wearing protective paint. Respond: How do you think the Indians and the American army each reacted to the results of this battle, and why?

The Battle of the Little Big Horn was a great victory for the Plains Indians. It was also their last major victory. Soldiers pursued the Sioux without mercy. Sitting Bull fled with a few followers to Canada. Within a year, Crazy Horse and his people were forced to surrender.

The Last of the Buffalo

Chief Crazy Horse surrendered to the soldiers because his people were starving. There were no more buffalo to hunt. It was a pattern that would be repeated for most of the other Indian tribes as well. In the end, it was the slaughter of the buffalo that defeated the Plains Indians.

In 1860, there may have been as many as fifteen million buffalo. By the 1880s, the huge buffalo herds were gone. Railroad workers and trophy hunters killed many buffalo. Finally, United States soldiers searched out the remaining herds. By killing the buffalo, the soldiers quickly defeated the Plains Indians. The Indians could not go on fighting without a source of food. The Plains Indians were forced to move onto the reservations.

Fighters for Indian Rights

Not all Americans agreed with the government's treatment of the Indians. In 1881, **Helen Hunt Jackson** published *A Century of Dishonor.* Her book told a story of many broken treaties. She described how whites had robbed the Indians of their land. In another book, *Ramona,* Jackson wrote of the mistreatment of the California mission Indians.

Another person who fought hard for Indian rights was **Sarah Winnemucca**, daughter of a Paiute (PIE-ute) chief. An excellent student, she spoke both Spanish and English, as well as three Indian languages. Winnemucca traveled across the country giving lectures. She talked to many people about the injustices her people had suffered. She wrote a book about the Paiute tribe, published in 1883.

Think: Without thinking about the effects, American businesses killed vast numbers of bison, also called buffalo. Buffalo robes became popular in the East. A team of sharpshooters could destroy a thousand buffalo in a day. Usually, they took only the skins. In addition, people killed these magnificent animals for sport. Countless buffalo were left to waste. This painting shows passengers and the crew of a railroad shooting at a herd of buffalo to clear the tracks. Railroad companies accused the animals of damaging the tracks. Respond: What were the long-term effects of these actions?

The writings of Helen Hunt Jackson (1830–1885) resulted in a government appointment. However, her report had less impact than her books.

Sarah Winnemucca went beyond writing and lecturing on behalf of Indians. She risked her life once to keep her tribe out of battle.

HISTORY MAKERS

Chief Joseph

The Brokenhearted Peacemaker

It began to snow. The air was wintry, and the wind was harsh. The children wept with cold and hunger. The older people thought about their faraway home, about friends and relatives killed in the fighting. Then a colonel in the United States Army called for another talk. He promised to treat the Indians well and to send them home if they stopped fighting.

Chief Joseph rode out to meet the army. As he surrendered his rifle, he said, `` . . . I am tired of fighting. Our chiefs are killed . . . . The little children are freezing to death . . . . My heart is sick and sad. From where the sun now stands I will fight no more forever.''

Chief Joseph was a leader of the Wallowa (wah-LAH-wuh) band of Nez Perce (nez PURS) Indians. The Nez Perce lived in the Pacific Northwest. They were hunters and gatherers who raised and traded horses. They loved their land.

Chief Joseph worked hard to keep peace between the Wallowa Nez Perce and pioneers coming to the Pacific Northwest. He hoped the Wallowa would keep their land without fighting the white settlers. Some Nez Perce bands made treaties with the United States, gave up their land, and moved to a reservation in Idaho. The Wallowa band, however, refused to sign any treaties that gave away their land.

In 1876, the United States ordered the Wallowa Nez Perce to the reservation. If the Indians refused, the army would make them move. Chief Joseph counseled his band not to fight the army.

However, fighting broke out between Indians and settlers before the Wallowa reached the reservation. Joseph and other chiefs decided the band should try to escape to Canada. The army followed and attacked them. Finally, Chief Joseph surrendered to save his band.

The Army did not keep its word. It sent the Wallowa band to reservations in Kansas and Oklahoma, not to Idaho. Chief Joseph had tried to protect his people from harsh treatment by the army and government. But his people lost what was dear to them. Chief Joseph died on a reservation in 1904. The reservation doctor said he died of a broken heart.

Think: This 1891 photograph shows the Sioux's Pine Ridge Reservation in South Dakota. The Indians fought long and hard to keep their old lifestyle. But finally they were forced to live on reservations. Respond: Why were the Indians forced to live a lifestyle they neither wanted nor understood?

The Dawes Act

Many people were shocked to hear of so much Indian suffering. In response, Congress passed the **Dawes Act** in 1887. The law divided reservation land among Indian families. Each family received 160 acres. The government hoped that the Indians would become farmers. In this way, they would learn American ways.

The new law failed to help the Indians. Few Indians were farmers. They were hunters and traders. The land set aside for Indian reservations was poor. It was land that white settlers could not farm. Many Indians sold their land for very little money. They did not understand the idea of private ownership of land. In Indian culture, the land belonged to everyone. For many years, large pieces of Indian land slipped into the hands of outsiders.

Under the Dawes Act, Indians on reservations lived lives of poverty.

Today there are 269 reservations in the United States. Living conditions on most reservations are still poor. Many Indians have left the reservations to work in cities. However, no matter where they live, Indians are proud of their heritage.

Section Review

1. What was the reservation system? How well did it work?
2. Who won the Battle of the Little Big Horn? Why?
3. Who were Helen Hunt Jackson and Sarah Winnemucca?
4. What was the Dawes Act?

CHAPTER SUMMARY

The discovery of gold and silver brought miners to many unsettled parts of the West. Boom towns sprang up around the mines and often disappeared when the mines gave out. After the gold was gone, many miners stayed to settle large areas of the West.

Irish and Chinese immigrants built the first transcontinental railroad. The railroad brought thousands of settlers to the Great Plains. The railroad also made it possible for cattle ranchers to create a cattle kingdom on the plains. However, after farmers and sheepherders moved onto the plains, the cattle kingdom came to an end.

The Homestead Act of 1862 brought many thousands of farmers to the Great Plains. Farmers overcame many challenges and hardships to turn the Great Plains into a productive farming region.

Before the settlement of the last frontier, the Plains Indians and the buffalo roamed the grasslands of the West. As settlers moved into Indian territory, the Indians were crowded off their land. The Plains Indians fought many battles with the United States Army. When the buffalo disappeared, the Indians were finally defeated and moved to reservations.

Some people did not like the way the Indians had been treated. They fought for Indian rights. The Dawes Act, passed in 1887, failed to help the Indians.

Key Words

Write a sentence to explain the meaning of each of these terms.

boom town	*dry farming*
vigilantes	*reservation*
Comstock Lode	*Homestead Act*

Major Events

Choose the answer that best completes the statement.

1. In 1859, Pikes Peak became famous because

   a) it was a landmark for pioneers.
   b) miners discovered gold there.
   c) sheep ranchers claimed it.

2. Between 1863 and 1869, work crews built the

   a) transcontinental railroad.
   b) cattle kingdom.
   c) Indian reservations.

3. Cattle ranchers controlled the Great Plains

   a) during the Civil War.
   b) during the Gold Rush.
   c) from 1865 through 1885.

4. The Battle of the Little Big Horn was the

   a) last time the army fought the Indians.
   b) last major Indian victory over the army.
   c) only time the Indians ever retreated.

5. The Dawes Act of 1887 tried to get Indians to become

   a) ranchers.
   b) miners.
   c) farmers.

Review

Important Facts

Answer each question with at least one complete sentence.

1. Which immigrant groups helped to build the transcontinental railroad?

2. What part did miners play in the settlement of the last frontier?

3. Name two things that Congress did to open up the West.

4. Why did mining companies replace the miners by the 1870s?

5. What did the cowboy on the Great Plains learn from the Mexican vaquero?

6. What was the Chisholm Trail? Why was it important?

7. What brought about the end of the cattle kingdom?

8. How did farmers practice "dry farming" on the Great Plains?

9. How did new kinds of farm machines help the farmers on the Great Plains?

10. What caused fighting to break out between the settlers and the Plains Indians?

11. After the Battle of the Little Big Horn, how did the army treat the Indians on the plains?

12. How did the slaughter of the buffalo bring about the final defeat of the Plains Indians?

13. What did Helen Hunt Jackson describe in *A Century of Dishonor?*

Skill Review

Study the bar graph, then answer the following questions.

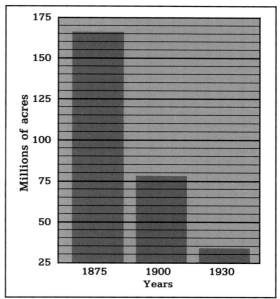

Reservation Lands

1. How much land did the U.S. government reserve for Indians in 1875? In 1900? In 1930?

2. Did the amount of land increase or decrease?

3. What reasons might explain this change in the amount of reservation lands?

Critical Thinking

Write a paragraph to answer each question.

1. What part did the railroad play in the settlement of the last frontier?

2. Compare General Custer's reasons for fighting the Battle of the Little Big Horn with those of Chiefs Sitting Bull and Crazy Horse.

18

Becoming an Industrial Nation

Years 1856–1900

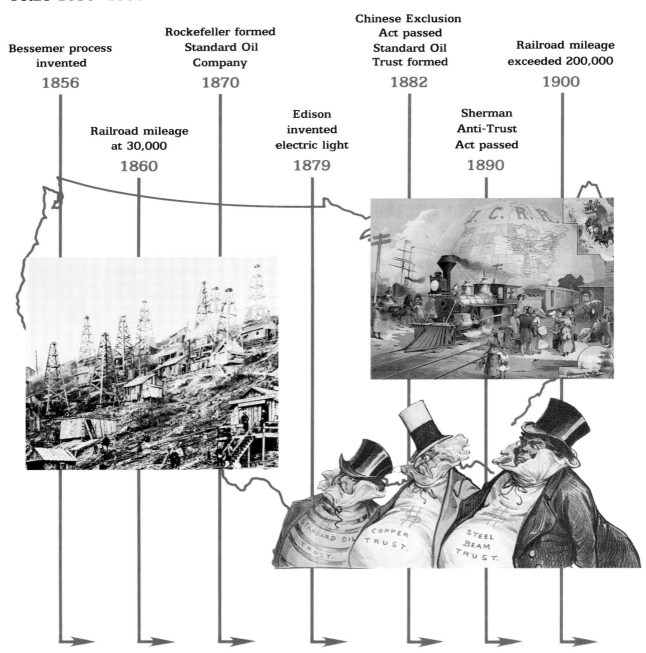

Bessemer process
invented
1856

Railroad mileage
at 30,000
1860

Rockefeller formed
Standard Oil
Company
1870

Edison
invented
electric light
1879

Chinese Exclusion
Act passed
Standard Oil
Trust formed
1882

Sherman
Anti-Trust
Act passed
1890

Railroad mileage
exceeded 200,000
1900

1. The Growth of American Industries

Learn these important terms:

consumer goods
heavy industry
corporation
capital
raw materials
Bessemer process
stockholders

Remember the main idea:

The rapid growth of industry after 1865 turned the United States into a great industrial nation.

Look for answers to these questions:

1. Why did heavy industry grow rapidly after 1865?
2. Why were natural resources and a large population important to industrial growth?
3. How did new inventions help the growth of industry?

During the years between 1865 and 1900, the United States changed very rapidly. It changed from a farming nation into an industrial nation. New factories sprang up in cities and towns. Miles and miles of new railroads were built.

None of these changes would have been possible without the American people. The population was growing quickly. Between 1865 and 1900, twelve million immigrants poured into America from Europe and Asia. And these new Americans were ambitious. They wanted to work hard and become successful.

As you will see as you read this chapter, success in America was not achieved by all. A few Americans built huge industries and became quite wealthy. Other Americans earned very little money. And some Americans invented things that made life and the development of industry easier for all.

Before 1865, most American factories made *consumer goods* (kuhn-SOO-muhr). These products were sold directly to the public, the consumers. Clothing and shoe factories, meat-packing plants, and flour mills produced consumer goods. Most of these factories were small and hired only a few workers.

In the late 1850s, *heavy industry* began to grow. Heavy industries produced machinery, iron rails, and engines. These products were bought by other factories or other industries. The Civil War helped both the consumer goods and the heavy industries to grow. Factories

Think: In this advertisement for the Illinois Central, the railroad is shown as being superior to all other forms of transportation. Respond: Tell how this ad makes each of the other forms look inferior.

became larger and employed many more workers. After the war, American industry continued to expand rapidly.

Railroads Help Industry to Grow

In 1869, the transcontinental railroad connected the eastern and western parts of the country. By the 1890s, four more railroads crossed the United States. Many smaller railroads were built in the Midwest and in the East. A network of railroads connected all parts of the nation. In 1860, there were about 30,000 miles of railroad in America. By 1900, railroad mileage had increased to over 200,000.

The growth of the railroad system made other industries grow. The railroad companies needed iron and steel for rails and engines, and they needed coal for fuel. Industries that provided railroad equipment and coal expanded as the demand for their products increased.

Railroads also served industry by providing a cheap means of shipping raw materials and finished goods over long distances. Railroads made it possible to haul coal and iron ore to the steel mills and power plants. Meat from Chicago, corn from Iowa, and flour from Minnesota could be shipped from the Midwest to eastern cities. Manufactured goods from the eastern cities could be shipped to people in the West. Railroads were soon carrying most of the passengers and freight in the nation.

Resources and Population

The growth of industry in America also depended on a supply of *raw materials*. Raw materials are needed to make manufactured, or finished, goods. These raw materials include coal, iron ore, oil, and lumber. America had large supplies of raw materials. Gold and silver and other important metals were mined in the West. There were large coal deposits in West Virginia, Pennsylvania, and Kentucky.

Very high quality iron ore came from Minnesota and Michigan. Oil, which was first used for lighting and greasing machinery, was discovered in Pennsylvania and Ohio. Lumber came from the nation's forests.

America was rich in another resource. The United States had a large and growing population. There seemed to be an endless supply of workers for the factories. Many of these workers came to the United States as immigrants. Others were Americans who had moved from farms to cities to find jobs. Still others were southern blacks moving north in search of better opportunities.

Capital and Corporations

Business leaders needed large amounts of money, or *capital*, to build factories, dig coal from the ground, or mine iron ore. The federal government encouraged the growth of industries by keeping taxes low. And Americans and wealthy people from other countries provided the capital that was needed.

Usually, these individuals invested their money in a new type of business organization called a *corporation*. A corporation is a company that is owned by many people called *stockholders*. They buy stocks, or shares, of the company. After 1865, many corporations were formed. These large businesses were important to the growth of American industry.

Inventors

Railroads, raw materials, workers, and capital made America's industries grow. But America also had another important resource—many talented inventors and scientists. These clever individuals invented labor-saving machines and new products. They improved methods of manufacturing. The inventions of the late 1800s changed American industries and American life.

One of the most important early inventions was a new method for making steel. A tougher metal than iron, steel had been too costly to make. In 1856, two inventors, working separately, developed a new and cheaper way to make it. They

Think: This picture from an advertisement for the H.C. Frick Coke Company shows coal being mined. The coal is heated in airtight ovens, where it becomes coke. Respond: What things in the ad tell you the public was not interested in the environment at the time?

Think: In a Bessemer converter, air added to molten iron could make steel cheaply. Respond: How did this cheaper steel affect the building industry in the mid-1800s?

Think: In 1879, boys and girls worked as telephone operators. Respond: What changes did the telephone bring to America?

were William Kelly, an American, and Henry Bessemer, an Englishman. Their method, known as the **Bessemer process,** gave rise to an important new industry.

Another invention, the refrigerator car, helped the meat-packing industry grow. Before the refrigerator car was invented, only live animals were shipped to market. A railroad car that could be kept cold inside allowed ranchers to slaughter their cattle near home and ship only the meat to market.

Many other inventions changed American industry and American life. The telegraph, invented by Samuel F. B. Morse, allowed Americans to send messages quickly over long distances. Alexander Graham Bell invented the telephone. In 1879, Thomas A. Edison, America's most famous inventor, invented the electric light. Edison also perfected the electric dynamo. It produced electric power to run trolley cars, subway trains, and elevators. In addition, Cyrus W. Field oversaw the placement of a cable at the bottom of the Atlantic Ocean. This cable allowed telegraph signals to be sent between the United States and Europe.

Section Review

1. How did railroads help the growth of industry?
2. What raw materials were necessary for America's industries?
3. Why was a growing population important to industrial growth?
4. Name three inventions of the 1800s that changed American life and industry.

PRODUCTS OF AGRICULTURE AND INDUSTRY IN 1890

This thematic map gives you information about the products of agriculture and industry in the United States in 1890. Remember that railroads criss-crossed the country. Food could be refrigerated, and the process of forming steel from iron ore had been developed. Look at the symbol key on the map. How many products are shown on the map? Find on the map itself at least one location of each product.

The products on the map can be classified into three groups: raw materials, consumer products, and heavy products that are sold to other industries. Make three lists classifying each product on the map under one of these groups.

Using your text and the map, answer the following questions.

1. Which consumer industries in 1890 were located in the South, including Texas and Oklahoma? Which raw materials were found in the South? Which heavy industry existed in the South?

2. Which two cities west of Chicago were industrial centers?

3. Which cities were centers of printing and publishing?

4. In which cities would you expect to find the newly-invented refrigerated railway cars being loaded? In which cities would you expect to find them being unloaded?

5. Which raw materials are used in each heavy industry shown?

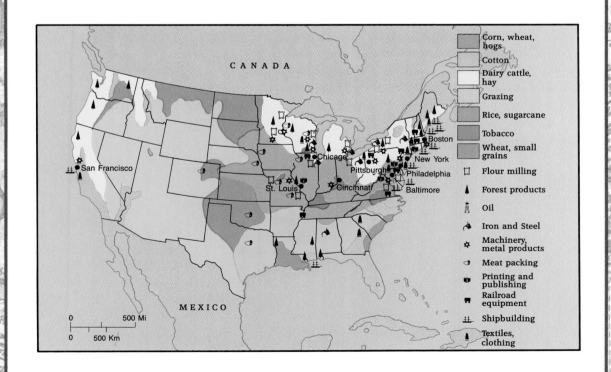

2. Captains of Industry

Learn these important terms:

integrated industry
Sherman Anti-Trust Act
trust
regulate
monopoly
rebates

Remember the main idea:

Between 1865 and 1900, powerful businesspeople gained control of entire industries. The government passed laws to control big business.

Look for answers to these questions:

1. How did Andrew Carnegie gain control of the steel industry?
2. How did monopolies develop during the late 1800s?
3. What did the government do to control the trusts?

The story of Andrew Carnegie shows the opportunities that America offered in the 1800s. Andrew Carnegie came with his parents from Scotland when he was a young boy. At the age of thirteen, he got his first job as a bobbin boy in a textile mill, changing spools of yarn. He earned $1.20 a week, working six days a week from sunrise to sunset. Later he became a telegraph operator for the Pennsylvania Railroad. Because Carnegie worked hard and learned as much as he could, he was promoted to better-paying jobs. Carnegie worked for the railroad for twelve years. He studied business and carefully invested his money.

Andrew Carnegie left the Pennsylvania Railroad in 1865. First, he invested his money in small factories that made iron products. After becoming successful in the iron business, Carnegie paid a visit to England. There he observed the Bessemer process of steelmaking. Carnegie knew that low-priced steel would quickly replace iron. He was determined to seize the opportunity to start a new industry.

After he returned to America, Carnegie built a steel plant in Pittsburgh, Pennsylvania. His factory produced steel rails. Steel rails lasted twenty times longer than iron rails. It was only a short time before the orders from the railroad companies came pouring in.

Gaining Control of the Steel Industry

Carnegie's company was much larger than any other steel company. Because of its great size, Carnegie's company could make steel more cheaply than other companies. By lowering his prices, Carnegie could outsell the other companies. Because he shipped so much steel by rail, he received ***rebates***, or refunds, from the railroad companies. Many steel companies were forced out of business because they just could not compete with Carnegie's company.

Carnegie put the profits he made back into his business. He began to buy companies that were connected with steel manufacturing. He bought the iron and coal mines that supplied the raw materials he needed. Carnegie then gained control of the plants that made iron and steel from the iron ore. He began to take over some of the shipping lines that transported his steel. He bought warehouses in which to store the steel. Then he gained control of the factories that manufactured products such as rails and machines.

By doing these things, Carnegie created an ***integrated industry***. An integrated industry controls everything from the raw materials to the finished product. By owning an integrated industry, Carnegie was able to keep his costs down. In this way, he could produce more steel at a lower price than his competitors. As the leader of the steel industry, Carnegie turned the United States into the largest steel producer in the world.

Creating a Monopoly

When a company becomes so strong that it controls an entire industry, it is known as a *monopoly* (muh-NOP-uh-lee). The Carnegie Steel Company was very powerful, but it did not have a monopoly on the steel industry. J. P. Morgan, a very powerful banker, supported several other big steel companies. He prevented Carnegie from controlling the entire industry.

Finally, in 1901, J. P. Morgan bought Carnegie's steel company for $225 million. The large steel companies were joined together to form the United States Steel Corporation. It was the first billion dollar business in America. When Carnegie left the steel business, he was a very rich man. He spent the rest of his life giving his money away to worthy causes.

John D. Rockefeller and the Oil Industry

John D. Rockefeller was twenty-three years old when he first invested in an oil refinery. In 1870, seven years later,

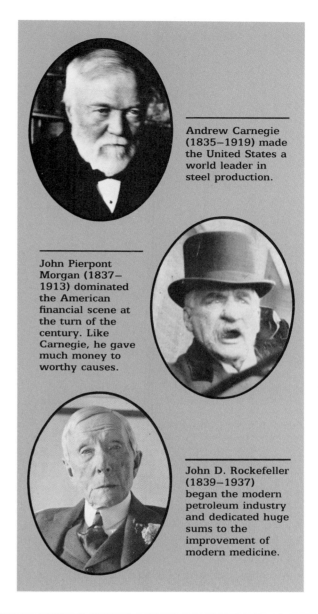

Andrew Carnegie (1835–1919) made the United States a world leader in steel production.

John Pierpont Morgan (1837–1913) dominated the American financial scene at the turn of the century. Like Carnegie, he gave much money to worthy causes.

John D. Rockefeller (1839–1937) began the modern petroleum industry and dedicated huge sums to the improvement of modern medicine.

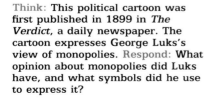

Think: This political cartoon was first published in 1899 in *The Verdict*, a daily newspaper. The cartoon expresses George Luks's view of monopolies. Respond: What opinion about monopolies did Luks have, and what symbols did he use to express it?

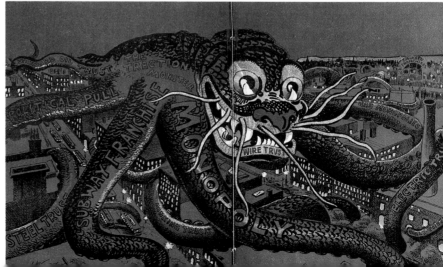

Think: **It has been said that, without oil, the enormous industrial growth of the 1800s would not have been possible.** Respond: **Give reasons why you agree or disagree with this.**

Rockefeller formed the Standard Oil Company. He set out to gain control of the entire oil industry through the refining business. He bought the pipelines that carried his oil from the wells to the refineries. He bought the storage tanks that sold the oil. Rockefeller also saved money by building his own warehouses.

By doing all these things, Rockefeller could sell oil for less than the other oil companies. The less fortunate oil companies had to sell out to Rockefeller or go out of business. By 1879, the Standard Oil Company controlled almost 90 percent of the country's oil refining business. In 1882, the Standard Oil Company became the Standard Oil Trust. A *trust* is a company that controls many smaller companies in the same industry.

Public Reaction to the Trusts

Other industries followed Rockefeller's lead and developed trusts of their own. Giant corporations ran the sugar, leather, and tobacco industries. Huge flour mills bought out the smaller local millers.

Some large corporations used their power to improve their products. Also, large corporations could sell their products to the consumer for less than the smaller companies could. These were some of the ways big business benefited the public. However, the trusts also acted in unfair ways. They often raised the prices of their products. They could charge whatever prices they wanted because they did not have to compete with other companies. Many people began to feel that the trusts were too big. They worried that big business was destroying competition, which had always been important in America.

SKILLS FOCUS: Summarizing

"Hull House." Social worker Jane Addams founds a community center for the poor of Chicago in 1889. In her struggle against poverty, she becomes a supporter of laws protecting children. Later she becomes the first woman to win the Nobel Peace Prize.

The paragraph above is a short *summary* of the movie *Hull House.* The summary does not contain all the details of the movie. It does not, for example, tell about Jane Addams's concern about the large number of children in prison. Nor does it tell how her efforts resulted in special courts for underage persons who broke laws. However, the summary does tell the most important parts. It tells who the movie is about and something about the most important events. If you had seen the movie and were telling a friend about it, you might give such a summary.

Each chapter in this book is followed by a summary that tells only the main points of the chapter. You can use the summary to help you remember the details of a chapter.

Look at the summary on page 400. The second paragraph summarizes Section 2, "Captains of Industry." Notice that the summary does not tell about Andrew Carnegie as a boy, for example. Details about how Carnegie started at a low-paying job are interesting, but they do not belong in the summary because they are not the most important facts.

One way to summarize the two paragraphs under the heading "Public Reaction to the Trusts" is to turn the heading into a question: What was the public reaction to the trusts? The answer to this question could be this summary sentence: People began to worry that the trusts were too big and were destroying competition in American business. Notice that the summary does not include information about the ways in which big business used its power. Such information is made up of details which are not necessary to the summary.

Summarize in one sentence the paragraphs under the heading "The Government Tries to Control the Trusts."

1. First, turn the heading into a question.
2. Now write a sentence that answers the question and summarizes the paragraph.

Summarize what you learned in this section about three leaders of industry.

3. First, reread the section and the three portrait captions. Form a question which relates to the three men.
4. Now write a sentence that answers the question and summarizes what you learned about the men.
5. Why are these three men discussed in the same section?

The Government Tries To Control the Trusts

At first, the state governments tried to *regulate*, or control, the trusts. However, they were not successful. Then, in 1890, Congress passed the **Sherman Anti-Trust Act**. This law made it illegal to organize a trust to gain a monopoly in any industry. However, many companies got around the new law by forming new types of monopolies. The new types of monopolies were not covered by the Sherman Anti-Trust Act.

Although monopolies continued to grow, many small businesses also got started during this time. In 1880, there were about 759,000 small business companies in the United States. By 1900, the number of small businesses grew to over one million. Some of these small companies manufactured products. Others sold products or provided services.

Section Review

1. What personal qualities helped Andrew Carnegie become a leader of industry?
2. What is an integrated industry?
3. What is a trust?
4. Why did many people feel that the trusts were too powerful?
5. Why did the Sherman Anti-Trust Act fail to stop the growth of monopolies?

Think: *Bosses of the Senate* by Joseph Keppler shows an opinion shared by many Americans in 1889.
Respond: What does the cartoon say about trusts and the Senate?

3. Problems of American Workers

Learn these important terms:

skilled workers
Chinese Exclusion Act
unskilled workers
old immigrants
new immigrants

Remember the main idea:

Between 1865 and 1900, unskilled workers received low wages and worked long hours. Many immigrants and blacks were among these unskilled workers.

Look for answers to these questions:

1. Why was life hard for unskilled workers during the late 1800s?
2. From where did most immigrants come during the late 1800s?
3. What problems did black workers face?

Think: **These unskilled Russian immigrants worked in the steel industry.** Respond: **What were the benefits and problems brought on by immigrants' willingness to work for low pay?**

America's workers in the late 1800s were divided into two groups. They were the *skilled workers* and the *unskilled workers*. Skilled workers had learned trades and were printers, carpenters, bricklayers, and machinists. They usually earned high wages and enjoyed good working conditions.

Unskilled workers had no skills and little education. Many unskilled workers ran machines in factories. These jobs required little skill and offered low wages. Unskilled workers were paid by the hour.

They earned about four hundred dollars a year and usually worked ten hours a day for six days a week. When business was slow, the unskilled workers were the first to be fired.

Immigrant Workers

Many of the unskilled workers were immigrants. Since many Chinese immigrants helped build the railroads, they settled in large communities in the West. Here, they continued to be labeled unskilled workers. Other immigrants came from all over Europe and settled throughout America. Many German and Scandinavian farmers settled on land in the Midwest. Immigrants with skills and those too poor to buy a farm stayed in the cities of the Northeast. They took whatever jobs they could get and were willing to work for low wages. These immigrants dug ditches, paved roads, and mined coal. They worked in meat-packing plants and textile mills. They did the heavy work in the iron and steel mills.

Think: **Women worked in industries, such as this candy factory where chocolate eggs were made.**
Respond: **How did hiring women affect the wages paid by factories in the late 1800s?**

In the 1880s, more immigrants began to arrive from the countries of southern and eastern Europe. Many of these immigrants were from Italy, Russia, Hungary, and Poland. These groups of people became known as the *new immigrants*.

Immigrants from the countries in northern and western Europe were called the *old immigrants*. The new immigrants accepted the very low wages factory owners offered them. The older group of workers from northern and western Europe disliked the newcomers. They felt that the new immigrants took away their jobs and made wages lower.

Other Americans became concerned about the steady stream of new immigration into the country. These Americans believed that the new immigrants tended to stay together longer and to adopt American ways more slowly than the earlier immigrants. They became concerned that their American way of life and their values were being threatened by too many foreigners.

Groups of Americans who wanted to restrict immigration started to organize. Their first target was the Chinese. In the 1870s, riots against the Chinese broke out in Los Angeles, San Francisco, and Denver. And in 1882, Congress passed the *Chinese Exclusion Act*. This law stopped Chinese immigration. After 1882, Congress continued to pass laws that restricted immigration.

Think: **Political cartoons illustrated the fears that many Americans had about the number of immigrants entering the country.** Respond: **Were these fears justified? Explain.**

THE GREAT FEAR OF THE PERIOD
THAT UNCLE SAM MAY BE SWALLOWED BY FOREIGNERS.

HISTORY MAKERS

Booker T. Washington
Believer in Education and Hard Work

"Sugar for your coffee, Mr. Washington? Or cream?"

"I'll have both, thank you."

"Now, tell me, Mr. Washington, did you really live in a log cabin in America?

"I was born and raised in a one-room log cabin, Ma'am. We had only a table and two benches, so our beds were bundles of rags on the dirt floor. There was no stove, so my mother, the plantation cook, cooked over the fireplace. My stepfather didn't belong to our owner. During the war he managed to escape from his master. After emancipation we joined my stepfather. I worked in a salt mine and a coal mine, and then, your Majesty, I was finally able to go to school."

The hostess smiled at her guest across the tea table. Like many people, Victoria, Queen of England, was interested in Booker T. Washington's life. Born a slave in the late 1850s, he had become a leading educator and spokesperson for black Americans.

Booker T. Washington was one of thousands of freed slaves who wanted an education. When he was sixteen, Booker T. Washington went to Hampton Institute, a school for poor black students. He paid his way by working as the school janitor. After he graduated, Washington taught. In 1881, he opened the Tuskeegee Institute in Tuskeegee, Alabama. There, black students were educated and trained as teachers, skilled tradespeople, and farmers. Washington thought black Americans could win acceptance in white America by becoming independent workers. Blacks who worked hard and helped themselves financially would slowly be integrated into American society, he felt.

Other black leaders disagreed, thinking it important to establish black political and civil rights as the law of the land. The National Association for the Advancement of Colored People (NAACP) was created to fight segregation and discrimination through the courts.

Booker T. Washington believed that education and hard work would integrate society. He devoted his life to creating educational and job opportunities for black Americans.

Think: Blacks were given the worst jobs and the lowest pay. They tried to stop this discrimination. Respond: How were the people in the photograph trying to improve their lives?

Black Workers

Black Americans in the North formed another large group of unskilled workers. After the Civil War, many black families headed for the cities of the North. Here they were often paid even lower wages than the unskilled workers from Europe. These two groups competed against each other for jobs in the factories.

Black workers also had problems finding jobs in the South. After the Civil War, jobs there were scarce. White skilled workers began to take over many of the jobs that skilled black workers, such as tailors, carpenters, cooks, and barbers, had held before the war. Often, black workers were forced to take the unskilled jobs. Black workers did get jobs in southern factories. But they were given the worst jobs, and they were paid the lowest wages.

In the late 1800s, many black Americans were losing both their jobs and their rights as citizens. A black leader, Booker T. Washington, tried to help blacks become workers and businesspeople. Washington believed that the best way for black citizens to advance was to get an education. He also thought they should train themselves to be good workers. He believed that when blacks had accomplished these things, they would be treated as equals. At his school, Tuskegee Institute, Washington taught job skills to black students.

Many white and black Americans agreed with Washington's ideas. However, there were also many black Americans who disagreed. They felt that blacks needed to fight for equal rights. They believed that when black citizens finally had the same rights as white citizens, their lives would improve.

Section Review

1. Why did factory owners find so many workers willing to work for low wages?
2. Why did the old immigrants dislike the new immigrants?
3. What advice did Booker T. Washington give blacks?

CHAPTER SUMMARY

After 1865, America experienced tremendous industrial growth. The building of railroads created a demand for rails and engines. The railroad also provided an inexpensive way to ship raw materials and finished products. Natural resources, a large population, capital, and many talented inventors contributed to America's rapid growth.

In the late 1800s, Andrew Carnegie built up the steel industry until it was the largest of any in the world. During the same period, John D. Rockefeller gained control of the oil industry. In 1882, Rockefeller's company was turned into a trust. As other corporations became trusts, competition among businesses was harmed. In 1890, Congress tried to control the power of the trusts by passing the Sherman Anti-Trust Act. However, business leaders simply created new types of monopolies.

America's growing industries were fueled by a seemingly endless stream of unskilled workers. Many of these workers were immigrants from Europe and Asia. In the late 1800s, immigrants came from countries in eastern and southern Europe. Many black workers competed with immigrants for jobs in the northern factories. Blacks in the South were forced to take the worst jobs at the lowest pay.

Key Words

Write a sentence to explain the meaning of each of these terms.

raw materials corporation
heavy industry skilled workers
regulate monopoly

Major Events

Choose the answer that best completes the statement.

1. After 1865, the growth of railroads

    a) decreased in the East.
    b) helped other industries grow.
    c) provided fewer consumer goods.

2. American investors contributed to industrial growth by

    a) providing capital.
    b) selling their railroads.
    c) encouraging immigration.

3. Carnegie built up the steel industry by

    a) supporting small companies.
    b) raising steel prices.
    c) owning an integrated industry.

4. The Sherman Anti-Trust Act of 1890

    a) forced all of the major trusts out of business.
    b) was not successful in controlling the trusts.
    c) ended Rockefeller's control of the oil industry.

5. Between 1865 and 1900, unskilled workers

    a) held good factory jobs.
    b) received low wages.
    c) worked mostly in the South.

Review

Important Facts

Answer each question with at least one complete sentence.

1. Why is a large supply of raw materials important to industrial growth?

2. Why was a large and growing population important to the growth of American industry?

3. How did the development of the Bessemer process change the steel industry?

4. What invention helped the meat-packing industry to grow?

5. What is an integrated industry?

6. Why was Rockefeller able to sell oil for less than his competitors?

7. Name two ways in which trusts acted unfairly.

8. Why did many Americans worry about the trusts?

9. Into what two groups were American workers divided in the late 1800s?

10. What was the difference between immigration before and after the 1880s? Why did the old immigrants dislike the new immigrants?

11. Why were immigrants important to the growth of industry in the late 1800s?

12. What were the special problems of black workers during the late 1800s?

13. How did Booker T. Washington think blacks could improve their lives in America?

Skill Review

Study this map, then answer the following questions.

1. Which industries in 1890 were principally located near Lake Erie? Of what advantage was location near the Great Lakes?

2. Which industry was developed by John D. Rockefeller?

3. Write one sentence to summarize the types of industry in Ohio in 1890.

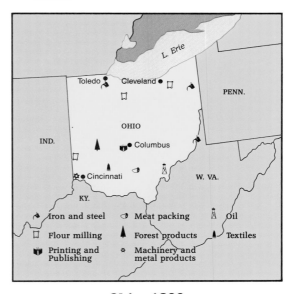

Ohio, 1890

Critical Thinking

Write a paragraph to answer each question.

1. Why were powerful business leaders able to gain control of entire industries during the late 1800s?

2. Explain the role of inventors during the late 1800s.

CHAPTER
19
American Life 1860–1900

Years 1860–1900

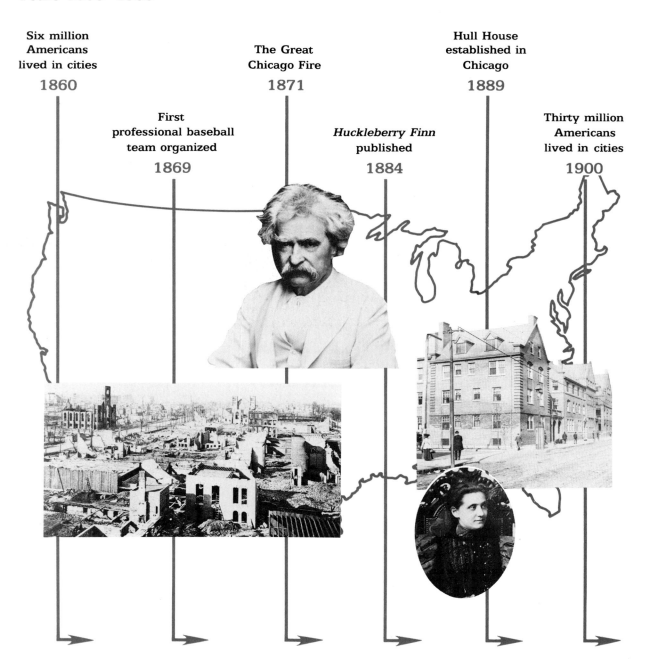

Six million
Americans
lived in cities
1860

First
professional baseball
team organized
1869

The Great
Chicago Fire
1871

Huckleberry Finn
published
1884

Hull House
established in
Chicago
1889

Thirty million
Americans
lived in cities
1900

1. The Growth of American Cities

Learn these important terms:

tenements

sanitation

Remember the main idea:

Immigrants and Americans who moved away from the farms helped cities grow rapidly after 1865. Overcrowding in the cities caused many problems.

Look for answers to these questions:

1. What made cities grow rapidly in the late 1800s?
2. Where did most of America's immigrants settle?
3. How did a fast-growing population cause problems in the cities of America?

The population of the United States more than doubled between 1860 and 1900. In the late 1890s, a new wave of immigrants arrived on the shores of America. They came to the teeming cities of America to escape poverty, tyranny, and starvation. They came with families or alone, almost always without skills or money. For most immigrants, life in America was a difficult adjustment.

In this chapter, you will see the problems immigrant families faced as they began new lives in America. You will read about some attempts to solve these problems. You will also read about other Americans. You will read about the farmers who moved to the cities. You will read about the more fortunate Americans as well.

As you read about the people, you will learn about many changes in their lives. Cities changed as people's needs changed. This affected the American way of life. More leisure time also affected Americans. You will read about some new interests Americans discovered.

In the years after 1865, American cities started to grow very rapidly. In 1860, there were approximately six million people living in city areas. That number was 16 percent of all Americans. By 1900, almost 40 percent of the population, more than thirty million people, lived in cities. Cities did not grow at the same rate all over the United States. The fastest growing cities were in the Northeast and the Middle West. New York, Chicago, and Philadelphia were the largest cities, with populations in the millions.

Many cities grew because they were transportation centers. Chicago grew rapidly because it was a major railroad center, and Philadelphia and St. Louis were

Think: This 1880 cartoon by Joseph Keppler shows immigrants arriving in the United States. Notice the signs posted for the immigrants to read. When the cartoon was created, immigrants were still accepted. Soon after, things changed. Respond: Why did things change?

located on rivers. Many of the fast-growing cities were also located near the natural resources needed by industry. The rich iron ore deposits near Lake Superior in Michigan made Detroit a center of iron and steel manufacturing. Iron and coal from the Appalachian Mountains fed the steelmaking plants of Pittsburgh.

As the new industrial cities grew, more workers were needed for the factories and mills. Large industries drew many job-seekers to the cities. One group of people looking for work in the cities came from the farms of America. It had become difficult to make a living in farming. By the late 1800s, farm machines had replaced many farm workers. Prices for farm products were low, and many farmers were so deeply in debt that they lost their farms. Tens of thousands of farm families sadly left their homes and moved to the cities. There they hoped to earn more money and find an easier life.

Immigrants Make the Cities Grow

By the end of the 1800s, foreigners were a large part of the population of any big city. They were the twelve million immigrants who arrived in the United States between 1865 and 1900. Most immigrants settled in the cities of the Northeast or Middle West. The largest group settled in New York City. Many immigrants arrived at New York Harbor without money, and they could not afford to travel farther.

The immigrants in the big cities chose to settle with people like themselves. City life was a colorful mixture of nationalities. Each neighborhood—Polish, Greek, Italian, Jewish—could be easily identified by the clothing, the shop signs, and the language spoken. The neighborhood streets became the center for almost all daytime activity. Men, women, and children escaped to the streets from their tiny, dark rented rooms. There they could find pushcarts filled with vegetables, fruits, pots and pans, and clothing. Families also used the neighborhood streets to visit with friends. And the streets served as playgrounds for the children.

Life in immigrant neighborhoods was very hard. Immigrants earned such low wages that everyone in the family had to work. Children worked long hours alongside their parents at the factories. Some children worked all day in windowless rooms surrounded by dangerous machinery. Other children worked at home with their parents, sewing clothing or making small items to sell.

Problems of the Cities

As cities grew and neighborhoods became more crowded, many new problems developed. Poor people were forced to live in slums, or run-down city neighborhoods. The slums spread rapidly as *tenements* (TEN-uh-ments) were built to house the continual flood of newcomers. Tenements were usually wooden buildings five or six stories high that were divided into tiny rooms. They were poorly built and poorly maintained. Large families often crowded together in one-room apartments. Many tenement apartments had no windows, heat, or water.

Some tenement residents collected water in buckets from public pumps in the streets. Wells under the streets held the water supply. However, this water was often polluted by garbage from the

Think: **Living and working conditions for many immigrants were not as easy as they had hoped. This photograph shows a family making a living by sewing clothes. Notice how small their home is and that all members of the family worked.** Respond: **How does the life of this family differ from family life today?**

MAP WORKSHOP DRAWING INFERENCES

GROWTH OF CITIES

When you compare the two maps below, you will find direct information about the growth of cities in the United States between 1860 and 1900. You can then go on to use the text to help you to infer additional information. (When you draw an inference, you come to a conclusion based upon all the general information you were able to gather.) For example, you could infer why some cities grew up where they did, or why some cities grew larger than others.

Look at the map of cities in 1860.

1. How many cities had a population of over one million people in 1860? How many had over 100,000?

2. How many of these large cities were in the South? How many were in the West?

Now look at the map of cities in 1900.

3. How many cities had over one million people? Which cities are they? Which of these cities grew the most in forty years?

4. How many cities were over 100,000? How many of these were in the South or in the West? Which cities are they?

5. Which states had the most cities over 100,000? What western state had two cities over 100,000?

Answer the following questions by drawing inferences.

6. Cities in what area were most affected by immigration from Europe? Why?

7. Which cities show the importance of water transportation?

8. What effect did the development of transcontinental railroads have on the growth of cities?

9. Cities often spring up around centers of industry. What can you infer about the development of industry in the South after the Civil War?

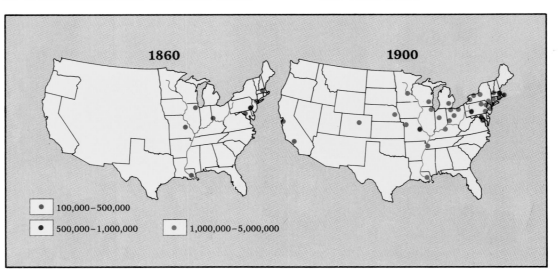

1860   1900

- 100,000–500,000
- 500,000–1,000,000   • 1,000,000–5,000,000

Think: **Wagon venders sold vegetables, fruits, and other goods on Hester Street in New York's Lower East Side. The living conditions shown here were typical of many immigrant sections of large cities. Notice the number of people cramped together.** Respond: **What problems were caused by this overcrowding?**

streets. This lack of *sanitation*, or clean and healthful conditions, caused outbreaks of disease. In the overcrowded living conditions of the tenements, illnesses spread rapidly. Many people died from smallpox and other serious diseases.

Crime also spread rapidly through the tenement neighborhoods. Most immigrant families struggled daily to get by, even with every member of the family working. Many adults and children were often unemployed, and sometimes homeless as well. With so many people living so closely together, stealing was a constant problem for many slum dwellers.

Section Review

1. Which three American cities had the largest populations during the late 1800s?

2. Why did people leave the farms to move to the cities?

3. What were the living conditions of immigrants in the cities?

4. Why did serious diseases kill many people in the cities of the late 1800s?

2. Cities Try To Solve Their Problems

Learn these important terms:

political machine
settlement house
party boss
Hull House

Remember the main idea:

During the late 1800s, overcrowding caused many problems in the cities. Both city governments and private groups tried to solve some of these problems.

Look for answers to these questions:

1. What did city governments do to improve services in the city?
2. Who ran the city governments?
3. How did private groups help poor people in the cities?

On the night of October 8, 1871, a fire broke out in Chicago. A high wind spread the blaze from building to building until the central part of the city was a mass of flames. This fire destroyed seventeen thousand buildings. It killed more than three hundred people and left ninety thousand homeless.

The Great Chicago Fire, as it came to be known, called attention to the problems of city life. Tens of thousands of immigrants and farmers were flooding the city. They could only afford to live in seriously overcrowded areas. This overcrowding led to the danger of not only fire, but also of disease and crime.

Improvements in City Services

Solving these problems presented a major challenge to city governments. After the Chicago fire, cities realized that they could no longer depend on volunteers to fight fires. They organized fire departments staffed with trained firefighters. They also bought fire engines and other firefighting equipment.

Poor sanitation was a more difficult problem to solve. City-owned waterworks replaced neighborhood wells, but city water was still not always fit to drink.

Think: The Great Chicago Fire raged for 24 hours, wiping out the city's central business district. The fire destroyed over 17,000 buildings, leaving 90,000 homeless and consuming 200 million dollars worth of property. **Respond:** What positive changes did this destructive fire help bring about?

Courtesy of Chicago Historical Society.

Dusty, dirty streets were also a health hazard. In the late 1800s, many cities started to pave their streets with bricks or asphalt. These materials were easier to clean than dirt or cobblestone streets.

Crime ranked as a major city problem. To make city streets safer during the 1880s, many cities replaced gas and oil lamps with electric streetlights. Electric lighting proved to be one of the most important improvements in city life.

New Transportation Helps Cities To Grow

Electricity also helped to solve the problem of transportation within cities that were rapidly expanding. Horse-drawn streetcars were too expensive, too slow, and too small to carry large numbers of passengers. By 1895, most large cities had replaced these horse-drawn cars with electric streetcars.

Soon subways and elevated railway lines, called els, were built in some cities. These new ways to travel were fast and cheap, and they allowed cities to expand more rapidly. People could travel to work from areas farther away from the central city. For this reason, wealthy and middle-class people began moving out to newer, more expensive neighborhoods. The city was no longer the only place to live. However, for some people there was no choice. Newly arrived immigrants and the poorest people became more concentrated in the older central districts.

Dishonesty in Big City Government

New fire departments, waterworks, paved streets, electric streetlights, and transportation systems did improve city life somewhat. However, they did not do enough. For one thing, the problems of growing cities were overwhelming. For another, many big city governments were run by corrupt, or dishonest, officials.

Think: **The electric streetcar above moves through the uncrowded Chicago suburb of Oak Park.** Respond: **How did the electric streetcar influence where people could live and work?**

Courtesy of Chicago Historical Society.

Think: **The elevated railroad ran on tracks above the ground, easing the crowded conditions on the roads below.** Respond: **Why were new forms of transportation needed in cities?**

These officials stayed in office by making deals with a *political machine*. A political machine was a smoothly run political organization. It was usually headed by a *party boss*, or strong party leader. The machine controlled city government by guaranteeing votes for officials. In return for these votes, the city officials awarded contracts for city services to friends or members of the machine.

For example, a city might be planning to pave its streets or put in new sewer lines. Businesspeople interested in these contracts might pay the local machine thousands of dollars. The machine would then use its influence with city officials to get the city contract for them. And at election time, the machine also had influence. It would get certain officials elected with thousands of immigrant votes.

To get these votes, the political machine provided many needed services for immigrants. The machine fed people when they were hungry. It found them jobs when they were out of work. It provided coal for people who could not afford it. Sometimes the machine even paid for boys from immigrant families to go to college or trade schools.

To show their appreciation, immigrants voted for candidates supported by the machine. Although it was a bad influence on city government, the machine did help poor immigrant families meet their daily needs. With its money, votes, and power, the political machine was almost impossible to beat in elections in most cities.

Helping the Poor

Even the machines could not take care of everyone's needs. One of the most difficult problems in the cities was easing the suffering of the poor and homeless. Immigrant families had to survive on the low wages they earned in the factories. When times were bad and factories laid off workers, many families suffered. During these times, thousands of people were left homeless.

City governments did not have enough employees or money to solve these problems. The political machines helped only those people who supported them. Private groups, such as churches and charities, did provide some help for the poor.

The most effective attempt to help the poor was the *settlement house*. A settlement house provided services for immigrants in their own neighborhoods. It offered English classes, taught job skills, and provided medical care. One of its

Courtesy of Chicago Historical Society.

Think: In 1889, Jane Addams (left) founded Hull House (photographed here in 1910) to help Chicago's immigrants. The settlement house was like a neighborhood center, or club. **Respond:** Are such programs still necessary? Explain.

most important services was caring for the young children of working parents.

The most famous settlement house was started by Jane Addams. She was a college graduate who wanted to make life better for those who were less fortunate. In 1889, Jane Addams set up a settlement house in Chicago. This house, called *Hull House*, served as a model for other settlement houses throughout the country.

Section Review

1. Why were fires a problem in the cities during the late 1800s?
2. How did cities spread out?
3. How did political machines stay in power?
4. What kinds of services did settlement houses offer the poor?

HISTORY MAKERS

Thomas Alva Edison

The Wizard of Menlo Park

''How long has it been? I have lost track of time.''

''It's been twenty-four hours, Mr. Edison, and it's still burning as brightly as we had hoped!''

''Wonderful! We'll keep checking on it. So far this model has burned longer than any other. I think it's because I used a different material for the wick inside the glass bulb. Horsehair didn't work. Neither did straw, cornsilk, wood splinters, or human hair. Those materials burned up or were broken. This cotton thread which I coated with lampblack and then baked seems to be holding up. If it works, we'll have found a light that's cleaner, safer, steadier, and even brighter than gas!''

Edison's electrically powered bulb burned for forty hours. Once again the inventor had made a breakthrough in technology.

Thomas Alva Edison had always been curious about how things work. When he was a child, his mother explained that hens hatched their eggs by sitting on them. Later in the day she found her son sitting on goose eggs, trying his best to make them hatch! Edison's teachers thought he was a nuisance because he always asked questions and only learned about what interested him. His mother took him out of school. She taught him herself at home. Perhaps she hoped the chance to learn by experimenting was what he needed.

When he was a teenager, Thomas Edison worked on the Grand Trunk Railroad selling candy, peanuts, and sandwiches. He also sold newspapers. He bought an old printing press and wrote and published a weekly paper. He even learned to use a railway telegraph. However, Edison lost his job when the conductor found flames sweeping through a small laboratory Edison had set up in a baggage car.

The electric light bulb, the motion picture, the storage battery, and electric motors are just a few of the hundreds of Edison's discoveries. His own favorite invention was the phonograph. Thomas Edison's discoveries changed the way people live all over the world.

3. Changes in American Life and Thought

Learn these important terms:

spectator sports
melodrama
realistic novel
ragtime

Remember the main idea:

City life brought about changes in the way Americans lived. Sports, theater, reading, and music became very popular.

Look for answers to these questions:

1. How did having more free time change the lives of city people?
2. What new music had its beginning in New Orleans?
3. What kind of books did Americans like in the late 1800s?

Industrial growth meant miserable living conditions for many unskilled workers in the cities. But industrial growth also brought a comfortable way of life to others. Many people from the new and growing middle class lived in good apartments or small homes. Some wealthy people built huge houses in the cities and filled them with imported furniture and art.

City life also brought many important changes to American families. City families were smaller than farm families, and they spent less time together. Fathers spent many hours away from home working at their jobs. Children attended school most of the day.

City life and new inventions changed the way women lived. Women in the city had more free time than farm wives. Sewing machines, washing machines, and carpet sweepers saved time and made work easier for women. Grocery markets offered fruits and vegetables. Ice boxes made it possible to store foods easily. And the iceman delivered ice to houses all year long.

Sports Become Popular

As city dwellers gained more leisure time, they looked for new ways to spend it. Bicycling became the favorite pastime for many people in the city. Americans also enjoyed *spectator sports*, or games to be watched. Baseball became America's most popular spectator sport and "national pastime." The first professional baseball team, the Red Stockings, was organized in Cincinnati in 1869. By 1903, there were enough baseball teams to play the first World Series.

Football was also a popular spectator sport in the 1800s. At that time, football was a rough sport with only a few simple rules. Crowds loved the game, and football soon became the favorite sport of college students.

Americans Enjoy Music and Theater

Two new inventions helped bring music into many homes. They were the phonograph, invented by Thomas Edison, and the player piano, a piano which played by itself.

Both inventions brought a new and exciting form of music to the American public. Black Americans in New Orleans had invented a new style of music called *ragtime*. Scott Joplin was one of the most famous of the ragtime musicians. His "Maple Leaf Rag" and other tunes soon made ragtime the most popular type of music among young Americans.

Think: Hoping to attract followers, the Chicago and All-American baseball teams played each other throughout the world. They are shown here in Rome. Respond: Why is this game so popular in America?

Americans also enjoyed going to the theater. **Melodramas** were their favorite plays. Melodramas always had a hero who was poor but honest, a heroine who was beautiful and brave, and a villain who was mean and rich. The audiences often cheered the hero and heroine and hissed at the villain.

Books and Education

New American writers appeared in the late 1800s. Some of them wrote *realistic novels*, or books that describe people, places, and events as they are in real life. Stephen Crane wrote one of the best-known of these novels, *The Red Badge of Courage*. Crane's book gave a true-to-life account of a soldier's feelings during the Civil War.

Think: This Stroberg print served as a theater advertisement in the early 1900s. Respond: What story is being told in the ad, and who might go to see this play?

SKILLS FOCUS: Identifying Fact and Opinion

The two sentences below are about the same topic, but one is a fact and the other is an opinion.

A. The Chautauqua Movement was founded at Chautauqua Lake, New York, in 1874.

B. The Chautauqua Movement was the best thing that happened in the last part of the 19th century.

The first sentence is a *fact*. It gives information that can be proven true by checking an encyclopedia or other reference.

The second sentence is an *opinion*. It states what someone thought about the Chautauqua Movement, but what it says cannot be proven true or false or checked in any reference. Another person might have had quite a different opinion of Chautauquas or thought that some other event at that time was much more important. Opinion statements often contain words such as *best, most important, I think, all, everyone,* or *never*.

It is a fact that the Chautauqua Movement did bring education and entertainment to thousands of people across America. In the late 1800s, there were no radios or televisions. People living in small towns eagerly hoped a traveling Chautauqua would set up its tents in their town. When a Chautauqua did come, a town became festive. For a week, all activities in the town centered around the grassy spot under the canvas. Writers, explorers, politi-cians, musicians, and storytellers took the stage to tell people of a world outside their community.

The following sentences are some that people may have heard while sitting at a traveling Chautauqua. Write the sentences. In front of each sentence, put an *F* if you think the sentence is a fact. Put an *O* if you think it is an opinion. Underline words in a sentence that make you think it is an opinion.

___ **1** Now I'll sing the most beautiful song that has ever been written about love.

___ **2** I think that once a man has lied to you, you can never trust him again.

___ **3** Everyone can afford to attend a Chautauqua.

___ **4** Iowa farmers are selling a bushel of corn today for thirty-six cents.

___ **5** The Spanish-American War ended in victory for the United States.

___ **6** The search for money causes all the trouble in the world.

The traveling Chautauquas disappeared when towns grew, transportation improved, and communication became faster. Think of a kind of entertainment that is popular today, such as movies, videos, or professional sports. Write one fact sentence and one opinion sentence about it.

Samuel L. Clemens (1835-1910), better known as Mark Twain, was a hard-working writer. Clarity, humor, and the use of truly American language mark his work.

One of the most important jobs of the schools was to prepare immigrants and their children for American life. Schools offered special classes for immigrants. These schools taught immigrants to speak English. They also taught immigrants the rights and duties of American citizens. By attending public school, children of immigrants learned about American life more quickly than their parents had.

Think: Below, an immigrant fills out the necessary forms for citizenship. Respond: Why did so many people want to become American citizens?

America's most famous realistic writer was Mark Twain, whose real name was Samuel L. Clemens. In 1884, Twain wrote his best-known book, *The Adventures of Huckleberry Finn*. This novel describes the friendship between a young boy and a runaway slave.

Americans read more in the late 1800s because they had more free time and were better educated. Between 1865 and 1900, an increasing number of American children attended public schools. Many states passed laws that required all children to attend elementary schools for a certain number of years.

Section Review

1. How did new inventions help change women's lives? Name two of these inventions.
2. What became America's most popular sport in the late 1800s?
3. What popular style of music was invented by black musicians in the late 1800s?
4. What is a realistic novel?

CHAPTER SUMMARY

From 1865 to 1900, American cities grew rapidly. Immigrants and Americans from rural areas moved into cities in great numbers. The rapid growth of cities led to many problems. Overcrowding in city tenements caused fire hazards, outbreaks of disease, and other types of suffering.

City governments improved the water supply, streets, and fire protection in some cities. New forms of transportation allowed cities to expand. However, in the late 1800s, cities were run by political machines that served their own needs more than those of the people. With the support of the immigrants, political machines controlled elections.

City governments offered few services for the poor. To meet the need, private organizations opened settlement houses in city neighborhoods. They offered language classes, child care, and other services to the poor.

City life in the late 1800s also brought new opportunities for leisure activities, such as sports, music, and the theater, for wealthy and middle-class Americans. Labor-saving inventions made life much easier for women. Education improved as states set requirements for school attendance. Schools also began offering special classes for immigrants so they could enter American life more easily.

Key Words

Write a sentence to explain the meaning of each of these terms.

tenements   sanitation
political machine   settlement house
spectator sports   realistic novel

Major Events

Choose the answer that best completes the statement.

1. Most problems in the cities of the late 1800s were caused by

   a) unemployment.
   b) overcrowding.
   c) lack of transportation.

2. Political machines won elections by

   a) controlling the candidates of both parties.
   b) threatening voters.
   c) winning the support of the immigrants.

3. Many city governments in the late 1800s improved

   a) city streets.
   b) services for the poor.
   c) city housing.

4. Immigrants in the cities of the late 1800s were helped by

   a) government services.
   b) labor-saving devices.
   c) private organizations.

5. People read more in the late 1800s mainly because

   a) there were more books.
   b) they were better educated.
   c) there were fewer jobs.

Review

Important Facts

Answer each question with at least one complete sentence.

1. Why did many people leave the farms for the cities during the late 1800s?

2. Why did some cities grow faster than others?

3. What was it like to live in a tenement?

4. Why were outbreaks of disease a constant danger in the slums?

5. What lessons did city governments learn from the Great Chicago Fire of 1871?

6. Name two problems of the cities in the late 1800s that city governments tried to solve. How did they try to solve them?

7. How did new forms of transportation change the cities?

8. Why did businesspeople support political machines in the cities?

9. What services did the political machines offer the immigrants?

10. What was the purpose of Chicago's Hull House?

11. Name two inventions of the late 1800s that changed the way people lived.

12. Name two leisure activities enjoyed by wealthy and middle-class city dwellers during the late 1800s.

13. Why did Americans read more in the late 1800s? Who was America's most famous realistic writer?

Skill Review

Compare these maps. Then tell whether each statement is a fact or an opinion and why.

1. None of these cities had fewer than 50,000 people in 1900.

2. Syracuse always had uglier slums than Rochester.

3. With so many immigrants, New York had to have the most corrupt political machine.

4. Albany grew the slowest.

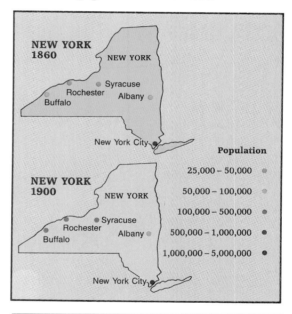

Critical Thinking

Write a paragraph to answer each question.

1. Why did the rapid growth of cities during the late 1800s cause so many problems?

2. Compare the lives of the wealthy and the poor in the cities of the late 1800s.

20
Tackling the Nation's Problems

Years 1865–1900

Knights of
Labor founded

1869

Garfield assassinated
Chester Arthur
became president

1881

Grover Cleveland
elected president

1884

Benjamin Harrison
elected president
(by electoral
votes)

1888

James A. Garfield
elected president

1880

Pendleton
Civil Service
Act passed

1883

American
Federation of
Labor founded

1886

William McKinley
elected president

1896

1. The American Government, 1865–1900

Learn these important terms:

Pendleton Civil Service Act
popular votes
civil service
merit system

Remember the main idea:

From 1865 to 1900, the federal government supported business interests. During that time, it had to make decisions about filling government jobs and about tariffs.

Look for answers to these questions:

1. What was unusual about the presidential election of 1876?
2. Why was the federal government forced to reform the civil service system?
3. Why was the tariff an important issue between Democrats and Republicans?

From 1865 to 1900, the federal government was challenged by many problems caused by the growth of cities and industries. Government decisions during this period were strongly influenced by the interests of big business. Business leaders in the Northeast controlled most of the manufacturing, trading, and banking in the nation. Their power was felt at all levels of government.

Farmers and workers began to resent the power of big business. They felt much of this power was gained at their expense. The profits of big business also seemed out of line. The people actually producing the goods had to struggle to get by.

As workers realized that government would not help them solve their problems, they formed labor unions. Farmers also joined together to solve their problems. As you read this chapter, you will find out how government viewed the relationship between workers and employers. You will also see some reforms made in government. The demands of the people of America made a difference.

After the Civil War, businesspeople in the Northeast controlled most of the manufacturing, trading, and banking in the nation. They also had the most power in the nation's two main political parties, the Democrats and the Republicans. As a result, the government often favored businesspeople over workers and farmers between 1865 and 1900.

Postwar Politics

General Ulysses S. Grant, elected president in 1868, was not a strong leader.

James A. Garfield
(1831-1881) was
assassinated only four
months after becoming
president. Many feel this
successful Congressman
would have made a fine
president.

Chester A. Arthur
(1829-1886), "The
Gentleman Boss," became
president when Garfield
was killed. He was a
steady and conscientious,
if unexciting, leader.

Historians praise Grover
Cleveland (1837-1908) for
his accomplishments and
his character. He worked
to lower the tariff, keep
the gold standard, and
return honesty to
government.

Many people he appointed to government jobs were poor choices. Some of these people, including several members of the Cabinet, made dishonest business deals. However, President Grant was not involved in this and was elected for a second term in 1872.

As Grant's second term came to a close, the Republican Party chose Rutherford B. Hayes as candidate for the 1876 presidential election. Hayes was then governor of Ohio. Samuel J. Tilden, the governor of New York, was the Democratic candidate. The majority of the *popular votes*, or votes of the people, were for Tilden. However, the presidential election is decided by the electoral votes, not by the popular votes.

When the electoral votes were counted, twenty of them were undecided. All but one of these electoral votes were from three Southern states. Congress set up a special commission of fifteen men to decide who would be president. The Southerners allowed their votes to go to Hayes. In exchange, the Republicans agreed to remove the last federal troops from the South. As a result of this deal, the commission voted to give the undecided electoral votes to Hayes. That's how he became president.

Civil Service Reform

In 1880, James A. Garfield, a Republican senator from Ohio, was elected president in a very close election. After a few months in office, Garfield was killed by a job seeker who was refused a government job. Garfield's death made Americans more concerned about how people received *civil service*, or government jobs.

Starting with Andrew Jackson, presidents had awarded government jobs on the spoils system, a reward to party supporters. Government jobs were considered the spoils, or prizes, that went to members of the winning party.

After President Garfield's death, many citizens demanded reform of the civil service system. Finally, Congress passed the *Pendleton Civil Service Act* in 1883. This law set up a Civil Service Commission to test people for government jobs. Only those with the highest grades were given jobs. This new plan for choosing government workers was known as the *merit system*. The new law applied only to 14 percent of all government jobs. However, the president was given power to extend the law to cover additional positions. President Chester Arthur, who had been Garfield's vice president, fully supported the new law.

President Arthur was followed in office by Grover Cleveland, elected in 1884. Cleveland became the first Democrat to be elected president since 1856. He also supported the merit system and promised to fill all appointments with qualified people. Cleveland extended the law to cover more workers. Other presidents continued to add more government positions. Today, over half of the federal employees are part of the civil service system.

The Problem of the Tariff

Between 1860 and 1900, the Democratic Party and the Republican Party agreed on many issues. However, Democrats and Republicans did not agree on the tariff. A tariff is a tax on goods imported from other nations. Most Republicans favored a high tariff. They claimed that a high tariff was necessary to protect American industry. Leaders of industry wanted high tariffs as well, so they could limit foreign competition.

Most Democrats wanted the tariff to be lowered because they believed that American industries no longer needed protection. They also felt that the high tariff hurt the farmers in the South and West. Farmers needed many goods that were manufactured in other countries.

Think: President Cleveland uproots the spoils system in this political cartoon by Joseph Keppler. Respond: Why, despite the difficulties, was Cleveland determined to do away with the spoils system?

Think: In December 1887, the Treasury had over $100 million in surplus. Taxes and tariffs had brought in more money than was needed. Grover Cleveland wanted to reduce the amount collected by lowering the tariffs. Joseph Keppler's cartoon depicts the issue in Congress. Respond: What symbols does Keppler use to tell his point of view?

In the years following the Civil War, Congress continued to raise the tariff. When Cleveland became president, he and his Democratic supporters tried to lower the tariff. However, the Republicans in Congress refused to pass a lower tariff law. When President Cleveland ran for a second term, he won a majority of the popular votes. But the Republican candidate, Benjamin Harrison, won more electoral votes and became president.

Under President Harrison, the Republicans in Congress passed a still higher tariff. Many Americans began to believe that higher tariffs only meant higher prices for the consumer. In the election of 1892, Grover Cleveland ran again for the Democrats. During his campaign, he promised to lower the new tariff rates. Cleveland defeated Harrison and again became president. He is the only president to have served terms that were not back-to-back.

Benjamin Harrison (1833-1901) was called "Little Ben" because of his size (5 feet, 6 inches), but he was a big war hero and an active president.

Section Review

1. How did Samuel J. Tilden lose the election of 1876?

2. What was the spoils system? What problem did it cause?

3. What was the Pendleton Civil Service Act?

4. Why did Republicans and businesspeople favor high tariffs?

HISTORY MAKERS

Mother Jones

Heroine of the American Labor Movement

"Are we ready, ladies? Have you got a bucket of water? A dishpan? A mop or a broom?"

The crowd of women nodded. Some waved their brooms and mops in the air.

"Good! Then we're ready. Now here's the plan. We march together to the mine. Make as much noise as you can! Bang your pails, yell and holler! When we get there, let those scabs know we're ready to mop up the floor with them. Let 'em know we're going to sweep 'em clean out of the mine! They're taking our men's jobs away, and we won't stand for it. We can't win this strike if the mines keep operating, so we must keep the strikebreakers out of the mines! Now ladies, let's march and go get 'em!"

The angry group of women moved toward the mine, banging on dishpans and buckets, waving their mops and brooms, screaming and yelling at the top of their lungs. The noise and fury of the miner's wives frightened the strikebreakers mining coal and the mules pulling the coal wagons. Once again, Mother Jones was leading a successful labor demonstration.

Mary Harris Jones was a teacher and a seamstress. Her husband and four children died in a yellow fever epidemic. She lost her sewing business four years later in the great Chicago fire. But she didn't give up on life. She became interested in the American Federation of Labor and spent the rest of her life as a labor organizer.

Mother Jones, as she was called, was most concerned about child labor. In 1903, she led a group of striking children from Pennsylvania textile mills to President Theodore Roosevelt's home in New York. Roosevelt would not see the children, but many people along the route became sympathetic to the hard lives of working children.

In 1930, Mother Jones celebrated her one hundredth birthday. She made a rousing speech that day. Mother Jones fought long and hard to abolish child labor and to create better conditions for American workers. She is one of the heroines of the American labor movement.

2. American Workers Organize Labor Unions

Learn these important terms:

Knights of Labor
Haymarket Riot
American Federation of Labor
injunction
strike
yellow dog contract
lockout
strike breakers
picket line

Remember the main idea:

In the years between 1865 and 1900, American workers formed labor unions. They fought to improve their working conditions.

Look for answers to these questions:

1. Why did workers organize labor unions in the late 1800s?
2. How did public opinion hurt the Knights of Labor?
3. What made the American Federation of Labor a new type of labor union?

In the 1800s, business owners believed that they had the right to decide what to pay workers. It was also their right, they believed, to decide what kind of working conditions to provide. They felt that if workers were dissatisfied with wages or working conditions, they could find jobs somewhere else. Government in the 1800s sided with business interests.

Political leaders believed that industry was good for the country, so they ignored the issue.

Without help from the government, workers had to find other ways to solve their problems. Most workers were concerned about long working days and low wages. Factory workers earned ten dollars or less for working sixty hours or more a week. For a family to survive, the mother, father, and older children had to work. Sometimes, jobs were hard to find. Machines had begun to take over the jobs of skilled workers. And when businesses hit slow periods, workers were laid off.

Working conditions presented another problem for workers. Employers were not required by law to provide safe working conditions. During the late 1800s, thousands of workers were killed or injured on the job.

Americans were also concerned about child labor. In 1900, over one million children under the age of sixteen worked full time. They worked in coal mines, textile mills, and in small rooms called sweat shops. Women and children worked the same hours as men, but they were paid much less.

The Knights of Labor

Workers tried to solve these problems by forming labor unions. One of the earliest national labor organizations was the ***Knights of Labor***. It was organized in 1869 in Philadelphia. The Knights of Labor was the first union to include workers from all over the nation. It accepted skilled and unskilled workers, women, and blacks. Many local unions did not allow women or blacks to join. The Knights of Labor wanted an eight-hour working day and an end to child labor.

In 1879, Terence V. Powderly became the leader of the Knights of Labor. Under his leadership, the union grew very rapidly. By 1886, the Knights of Labor had

Think: **Members of the Women's Trade Union League demonstrated in the Murray Hill section of Manhattan in the early 1900s. Read the signs held by the women. Think about what they were hoping to accomplish.**
Respond: **Tell why you agree or disagree with them.**

700,000 members. Powderly was against using the union's most powerful weapon, the *strike*. When union members go on strike, they stop work until the employer meets the union's demands.

Oddly enough, it was a successful strike that brought the Knights of Labor many new members. In 1885, the Knights of Labor called a strike against the Missouri Pacific Railroad. The owner, Jay Gould, had ordered a cut in pay for workers. Union leaders stopped work all along the Missouri Pacific line. Gould was forced to meet union demands and cancel the wage cuts.

One year later, this victory was erased by the *Haymarket Riot* of 1886. A union in Chicago went out on strike against the McCormick Harvester Company. During the strike, police attacked the strikers and shot several workers.

Think: **Notice that a worker is trying to reach the food at the top of a pole smeared with *monopoly grease*.** Respond: **What point of view does this political cartoon reveal?**

The next day, many workers held a peaceful meeting in Haymarket Square to protest the shootings. Many of these workers were members of the Knights of Labor. The police tried to break up the meeting. Someone threw a bomb that killed several police officers. Although the bomb thrower was never found, union leaders were arrested and put in prison. Some were hanged. Many people blamed the labor unions for causing trouble. As a result, the Knights of Labor lost most of its members.

The American Federation of Labor

In the same year as the Haymarket Riot, a new labor organization was formed. Samuel Gompers called his union the *American Federation of Labor*, or AFL. The AFL joined together several separate unions of skilled workers. Each union represented a particular group of workers, such as machinists, carpenters, or cigar makers. Unlike the Knights of Labor, the AFL did not include unskilled workers.

Samuel Gompers believed that his union should work for specific goals. He believed that the first goals should be shorter hours, more pay, and better working conditions. Gompers also believed that the strike was the union's most powerful weapon. He planned to use strikes, if necessary, to get what the workers needed. Gompers also favored bargaining with employers. He announced that he would cooperate with any company willing to talk with his union. Under Gompers's leadership, the American Federation of Labor grew from 150,000 members in 1886 to over 500,000 by 1900.

Think: **These representatives of the craft unions became the executive council of the American Federation of Labor.** Respond: **What were the first goals of the AFL?**

Think: **Look closely at the details in this political cartoon by J. A. Wales. Notice the words on the various objects. The little man in the center is Terence Powderly, who, like Samuel Gompers, believed strongly in arbitration.** Respond: **What do the two large men represent?**

Unions and Employers Struggle

For the most part, employers refused to bargain with unions. They had weapons, too. Some employers refused to hire union members. They made workers sign an agreement, a *yellow dog contract*, saying they would not join unions.

When workers went on strike, owners hired *strike breakers*, people not in the union, to take their jobs. Another method was the *lockout*. Workers were locked out of the workplace until they agreed to company terms.

During this period, the federal and state governments backed the factory owners. When workers went on strike, they walked outside the factory in a

Think: **Federal troops protected trains during a strike. Strikers and owners accused each other of damaging the cars.** Respond: **Why would either side damage the trains?**

picket line. Picket lines kept people from going in. Employers could stop strikers from picketing by asking a judge to issue an *injunction* (in-JUNK-shun), or court order, against the strike. If the workers disobeyed, state and national troops enforced the injunction.

These methods often led to violence. More than one thousand strikes a year occurred from 1880 to 1890. Many people were wounded or killed as troops and strikers clashed.

Section Review

1. What were the main goals of the labor unions in the late 1800s?
2. What was the Haymarket Riot? What effect did it have on the Knights of Labor?
3. How were the Knights of Labor and the American Federation of Labor different?
4. Name two ways employers fought against union members during the late 1800s.

If you had read a newspaper in May 1886, you might have seen these headlines:

Labor Movement Gains Membership

Growing Labor Movement Aims To Destroy Strength of America

The first headline is from a news story about labor. A news story states facts about an event without giving an opinion. It contains information that answers who, what, where, when, why, and how questions. You can tell from the headline that the news story presented only facts.

The second headline is from an editorial. The article that followed it gave the writer's opinion about the increasing strength of labor. It tried to convince readers to accept that opinion. You can tell from the headline that the editorial writer was against labor.

Read the following news story and editorial about the Haymarket Riot, then answer the questions.

Eleven Die in Haymarket Square

Chicago, May 5, 1886
A bomb thrown by an unknown person disrupted last night's rally in support of labor in Haymarket Square. Seven police officers were killed and sixty-seven were wounded by the blast. Police responded with gunfire, resulting in the deaths of at least two people. Thirty-six anarchists have been held as suspects in the bombing incident.

Big Business and Police Murder Workers

Chicago, May 5, 1886
Last night's peaceful rally in Haymarket Square was shattered by ranks of marching police officers led by their vicious anti-labor captain, Black Jack Bonfield. A bomb, probably thrown by McCormick spies in order to make the rally look violent, landed near the police ranks. The police, eager for a chance to attack the rallying workers, opened fire. Many innocent people were injured, and at least two were killed. Obviously, the police are on the side of big business. Together these two groups are working to destroy the labor movement. Every clear-thinking citizen can see the plot, and we must join together to stop it!

1 What essential facts does the news story contain?
Who?   When?
What?   Why?
Where?   How?

2 What opinion does the news story present?

3 What opinion does the editorial writer have about who caused the Haymarket Square tragedy?

4 What feelings does the editorial writer want the reader to have about the McCormick company, the strikers, and the police?

3. American Farmers Protest

Learn these important terms:

cheap money hard money
Grange   cooperatives
alliance   Populist Party

Remember the main idea:

Between 1865 and 1900, farmers found it hard to make a living. They formed farmers' groups and a third political party to help them solve their problems.

Look for answers to these questions:

1. Whom did farmers blame for their troubles. Why?
2. How did farmers try to solve their problems?
3. What changes did the Populist Party want to make?

By 1890, American farmers were producing twice as much corn, wheat, and cotton as they had in 1860. In part this growth happened because hundreds of millions of acres in the west were turned into farms. But farm production could not have grown so much without the introduction of new farm machines.

Farm Problems

Both land and machines cost money, however. Bankers were eager to lend money. Moreover, farmers were eager to borrow it when farm prices were high.

Lending was common and prices were high during and after the Civil War. But by the mid-1870s, the country was in a depression. People had less money to spend on food, even though farmers were turning out large crops. The combination of this large supply and a lower demand meant farmers received very low prices for their products.

Many farmers could not make enough money to pay their costs or repay their loans. As a result, hundreds of thousands of small farmers had to give up their land and become tenant farmers.

Farmers blamed most of their troubles on the people who helped bring farm products to market. These people included the railroad companies, millers, owners of grain warehouses, stockyard owners, and bankers. Farmers felt that these people, especially the railroads, charged too much. This made it almost impossible to make a living in farming.

To solve their problems, farmers looked to the government. They wanted the government to regulate the railroads and thereby lower their costs. They also wanted the government to issue more **cheap money**, or money not backed by gold. There was less currency in circulation than there had been, farmers pointed out. As a result, people had less money to spend. Farmers reasoned that with more currency in circulation, people could afford to pay higher prices. Then farmers would be able to make a profit.

The federal government had first issued cheap money during the Civil War. It printed paper greenbacks that were not backed by gold. After the war, Congress decided to replace greenbacks with **hard money**, or money backed by gold. Bankers wanted to be paid back in hard money. Since gold was scarce and more valuable than greenbacks, it became difficult for farmers to pay off their debts.

Think: Farmers formed cooperatives, often combining their resources to buy large farm machines. Most of the equipment they bought together was that which would be used only for a short period each year. Respond: **Why was forming cooperatives a good plan for many farmers?**

Farmers Organize

Farmers, like factory workers, began to join together to solve their problems. The *Grange* was the first farmers' group to be organized. In the 1870s, the Grange worked to get many states to pass laws to regulate the railroads. The Grange also formed farmers' *cooperatives*. Cooperatives were groups of farmers who joined together to sell their farm products and to buy farm machines.

In the 1880s, the Grange was replaced by two new farmers' *alliances*, or groups. These were called the Northern Alliance and the Southern Alliance. In the South

there was also a separate Colored Farmers' Alliance for black farmers. These organizations formed cooperatives and worked for laws to help the farmers.

However, farmers were disappointed by many of the political candidates they had helped to elect. Members of the alliances met together and decided to start a third political party. They called it the *Populist Party*, or the People's Party. Most

Think: **In 1867, the Grange was formed to ease the isolation of rural Americans. It intended to educate the farmers so they could avoid being taken advantage of. The Grange reached its peak in 1876.** Respond: **The Grange issued this poster in the 1870s. How does the poster idealize the farmer?**

GIFT THE GRANGERS.

"I PAY FOR ALL."

FAITH
HOPE

CHARITY
FIDELITY

THE ELECTION OF 1896

Election maps tell you for which president and for which political party each state casts its electoral vote. Election maps also tell you how many electoral votes each state has. Circle graphs like those below can show you percentages of a whole.

Study the map and the map key.

1. Colors are symbols on this map. What do the two colors stand for?

2. How many states voted Republican in the election?

3. How many states voted Democratic?

4. What do the numbers on the states stand for?

Now look at the circle graphs.

5. Which presidential candidate won the election of 1896? How do you know?

6. What percentage of the electoral vote went to the Republicans? What percentage went to the Democrats?

7. What percentage of the popular vote went to the Republicans? What percentage went to the Democrats?

Use your text to help you answer these questions.

8. In what areas of the country were the Populist/Democratic Party and Bryant strongest? Why were Populist ideas strongest in these areas?

9. In what areas of the nation were the Republicans strongest? Why?

10. Are the percentages of electoral votes the same as the popular votes? Why can they be different?

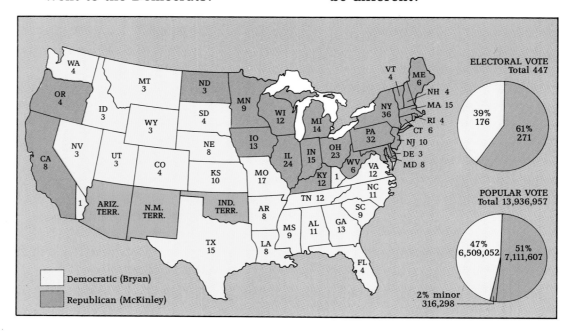

ELECTORAL VOTE
Total 447

39% 176

61% 271

POPULAR VOTE
Total 13,936,957

47% 6,509,052

51% 7,111,607

2% minor 316,298

Democratic (Bryan)

Republican (McKinley)

of its members were farmers. Other workers also supported the new third party. Many people who felt that big business was too powerful also joined.

In 1892, the Populists decided to run a candidate for president. They nominated James B. Weaver of Iowa. The Populists did not win the presidential election. However, they elected three governors, five senators, and ten members of the House of Representatives.

A Strong Populist Program

The Populists wanted to reform the government. These were the most important changes they wanted to make:

1. Government ownership and operation of all railroad and telegraph systems. Populists wanted these systems to be run in the best interests of the people.

2. A graduated income tax. Populists wanted people who earned higher incomes to pay a larger percentage in taxes. In 1892, everyone paid an income tax of 2 percent.

3. Voting by secret ballot. In many states, how a person voted was public information. Populists wanted this to end.

4. Direct election of senators. Populists wanted voters, not state legislatures, to elect senators.

5. Limits to immigration. Populists especially wanted to limit those immigrants they felt were "undesirable."

6. An eight-hour day for workers.

7. Government issue of more silver dollars to increase the amount of money available.

The Election of 1896

In 1896, the Democratic Party borrowed some of the Populist Party's ideas. Both the Democrats and the Populists decided to back William Jennings Bryan for president. The Populists wanted the

When **William McKinley (1843-1901)** was assassinated in 1901, the nation mourned for days. His first term as president had shown him to be a powerful and practical leader.

government to make an unlimited amount of silver available for circulation. Bryan was a strong supporter of this free coinage of silver.

The Republican candidate was William McKinley of Ohio. He was backed by wealthy business leaders and bankers. Large amounts of campaign money helped McKinley win the election. Although the Populists did not win this election, many of their ideas were eventually accepted by both the Democratic and Republican parties.

Section Review

1. What problems did farmers have? How did they want the federal government to help them?

2. What were farmers' cooperatives? Why were they formed?

3. Why did farmers form a third political party?

4. Whom did the Populists back for president in 1896? What issue did he support?

CHAPTER SUMMARY

In the years following the Civil War, the federal government supported business interests. President Garfield's death in 1881 led to a reform of the civil service system. A merit system based on hiring qualified people replaced the old spoils system. Between 1860 and 1900, the tariff was a major issue. Republicans kept the tariff high while they were in power.

In the late 1800s, workers organized labor unions to improve working conditions. Terence Powderly led the Knights of Labor in a successful strike against the Missouri Pacific Railroad. Public opinion turned against labor unions after the Haymarket Riot of 1886. As a result, the Knights of Labor lost their membership. The American Federation of Labor, started by Samuel Gompers, used strikes against employers to achieve its goals. Violence often broke out during strikes.

During this period, farmers joined together to demand reforms. They formed cooperatives and supported candidates who would serve their interests. However, unhappy with these candidates' efforts, farmers formed the Populist Party in 1892. Although the Populists did not elect a president, they elected many other candidates to office. Both the Democrats and Republicans adopted many Populist ideas.

Key Words

Write a sentence to explain the meaning of each of these terms.

popular votes merit system
Knights of Labor injunction
cooperatives lockout

Major Events

Choose the answer that best completes the statement.

1. The Pendleton Civil Service Act of 1883
   a) prohibited any sort of dishonest business deals.
   b) increased government employment.
   c) replaced the spoils system.

2. After the Haymarket Riot of 1886,
   a) farmers began to organize.
   b) employers improved working conditions.
   c) labor unions lost members.

3. During the late 1800s, large businesses
   a) enjoyed government support.
   b) bargained with unions.
   c) fought for low tariffs.

4. In the 1870s, the Grange was organized to
   a) help farmers.
   b) raise the prices of crops.
   c) elect Populists to office.

5. The Populists and Democrats backed the same candidate in the
   a) election of 1884.
   b) election of 1892.
   c) election of 1896.

Review

Important Facts

Answer each question with at least one complete sentence.

1. What was unusual about the presidential election of 1876? Who won? Why?

2. How were government jobs awarded before civil service reforms were passed?

3. Why were Democrats against high tariffs?

4. What was Cleveland's campaign promise when he ran against Harrison in the 1892 election?

5. Name two problems of workers during the late 1800s.

6. What was a yellow dog contract?

7. What event increased the membership of the Knights of Labor? How did they lose their membership?

8. What were the goals of the American Federation of Labor?

9. What weapons did employers use against organized labor during the late 1800s?

10. Whom did farmers blame for their problems?

11. What organizations helped farmers in the late 1800s? What were their methods?

12. Why did farmers start a third political party?

13. Name two demands of the Populist Party.

14. In which elections did Populist candidates run for president?

Skill Review

Read these newspaper articles, then answer the following questions.

DEMOCRATIC DEFEAT DOOMS NATION

The outcome of this month's election spells defeat not just for the Democratic Party or even for the Populist Party. The failure of William Jennings Bryan to capture the presidency from the selfish interests of bankers and businessmen means continued hardship for the good working people of America. And when honest farmers and laborers cannot earn a decent living, the entire nation suffers.

McKINLEY MEANS A STRONG AMERICA

Americans in all walks of life can breathe easier with the election of William McKinley. Under McKinley we will not have to fear the damage that the free coinage of silver would do to our economy. McKinley's sound money policies will protect rich and poor alike from the horror of inflation.

1. What facts does the first article present? What opinions?

2. Is the first article a news story or an editorial? Why?

3. What facts does the second article present? What opinions?

4. Is the second article a news story or an editorial? Why?

Critical Thinking

Write a paragraph to answer each question.

1. Why did workers and farmers organize in the late 1800s?

2. Why was the free coinage of silver an important issue to the Populists?

Important People

Choose the answer that best completes the statement.

1. Helen Hunt Jackson wrote about

   a) tenement housing.
   b) the mistreatment of Indians.
   c) child labor in factories.

2. In 1856, William Kelly and Henry Bessemer invented

   a) the refrigerator car.
   b) the electric streetcar.
   c) a new way to make steel.

3. During the late 1800s, Andrew Carnegie became known as

   a) the oil king.
   b) a famous inventor.
   c) a captain of industry.

4. Jane Addams started Hull House in Chicago to

   a) find jobs for black workers.
   b) provide services to the poor.
   c) fight the political machines.

5. *Huckleberry Finn,* a realistic novel, was written by

   a) Mark Twain.
   b) Scott Joplin.
   c) Stephen Crane.

6. In 1886, Samuel Gompers organized a

   a) farmers' cooperative.
   b) new political party.
   c) union of skilled workers.

7. The Populist candidate in the 1896 presidential election was

   a) James B. Weaver.
   b) William McKinley.
   c) William Jennings Bryan.

Main Ideas

Choose the answer that best completes the statement.

1. Miners seeking gold in the 1800s

   a) replaced the cattle ranchers.
   b) opened up lands in the West.
   c) destroyed the buffalo herds.

2. The settlement of the Great Plains brought an end to the

   a) boom towns.
   b) cowboys' long drives.
   c) Plains Indians' way of life.

3. The purpose of the Homestead Act of 1862 was to

   a) encourage settlement of the Great Plains.
   b) place Indians in reservations.
   c) teach Indians on reservations to be farmers.

4. From 1865 to 1900, America experienced great changes from

   a) industrial growth.
   b) the discovery of gold.
   c) new forms of transportation.

5. Business leaders such as John D. Rockefeller

   a) helped companies get started.
   b) controlled entire industries.
   c) kept consumer prices low.

6. During the late 1800s, government was unable to stop

   a) the growth of labor unions.
   b) the growth of trusts.
   c) the flood of immigrants.

7. During the 1800s, unskilled workers

   a) could always get jobs.

Review

b) earned low wages.

c) worked mostly in the South.

8. Many of the problems of the city slums during the late 1800s were

   a) solved by city governments.
   b) caused by political machines.
   c) caused by overcrowding.

9. Subways and other new forms of travel allowed

   a) cities to spread out.
   b) the poor to move to new areas.
   c) city dwellers to have more leisure time.

10. Industrial growth meant a more comfortable life for

   a) factory workers.
   b) the middle class.
   c) the Old Immigrants.

11. Presidents Chester Arthur and Grover Cleveland supported

   a) a higher tariff.
   b) labor unions.
   c) civil service reform.

12. During the late 1800s, the injunction was often used by

   a) employers.
   b) city governments.
   c) labor unions.

13. Populists were mainly

   a) farmers.
   b) immigrants.
   c) city dwellers.

14. One of the main goals of the Populist Party was to

   a) help the poor.
   b) prohibit child labor.
   c) gain control of the currency.

History Skills

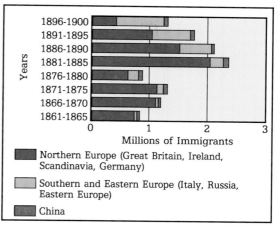

Immigration to the United States 1861–1900

Choose the answer that best completes the statement.

1. Immigration was greatest between

   a) 1886 and 1890.
   b) 1881 and 1885.
   c) 1861 and 1865.

2. More people came from southern Europe than northern Europe from

   a) 1881–1885.
   b) 1891–1895.
   c) 1896–1900.

3. Which statement is an opinion?

   a) Chinese immigration should not have been limited.
   b) China forbade emigration.
   c) Chinese immigrants were vastly outnumbered.

4. You can infer that between 1891 and 1900, living conditions were not good in

   a) southern and eastern Europe.
   b) China.
   c) New York.

Changes Abroad and at Home

UNIT 7
1865–1921

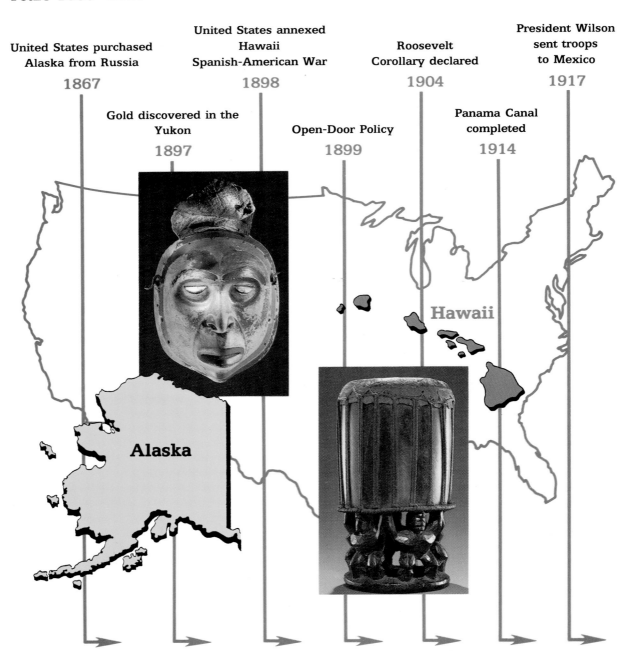

United States purchased
Alaska from Russia
1867

Gold discovered in the
Yukon
1897

United States annexed
Hawaii
Spanish-American War
1898

Open-Door Policy
1899

Roosevelt
Corollary declared
1904

Panama Canal
completed
1914

President Wilson
sent troops
to Mexico
1917

Hawaii

Alaska

1. The United States and the World, 1865–1900

Learn these important terms:

Monroe Doctrine
imperialism

Remember the main idea:

Between 1865 and 1900, America was becoming a world power. During these years, the United States gained new territories.

Look for answers to these questions:

1. How did the United States help Mexico and Venezuela during the late 1800s?
2. Why did Americans want to acquire overseas territories?
3. How did Hawaii become a part of the United States?

By the turn of the century, Americans were feeling patriotic about their country. The United States had become a great industrial power. The young country had emerged from the Civil War with a strong and secure government. It seemed only natural that America should take its rightful place among the powerful nations of the world.

In this chapter you will learn what actions the United States took to become a world power. Other nations had already acquired colonies in the undeveloped areas of the world. Nations with colonies gained power, wealth, and new sources of trade. To compete with these nations, Americans reached beyond their shores to acquire new territories, power, and influence overseas.

As you read, you will learn about laws, old and new, that stated the right of America to become involved in other countries. You will read about a war that started, in part, because of such involvement. You will also read about some battles that could have become wars but didn't. Finally, you will learn about the new American territories gained between the years of 1865 and 1917.

The *Monroe Doctrine* of 1823 warned European nations to stay out of the Americas. Until the 1860s, the United States was ready to enforce this doctrine whenever necessary.

However, once America became occupied with the Civil War, it could not look beyond its own borders. To the south, the Mexican government had little money after its own civil war. The Mexican leader, Benito Juarez (HWAH-rez), stopped payment on Mexico's debt to France. In return, French troops invaded Mexico. The French then replaced Juarez with an emperor, the Austrian archduke Maximilian (MAX-suh-MIL-yun). President

Think: *Purchase of Alaska* was created by the American-history painter Emanuel Leutze to commemorate the signing of the contract in 1867. William Seward, Secretary of State, offers his pen to the Russian representative, shown touching the globe. Respond: Why were Seward's critics wrong about the purchase?

Lincoln did not try to stop France because American troops were needed in the Civil War. But when the war ended, fifty thousand American soldiers were sent to the Mexican border. France did not want war with the United States. The French troops left Mexico in 1867, and Mexico was again an independent nation.

In 1895, the United States once again found it necessary to enforce the Monroe Doctrine. The cause of the problem was the boundary between British Guiana (gee-AN-uh) and Venezuela (VEN-uh-ZWAY-luh). In 1895, Venezuela asked the United States to help solve its dispute with Great Britain.

President Grover Cleveland wanted to form an international commission to solve the problem. Great Britain refused. Presi-dent Cleveland threatened to appoint an all-American commission to decide the boundary. This made it clear that the United States was ready to enforce a decision, if necessary. Great Britain gave in, and a special commission was formed to solve the boundary dispute.

America Acquires New Territories

Many Americans laughed when the secretary of state, William Seward, purchased Alaska from Russia in 1867. They called the purchase Seward's Folly or Seward's Icebox. Secretary Seward paid seven million dollars, or about two cents per acre, for this vast land. About thirty years later, Americans realized what a great bargain this was.

In 1897, gold was discovered in the Yukon territory near the border of Canada and Alaska. A great gold rush started. Thousands of miners struggled across the dangerous Chilkoot Pass to get to the Yukon. Many died of starvation or extreme cold. Some struck it rich. Later on, Americans began to settle Alaska. They discovered rich supplies of fish, furs, lumber, coal, and oil. Buying Alaska turned out to be one of the best deals ever made by the United States.

At the time of the Alaskan gold rush, some European nations were developing overseas empires. Nations such as Great Britain, France, and the Netherlands had taken over large areas of Africa and Asia. An increasing number of Americans believed that the United States should also acquire overseas territories. By the 1890s, some Americans began to believe in *imperialism* (ihm-PIHR-ee-ul-iz-um). Imperialism is the idea that a nation needs many colonies and territories to be rich and powerful.

It was felt that the United States needed colonies to take its place alongside other world powers. Moreover, undeveloped lands were often rich in raw materials. American industries needed these raw materials for their factories. Colonies also provided a market, or selling place, for American products.

Those who wanted to expand said the United States needed islands in the Pacific Ocean. Trading ships and navy ships needed places to stop for fuel, water, and other supplies. In 1867, the United States acquired Midway Island in the Pacific. In 1887, the United States also built a naval base at Pearl Harbor, in Hawaii.

Think: **In the political cartoon below, Carl Schurz, a political reformer, tries to give Uncle Sam some anti-expansion medicine. Look for clues that show the cartoon's attitude about expansion.** Respond: **What views does the cartoon express, and what symbols does it use to express them?**

HISTORY MAKERS

Lydia Kamekeha Liliuokalani

The Last Queen of Hawaii

"Now, Madam, here are our terms. If you will agree to give up any and all claims to the throne, we will pardon the rebels. If you will not agree, we will shoot them. The fate of two hundred prisoners is in your hands. You have the power to free them or to end their lives."

The room was very still as the Queen considered the offer. The only sounds were made by guards marching back and forth in front of her door. Since she had been brought to the palace ten days earlier, no one, not even the Bishop, had been allowed to see her. She had not encouraged the uprising to restore her to the throne, but once it started, she had hoped it might succeed without any bloodshed. The rebels had fought hard, but they were not well organized or well trained.

She sighed deeply. There was only one answer she could give the Provisional government. The men who had risked their lives for her and for their country could not be left to die. Slowly she looked around the small room that was her prison.

"Very well, gentlemen. I accept your terms. I renounce all claims to the throne of Hawaii, now and forever."

Queen Liliuokalani was the last ruling member of Hawaiian royalty. In 1893, a group of American businesspeople living and working in Hawaii had seized control of the government. They wanted Hawaii to become a possession of the United States. The United States, however, did not cooperate, and in 1894 the Americans established the Republic of Hawaii. Most Hawaiians were unhappy with the new government. Early in 1895 a group of Hawaiians rebelled, trying to restore Queen Liliuokalani to the throne. The rebellion was short and unsuccessful, and the queen gave up the throne in exchange for her supporters' lives.

In 1898, when the United States annexed Hawaii, Queen Liliuokalani wrote the song, "Aloha Oe" (Farewell to Thee). She and her people were saddened by the change in Hawaiian government. As a United States territory, Hawaii had only partial self-government. However, sixty-one years later, Hawaiians joyfully regained self-government when Hawaii became the fiftieth state of the Union.

Hawaii Becomes a Part of the United States

Americans had been interested in the Hawaiian Islands for many years. Since the early 1820s, American trading ships had stopped in Hawaii. Many American missionaries had settled there to convert Hawaiians to Christianity. Their descendants built cattle ranches and huge sugar plantations. It was not long before the suger planters became quite powerful.

In 1893, Queen Liliuokalani (lih-LEE-uh-woh-kah-LAH-nee), tried to bring her country back under the rule of Hawaiians. She introduced government reforms to take away the power of the planters. Alarmed, the Americans revolted. Backed by marines from the *U.S.S. Boston*, the Americans took control of the government. They asked President Cleveland to take over Hawaii.

President Cleveland turned down their request and ordered the marines to leave Hawaii. The Americans in Hawaii stayed in control of the government, however. They declared Hawaii a republic. Finally in 1898, Congress voted to make Hawaii part of the United States.

Section Review

1. How did the United States use the Monroe Doctrine to help Mexico? How did President Cleveland use the Monroe Doctrine?
2. Why was having colonies important to a nation?
3. What caused Americans to change their minds about the purchase of Alaska?
4. Why did Americans in Hawaii take control of the Hawaiian government?

2. The Spanish-American War

Learn these important terms:

sensationalism
Rough Riders
Platt Amendment

Remember the main idea:

In 1898, the United States fought and won the Spanish-American War. As a result, the United States gained many new territories.

Look for answers to these questions:

1. Why were Americans eager for war with Spain?
2. What new territories did the United States gain after the Spanish-American War?
3. How did the United States govern each of these new territories?

In 1895, the people of Cuba revolted against Spanish rule. Cuba, an island ninety miles from Florida, was Spain's most prized colony. To crush the revolt, the Spanish government put many Cubans into prison camps. Thousands of them died from disease and hunger.

Americans learned about the rebellion in Cuba from the newspapers. The news stories contained many examples of violent acts against the Cubans by the Spanish soldiers. It was true that the Spanish were cruel in putting down the revolt. However, many newspaper stories were exaggerated. Exciting headlines

YELLOW

JOURNALISM

Drawn by E. W. Kemble for *Leslie's*

YOU ARE THE ENEMY I FEAR MOST

Think: E. W. Kemble's cartoon takes a strong stance against sensational news, or yellow journalism.
Respond: Why do you think yellow journalism is something to be feared?

sold more papers, and newspapers competed with one another for customers.

There were two main rival newspapers in New York, the *New York Journal* and the *New York World.* Each relied heavily on **sensationalism,** or appealing to people's emotions, to sell newspapers. William Hearst, publisher of the *Journal,* was sure the United States would declare war on Spain. He sent a reporter and an illustrator, the great Frederic Remington, to Cuba to report on the fighting.

From Cuba, Remington sent a telegram to Hearst saying that things were quiet and he wanted to come home. Hearst sent back a reply ordering him to stay. The telegram said: "You furnish the pictures and I'll furnish the war."

On February 15, 1898, the American battleship *Maine* blew up in the harbor of

Havana, Cuba. The cause of the explosion was unknown. However, Hearst's newspaper, and many other American papers, immediately called for war with Spain.

The United States Goes to War

The *U.S.S. Maine* had been sent to Cuba to protect the lives and property of Americans. The explosion killed 260 American sailors. No one ever found out how the *Maine* blew up, but most Americans blamed the Spanish government.

This was the least likely explanation, because Spain was trying desperately to avoid war with the United States. A more likely explanation is that Cuban rebels planted the bomb. It is possible that these rebels wanted to push the United States into a war with Spain. Eager for a colonial empire and encouraged by the newspapers, many Americans called for war.

President McKinley tried to keep the United States out of war. In March of 1898, he sent a note to the Spanish, demanding an end to the fighting in Cuba. On April 9, the Spanish government agreed to McKinley's demands, but it was too late. The American public was too angry and demanded war. President McKinley gave in to the spreading war fever. On April 11, he asked Congress to declare war on Spain. Thus, the Spanish-American War began. Fighting broke out on two fronts, Cuba and the Philippine Islands (FILL-uh-PEEN).

The War on Land and at Sea

The first battles of the war took place in the Philippines. On May 1, 1898, the Spanish fleet was destroyed in Manila Bay. The Americans lost no men or ships.

While fighting was taking place on the sea in the Philippines, fighting on land was beginning in Cuba. The American army was small and unprepared for war.

Think: Although the cause of the blast that sunk the *USS Maine* was never discovered, some American newspapers were quick to blame Spain. But Spanish efforts to rescue the ship's crew were not reported in any American papers. Respond: Why did the newspapers act as they did? Do you agree with their reasons?

Think: American and Spanish ships exchange fire in James Tyler's dramatic painting, *The Battle of Manila Bay.* The United States had joined the war to free the Cubans, but gained Guam, Puerto Rico, and the Philippine Islands. Respond: Why did some Americans think it was wrong to take these islands?

Only eighteen thousand soldiers, including four black regiments, were sent to Cuba. Many of the soldiers were volunteers who had enlisted as war began.

One of the volunteer units was led by Theodore Roosevelt, who had resigned as assistant secretary of the navy. Roosevelt's volunteer unit, which included personal friends and cowboys, was called the **Rough Riders.** The Rough Riders took part in the most famous battle of the war, the Battle of San Juan Hill. [San Juan Hill was used by the Spanish to defend Santiago (SAHN-tee-AH-goh), a city on the southern coast of Cuba. Most of the Spanish troops in Cuba were stationed there.]

On July 1, 1898, American soldiers attacked the Spanish army defending San Juan Hill. A regiment of black soldiers led a fierce attack on one side of the hill. The Rough Riders, led by Theodore Roosevelt, charged up the center of the hill. Thus, the Spanish troops were defeated and San Juan Hill was captured. By the next day, the American army had forced the Spanish troops back down to the city of Santiago. The Battle of San Juan Hill made Teddy Roosevelt a popular hero.

On July 3, Spanish ships tried to escape from the Santiago harbor. These ships were stopped by an American fleet, which completely destroyed the Spanish fleet. On July 17, the Spanish commander surrendered and the war in Cuba was over. The United States immediately went on to capture Puerto Rico.

In August of 1898, American troops again turned their full attention to the

SPANISH-AMERICAN WAR, 1898

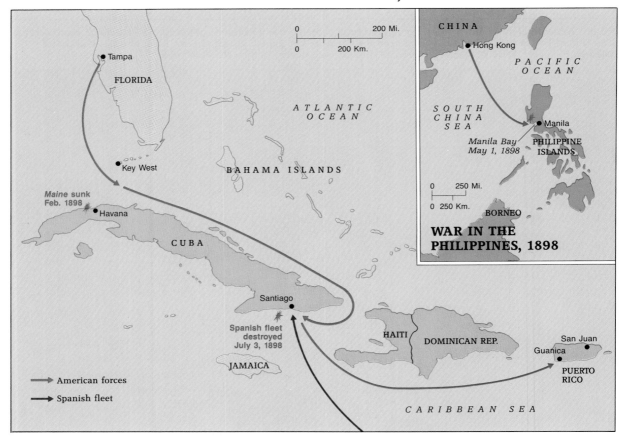

WAR IN THE PHILIPPINES, 1898

Think: **Theodore Roosevelt and his Rough Riders were considered heroes after their victory at San Juan Hill. The print above, from a watercolor by W. G. Read, is a fictionalized account of what happened. The real event was less sensational.** Respond: **Who are some of today's heroes, and what have they done?**

Philippines. This time they fought successfully on land. They immediately captured the Spanish fort. The Spanish-American War was over on both fronts.

The war had lasted only four months, but unsanitary conditions and tropical diseases in Cuba killed many American soldiers. Of the Americans killed in the war, 379 died in combat and 5,083 died of diseases.

The United States Gains Many New Territories

In the peace treaty that ended the war, Spain gave Cuba its independence. The United States acquired Puerto Rico, the islands of Wake and Guam, and the Philippine Islands. In return for the Philippines, the United States paid Spain twenty million dollars.

Think: **This political cartoon shows the United States as a protector of the Philippine Islands.** Respond: **What did the creator of the cartoon want people to think?**

Dr. Walter Reed discovered that mosquitoes carried the disease. By having the mosquitoes destroyed, the doctors were able to wipe out yellow fever.

Cuba became independent in 1902, but it was a conditional independence. To get American troops to leave, Cuban leaders had to approve the *Platt Amendment.* This law was passed by Congress in 1901. It gave the United States certain rights in Cuba. Most importantly, it allowed the United States to intervene whenever political troubles threatened Cuba's independence.

Governing the Philippines was a much more difficult task. Before the Spanish-American War, Filipino rebels were fighting for independence from Spain. After the Spanish left, the rebels were determined to gain independence. Led by Emilio Aguinaldo (ah-gwee-NAHL-doh) the rebels started a new revolt, this time against the Americans. By 1900, American forces in the Philippines had to be increased to seventy thousand. It was a long and bloody struggle. Finally, in March 1901, Aguinaldo was captured. The revolt was over. A new government under the control of the United States was established.

Americans did not agree on what to do with their new colonies. Some Americans wanted to take over all of the Spanish colonies and govern them as an American empire. Many other Americans felt that ruling other lands was violating the principles of the Constitution.

The people who lived in America's new territories did not become citizens of the United States. They enjoyed only those rights given to them by Congress. The island of Guam, for example, was governed by the navy.

From 1898 to 1902, the United States governed Cuba, and American soldiers were stationed there. American and Cuban doctors worked together to find a cure for the deadly disease, yellow fever. Major William Gorgas (GORE-gus) and

Section Review

1. How did newspaper stories about the Cuban revolution influence Americans?

2. Why was the Battle of San Juan Hill important? Who led the U.S. soldiers?

3. Who governed Cuba after the Spanish-American War?

4. What happened in the Philippines after the Spanish were defeated?

Here is an advertisement from an 1897 San Francisco newspaper.

> Sensible People Will Not Accept Substitutes
>
> ## Pond's Extract The Old Reliable Remedy
>
> Can Be Used With Perfect Safety For Insect Bites, Sunburn, and Summer Complaints
>
> ### IT IS UNEQUALED
>
> From a prominent druggist's journal: "Beware of worthless imitations said to be just as good as Pond's."

Although the 1897 advertisement doesn't have today's bright artwork and catchy jingles, both old and new advertisements represent a form of *propaganda*. Propaganda is any information distributed to convince people that an idea is right.

The Pond's advertisement claims that *sensible* people will not use anything else, and who wants to be thought insensible? The ad also reassures people about the product's safety and quotes an unnamed expert. Think about how the advertisements of today are similar to the Pond advertisement.

Today, most propaganda comes in the form of advertising, but it also comes in other forms. Some newspapers print articles that present only one side of an issue.

Today's newspapers more often present facts than propaganda. Newspapers of the 1890s were different, however. In that time some rival newspapers tried to increase readership by using unfair methods. Those methods often included printing stories that were exaggerated or even untrue. Newspaper owners hoped curiosity about such headlines as "Spanish Feed Cuban Prisoners to Sharks" would make people want to read their newspapers. William Randolph Hearst was the owner of such a newspaper, the *New York Journal*. Hearst believed that the United States should fight against Spain to free the nearby island of Cuba. He used propaganda in his newspaper to convince his readers that war was indeed necessary.

When a reporter for Hearst's rival paper wrote the following article, Hearst at once hired him, at an increased salary, to work for the *New York Journal*.

> No man's life, no man's property is safe. American citizens are imprisoned or slain without cause. American property is destroyed on all sides. . . . Blood on the roadsides, blood in the fields, blood on the doorsteps, blood, blood, blood! . . . A [battlefield] lies within eighty miles of the American coast. Not a word from Washington! Not a sign from the president!

1. What country is the article talking about?

2. What word is repeated in the article to stir up people's feelings?

3. What do you think the writer of article wants the reader to do?

3. The United States and the World, 1900–1917

Learn these important terms:

Open-Door Policy
Isthmus of Panama
Roosevelt Corollary
Boxers
Canal Zone
dollar diplomacy

Remember the main idea:

In the early 1900s, Americans took an interest in the rest of the world. They were involved in China, built the Panama Canal, and used their influence in Latin America.

Look for answers to these questions:

1. What was America's Open-Door Policy? Whose idea was it?
2. Why was the Panama Canal important to the United States?
3. How did Theodore Roosevelt use the Monroe Doctrine in Latin America?

While the United States was gaining new territories, other nations were trying to gain control of China. Britain, France, Germany, Russia, and Japan had each claimed a part of China for trade and investment. The United States did not want China to be seized and divided into colonies. Nor did it want to lose its own trade with China.

In 1899, John Hay, the American secretary of state, sent a note to the European nations. He asked them not to seize territory in China and to agree to equal trading rights for all nations. This agreement was called the **Open-Door Policy**. Only Great Britain agreed to Hay's request. The other European nations were not willing to agree completely. Nevertheless, John Hay hoped they might support his Open-Door Policy.

The Boxer Rebellion

The Chinese did not want to be ruled by European nations. Many of them formed a group called the **Boxers** to lead a movement against all foreigners in China. In 1900, the Boxers tried to force all foreigners to leave China. Some westerners were murdered. Seven nations, including Great Britain, France, and Japan, joined the United States in sending troops to China. This international force quickly ended the Boxer Rebellion.

Afterwards, several European nations wanted to take over China completely.

Think: The print below shows the Boxer troops fighting successfully. **Respond:** Why do you think the Chinese artist showed the Boxers as victorious when they lost the war?

Think: The labor of 35,000 men resulted in the Panama Canal. Engineering expertise came from John Stevens and George Goethals. William Gorgas removed the threat of yellow fever. Respond: How did President Roosevelt contribute to the Canal's completion?

But Secretary Hay refused to agree to this. Instead, he suggested that China repay European nations for their losses, rather than give up its land. The European nations accepted Hay's suggestion. China remained an independent nation.

Building the Panama Canal

After the Spanish-American War, the United States owned many new territories in both the Atlantic and Pacific Oceans. For ships to get from one ocean to the other, however, they had to sail around South America. This was a long and difficult journey. The French had tried to build a canal across the *Isthmus of Panama*, a narrow strip of land joining North and South America. The isthmus was then a part of Colombia. Building the canal was a difficult job, and the French finally gave up.

When Theodore Roosevelt became president in 1901, he convinced Congress that the United States should build the canal. America offered Colombia ten million dollars for the right to build the canal. Colombia refused the offer.

However, revolution soon broke out in Panama. Panama declared its independence from Colombia. Roosevelt then

THE UNITED STATES AS A WORLD POWER

In this section of the text, you read that in the years between 1867 and 1915 the United States became a world power. By using your map skills, you can find on the map below the countries that the United States came to control or to influence. In the text you can read about the different ways in which   power was achieved.

Look at the map and find the areas that the United States controlled.

1. Which of these United States possessions is the largest? How far is it from the United States?

2. What small Pacific island was acquired in 1867? Why was it acquired?

3. Which Pacific island group lies closest to the United States mainland? How far is its closest island from the mainland? On what date did it become a part (not a state) of the United States? In what ways did United States business interests, military forces, and government bring this about?

4. Which Pacific possessions were gained in a war that started in the Atlantic? How and where did the United States Army perform in that war? What two naval victories took place? Where did they take place?

5. What role did the United States play in Cuba?

Now look at the countries where the United States had influence.

6. Where in Asia did the United States have influence? How was this gained?

7. What role was played by the Monroe Doctrine?

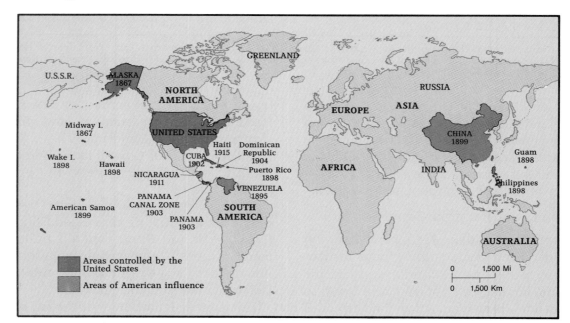

ordered the navy to Panama to assure the revolution's success. Within three months, the United States signed a treaty with Panama to build the canal. The strip of land rented to the United States by Panama was called the *Canal Zone*.

The great task of building the canal began in 1906. First, the mosquitoes in the Canal Zone were destroyed to get rid of malaria and yellow fever. Then, using enormous earth-moving machines, fifty thousand workers began to dig. It took eight years to dig a fifty-mile ditch across the hot jungles and mountains of Panama. Finally, in August 1914, the canal was completed. The Panama Canal shortened the distance between the Atlantic and Pacific coasts of the United States. The journey between New York and San Francisco was now eight thousand miles shorter. The Panama Canal quickly proved valuable for world trade and for the defense of America as well.

Roosevelt and the Monroe Doctrine

President Roosevelt believed that Latin America was under the influence and protection of the United States. His first opportunity to take a firm stand on this issue came in 1904. Several European nations wanted to send troops to the Dominican Republic (do-MIN-ih-cun). This tiny island in the Caribbean owed money to the European nations. Roosevelt was determined to prevent those nations from invading any Latin American country. He declared the *Roosevelt Corollary* (KAWR-uh-lair-ee), an addition to the Monroe Doctrine. The Roosevelt Corollary allowed the United States to take over the affairs of Latin American nations to prevent European invasions.

In 1904, Roosevelt sent the United States marines to the Dominican Republic. Their job was to see that the European nations were paid back. The marines took over the collection of customs and paid back the countries that were owed money. Many times, the United States sent soldiers into Latin America to keep European nations out.

The United States Loses Friends in Latin America

Many Latin American nations resented Roosevelt's policies. They were angry about American troops landing on their soil. William Howard Taft changed American policy toward Latin America when he became president in 1908. President Taft tried to influence Latin Americans with *dollar diplomacy*. Dollar diplomacy is the use of investments to influence governments. Taft encouraged American business leaders to build railroads and plantations in Latin American countries. This improved relations with Latin America.

However, relations with Mexico worsened in 1917 when President Wilson ordered troops into Mexico. They were searching for Pancho Villa, a Mexican general who had shot a number of Americans. General John J. Pershing led six thousand soldiers on a fruitless chase through Mexico. The American troops never found Villa. But they succeeded in injuring America's relationship with Mexico for many years.

Section Review

1. What was the Boxer Rebellion?
2. Why was the Panama Canal valuable to the United States and other countries?
3. What was the purpose of the Roosevelt Corollary?
4. What was President Taft's policy toward Latin America?

CHAPTER SUMMARY

Between 1865 and 1900, the United States joined other countries in the rush for colonies. The United States acquired Alaska, Hawaii, and several small islands in the Pacific. During this period, America used the Monroe Doctrine to resolve a border dispute between the countries of Venezuela and British Guiana.

The explosion on the *U.S.S. Maine* and newspaper stories about Spanish cruelty in Cuba led to war against Spain in 1898. American victories in Cuba and in Manila Bay in the Philippines quickly ended the Spanish-American War. The United States acquired Puerto Rico, Wake Island, Guam, and the Philippine Islands. The United States governed Cuba until 1902. After capturing the Philippine rebel leader, Emilio Aguinaldo, the United States took over control of the Philippines.

American Secretary, John Hay, tried to keep trade open in China with his Open-Door Policy. In 1900, the United States joined other nations to put down the Boxer Rebellion in China.

President Theodore Roosevelt succeeded in getting the Panama Canal built in 1914. He took a firm stand in Latin America, using United States troops to back the Monroe Doctrine. President William Taft replaced Roosevelt's policy toward Latin America with dollar diplomacy.

Key Words

Write a sentence to explain the meaning of each of these terms.

imperialism
Platt Amendment
Boxers
sensationalism
Open-Door Policy
dollar diplomacy

Major Events

Choose the answer that best completes the statement.

1. The United States used the Monroe Doctrine in 1867 to
   a) keep trade open with China.
   b) defeat the Philippine rebels.
   c) support Mexico in its efforts to get rid of French troops.

2. Americans in Hawaii disliked
   a) Cleveland's policies.
   b) new government reforms.
   c) the sugar planters.

3. The explosion on the *Maine* led to
   a) the annexation of Hawaii.
   b) war with Spain.
   c) the Roosevelt Corollary.

4. The building of the Panama Canal
   a) hurt America's relationship with Mexico.
   b) improved world trade.
   c) was Taft's biggest success.

5. Roosevelt's actions in the Dominican Republic
   a) kept European countries out.
   b) improved America's relations with Panama.
   c) were generally disliked.

Review

Important Facts

Answer each question with at least one complete sentence.

1. How was the Monroe Doctrine used in 1895?

2. What happened in 1897 to turn Seward's Folly into a good deal?

3. Why did Americans favoring imperialism say America needed colonies?

4. Why were islands in the Pacific important to the United States?

5. What did Americans in Hawaii want President Cleveland to do?

6. How did the newspapers get Americans involved in Cuba's revolt against Spain?

7. Who were the "Rough Riders"? How did they become famous?

8. What did many American soldiers die from during the Spanish-American War?

9. What territories did the United States gain from Spain after the Spanish-American War?

10. What did American and Cuban doctors accomplish in Cuba?

11. Why was governing the Philippines a difficult task for the United States?

12. Why was the United States interested in the affairs of China?

13. What problems made building the Panama Canal so difficult?

14. What was the Roosevelt Corollary?

15. What action did President Wilson take in 1917 that caused problems with Mexico?

Skill Review

Study this cartoon, then answer the following questions.

1. What does the woman in the pan represent?

2. What problem does she have if she stays in the pan?

3. What problem will she have if she jumps out?

4. How might this cartoon have been used for propaganda in 1898?

The caption of the cartoon is "The Duty of the Hour—To Save Her Not Only from Spain, but from a Worse Fate."

Critical Thinking

Write a paragraph to answer each question.

1. Why did the United States want to acquire overseas territories? What were advantages and disadvantages of having overseas territories?

2. Why did Theodore Roosevelt interfere in Latin America during his term as president?

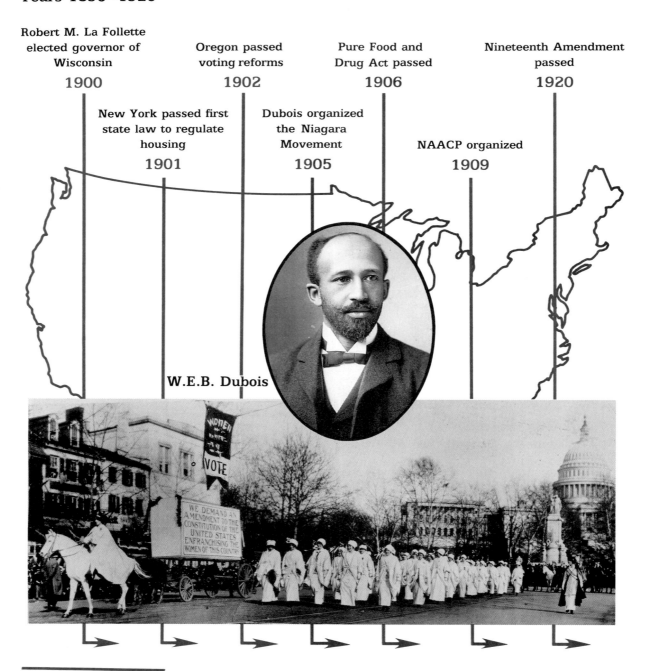

Robert M. La Follette
elected governor of
Wisconsin
1900

Oregon passed
voting reforms
1902

Pure Food and
Drug Act passed
1906

Nineteenth Amendment
passed
1920

New York passed first
state law to regulate
housing
1901

Dubois organized
the Niagara
Movement
1905

NAACP organized
1909

W.E.B. Dubois

1. New Reformers and Their Goals

Learn these important terms:

Progressives
Niagara Movement
National Urban League
National Association for the Advancement of Colored People

Remember the main idea:

The Progressive Movement adopted many Populist ideas about improving conditions in America. Black Americans formed groups to work for their rights.

Look for answers to these questions:

1. What were the main goals of the Progressives?
2. How were the Progressives different from the Populists?
3. What groups were formed in the early 1900s to help black Americans gain equality?

By the turn of the century, the people of America realized that the problems created by the growth of industries and cities had not disappeared. It was not a good time to be poor, and only a few were rich. There was, however, a large and well-educated middle class. Members of the middle class introduced a new spirit of reform, the Progressive Movement, and it spread throughout the country.

In this chapter, you will read about the Progressives and their goals. They attacked dishonesty in government and business. They protested the working conditions of women and children. They tried to improve the living conditions of the poor. Moreover, the Progressives demanded that government accept responsibility for solving these problems.

The Progressives found much support for their ideas. Writers helped spread the word. As you will see, politicians soon responded. Important new laws were passed. Americans again saw their demands being met.

By the end of the 1890s, Americans were thinking about their country in new ways. Most people were very proud of the United States' rise to power among the nations of the world. Prosperity had returned, and the nation was becoming an industrial giant as well. However, the Populists had made people realize that serious problems existed within the "Land of Plenty."

Populists and Progressives

Many Populists were debtor farmers from the South and the West. They wanted government help in solving their economic problems. To achieve their goals, they formed a political party and focused on specific issues. In 1896, they "put all their eggs in one basket" by concentrating on the free silver issue and backing its spokesperson for president. After William Jennings Bryan lost, the Populist Party withered away.

The spirit of reform did not die, however. New groups seeking to improve society gained national attention. The new reformers were called *Progressives*. They believed in making progress toward the ideals of a democratic society. Like the Populists, the Progressives believed that government could and should solve the country's problems. The two groups also shared a desire to control big business.

However, the Progressives differed from the Populists in several ways. Unlike the rural Populists, the Progressives came from the growing urban middle class. They were lawyers, small business owners, social workers, teachers, and homemakers. They were neither rich nor poor, but comfortable and well-educated citizens of the cities.

Think: Slum conditions in New York City's Lower East Side are shown in this 1915 photograph. Respond: **According to Progressives, whose responsibility was it to clean up the slums?**

Think: **The Henry Street settlement house gave help to lower Manhattan's poor and needy.** Respond: **Why were these nurses considered part of the Progressive Movement?**

The Progressives were not an organized political party like the Populist Party. They were not a unified group that concentrated on achieving a few specific demands. Instead, the term *Progressive* was applied to a large number of groups with a great variety of concerns. These groups often did not agree on what methods to use to achieve their goals. Nevertheless, the various groups came to be known as the Progressive Movement.

Targets of Progressive Reform

The Progressive Movement had three main goals. First, Progressives worked to improve the lives of the poor. They sought to get rid of slums and improve working conditions in factories. Second, Progressives wanted to control big business in the interest of the average citizen. They

PROGRESSIVE ACTION: WORKMEN'S COMPENSATION

You can use a map like this to answer a research question. On the map, you see dates on which most of the states passed a workmen's compensation law. These laws were a result of action by Progressives. Why did some states pass these laws years ahead of others? Was it a regional matter? Were industries involved? Study the map to find out.

Look at the map, and on a separate sheet of paper list the states that were the first to pass a workmen's compensation law. Next to that list, list the states that followed a year later. In a third column, list states that had *not* passed one of these laws by 1916. Then answer these questions.

1. What was the first year in which workmen's compensation laws were passed? Are the states that passed one of these laws in the first year from any one region in particular?

2. Are the states that passed laws in the second year from any one region in particular?

3. Are there any regional patterns in the states that had not passed one of these laws by 1916?

Look now at the Chapter 18 Map Workshop, "Agriculture and Industry in 1890."

4. Do the southern states with textile industries match the states that were slow to pass workmen's compensation laws?

5. In which western states are large grazing areas found? Were these states slow to pass workmen's compensation laws?

6. Write a sentence explaining which states were slow to pass these laws.

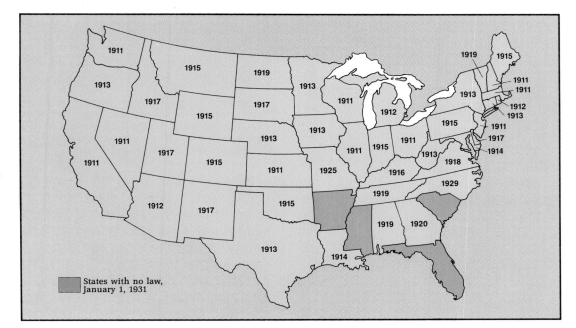

States with no law, January 1, 1931

Think: Work conditions for many people, especially women and minorities, remained poor. Respond: What do you think it was like to sew clothes all day in a sweat shop?

wanted to break up trusts and monopolies and restore economic competition. Third, Progressives wanted to erase corruption in government at all levels. They wanted to take power away from the political machines and give it to the voters.

Gains and Losses in Voting Rights

One way to increase the power of voters was to increase the number of voters. Some Progressives worked to give women the right to vote as a means of getting other reforms passed. But many women worked for the right to vote as a reform in itself. Women gained the right to vote in the Territory of Wyoming in 1869. The

Think: Closely examine the inside of this New York tenement house. Notice how many people were living in it. Respond: What problems can result from such living conditions?

struggle continued until 1920, when the Nineteenth Amendment to the Constitution was passed. It guaranteed women's right to vote in all states.

While women were gaining the right to vote during the Progressive Era, southern blacks were losing it. After the Populist Party died, white Southerners went back to the Democratic Party. Political cooperation between whites and blacks stopped. Blacks in the South faced stricter segregation, and most black citizens lost their right to vote.

Think: Support for women's suffrage, the right to vote, was growing. Notice the banner carried in this parade. Respond: Why were women finally getting the support they needed?

When blacks tried to demand their rights, some whites used force to stop them. During the 1880s and 1890s, mobs sometimes took the law into their own hands. Particularly in the South, mobs were known to seize blacks suspected of committing crimes. These mobs would hang their victims without trials. Progressives did not actively protest such actions. Most Progressives were not interested in the problems of minorities.

W.E.B. Dubois (1868–1963) tried many different methods for bringing about equal rights for blacks in his lifetime. He was always outspoken in his views.

Black Reformers

It became clear that black Americans would have to work together to help themselves. In 1905, W.E.B. DuBois (doo-BOYS) and other black leaders founded the *Niagara Movement* (neye-AG-ruh). The Niagara Movement stated the goals of black Americans. These goals included the right to vote, the right to be educated, and the right to be admitted to all public places.

DuBois, leader of the Niagara Movement, was a graduate of Harvard University and was a college professor. DuBois challenged the teachings of Booker T. Washington, another leader of black Americans. Washington believed that blacks should improve their lives through job training. DuBois argued that job skills were not enough. He wrote that ''. . . we must strive for the rights which the world accords to men. . . .''

In 1909, the Niagara Movement became part of a new, larger organization. DuBois and his followers joined with a group of white Progressives to form the *National Association for the Advancement of Colored People*.

By 1914, the NAACP had six thousand members. The organization fought to win equal rights for black citizens. They started a program of legal action that took their fight to the nation's courts. In 1911, the *National Urban League* was organized. The Urban League was formed to help black Americans in northern cities find jobs.

Think: This 1924 photograph of blacks picking cotton proves that conditions for many blacks had not improved. Respond: Why were things so bad for southern blacks?

Section Review

1. Who were the Progressives?
2. What kinds of reforms did Progressives propose?
3. What were the problems of black Americans in the early 1900s?
4. How did the NAACP help black Americans?

2. Muckrakers and Reforms

Learn these important terms:

muckrakers
Meat Inspection Act
Pure Food and Drug Act
child labor laws

Remember the main idea:

Progressives informed the public about the problems of American life. They used public opinion to persuade lawmakers to solve some of these problems.

Look for answers to these questions:

1. How did the muckrakers affect the Progressive Movement?
2. What was the Pure Food and Drug Act?
3. How did Progressives help workers and the poor?

In some ways, the problems of American life in the early 1900s were like the muck along a dirty stream. Just like muck, they were unpleasant and easy to ignore. However, not everyone was willing to ignore these problems. Some reformers, who were also writers, wanted to expose the problems of American life. They were called **muckrakers** because they raked up the muck of unpleasant problems.

Muckrakers wrote about many subjects. Their articles were published in magazines such as *McClure's* and *Collier's*. These writers looked for evidence of dishonesty in industry and in the government. Their articles became so popular that magazine editors began to focus on muckraking.

Ida M. Tarbell and Lincoln Steffens, two famous muckrakers, were hired by the editor of *McClure's*. Their job was to find corruption and write articles telling about it. Ida Tarbell wrote a series of articles that showed how the Standard Oil Company took control of the oil industry. Her articles accused Standard Oil of using unfair methods to crush its competitors. Tarbell revealed how company officials and government employees made deals favorable to Standard Oil.

Lincoln Steffens wrote about dishonest leaders in city and state governments. His series of articles was called *The Shame of*

Think: **During the early 1900s, magazines like** *McClure's* **(cover shown below) published articles by muckrakers.** Respond: **How did muckrakers demonstrate American freedom of the press?**

McCLURE'S MAGAZINE
FEBRUARY 1910 · FIFTEEN CENTS

HISTORY MAKERS

Ida Tarbell

Lady Muckraker

The dining room at the home of Alexander Graham Bell was ready for a dinner party. Silver and candles glowed on the table as the guests entered the room. Frank Vanderlip, a vice president of National City Bank, spoke softly to the guest at his right.

"Miss Tarbell, I understand you're researching John D. Rockefeller and the Standard Oil Company."

"Yes, indeed, Mr. Vanderlip. It promises to be a most interesting series of articles for my magazine."

"I think you should know, Miss Tarbell, that my bank is very concerned about these proposed articles. Very concerned."

"If I am not mistaken, Mr. Rockefeller owns a controlling interest in your bank, Mr. Vanderlip."

"That is true, Miss Tarbell."

"You know, Mr. Vanderlip, when I began my research on John D. Rockefeller and the Standard Oil Company, I was warned that the company might try to stop me. People said Standard Oil wouldn't cooperate with me, and might try to hurt me. I am sorry that Standard Oil or Mr. Rockefeller would threaten me in any way, but it makes no difference. I will continue to do my job as usual."

Ida Tarbell did such a good job of investigating Standard Oil that her research was published both as a series of articles in *McClure's* magazine and as a two-volume book, *The History of the Standard Oil Company.* Partly as a result of her writing, the Standard Oil trust was broken up by the United States government.

Ida Tarbell was one of a group of reporters called muckrakers. Muckrakers investigated big business in the late nineteenth and early twentieth centuries. They fought against the corruption they found there and in government. Their fighting took the form of articles carried by popular magazines.

In addition to working as a reporter, Ida Tarbell wrote biographies, edited magazines, lectured, and took part in White House conferences on industry and unemployment. Her wide range of interests and writing made her one of the most popular women in America.

Lincoln Steffens (1866–1936) believed businesspeople were responsible for political corruption. As a journalist, he used his sharp mind to expose political wrongdoings.

the Cities. Steffens showed that corruption was part of every large city government in every state. In one article, he reported on the deals a city mayor and his police chief had made with criminals. Other muckrakers wrote articles about the unfair practices of the railroads, banks, and insurance companies.

Millions of Americans read these articles in the magazines. For the first time, middle-class Americans learned about some serious problems in America.

The Pure Food and Drug Act

In 1906, a famous muckraker, Upton Sinclair, published *The Jungle*. In this book, Sinclair revealed the shocking facts about the meat industry. Meat was packed in extremely dirty conditions. Some companies allowed spoiled meat to be packaged and sold.

Other muckrakers revealed that canned vegetables were sometimes treated with dangerous chemicals to make them look fresh. The public also learned that some medicines contained alcohol and dangerous drugs. Some of these medicines were given to babies.

Thousands of Americans read these accounts of conditions in the food and

Upton Sinclair (1878–1968) is best remembered for his novels calling for social reform. However, his nonfiction works serve as a clear record of America during his time.

drug industries. They were outraged. President Theodore Roosevelt, a leader of the Progressives, urged Congress to act on this problem. In 1906, Congress passed the *Pure Food and Drug Act*. This law set standards for processed foods and medicines. Congress also passed the *Meat Inspection Act*. This law required federal inspectors to check all meat, fresh and canned, to make sure it was safe to

Think: After the Pure Food and Drug Act and the Meat Inspection Act were passed in 1906, meatpacking plants were closely watched. Respond: Why were these laws necessary?

eat. These important laws helped to protect the health of Americans.

Progressives Improve Housing

Progressives also found many conditions that needed to be improved in the cities. The stories and photographs of Jacob Riis (REES), a newspaper reporter, showed Americans the miserable living conditions of the poor in the cities. Due largely to Riis's efforts, one of the worst tenement sections in New York City was torn down. In his book, *How the Other Half Lives*, Riis showed how tenement living produced crime, disease, and misery among poor families.

Progressives demanded that state governments improve housing conditions. In 1901, New York passed the first state law to regulate the building of apartment houses. The new law required buildings to have more windows, more running water, and fire escapes. By 1910, most of the other states had also passed laws to improve housing for the poor.

Progressives Help Workers

Progressives also improved working conditions in factories. Progressives helped pass laws requiring factory owners to make machines safer and to pay

Think: This man was hurt on the job, but received no money for medical care or food. Respond: What changes did the Progressives make, and why were these changes important?

Think: **These young boys worked in a coal mine, breaking coal. Closely examine their faces. Notice how sad the boys look and how young they are. Think about what you were doing at their age. Progressives passed laws to protect children from this kind of abuse.** Respond: **Why are child labor laws important?**

workers who were hurt on the job. Some states passed laws that cut the workday for women from twelve or fourteen hours to ten hours a day.

Progressives also wanted laws to protect children employed in factories. In the early 1900s, most states began to pass **child labor laws**. These laws made it unlawful for factory owners to hire children younger than twelve years old. By 1917, most states had laws prohibiting children under sixteen to work at night.

Section Review

1. How did muckrakers help the Progressive Movement?
2. What laws set standards for the food and drug industries?
3. Who wrote a book about life in city tenements?
4. What were child labor laws?

3. Progressives Seek Better Government

Learn these important terms:

initiative
direct primary elections
referendum
recall

Remember the main idea:

Progressives reformed city and state governments. Their reforms destroyed the political machines, gave voters more power, and limited the influence of big business.

Look for answers to these questions:

1. How did Progressives break the power of the political machines?
2. What new voting laws improved state governments?
3. What were the Progressive reforms of Robert La Follette?

When the Progressives tried to improve conditions in the cities, they had to fight the political machines. They knew that the machines got most of their money from businesses that supplied gas, electricity, water, and streetcar service for the city. The Progressives believed that the way to beat the political machines was to have the city take over these services.

The Progressive mayor of Cleveland, Tom L. Johnson, tried this plan, and it worked. The city paid the owners a fair price for their businesses and took control of the services. Without money, the political machine in Cleveland lost much of its power. Many other cities followed Cleveland's example and took over city services. As a result, the power of political machines was weakened.

Reformers in some cities tried different forms of government. One successful reform was the city manager system. The city council hired a city manager to run the day-to-day affairs of the government. The city manager kept the job if the duties were performed well. The city manager did not have to run for reelection. Because of this, the city manager was less likely to be influenced by the political machine. This system worked well and was adopted by many small cities.

Think: **Mayor Tom Johnson of Cleveland (seated next to driver) had his city buy the businesses and services which had been controlled by the political machines.** Respond: **Why did this plan work?**

In 1890, Jacob Riis, a newspaper reporter, wrote a book about the poor in New York City. Called *How the Other Half Lives*, it gave many wealthy people their first look at the daily lives of ''the other half.'' The book is a primary source since it was written by a person who observed first-hand the conditions of the times. The book's photographs and pictures are also primary sources. They were made in the places and at the times of Riis's observations. These primary sources can be used today to see how some people of the 1890s lived.

A family's single-room home with a common bed of rags

You can tell from the picture that this family's daily activities, such as sleeping and eating, had to take place in one room. Many objects in the room were probably used for several purposes. For example, the chairs may have been pulled together to form a bed.

Look at the photographs below from Riis's book, and read the captions under them. Then use this primary source to answer the questions.

Lodgers in a crowded Bayard Street tenement—five cents a spot

1 The lodgers were probably unrelated people. What can you tell from the picture about the amount of privacy each person had in the tenement?

Street children in sleeping quarters

2 Why do you suppose the children are sleeping over a heating grate?

The Oregon System

State governments were also controlled by the political machines. Progressives such as William S. U'ren, the governor of Oregon, made the first state government reforms. U'ren believed that corruption in state governments could be stopped by giving the voters more power. In 1902, the Oregon legislature passed new voting laws to destroy the power of the machines. These laws put more power directly in the hands of the voters.

These new laws were the *initiative*, the *recall*, and the *referendum*. The initiative gave voters the right to suggest new laws to the state legislature. The recall gave voters the right to remove dishonest officials from state government. The referendum allowed voters to accept or reject a law passed by a city council or state legislature.

Oregon was also one of the first states to set up *direct primary elections*. Direct primary elections allowed voters to choose their own candidates for office. Before this law was passed, the political machine often chose which candidates would run for office. With these reforms, Oregon's voters gained power to make their government more democratic.

Wisconsin's Progressive Governor

One of the most famous Progressive governors was Robert M. La Follette of Wisconsin. When La Follette was elected governor in 1900, he promised to give voters more power, and he did. Under La Follette, Wisconsin adopted direct primary elections, the initiative, the recall, and the referendum.

La Follette continued the battle for reform in other areas as well. He believed that the public needed to be protected against big business and other powerful interests. After a hard battle with anti-reform forces, La Follette signed a law

Robert La Follette (1855–1925) earned the name "Fighting Bob" because he refused to compromise on his Progressive ideas.

that increased taxes on the railroad companies. La Follette reformed the state civil service and established a railroad commission to regulate the railroads more closely. He was elected three times as governor of Wisconsin.

Many other governors followed La Follette's example and passed similar reforms. The governors ended the power of the political machines. They made their state governments more responsive to the needs of the people. Many states passed laws to regulate big businesses. Businesses were also forced to pay their fair share of state taxes.

Section Review

1. How did Cleveland's mayor, Tom Johnson, take away the power of the political machines?

2. What are the initiative, the referendum, and the recall?

3. What allowed voters to choose their own candidates for office?

4. How did Robert M. La Follette protect the public against big business interests?

CHAPTER SUMMARY

During the 1890s and the early 1900s, middle-class Americans became concerned about the many problems caused by industrial growth. Their demand for reform was called the Progressive Movement. The Progressives adopted some Populist demands, such as reforming government and controlling business, but they also had many concerns of their own.

Most Progressives were not concerned with the problems of minorities. Black Americans formed various organizations to help themselves. W.E.B. Dubois started the Niagara Movement, which later became the NAACP. This organization fought for equal rights for black Americans.

By exposing corruption in industry and government, muckrakers aroused the public to demand reforms. Their investigations led to new laws, such as the Pure Food and Drug Act and the Meat Inspection Act. Progressives also improved housing for the poor and pushed through state labor laws to improve working conditions.

City governments began working to beat political machines. State political reforms such as the recall, the referendum, and the initiative also took power away from the political machines and put it in the hands of the voters. Robert La Follette and other Progressives supported state reforms that limited the power of big business.

Key Words

Write a sentence to explain the meaning of each of these terms.

initiative *recall*
Niagara Movement *referendum*
muckrakers

Major Events

Choose the answer that best completes the statement.

1. In 1890, Wyoming was the first state to
   a) control big business.
   b) elect a Progressive governor.
   c) allow women to vote.

2. In 1909, the Niagara Movement became part of the
   a) Progressive Movement.
   b) NAACP.
   c) child labor laws.

3. In 1906, Upton Sinclair's *The Jungle* exposed conditions in
   a) the meat industry.
   b) city tenements.
   c) factories.

4. The Oregon System of 1902
   a) gave voters more power.
   b) took power away from the labor unions.
   c) gave cities new systems of self-government.

5. In 1906, Wisconsin elected one of the most famous Progressive governors,
   a) Lincoln Steffens.
   b) Tom Johnson.
   c) Robert La Follette.

Review

Important Facts

Answer each question with at least one complete sentence.

1. Name two goals of the Progressives.

2. What did the Progressives believe was the responsibility of government?

3. What did women gain during the Progressive Era?

4. What was the purpose of the NAACP? Who were the founders?

5. What part did the muckrakers play in the Progressive Movement?

6. What did the investigations of Ida Tarbell reveal about the oil industry?

7. What did Americans learn from the series of articles called *The Shame of the Cities*?

8. Name two laws passed in 1906 that protected consumers. What did they do?

9. What labor laws did Progressives pass to help women and children?

10. How did the political machines control city governments?

11. What did Tom L. Johnson do?

12. How did the city manager system reform city governments?

13. What laws to reform state government did William S. U'ren and the Oregon legislature pass?

14. How did some Progressive states protect the public against the interests of big business?

Skill Review

Study this map, then answer the following questions.

1. In which part of the country did women have the most voting rights?

2. In which parts of the country did women have no voting rights?

3. How might you explain the difference in voting rights between regions?

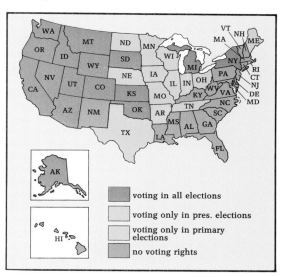

Voting Rights for Women, 1920

Critical Thinking

Write a paragraph to answer each question.

1. Compare the Populists and the Progressives. Who made up each group? Why were the Progressives more successful?

2. How did the views of W.E.B. Dubois differ from those of Booker T. Washington? What views did they share?

23
Reformers in the White House

Years 1901-1916

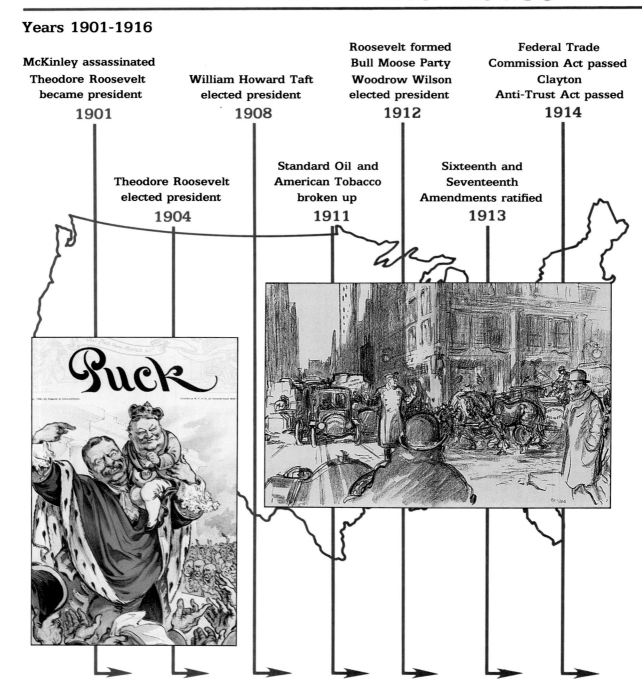

McKinley assassinated
Theodore Roosevelt
became president
1901

Theodore Roosevelt
elected president
1904

William Howard Taft
elected president
1908

Standard Oil and
American Tobacco
broken up
1911

Roosevelt formed
Bull Moose Party
Woodrow Wilson
elected president
1912

Sixteenth and
Seventeenth
Amendments ratified
1913

Federal Trade
Commission Act passed
Clayton
Anti-Trust Act passed
1914

The Progressives had successfully pushed through reforms in city and state governments. However, there were many problems that had to be solved at the national level. The Progressives were fortunate. In 1901, Theodore Roosevelt became the first president to champion the cause of the Progressives. He was followed in office by two presidents, William Taft and Woodrow Wilson, who continued his active support of the Progressive Movement.

As you read this chapter, you will find out how three Progressive presidents curbed the power of big business, defended labor, conserved natural resources, and reformed the income tax. Of course, they did not do these things alone. Congress supported Progressive ideas by passing many important laws. The Democrats and the Republicans agreed on most issues during the Progressive era. In short, the period from 1901 to 1916 was a time when the government began to work on improving life within the United States.

1. Teddy Roosevelt and the Square Deal

Learn these important terms:

Square Deal
conservation
Hepburn Act
arbiters
Elkins Act
Newlands Reclamation Act

Remember the main idea:

Theodore Roosevelt was a great national leader of the Progressives. During his presidency, many Progressive ideas became laws.

Look for answers to these questions:

1. How did President Roosevelt earn his nickname, the "trust-buster"?
2. What did President Roosevelt mean by the Square Deal?
3. What did President Roosevelt do to protect the nation's natural resources?

Shortly after his reelection, President William McKinley was assassinated. In 1901, Vice President Theodore Roosevelt became president.

Roosevelt was an enthusiastic and energetic individual. A sickly and weak child, Roosevelt had strengthened his body through will power and rugged exercise. One of the most well-read presidents, Roosevelt had also written more than a dozen books. Roosevelt was a war hero, as well. He led the famous Rough Riders during the Spanish-American War.

APOSTLE OF PROSPERITY.

HE WHO SOWS WIND WILL REAP STORM —
BUT FROM GOOD SEED SPRINGS PROSPERITY!

STRIFE
T.R.

PROSPERITY

AGRICULTURE
FORESTRY.
MINING.

INDUSTRY
COMMERCE.
NAVIGATION.

ARBITRATION
JUSTICE.
LAW.

LITERATURE
SCIENCE
ART.

TAKE SPADE AND HOE THYSELF; DIG ON —
GREAT SHALT THOU BE THROUGH PEASANT TOIL.

GOETHE'S FAUST II PART.

Think: Theodore Roosevelt is portrayed as a farmer sowing seeds of prosperity. Many of the programs he supported are listed on the sacks of seed. **Respond:** What reasons does the creator of the artwork give for supporting Roosevelt?

His popularity as a war hero carried over to the White House. He quickly established himself as a strong leader and a man of action.

During his first years in politics, Roosevelt had become interested in the problems of the poor. As president, Roosevelt believed that he must serve all the people of the United States. When he became president, Roosevelt said he wished to give all Americans a *Square Deal*. By this, he meant that he wanted the federal government to pass laws to help all Americans, not just some special groups. At last, the Progressives had found a national leader for their movement.

President Roosevelt as "Trustbuster"

President Roosevelt became known as the "trustbuster" during his first term. He earned this title by going after several of the nation's biggest trusts. His first action was against the Northern Securities Company, which controlled the three

476 *UNIT 7*

major railroads serving the Northwest. In Roosevelt's opinion, the unfair practices of this railroad monopoly were violating the Sherman Anti-Trust Act.

Roosevelt pursued the case to the Supreme Court. In 1904, the Court ruled that the Northern Securities Company was in violation of the Sherman Anti-Trust law. Under Roosevelt's leadership, the government also took action against forty-four other large corporations.

Taking the railroads to court was not enough, however. In the early 1900s, many railroads still charged unfair rates and gave rebates to certain businesses. President Roosevelt wanted new laws to control the railroads. Encouraged by the president, Congress passed the **Elkins Act** in 1903, which made rebates unlawful. The **Hepburn Act**, passed in 1906, gave the Interstate Commerce Commis-

As president and long-time politician, Theodore Roosevelt (1858-1919) worked steadily for various reforms. He was a popular and controversial leader and a fine writer.

sion the right to regulate the rates that railroads were allowed to charge.

Roosevelt did not want to simply destroy trusts. He realized that big business was here to stay. Therefore, Roosevelt believed that government should control big businesses. He wanted to regulate large corporations to keep them from becoming too strong, not destroy them.

Roosevelt Gives Workers a Square Deal

In the spring of 1902, President Roosevelt applied his idea of the Square Deal to workers. More than one thousand coal miners went on strike in Pennsylvania. They wanted higher pay and shorter hours. The mine owners refused even to talk with the strikers. By October, the strike was still not settled. Americans were facing the coming winter without coal for heat.

Roosevelt wanted a group of **arbiters** (ARE-bit-turs), or people with the power to decide a dispute, to settle the strike. When the mine owners refused this suggestion, Roosevelt said that he might send troops to operate the mines. The employers agreed to let the arbiters settle the strike. The workers received a raise and a nine-hour workday. It was the first time government had supported labor.

After his election in 1904, Roosevelt asked Congress to pass laws to improve

Think: **Roosevelt is shown washing the American eagle with anti-trust soap in this political cartoon.** Respond: **What is the cartoon telling us, and what symbols does it use?**

Think: **The above coal miners went on strike, protesting harsh working conditions. The mine owners did not want to sign long-term agreements.** Respond: **List arguments of each side.**

working conditions. He wanted to regulate child labor and to provide health and safety laws for factory workers. However, Congress did not respond right away to Roosevelt's proposals.

Roosevelt's Concern for the Environment

Roosevelt loved the outdoor life. He liked to camp, hunt, and hike in the wilderness. One hiking companion, John Muir, expressed his concerns about the country's vanishing wilderness areas. Muir believed in **conservation**, or the protection of natural resources. He wanted to preserve the nation's wilderness and natural wonders for all Americans to enjoy. Roosevelt was the first president to listen to the views of people like John Muir.

Other conservationists feared that lumber and other valuable resources would be destroyed by greedy companies. For years, lumber companies had cut down entire forests without replacing them. Ranchers had allowed sheep and cattle to eat away the grasslands of the Great Plains. Without plant roots to hold it in place, the topsoil was being blown away.

Much of this land had turned into useless "dust bowls."

Roosevelt pushed for measures to save these valuable resources. In 1902, Congress passed the **Newlands Reclamation Act**. This law allowed funds from the sale of federal lands to be used to irrigate or reclaim damaged land. In addition, President Roosevelt asked Congress to set aside more than 100 million acres of public land as national forests. Roosevelt also established six new national parks, including Crater Lake, Petrified Forest, and the Grand Canyon national parks.

Roosevelt was the first president to make Americans realize the importance of conserving the nation's resources.

Section Review

1. How did President Roosevelt view the trusts?
2. What was the Elkins Act?
3. How did President Roosevelt handle the Pennsylvania coal miner's strike of 1902?
4. What measures did President Roosevelt take to protect the

Think: **Theodore Roosevelt and John Muir behold the beauty of Yosemite.** Respond: **Why is the work of these two men so important to all generations who follow them?**

NATIONAL PARKS THROUGH THE PROGRESSIVE ERA

In this section, you read how Progressives enlarged the National Park System. This map shows where and when the parks were created, up through 1916. The map and the table above it help you to understand how much land was set aside for national parks. Notice also the size of each National Park.

Study the map and the map key.

1. What was the first national park? When was it created?

2. In what sections of the country were most of the national parks?

3. What kinds of geographic features tend to become part of national parks?

Now study the table at right.

4. Roosevelt was president from 1900 to 1908. How many acres of national parks did he create?

5. How many acres were in national parks before Roosevelt came into office?

6. How many acres of land did the second and third Progressive presidents turn into national parks? How many square miles? (A square mile is 640 acres.)

National Parks Through the Progressive Era

Park	Acres	Park	Acres
Acadia (ME) 1916	39,056	Mt. Rainier (WA) 1899	235,404
Crater Lake (OR) 1902	160,290	Olympic (WA) 1909	915,426
Glacier (MT) 1910	3,020,396	Petrified Forest (AZ) 1906	93,493
Grand Canyon (AZ) 1908	1,218,375	Rocky Mountain (CO) 1915	266,943
Hawaii Volcanoes (HI) 1916	229,177	Sequoia (CA) 1890	402,488
Hot Springs (ARK) 1832	5,826	Wind Cave (SD) 1903	28,292
Kings Canyon (CA) 1890	460,136	Yellowstone (ID, MT, WY) 1872	2,219,823
Lassen Volcanic (CA) 1907	106,372	Yosemite (CA) 1890	760,917
Mesa Verde (CO) 1906	52,085	Zion (UT) 1909	146,451

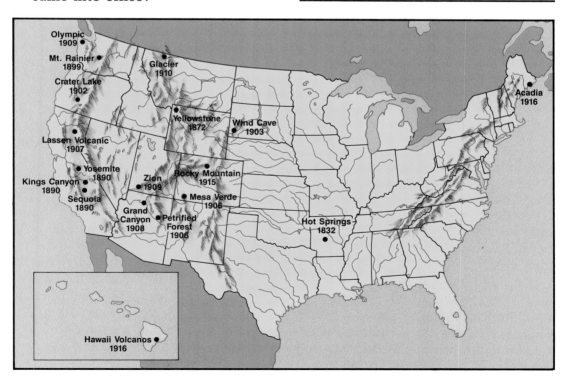

2. The Nation Under President Taft

Learn these important terms:

Mann-Elkins Act
Sixteenth Amendment
Bull Moose Party
Seventeenth Amendment

Remember the main idea:

Although President Taft supported many of the ideas and policies of President Roosevelt, he was a great disappointment to the Progressives.

Look for answers to these questions:

1. What did President Taft achieve during his term?
2. Why were the Progressives disappointed with President Taft?
3. Why did Theodore Roosevelt start his own political party?

Theodore Roosevelt was easily elected president in the election of 1904. He was an extremely popular president and could have run for reelection in 1908. However, Roosevelt believed at that time that two terms were enough for any president. He refused to run again. Roosevelt suggested the Republicans choose William Howard Taft, his secretary of war, as their candidate. Roosevelt was sure that Taft believed in Progressive ideas.

The Democrats again chose William Jennings Bryan as their candidate. During the campaign, the Democrats accused the Republicans of favoring big business. They promised to defend the interests of the common people.

The Republicans also appealed to the average American. They promised to lower the tariff, to regulate big businesses, and to continue the conservation of natural resources. With the enthusiastic support of popular President Roosevelt, Taft easily won the election of 1908. However, his term was a difficult one.

William Howard Taft was not at all like Theodore Roosevelt. Roosevelt believed the president had the right to do anything not forbidden by the Constitution. Taft, on the other hand, believed the president should do only what the Constitution required of him. Taft was not a strong leader, nor did he have Roosevelt's energy and personal style. He was slow in making decisions. Yet, Taft passed twice as much Progressive legislation as Roosevelt. This fact was overlooked by many people because Taft lacked the strong leadership qualities of Roosevelt. Even the Progressives distrusted Taft from the beginning. And he soon confirmed some of their suspicions.

Taft Disappoints the Progressives

One of the issues the Progressives had supported was lowering the tariff. Republicans traditionally voted for high tariffs because they wanted to protect American industry from overseas competition. However, tariff rates were so high in 1909 that there was little competition among American industries. As a result, prices on American goods were too high. President Taft asked Congress to lower the tariff to promote competition. Congress, however, passed a higher tariff bill. The Progressives urged Taft to veto the bill. Instead, Taft signed the bill into law. The Progressives felt Taft had let them down.

Another disappointment for the Progressives was President Taft's conservation policies. Taft allowed his secretary of the interior, Richard Ballinger, to open up

some government lands for use by private companies. These lands had been set aside by the Roosevelt administration. Gifford Pinchot, chief of the Forest Service, attacked Ballinger's actions. After Pinchot wrote an angry letter to Congress, Taft fired him for openly criticizing the secretary. Progressives immediately labeled Taft an enemy of conservation. However, Taft believed in conservation and continued many of Roosevelt's policies. He set aside more public land as national forests than Roosevelt had.

Taft's Achievements

The Progressives also labeled President Taft a friend of business. Yet Taft's administration brought ninety anti-trust suits against big business, twice as many as Roosevelt. In 1911, two large trusts, the Standard Oil Company and the American Tobacco Company, were broken up.

During Taft's term, Congress passed the **Mann-Elkins Act**. This law, which was strongly backed by Taft, was a blow to the railroad monopolies. It gave the Interstate Commerce Commission the power to regulate railroad rates. The Commission also gained the power to regulate the telephone and telegraph companies.

Under Taft, many other Progressive ideas were made into laws. New labor laws provided safety regulations for railroad employees and an eight-hour day for federal employees. Taft also created a Children's Bureau within the Department of Labor to gather information on working children. In another Progressive victory, Congress passed a law that required its members to make public their source of campaign funds. Congress also set up the parcel post system.

During Taft's term, Congress proposed the Sixteenth and Seventeenth Amendments to the Constitution. The **Sixteenth Amendment** gave the federal government the right to pass an income tax law. The **Seventeenth Amendment** gave the voters the power to elect senators directly. President Taft backed both these amendments, which became laws in 1913. In

William Howard Taft (1857-1930) is the only man in history to serve both as president and as chief justice of the United States. He enjoyed the latter office much more.

SKILLS FOCUS: Planning a Report

When you are asked to write a report, remember to plan. The more planning you do, the better your actual writing will be.

The first step in planning a report is to choose a topic. The topic, of course, should be one that is interesting to you. Your interest will help pull you through hours of research and writing. Your choice of topic is also determined by the length of the assigned report. The topic should be neither too broad nor too narrow to cover in the length of the report assigned. A five-page report on the topic of the Progressive Movement would be a difficult assignment because there is too much material to cover effectively. On the other hand, a person doing a report of the same length on President Taft's sense of humor might not find enough information on the topic.

After you choose your topic, you need to plan how and where you will locate information on your topic. Library research can yield facts about most topics. Start by browsing through your school library or the public library. Also consider talking to, or interviewing, resource persons who might know about your topic.

An important step in planning a report is making a schedule for each step of the process. Here are the steps you might take:

a. Locating information.
b. Taking notes. (Write one fact per card. List the source of information on each card.)
c. Making an outline. (Organize facts into categories. Decide which facts are main ideas and which facts are supporting details. Arrange them logically.)
d. Writing the first draft. (Write in paragraphs. Be sure the report has a beginning, a middle, and an end.)
e. Revising. (Rearrange information if necessary to make better sense. Correct all spelling and grammar errors.)

Plan a five-page report on some aspect of Roosevelt as an effective Progressive leader, as discussed in Section 1 of Chapter 23.

1 What topic will you choose? Remember to make it neither too broad nor too narrow and to choose a topic that truly interests you.

2 What sources can you use for your information?

3 Make a schedule for your report. Write down the amount of time you think it will take for each step of the process.

a. Locate information.
b. Take notes.
c. Make an outline.
d. Write the report. (Usually this is only about one-third of the total time.)
e. Revise the report. (Revision should take as long as writing the first draft.)

spite of Taft's achievements, his many critics continued to believe that he was a poor replacement for Roosevelt.

Roosevelt Breaks with Taft

In the election of 1910, the Democrats won control of the House of Representatives. The Democrats also gained seats in the Senate. The Progressives, who were mostly Republicans, blamed these losses on President Taft. Theodore Roosevelt, too, felt that his old friend had let down the Progressives. Roosevelt did not want Taft to be reelected.

Taft, however, was the leader of the Republican Party and won the nomination at the convention in June 1912. As a result, Roosevelt and the Progressives left the Republican Party. They formed their own political party and named it the Progressive Party, or **Bull Moose Party**. It was nicknamed the Bull Moose Party because Roosevelt boasted that he was as strong as a "bull moose."

In the election, Roosevelt got more than four million votes. Taft trailed Roosevelt by more than 600,000 votes. This split in the Republican vote handed the election to the Democrats. Their candidate was Woodrow Wilson, the reform governor of New Jersey. Wilson received over six million votes and was elected president.

Section Review

1. How did President Taft view his role as president? How was it different from Roosevelt's view?
2. What was the purpose of the Mann-Elkins Act?
3. Why did Theodore Roosevelt refuse to back President Taft for reelection?
4. What helped Woodrow Wilson win the election of 1912?

---

3. Wilson and the New Freedom

Learn these important terms:

New Freedom
Federal Reserve Act
Federal Reserve System
Clayton Anti-Trust Act
Federal Trade Commission Act
Underwood Tariff
graduated income tax
interest
Adamson Act
Keating–Owen Act
Federal Farm Loan Act

Remember the main idea:

Woodrow Wilson achieved most of his goals for the nation during his first term as president.

Look for answers to these questions:

1. What was President Wilson's New Freedom?
2. How did President Wilson handle the trusts?
3. What new laws helped farmers and workers?

Two Republican presidents, Theodore Roosevelt and William Howard Taft, carried the Progressive Movement to the White House. However, many Democrats were Progressives, too. Woodrow Wilson, elected president in 1912, brought a new and more ambitious Progressive program to the White House.

Woodrow Wilson (1856-1924) was governor of New Jersey before becoming president of the United States. He led America through World War I, a trying time.

President Wilson, like Roosevelt, believed that the president must be a strong leader. Woodrow Wilson's campaign plans for running the government were called the **New Freedom**. The New Freedom included lowering the tariff, reforming the nation's banks, and breaking up the monopolies. Now that Congress was controlled by Democrats, most of Wilson's program became law.

President Wilson wasted no time in asking Congress to lower the tariff. A lower tariff would increase competition by lowering the price of imports. Wilson knew that increased competition would help break up the monopolies. In 1913, Congress passed the **Underwood Tariff**. This law lowered the tariff for the first time since the Civil War. Many new items, such as iron, steel, and farm machinery, were added to the tax-free list.

Congress knew the new tariff would reduce the government's customs revenue. Therefore, they included a tax reform measure in the Underwood Tariff law. This reform called for a **graduated income tax**. Under this law, the wealthy paid taxes at a higher rate than people with low incomes. Americans earning less than $4,000 a year paid no taxes.

Think: This scene shows a line to income tax windows in 1918. When the Sixteenth Amendment, allowing graduated taxes, passed, many people had to pay no tax at all. The wealthiest people paid the most tax, 6 percent for those earning over $500,000. Respond: What do you think of graduated taxes?

Fighting the Trusts

Unlike Roosevelt, President Wilson wanted to break up the trusts, not just regulate them. Only when the trusts were broken up, Wilson believed, could competition really exist. Congress supported Wilson's anti-trust policies by passing two laws in 1914. They were the **Clayton Anti-Trust Act** and the **Federal Trade Commission Act**. The purpose of these two acts was to end the control of any industry by a few big companies.

The Clayton Anti-Trust Act clearly listed the things big companies were not allowed to do. It particularly prohibited unfair business practices that limited competition. For example, fixing prices for an entire industry was outlawed. The law also stated the conditions under which injunctions, or court orders, could be used to stop strikes.

The purpose of the Federal Trade Commission was to regulate business activities. A five-member commission was set up to make sure the Clayton Anti-Trust Act was obeyed. The commission had the power to tell a corporation to stop its unfair practices. Its power was limited to overseeing the trusts, however. The commission could not break up trusts.

Breaking Up the Banking Trust

President Wilson was interested in breaking up one of the biggest trusts, the nation's banking system. The banking system was controlled by a few powerful bankers. They regulated the flow of money and decided what rates of **interest** to charge. Interest is the fee charged by banks for lending money. To solve this problem, President Wilson asked Congress to pass the **Federal Reserve Act**.

The Federal Reserve Act greatly improved America's banking system and is still in operation today. This law, passed in 1913, developed the **Federal Reserve System**. The Federal Reserve System consists of twelve Federal Reserve Banks located throughout the country. The Federal Reserve System controls the flow of money by setting the interest rate at which smaller banks can borrow money from the twelve Federal Reserve Banks. The Federal Reserve System also issues paper money and handles all the federal government's money.

Wilson Helps the Farmers and Workers

In the Congressional elections of 1914, the Republicans made important gains. To win more support, Wilson realized he had to help America's farmers and workers. Farmers needed money to run their farms. Most farmers could not borrow money from banks because banks charged very high rates of interest on loans. So President Wilson asked Congress to pass the **Federal Farm Loan Act**. This law set up special banks to provide easy loans to farmers.

Under Wilson's leadership, Congress also passed laws that helped workers. The **Adamson Act** gave railroad workers on interstate lines an eight-hour workday. By passing this law, Congress helped to prevent a nationwide railroad strike. The **Keating–Owen Act**, passed in 1916, strictly regulated child labor. However, the Supreme Court later declared this law unconstitutional.

By 1916, the Progressive era was coming to an end. Although many social reforms were passed, the Progressives did not achieve all their goals. Stronger anti-trust laws were passed, but big business was still very powerful. Some workers were helped by Progressive reforms. But for many workers, labor conditions remained the same. Political reforms improved city and state governments.

HISTORY MAKERS

Louis D. Brandeis

The People's Attorney

"Gentlemen of the Court, I ask you to examine the figures. Twenty states have passed laws which limit working hours for women and protect their health and safety on the job. Why? Because the numbers show that women who work more than ten hours a day become exhausted. Exhaustion leads to illness, and illness leads to a drop in factory production. A shorter working day means greater profits for manufacturers and for our whole society. Women who work only ten hours a day have more time to do the cooking, cleaning, laundry, and sewing, and to raise their families."

It was 1908, and legal history was being made. Louis D. Brandeis was arguing a case, *Muller v. Oregon*, before the Supreme Court. Oregon was being sued by a manufacturer over a recent state law which limited the working hours of women. Louis D. Brandeis used human rights issues and numerical information on working conditions to prove his case. Until this argument, known as the "Brandeis Brief," court cases were argued on the basis of past cases and decisions. Brandeis's use of figures and human rights introduced a different way of presenting, arguing, and deciding court cases.

Louis Brandeis felt that monopolies of any kind were undemocratic. He fought in the courts against transportation and insurance trusts, often refusing to accept any payment for his work. He worked with labor unions and management to arbitrate disputes, settle strikes, and create fair working conditions.

Brandeis's philosophy became the basis of Woodrow Wilson's "New Freedom" platform in the 1912 presidential campaign. Wilson was impressed by Brandeis's ideas. He called for new anti-trust laws, government regulation of big business and of working conditions, and federal money for education.

In 1916, President Wilson nominated Brandeis to the United States Supreme Court. He became the first Jewish Supreme Court Justice. Louis D. Brandeis wanted to make America a better place for everyone. He believed in equality of opportunity for men and women, and he devoted his life to an earnest pursuit of social justice.

Think: In the cartoon above, President Wilson is shown directing the "traffic" of American businesses. Note that he is giving "Legitimate Business" the right-of-way while holding up "Monopoly." He took a typically Progressive stance against big business. Respond: What other Progressive ideas did President Wilson agree with?

Yet, women had not yet received the vote. And child labor was still legal.

Nevertheless, the Progressive Movement brought about many changes in American government in a very short period. Americans had accepted the Progressive idea that the federal government was responsible for the welfare of all the people. And government no longer protected the interests of all big businesses at the expense of the public good.

President Wilson had achieved most of the Progressive goals of his New Freedom program during his first term. By 1916, however, he had less time to devote to social reforms. World attention was fo-cused on Europe. A great war had begun, and Wilson needed to protect the interests of the United States.

Section Review

1. How did President Wilson try to break up the trusts?
2. What was the purpose of the Federal Reserve Act?
3. How did President Wilson help the farmers?
4. What did the Keating–Owen Act call for?

CHAPTER SUMMARY

Theodore Roosevelt became president in 1901 after the assassination of President McKinley. He represented the Progressive Movement. His actions against the big trusts earned him the name "trustbuster." Under him, Congress passed laws to regulate the railroads. Roosevelt's settlement of the coal miners' strike showed that he would give labor a fair deal. Roosevelt was the first president to support conservation.

William Howard Taft was elected president in 1908. He continued the Progressive policies of Roosevelt, but his cautious manner irritated the Progressives. During Taft's term, Congress passed amendments providing for an income tax and the direct election of senators. Roosevelt refused to back Taft for reelection in 1912. He split away from the Republicans and started his own party, with himself as candidate. However, the Democrat, Woodrow Wilson, won the election.

President Wilson's New Freedom program lowered the tariff, introduced a federal income tax law, and reformed the banking system. The Federal Reserve System was set up in 1913. Two strong anti-trust laws were passed in 1914, the Clayton Anti-Trust Act and the Federal Trade Commission Act. Under Wilson, Congress also passed laws that helped farmers and workers.

Key Words

Write a sentence to explain the meaning of each of these terms.

Square Deal   *New Freedom*
Bull Moose   *Clayton*
  Party   *Anti-Trust*
arbiters   *Act*
conservation

Major Events

Choose the answer that best completes the statement.

1. The Supreme Court supported "trustbusting" in 1904 by

   a) approving the Adamson Act.
   b) regulating the banks.
   c) acting against the railroads.

2. Government supported labor for the first time

   a) with the Hepburn Act of 1903.
   b) while Taft was president.
   c) during the coal strike of 1902.

3. The Mann-Elkins Act passed during Taft's term

   a) helped farmers.
   b) limited child labor.
   c) regulated the railroads.

4. The Federal Reserve Act of 1913
   a) prevented a nationwide railroad strike.
   b) improved the banking system.
   c) prohibited unfair business practices.

5. Between 1901 and 1916, Congress

   a) passed Progressive reforms.
   b) was always controlled by Republicans.
   c) supported the railroads.

Review

Important Facts

Answer each question with at least one complete sentence.

1. According to Roosevelt, what was government's role in dealing with the trusts?

2. What was the purpose of the Elkins and Hepburn Acts?

3. What problems concerned John Muir and other conservationists?

4. Name two ways Theodore Roosevelt helped America's conservation effort.

5. Why did Roosevelt refuse to run in 1908? Why did he recommend Taft as a candidate?

6. In what ways did Taft disappoint the Progressives?

7. Why didn't Roosevelt support Taft for reelection? Who ran for president in 1912?

8. What were the Sixteenth and Seventeenth Amendments?

9. Name two things Taft accomplished.

10. Why did President Wilson push through the Underwood Tariff?

11. What was President Wilson's attitude toward the trusts? How did he differ from Roosevelt?

12. What was the purpose of the Federal Trade Commission?

13. How did the Federal Farm Loan Act help farmers?

14. How did the Federal Reserve System work? Why were these reforms necessary?

Skill Review

Study this map and table, then answer the following questions.

1. Which national forests lie entirely within Arizona? How many acres do they have in total?

2. Which national forests extend beyond Arizona's borders? How many acres do they have?

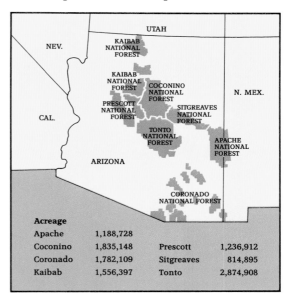

Acreage			
Apache	1,188,728		
Coconino	1,835,148	Prescott	1,236,912
Coronado	1,782,109	Sitgreaves	814,895
Kaibab	1,556,397	Tonto	2,874,908

Arizona National Forests

Critical Thinking

Write a paragraph to answer each question.

1. Compare the leadership qualities of Roosevelt and Taft. How did these qualities influence their popularity?

2. What were the goals of Wilson's New Freedom? What did these goals have in common with the Progressive Movement? How were they different?

CHAPTER
24
Becoming a World Power

Years 1914–1921

World War I began	*Lusitania* sunk by Germans	United States declared war on Germany Selective Service Act passed	World War I ended	United States Senate voted against the Versailles Treaty
1914	1915	1917	1918	1920

1. The United States Tries To Remain Neutral

Learn these important terms:

alliances
Central Powers
Allied Powers
submarine

Remember the main idea:

When World War I broke out in Europe, the United States tried to remain neutral. Germany's repeated attacks on American ships finally forced the United States to enter the war.

Look for answers to these questions:

1. What events led to the outbreak of war in Europe in 1914?
2. How did President Wilson try to keep America neutral?
3. What events finally brought the United States into the war?

In the early 1900s, the United States expanded its boundaries and began to play a role in world affairs. The United States acquired new overseas territories, including Spain's former colonies of the Philippines and Puerto Rico. It also became involved in China and Latin America. And by 1914, the United States had built the Panama Canal. Meanwhile, European nations were also building overseas empires. By the early 1900s, competition for colonies among the European powers had grown fierce. Great Britain, France, Russia, and Germany had built up huge armies. As the European nations struggled for economic and military power, the stage was set for war.

In this chapter you will read about World War I. You will find out how war broke out in Europe and why the United States became involved. Once the United States entered the war, Americans joined together to support the war effort. When World War I was over, life in America had changed, and the United States had become a leading world power.

By the early 1900s, all of the major European powers had built up huge armies. They also formed **alliances**, or treaties, to protect one another. Great Britain, France, and Russia joined together to form the **Allied Powers** (Allies). Germany joined with Austria-Hungary to form the **Central Powers**. Later, they were joined by Turkey and Bulgaria. The countries in each alliance agreed to fight to defend any members which were attacked. An uneasy peace existed in Europe.

The peace was broken suddenly on June 28, 1914, in the town of Sarajevo

EUROPE IN 1914

Think: **In 1882, Italy signed a Triple Alliance with Germany and Austria-Hungary. Each would support the others in case of attack. When World War I began, the Central Powers looked to Italy for help. But Italy remained neutral, saying the Central Powers were the attackers. In 1915, Italy joined the Allies.** Respond: **Why do you think Italy supported the Allies?**

in Austria-Hungary. Archduke Franz Ferdinand, heir to the throne of Austria-Hungary, and his wife were visiting the province of Bosnia. Bosnia was one of many territories controlled by the Austro-Hungarian empire. A large number of Serbs lived in Bosnia. They wanted to break away from Austria-Hungary and join the neighboring country of Serbia.

As Archduke Franz Ferdinand and his wife drove past the crowds in Sarajevo, two shots rang out. They were fired by Gavrilo Princip, a discontented young Serbian. The assassination of the Archduke and his wife set off a chain reaction that eventually led to a long, costly, and

terrible world war. First, Austria declared war on Serbia. Because Russia announced it would defend Serbia, Germany declared war on Russia. France and England were drawn into the dispute because they were allied with Russia. By August 1914, World War I had begun.

America Tries To Stay Out of War

Both the Allies and the Central Powers tried to win America's support. However, Americans did not want to be involved with the war in Europe. Still, many Americans sympathized with the Allies because they shared the same language and culture with the British. On the other hand, Americans of German heritage favored the Central Powers.

Both the Allies and the Central Powers used propaganda to win American support. Great Britain was especially successful at stirring up hatred for the Germans. It accused the Germans of cruelly attacking innocent people. Although there was no evidence behind these stories, many Americans believed them.

Nevertheless, President Woodrow Wilson declared that the United States intended to remain neutral. This meant that the United States was not going to favor either the Allies or the Central Powers. It also meant that the United States was willing to sell supplies to nations on both sides.

The Sinking of the Lusitania

Both Great Britain and Germany tried to stop American ships from carrying supplies to the enemy. Germany used a new weapon, the **submarine**, which attacked while under water. Submarines depended on a surprise attack, and they gave no warning before attacking a ship.

In 1915, the British passenger ship *Lusitania* (loos-uh-TAYN-yuh) was sunk by a German submarine. The British ship was carrying ammunition as well as passengers. Although they had been warned of the dangers, some Americans still chose to travel on this ship. When the *Lusitania* sank, 1,198 people were killed, 128 of them Americans. People in the United States were shocked and angry over this sinking.

President Wilson demanded that Germany stop sinking passenger ships without warning them first to surrender. President Wilson also asked for a money payment for the Americans who died. The Germans agreed to all these demands. This promise kept President Wilson from asking Congress to declare war.

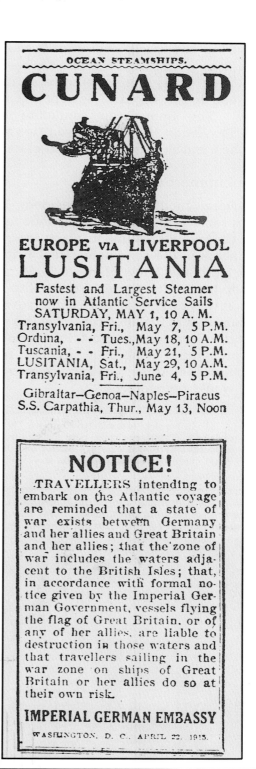

Think: **Read this warning issued by the Germans before they sank the *Lusitania*. Years later it was discovered that weapons were on board.** Respond: **Was this a fair warning? Explain.**

During the crisis over the *Lusitania*, President Wilson was running for reelection. His party, the Democrats, campaigned on the slogan, "He kept us out of war!" The Republican candidate was Charles Evans Hughes. Wilson defeated Hughes, but it was a very close election.

The Zimmerman Note

Several months after President Wilson's reelection, the Germans announced that they would resume firing on any neutral ships in the seas near Great Britain. The Germans knew that their decision might bring the United States into the war. It was a risk they were willing to take because Great Britain's control of the seas hurt the German war effort. Furthermore, by preventing American supplies from reaching the Allies, Germany hoped the war would be over quickly.

Think: In his war message to Congress, Wilson declared, "Property can be paid for; the lives of peaceful and innocent people cannot be." **Respond:** What made Wilson support going to war?

In February of 1917, shortly after Germany's announcement, the British sent President Wilson a copy of a telegram they had intercepted. The telegram was sent by Arthur Zimmerman, the German foreign minister, to the Mexican government. In this note, Germany promised to help Mexico regain New Mexico, Texas, and Arizona. Mexico had only to agree to fight with the Central Powers if the United States attacked Germany.

Think: Many Americans wanted the United States to stay out of the war. The photograph below shows demonstrators carrying signs during a May Day parade. Some people believed the United States was profiting by the war in Europe. **Respond:** Do you agree or disagree with these accusations? Why?

Major events like World War I do not have one simple cause. Two deaths in a remote corner of Europe do not explain the outbreak of global war. To understand the causes of World War I, you need to look at the chain of events which led up to it.

Think of this series of events as a row of dominoes. Something causes the first domino to fall. It then causes the next one to fall. Each event in the chain has a cause and an effect. The effect, in turn, may become the cause of the next event.

The chart below shows some of the events leading up to the entry of the United States into World War I. Copy the chart on a separate sheet of paper. Then fill in the correct cause and effect for each event. Choose your answers from the lists above the chart. Write the letter of the correct answer in the blank.

Causes

a. Germany seeks allies in North America.

b. Russia promises to aid Serbia.

c. The British control the seas and the flow of supplies to Europe.

d. Serbs in Bosnia do not want to be controlled by Austria-Hungary.

e. Germany needs to destroy ammunition going to the Allies.

f. The Central Powers do not want the U.S. to enter the war.

Effects

g. The United States enters the war on the Allied side.

h. President Wilson demands that Germany pay reparations and stop sinking ships without warning.

i. Austria declares war on Serbia.

j. President Wilson maintains American neutrality.

k. France and England enter the war to help Russia.

CAUSE	EVENT	EFFECT
_____	**1** A Serbian kills the Archduke and Archduchess of Austria-Hungary.	_____
_____	**2** Germany declares war on Russia.	_____
_____	**3** Germany sinks the British ship *Lusitania*.	_____
_____	**4** Germany agrees to President Wilson's demands.	_____
_____	**5** Germany resumes firing on neutral ships and sinks three American vessels.	_____
_____	**6** Germany sends the Zimmermann note to Mexico.	_____

Think: Notice the symbols for America on the front page of this newspaper, dated April 6, 1917. Read the paper's headlines. Respond: How can you tell that most Americans supported the war?

The Zimmerman note and the sinking in March of three American ships ended America's neutrality. Wilson could no longer keep the United States out of the war. He asked Congress to declare war on Germany. "The world," he said, "must be made safe for democracy." Congress agreed and declared war on Germany on April 6, 1917.

Section Review

1. Which countries joined together to form the Allied Powers? Which countries formed the Central Powers?

2. Why did some Americans support the Allies even though America remained neutral?

3. How did President Wilson handle the sinking of the *Lusitania*?

4. What combination of events led the United States to declare war on Germany?

2. The United States Goes to War

Learn these important terms:

convoy
War Industries Board
Selective Service Act
armistice

Remember the main idea:

The United States played an important role in winning World War I. Americans at home supplied weapons and food. American soldiers helped defeat the German army on the battlefield.

Look for answers to these questions:

1. How did Americans contribute to the war effort at home?

2. What important contributions did American women make during World War I?

3. What major battles stopped the German advance on the Western Front?

When the United States entered the war in 1917, the Allies and Central Powers had been fighting for almost three years. With enemies on both eastern and western borders, the Central Powers had to fight on two fronts. At the beginning of the war, Germany had hoped to conquer France quickly after invading Belgium. This plan did not work, however. Fighting continued on the Western Front.

Both the Allies and the Central Powers dug trenches for six hundred miles across

Belgium and France. From inside the trenches, the two sides shot at each other. Sometimes, one side tried to attack the other side by crossing the area between the two sets of trenches, called "no-man's land." The attackers faced a steady stream of machine gun fire that killed hundreds of soldiers at a time. These attacks were costly for both sides. After three long years, the Allies and the Central Powers had fought to a stalemate on the Western Front.

Control of the Eastern Front did not belong clearly to either side. The Central Powers had originally planned to concentrate on the eastern campaign after quickly defeating France. But the Germans could not take France. Nor could they gain a victory over Russia.

The Russian army fought on for three years, despite a number of problems. When Turkey joined the Central Powers in 1914, Russia had another enemy on its borders. Moreover, the Russian army was a poor match for the well-equipped German troops. It lost millions of soldiers in the first three years of fighting. These staggering losses led to the downfall of the Russian government in March 1917.

Think: Chemical and gas warfare caused massive casualties in World War I. Respond: What feelings does the artwork by French artist de Groux convey about this type of warfare?

Musée des Deux Guerre Mondiales

Think: *Troops Waiting To Advance* **by W.J. Aylward shows soldiers relaxing as best they could between battles. Their relief upon escaping the awful conditions of trench warfare was short-lived. Later, marching through the rubble of a once-active city, the troops took St. Mihiel. Respond: What thoughts might these soldiers have?**

Think: Newton Baker, Secretary of War, drew the first draft number of World War I. Respond: Why was the Selective Service Act passed on May 18, 1917?

As the United States entered the war in the spring of 1917, the Allied position looked weak. It appeared that the Russians might surrender to the Germans. Furthermore, the Allies had run short of food and supplies. In an effort to end British control of the seas, German submarines had sunk many ships. Fewer and fewer supplies were reaching the Allies.

The United States rushed to raise and train an army to send overseas. In May of 1917, Congress passed the *Selective Service Act*. This law required all men between the ages of 21 and 30 to register to serve in the armed forces. Almost three million men were drafted. Two million more volunteered. By the end of the war, almost five million Americans served in the army and navy, including thousands of women. Women served as nurses, telegraph operators, and clerks.

Once the soldiers were trained, they were sent to Europe by *convoy*. A convoy was a group of ships carrying men and supplies guarded by navy warships. The convoys worked so well that only two American troop ships were sunk by the German submarines.

The War Effort at Home

As American soldiers were shipped overseas, Americans at home prepared for the war effort. They needed to provide both the Allies and American troops with food and supplies.

President Wilson asked Herbert Hoover to take charge of food collection. Under Hoover, American farmers were asked to raise more food for the war effort. The government encouraged their efforts by raising the prices of farm products. Hoover also asked Americans to give up bread and meat one day a week. These days were called ''Wheatless Mondays'' and ''Meatless Tuesdays.'' The program worked so well that the government raised enough food to supply both the Allies and the American troops.

Think: The first U.S. Savings Bonds were issued during World War I. Below is a bond rally on Wall Street. Respond: Why were bonds a good way to help pay for the war?

On the Job for Victory, The Museum of Modern Art

Think: Merchant marine ships were among the war products being built in American factories. These products were sold for great profits to both sides at the beginning of the war. Later, only the Allies received American goods. **Respond: Of** what does this poster by Jonas Lie try to convince its viewers?

ON THE JOB FOR VICTORY

UNITED STATES SHIPPING BOARD   EMERGENCY FLEET CORPORATION

Meanwhile, Americans worked extra hours in the factories producing goods needed for the war. A **War Industries Board** was formed in July 1917 to direct factory production. Within a year, nearly all American factories operated day and night producing ammunition, rifles, clothing, and other military supplies. With so many men drafted for the war, women took over many of the jobs that only men had been allowed to hold before the war. They worked in factories, drove tractors, and ran businesses. Others worked for organizations such as the Red Cross. Their contributions to the war effort were recognized and appreciated.

Fighting the War

While Americans at home showed their patriotic spirit, American navy ships were destroying German submarines. In 1917 and 1918, many German submarines were sunk when the navy laid thousands of mines in the North Sea. These efforts seemed to be working. The flow of food and supplies to Germany almost stopped. The Germans were weakening.

Then, in November 1917, a revolution took place in Russia and a new government came to power. The Russian army was exhausted and without food or supplies. In March 1918, the new government signed a treaty with Germany and withdrew from the war. Germany quickly moved its soldiers from Russia to the Western Front in France.

Think: With so many job opportunities, women were getting the chance to prove themselves. Respond: **What other changes for women came about during World War I? Why?**

Think: **On May 31, 1918, the Germans were on the banks of the Marne, near Paris. But American troops blocked the enemy at Château-Thierry. George Harding's drawing captures the movement of American soldiers toward Château-Thierry.** Respond: **What might have resulted had the Americans not joined the war?**

As the new wave of German soldiers attacked the Allied lines in France, American troops arrived. They were just in time to help the sagging British and French lines. At the battles of Cantigny (kahn-teen-YEE), Chateau-Thierry (sha-TOH-tye-REE) and Belleau Wood (BEL-oh), American soldiers forced the Germans to withdraw. There were tremendous losses on both sides.

In July 1918, the German army attacked Paris. The American forces, led by General John Pershing, stopped the attack and pushed the Germans back. For the next several months, German troops continued to retreat. On November 7, 1918, Germany asked for an *armistice* (AHR-muh-stuss), or an end to the fighting. On November 11, 1918, the Allies agreed to an armistice.

World War I took more lives than any previous war. Almost twelve million soldiers were killed, and twenty million were severely wounded. In the rest of this chapter, you will read about President Wilson's peace plan after "the war to end all wars."

Section Review

1. What was the Selective Service Act of 1917?
2. What contributions did women make to the war effort?
3. How did the Russian revolution help the Germans?
4. Where did the Allied troops stop the German advance?

MAP WORKSHOP USING MAP AND READING SKILLS

WORLD WAR I

You can combine your map skills with your reading skills to get information. After you have read Section 2 of the text about World War I, study the map below and its *inset*. Maps often have insets to give you a close-up view of a part of the larger map. Notice the battles and Armistice Line on this inset.

Use the map and the text to answer these questions.

1. Which European nations were neutral?

2. Which non-European nation was a Central Power?

3. Which side, the Allies or the Central Powers, advanced beyond the stabilized front in France?

4. In which battles did American soldiers take part?

5. How do you explain the fact that the war lasted much longer than expected?

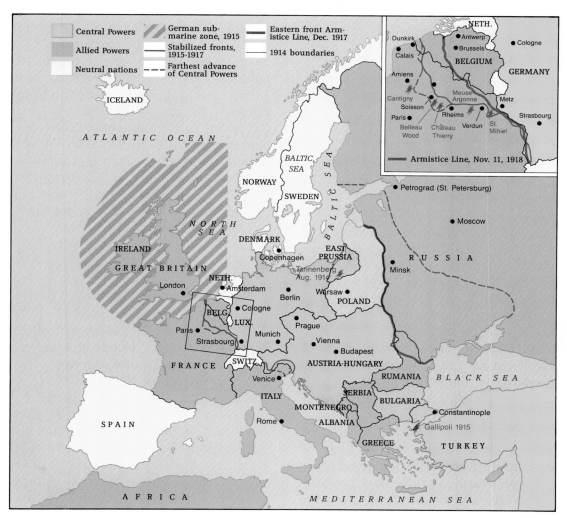

3. Peacemaking After World War I

Learn these important terms:

Fourteen Points
League of Nations
reparations
Treaty of Versailles

Remember the main idea:

Allied leaders turned down most of President Wilson's peace plan. The United States Senate refused to accept the Treaty of Versailles.

Look for answers to these questions:

1. What was President Wilson's plan for peace?
2. Why did President Wilson accept most of the Allies' demands?
3. Why did the Senate refuse to accept the Treaty of Versailles?

President Wilson believed that by fighting World War I, the United States had made "the world safe for democracy." He wanted the peace to be fair to both the losers and the winners of the war. He did not wish to punish the Central Powers or take away their territories.

In 1917, President Wilson announced the *Fourteen Points*, or his plan for peace. His Fourteen Points included an end to secret treaties, freedom of the seas, a reduction of military forces, and the right of all people to choose their own government. The fourteenth point, and the most important to President Wilson, called for all nations to join a *League of Nations*. Its purpose was to keep the peace and to settle problems among nations. President Wilson believed that a League of Nations could prevent future wars.

In December 1918, President Wilson sailed for Europe to attend the peace conference at Versailles (ver-SY), in Paris. Wherever he went in Europe, huge crowds turned out to greet him as a hero. At the peace conference, Wilson was joined by David Lloyd George of Great Britain, Georges Clemenceau (KLEM-un-SOH) of France, and Vittorio Orlando (or-LAN-doh) of Italy. These leaders were known as the "Big Four" because they dominated the peace talks. The Russians were in the midst of a civil war and did not attend the peace conference.

President Wilson presented the Allied leaders with his plan for peace. But the Allies turned down most of the Fourteen Points. Britain and France wanted Germany to be punished. They wanted *reparations* (REP-uh-RAY-shuns), or large amounts of money from Germany to pay for the lives and property destroyed in the war. President Wilson had to accept most of their demands in order to get the Allies to form the League of Nations.

The Treaty of Versailles

The peace treaty that ended World War I, the *Treaty of Versailles*, was signed on June 28, 1919. Germany and all of the European Allies, except Russia, signed the treaty. The treaty was not what Wilson had hoped for. His plea for a "peace without victory" was not honored. France and Great Britain won their revenge by making Germany fully responsible for $15 billion in reparations to the Allies. Germany was also required to pay an unspecified amount in other compensations. In effect, the Germans were asked to sign a blank check. That amount totalled almost $33 billion by 1921! In

Think: The Big Four met at Versailles in Paris to discuss peace terms. None of the representatives achieved all of his goals. Pictured left to right are Vittorio Orlando, David Lloyd George, Georges Clemenceau, and Woodrow Wilson. Respond: Why didn't Russia have a representative at the Versailles conference?

EUROPE IN 1919

Think: When World War I ended, new national boundaries were drawn in Europe. Many new nations were formed. Most of the Allies gained territory, although Russia lost a great deal of territory. The Central Powers also lost much territory. Respond: Why were the new boundaries drawn? Do you think they were fair?

addition, Germany lost all of its overseas colonies. It was also forbidden to rebuild its army and navy.

Two points that were important to President Wilson were included in the Treaty of Versailles. Borders were redefined and new independent nations were created, including Poland and Yugoslavia (yew-goh-SLAHV-ee-uh). Most important of all, the treaty called for a League of Nations to be formed. Its purpose was to solve peacefully any problems among nations that threatened world peace.

Americans Debate over the League

When President Wilson returned to the United States, he was confident that the treaty would be approved. However, President Wilson had overlooked a growing desire among Americans to pull back from European affairs. A powerful spokesman for this position was Henry Cabot Lodge, Republican senator from Massachusetts.

Lodge was determined to stop Wilson's plan for a League of Nations. He argued that the United States might get involved in future wars in Europe by protecting nations in the League. Lodge and many other senators refused to approve the treaty. They wanted changes made in the plan for the League of Nations.

President Wilson refused to accept any changes in his plan. In September 1919, Wilson traveled across the United States to urge Americans to support the Treaty of Versailles. Opponents of the treaty also toured the country to speak out against it. Feelings ran high on both sides.

Think: **President Wilson worked hard trying to convince Americans to accept the Treaty of Versailles, which called for a League of Nations.** Respond: **Why did the Senate refuse?**

While on this speaking campaign, President Wilson suffered a stroke in Colorado. He was unable to continue his tour. Twice while President Wilson was still sick the Senate voted to turn down the treaty. The Senate refused to accept the treaty as long as the League of Nations was included.

President Wilson expected the presidential election of 1920 to show that Americans favored the treaty and the League. Instead, the Democratic Party lost the election to the Republicans. The United States never joined the League of Nations. A separate treaty was signed with Germany in 1921. Wilson's plan for a lasting world peace had failed.

Think: **Sir William Orpen captured an historic moment in** *The Signing of the Versailles Treaty in the Hall of Mirrors*. **The treaty reflected the anger felt by the Allies.** Respond: **Do you think the Allies needed to take such strong measures against Germany? Explain.**

HISTORY MAKERS

Jeanette Rankin

America's First Congresswoman

The roll call began for the final vote on President Wilson's Declaration of War. The House of Representatives was silent as the clerk polled the members. A new member had not voted on the first roll call. This was the last chance to vote. Would the vote be for war or for peace? As the new member rose, the hush in the House deepened.

"I want to stand by my country," she said, "but I cannot vote for war. I vote *no*."

Jeanette Rankin, the first woman elected to the United States Congress, was one of fifty members of Congress voting against entry into World War I.

Jeanette Rankin was well qualified for office. She had worked all over the country for women's right to vote. In Montana she led the campaign that won the vote for women there in 1914. As a result, she was well known throughout the state and decided to run for Congress. Jeanette Rankin traveled all over the state to speak to as many people as she could. She received enormous support from women, and in 1916, she was elected.

During her first term in Congress, Jeanette Rankin had goals. She wanted to protect the working rights of women and children. She was concerned about civil liberties, and she wanted a constitutional amendment allowing everyone to vote.

Rankin ran for Congress again in 1918. This time she lost, probably because of her anti-war vote. In the 1920s and 1930s, she was a social worker and a peace activist. In 1940, she was reelected to Congress, and on December 8, 1941, Rankin was the only member of Congress to vote against entry into the second World War. Since she could not go to war, she said, she would not send anyone else to fight.

After her second term in Congress, Jeanette Rankin returned to peace and social work. In 1968, she led the Jeanette Rankin Brigade of five thousand women in an anti-war march in Washington, D.C. She was eighty-seven years old. Jeanette Rankin was a patriot who worked throughout her life for human rights, human values, and world peace.

Think: On August 26, 1920, the National Women's Party had a grand celebration—women had finally won the right to vote. The Nineteenth Amendment, ratified that day, clearly states: The right of citizens of the United States to vote shall not be denied . . . on account of sex. Respond: What helped women get the vote?

Changes for Women

After the war, Americans turned their attention to life at home. The war had brought many changes, especially for women. As a result of their contributions to the war, women had gained self-esteem. Leaders for women's rights, such as Carrie Chapman Catt, encouraged women to work more vigorously for their rights. Their efforts were finally successful. On June 4, 1919, Congress passed the Nineteenth Amendment, granting women the right to vote. Many more big changes would come in the 1920s as Americans recovered from the war and rejoiced in their country's victory.

Section Review

1. How did President Wilson want to deal with Germany after the war? What were the views of the Allies?
2. Which parts of President Wilson's peace plan were included in the Treaty of Versailles?
3. Who led the fight in the Senate against the treaty? How did the Senate vote?
4. What was the Nineteenth Amendment?

Chapter

CHAPTER SUMMARY

World War I began with the assassination of Archduke Franz Ferdinand in Europe in 1914. Although the United States tried to stay out of the fighting, the sinking of American ships and the interception of the Zimmerman note brought America into the war in 1917.

Under the Selective Service Act of 1917, men were drafted for the army. Men and women at home helped the war effort by working in factories to produce war supplies and by saving food. American soldiers arrived in Europe in time to stop the German advance on France. After several major battles, the German army retreated, and an armistice was signed on November 11, 1918.

President Wilson presented his peace plan, the Fourteen Points, at the peace talks in Versailles. Allied leaders, however, wanted to punish the Germans and refused to accept most of Wilson's plan. But Wilson's plan for a League of Nations was included in the Treaty of Versailles.

In spite of Wilson's efforts, the Senate refused to accept the Treaty of Versailles. The United States did not join the League of Nations, but later signed a separate treaty with Germany.

After the war, women worked harder for their rights and won the right to vote in 1919.

Key Words

Write a sentence to explain the meaning of each of these terms.

alliances
armistice
Fourteen Points
convoys

Selective
  Service Act
reparations

Major Events

Choose the answer that best completes the statement.

1. World War I began after

   a) the sinking of the *Lusitania.*
   b) the assassination of Archduke Franz Ferdinand.
   c) German submarine attacks.

2. After the revolution in 1917, Russia

   a) joined the Central Powers.
   b) withdrew from the war.
   c) surrendered to Germany.

3. The Germans were forced to retreat after the

   a) battle at Cantigny.
   b) Americans landed in France.
   c) attack on Paris failed.

4. In 1919, the Treaty of Versailles required Germany to

   a) give its colonies to Russia
   b) be governed by the League of Nations.
   c) pay for all war damages.

5. The U.S. Senate rejected the Treaty of Versailles because

   a) it included a League of Nations.
   b) Lodge voted against it.
   c) it was not signed by all of the Allies.

Review

Important Facts

Answer each question with at least one complete sentence.

1. How were France and England drawn into World War I?

2. Why did many Americans sympathize with the Allies?

3. What brought an end to America's neutrality during World War I?

4. In what condition were the Allies when the United States entered the war?

5. What was the purpose of the War Industries Board?

6. What contribution did Herbert Hoover make to the war effort?

7. Why were the Germans able to move large numbers of soldiers to the Western Front in 1917?

8. Why did the U.S. Navy plant mines in the North Sea in 1917 and 1918?

9. What was General John Pershing's role in World War I?

10. Which part of the Fourteen Points did President Wilson value most?

11. Which countries did the "Big Four" represent? Why were the leaders from these countries known as the "Big Four"?

12. In what ways did some Americans disagree with President Wilson's plans for world peace?

13. What was the Nineteenth Amendment?

Skill Review

Read these sets of events, then answer the following questions.

A. stalemate on the western front
   trench warfare

B. Zimmerman note
   sinking of 3 American ships
   U.S. entry into World War I

C. new German attacks in France
   Russian-German peace treaty

D. Germany declares war on Russia.
   Austria declares war on Serbia.
   France and England declare war on Germany.
   Russia defends Serbia.

1. In set A, which fact was cause? Which was effect?

2. Which event was the result of the other two in set B?

3. Which event in set C caused the other?

4. List the events in set D in cause-and-effect order.

Critical Thinking

Write a paragraph to answer each question.

1. In what ways did women's lives change during the war and after it was over?

2. Compare President Wilson's plan for peace with the peace treaty that ended World War I.

Important People

Choose the answer that best completes the statement.

1. The first president to expand the Monroe Doctrine was

   a) Woodrow Wilson.
   b) Theodore Roosevelt.
   c) William McKinley.

2. W.E.B. Dubois fought for

   a) an end to child labor.
   b) equal rights for blacks.
   c) state government reform.

3. In his book *The Jungle,* Upton Sinclair wrote about

   a) city slums.
   b) the oil industry.
   c) meat-packing plants.

4. John Muir was a famous

   a) conservationist.
   b) Progressive mayor.
   c) muckraker.

5. Robert M. La Follette used his office to obtain

   a) better housing for the poor.
   b) state government reforms.
   c) tougher anti-trust laws.

6. President Woodrow Wilson believed strongly in

   a) a high tariff.
   b) a plan for world peace.
   c) equal rights for women.

7. At Paris, victorious Allied troops were led by

   a) General John J. Pershing.
   b) General Douglas MacArthur.
   c) Commodore George Dewey.

Main Ideas

Choose the answer that best completes the statement.

1. In the late 1800s, Americans believed in imperialism, or

   a) a policy of staying out of world affairs.
   b) a policy of acquiring new territories.
   c) a policy of supporting the independence of all nations.

2. After the Spanish-American War, the United States gained

   a) Puerto Rico and the Philippines.
   b) Cuba, Puerto Rico, and the Philippines.
   c) Wake, Guam, and Puerto Rico.

3. The Open Door Policy of 1899 showed America's interest in

   a) alliances with Latin America.
   b) immigration from all nations.
   c) equal trading rights in China.

4. In the late 1890s, the Progressives

   a) fought for equal rights.
   b) formed a political party.
   c) worked for social reforms.

5. Muckrakers were

   a) reformers.
   b) corrupt city officials.
   c) Progressive governors.

6. The initiative, referendum, and recall gave more power to

   a) voters.
   b) city councils.
   c) members of Congress.

7. The first president to give labor a "square deal" was

    a) Woodrow Wilson.
    b) William Howard Taft.
    c) Theodore Roosevelt.

8. President William Taft

    a) disappointed the Progressives.
    b) defended the trusts.
    c) reformed the schools.

9. During President Wilson's term, Congress passed the

    a) Mann-Elkins Act.
    b) Selective Service Act.
    c) Sherman Anti-Trust Act.

10. The Central Powers included

    a) Austria-Hungary and Turkey.
    b) Germany and Russia.
    c) France and Italy.

11. America's neutrality during World War I was ended by the

    a) success of British propaganda.
    b) sinking of the *Lusitania.*
    c) attacks on American ships.

12. The Fourteen Points called for

    a) reparations from Germany.
    b) a European alliance.
    c) a League of Nations.

13. The Treaty of Versailles was signed by

    a) some of the Allies.
    b) all of the Allies.
    c) none of the Central Powers.

14. Women gained the right to vote when Congress passed the

    a) Sixteenth Amendment.
    b) Eighteenth Amendment.
    c) Nineteenth Amendment.

History Skills

Choose the answer that best completes the statement.

1. In the "Woman's Land Army of America," women serve as

    a) farmers.
    b) soldiers.
    c) factory workers.

2. The purpose of this poster is to get women to

    a) enlist in the United States Army.
    b) grow their own food to make more food available to send to the Allies.
    c) work on farms so that they will not take factory jobs away from American men.

3. This poster is an example of

    a) an editorial.
    b) wartime propaganda.
    c) exaggeration.

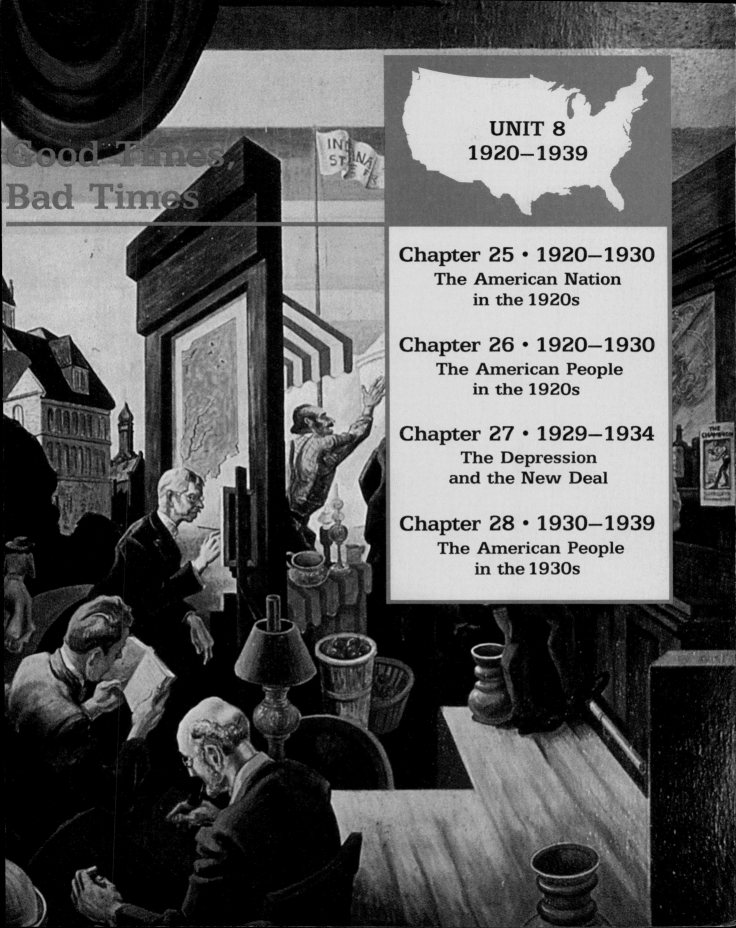

Good Times,
Bad Times

25
The American Nation in the 1920s

Years 1920–1930

Eighteenth Amendment
(Prohibition) went into effect
Warren G. Harding
elected president

1920

McNary-Haugen Bill
came before Congress
Coolidge elected president

1924

Herbert Hoover
elected president

1928

Harding died
Calvin Coolidge
became president

1923

A mass-produced
Model T
cost only $290

1925

1. American Government in the 1920s

Imagine you are a reporter in 1917. Your assignment is to write about the economy of the United States as it enters World War I.

Your story describes how factories build ships faster than German submarines can sink them. Almost half a million new railroad cars are built to carry farm produce and factory goods. High farm prices and food conservation help farmers feed Americans and their European allies.

You write about the army on the home front—millions of workers striving to meet wartime goals. Agreements between government and unions prevent most strikes. The federal government insists on higher wages and an eight-hour day for many workers. There seems to be a job for almost everyone, including women and minorities.

Then the war ends. In your "follow up" story, you tell how Americans are coping with the challenges of peace. Millions of jobs disappear overnight. Factories struggle to change over to producing consumer goods. Unemployment leads to strikes. Plunging farm prices throw many farmers into debt. Eventually, however, the economy adjusts, and prosperity arrives.

In this chapter, you will read about these changes and more. The growth of industry helped many people, but all did not share in the good times. By the middle of the 1920s, American business was growing by leaps and bounds. How did it happen?

Learn these important terms:

Veteran's Bureau
Teapot Dome

Remember the main idea:

The three Republican presidents elected in the 1920s wanted to help business grow. They thought that the government should help business but not control it.

Look for answers to these questions:

1. What were most Americans concerned about at the beginning of the 1920s?

2. How did the Republicans want to help business?

3. What happened to government regulation of business during the 1920s?

Before World War I, many Americans supported the ideas of the Progressives. The Progressives wanted to change government and business and make them more fair for everyone. After the war, however, most people had other concerns. They looked for better jobs and business opportunities. They wanted to bring back the "good old days" of peace and prosperity.

The Republican candidate for president in 1920 was Warren G. Harding, a senator from Ohio. The Democrats' candidate was James M. Cox, the governor of Ohio.

The ambition of Warren G. Harding (1865-1923) was to be America's "best-loved" president. Unfortunately, scandal and his lack of leadership made this impossible.

Harding's promises of lower taxes, a higher tariff to protect American business, and a "return to normalcy" appealed to many Americans. Most Americans were much more interested in business at home than in the League of Nations and foreign affairs. Harding was elected president by a large majority.

Congress Helps Business

Harding was not a strong leader. He had ideas he wanted to put into action. But he let Congress run the nation. Controlled by Republicans, Congress passed laws designed to help business. It lowered taxes and raised the tariff. Lower taxes gave companies more profits and more money to spend on growth. Lower income taxes rewarded those who had earned fortunes. Lower taxes also gave people more money to spend on the products of the factories. Higher tariffs helped American industry by making foreign goods sold in America cost more than American goods.

Scandals Under President Harding

President Harding caused problems for himself. He chose government officials because they were friends, not because they would do a good job. Some of his highest officials were dishonest. One official stole money from the **Veteran's Bureau**, an organization set up by Congress to help soldiers and sailors after the war. Another friend of Harding's sold government jobs and other favors.

The worst scandal of all involved the **Teapot Dome**, a large deposit of oil in Wyoming that belonged to the government. To get this oil cheaply, some oil companies bribed the secretary of the interior with a large amount of money. This man, Albert Fall, was a close friend of President Harding. Despite this friendship, Fall let the oil companies drill for oil on the Teapot Dome and other government lands.

These scandals shocked the president when he learned of them. In the summer of 1923, Harding became ill and died.

Think: This cartoon shows steam from the investigation that caused three oil company presidents to resign. **Respond:** What other results did the Teapot Dome scandal have?

Keeping Cool with Coolidge

Calvin Coolidge, the vice president, finished out Harding's term. In 1924, the Republicans chose him as their candidate for president. They told Americans to ''Keep cool with Coolidge.'' The Democrats ran John W. Davis, a rich lawyer from New York.

The Progressive Party appeared once again and ran as a third party against the Republicans and Democrats. Their candidate was Senator Robert La Follette of Wisconsin. The Progressives wanted to help the farmers, tax rich people and big businesses, and have the government take over the railroads. The Progressives won five million votes, mainly from farmers and workers. However, Coolidge won the election easily.

Calvin Coolidge (1872-1933) had a full life as a politician. He served as mayor, Massachusetts state senator, governor, vice president, and—finally—president. His terms were all marked by quiet efficiency.

Under President Coolidge, the Republicans went on helping business. Laws to regulate big business, such as the Clayton Anti-Trust Act, were not enforced. Congress continued to lower income taxes and raise tariffs. Business grew rapidly. After the troubles of the Harding years, many Americans were glad to have ''Silent Cal'' in the White House. The nation was prosperous again, and his administration was free of scandal.

WHAT A FRIEND WE HAVE IN COOLIDGE!

THE CASH REGISTER CHORUS.

Fitzpatrick in the St. Louis Post-Dispatch.

Think: Cartoonist Fitzpatrick created this political cartoon during the 1924 presidential race. Respond: According to the cartoon, who has a friend in Coolidge?

Hoover Supports Business

In 1928, President Coolidge decided not to run again. The Republicans chose Herbert Hoover, the secretary of commerce, as their candidate for president. Hoover, born in the farm country of Iowa, had become a successful engineer and businessman. During and after the war, Hoover ran programs that distributed food to Europe and helped its nations recover from the war.

The Democrats ran Alfred E. Smith. His background was different from Hoover's. Smith had grown up in a slum neighborhood of New York, but he worked hard to get ahead. He had been elected governor of New York four times.

Hoover and Smith also had different ideas. Hoover, like Harding and Coolidge, favored big business. He promised to keep the tariff high. Smith had spent much of his time dealing with working

Think: **Alfred Smith (wearing a bow tie) lost the election of 1928 to Herbert Hoover. Religion and prohibition were major issues in the 1928 campaign. Some say Smith lost because he was a Catholic and because he was against prohibition.** Respond: **Would you have supported prohibition? Why, or why not?**

people's problems. He promised to help America's workers and farmers.

Hoover easily defeated Smith. Many Americans were enjoying good times in 1928. They felt Hoover was more likely to keep the good times coming. Some Americans voted for Hoover as a way of voting against Smith. These people were threatened by Smith's religion. Smith was the first Catholic to run for president. There was strong anti-Catholic feeling in some parts of the country.

Herbert Hoover (1874-1964) is remembered for more than his term as America's thirty-first president. He was a successful engineer, a dedicated worker for international relief, and a fine author.

Republican Ideas in the 1920s

All three Republican presidents had similar ideas about government and the economy. They believed the government should actively help business. Their main way of helping business was to keep taxes low and tariffs high.

The Republicans did not feel that government should regulate or control business. Under the Republican presidents, the Progressive laws against trusts or monopolies were not enforced. People who favored big business were appointed to the Interstate Commerce Commission and the Federal Trade Commission. They seldom brought cases against big business to court. Sometimes the government actually encouraged trusts to grow.

Section Review

1. How did President Harding's officials bring trouble to him?

2. How were Herbert Hoover and Alfred E. Smith different?

3. How did the Republicans help big business in the 1920s? Did they regulate business?

You learned in Section 1 of this chapter that President Calvin Coolidge was often called "Silent Cal." Do you wonder how he got that nickname? If you are curious, an encyclopedia might be the place to begin looking for information.

You might start your search in the encyclopedia under the entry "Presidents of the United States." As you look through the entry, you find a chart about the presidents. Here's part of what it says for Calvin Coolidge, the thirtieth president.

President	Born	Birthplace
Calvin Coolidge	7/4/1872	Plymouth Notch, VT

Political Party	College	Occupation
Republican	Amherst	Lawyer

This information gives several facts about Coolidge but does not tell about his nickname. As you look through the rest of the article, you find headings such as "Role of the President" and "Development of the Presidency." You realize this is not the place to find out about Coolidge's nickname. At the end of the article, you find this:

Related articles in this encyclopedia. See separate encyclopedia entries for each president.

When you look in the encyclopedia under "Coolidge, Calvin," you find more information. Here is part of the encyclopedia entry.

Coolidge rarely smiled, laughed, or even talked. People wondered why. At an important government dinner, a woman told Coolidge that she had bet that she could get him to say more than two words. Coolidge replied, "You lose."

When Coolidge left the White House in 1927, reporters for several newspapers asked him to comment upon his years as president. They may have expected a lengthy story for their papers, but Coolidge said only, "Good-bye. I have had a very enjoyable time in Washington."

At the end of the encyclopedia entry is this helpful information:

Related articles in this Encyclopedia: PRESIDENTS OF THE UNITED STATES; HARDING, WARREN G.; ROARING TWENTIES. Additional resources: *Calvin Coolidge, The Man From Vermont*, by Claude M. Fuess.

Use the information above to answer the following questions.

1 In which volume of the encyclopedias pictured above would this article appear?

2 What did you learn from the article about how Coolidge got his nickname?

3 Which of the related articles probably tells about Coolidge's years as vice president?

4 Where does the encyclopedia suggest that you look for more information about Coolidge?

2. American Businesses Grow

Learn these important terms:

mass production
standard parts
assembly line
credit plans
chain stores
trade associations

Remember the main idea:

New ways of manufacturing helped American industry grow. New industries were started and American businesses grew larger.

Look for answers to these questions:

1. What helped industry make more goods more cheaply?
2. What new industries became important in the 1920s?
3. How did American businesses grow larger?

In the 1920s, automobile manufacturing became America's largest industry. Millions of Americans bought cars.

New industries can make new jobs. They can create more new industries as well. The automobile industry is a good example. The industry needed people to make parts for cars and to put them together. But this was only the beginning. Many other people were needed to work in gasoline stations and garages. The oil industry boomed because of the demand for gasoline. People wanted modern roads, so billions of dollars were spent to crisscross the country with highways.

New businesses, such as roadside restaurants and motels, sprang up along the roads. Many areas attracted streams of tourists. This meant new jobs for the people living there.

Think: In 1913, the Ford Motor Company had 12,000 employees at its Highland Park plant alone. Respond: What other jobs were created by the availability of automobiles?

CADILLAC *Custom-Built* **BODIES**
~ *at prices consistent with wise investment*

Cadillac invites you to give free rein to your individual preferences when you purchase a V-63 Cadillac with Custom Body by Fisher.

From among the twenty-four master color harmonies, select the one which pleases you above all others. Choose the particular style of upholstery, in

mohair or cloth, which appeals to you as being most beautiful.

In this way, your Custom-Built Cadillac will faithfully reflect your personal ideal of beauty just as it represents the highest standard of dependable, vibrationless eight-cylinder performance.

CADILLAC MOTOR CAR COMPANY, DETROIT, MICHIGAN
Division of General Motors Corporation

Think: Early Cadillacs received acclaim for technical achievements like standardized parts and electric starters. Respond: What does Cadillac seem to stand for in this 1920s advertisement?

New Ways of Manufacturing

Several things helped industries grow in the 1920s. One was *mass production*, or making large quantities of a product. When a factory makes large numbers of one product, each item costs less to make. Consider, for example, automobile manufacturing. Automobile factories have to spend a certain amount of money on machines and other operating expenses. However, making a thousand cars does not cost much more than making a hundred cars. When many cars are made, the fixed cost per car is much less.

The results of mass production are lower prices for the products. This means greater consumer demand. For example, Henry Ford's Model T car cost $950 when it first came out in 1908. In 1925, however, mass production made it possible to sell a Model T for only $290. Many more people could now afford cars.

Mass production required two other things. One was *standard parts*. A standard part fits into any machine of the same model. In the 1920s, the use of standard parts made the *assembly line* popular. The assembly line moved the parts from worker to worker to be put together. Each worker was trained to do a particular job and did that same job over and over again. The assembly line used labor more efficiently. It cut the time needed to make a car from twelve hours to about an hour and a half. Assembly lines also worked efficiently in other industries.

Americans Use Electricity

Another thing that changed many Americans' lives and created new industries was the growing use of electricity. At the end of World War I, few American homes had electricity. But the electric industry grew rapidly. By the end of the 1920s, almost two-thirds of all American homes used electricity for lighting.

Think: The picture above shows only part of the cars produced in the Highland Park plant in one day.
Respond: Why was it possible to make so many cars in such a short time?

Think: Unprepared for the number of cars to take to the road, city streets were often jammed with traffic.
Respond: Why were so many people able to buy a car after 1913?

MANUFACTURING IN THE UNITED STATES, 1920

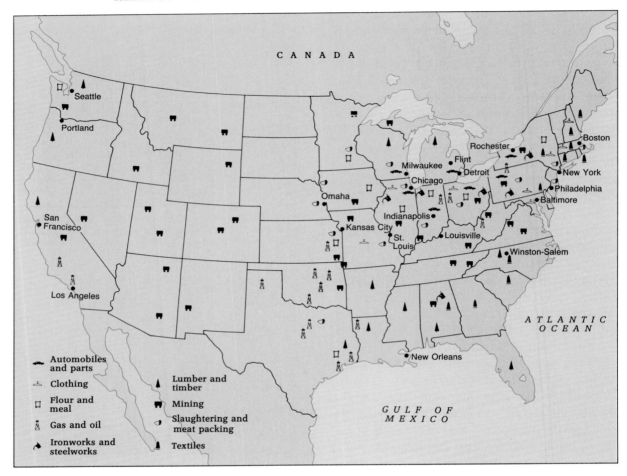

Automobiles and parts | Lumber and timber
Clothing | Mining
Flour and meal | Slaughtering and meat packing
Gas and oil | Textiles
Ironworks and steelworks

With electricity available in more homes, many Americans started to buy electrical appliances, such as irons and vacuum cleaners. This demand created a new industry of consumer electric products. As the amount of electricity needed increased, the power industry grew.

All of this electricity was produced by a few very large power companies. They kept the price of electricity high. The government made little attempt to control the electric power industry.

Some people in Congress wanted the government to buy some electric power companies. They believed that government ownership might force the other power companies to lower their prices.

This idea was not accepted by most Americans during the 1920s, however.

New Industries Become Important

Many new industries appeared and grew rapidly in the 1920s. There were many new things to buy and do. Movies and the phonograph, invented around 1900, now grew into big industries. Radio became an important new industry as well.

The transportation industry started to change. Buses and trucks began to move passengers and freight around the country. Airplanes started to carry the mail, but they did not carry many passengers.

HISTORY MAKERS

—— Henry Ford ——

Creator of the Tin Lizzie

"I am going to democratize the automobile. When I'm through, everybody will be able to afford one. And almost everyone in America will have one, too."

"Nonsense, Mr. Ford! Automobiles are for rich people. They are expensive to make and expensive to repair. A working person can't possibly afford to buy an automobile and keep it in good running order. It simply is not practical. The thought really is quite absurd!"

"It may be absurd, sir, but I am going to do it. I'm going to manufacture an automobile that is reasonably priced and easy to maintain. I'm going to give every American a car to drive!"

Henry Ford was as good as his word. He designed an automobile that was easy to make, easy to operate, and easy to repair. He called it the Model T, and he sold it to the nation. The car was nicknamed "The Tin Lizzie."

The Model T Ford was a simple automobile, unlike most other early cars. It was big enough to carry a family, and small enough to take care of without too much expense. The car sat up high on its wheels so it wouldn't get stuck on roads built long before the automobile appeared. Most Model T's were plain black—definitely not fancy! They were built to run well and cost little, not to look good.

Ford used the idea of a moving assembly line to cut down product costs. Building one automobile at a time took about fourteen hours. A car built on an assembly line could be built in about an hour and a half! Standardized, interchangeable parts made manufacture and repair easier and less costly.

By the mid-1920s, Tin Lizzies cost less than three hundred dollars. The average American could afford a Model T. Many people bought Model T's on installment plans. In nineteen years of production, fifteen million Model T's were made and sold. Ford's Tin Lizzie put Americans on wheels.

Problems for Old Industries

When new industries become important, old ones are often hurt. This happened in the 1920s. The coal industry became less important as more electricity was used. Other industries began to suffer from foreign competition. The cotton industry had trouble because many foreign nations now grew their own cotton. Silk and rayon also began to replace cotton. American shipping companies began to lose business as foreign ships became faster and cheaper.

Railroads began to lose business to truck and bus companies. They fought back by making their trains faster and more modern. Small railroads joined together to make one large company. In this way, the railroads did not compete with one another for business. They also were able to charge lower prices and provide better service.

Growth of Big Businesses

In the 1920s, many American companies started to grow larger. When the United States Steel Corporation was formed in 1902, it was the only company in America worth a billion dollars. By the end of the 1920s, many companies had become billion-dollar companies.

Up until this time, most stores were small and were owned by families or small companies. During the 1920s, companies such as Woolworth's opened **chain stores**. These companies owned stores in many parts of the country. They could sell goods cheaply because they could buy them in large amounts from the manufacturers.

Companies looked for new ways to increase the demand for their goods. They used more and more advertising to make people want to buy the biggest, best, and latest models. Stores made it easier for

Think: **Nearly 90 percent of all the pianos, sewing machines, washing machines, vacuum cleaners, radios, and refrigerators were bought on credit in the 1920s. Also high on the list of items bought on credit were furniture and automobiles.** Respond: **What are the pros and cons of buying on credit?**

people to buy by offering *credit plans*. Using a credit plan, people could buy a car, for example, for a small amount of money paid at the time of purchase. They could take it home right away, and pay the rest of its cost in monthly payments.

Some changes in the 1920s did not help the American buyer. As industries got bigger, some came under the control of a few very large companies. These companies decided how to run the industry. They set prices and determined how much would be produced each year. Other industries were run by groups of businesspeople who joined together to form *trade associations*.

There were two sides to the change and growth in American business and industry in the 1920s. Larger businesses could make goods more cheaply than small ones. They offered the consumer new conveniences. However, as a few companies or people controlled an industry, prices often became higher. Companies that might have charged lower prices were forced out of business. Workers in such industries had a hard time forming unions or gaining better wages and working conditions. In the rest of this chapter, you will read about these workers. You will also read about other groups of people who had problems.

Section Review

1. How did mass production work? How did it help industry?
2. How did the automobile industry create new jobs?
3. What industries had trouble in the 1920s?
4. How did businesses and industries change the way they were run during the 1920s?

3. Changes in America During the 1920s

Learn these important terms:

McNary-Haugen Bill
bootlegging
Eighteenth Amendment
Prohibition

Remember the main idea:

Some groups of people had trouble in the 1920s. Unions became weaker. Farmers and unskilled workers did not share in the good times. Prohibition also caused problems.

Look for answers to these questions:

1. What problems did workers have after World War I ended?
2. What happened to unions during the 1920s?
3. Why did farmers have problems in the 1920s?
4. What was the Eighteenth Amendment? What effect did it have on America?

As soon as World War I ended, most American soldiers and sailors left the army and navy. Many of them had trouble finding jobs.

During the war, the government had controlled certain businesses. These businesses were later returned to their owners. But factories no longer got orders for war supplies, and many workers lost their jobs. It took time for factories to change over to making consumer goods. Prices for food and clothing went up faster than

Think: Textile workers throughout the South were dissatisfied with the long hours and low pay in the late 1920s. Above, mill hands in Gastonia, North Carolina, finally went on strike. They fared better than strikers in nearby Gaston, many of whom were shot. Respond: Why were unions losing their power?

wages did. In 1919, many groups of workers went on strike for higher wages and better working conditions.

At first, these strikes were successful. Then factory owners fought back. They often got the government to help them put down strikes. When coal and steel workers went on strike, the factory owners refused to talk to them. Instead, they asked for injunctions, or court orders, to end the strikes.

Problems for Unions

By the end of 1923, good times had returned to the nation. Factories ran at full capacity again. Expanding businesses needed more workers to meet the demand for consumer goods. Skilled workers could find plenty of high-paying jobs. Some companies began to treat workers better. They offered higher wages, a shorter workday, paid vacations, and pension plans. All of these things made skilled workers lose interest in unions. Some companies, feeling that unions could no longer hurt them, simply refused to hire union workers. In turn, unions became weaker and had a hard time fighting back.

Unskilled workers did not share in improved working conditions. Many still worked twelve-hour days and earned low wages. Most blacks and Mexican-Americans, when they could get jobs at all, could only get unskilled work.

Problems for Farmers

Farmers were another group that did not share in the good times of the 1920s. During the war they made much money selling food to Great Britain and France. When the war ended, these countries went back to growing their own food. American farmers grew more crops than they could sell, and farm prices fell sharply. Meanwhile, prices rose for the machines and manufactured goods that farmers needed.

During the war when farming was profitable, many farmers had bought extra land. They hoped to farm it and to make even more money. When farm prices fell, farmers could no longer make their payments on this land. They went into debt, and many lost their farms. Some farmers went to work for others as tenant farmers. Others gave up farming and moved to the cities.

Government and Farmers

In 1924, the **McNary-Haugen Bill** came before Congress. It ordered the government to buy any crops the farmers could not sell. The government was to sell the crops to foreign countries. At first, Congress turned down the McNary-Haugen Bill. Later, Congress passed the bill twice, but President Coolidge vetoed the bill both times.

Problems with Prohibition

A different kind of problem was caused by **Prohibition**, or the outlawing of alcohol. The abuse of alcohol caused problems for many American families. Since the nineteenth century, groups of Americans had tried to make drinking illegal. In 1919, the **Eighteenth Amendment**, often called the Prohibition Amendment, was approved by Congress. It changed the Constitution to make it unlawful to buy or sell alcoholic drinks.

Fitzpatrick in the St. Louis Post-Dispatch.

Think: **A farmer, forced to sell his land, gazes at the smokestacks of a city's profitable factories.** Respond: **What does Fitzpatrick, the cartoonist, want us to think?**

Carrie Nation (1846-1911) used violent tactics, including swinging a hatchet, to wreck saloons. She also protested short skirts and smoking, and she worked for women's voting rights.

MAP WORKSHOP COMBINING MAP AND GRAPH SKILLS

AGRICULTURE IN THE UNITED STATES, 1920–1930

Using graph skills, you can learn about economic development. Graphs like the bar graph below tell what happened over time. This graph shows how prices of agricultural products changed from 1920 to 1930. Using your map skills, you can then see what the effect of these price changes was in different areas and states of the nation.

Look at the bar graph.

1. On a separate sheet of paper, list the agricultural product that had the biggest drop in price. Beneath it, list the product with the next biggest drop, and so on, listing all products.

2. What was the effect of these falling prices on farmers?

Look at the map and its keys.

3. Which agricultural products were important to Kansas? Which were important to California?

Use both the graph and the map to answer these questions.

4. Which agricultural product dropped the most in price? Which states did this harm?

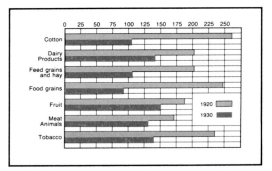

U.S. Agricultural Products 1920-1930

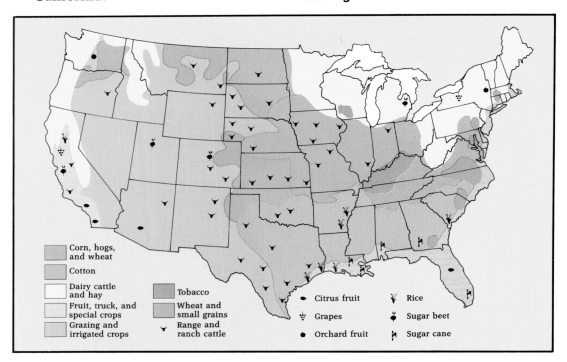

Corn, hogs, and wheat

Cotton

Dairy cattle and hay

Fruit, truck, and special crops

Grazing and irrigated crops

Tobacco

Wheat and small grains

Range and ranch cattle

Citrus fruit   Rice

Grapes   Sugar beet

Orchard fruit   Sugar cane

Think: **Federal agents empty barrels of beer into Lake Michigan.** Respond: **Why were the agents never able to completely wipe out the drinking of alcoholic beverages?**

This law did not work well since many Americans wanted to keep drinking. They bought "bootleg" or illegally produced liquor. *Bootlegging* became a big business, and it made some people rich and powerful. It led to much corruption in local government. Sometimes bloody "gang wars" were fought over control of the bootleg liquor business in a city. Organized crime was widespread. The growth in crime made many people feel that the Prohibition Amendment was a failure and should be repealed.

The problems of unskilled workers and farmers during the 1920s show that periods of economic growth do not help everyone. The results of Prohibition show that reforms do not always bring the changes reformers want. The 1920s were a time of great economic and social change. In the next chapter, you will learn what Americans thought about the changes going on around them.

Section Review

1. What happened when workers went on strike after the war?

2. Why did fewer workers support unions in the 1920s?

3. How did the McNary-Haugen Bill propose to help farmers?

4. What was bootlegging? What problems did it cause?

CHAPTER SUMMARY

The 1920s brought many changes in American industry and business. After factories converted from war production to consumer goods, America "got down to business." Under three Republican presidents, the government supported big business. Congress voted for lower income taxes and higher tariffs.

Serious scandals arose during Harding's administration. Calvin Coolidge and Herbert Hoover continued the Republican policy of helping big business.

The tremendous growth in American business and industry during the 1920s came from several sources. The automobile industry grew rapidly and helped create new industries. Mass production made it possible to make goods more cheaply. Chain stores spread across America. Credit plans encouraged more people to buy expensive goods. Many Americans bought electric home appliances. Businesses grew larger, and some industries were taken over by small groups.

Not everyone shared in the good times. Some industries lost business. Unions were weakened, and conditions for unskilled workers did not improve much. Farmers suffered from low farm prices and debt. Prohibition also caused problems. It did not stop Americans from drinking, and it led to crime and corruption.

Key Words

Write a sentence to explain the meaning of each of these terms.

assembly line
McNary-Haugen Bill
Eighteenth Amendment
Teapot Dome
trade associations
mass production

Major Events

Choose the answer that best completes the statement.

1. Most Americans in the 1920s were interested in
   a) foreign affairs.
   b) business opportunities.
   c) social problems.

2. Republicans in the 1920s wanted
   a) to help business.
   b) to regulate business.
   c) to raise taxes.

3. The U.S. industry that became the largest was
   a) steel.
   b) automobiles.
   c) railroads.

4. Industries that had problems in the 1920s included
   a) oil and gas.
   b) electricity and radio.
   c) coal and overseas shipping.

5. Farmers had problems during the 1920s because of
   a) unusually bad weather.
   b) surplus crops and low prices.
   c) an increase in food imports.

Review

Important Facts

Answer each question with at least one complete sentence.

1. What did Warren G. Harding promise Americans when he ran for president in 1920?

2. What did Congress do to help business during the Harding Administration?

3. Why did Herbert Hoover defeat Alfred E. Smith in 1928?

4. What happened to government regulation of business during the 1920s?

5. Which industries were helped by the popularity of the automobile? Which new industries did the automobile create?

6. What effect did bringing electricity to more homes have on the American economy?

7. What problem did the railroads have during the 1920s? How did they try to solve it?

8. How did businesses encourage Americans to buy more goods?

9. How did the way big businesses were run change in the 1920s?

10. Why did many workers go on strike after World War I?

11. Why did unions become weaker during the 1920s? Which workers did not gain much in the 1920s?

12. Why did the ending of World War I hurt farmers?

13. What was Prohibition? Did it work? Why, or why not?

Skill Review

Look at the map and graphs, then answer the following questions.

1. What were the main industries of Illinois in the 1920s?

2. Which part of the state was enjoying prosperity? Why?

3. Which part of the state was not doing well? Why not?

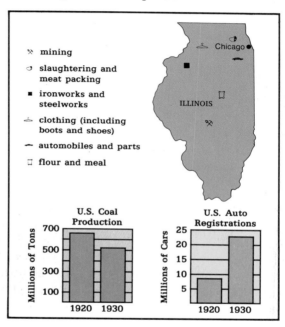

Illinois, 1920s

Critical Thinking

Write a paragraph to answer each question.

1. How would a prosperous American home of the 1920s look different from one of the 1890s?

2. In what ways did changes in the ways factories were run help workers? In what ways did the changes hurt workers?

CHAPTER

26

The American People in the 1920s

Years 1920–1930

Sacco–Vanzetti
case
1920

Strict controls on
immigration passed
1924

Charles Lindbergh
crossed the Atlantic
1927

First "talking picture"
released
1927

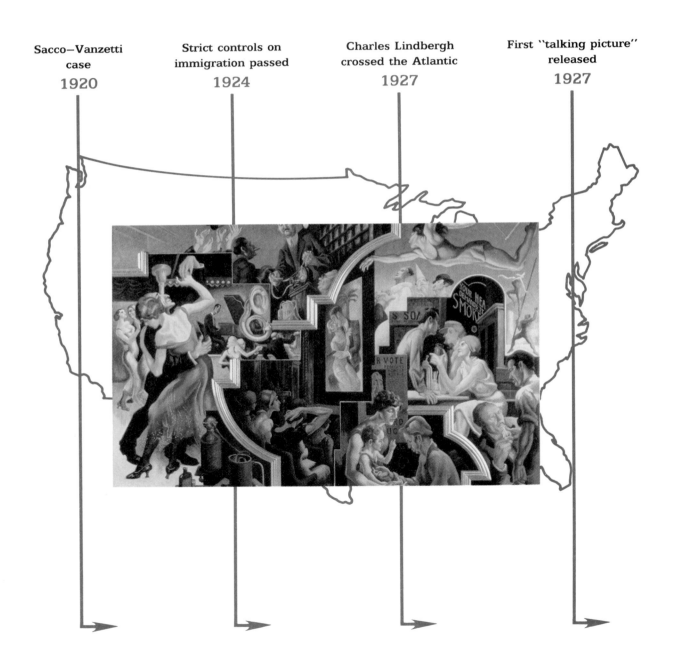

Changes in business and labor made up only part of the story of America in the 1920s. Just as important were changes in the ways Americans looked at themselves, one another, and the world around them.

New people and new ideas can be threatening as well as exciting. In this chapter you will read about some Americans' efforts to stop the flow of immigrants to America. They disliked the immigrants' foreign languages and customs. They also feared losing their jobs to the newcomers. Meanwhile, as blacks continued to struggle for their rights, some whites fought to keep them *segregated*, or separate from whites, and under control.

New ideas also met with resistance. Music, writing, and art expressed thoughts and feelings that challenged old beliefs. Science offered a new picture of the world and human life. Many scientific discoveries disturbed people with traditional ideas.

At the same time, however, others were excited by the new ideas. Young people found they had new freedom. Women declared their independence in the ways they dressed and acted. The pulsing rhythms of jazz music filled the air. The 1920s became known as "the Jazz Age."

1. New Americans and Old Fears

Learn these important terms:

Universal Negro Improvement Association
quota system
Communists
anarchists

Remember the main idea:

After World War I, many Americans feared people different from themselves. As a result, immigration was restricted during the 1920s. Blacks continued to run into obstacles in their struggle for freedom.

Look for answers to these questions:

1. What led to the restriction of immigration in the 1920s?
2. What approaches did blacks take in their struggle for freedom?
3. What did the Ku Klux Klan try to do? Was it successful?

The United States is often called a nation of immigrants. Between 1820 and 1890 about fifteen million immigrants came to America. They were mostly Irish, Germans, and other people from countries of northern Europe.

Immigrants were not always welcomed right away. Some Americans looked down on them because of their foreign customs. Gradually, however, these groups of European immigrants became part of American society. On the other hand, people from completely unfamiliar cultures were not readily accepted. By the 1870s,

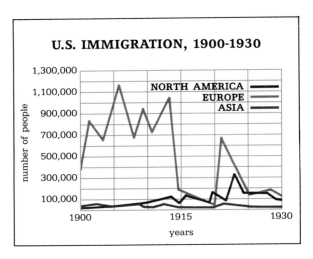

U.S. IMMIGRATION, 1900-1930

NORTH AMERICA
EUROPE
ASIA

number of people

1,300,000
1,100,000
900,000
700,000
500,000
300,000
100,000

1900   1915   1930

years

about 100,000 Chinese had come to America. These people faced anti-Chinese riots in some western cities. And in 1882, Congress passed a law preventing further immigration from China. In 1910, Japanese immigration was also halted. About 130,000 Japanese had come to America by that time.

Between 1890 and 1924 a great new wave of immigrants, more than twenty million of them, came to America. Some of these immigrants came from northern and western Europe. But huge numbers

Think: **Nearing the end of their journey, immigrants attempt to get a glimpse of their new home.**
Respond: **What reasons might these immigrants give for coming to America?**

also came from Italy, eastern Europe, and Greece. About a million Jews arrived from eastern Europe, many fleeing religious persecution.

Like the Asians who had come earlier, many of these new groups of immigrants did not fit easily into American society. Their languages and cultures were quite different from those Americans already knew. New immigrants often kept to themselves and lived together in their own communities. Since they did not become Americanized quickly, the new immigrants often faced discrimination.

Closing the Gate

In the early 1920s, anti-immigrant feelings grew stronger. Several things contributed to this dislike and fear of foreigners. During World War I, the government encouraged support for the war by picturing Germans as evil brutes. While this attitude helped the war effort, it also encouraged a dislike of people from non-Allied countries.

After the war ended, there was a time of high unemployment and labor troubles. Many Americans feared losing their jobs to immigrants who would work longer hours for lower wages.

Responding to this anti-immigration feeling, Congress in 1921 set up a *quota system*. This law limited the number of immigrants entering the country each year. In 1924, Congress passed an even stricter law. This law limited immigration levels to those recorded over thirty years earlier. Immigrants from each country could not number more than they did in 1890. Thus, the number of immigrants coming from southern and eastern Europe was even more restricted. A 1929 law adjusted these quotas to make them more fair. But this law also reduced the total number of immigrants per year to only 150,000. Asians still were kept out almost completely.

Collection, The Museum of Modern Art.

Think: Artist Ben Shahn made his mark with this painting, *The Prisoners Sacco and Vanzetti*. The trial and execution of these two anarchists caused an uproar throughout America. The evidence against the men was only circumstantial, not solid. Respond: Had Sacco and Vanzetti not been immigrants and anarchists, how might they have been treated?

The Red Scare

In 1917, a revolution in Russia had brought **Communists**, or "Reds" as they came to be called, to power. The Communists wanted to overthrow present governments and replace them with a new system of organizing society. They felt a few rich people controlled industries, and they wanted the government to run all businesses for the benefit of workers. The Communists called for a worldwide revolution to bring about these changes.

Even before 1917, some Communists had immigrated to the United States. **Anarchists**, revolutionaries who did not believe in having any type of government at all, also entered the United States. After World War I, some Americans feared that Communists or anarchist immigrants were trying to take over the country. They blamed the labor troubles of the early 1920s on "foreign agitators." Attorney General A. Mitchell Palmer even claimed that there was a plot to destroy

America. On New Year's Day 1920, he had the police round up about six thousand people from thirty-three cities. There was little evidence against most of these people, and most of them were later released without trial. When the predicted revolution did not come, Palmer's influence on government faded. Many people still wanted to isolate America from foreigners, however.

Sacco and Vanzetti

In 1920, two Italian immigrants, Nicola Sacco and Bartolomeo Vanzetti, were accused of killing a man during a robbery. Not only were they foreigners, but they were also anarchists. Sacco and Vanzetti seemed to symbolize the worst fears of some Americans. They were tried and sent to the electric chair. Many people felt they were innocent and had not received a fair trial. These people saw Sacco and Vanzetti as victims of the Red Scare.

A New Black Freedom Struggle

Even more than immigrants, blacks continued to face discrimination, sometimes in the form of outright violence. About 400,000 blacks had joined the armed forces during the war, and about half of them had gone to Europe. Other blacks had moved from the South to the North to take factory jobs during the war. This movement continued during the 1920s. It allowed many blacks to see a wider world with new possibilities. They became less content than ever with the boundaries white America had set for them. Having served their country, blacks thought America would finally accept them as equals.

They were wrong. Although they found some opportunities, blacks also found dis-crimination and low wages. When hard times came after the war, they were usually the first to lose their jobs. As more blacks competed with whites for jobs and housing, racial tensions mounted. Race riots broke out in some cities. In 1919, six days of rioting in Chicago left thirty-eight dead and more than five hundred injured. In addition, fires set by rioters left about one thousand homeless.

Black Groups Choose Different Paths

As blacks continued to struggle for their rights, they became divided over the best way to gain freedom. Groups such as the NAACP (National Association for the Advancement of Colored People) and Urban League fought for the rights of blacks as American citizens. These

Think: The prominent black artist, Jacob Lawrence, did a series of sixty paintings on *The Migration of the Negro*. Below is panel one from the series (1940). It shows blacks moving from the South to the North. Respond: Why were many blacks moving to the North, and what did they find when they got there?

The Phillips Collection, Washington D.C.

PERSONS PER MOTOR VEHICLE

By comparing the maps below, you can see how quickly Americans took to the automobile. The figures on these maps show how many people there were for each vehicle in the state. To get the figures, the mapmaker divided a state's total population by its total number of registered vehicles. What led to the increase in cars? Prosperity, mass production, and a national love for the automobile are the answers.

Look at the map for 1913.

1. Which state had the fewest persons per car? Which state had the most persons per car?

2. Which area of the country seemed to have had the least interest in the automobile? Which areas seemed to have had the greatest interest?

Now look at the map for 1930.

3. Which states had the fewest persons per car? Which states

had the most? Did the states with the most persons per car change since 1913? Which area of the nation had the fewest persons per car? Did this change since 1913?

4. What happened to the popularity of the automobile in Oklahoma from 1913 to 1930? Compare the difference between California and Oklahoma in 1913 with the difference between these two states in 1930. What happened?

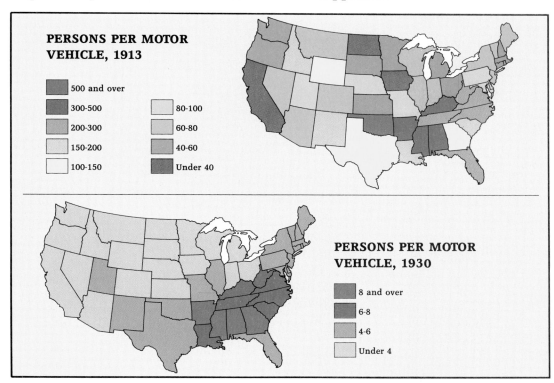

PERSONS PER MOTOR VEHICLE, 1913

- 500 and over
- 300-500
- 200-300
- 150-200
- 100-150
- 80-100
- 60-80
- 40-60
- Under 40

PERSONS PER MOTOR VEHICLE, 1930

- 8 and over
- 6-8
- 4-6
- Under 4

Think: The original Ku Klux Klan died out after southern whites regained control of their governments. But when fear and anger toward immigrants grew in the early 1900s, the organization reappeared in 1915. Respond: Why did many Americans disagree with the Klan's methods?

Return of the Ku Klux Klan

Garvey's plan pleased some whites who wanted to drive blacks out of the country. Their dislike of blacks and immigrants provided support for a new Ku Klux Klan. The original Klan was started by some southern whites to control blacks after the Civil War. The new Klan was started in 1915. By 1925 there were almost five million Klan members all over the United States.

Their targets were Catholics, Jews, immigrants, and especially blacks. They used whippings, cross-burnings, even murder to frighten these people. They held big marches and gained political power in several southern states. But most Americans, even those who agreed with some of the Klan's ideas, did not support their violent methods. Their leaders fought among themselves. By the end of the 1920s, the Ku Klux Klan had lost most of its power.

The Klan seemed like a remnant of an earlier America. All around it, American life was changing in many different ways. You will read about these changes in the next section.

groups were not very successful, however. Many blacks turned to a new group called the **Universal Negro Improvement Association**, or U.N.I.A. It was led by a Jamaican immigrant, Marcus Garvey. He said that it was impossible for blacks ever to win their rights in America. He said that blacks should be proud of their culture and history. Garvey wanted blacks to return to Africa to build a new country there. Although his project failed, many blacks welcomed his message of pride.

Section Review

1. How were the later groups of immigrants different from the early ones?
2. What was the purpose of the immigration laws passed during the 1920s?
3. What problems did blacks face in the 1920s? What were two strategies they developed to deal with them?
4. Who were the targets of the new Ku Klux Klan? How did most Americans respond to the Klan?

2. American Life in the 1920s

Learn these important terms:

flapper   *nickelodeon*
suburb

Remember the main idea:

Life changed for Americans during the 1920s. American women became more independent. The ways American families lived began to change. Americans enjoyed new kinds of entertainment.

Look for answers to these questions:

1. In what ways did American women become more independent in the 1920s?
2. How did new inventions change American family life during the 1920s?
3. What new kinds of entertainment became popular in the 1920s?

The 1920s brought changes to business and to labor. The decade also brought struggles to blacks and immigrants. However, the 1920s are perhaps best known as the years during which American life entered the modern age.

The radio began to bring political debates, sports, and other entertainment directly into American homes. The automobile made it possible to visit more places and to do more things. The movies and the news offered heroes and heroines to admire. Life seemed to move faster and to be more exciting. From this excitement came a nickname, the ''Roaring Twenties.'' During this lively decade, a new national culture was being born.

American Women Become More Independent

Many American women had worked during World War I. In 1920, the Nineteenth Amendment gave women the right to vote. In the 1920s, a growing number of women supported themselves. More women went to college.

Many women also began to do things that had been reserved for men. They drove cars and played tennis and golf. They joined clubs and became involved in civic activities. A modern American woman of the 1920s enjoyed life, and her pleasure showed. She was known as a *flapper*. She wore a short skirt, cut her hair into a boyish bob, and used lipstick and rouge.

FEBRUARY 18, 1926   Teaching old Dog new tricks   PRICE 15 CENTS

Think: Examine the flapper and her dancing partner on the cover of this 1926 magazine. **Respond:** How did the modern woman of the 1920s differ from American women before 1920?

Think: Although more women worked in the 1920s, most were in low paying jobs, like these fruit packers. Respond: Why were more women able to work, and why was their pay low?

Women made important gains in the 1920s. It is important to note, however, that women still were paid less than men. Many jobs were all but closed to women. Like blacks, women would continue to struggle for equality.

Changes in Ways of Living

American family life changed during the 1920s. With the invention of machines such as vacuum cleaners and electric washers, housework took up much less of a woman's time. Many women were able to go to work or to join clubs. Many families had fewer children.

The kinds of places in which people lived also changed. In the cities, more and more people lived in apartment buildings. Many other people began to move to the **suburbs**, or towns on the edge of large cities. Before the 1920s, only the rich were able to live in the suburbs. But during the 1920s, many suburbs had large numbers of low-cost, one-story homes for sale. Whole new towns sprang up in what had once been countryside.

It was the automobile that made much of this new way of life possible. With cars, people could work in the city and live in the suburbs. An automobile made it easy to travel hundreds of miles to beaches and mountain resorts, or even to travel across the country. Farmers and other people living in the country could come to the city more often, too. The modern way of dating came into being as teenagers asked parents, "May I have the car tonight?"

Think: The picture above definitely depicts its time. Note the woman's "flapper" look and the grafitti on the car. Respond: Why should a true picture of the time include an automobile?

Going to the Movies

Americans in the 1920s enjoyed going to the movies. Motion pictures had first been developed in the 1890s. The early movie theaters were called **nickelodeons** (NIK-ul-OH-dee-uhns) because admission cost five cents.

Most of the earliest films were short, and many featured real life. Gradually, films became longer and more creative. Some even used tricks of the camera. In 1915, David Wark Griffith created *The Birth of a Nation.* This three-hour-long movie proved that films could affect viewers and hold their attention. From this point, there was no stopping the love affair between Americans and movies.

In the 1920s, nickelodeons were replaced by large movie theaters. About eighty million Americans went to the movies every week. All of the early movies were silent. Many of the most popular were comedies, featuring such stars as Charlie Chaplin, Buster Keaton, and Laurel and Hardy. However, Americans could choose to see other types of movies as well. The Western, a truly American type of film, had loyal followers who liked to see "good guys" like Tom Mix win. Other moviegoers preferred movies featuring romance. Still others went to the movies simply to see their favorite stars—Mary Pickford, Douglas Fairbanks, and Lillian Gish, among others. As Americans grew more fascinated with movies, the once-tiny village of Hollywood near Los Angeles became world famous. And in 1927, another breakthrough occurred in filmmaking. The first movie with a sound track, *The Jazz Singer,* was released, starring Al Jolson.

In addition to bringing entertainment, movies helped to shape American culture. They created new images of heroism and villainy. Movies also showed Americans more of their own country and opened their eyes to the world at large.

Think: People eager to see and hear an early talking picture, *Lights of New York*, line the streets of Hollywood, California. In 1927, Warner Brothers produced the first talking movie. They called their sound device the Vitaphone. Respond: How have motion pictures changed the way people live?

Radio Brings the World to the Living Room

Radio first became an important part of American life in the 1920s. The first commercial radio station, KDKA, was opened in Pittsburgh in 1920. The few people who had radios and lived nearby could follow the results of the Harding-Cox election. Only seven years later, there were more than seven hundred radio stations and about twelve million radios in the country. For the first time people could hear about news as it happened. Radio also brought music, sports, drama, variety shows, and many commercials into American homes.

Think: **Using earphones, Cornelius Vanderbilt, Jr. listens to an early radio program. When radios first came out, they were expensive. Only wealthy people, such as Mr. and Mrs. Vanderbilt, could afford them. But soon nearly every family had a radio to gather around.** Respond: **What changes did the radio bring?**

Think: **Perhaps the most interesting live programs were the dramas, comedies, and mysteries of radio theater. Along with the spoken words, props provided the background noises that helped listeners *imagine* the story. For example, the tinkling of the glasses would let listeners know these characters were toasting each other.** Respond: **What important role did early radio play in the lives of most Americans?**

Think: Charles Lindbergh was hailed as one of America's greatest heroes after his solo cross-Atlantic flight. **Respond:** What characteristics did Lucky Lindy possess?

The Roar of the Crowd

During the 1920s, sports events became very popular. More Americans had time and money to spend on watching sports. Baseball, the "national pastime," gained many new fans. Large crowds came to Yankee Stadium in New York to watch Babe Ruth hit record-breaking home runs. "Red" Grange of the University of Illinois and other famous football stars helped make football a second national pastime.

There were also many excellent black baseball players, boxers, and other athletes. But they were not allowed to play with whites.

Americans had other kinds of heroic figures, too. In 1927, Charles Lindbergh flew his airplane, the "Spirit of St. Louis," alone on a nonstop flight from New York to Paris. He was in the air more than thirty-three hours.

There was something about Lindbergh's flight that appealed to Americans. He was not the first person to fly to Europe from the United States. But he was the first person to make the flight alone, in a tiny plane, over a vast ocean. Whether it was Babe Ruth or Charles Lindbergh, Americans loved the idea that a single person could face great odds and do something better than ever before. Lindbergh, especially, captured the spirit of the times. When he returned from France, cities all over America held parades and celebrations in his honor.

The Music Goes Round

The record player also became a common household item in the 1920s. The first record players had to be wound by hand and provided a rather thin, scratchy sound. The new record players of the 1920s were powered by electricity and offered much better sound. In the 1920s, people could hear opera, their favorite symphony orchestra, country music, and a new American music—jazz.

Think: **Thomas Hart Benton painted** *Contemporary America* **(portion shown above) in 1930. He meant the mural to show real people in real situations of the 1920s. He included his wife and son (middle bottom) and himself (standing, bottom right).** Respond: **What popular activities of the 1920s are depicted?**

A National Culture

The new American culture emerging in the 1920s came about because of new ideas and new ways of spreading them. Radio networks began to bring the same issues and ideas to people all over the country. People often heard about news events while they were still happening, rather than days later. People all over the country watched the same movies and played the same records. Heroes like Babe Ruth and Charles Lindbergh did not belong to one city or state, but to the whole country.

Americans still had differences. For example, farmers and city dwellers still had very different ways of life. Many blacks, Asians, and Hispanic Americans felt rejected by an America that seemed to be for whites only. Some parts of American life had changed, but others had not. As you read the next section, you will see how artists and educators felt about the changes in American life during the Roaring Twenties.

Section Review

1. How did life change for many American women in the 1920s?
2. How did entertainment change in the 1920s?
3. What did Charles Lindbergh represent to Americans?
4. What helped create a new, widespread American culture?

HISTORY MAKERS

George Herman "Babe" Ruth

The Sultan of Swat

The youngster could hardly believe it. A new world was opening before his eyes. The journey to the training camp was his first train ride. Now his teammates were telling him to order whatever he wanted for breakfast. The Baltimore Orioles would pay for all his meals during spring training, they told him. Three orders of ham and pancakes later, he was full.

His teammates were amused. They decided their new rookie was as innocent as a baby, so they called him Babe. The nickname lasted, and so did the rookie. George Herman Ruth, better known as Babe, became one of the great baseball players of all time.

Babe Ruth was an American hero. Not only was he a great baseball player, he was a classic American success story. George Herman Ruth was born and raised on the tough Baltimore waterfront. His parents sent him to Saint Mary's Industrial School for orphans, delinquents, and runaways when Babe was seven years old. It was at Saint Mary's that Babe learned to play baseball. And it was from Saint Mary's that Babe began his baseball career. The last entry in his Saint Mary's records reads, "He is going to join the Balt. Baseball Team."

Between 1914 and 1920, Babe played for the Boston Red Sox. He pitched three World Series games for the Red Sox and won them all. During his last year with Boston, Babe moved to the outfield. He also began concentrating on his hitting.

In 1920, Babe Ruth was traded to the New York Yankees. Until he retired in 1935, Babe was one of the most popular Yankee players. Yankee Stadium was nicknamed "The House That Ruth Built." His power hitting made the home run popular. His home run record of 714 stood until 1974.

Babe Ruth had a fantastic career. He was the type of hero Americans in the "roaring twenties" were looking for. His athletic abilities, enthusiasm, and rise from rags to riches reflected the spirit of the 1920s. In 1930, the poor kid from Baltimore earned a larger salary than the president of the United States! The Babe said he owed everything to baseball—"the best game ever invented."

3. American Art and Thought in the 1920s

Learn these important terms:

Harlem Renaissance
progressive education
vocational courses
traditionalists

Remember the main idea:

The 1920s was a creative time in music, literature, and art. Blacks made important contributions. New kinds of education were developed.

Look for answers to these questions:

1. How did jazz develop?
2. What did people write about during the 1920s?
3. What contributions did blacks make to the arts?
4. How did education change during the 1920s?

Edward Kennedy "Duke" Ellington (1899–1974) committed his life to music. He wrote music, played the piano, and conducted his own orchestra. Still popular, the Duke's jazz seems timeless.

The 1920s got the name "the Jazz Age" from the energetic, creative, constantly changing sounds of jazz music. Jazz grew out of the popular ragtime music of the early 1900s in America. It also combined sounds from African and Latin American traditional music, and even used some sounds from classical music. Most of the earliest and most creative jazz performers were blacks. Louis Armstrong and Duke Ellington were two of the most famous. Talented white performers such as Bix Beiderbecke added their own sounds. Jazz became a music for all Americans.

Blacks also continued to develop their tradition of the blues, a music that spoke of the troubles and concerns of everyday life. With the invention of phonograph recording, millions of people in the 1920s enjoyed jazz and blues music. Records also preserved the unique styles of different musicians for later generations to hear.

Writers Describe a Changing America

The 1920s was also an exciting decade for American literature. American writers wrote about the changes in the nation and how they affected people. Ernest Hemingway's *A Farewell to Arms* looked at the war and what it had done to those who had faced it. The novels of Sinclair Lewis attacked the shallow values of Americans who were only interested in making money. F. Scott Fitzgerald described the problems that young people faced because of the changes in American life. One group of novelists called the Naturalists put modern scientific ideas into their books. Eugene O'Neill, the most famous playwright of the 1920s, wrote about troubled people and their problems. And poets like Robert Frost and Carl Sandburg used vivid, direct language from everyday life.

Ernest Hemingway (1899–1961) wrote six novels and more than fifty short stories. Using a simple style, he wrote of life's struggles. His idol was Mark Twain.

Black Artists in the 1920s

Music was not the only area in which black Americans helped create the new American culture. In the Harlem district of New York, talented black writers and artists came together. Their movement was called the **Harlem Renaissance** (REN-uh-SANS), or rebirth. Blacks from other parts of the country participated, too.

Claude McKay's *Harlem Shadows* was one of the earliest works of this Renaissance. He was soon joined by other great poets such as Countee Cullen, Langston Hughes, and James Weldon Johnson. Their poems told of black life and problems and looked forward to a better way of life. Black painters and sculptors created works that found homes in art museums all around the world. Other blacks

Paul Robeson (1898–1976) became famous as an actor and singer. He is considered one of the greatest performers of the 1920s. He also fought for black civil rights.

SKILLS FOCUS: Using a Dictionary

In 1925, Ms. West was a German emigrant and an American immigrant. To be sure which country the woman moved *from* and which country she moved *to*, you can refer to a dictionary.

Look at the dictionary entries below. The word *emigrant* is listed first, because it comes before *immigrant* in alphabetical order. In parentheses after each entry word is a respelling that shows how to pronounce the word. The letter *n.* that follows shows that each word is a noun. The definitions of the words and the sample sentence help you see that Ms. West is an emigrant from Germany, or has left Germany. She is an immigrant to the United States, or has come to the U.S.

em • i • grant (em´-uh-gruhnt) *n.* one who leaves his or her country to settle in another.—*adj.* leaving one's country to settle in another.

im • mi • grant (im´-uh-gruhnt) *n.* one who enters a foreign country and plans to settle there: *Mexico has many immigrants from other Central American countries.*—*adj.* immigrating.

In the early years of this century, an immigrant to America might live in a ghetto.

Look at the dictionary entry for *ghetto* and answer the questions that follow.

ghet • to (get´-oh) *n., pl.* -tos. 1. a section of a city in which many members of the same race or nationality live. 2. (formerly) a section of some European cities where Jews had to live.

1. Does the word *ghetto* come before or after the word *immigrant* in the dictionary?

2. Does the first syllable of the word *ghetto* rhyme with *set* or with *seat*?

3. How do you spell the plural form of *ghetto*?

4. What group of people did the word *ghetto* formerly apply to?

5. What does the word *ghetto* mean today?

Use a dictionary to look up the underlined words in the following sentences. Write down each word's pronunciation, part of speech, and meaning.

6. Some American families have a custom of taking two-week summer vacations.

7. Exchanging holiday gifts is a lasting tradition for many Americans.

8. The culture of America has been shaped by ideas from people of many other countries.

9. American cuisine has been greatly affected by people from many countries.

Marian Anderson (1902–) was a concert singer who toured Europe and America. Her rich voice lent itself to everything from simple songs to complex opera.

became famous actors, singers, and musicians. Among them were Paul Robeson, Bessie Smith, and Marian Anderson.

Education for a New Age

Americans were also very much interested in education during the 1920s. Increased prosperity meant that more children were able to go to school through high school. The subjects taught in high school changed. More *vocational courses* were offered. These taught skills to prepare students for jobs in places such as offices and machine shops.

New methods of education were also explored in some schools. John Dewey developed the ideas behind *progressive education*. This kind of education tried to match school work to students' needs, abilities, and interests.

New Ideas and Old Traditions

When ways of living change as rapidly as they did in the 1920s, there is bound to be conflict between old ways and new. Many people in the 1920s felt threatened by all the changes they saw around them. *Traditionalists*, people who were against change, did not like what they saw in the 1920s. They were shocked by the new ways women dressed and acted. They were afraid young people had no morals. They also worried about the role movies played in America. When one famous actor died, thousands came to the funeral and wept. Traditionalists worried that Americans were too caught up in the unreal world of movies.

Other Americans felt threatened by new ideas. Scientists had new theories about many things. Some theories put forth new ideas about the origins of human life. These ideas dismayed many people. They fought to keep any ideas of this type out of schools.

Many Americans wanted their children to grow up having the same ideas and traditions they had. However, the nation was changing. Out of the struggle between old and new, a richer, more varied American culture would arise.

Section Review

1. What different kinds of music did jazz draw upon?
2. What happened during the Harlem Renaissance?
3. What changes took place in American education in the 1920s?

Chapter

CHAPTER SUMMARY

The 1920s were one of the most interesting times in American history. In some ways, America became less open to new people and ideas. Immigration was restricted. People feared new political ideas after the Communist revolution in Russia. The Ku Klux Klan tried to oppress or drive away blacks and other members of minorities.

In other ways, the 1920s opened up many new possibilities for Americans. It was a time of many changes in the ways Americans lived. Women gained a new sense of independence through voting, working, and having more leisure time. While blacks did not gain their full rights or opportunities, they succeeded in making important contributions to American culture. The sound of jazz music and the vivid works of writers and artists became the symbols of a changing America.

During the 1920s, much of what we think of as modern American culture came into being. The automobile brought many changes in its wake. Cities spread out into suburbs, and people traveled more. The nation's prosperity gave many people more leisure time and new ways to spend it. Radio news brought the nation closer together. The movie screen showed heroes that millions of Americans could admire. Live heroes also captured the people's imaginations.

Key Words

Write a sentence to explain the meaning of each of these terms.

quota system
Universal Negro
  Improvement
  Association
flapper

suburb
Harlem
  Renaissance
progressive
  education

Major Events

Choose the answer that best completes the statement.

1. Under the immigration law of 1921, the number of immigrants coming into the United States was

   a) limited.
   b) unlimited.
   c) kept the same.

2. The arrest of 6,000 people on January 1, 1920, was caused by

   a) fear of Communists.
   b) fear of Indians.
   c) fear of Italians.

3. The Nineteenth Amendment, taking effect in 1920, gave women

   a) the right to work in any job.
   b) the right to earn as much money as men.
   c) the right to vote in all elections.

4. The 1920s became known as the

   a) Jazz Age.
   b) Progressive Age.
   c) Age of Invention.

5. By 1925, the Ku Klux Klan was quite large because

   a) Prohibition was unsuccessful.
   b) whites feared minorities.
   c) the Red Scare had failed.

Review

Important Facts

Answer each question with at least one complete sentence.

1. Why did some Americans not get along well with immigrants? What resulted from these strong feelings against immigrants?

2. Who were Sacco and Vanzetti? What happened to them?

3. Why did race riots break out after World War I?

4. What were the goals of the new Ku Klux Klan? Was the Klan successful?

5. What new things did women do in the 1920s? Did women become completely equal with men?

6. What things did the automobile help families to do?

7. How did the movies change in the 1920s? What kinds of movies were popular?

8. What kinds of things could Americans hear on the radio by the late 1920s?

9. What sports were popular in America during the 1920s? Who played them?

10. Why did Charles Lindbergh become a great American hero?

11. Who were some writers of the 1920s who wrote about changes in American life?

12. Who were some important black writers, artists, and singers?

13. What new kind of courses did high schools begin to offer?

Skill Review

Read these dictionary entries, then answer the following questions.

1. What part of speech are these three words?

2. Which type of music appears to be the oldest?

3. Where does the word *jazz* come from?

4. What generalizations can you make about these three kinds of music?

blues (blooz), *n.* 1. A condition of depression or sadness. 2. A style of jazz which developed out of southern American black songs and usually having a slow tempo and flatted thirds and sevenths.

jazz (jaz), *n.* A kind of American music first played unrehearsed by black bands in southern towns at the turn of the century. Jazz has a strong rhythm and variations on basic tunes and chords performed by one or more musicians. [origin uncertain.]

ragtime (RAG tym), *n.* A kind of American dance music, popular between 1890 and 1915, having a fast tempo and shifts in rhythmic beats. It is thought of as an early form of jazz. [from *ragged time*, name first given to New Orleans music as played by black musicians on Mississippi river boats.]

Critical Thinking

Write a paragraph to answer each question

1. Compare the goals and approaches taken by the Universal Negro Improvement Association and the Ku Klux Klan.

2. In what way is jazz a truly American music?

27
The Depression and the New Deal

Years 1929–1934

Stock market crashed

Emergency Banking Act
passed
National Recovery
Administration passed

Social Security Act passed
Works Progress
Administration set up

1929

1933

1935

Franklin D. Roosevelt
elected president

Securities Exchange Act
passed

Wages and Hours Law
passed
Worst of depression over

1932

1934

1938

NRA
MEMBER
U.S.
WE DO OUR PART

1. The Great Depression

In early 1929, most Americans looked forward to continuing good times. Factories poured out increasing numbers of consumer goods. Advertising described wonderful new products and offered easy credit. Most of all, Americans were very hopeful about the future. There seemed to be endless opportunities to get rich. Stock prices were soaring. Even people with modest incomes bought stock. They planned to make big profits by selling it when the prices went even higher.

The United States at the end of 1930, less than two years later, was a very different place. Four million people had lost their jobs, and many soon lost their homes. Some people were starving, and many people waited in long lines for the free soup provided by charities. Meanwhile, farmers burned or buried food that they could not sell. Many lost their farms. America looked like it had been conquered and looted by an invisible enemy.

Yet America had not been invaded. The disaster that struck the nation was the result of economic forces. It was the worst economic depression in American history.

In this chapter you will learn some of the reasons why the Great Depression happened. You will see how it changed the lives of ordinary Americans. You will also see how Franklin Roosevelt's New Deal put the nation back on the road to prosperity.

Learn these important terms:

stock market
Reconstruction Finance
 Corporation
speculation
dividends
margin

Remember the main idea:

A fall in demand for consumer goods and speculation in the stock market helped cause the Great Depression. President Hoover was not able to end the depression.

Look for answers to these questions:

1. What were some causes of the Great Depression?
2. How did the depression affect Americans?
3. What did President Hoover do to try to end the depression?

The American *stock market* was important for the growth of business. Since the nineteenth century, Americans with money to invest bought stocks, or shares in businesses. A business sold stock to raise money for expansion. If the business was successful, it paid *dividends*, or portions of its profits, to its stockholders.

In the 1920s, however, the stock market started to change. Since businesses were making so much money, more and more people wanted to own stocks. This increased demand made stock prices rise. People could now make money by using *speculation*. This meant buying some stock, waiting for the price to rise, and then selling it. People wanted to make money buying and selling stock rather than keeping stock to get dividends.

More people could own stocks in the 1920s because they could buy stock on *margin*. To do this, they would make a down payment on the stock. Then they would borrow the rest of the stock's price from the broker, or stock trader. By buying on margin, people could buy many more shares of stock than they could pay for. The buyer could hold the stock a short time, then sell it. In this way a big profit could be made even after repaying the loan. But this only worked if stock prices continued to go up. If prices went down, most margin buyers would have to sell to pay for their loans. Even still, 1,500,000 Americans were playing the stock market by 1929.

Businesses Start To Have Problems

The basic value of stocks, however, depends on the success of the businesses they represent. By the late 1920s, a number of things had started going wrong with the economy.

Many Americans did not share in the good times of the 1920s. The bills designed to help farmers were vetoed, and farm prices continued to go down. Farmers could not buy many consumer goods. People with unskilled jobs still made low incomes. And many blacks and other minorities had never shared in the postwar prosperity. The market for expensive consumer goods was limited to a relatively small number of people.

Many American business owners, however, thought that demand was unlimited. They kept expanding their factories and making more goods, believing that this would increase their profits. But factories were making more goods than they could sell. Eventually, workers began to lose their jobs as industries reduced their production. In turn, people without jobs could not buy much. Fewer sales for businesses meant still fewer jobs.

The Stock Market Crashes

In September 1929, some people became afraid that conditions were going to get worse. They began to sell their stock. As stock prices started to go down, more people were forced to sell their stock to pay their margin loans. In turn, this pushed prices down still further. Other people thought the problems were only temporary. So, they bought stock and waited for the price to go up again. For about a month, prices moved up and down. Some people thought things would settle down and prices would start to climb again.

Instead, in October 1929, panic broke out, and the stock market crashed. On October 24, Black Thursday, thirteen million shares of stock changed hands, and prices went lower and lower. On October 29, nearly everyone tried to sell stock, no matter how low the price. In the next two weeks, stocks lost more than thirty billion dollars of their value. By 1930, many stocks were worth almost nothing.

Think: On October 24, 1929, Black Thursday, the streets surrounding the New York Stock Exchange were crowded with people trying to sell stock. Respond: What was the result?

Think: When some banks closed, people panicked. Nearly everyone started withdrawing savings. Respond: Why did this cause problems for the banks?

The Depression Begins

When the stock market crashed, thousands of Americans lost their savings. In addition, many businesses lost the money they needed to operate. Most of the people who had been buying expensive goods also lost their money. Those who had money were spending it very cautiously. As a result, the demand for consumer goods fell. This caused thousands of workers to lose their jobs. These jobless workers could no longer pay for the goods they had bought on credit. The loss of these credit payments hurt businesses even more.

To make matters worse, banks had lent many millions of dollars to stock brokers to make margin loans. Many of these banks had to close. By the end of 1932, more than five thousand banks had failed. As the news of bank failures spread, people tried to withdraw their savings. Banks without enough cash on hand had to close. As a result, many people lost all they had saved.

Like a house of cards, the whole system collapsed. By the end of 1932, thirteen million Americans, or about one-fourth the nation's workers, had lost their jobs. Most people who still had jobs had to take sharp cuts in pay.

Americans hit by the depression struggled to find a way to make a living. Some people hitched rides on railway freight cars, hoping to reach a place where there was work. In addition, many farmers left their farms.

In the cities, the homeless built shacks. City governments and charities struggled to feed the hungry. Some people sold apples on street corners.

Think: A man whom you'd expect to see sitting behind a desk is instead selling apples, trying to earn some money. Respond: Why were people so unprepared for the depression?

Think: **In 1932, thousands of bonus army marchers protested in Washington.** Respond: **Tell why you think these veterans were right or wrong for demanding money when times were so hard.**

The Federal Government Fails To End the Depression

At first, President Hoover thought that business just needed some help to get started again. Hoover established the *Reconstruction Finance Corporation* in 1932 to lend money to railroads, banks, and other businesses. Taxes were cut, and the tariff was increased. The government made it easier for businesspeople to borrow money. Money was also loaned to state and local governments for building roads, bridges, and buildings. Hoover also set up a Farm Board to buy some of the farmers' crops. The Board also tried to keep farm prices from falling.

Most of Hoover's programs did not provide immediate jobs for people. Nor did his programs give money or other help directly to people. Hoover believed, instead, that Americans should rely on themselves. However, his policies failed to bring about recovery.

President Hoover Becomes Very Unpopular

Not surprisingly, many Americans blamed President Hoover for failing to stop the depression. They felt he had done far too little to help the people who were suffering. Lower taxes and business loans did not shelter the homeless or feed the hungry. Local governments and charities could not meet the needs of so many people. Bitter people began to call their shack towns Hoovervilles. The newspapers people huddled under in the cold were called Hoover blankets.

The Bonus Army

Congress in 1924 had passed a law to pay pensions to World War I veterans. However, veterans were not to receive any payments until 1943. Suffering from the depression, thousands of veterans demanded immediate payment. Hoover refused to make the early payments.

In the summer of 1932, thousands of veterans marched on Washington. Some of these bonus marchers set up a camp on the lawn of the Capitol and refused to leave. Hoover ordered the army to remove the marchers. As some of the veterans fought back, three people were killed. Hoover's treatment of the veterans made him even more unpopular.

Section Review

1. What caused the stock market crash of 1929?

2. What major mistake did American business owners make in the late 1920s?

3. How did the Great Depression affect Americans?

4. How did President Hoover try to end the depression? What was the result?

SKILLS FOCUS: Using an Almanac

During the Great Depression, unemployment was one of the United States' biggest problems. Today, unemployment is not as high, but it is still a concern. To find out how many people are unemployed today, you could look in an *almanac*, which is a book of facts and figures published every year. An almanac is a gold mine of information on subjects from sports and national parks to space flights and presidential elections. Because it is published every year, an almanac has more up-to-date statistics than other sources.

Here is part of the quick reference index of an almanac. You can see that facts about employment appear on pages 63, 64, and 107–109.

On page 108, you would find information about the percentage of unemployment in the United States. Here is part of that page.

U.S. Unemployment Rates*

	1981	1982	1984
TOTAL, 16 YEARS AND OVER	7.6	9.6	7.5
MEN, 20 YEARS AND OVER	4.2	8.9	6.6
WOMEN, 20 YEARS AND OVER	6.8	8.1	6.8

*Figures are percentages of the civilian labor force.
Source: Bureau of Labor Statistics, U.S. Labor Department

You can see that of the three years listed, 1982 had the highest unemployment rates.

1 Look in an almanac for the present year and find the latest unemployment rates. Compare them to the rates above.

On page 63 of the same almanac, you would find the chart below. Answer the following questions about it.

2 What three jobs are expected to increase the most by 1995?

3 What job shown on the chart has the highest salary?

4 What job is expected to decrease in number of openings?

Jobs: Job Openings to 1995 and Current Earnings

Occupation	Est. No. of Jobs, 1982	% Change, 1982-1995	Average Weekly Earnings
Construction			
Carpenters	863,000	+20-29	$340
Electricians	542,000	+30-49	$430
Painters	362,000	+20-29	$295
Plumbers	388,000	+30-49	$420
Roofers	102,000	+20-29	$310
Educational			
K-6 teachers	1,366,000	+30-49	$385
H.S. teachers	1,024,000	+3-9	$405
College teachers	744,000	−6	$490

Source: Bureau of Labor Statistics, U.S. Labor Department

2. Franklin D. Roosevelt and the New Deal

Learn these important terms:

New Deal
Emergency Banking Act
National Recovery Administration
Civilian Conservation Corps
lame duck
fireside chats
Agricultural Adjustment Act
Public Works Administration
Home Owners Loan Corporation

Remember the main idea:

President Roosevelt acted quickly to restore the confidence of Americans. He had Congress pass many laws to help farmers and provide jobs and relief.

Look for answers to these questions:

1. How did Roosevelt try to restore the confidence of the American people?
2. How did the New Deal help farmers?
3. How did the New Deal create new jobs?

The Democratic Party chose Franklin D. Roosevelt, the governor of New York, as their candidate for president. Roosevelt had been raised in an established, wealthy family. He had served in Woodrow Wilson's administration as assistant secretary of the navy. As the 1920s began, Roosevelt seemed to be on the road to high office.

In 1921, however, he was struck by polio. The disease left him unable to walk without crutches. He fought back, however, and exercised until he could walk slowly and painfully with braces and a cane. He was determined to continue in politics. He would need that determination to lead a nation suffering from a kind of economic polio.

Think: The press was always careful to show Roosevelt as a strong man able to stand without help from others. Respond: How has the attitude of the press changed toward presidents?

Roosevelt Offers a New Deal

In the campaign of 1932, Roosevelt promised voters a *New Deal*. This New Deal was a plan to lead the nation out of the depression. Roosevelt gathered a group of experts to work out the details of the plan.

In the election of 1932, the Republicans decided to stay with President Hoover. Hoover told Americans that his plans to help the country were starting to work. He also told Americans that he favored letting states decide whether they wanted prohibition laws.

An optimistic president, Franklin Delano Roosevelt (1882-1945) worked hard to end the Great Depression. His policies, though controversial, were shrewd, and his historical reputation is solid.

The main features of the New Deal included: 1) a large program of public works, or government building projects, to provide jobs; 2) direct federal relief payments for Americans without jobs; 3) old age pensions, or payments; 4) a lower tariff; and 5) higher prices for farm products. In addition, Roosevelt wanted to regulate banks and the stock market. In this way, he could prevent the problems that had helped cause the depression. Finally, he supported an end to Prohibition.

Roosevelt won the election by a landslide of more than seven million votes. In addition, the Democrats won control of both houses of Congress. With such strong support, Roosevelt was sure to have his New Deal laws passed quickly.

The Twentieth Amendment

Franklin D. Roosevelt was elected in November 1932. But, under the Constitution, he was not able to take office until March 1933. For almost five months Roosevelt was unable to put his ideas and policies into action. President Hoover, on the other hand, no longer had support.

To prevent future *lame duck* periods such as this, Congress passed the Twentieth Amendment to the Constitution. This amendment moved up the beginning of a president's term in office from March to January. However, this amendment was not passed in time for Roosevelt's first swearing-in ceremony.

Restoring Confidence

On March 4, 1933, millions of Americans waited to hear what their new president would do. Roosevelt knew that he had to give Americans a reason to hope and work for recovery. In his inauguration speech, Roosevelt told Americans that "the only thing we have to fear is fear itself." He also began a series of *fireside chats*—radio talks with the American people. Many Americans appreciated how Roosevelt talked to them directly and seemed to care about their daily needs.

Think: Roosevelt became the first president to use the radio to communicate directly to the American public. Respond: How did Roosevelt's fireside chats affect people?

The first thing that had to be done was to save the banking system. Many banks had been forced to close following the stock market crash. As the news of these closings spread, people rushed to their banks to withdraw their savings. Even those banks still in good condition were being forced to close as they ran out of money during this panic.

Roosevelt quickly put the **Emergency Banking Act** through Congress. This law declared a bank holiday that closed all banks for four days in March 1933. During this time, federal inspectors examined the banks. The banks that could be saved were then reopened with the aid of the government. With their confidence restored, Americans put over a billion dollars back into the banks.

Roosevelt's Plans To Help the Farmer

Farmers, already hurting in the 1920s, suffered badly during the depression. By 1933, prices for crops were so low that many farmers lost their farms. They had been unable to make enough money to repay their loans. To help the farmers, Congress passed a law that allowed farmers to borrow money from the government. This money had to be used to pay back the banks.

To help the farmers receive higher prices for their crops, Congress passed the **Agricultural Adjustment Act** (AAA) in 1933. This New Deal law paid farmers who agreed to grow smaller amounts of crops. Reducing the supply of crops would tend to raise farm prices. In 1936, the Supreme Court ruled that the AAA was unconstitutional. To counter this, Congress passed a new version in 1938.

Think: Shopkeepers displayed the Blue Eagle in their windows to show that they complied with the NRA codes. Respond: **What was the aim of the NRA, and why did it fail?**

Help for Industry

Roosevelt felt that business owners and workers would have to cooperate in order to start business moving again. Such cooperation under government supervision had helped industry meet the challenge of World War I. So, in 1933, Congress established the **National Recovery Administration** (NRA) to set up codes, or rules, for each industry. These codes cut down working hours, raised wages and prices, and limited the amount of goods produced. However, the NRA came to an end in 1935, when the Supreme Court ruled it unconstitutional.

Think: **Despite the overwhelming support the NRA received when it started, consumers, workers, and small businesses came to distrust the NRA codes. One complaint was that the codes supported monopolies.** Respond: **What programs did Roosevelt start to replace the NRA?**

MAP WORKSHOP DRAWING CONCLUSIONS

THE RELIEF PROGRAM

This map shows two different types of information. Using different colors, it tells changes in population for each state. Using different colors of houses as symbols, it shows what percentage of families within each state were on relief as of October 1933. From these two types of information you will be able to draw some conclusions about the effects of the Great Depression on each state and on the nation as a whole.

Use the color code in the map key to find changes in state populations.

1. Which states were losing people? Why do you think this was happening?

2. Which states were growing the fastest? What caused their population growth?

3. Which states were growing at a rate of 5 percent or less? What reasons can you offer for their slow growth?

Match the house in each state to the house in the map key to find out what percentage of a state's families were on relief.

4. Which states had the highest relief rate?

5. Which states had the lowest relief rate? What reasons might explain a low relief rate?

Think about both population changes and relief rates.

6. Which states seem hardest hit by the depression? Why?

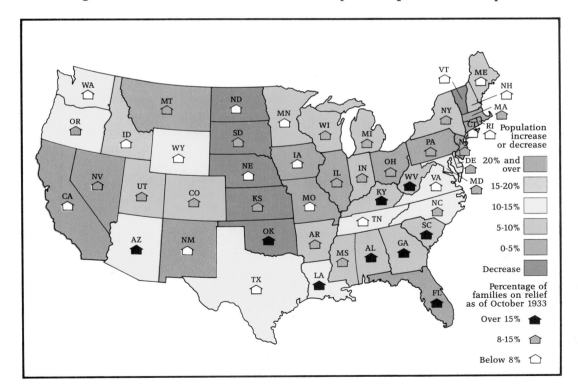

Providing Jobs and Relief

As long as so many people were unemployed, no recovery was possible. If people were put back to work, even at government expense, they would have money to spend on goods. This would make it possible for industries and businesses to recover and begin hiring more workers.

Roosevelt asked Congress to set up the *Public Works Administration* (PWA). This agency put thousands of Americans to work constructing government projects such as buildings, bridges, and dams. But this was not the only New Deal program that created jobs.

The government also established the *Civilian Conservation Corps* (CCC) in 1933. This organization provided jobs for young people between the ages of eighteen and twenty-five. These people lived in camps and were organized like a peaceful army. They planted trees, built roads, and improved the national parks. About two million young Americans eventually served in the CCC.

To provide help for the many Americans who were still unemployed, Congress passed a law to provide relief payments. People who still owned homes were helped by the *Home Owners Loan Corporation* (HOLC), begun in 1933. Homeowners could borrow money from the HOLC to pay off their bank loans. In this way, people prevented their homes from being taken back by banks.

The Repeal of Prohibition

Roosevelt also urged that the Twenty-first Amendment be passed. This amendment would repeal the Eighteenth Amendment and end Prohibition. The Twenty-first Amendment was ratified by the states only nine months after it was presented to them.

Section Review

1. What were the main features of the New Deal?
2. Which New Deal law tried to help farmers?
3. Which New Deal programs provided jobs?
4. Which New Deal law regulated business and labor conditions?

3. New Laws and Challenges

Learn these important terms:

Tennessee Valley Authority
Congress of Industrial
Organizations
Social Security Act
Wages and Hours Law
Securities Exchange Act
Works Progress Administration
National Labor Relations Act

Remember the main idea:

As time passed, more New Deal laws were needed. President Roosevelt withstood challenges and remained popular. After 1938, the worst of the Great Depression seemed to be over.

Look for answers to these questions:

1. What challenges did President Roosevelt and the New Deal laws face?

2. What important benefits did workers and unions gain from the New Deal?

3. How did the Great Depression and the New Deal affect women and minorities?

Some New Deal laws began to help workers and farmers. Other laws did not work so well. Still others were declared unconstitutional by the Supreme Court. President Roosevelt believed in trying many different things. If a program worked, he continued it and made it larger. If something did not work, he tried something else.

In the election of 1934, more supporters of the New Deal were elected to Congress. Lawmakers continued to give Roosevelt's policies strong support. As the 1930s continued, many more New Deal laws were passed.

The New Deal and Public Works

The area around the Tennessee River was often subject to floods. The same waters that were so destructive, however, could be harnessed to generate electricity. So, in 1933, Congress set up the *Tennessee Valley Authority* (TVA). The TVA was the biggest public works project of the New Deal. It built dams that generated a large amount of electricity.

Think: **Under the TVA, a system of dams was built in the Tennessee River Valley. Construction of the Fort Loudoun Dam is shown here.** Respond: **What benefits did the TVA dams bring?**

The TVA provided several benefits. For example, building and operating the dams provided jobs. In addition, the TVA provided cheaper electricity and helped to break up electric power monopolies.

Dams were not the only kind of public works projects. In 1935, Roosevelt asked Congress to set up the **Works Progress Administration** (WPA). The WPA was an even larger program than the Public Works Administration had been. In addition to completing construction projects, the WPA hired writers, artists, and musicians. This encouraged the creative expression of American culture.

The Stock Market Is Regulated

You may remember that the stock market crash was caused by too much buying and selling for quick profit. To prevent future crashes, Congress passed the **Securities Exchange Act** in 1934. This act set up a commission to regulate the way stocks were bought and sold.

Unions Become Stronger

In 1935, Congress passed the **National Labor Relations Act**. This act made it unlawful for a business to refuse to deal with a labor union. It provided for elec-tions where workers could vote to form a union. If the union won the election, the employer had to recognize the union. Thus, the National Labor Relations Act gave labor unions the protection they needed to grow stronger.

The American Federation of Labor (AFL) used the new protections to organize previously nonunion workers. In

Think: Because of the National Labor Relations Act, this steelworker and other laborers could vote for their chosen unions. Respond: What other changes did the act bring?

TENNESSEE VALLEY AUTHORITY

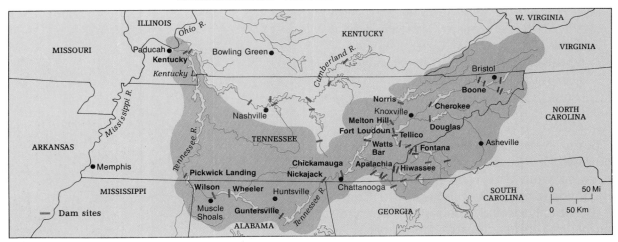

Think: *We Demand,* a painting by Joe Jones, shows picketing workers. Respond: What feelings are conveyed in the painting?

addition, a group of AFL leaders decided to organize unskilled and semi-skilled workers. In the past, these workers were not asked to join unions. When other AFL leaders objected, John L. Lewis and leaders who agreed with him formed a separate group. That group eventually became a separate union called the *Congress of Industrial Organizations* (CIO). The CIO tried to organize all the workers in an industry regardless of skill. By 1940, the AFL and CIO together had about nine million members.

Because the New Deal supported the rights of workers, many workers joined the Democratic Party. This gave the Democrats a large number of voters whom they could count on for many years.

More Laws Help Workers

In 1938, workers gained better working conditions under a law called the *Wages and Hours Law*. This law set a minimum hourly wage for most jobs at twenty-five cents. The law limited the work week to forty-four hours and required overtime pay.

One of the most important of all the New Deal laws was the *Social Security Act* of 1935. This law required both businesses and workers to make regular payments to the government. Then when most workers reached the age of sixty-five, they would receive regular pension payments. The Social Security Act also provided payments to workers who lost their jobs or became disabled.

Challenges to the New Deal

Roosevelt continued to be very popular. In 1936, he defeated the Republican candidate, Alfred M. Landon, by more than eleven million votes.

On the other hand, not everyone supported the New Deal. Many conservatives believed that the New Deal would lead to an America controlled by an all-powerful government.

The strongest challenge to Roosevelt and his New Deal came from the Supreme Court, however. Many New Deal laws extended the power of the federal government into new areas. For example, busi-

Think: On November 24, 1936, the first social security forms were processed in the New York City Post Office, below. Respond: Why was social security set up?

HISTORY MAKERS

Frances Perkins

The First Woman Cabinet Member

"He's done what? Appointed who? Nonsense! Franklin Delano Roosevelt has some strange ideas, but he's not that irresponsible! Surely he is not so foolish as to appoint a woman as Secretary of Labor! How could a woman possibly handle a Cabinet position? And just who is this Frances Perkins, anyway? Does anyone know her?"

Frances Perkins was well prepared to be Secretary of Labor. Both business and labor were upset at first by her appointment in 1933, but the first woman Cabinet member proved to be an effective leader. She was a capable administrator of the Department of Labor.

Frances Perkins began her career in public service as a teacher and a social worker. In 1910, Frances Perkins was appointed to a commission investigating a fire at the Triangle Shirtwaist Factory in New York City. The fire had killed over one hundred women. As part of the investigation, Perkins took other commission members and politicians through sweatshops to show the dangerous conditions in which women had to work. After this, Frances Perkins successfully worked to get laws for safety standards in the workplace, a shorter workday for women, and an end to child labor.

Frances Perkins was also a member of New York state commissions on industry and labor. Later she was appointed state industrial commissioner by Governor Franklin D. Roosevelt. Frances Perkins believed strongly in helping the unemployed. She helped to convince Governor Roosevelt that state aid for people who were out of work was a social duty, not an undeserved handout.

As Secretary of Labor, Frances Perkins greatly increased the department's research, social services, and enforcement of fair labor standards. She also worked hard for some form of social insurance. The result was Social Security.

Frances Perkins was a social worker, economist, and public servant. As the first woman Cabinet member, she served the Department of Labor, and her country, well.

nesses were told how to pay and treat their workers and, sometimes, how much to produce. Most of the Supreme Court justices believed in a strict interpretation of the Constitution. They supported its limits on government power. The Supreme Court declared both the Agricultural Adjustment Act and the National Recovery Act unconstitutional.

Roosevelt was afraid that the court would throw out more of the New Deal laws. So, he came up with a plan to add judges who would favor the New Deal. He wanted to add a new justice for each existing justice who refused to retire after reaching age seventy. This would increase the size of the Supreme Court from nine to fifteen justices.

While Congress still supported Roosevelt and the New Deal, it refused to support this plan. Even his strongest supporters were afraid to give the president such power. They feared it would destroy the constitutional system of checks and balances among the branches.

Roosevelt lost this battle, but eventually got Supreme Court support. As justices died or retired, Roosevelt appointed replacements who supported his ideas. The Supreme Court began to uphold New Deal laws.

The New Deal Draws to a Close

The New Deal helped keep hope alive in America during the depression. Although the New Deal helped many people, recovery was painfully slow. Then business began to improve in 1936 and 1937. In response, Congress began to cut back on the amount of money spent on public works and relief. Congress hoped to keep the government from going farther into debt. But business was not ready to hire all the people who lost government-supported jobs.

In October 1937, things took a turn for the worse. At the beginning of 1938, ten

Think: **After the Supreme Court found some of his programs unconstitutional, Roosevelt tried to control the court by adding judges.** Respond: **How does this cartoon show his action?**

million people were again unemployed. As a result, Roosevelt asked for government spending to be increased again. Finally, by the end of 1938, the worst of the depression seemed to be over. As a result, no more New Deal laws were passed. President Roosevelt continued to be popular. He was reelected in 1940 and again in 1944.

Section Review

1. How did the New Deal help labor unions and workers?
2. How did the Supreme Court challenge the New Deal? How did Roosevelt respond?
3. What was the Tennessee Valley Authority? Why was it an important part of the New Deal?

CHAPTER SUMMARY

Although many Americans had good times during the 1920s, there were some hidden problems. Business could not keep selling more and more goods, because there was a limited number of buyers. As business began to slow down, stocks could not keep going up. When the stock market crash came, many businesses closed or were cut back, many banks were closed, and many people lost their jobs. President Hoover was not able to deal with this severe depression, and he became very unpopular.

Franklin D. Roosevelt offered a New Deal to fight the depression. As president, he had many laws passed to help business, labor, and farmers. Many people were hired by public works projects. People without jobs received direct help, or relief. Laws were passed to improve working conditions and to protect labor unions. The Social Security Act gave workers pensions and other benefits. Blacks and other minorities suffered very badly during the depression, although the New Deal gave them some help.

The Supreme Court at first declared some New Deal laws unconstitutional, but eventually became favorable to the New Deal. By 1938, the worst of the Great Depression had ended, although real prosperity did not return until World War II.

Key Words

Write a sentence to explain the meaning of each of these terms.

speculation

New Deal

National Recovery Administration

Works Progress Administration

National Labor Relations Act

Major Events

Choose the answer that best completes the statement.

1. Soon after the stock market crash
   a) most workers went on strike.
   b) many banks and businesses closed.
   c) stock prices went back up.

2. President Hoover lost the election of 1932 because voters felt
   a) he had caused the depression.
   b) he was unable to end the depression.
   c) he had ignored the depression.

3. Starting in 1933, the New Deal provided many jobs by
   a) starting public works projects.
   b) drafting the unemployed.
   c) paying companies to hire more workers.

4. The Social Security Act of 1935
   a) provided jobs for all workers.
   b) set a minimum wage.
   c) set retirement pensions.

5. In 1936, the main opposition to the New Deal came from
   a) Congress.
   b) the Supreme Court.
   c) labor unions.

Review

Important Facts

Answer each question with at least one complete sentence.

1. Why did businesses start to get into trouble in the late 1920s?

2. How did the buying of many stocks on margin make the stock market crash worse?

3. How did the stock market crash lead to many Americans losing their jobs?

4. How did Hoover try to end the depression? Did his programs help most people?

5. How did the Bonus Army affect Hoover's popularity?

6. What were the main features of the New Deal?

7. Why was Roosevelt able to get so many New Deal laws passed so quickly?

8. How did Roosevelt try to restore Americans' confidence in the banking system?

9. How did the New Deal help farmers?

10. How did the New Deal help workers?

11. How did Congress try to prevent future stock market crashes?

12. How did Roosevelt deal with Supreme Court opposition to the New Deal? What was the reaction to his plan?

13. Why did depression conditions return in 1937? How did Roosevelt react?

Skill Review

Look at this graph, then answer the following questions.

1. In which year was unemployment lowest? When was it highest?

2. What percentage of the workforce was unemployed in 1937?

3. Where would you look in an almanac to compare this year's rate of unemployment with the rate in 1937?

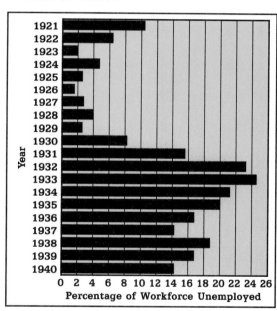

Unemployment 1921-1940

Critical Thinking

Write a paragraph to answer each question.

1. How did the New Deal change the way most Americans thought about their government?

2. Do you think a depression as bad as the one of the 1930s could happen again? Why, or why not?

28
The American People in the 1930s

Years 1930–1939

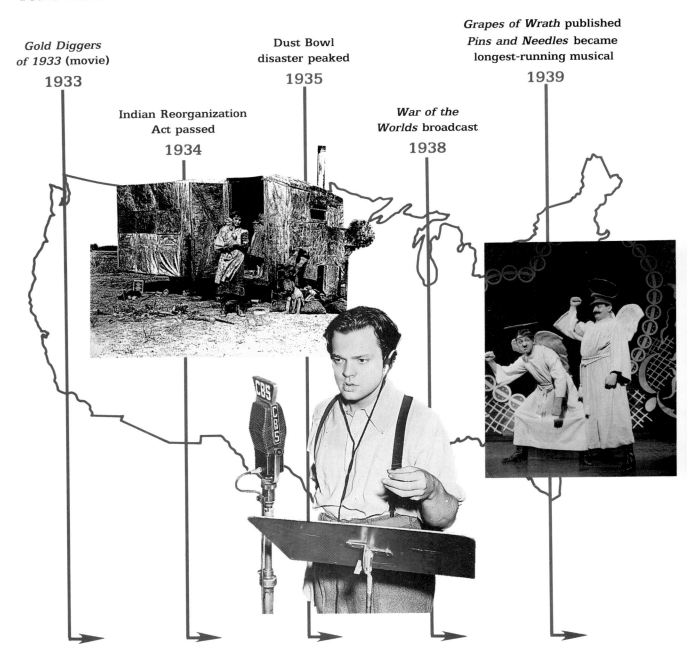

Gold Diggers of 1933 (movie)
1933

Indian Reorganization Act passed
1934

Dust Bowl disaster peaked
1935

War of the Worlds broadcast
1938

Grapes of Wrath published
Pins and Needles became longest-running musical
1939

Imagine you are a man with a wife and two children in 1933. Until 1930, you worked at the Ford plant. You were proud of your own new car and your new home.

Then, after the stock market crash, everything changed. Fewer people could afford new cars. The Ford factory laid off workers. You worked part-time for a while. Then you, too, lost your job.

Your family lived on your savings at first. You let the bank take back the car so you could keep up payments on the house. You looked for work, of course. Sometimes you found a job that lasted a few weeks. Mostly you found nothing.

Today is Saturday. You count the money in your wallet and announce that it's time for a treat: the family will go to the movies.

The movie is called *Gold Diggers of 1933.* Its romantic story isn't very believable. But one song, "Remember My Forgotten Man," could have been written for you. It tells about soldiers who fought for their country but are forgotten and jobless today.

Best of all is the song that opens the movie. Girls in costumes made of gold coins sing: "We're in the money! We've got a lot of what it takes to get along." As you listen, you feel better. You decide you were right to spend your money on this treat. It gives you something you need almost as much as food or a job; it gives you hope.

Learn this important term:

mural

Remember the main idea:

People learned to do without things during the Great Depression. Families had a hard time, and many young couples put off starting families. People came to value cooperation and to believe that government should help those in need.

Look for answers to these questions:

1. How did people "stretch a dollar" during the depression?
2. How did the depression change American family life?
3. What common American beliefs changed during the depression?

During the 1920s, many Americans were able to lead more comfortable lives than ever before. They bought new homes, cars, and appliances. When the Great Depression struck, they lost these comforts and the improved social position that went with them. They were often forced to return to a poorer style of life. Many tried hard not to let their neighbors see their misfortune. They did not realize that most of their neighbors were pretending in just the same way.

Doing Without

People in almost every income group learned how to make their money go

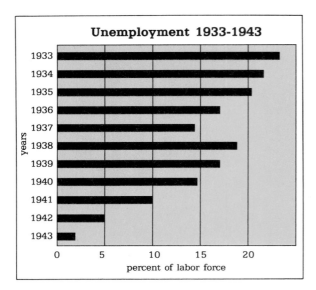

Unemployment 1933-1943

percent of labor force

farther. They learned to make the things they owned last longer. People mended their clothes—sometimes over and over—instead of buying new ones. When older children outgrew their clothes, the clothes were passed down to younger members of the family. Advertisements sold products by showing how they would "stretch a dollar."

Food prices fell, but wages fell even faster—and many people had no wages at all. Meat disappeared from many tables or was seen there only as a special treat. Mothers saved and reused every bit of leftovers and ordered their children to "clean their plates." The poorest people searched through garbage cans or under vegetable-sellers' pushcarts for food that was thrown away. Others stood for hours in lines to receive bread or soup. Many families went to bed hungry, and a few actually starved.

Housing was another big problem. Some people lost their homes when they fell behind in mortgage payments. Others hung onto theirs only with the help of friends. People gave "house-rent parties," charging for admission and food to raise rent money. Those who lost their homes might move in with relatives or friends. If they had no one to move in with, they might be forced to live in shacks of boards and tar-paper. Some moved from place to place and had no homes at all.

Changes in Family Life

Some families were drawn closer together by the hard times. Others were torn apart. Trapped together at home all day, husbands and wives got on each other's nerves. Often relatives moved in with them, adding to the tension.

Think: Breadlines formed in cities throughout the nation. Free or cheap bread and soup fed thousands. Respond: Why were so many people nearly starving?

Think: At first people with jobs could not understand the plight of those without. The jobless were thought to be lazy and unwilling to work. But as the Great Depression dragged on, attitudes toward the jobless changed.
Respond: What do you think it was like to be without a job during the depression?

In spite of these strains, the divorce rate dropped. The reason in many cases was simple: divorces were expensive. Most people could not afford them.

It was so hard to make a living during the depression that many young people put off getting married. Those who were married often put off starting families. The population growth rate slowed down. Only about half as many babies were born during the 1930s as had been born during the 1920s.

Changes in Attitudes

Most people in the 1930s had grown up believing that, with a combination of hard work and luck, anyone could be successful. They also believed that any good and willing worker could find work. They had trouble understanding that this was no longer true. As a result, people who still had jobs or money sometimes looked down on those who did not. They believed unemployed people simply did not want to work and therefore did not deserve any type of help.

People who could not find work after months of trying blamed themselves for failing. They were ashamed to ask for charity or government help. Some would not apply for relief until their families were almost starving.

However, many people began to feel differently as the Great Depression dragged on. Both employed and unemployed people came to believe that people in need had a right to get help from the government. They came to believe, too, that the government had both the right and the duty to control parts of the economy in order to protect citizens.

Think: The great Mexican muralist Diego Rivera painted *Detroit Industry* in the early 1930s. Like many of his murals, this work celebrated the triumph of labor. Carefully study this detail of the mural, "Body Presses and Assembly of Chassis." **Respond:** What do you think Rivera was trying to tell us about people and industry?

Along with these changes came changes in people's attitudes toward business and wealth. Most people in the 1920s had admired rich, successful businesspeople and had wanted to be as successful as possible themselves. Now they blamed these same businesspeople for all their troubles. Cartoons, movies, and radio shows made fun of rich people or showed them as villains. People came to feel that fairness and honesty in business were as important as making money.

Many middle-class people felt a new interest in and respect for workers. Stories and plays celebrating lives of "honest toil" became popular. Workers were often the main figures in the *murals,* or large wall paintings, done by WPA artists to decorate public buildings. Many of these murals were inspired by the work of Mexican artists such as Diego Rivera.

People still felt that individuals had both the right and the responsibility to take care of themselves. At the same time, working together and sharing became more common. Families helped friends or relatives who had been harder hit by the depression than they were. Workers recognized that they had a better chance to gain decent wages if they banded together. Labor unions became more popular and respectable.

Section Review

1. How did people help one another keep their homes during the Great Depression?

2. What happened to divorce and birth rates during the depression? Why?

3. How did many people's feelings about business and workers change during the depression?

THE DUST BOWL

Sometimes you must go to several sources to find the information that you want. Here you can combine information from the two maps and the table to learn about a cause of the Dust Bowl.

Study the map on the left.

1. Which states were part of the Dust Bowl? Which were worst hit by the disaster?

Now study the other map.

2. Which states have the highest average yearly precipitation? Which states have the lowest?

3. What is the average yearly precipitation of the Dust Bowl states? On a separate sheet of paper, list these states and figures one by one.

Next study the table.

4. On a separate sheet of paper, write down the average annual precipitation for each of the Dust Bowl states except Kansas for the years 1934–1939. Are

these averages higher or lower than the averages on the map? Answer for each state. (Remember that precipitation averages are for the whole state, not just the Dust Bowl area.)

	'34	'35	'36	'37	'38	'39
Colorado	7.9	7.2	7.6	7.0	13.3	6.4
Nebraska	17.2	26.8	12.4	21.7	28.0	18.3
New Mex.	4.6	12.7	9.5	7.0	9.3	5.8
Oklahoma	14.3	11.7	9.7	11.3	14.9	13.6
Texas	32.1	33.2	34.9	23.3	21.7	16.7
Kansas	(Figures not recorded)					

**Dust Bowl Annual Precipitation
1934-1939**

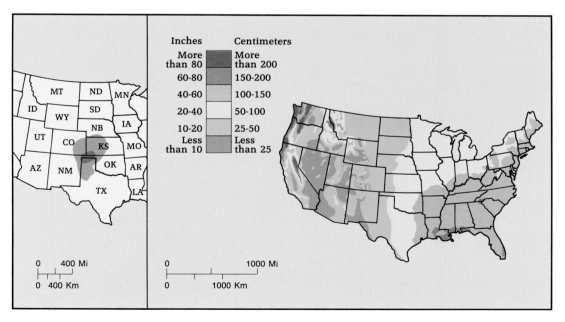

2. Groups with Special Problems

Learn these important terms:

Dust Bowl
Rural Electrification Administration
Black Cabinet
Indian Reorganization Act

Remember the main idea:

During the Great Depression, falling prices and natural disasters made life especially hard for farmers. Women were discriminated against but held onto traditional "women's jobs." Blacks and other minorities suffered even more than whites during the depression, but some New Deal programs helped these groups.

Look for answers to these questions:

1. What special problems did farmers have during the depression?
2. What happened to women who tried to seek work?
3. What gains and losses did minority groups have during the Great Depression?

White men in America's cities suffered badly during the depression. Other Americans, however, suffered even more. Farmers, whether white or black, had special problems. Women, blacks, and other minorities still faced unfairness as they tried to compete with white men for work.

Special Problems of Farmers

Prices for farm products were very low during the depression. Some farmers were so angry and discouraged that they destroyed what they had grown rather than trying to sell it. They burned crops, slaughtered healthy pigs and cattle, and poured milk onto roadways. This was an especially painful sight to those who knew that people were starving in the cities of America.

A natural disaster, in addition to falling prices, destroyed many farmers' way of life. From 1932 to 1939, a long spell of dry weather and high winds turned Kansas, Oklahoma, and other midwestern states into what was known as a *Dust Bowl*. Wheat and other farm crops did not hold down topsoil the way the prairie grasses had. When the winds came, the soil simply blew away. Unable to grow more crops, more farmers than ever lost their farms.

Many of the homeless came from Oklahoma. "Okies," as they were called, packed everything they had into the family car and headed for the far West. There they hoped to find jobs. Often they found nothing but disappointment and harsh treatment when they arrived. As migrant workers, they went from farm to farm, searching for a day's work. They lived in makeshift shacks or in their cars.

Sharecroppers and tenant farmers also had special problems. Most of these were blacks living in the South. They worked on farms owned by others. They were supposed to get part of the profits from the crops they grew. Often, however, the money was completely used up in paying rent for the land or in buying the seeds and tools they needed. When the Agricultural Adjustment Administration told farmers to cut back crops, many farm owners forced most of their tenants or sharecroppers off the land.

Some government agencies did try to help these groups. There were experiments with buying land and giving it as homesteads to people who had been tenant farmers. The Farm Security Administration set up clean camps for migrant workers. And the **Rural Electrification Administration**, or REA, gave loans to farm cooperatives so that inexpensive electric power could be brought to farms. Electricity brought lights and appliances that eased the burden of life for those who had managed to keep their farms.

Think: The work of artist Ben Shahn is filled with social statements. Shahn was a social realist. He portrayed things as harshly as he saw them. At the same time, Shahn wanted things to be better. Respond: Why was it important for artists to record what they saw and felt during the Great Depression?

Think: Throughout the Great Plains, farm families had to make tough choices. Abandoned farms dotted the Dust Bowl. Many farmers moved west, hoping to find work. Some stayed, only to watch their farm land be reduced to dust. Respond: What caused a large portion of the Great Plains to become a dust bowl?

Think: In the 1930s, some people thought of certain jobs as being only for men or only for women. Respond: How did this way of thinking stop men from getting work?

"Women's Work"

More women than ever before, both married and single, left home to look for work during the depression. Sometimes they had better luck as job hunters than men. Most men would not apply for "women's work," jobs such as domestic service, clerical work, or teaching. Thus these jobs, low-paying as they were, remained open to women even when many men were unemployed.

Even so, society often discouraged women, especially married women, from seeking jobs. Many people believed that women took jobs away from men. Half of the country's schools would fire a woman teacher if she got married, for example. When women did the same work as men, the women were paid less, even by government agencies.

Women made some gains under the New Deal, however. President Roosevelt's wife, Eleanor, spoke out for women's rights and urged her husband to appoint more women to government office. More than one hundred women were appointed to high government positions, including Frances Perkins, the U.S. secretary of labor. She was the first woman Cabinet officer.

"Last Hired, First Fired"

Blacks, like women, had held some jobs that most white men did not want. Unlike women, however, blacks often were not able to hold onto these jobs during the depression. All over the country, blacks were "last hired and first fired." Twice as many blacks as whites were unemployed during the depression. Those who were tenant farmers or sharecroppers often lost their land and homes. They crowded into the cities to join the equally unemployed blacks who lived there.

Many New Deal programs helped blacks. President Roosevelt appointed a number of blacks to help him understand the needs of black people. This so-called

Think: The depression created more than financial problems throughout the nation. Here, out-of-work Texans wile away the hours. Respond: How were people's self-images affected by the depression?

HISTORY MAKERS

——Woody Guthrie——

A Songwriter for all Americans

On a Sunday in 1935, the weather in Pampa, Texas, was hotter than usual for April. Late in the day, people sitting outside, trying to cool off, saw a huge dark cloud off to the north. As the cloud came closer to town, it grew bigger and darker until it filled the horizon. Birds flew in front of it, trying to escape the storm. The black sky was streaked with red. The cloud descended on the town with a roar as the temperature dropped fifty degrees. But no rain fell. The black cloud filling the sky was made of dust and clay, topsoil blown away from Texas, Nebraska, and the Dakotas. While the wind blew, people covered their faces with wet rags so they could breathe through the dust. Many thought that the end of the world had come. They gathered together to talk of what was happening. The storm lasted into the night. The next afternoon the dust began to blow again. When it finally stopped, people took dirt out of their houses by the shovelful.

Woody Guthrie lived in Pampa when the great dust storm blew. He saw people, already hurt by the Great Depression, leaving their now worthless land and struggling to find work, handouts, or some way to stay alive. Woody Guthrie wrote a song about the storm and what it did to people's lives. He called his song "Dusty Old Dust." It became known as the theme song of the Great Depression.

Woody Guthrie composed and sang songs about America and Americans. He wrote about labor unions, the Bonneville Dam, patriotism, and Einstein's theory of relativity. Woody's sympathy was for the "little guy," the underdog. His most famous song, "This Land Is Your Land," written toward the end of the Great Depression, is about an America that should belong to everyone— rich and poor alike.

Woody Guthrie influenced American music into the mid-1980s. Pete Seeger, Bob Dylan, and Woody's son Arlo all carried on the Guthrie tradition of music that is for and about all the people. His songs, Woody Guthrie once said, sing America's history.

Black Cabinet gave blacks a voice in the Roosevelt administration. One member, Mary McLeod Bethune, worked especially hard to get jobs and education for young blacks. Because of the help they received, many blacks became supporters of Roosevelt and the Democratic Party.

Other Minorities

In the 1920s, many immigrants from Mexico had worked on farms in the Southwest. These jobs became more in demand in the 1930s, however. To cut down on job competition, the government forced between a quarter million and a half million ''Mexicans'' to move to Mexico. Some of these people were really citizens of the United States.

Indians had even worse luck finding work during the depression than did blacks or Mexican-Americans. They did make one gain during the New Deal days, however. The **Indian Reorganization Act** of 1934 stopped the government policy of dividing reservations into small parcels of farm land. It also recognized the Indians as tribes and gave them a little more say over their future. The approval of this act showed that Americans finally were gaining respect for the Indians' traditional way of life.

Section Review

1. What caused the natural disaster that destroyed many midwestern farms in 1934 and 1935?
2. What kinds of jobs were women able to keep during the Great Depression?
3. How did the Indian Reorganization Act of 1934 show recognition of the Indians' traditional way of life?

3. Entertainment and the Arts in the 1930s

Learn these important terms:

musicals   *swing music*

Remember the main idea:

People found inexpensive ways to entertain themselves and forget their troubles during the 1930s. Serious writers and artists explored the causes and sufferings of the Great Depression.

Look for answers to these questions:

1. What kinds of movies and radio shows did people enjoy in the 1930s?
2. What plays and novels described problems in particular parts of the country?
3. How did the government help writers and artists during the depression?

Whether they wanted it or not, many Americans in the 1930s found themselves with more free time than ever before. As businesses cut back work to save money, the five-day work week became common. People without jobs, of course, had no work week at all. People looked for inexpensive ways to amuse themselves and raise their spirits during their free time.

Many people turned to bicycling, softball, and other sports. New Deal work projects built many new public swimming pools, playgrounds, and other places for

Think: With so many people out of work, recreation became a way of life. Parks, playgrounds, and beaches were often crowded with people who had plenty of spare time, but no money to spend. Imagine trying to find a spot on this Coney Island Beach. Respond: What changes were made because so many people had leisure time?

outdoor activities. Sports became something for everyone, not just for a few rich or talented people. Instead of paying to watch others play, people became active players themselves.

Americans Watch Movies

Movies were another inexpensive amusement. Extravagant movie *musicals*, or shows featuring singing and dancing, were especially popular. Movies like *Forty-Second Street* and *Footlight Parade* showed hundreds of dancing women, photographed in ways that turned them into stars, flowers, and other fantastic designs. In other movies, the famous comedian Groucho Marx and his brothers tricked wealthy people into giving them anything they wanted. Child star Shirley Temple and Walt Disney's cartoon characters charmed their way to equal success. Happy movies like these helped people forget their troubles.

In the late 1930s, color brought almost as big a change to the movies as sound had. In 1939, color helped make *The Wizard of Oz* magical and the Civil War South of *Gone with the Wind* thrilling.

Think: Edgar Bergen and Charlie McCarthy reached millions with their radio act. Respond: How did radio entertainment affect the lives of Americans during the depression?

Americans Listen to Their Radios

Millions tuned in their radios each week to hear Edgar Bergen and his wisecracking dummy, Charlie McCarthy. They also enjoyed other comedians such as Fred Allen and Jack Benny. Radio dramas encouraged people to "make movies in their heads" with their own imaginations. One, a story about an invasion from Mars called *War of the Worlds* that was broadcast in 1938, was so effective that millions of people believed it was real. Some even fled from their homes, sure that the Martians would find them and kill them if they remained.

Americans Read Newspapers and Magazines

Newspapers got bigger, but there were fewer of them. Rival newspapers in the same city often joined together. Many cities came to have only one morning and one afternoon paper—and sometimes both were owned by the same company. Sunday editions grew larger, often including a magazine section and comics pages in color.

More and more Americans read magazines. *Life* and *Look* were made up mostly of photographs. Weekly magazines such as *Time* and *Newsweek* kept people up to date on the news, often describing important events in more depth than newspapers could. *Reader's Digest* allowed people to sample shortened forms of articles that had first appeared in other magazines. People also read magazines that carried special kinds of stories, such as mysteries, westerns, or science fiction.

Americans Dance and Listen to Music

Dancing was another popular way to spend time. Big bands, mostly with white musicians, replaced the smaller jazz groups of the 1920s. Their *swing music*

Think: Jitterbugging was active, cheerful dancing that didn't reflect the hard times. Jitterbugs danced to swing music playing by big bands. Respond: How do today's music and dances relate to the times?

Think: **Examine the people in Edward Hopper's *Nighthawks*. Imagine what they are saying or thinking. Consider the deserted streets outside the restaurant.** Respond: **Why was loneliness a part of the depression?**

was sweeter and easier to dance to than jazz. It owed a lot to jazz, however. Like jazz, it let individual musicians invent their own variations on each basic tune that the band played. Some of the most popular bands were those of Benny Goodman, Glenn Miller, and the two brothers Jimmy and Tommy Dorsey. During the "Swing Era," jazz truly entered the mainstream of American culture. Young "jitterbugs" sometimes waited in line all night to get into one of the big bands' concerts.

Writers and Artists Show Problems of Depression America

While popular entertainers usually tried to help people forget the depres-

sion's hard times, serious writers and artists described conditions in the United States as they really were. In his 1939 novel *The Grapes of Wrath*, John Steinbeck told the story of a family whose farm was destroyed by the Dust Bowl disaster. This book was made into a popular movie in 1940. A three-volume book by John Dos Passos, *U.S.A.*, and a popular novel by Ernest Hemingway, *To Have and Have Not*, also pictured the horrors of depression life in the United States. Many of these books featured people whose lives were destroyed by economic problems that were not their fault. James Farrell's *Studs Lonigan* went further; it portrayed the death of an American era.

To find one famous novel about the Great Depression, John Steinbeck's *The Grapes of Wrath*, you can look in the *card catalog* of your library. A card catalog contains information about each book in the library. Usually the information is listed on cards. Here are the two cards you would find for *The Grapes of Wrath* if the library has a copy.

Author card

```
FIC       Steinbeck, John, 1902-1968
STE          The grapes of wrath/John Steinbeck
          New York: Viking Press, 1958, c 1939. 619 p.
```

Title card

```
             The grapes of wrath
FIC       Steinbeck, John, 1902-1968.
STE          New York: Viking Press, 1958, c
          1939. 619 p.
```

From the cards, you can see that John Steinbeck lived from 1902 to 1968 and wrote the book in 1939. Viking Press published this edition, which has 619 pages, in 1958.

Because *The Grapes of Wrath* is *fiction*, or an imaginary story made up by the author, you will find the book in the fiction section of a library. All the fiction books are arranged alphabetically by the last names of the authors.

If *The Grapes of Wrath* interests you and you want to find out more about the hard lives of the American farmers during the depression, you might look for another book on the subject. A *nonfiction*, or true, book could give you facts about the Great Depression.

Each nonfiction book has three cards in the card catalog: an author card, a title card, and a subject card. Here is one card you might find if you looked in the card catalog under the subject "Depressions."

Subject card

```
          DEPRESSIONS – 1929 – United States
978     Bonnifield, Matthew Paul, 1937 –
BON        The Dust Bowl: men, dirt, and depres-
        sion/Paul Bonnifield. Albuquerque: University
        of New Mexico Press, c 1978, 232 p.
        Bibliography
        Includes index
        1. Great Plains – history. 2. Great Plains –
        Economic Conditions. 3. Great Plains – Climate
        4. Depressions – 1929 – United States. 5.
        Droughts – Great Plains – History. 6. Agricul-
        ture – Great Plains – History.
```

The number to the left on a subject card is the *call number* of the book. Call numbers help you find a book in the library. You will find this book on the shelves with other books that have the same call number.

Use the card to answer these questions.

1 What is the title of the book?

2 In what year was the book written?

3 When did the author live? Could the book have been a primary source, one written by someone who lived during the Great Depression? Why, or why not?

4 How many pages does the book have?

Plays also dealt with the problems of working or unemployed people. Clifford Odets wrote a play about labor unions called *Waiting for Lefty*, for example. A musical show that praised labor unions, *Pins and Needles*, was put on in 1937 by a company of actors who were also garment workers. By 1939 it had run longer than any other American musical.

Poets and artists showed the sufferings of depression America as well. Stephen Vincent Benet wrote about the hardships of city life in a book of poems he called *Burning City*. Archibald MacLeish, in a long poem called *Land of the Free*, summed up many people's feelings of helplessness with the repeated words, "We don't know—we can't say—we're wondering. . . ." Artist Edward Hopper pictured the glaring lights and lonely people of America's cities.

Other books and plays described problems in particular parts of the country. Erskine Caldwell's play *Tobacco Road* showed the terrible living conditions of poor southern farmers. William Faulkner's novels also described the South. Meyer Levin and Henry Roth described Jewish life in American cities. And Richard Wright in *Native Son* described the lives of black Americans living in a Chicago slum.

American Strengths and Values

At the same time they pictured American problems, writers and artists of the 1930s showed the strengths of the American people. Steinbeck's novel showed how the members of the Joad family helped one another survive. Carl Sandburg's poems called for improvements in American life, but they also described the power of America's working people. Grant Wood and Thomas Hart Benton painted pictures showing the life and people of the Midwest. Robert Gwathmey painted some outstanding pictures show-

ing the typical life of black Americans. Many writers and artists of the 1930s called for a return to the values of an earlier time, when people had been closer to the land and more willing to help one another through hardship.

Government Help for Writers and Artists

The Works Progress Administration gave jobs to many artists and writers. Members of the Federal Art Project painted thousands of pictures that were loaned to schools and libraries. Other artists painted murals in public buildings. Fifteen thousand musicians in the Federal Music Project put on concerts and gave music lessons to children. The Federal Theater Project gave jobs to more than twelve thousand actors, who put on plays seen by millions of Americans.

Some writers visited people in the country and recorded folk stories and customs that were dying out. Others prepared guidebooks describing the important features of each state and major city. The Farm Security Administration paid photographer Dorothea Lange to take pictures of the poorest American people and their living conditions. Lange's photographs did far more than simply record facts. They left behind a deeply moving picture of people's sufferings, the true face of the Great Depression.

Section Review

1. What caused more people to take part in sports in the 1930s?
2. What did writers and artists of the 1930s tell and show about American life?
3. What jobs did the WPA create for writers and artists?

CHAPTER SUMMARY

During the Great Depression, people lost many of the comforts and the social position they had gained during the 1920s. They learned to make things last or to do without them. People put off marriage, children, and divorce. They changed values and attitudes, too. Many began to believe that government should protect citizens from the worst effects of economic changes. Middle-class people began to value working people, fairness in business, and cooperation.

Farmers suffered from low farm product prices and from the natural disaster of the Dust Bowl. Tenant farmers often were thrown off their land. Women kept traditional "women's work" but were paid less than men. Blacks were "last hired and first fired" but were helped by some New Deal programs. Mexican-Americans and Indians suffered perhaps worst of all in the depression.

Popular entertainment helped people forget their troubles. People played sports, watched movies, listened to the radio, read newspapers and magazines, and danced. Meanwhile, serious writers and artists described the sufferings of depression-era Americans in plain language.

The Great Depression greatly challenged Americans, but it also helped them to develop strengths needed for the future.

Key Words

Write a sentence to explain the meaning of each of these terms.

mural
Dust Bowl
REA
Black Cabinet
musicals

Major Events

Choose the answer that best completes each statement.

1. Dry weather in the Midwest in 1935 made many farmers
   a. build irrigation systems.
   b. leave their farms.
   c. grow crops that needed little water.

2. Americans during the depression came to believe that those in financial trouble
   a. deserved government help.
   b. caused their own troubles.
   c. should be helped only by friends and relatives.

3. The Indian Reorganization Act
   a. broke up Indian tribes.
   b. recognized Indian tribes.
   c. established new reservations.

4. In the late 1930s, movies improved by adding
   a. color.
   b. sound.
   c. bigger screens.

5. Many writers and artists got government jobs from the
   a. REA.
   b. NRA.
   c. WPA.

Review

Important Facts

Answer each question with at least one complete sentence.

1. How did people make their clothes last in the 1930s?

2. What things added to the strain on families during the Great Depression?

3. How did the depression change people's feelings about the job of government?

4. Who or what did people blame for the depression?

5. How did middle-class people feel about workers?

6. What did farmers do with products they could not sell?

7. What was life like for many "Okies"?

8. Why did women sometimes find jobs more easily than men?

9. In what way did black farmers suffer even more than white farmers?

10. What happened to some Mexican-Americans during the depression?

11. Why did people have extra free time in the 1930s?

12. What kinds of movies were most popular during the 1930s?

13. What was *War of the Worlds?*

14. How did most serious writers and artists react to the Great Depression?

15. How did Dorothea Lange show life during the depression?

Skill Review

Look at this graph, then answer the following questions.

1. What percentage of farms had electricity when the Rural Electrification Administration began in 1935? What was the percentage in 1940?

2. What headings would you check in the card catalog to compare farms with electricity to the nation as a whole?

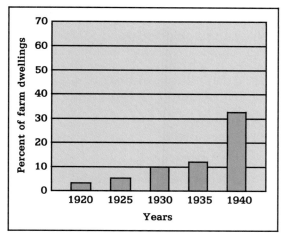

Farm Dwellings with Electricity 1920-1940

Critical Thinking

Write a paragraph to answer each question.

1. What might a family gain by telling friends about their depression problems? What might they lose?

2. What attitudes did depression writers and artists think were better in earlier times? Do you agree or disagree?

Important People

Choose the answer that best completes the statement.

1. The Teapot Dome scandal happened during the administration of

   a) Theodore Roosevelt.
   b) Warren G. Harding.
   c) Herbert Hoover.

2. The Universal Negro Improvement Association was founded in 1914 by

   a) Booker T. Washington.
   b) Langston Hughes.
   c) Marcus Garvey.

3. F. Scott Fitzgerald expressed the spirit of the Jazz Age in his

   a) novels.
   b) jazz music.
   c) movies.

4. The New Deal was offered by

   a) Herbert Hoover.
   b) Alfred E. Smith.
   c) Franklin D. Roosevelt.

5. John L. Lewis made important contributions as

   a) a labor union leader.
   b) head administrator of public works projects.
   c) the inventor of mass production methods.

6. The first woman to become a member of a president's Cabinet was

   a) Frances Perkins.
   b) Eleanor Roosevelt.
   c) Mary McLeod Bethune.

Main Ideas

Choose the answer that best completes the statement.

1. The main benefit gained from mass production and the assembly line was that

   a) fewer workers were needed.
   b) a better quality of goods could be made.
   c) goods could be made more cheaply and sold for lower prices.

2. In the 1920s, an investor would probably make the most money buying stock in

   a) railroad companies.
   b) automobile manufacturers.
   c) coal mines.

3. The rise of the Ku Klux Klan, the Red Scare, and restrictions on immigration showed that many Americans

   a) did not like people who were different from them.
   b) wanted a new kind of government.
   c) were open to new ideas.

4. The biggest difference between America in the 1920s and America in the 1930s was in

   a) relations with other nations.
   b) business and jobs.
   c) developments in technology.

5. The 1929 stock market crash was

   a) the main cause of the Great Depression.
   b) not really a cause of the Great Depression.

Review

c) a trigger that started the collapse that became the Great Depression.

6. Franklin Roosevelt and Herbert Hoover differed most on

   a) the need to end the depression.
   b) the role of government in solving the nation's economic problems.
   c) the importance of industry to the nation.

7. The New Deal did *not* involve

   a) public works programs.
   b) government ownership of all businesses.
   c) relief for the unemployed.

8. One thing that did not change much for Americans when the Great Depression came was

   a) admiration for successful businesspeople.
   b) the importance of sharing and cooperation.
   c) interest in the movies and sports.

9. The depression ended

   a) only gradually, as World War II approached.
   b) soon after the New Deal began.
   c) after World War II.

10. A New Deal program that continues today is

    a) the National Recovery Administration.
    b) the Works Progress Administration.
    c) Social Security.

History Skills

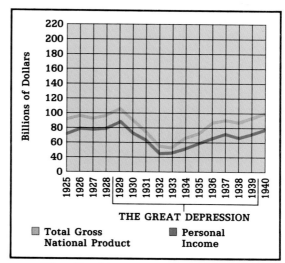

THE GREAT DEPRESSION

■ Total Gross National Product ■ Personal Income

The Decline and Recovery of the National Economy

Choose the answer that best completes the statement.

1. Personal income was highest in

   a) 1928.
   b) 1929.
   c) 1940.

2. The worst year of the depression was

   a) 1932.
   b) 1933.
   c) 1934.

3. To find the meaning of "gross national product," look in

   a) an encyclopedia.
   b) an almanac.
   c) a dictionary.

4. To compare personal income of 1933 with that of today, look in

   a) an almanac.
   b) the card catalogue.
   c) an encyclopedia.

The United States in a Turbulent World

UNIT 9
1920–1945

Chapter 29 • 1920–1940
The U. S.
and the World
1920–1940

Chapter 30 • 1940–1945
The U. S.
Fights in
World War II

CHAPTER
29
The U. S. and the World 1920–1940

1920–1940

Washington Naval
Conference

1921

Japan invaded
Manchuria

1931

Hitler took over German
government

1933

German army entered
Rhineland
Civil war in Spain

1936

Germany invaded
Czechoslovakia and Poland
World War II began

1939

Congress passed draft law
Germany attacked Britain

1940

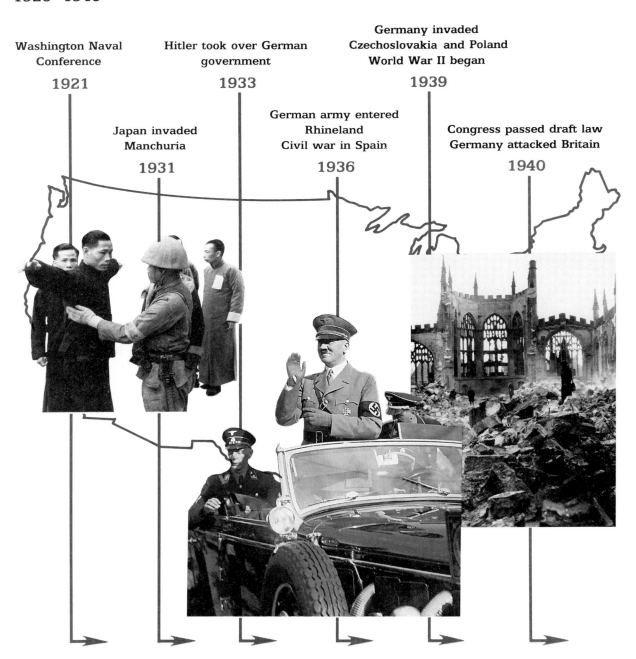

In the years following World War I, most Americans did not pay much attention to what was going on in the rest of the world. In the 1920s, many Americans were interested in business opportunities. Most of the money to be made was at home, rather than abroad. And during the Great Depression of the 1930s, most Americans worried about keeping or getting a job. Problems of nations in Europe or Asia seemed far away indeed.

When American soldiers returned home from the "war to end all wars" in 1919, they probably thought the job had been done. The world had been, in Woodrow Wilson's words, "made safe for democracy."

It seems democracy is never truly safe, however. In the 1930s, Italy, Germany, and Japan became dictatorships. They built up their armies and navies and began to carve out empires. Their method was invading and taking over weaker countries.

Gradually, the actions of the dictators began to threaten American interests. And the sympathy of Americans was drawn to countries that fought to keep their freedom.

In this chapter, you will learn how the United States attempted to deal with an increasingly dangerous world. Despite efforts to keep the peace, by the end of the 1930s the world was again at war. America was about to be drawn into the fight.

1. Relations with Other Nations

Learn these important terms:

Washington Naval Conference
Kellogg-Briand Pact
Dawes Plan
Young Plan
Good Neighbor Policy
reciprocal trade agreements

Remember the main idea:

The United States wanted to make agreements to help nations avoid future wars. It tried to help the nations of Europe pay their war debts. It also adopted a new "good neighbor" policy toward Latin America and prepared to give the Philippines independence.

Look for answers to these questions:

1. How did the United States try to keep peace in the world?
2. How did relations between the United States and Latin American nations change in the late 1920s?
3. How did the United States help improve world trade?

Since the beginning of the century, nations that wanted to be world powers had competed to build more and bigger battleships. The battleship, with its heavy armor and big guns, was the single most powerful and expensive weapon ever created. The nation with the most powerful fleet could control the seas.

Think: **Henry Reuterdahl showed the United States fleet as it passed through the Straits of Magellan on February 8, 1908. Battleships like these were important at the time—important enough to merit an artist's attention.**
Respond: **Would this same scene be appropriate in the late 1920s? Explain.**

There seemed to be no end to this expensive arms race. After World War I, the United States, Great Britain, Japan, and six other nations met in Washington, D.C., to reduce naval warfare. At this **Washington Naval Conference** in 1921, the nine nations agreed to limits on the size and number of large warships.

The Washington Naval Conference was not as successful at arms control as it seemed, however. Although many people did not realize it yet, the day of the great battleship was almost over.

In 1921, a test was arranged off the coast of Virginia, where a former German battleship was anchored. Airplanes flew overhead and dropped large bombs. Within half an hour, the battleship had been sunk.

The airplane and the submarine, not the battleship, would be the most important naval weapons in a future war. But the Washington Naval Conference did not regulate airplanes or submarines. Nor were the nations able to agree on a way to reduce their armies. Meanwhile, more powerful guns and tanks were being developed all the time.

When it became clear that arms control did not work, the United States tried to prevent another war. It worked for an international agreement. In 1928, the American secretary of state, Frank Kellogg (KELL-aug), and the French leader Aristide Briand (bree-AHN) invited other nations to sign an agreement called the **Kellogg-Briand Pact**. Sixty other nations signed the agreement, promising to settle all their problems peacefully. But such agreements were only as good as the intentions of the leaders involved. There was no way to stop a nation from breaking the agreement.

War Debts Cause Problems

During World War I, the United States had loaned almost $10 billion to its allies, particularly Britain and France. The countries had used most of this money to buy weapons and supplies in the United States. Because they had used the money for the allied war effort, they did not feel they should have to pay it back. The United States did not agree. However, the American government agreed to cut the interest on the loans and allow more time for payment.

These compromises did not solve the problem, however. In order to pay their war debts, the Europeans had to be able to sell their products in the United States. During the 1920s, however, the United States kept raising the tariff to protect its businesses. High tariffs made foreign goods more expensive in the United States. This meant it was hard for the Europeans to sell their goods in the American market.

Germany, in turn, owed payments, or reparations, to the European nations it had fought. Under the Treaty of Versailles, Germany owed large amounts of money for the damage that its armies had done. The European allies wanted to use this money to pay their debts to the United States. However, Germany suffered from hard times in the early 1920s and was not able to pay reparations.

The United States tried to help the European nations pay their war debts by helping Germany pay its debts to them. It developed two plans to help Germany pay its reparations. Under the **Dawes Plan** of 1924, the United States agreed to loan money to Germany. It also adjusted the reparations payments to make them easier for Germany. Later, the **Young Plan** reduced the payments further. These plans made it possible for Germany to pay its reparations and for the European nations to pay their war debts during the 1920s. During the 1930s, however, the depression struck Europe as well as the United States. Debt payments stopped.

Think: Before World War I, one German mark would have bought a loaf of bread. After the war, it took thousands of marks to buy bread. Respond: What caused the mark to lose its value?

Think: After World War I, living conditions in Germany were harsh. Prices kept going up, and jobs were hard to find. Respond: What reaction might the Germans have had to these conditions?

Think: After lending money to Nicaragua in 1911, American banks were given financial control of the country. American marines set up camps in Nicaragua to put down anti-American forces. Respond: How did the people of Nicaragua feel about the Americans' presence?

Better Relations with Some Countries

In the early 1900s, the United States had not had good relations with Latin American countries. Under President Wilson, the United States had tried to overthrow the Mexican dictator Victoriano Huerta (WER-tah). The Americans succeeded only in angering Mexicans on both sides of their civil war. And during the 1920s, United States Marines were sent at various times to Nicaragua, Honduras, Cuba, Haiti, and the Dominican Republic to protect American interests. Most Latin Americans resented such interference in their national affairs.

In the late 1920s, American policy toward Latin America began to change, however. In 1925, the Mexican government said that American oil companies could no longer own land in Mexico, but would have to rent it. Four large oil companies asked the United States government to send troops to protect their rights. The Senate, however, passed a resolution demanding a peaceful settlement of the problem. President Coolidge supported this peaceful approach. And in 1930, under President Hoover, the United States agreed to stop sending troops into the Latin American countries.

When President Roosevelt took office, he promised that the United States would be a "good neighbor" to Latin American nations. It would work with them to settle problems peacefully and would respect their rights. Although problems remained, this **Good Neighbor Policy** was very popular with Latin Americans.

The United States also faced demands from people living in American territories. The people of the Philippines, for example, demanded complete independence from the United States. While not granting immediate independence, the United States did agree to make the Philippines independent in 1946. However, a demand by the people of Puerto Rico for more self-government was refused.

Relations with the Soviet Union

In February 1917, a revolution broke out in Russia. Russia was taken over by Communists, and it became known as the Soviet Union. During the 1920s, the United States refused to deal with the

In 1925, the United States' relations with Mexico were strained. The Mexican government told American oil companies that they would have to rent land in Mexico that they had formerly owned. When this happened, many Americans probably took a closer look at their nearest southern neighbor. To find out about Mexico, they may have used an *atlas*, which is a book of maps.

Today's atlases offer other information besides maps. You could consult an atlas to find out a country's population, size, language, and other facts. Here is an atlas article about Mexico.

MEXICO

AREA: 761,601 sq. mi.

POPULATION: 59,200,000.

LANGUAGE: Spanish. Many Indian dialects also spoken.

RELIGION: Predominantly Roman Catholic.

ECONOMY: Grows 50% of world's sisal. Crops of cotton, coffee, beans, corn, rice, sugar, and wheat also important. Livestock. Rich in natural resources, including silver, coal, petroleum, sulfur, copper, lead, and iron. Tourism important.

MAJOR CITIES: Mexico City (pop. 7,768,033), capital; Veracruz, port; Monterrey, heavy industry.

CLIMATE: Tropical along coasts and in south; temperate in central plateau.

FOR INFORMATION: Mexican Govt. Tourist Bureau, 630 Fifth Ave., New York, N.Y. 10020.

Answer the following questions by referring to the atlas article.

1 What is the main language of Mexico?

2 What crops are grown in Mexico? What else, besides agriculture, does Mexico's economy rely on?

3 What is the main port city of Mexico?

4 What parts of Mexico are warmest?

5 What is the population of Mexico's capital?

6 What religion do most Mexicans follow?

7 Do you have to write to Mexico to find out more information?

Use an atlas to answer the following questions about America's other neighbor, Canada. (Your school or public library will have an atlas.)

8 What is the population of Canada?

9 What is the climate of Canada like?

10 What languages are spoken in Canada?

11 How many square miles does Canada cover?

12 What is the capital of Canada? What is its population?

13 Name three other major Canadian cities.

Soviet Union. Many Americans hoped the Communists would eventually fall from power.

By the 1930s, however, it was becoming clear that the Soviet Union was there to stay. In 1933, the United States agreed to recognize, or have diplomatic relations with, the Soviet Union.

This agreement was not as friendly as the United States had hoped. The Soviet Union refused to pay the money that the former Russian government owed to the United States. Also, trade between the United States and the Soviet Union did not increase very much.

World Trade Begins To Improve

The United States passed a very high tariff in 1930. This tariff proved to be damaging to trade. In the early 1930s, the United States tried to increase its trade with other nations. The American government agreed to lower the tariff on goods from nations that would lower their tariffs on American goods. These *reciprocal trade agreements* improved trade among the United States, Great Britain, Canada, and many other nations.

In general, American foreign policy during the 1920s and 1930s was most successful in dealing with Latin America and with world trade issues. Neither the United States nor other nations were very successful in reducing the chances of war, however.

Section Review

1. How successful were efforts to control the arms race?
2. Why did European nations have trouble paying their war debts?
3. How did the United States change the way it dealt with Latin American countries?

2. Moving Toward World War II

Learn these important terms:

dictatorship
Nazi
Rhineland
Axis Powers
isolation movement
Neutrality Act of 1935
Abraham Lincoln Brigade

Remember the main idea:

Japan, Italy, and Germany became dictatorships in the 1930s. They began to attack weaker nations. Although Americans were reluctant to get involved in these conflicts, the United States began to take steps to help defend freedom in Europe and Asia.

Look for answers to these questions:

1. What countries were invaded by countries ruled by dictators?
2. Was the League of Nations able to stop the invasions?
3. What did most Americans think the United States should do about European conflicts?

In the 1930s, Japan, Italy, and Germany became *dictatorships*. A dictatorship is a nation in which all power is in the hands of one person or a small group of people. The dictators lived for the sake of power. They soon turned their nations into military machines bent on extending their power to the nations around them.

JAPANESE INVASION OF MANCHURIA, 1931

Japan Attacks China

In the 1930s, the government of Japan fell under the control of a small group of military men. These leaders decided to conquer China in order to gain raw materials needed by Japanese industry. They hoped eventually to set up a great Japanese empire in Asia and the Pacific.

In 1931, the Japanese army attacked and took over Manchuria (man-CHOOR-ee-uh) in the northeastern part of China. China asked the League of Nations for help against Japan. But the League only warned Japan that it must get out of China. The Japanese ignored this warning and soon quit the League of Nations. By 1938, Japan had taken control of a vast portion of eastern China.

Italy Attacks Ethiopia

During the 1920s, Benito Mussolini (bun-NEET-oh MOO-soh-LEE-nee) became the dictator of Italy. In 1935, Mussolini attacked Ethiopia, an ancient nation in northern Africa. The people of Ethiopia fought bravely against the Italian armies, but they lacked modern military weapons. By 1936, Ethiopia was conquered.

Haile Selassie (HY-lee suh-LASS-ee), the emperor of Ethiopia, asked the League of Nations for help against Italy. The League ordered its members to stop selling war supplies to Italy, but this action was not very effective. Oil, the only thing Italy really needed to carry on the war, was not included.

Think: In 1935, Italian troops attacked Ethiopia. Italian officers were photographed entering Aduwa. Respond: What did Mussolini hope to gain by conquering the Ethiopians?

Think: During the 1930s, Japan seized various parts of China. Many of the Chinese people were forced to do labor. Respond: What did the Japanese hope to gain by conquering China?

Think: **Paul Goebbels worked to persuade German citizens to support the Nazis. He is shown here passing out Christmas presents to the poor. Nazis promised jobs and glory for Germans and their country. Nazi propaganda did not always tell the truth.** Respond: **Why did many German people choose to support the Nazis?**

Hitler Becomes Dictator of Germany

The most serious threat to peace developed in Germany. Many Germans felt that they had been unjustly treated by the Allied nations following World War I. In the Treaty of Versailles, Germany was stripped of part of its territory. Its army was reduced to 100,000 men. Germany also had to pay huge amounts of money in reparations. When the Armistice was signed at the end of World War I, Allied military leader Marshall Foch warned, ''This is not peace. It is an armistice for twenty years.'' But Britain and France did not seem to be concerned that their defeated enemy could rise again.

In the early 1920s, and again in the early 1930s, severe economic hardships struck Germany. The Germans grew desperate and angry. The democratic government that was elected in Germany in the early 1920s was weak. It could not govern effectively. Communists and other parties sent followers into the streets to fight one another.

One of the parties that battled for power was taken over by Adolf Hitler (AY-dawlf HIT-lur). His party was the National Socialist, or *Nazi* party. Hitler effectively played upon the frustrations of the German people. He told Germans that they were the ''master race'' and would eventually take over the world. He blamed the Jews for Germany's troubles and encouraged people to hate and persecute, or treat badly, the Jews. By 1933, Hitler became powerful enough to become the dictator of Germany.

Think: **A gifted speaker, Hitler found it easy to convince people, especially the young, to follow him. In his book *Mein Kampf*, Hitler told of his plans for Germany to conquer Europe. It seemed as if most European leaders weren't paying attention.** Respond: **Why did so many world leaders ignore the warnings of Hitler's war plans?**

Once he took power, Hitler began to rebuild Germany's army and navy. Secretly, he also built a powerful air force. Although these actions violated the Treaty of Versailles, France and Britain did nothing to stop Hitler. French leadership was weak, and France relied on its wall of fortifications along the German border. Many British leaders thought they could stay out of European problems.

In 1936, Hitler sent his army into the ***Rhineland***, the territory along the Rhine River in western Germany. Although this was another treaty violation, and France and Britain still had much more powerful armies than Germany, they again did nothing to stop him.

Hitler then signed an agreement with Mussolini. They called themselves the ***Axis Powers***, saying that power in Europe would soon revolve around an axis, or line between Berlin and Rome.

Most Americans Favor Isolation

While many Americans were uneasy about the actions of the new dictatorships, they did not want America to become involved. They were unhappy that American sacrifices during World War I had not led to a peaceful and free world. And they were suspicious about calls for war. Between 1934 and 1936, hearings held by Senator Gerald P. Nye of North Dakota seemed to suggest that the war had been started by bankers or weapons makers seeking profits. Seventy-one percent of the people interviewed in a 1937 Gallup poll said they thought it had

Think: **Most people wanted to believe that World War I was the war to end all wars. So when it looked as if the world was heading for another major war, many people were against it. The United States chose to isolate itself; European countries did not have that choice.** Respond: **Do you think the Americans were right? Explain.**

been a mistake for the United States to enter World War I.

Most of these Americans wanted the United States to isolate itself from the world. This *isolation movement* had considerable political power in America during the 1930s.

Neutrality Laws Are Passed

Responding to the isolationists, Congress passed the *Neutrality Act of 1935*. This law said that American factories could not sell weapons to any nation at war. American ships were not allowed to carry weapons to any nation at war. And American citizens were forbidden to travel on ships belonging to a nation at war. It was hoped that these laws would prevent incidents like the sinking of the *Lusitania* that had led the United States toward World War I.

In 1937, another Neutrality Act was passed. This law allowed nations at war to buy nonmilitary goods if they carried them away in their own ships. This helped trade, but it also meant that a nation with many ships, like Japan, would be helped more than one like China, which was poor and had few ships.

Some Americans Fight the Dictators

Although Americans who favored isolation were in the majority, some Americans wanted to do something about the threat of Hitler and Mussolini. In 1936, a civil war broke out in Spain. Spain was ruled by a king, but he was not a dictator. A general, Francisco Franco, wanted to take over the government and become dictator. Hitler and Mussolini supported Franco in his actions. The Soviet Union

HISTORY MAKERS

Albert Einstein

One of the World's Greatest Thinkers

"Honestly," complained the teacher, "it's clear the boy's a very slow thinker. I don't know why his parents sent him to school! He can't answer most questions without taking a long time to think. It must be quite difficult for him. His parents might as well face it—Albert Einstein will never amount to much!"

The teacher was wrong. Albert Einstein became a brilliant scientist, one of the greatest the world has ever known. He won the Nobel Prize for his research in physics. Einstein seemed slow in school because he would not answer a question until he had worked out the answer. He took his time, thinking through each question carefully.

Albert Einstein was born in Germany. He spent time in Switzerland, going to school, working, and teaching. Then he returned to Germany to teach and do research. When Hitler and the Nazi party gained power, Einstein decided to leave Germany. Hitler's anti-Jewish attitudes and his use of violence against Jews made Germany a dangerous place for Einstein and other Jews. In 1933, Einstein came to the United States to teach. In 1934, the Nazi government took away his German citizenship.

Germany's loss was the United States' gain. Einstein's scientific genius and his personal influence helped the United States and its allies win World War II. In 1939 Einstein wrote to President Roosevelt, warning him that German scientists were working on a new and powerful bomb. He urged researching and developing weapons using atomic power to end World War II. Einstein's Theory of Relativity helped scientists in the United States learn how to split the atom and ultimately develop the atomic bomb.

Albert Einstein's scientific theories changed the ways scientists think. His theories helped begin the Atomic Age. But Einstein was deeply concerned about the effect of nuclear weapons on world peace and human survival. He opposed the arms race and the development of more powerful nuclear weapons. "You cannot simultaneously prevent and prepare for war," Einstein believed.

Think: **Americans in the Abraham Lincoln Brigade fought against Franco in Spain.** Respond: **Why did these Americans choose to fight when their government did not?**

supported the Spanish government, or loyalists, against Franco's rebels. While the United States government remained neutral, a group of American volunteers calling themselves the ***Abraham Lincoln Brigade*** went to Spain to fight on the loyalist side.

The Spanish civil war showed a shift in military tactics, or ways of fighting. Many Spanish cities were savagely bombed from the air, showing the power of the airplane. Supported by massive aid from Germany and Italy, Franco won.

Section Review

1. What kinds of actions were taken by the dictators who took power in the 1930s? What kinds of things did they do?

2. How did Germany increase its power after Hitler took over? How did Britain and France respond?

3. How did the neutrality acts passed by Congress try to keep America out of future wars?

---

3. The Beginning of World War II

Learn these important terms:

Sudetenland
appeasement
racism
draft law
blitzkrieg
Lend-Lease Act

Remember the main idea:

Hitler continued to take over territory. Germany invaded Poland, and World War II began. By June of 1941, Hitler ruled nearly all of western Europe.

Look for answers to these questions:

1. What countries did Germany invade and conquer?

2. What happened when Hitler attacked Great Britain?

3. How did the United States prepare for war?

Encouraged by the lack of opposition to his actions, Hitler started to build a German empire. In March 1938, he annexed, or joined, Austria to Germany.

Next, in September 1938, he turned his attention to Czechoslovakia (CHEK-oh-sloh-VAK-ya). Hitler demanded that Germany receive the ***Sudetenland*** (soo-DAYT-un-land), a rich industrial part of Czechoslovakia where many Germans lived. Czechoslovakia wanted to fight to protect its territory. It could not resist Hitler effectively without help from Britain and France, however. These countries had promised to defend Czechoslovakia.

Neville Chamberlain, the British Prime Minister, and French Premier Daladier (dah-lah-dee-AY) met with Hitler in Munich. Hitler promised them that if he were given the Sudetenland, he would not demand any more territory. The British and French leaders were anxious to avoid war. They adopted a certain policy called **appeasement**. They gave in to demands in exchange for peace. This meant they gave Hitler what he wanted. Returning from the meeting, Chamberlain told the British people that he had gained "peace in our time." Unfortunately, he could not have been more wrong.

Think: British Prime Minister Neville Chamberlain told Hitler that England did not want war. Respond: Why was this an open invitation for Hitler to carry out his plans?

The United States Begins To Respond

Many Americans began to be alarmed at what was happening in Europe and Asia. Americans doubted that Hitler was going to be satisfied with what he had gained so far. Pictures of fanatic crowds and columns of Nazi soldiers became a common part of the weekly newsreels shown in movie theaters. Especially alarming was the Nazis' **racism**, or the false belief that one race, or group of people, is better than all others. Jews, the "inferior race," were harassed, beaten, and driven from their homes and businesses. Worse was to come.

When another poll was taken in February 1938, the majority of Americans now thought that the United States should help defend France and Britain if they were attacked. Most Americans still wanted to keep out of the fighting, but they were willing to give "all aid short of actual war."

President Roosevelt believed in giving such support. But America was not prepared even to defend itself. In the early 1930s, the United States had a very small army for a country its size. Roosevelt asked Congress for money to build up America's military forces, including the navy and air force.

World War II Begins

Ignoring the promises he made at Munich, Hitler continued to gobble up territory. In March of 1939, he took over the rest of Czechoslovakia. In August of 1939, Hitler signed a treaty with Joseph Stalin, the Soviet dictator. They agreed not to fight each other and secretly agreed to divide Poland between them.

Now free of the danger of attack from the east, Hitler was ready to take over Poland. On September 1, 1939, German dive bombers screamed out of the sky and smashed Polish military bases. Fast-moving tanks led columns of German troops across the Polish border.

Think: **Britain and France told Germany to withdraw from Poland or they would declare war. When Hitler refused, war was declared.** Respond: **Why was Europe unprepared for war?**

Great Britain and France finally realized that they had to fight. On September 3, 1939, Britain and France declared war against Germany, and World War II began. It was too late to help Poland, which surrendered within a few weeks.

The American government now had to face the possibility that the United States would be attacked or forced to enter the war eventually. In 1940, Congress passed the first peacetime *draft law* in history. This law required all men between the ages of twenty-one and thirty-five to serve in the army. The draft would provide a pool of trained men to meet wartime needs.

Hitler Attacks France

In April 1940, Germany attacked Denmark and Norway. The British and French sent forces to try to defend Norway, but they were unsuccessful.

In May 1940, German panzer (tank) divisions smashed into the Netherlands, Belgium, and Luxembourg. Soon they had moved deep into France. Although France had a strong army, the French were not able to react quickly enough to the German *blitzkrieg* (BLITS-kreeg), or "lightning war." The British sent an army to help, but they were soon pushed back to the town of Dunkirk on the English Channel. There, brave sailors and fishermen used a vast fleet of ships and tiny boats to rescue about 340,000 British and French troops and bring them back to Britain.

The United States Aids Great Britain

By the end of June 1940, Germany had conquered all of western Europe except Britain. Americans realized that if Britain fell, the routes across the Atlantic, and eventually the United States itself, would be in danger. More American assistance to the British seemed essential.

In 1939, Roosevelt had gotten Congress to change the Neutrality Act so that countries could buy weapons if they paid cash for them and took them away in their own ships. This plan was designed to help Great Britain, which had many ships. In addition, in 1940, Roosevelt arranged a deal in which fifty American warships were traded to Britain in exchange for leases on British naval bases. The British needed these ships to fight the German submarines.

In August 1940, Hitler began to prepare to invade Britain. First, though, the Germans had to destroy the British air force and navy. Waves of German bombers attacked coastal ports, airfields, and finally London itself. Americans heard

Think: **When France fell, the British sent a thousand boats to Dunkirk to bring the French and British soldiers to safety in England.** *The Withdrawal from Dunkirk, June 1940* **shows a part of the historic rescue.** Respond: **Why had France fallen so quickly?**

American Edward R. Murrow (1908-1965) began his dramatic radio broadcasts during the Battle of Britain with the words "This . . . is London."

AXIS AGGRESSION BEFORE WORLD WAR II

This map will add to your knowledge of the events that led to World War II. You already know from your text about Germany's invasion of Austria, Czechoslovakia, and the Rhineland. From this map and its inset, you will learn about Italy's invasions. These were led by the dictator Benito Mussolini.

Like other European nations, Italy controlled nations in Africa. These were Libya, Eritrea, and Italian Somaliland. Nearby Ethiopia was an old independent African kingdom. In a show of strength, Mussolini invaded Ethiopia. The Ethiopians' primitive weapons were no match for Italy's tanks and planes.

Look at the map and its inset.

1. To launch the invasion, the Italian forces had to sail over what bodies of water? On which body of water is Eritrea?

2. Mussolini had hopes of sharing in Hitler's conquests in Europe. He supported the Fascist forces in the Spanish Civil War. He also moved his troops toward the Austrian border. He gave Hitler little help, however. What European country did Mussolini invade? When? Was a navy needed? Was he successful? From what you know of him and of Albania's position on the map, what was his purpose?

Use your text to answer this question.

3. Explain the two arrows indicating invasions of Poland.

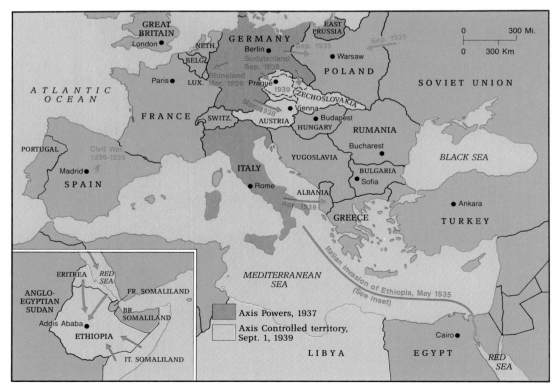

radio broadcaster Edward R. Murrow's reports from London, complete with the sound of air raid sirens and bombs.

The bravery of the British people and the words of Winston Churchill, the new British Prime Minister, appealed to Americans. The British air force, though outnumbered by the Germans, fought off the attacks. Hitler decided that it would be too costly to invade Britain.

Think: **For nearly a year, German planes bombed London and other English cities nightly. Coventry Cathedral was one of many churches hit.** Respond: **How did the British respond?**

Britain faced great hardships, however. By 1941, the British had run out of money to pay for American war supplies. Congress passed the *Lend-Lease Act*. This law allowed the United States to lend, rather than sell, war supplies to Britain, and later, to other countries fighting against Germany.

By the end of 1941, the United States was all but in the war. The American navy had begun to protect merchant ships delivering supplies to Britain, and American destroyers and German submarines began to shoot at each other.

By permission of Punch, 1/29/41

Think: **The Illingworth cartoon ''The Way of the Stork'' shows American aid in the form of the Lend-Lease Act of 1941.** Respond: **What types of aid does the cartoon show?**

In twenty years, American attitudes had gone from isolation to neutrality to active involvement in the defense of allies. Efforts to guarantee peace had failed, and the United States had to respond to the challenge. It now seemed only a matter of time before America would enter World War II.

Section Review

1. When and how did World War II begin?
2. How did the United States increase its strength and prepare for possible war?
3. How did the United States help Great Britain?

CHAPTER SUMMARY

During the 1920s and most of the 1930s, most Americans did not pay much attention to what was going on in Europe and Asia. American foreign policy dealt mostly with Latin America and the improvement of world trade. However, American leaders did join with other world leaders in trying to find a way to prevent future wars. Attempts to reduce the size of armies were unsuccessful. And although peace treaties were signed, there was no way to enforce them.

In the 1930s, Japan, Italy, and Germany became dictatorships. Japan began to take over parts of China. Italy tried to create an empire in Africa. Hitler took over the German government and then began to take over the countries near Germany. European leaders did not try to stop Hitler. Instead, they tried to appease him.

Many Americans wanted the United States to follow a policy of isolation, or separate itself from these conflicts. Congress passed neutrality laws that tried to prevent incidents that could lead the United States into war.

By the end of the 1930s, however, Europe was again at war. President Roosevelt and Congress began strengthening the American military forces and helping Britain directly. Obviously, there was no way America could avoid becoming more deeply involved.

Key Words

Write a sentence to explain the meaning of each of these terms.

reciprocal trade agreements

Good Neighbor Policy

Axis Powers

Neutrality Act of 1935

Sudetenland

Lend-Lease Act

Major Events

Choose the answer that best completes the statement.

1. In 1921, the United States and other major nations limited

   a) the size of their armies.
   b) the number of warships.
   c) the development of airplanes.

2. When Hitler entered the Rhineland, Britain and France

   a) did little to stop him.
   b) stopped trade with Germany.
   c) declared war against Germany.

3. During the 1930s, most Americans

   a) supported Hitler and Mussolini.
   b) wanted to avoid war.
   c) wanted the United States to oppose the dictators.

4. World War II began when

   a) the German army marched into the Rhineland.
   b) the Japanese invaded China.
   c) Germany invaded Poland.

5. By the end of 1940, the Germans had conquered

   a) most of western Europe.
   b) Great Britain.
   c) the Soviet Union.

Review

Important Facts

Answer each question with at least one complete sentence.

1. Why were efforts to control arms mostly unsuccessful?

2. Why did Britain and France have trouble paying their war debts to the United States? How did the United States try to help?

3. How did the way the United States dealt with Latin America change in the late 1920s?

4. How did the United States deal with the Philippines and Puerto Rico?

5. Was the League of Nations successful in protecting weak nations from attack? Why, or why not?

6. Why did Japan attack China?

7. How did Hitler gain the support of the German people?

8. What were the goals of the isolation movement?

9. What policy did the British and French use at Munich? Did it work?

10. How did the United States begin to prepare for war?

11. How did Roosevelt help Britain after France was conquered by Germany?

12. What happened when Hitler got ready to invade Britain?

13. As 1941 drew toward an end, how close was the United States to war?

Skill Review

Study this map, then answer the following questions.

1. When and why did Germany invade Poland?

2. When and why did the Soviet Union invade Poland?

3. Why didn't Germany and the Soviet Union go to war over Poland?

Invasions of Poland, 1939

Critical Thinking

Write a paragraph to answer each question.

1. Do you think World War II would have started if Germany had been treated differently after World War I? Why, or why not?

2. How did American attitudes toward involvement in World War II change between 1937 and 1941? Why do you think they changed?

30
The U.S. Fights in World War II

1940–1945

Battles of Coral Sea
and Midway
Allies invaded Africa
Battle of Stalingrad

Allies invaded France
Battle of the Bulge

Japan joined Axis powers

1940

1942

1944

Atlantic Charter signed
Japanese attacked
Pearl Harbor
United States entered war

Allies invaded Sicily
and Italy

Yalta Conference
Germany surrendered
Japan surrendered
United Nations set up

1941

1943

1945

HE'S
WATCHING
YOU

1. The United States Enters World War II

On the morning of December 7, 1941, a message came into Washington, D.C., on the teletype. An aide read the following words to President Roosevelt: "Air raid, Pearl Harbor. This is no drill."

Many Americans had expected war with Germany in the coming months. When war came at last to America, however, it was brought by Japanese airplanes out of a blue Pacific sky. It was a day that President Roosevelt said "would live in infamy."

In this chapter you will read how Americans worked to build the greatest military force the world had ever seen. Even more than World War I had, World War II reached into every part of Americans' lives. For many Americans, the war meant steady jobs. For the families of soldiers fighting in Europe and across the Pacific, it also meant dreading the telegram that began, "We regret to inform you . . ." For the soldiers, sailors, and fliers, it meant moments of terror and quiet courage, and, often, days of sheer exhaustion.

World War II was a turning point in modern history. It revealed the horrible torture and killing of millions of Jews and other people by the Nazis. It brought the atomic bomb, threatening that any future war would truly be a "war to end all wars." And it left us the world we live in today, divided between two superpowers, the United States and the Soviet Union.

Learn these important terms:

treaty of alliance
embargo

Remember the main idea:

The United States declared war on Japan after Japan attacked Pearl Harbor. Because Japan had joined the Axis powers, the United States also went to war against Germany and Italy.

Look for answers to these questions:

1. What did Japan want the United States to agree to do?
2. How did the United States try to put pressure on Japan?
3. When did the United States enter World War II?

In the 1930s, the Japanese government was taken over by a group of military leaders. These leaders wanted Japan to take over China and other parts of Asia for industrial resources and for glory. In the 1930s, the Japanese took over Manchuria and much of the coast of China.

The Japanese leaders wanted to be able to carry out their plans in China without interference from the United States. In 1940, therefore, Japan signed a *treaty of alliance* with Germany and Italy and joined the Axis Powers. The treaty said that if any of the three nations were attacked by a nation not already involved in the war in Europe, all three nations

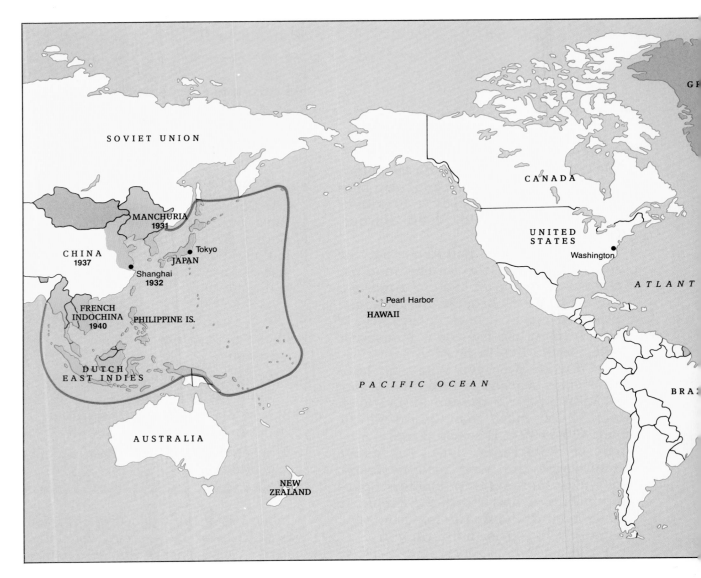

would fight together. This meant that if the United States declared war on Japan because of Japanese actions in China, then Germany and Italy would declare war on the United States.

In 1941, Japan continued to build its empire in Asia. It took over French Indo-China (the colony that would later become the nations of Vietnam, Laos, and Cambodia). The Japanese also prepared to take over nearby British and Dutch colonies.

These colonies could not count on any protection from their European rulers. The Netherlands had been taken over by Germany, and the British were fighting for their lives. Only the United States was in a position to stop the Japanese plans. To try to force the Japanese to stop their attacks, President Roosevelt declared an *embargo* against Japan. This embargo stopped all shipments of gasoline, oil, iron, and steel from the United States to Japan. Soon, all trade between the two nations was cut off.

ICELAND

GREAT
BRITAIN   GERMANY
London •   Berlin
FRANCE
1940

POLAND
1939

Leningrad •
• Moscow

SOVIET UNION
1941

INDIA

ETHIOPIA

INDIAN OCEAN

Territory controlled by Axis

Allied countries

Neutral countries

In March 1941, leaders of the United States and Japan held talks to try to find a solution to their conflict. The talks continued for many months, but the two sides could not reach an agreement. The Japanese wanted the Americans to let them have a free hand in China in exchange for agreeing not to attack other areas. The United States, on the other hand, wanted an independent China, in keeping with its Open Door Policy.

Japan Attacks Pearl Harbor

At the American naval base at Pearl Harbor, the morning of December 7, 1941, started out as just another peaceful Sunday. Although there had been reports that the Japanese were preparing to attack the United States, most experts felt that Japan would attack in east Asia or the Philippines first. But where were the Japanese aircraft carriers? No one was really sure where they had gone. When a radar operator near Pearl Harbor reported that there were two airplanes approaching Hawaii, officials thought they were American planes.

Think: **When Japanese pilots arrived in Pearl Harbor, they found the fleet unprotected and unprepared. The losses in American lives, ships, and planes were great. After twenty years of trying to avoid war, the American people then faced the need to defend themselves.** Respond: **Why did the attack on Pearl Harbor unite Americans?**

Think: The *Arizona* sank after being blasted with Japanese bombs. Five out of eight battleships were sunk or badly damaged. But only the *Arizona* and the *Oklahoma* never rejoined the fleet. The fleet's four aircraft carriers were not in the harbor. Respond: Why weren't the Americans prepared for the Japanese attack?

Actually, they were the advance scouts for a powerful fleet of Japanese aircraft carriers that had approached Pearl Harbor without being seen. At 7:55 A.M., swarms of Japanese planes began to dive out of the sky over the harbor. When the last bomb had fallen, most of America's powerful battleships had been sunk or badly damaged. Many airplanes had been destroyed on the ground. More than 2,500 Americans were killed in the attack. The Americans were lucky in one way, however. Their four aircraft carriers were not in port and escaped the attack.

The Japanese leaders had decided to gamble on delivering a knockout blow against the United States. If they could destroy most of America's naval power, they would have time to build and strengthen their Asian and Pacific empire. They also hoped that Americans would be so shocked and discouraged that they would make peace with Japan.

The United States Declares War

Americans were indeed shocked and angry at this attack that had been made without a declaration of war. The next day, Congress declared war on Japan. A few days later, carrying out their agreement with Japan, Germany and Italy declared war on the United States. The United States in turn declared war on Germany and Italy. The United States was now fighting in World War II.

Section Review

1. What areas had Japan taken over before launching the attack on Pearl Harbor?
2. Why was the attack on Pearl Harbor a surprise?
3. What were the effects of the attack on Pearl Harbor?

2. The Home Front

Learn these important terms:

Office of Production Management
War Production Board
Executive Order 8802
Nisei
*Fair Employment Practices
 Commission*
Office of Price Administration
rationing system

Remember the main idea:

America needed a tremendous amount of weapons, supplies, and food to fight the war. Many people, including women and blacks, went to work in factories. The government raised taxes, sold bonds, and contolled wages and prices to maintain the wartime economy.

Look for answers to these questions:

1. Why did many women and blacks get factory jobs?

2. How did the government pay for the war?

3. Why did the government control the economy during the war?

In some ways, the United States was better prepared for World War II than it had been at the start of World War I. When Japan attacked Pearl Harbor, the United States already had about two million men in its armed forces because of the draft law of 1940. The draft was soon expanded. More than sixteen million Americans served in the armed forces during World War II. This number is about five times as many as had served during World War I.

In addition, the **Office of Production Management** had been formed early in 1941. This office set up plans for helping American industry change over from peacetime to wartime production.

America's Huge War Needs

The army had to send millions of soldiers overseas. They would be fighting on three continents and two oceans. For these reasons the United States needed millions of tons of warships, cargo ships, and troop transports.

Think: Americans astonished the world with their productive energy. Thousands of war planes, ships, trucks, tanks, and guns were made. Respond: How did planning aid in the Americans' success?

In 1942, President Roosevelt set production goals for the year at about sixty thousand planes, forty-five thousand tanks, and eight million tons of shipping. In January 1942, the **War Production Board** was set up to oversee the change to war production in American factories. By the end of the war, American industry was producing twice as many war supplies and weapons as all of its enemies put together.

Americans Go Back to Work

World War II brought the last of the depression to an end. In 1942 alone, the government ordered more than $100 billion worth of war supplies. Factories began to work two or even three shifts a day. Labor unions promised not to slow down the production of war supplies by going on strike. Except for a long strike by the coal miners, most unions kept this promise and settled their problems without going on strike.

Farmers, too, had much work to do to provide food for the military and for America's allies. In spite of a lack of farm workers and parts for farm machines, American farmers grew the largest crops in America's history.

During the war, prices for farm products increased. Many farmers were able to get out of debt, and some were even able to buy more land and new farm equipment.

Opportunities for Women and Blacks

Since so many men were serving in the armed forces, women took over many of these factory jobs. Americans got used to seeing "Rosie the Riveter" doing heavy work that used to be reserved for men.

About one million blacks served in the armed forces. Many others were able to find jobs because of the demand for factory workers. Many blacks moved from the South to the industrial cities of the Northeast and Middle West, and to the shipyards on the west coast. Blacks still suffered discrimination, however, both in the armed forces and in civilian jobs. In the army, they were kept in separate units. In factories, they often were given only low-paying jobs.

Think: In factories throughout the United States, women were doing what before had been considered men's jobs. Songs like "Rosie the Riveter," "We're the Janes Who Make the Planes," and "The Lady at Lockheed" praised women in industry. Women not only worked in factories; they did every kind of work. They were farmers and government leaders, for example. Attitudes toward women began to change. Respond: Why did women and other minorities finally get the chance to prove themselves during World War II?

Black leaders were able to take advantage of the need for labor. They pressured the government to end discrimination. They also pointed out that America had declared war on Hitler's racism. Wasn't it time to end racism at home as well?

Responding to this pressure, President Roosevelt issued *Executive Order 8802.* This order made it unlawful for any factory producing war supplies to refuse to hire workers because of their race, color, or religion. A *Fair Employment Practices Commission* was formed to see that this order was carried out. While this effort was not completely successful, the end of the war saw about two million black workers in factories.

Japanese-Americans Are Mistreated

The anger Americans felt after the Pearl Harbor attack helped the war effort. Many Americans did not wait to be drafted, but volunteered to fight in the war. Government posters urged Americans to "Remember Pearl Harbor" and work hard every day.

This anger hurt one group of Americans, however. German-Americans and Italian-Americans were usually not blamed for the actions of Hitler and Mussolini. Japanese-American citizens, or *Nisei,* however, were treated very differently. Pearl Harbor inflamed the racist feelings that some Americans had toward Japanese. Some Americans also were afraid that the Japanese-Americans were spying for Japan and secretly trying to damage the war effort. As a result, more than 100,000 Nisei were rounded up and put into special camps.

Despite this mistreatment, the Nisei showed their loyalty to America. Thousands of Nisei were allowed to fight against the Germans. Many of them received medals for bravery.

Think: **During World War II, 100,000 Japanese-Americans were taken from their homes.** Respond: **What do you suppose these people were thinking as they were taken to relocation camps?**

Raising Money for the War

World War II cost more than any other war in American history. From 1941 to 1945, the United States government spent about $400 billion to pay for the war. This huge amount was more than twice the amount spent by the American government during all the years from 1789 to 1941. The government raised much of this money by increasing taxes. Since so many Americans were working, the earnings that could be taxed had increased tremendously. In addition, the government borrowed in excess of $100 billion by selling war bonds.

The Government Sets Up Controls

Another money problem that usually comes during wartime is inflation, or an increase in wages and prices. Inflation results when there is more money than there are goods to buy with the money. After America entered the war, a tremendous amount of money flooded into the

HISTORY MAKERS

Yoshiko Uchida

Member of Family Number 13453

The family was listed as number 13453. They had ten days to pack before they had to report to the Civil Control Station—ten days to decide what to take, what to give away, what to sell, and what to save. Friends took the piano and boxes of books. Some furniture went into storage, and some was sold. Their old collie, Laddie, was given away. On the last morning, neighbors brought breakfast, then drove them to the Civil Control Station at the First Congregational Church. As they entered the church, the family saw armed soldiers guarding the doors.

Family 13453, the Uchidas, lived in Berkeley, California. Dwight and Iku Uchida were Japanese immigrants who, because of their nationality, could not become citizens. Their daughters, Yoshiko and Keiko, were American citizens born in the United States.

After the bombing of Pearl Harbor, people feared Japanese-Americans might spy for Japan. President Roosevelt ordered the army to evacuate the entire Japanese-American community on the west coast to camps in the West and Midwest. From the camps, people were to be relocated to areas away from the west coast. Within two months, 110,000 American citizens and their alien parents lost their incomes, their property, and their civil liberties.

Yoshiko Uchida was a college student when her family was sent to Topaz, Utah. Like all the camps, Topaz was isolated. The housing barracks were quickly and badly built. Summers were hot and dry, and winters were cold and snowy. Always the air was full of dust. Yoshiko worked as a secretary and a teacher until 1943, when she left for graduate school at Smith College. Her sister Kay also moved east.

After the war, Yoshiko Uchida became a teacher and a writer. Several of her books are about Japanese-American life before and during the war. She writes for all Americans, she says, "with the hope that through knowledge of the past, they will never allow another group of people in America to be sent into a desert exile again."

Think: **Gasoline was in such short supply that gas trucks were often followed. Traffic jams in gas stations were common.** Respond: **Why was gasoline rationed during the war?**

economy because of war work. There were few consumer goods to buy, however, since many factories had changed over to producing war goods.

In World War I, this situation had led to steep price increases. To prevent this from happening again, the **Office of Price Administration** (O.P.A.) was set up. It was in charge of setting prices, wages, and rents. It also created the **rationing system** (RASH-uh-neeng). This system distributed scarce goods fairly. Each person or family was given a book of stamps that had to be presented along with cash to buy these goods. Among the products rationed were shoes, tires, sugar, gasoline, coffee, and meat.

Section Review

1. Why was the government better prepared for World War II than it had been for World War I?

2. How did World War II help the American farmers?

3. How did the government try to stop racial discrimination in war-related jobs?

3. The Battle Fronts

Learn these important terms:

Battle of the Bulge
Battle of Midway
Holocaust
Battle of the Coral Sea
concentration camps

Remember the main idea:

When the United States entered the war, Germany and Japan were winning. The United States made its main effort in Europe, but also stopped the Japanese advances in the Pacific. The United States and its allies defeated Germany. In the Pacific, the United States won back the territory Japan had taken and defeated Japan.

Look for answers to these questions:

1. What was the situation in Europe and in the Pacific in early 1942?

2. How did the Allies win the battles in Europe?

3. How did the United States defeat Japan?

As 1942 began, the Axis powers seemed to be winning the war. Japan quickly captured much American territory in the Pacific, including the Philippines and many islands in the south and central Pacific. Hong Kong, Malaya, Burma, and the Dutch East Indies also fell to the Japanese. Australia and India seemed to be next on the list.

Think: Notice the flags of the Allies placed on the gun barrels in this poster from the 1940s. **Respond:** What does the World War II poster promise?

In Europe, the Germans continued to capture territory, including Greece and Yugoslavia. And in June of 1941, Hitler had attacked his ally, the Soviet Union.

Allied War Plans

The United States needed time to train and equip its forces. Until this was done, it could not fight an all-out war against both Germany and Japan.

Allied leaders decided to direct their main effort against Germany while trying to slow down the Japanese in the Pacific. Germany had to come first, because the war in Europe was at a critical stage. Germany was threatening to cut Britain off from the United States. And the Soviet Union was also in danger of being overrun by the Germans.

WAR IN EUROPE AND AFRICA, 1939-1945

Think: German wolf packs, teams of two to forty submarines, worked together to blockade Britain and the rest of Europe. Respond: How did the Allies learn to fight these undersea menaces?

Winning the Battle of the Atlantic

Before America could help its allies, the sea route to Britain and Europe had to be secured. The Battle of the Atlantic was actually not one battle but months of individual battles between cargo ships and their defenders and the deadly German "wolf packs" of U-boats, or submarines.

At first, the U-boats got the best of it. The Americans were not used to fighting submarines. But American anti-submarine forces soon learned more effective tactics. Aided by airplanes, radar, and sound-detection equipment, they began to sink or drive off the submarines.

Allied Gains in Africa and Italy

To strike back against Germany, the Allies agreed to attack the Axis troops in North Africa. If they could secure North Africa, the Allies would have bases from which to attack Europe across the Mediterranean Sea.

In November 1942, a large army of American, Canadian, and British troops led by General Dwight D. Eisenhower (eye-zun-HOW-ur) landed on the northern coast of Africa. By May 1943, this Allied army forced the German and Italian armies in Africa to surrender.

The Allies next launched attacks on Sicily and Italy. In July of 1943, Allied troops captured Sicily, the island at the tip of Italy. Early in September, Allied troops landed in southern Italy. Many Italians no longer supported Mussolini, and he fell from power. The Italian government surrendered to the Allies. But Germany rushed troops into Italy, and fierce fighting continued.

The War in the Soviet Union

At first, the German invaders had overwhelmed the Soviet defenders. But Hitler did not realize the size of the Soviet forces or the problems involved in invading such a huge country. Also, the Germans were not prepared for the terrible winters they found in the Soviet Union.

The German advances began to slow down, and the Soviet defenders, aided by supplies from America, grew stronger. In September 1942, the Germans attacked the key city of Stalingrad (STAHL-un-grad). After months of fierce fighting, the Soviets held the city and then counterattacked, surrounding and capturing large numbers of Germans. The tide in the East turned. By the spring of 1944, the Soviet armies were pushing the Germans back toward Poland.

Think: American troops prepared for battle. After bitter fighting, German forces surrendered in North Africa in 1943. Respond: What was gained by defeating the Axis troops in North Africa?

Think: Landing craft tanks (LCTs) brought soldiers close to shore. The men had to face enemy fire and heavily mined beaches. Twenty-five hundred soldiers died at Omaha Beach. But the D-Day invasion was a success. The Allies had a foothold in France. **Respond:** Why was the success of the invasion so important?

The Allies Invade Europe

Meanwhile, the Allies were planning to invade western Europe. First, a massive bombing campaign was started against Germany. The bombing gradually weakened Germany's ability to defend its European empire.

Finally, on June 6, 1944, "D-Day," the greatest invasion ever launched, began to pour ashore on the beaches of Normandy in northwestern France. More than five thousand ships were used, and in two months, more than two million Allied soldiers were landed, the majority of them Americans.

By the end of July, Allied forces had broken through into the interior of France. On August 25, Paris was liberated, or set free, by the Allies.

Think: The French town of St.-Lô was left in ruins after Allied planes bombed the area, making way for tanks and troops. The liberation of Paris was soon to follow. Ogden Pleissner recorded the movement of an Allied tank column through the ruins. Consider the vast destruction of many of Europe's cities. **Respond:** What do you think it was like to live in France during World War II?

The War in Europe Ends

By late 1944, the Germans were being pushed steadily back on all sides. In the West, American and British forces raced toward the Rhine River and into Germany. In the East, the Soviets captured Rumania, Bulgaria, and Hungary. They also drove through Poland and Austria toward Germany.

At the *Battle of the Bulge* in December 1944, the Germans tried to stop the Allies in the West. The Allied advance was only slowed for a short time, however. In March 1945, the Allied armies poured into Germany from both sides. In April, Hitler and some of his top leaders took their own lives.

As Allied soldiers liberated the lands Hitler had occupied, they made a shocking discovery. They found terrible German *concentration camps*. Their purpose was to carry out Hitler's plan to completely destroy the Jewish people. People in the camps were victims of forced labor, starvation, torture, and murder. Six million Jews, as well as many other people Hitler hated, had died in these camps in what became known as the *Holocaust*.

Think: **When Americans entered Buchenwald Concentration Camp, they found thousands of prisoners near death. Thousands had already died.** Respond: **What stories do these faces tell?**

Think: **When Allied forces opened the prison gates at Bad Orh, Germany, the prisoners of war were set free. The expressions on their faces show how the Americans and other prisoners felt about their release.** Respond: **What emotions are they displaying?**

Think: During the Battle of Midway, the Japanese *Mikuma* collided with another Japanese ship while trying to avoid an American submarine. The *Mikuma* later was sunk by American planes. The Battle of Midway ended Japan's expansion eastward.
Respond: Why couldn't the Japanese afford to lose ships such as the *Mikuma*?

On May 8, 1945, Germany surrendered to the Allies. President Roosevelt did not live to see this great victory in Europe. He had died in April 1945. Harry S. Truman, the vice president, became president.

The Tide Turns in the Pacific

In 1942, the Japanese had become masters of a wide-ranging island empire. The United States was greatly outnumbered by the Japanese in aircraft carriers and battleships.

In May 1942, a Japanese invasion fleet moved toward New Guinea (GHIN-ee). Its object was to establish a base from which Japan could attack Australia. The Americans fought off the invasion. In the **Battle of the Coral Sea**, the two fleets never came within gun range of each other. Instead, each side's aircraft carriers sent airplanes to find and bomb the enemy. The Americans suffered the greater damage, but the Japanese fleet was forced to turn back.

The decisive naval battle of the Pacific war was fought in June 1942. The Japa- nese decided to invade Midway Island with a huge fleet. Midway was the key to control of the whole central Pacific.

The Japanese did not realize, however, that American code-breakers had discovered the Japanese plans and knew where the Japanese ships would be. In the **Battle of Midway**, the Americans surprised the Japanese and sank the four largest Japanese carriers, losing only one of their own. Lacking America's mighty industrial resources, the Japanese could not easily replace their losses. Japan was soon forced to take the defensive.

Island-Hopping to Japan

The United States began to recapture the territory the Japanese had taken. In August 1942, American marines landed on the island of Guadalcanal (GWAHD-ul-kuh-NAL) in the Solomon Islands. By the end of 1943, after fierce air, sea, and land fighting, the Americans had captured the Solomon Islands and much of New Guinea. The Americans began to capture key

Think: **After fierce fighting in Iwo Jima, 750 miles from Tokyo, Americans finally took the strategically located island.** Respond: **What does this artwork symbolize?**

islands and build bases from which to attack the Japanese Empire, including Japan itself.

In 1944, using this island-hopping strategy, the Americans captured Saipan (seye-PAN), Guam, Iwo Jima (EE-WO JEE-mah), and finally the island of Okinawa on the doorstep of Japan itself. American bombers pounded Japanese cities, starting terrible fires. But the Japanese government still would not surrender.

The War in Asia Ends

By the summer of 1945, it looked like the Americans would have to invade Japan itself. The Americans knew the Japanese would fight fiercely. The final battle would probably cost thousands of American and Japanese lives.

Something new then entered the picture. By the summer of 1945, American scientists had developed and tested an atomic bomb. Some of the scientists

Think: **On August 9, 1945, an American plane dropped an atomic bomb on the Japanese city of Nagasaki. Immediately, 40,000 were dead or missing; thousands more have since died of radiation.** Respond: **Do you agree or disagree with the decision to use atomic weapons to attack an enemy? Explain.**

WAR IN THE PACIFIC, 1942–1945

The United States had been at war with Japan since the attack on Pearl Harbor in December 1941. For over a year, Japan had moved steadily southward across the Pacific, island by island. Australia was next.

The United States fought back in the Pacific Ocean area. It did so with a new kind of warfare called "island hopping." Naval aircraft on huge carriers would attack a Japanese fleet. Then Marine or Army units would go ashore on an island. The islands were used as stepping stones to get within bombing range of Japan, using large, high-flying, long-range Army bombers.

Look at the map and the map scale.

1. Using the map scale, estimate how many square miles Japan controlled.

2. How near was Japanese control to Australia?

3. What nations had fallen to Japan? Which were threatened?

4. What was the strategy in taking the islands of Tarawa, Kwajalein, and Eniwetok?

The atomic bomb was flown from the small island of Tinian located between Guam and Saipan. Find this area on the map.

5. What other strategies for ending the war might have been used?

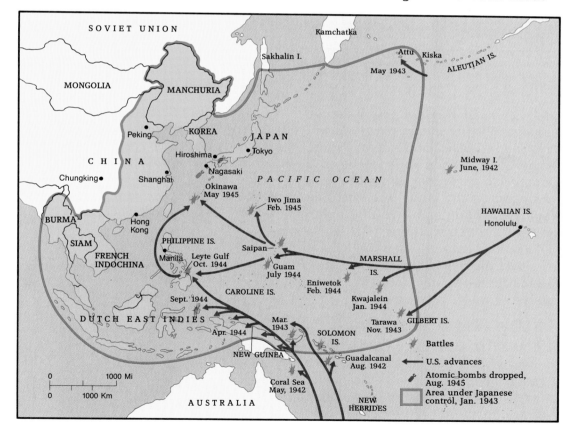

Think: On September 2, 1945, the Japanese formally surrendered aboard the battleship *Missouri* in Tokyo Bay. The surrender agreement was signed by General MacArthur for the Allies and General Umeza for the Japanese. Respond: Why is it appropriate that the surrender took place on an American battleship?

opposed using this terrible new weapon, but the possibility of saving many American lives made President Truman decide to use the bomb. When Japan refused a final demand to surrender, atomic bombs were dropped on the cities of Hiroshima and Nagasaki, killing about 150,000 people and injuring many others with radiation. The atomic attacks, combined with the news that the Soviet Union had decided to attack Japan, finally forced the Japanese government to surrender.

The Terrible Cost of World War II

World War II was over. More than twenty-five million people had died as a direct result of the war, with the Soviet Union and Germany losing the most. More than one million Americans were either killed or wounded. Large parts of Europe and Asia were destroyed.

The United States now faced the question of how to help the world rebuild. Many Americans realized their country could never again ignore the rest of the world. The United States would have to make a long-term commitment to maintaining peace and freedom.

Section Review

1. Why did the Allies decide to attack the Axis in North Africa?
2. Why did the United States win the Battle of Midway? What were the effects of this victory?
3. How did the war in Europe end? How did the Pacific war end?

4. Planning for Peace After World War II

Learn these important terms:

Atlantic Charter
United Nations
International Court of Justice
Big Three nations
Security Council
General Assembly

Remember the main idea:

The United States, Great Britain, and the Soviet Union made plans for fighting the war. They also agreed to organize the United Nations, and to divide Germany and occupy it after the war.

Look for answers to these questions:

1. What did the Big Three leaders agree to do with Germany after the war?

2. How was the United Nations organized?

3. After the war, what led to a disagreement between the United States and the Soviet Union?

Even before the United States was officially in World War II, President Roosevelt and Winston Churchill, the Prime Minister of Britain, drew up a statement that explained their war aims. This *Atlantic Charter*, as it was called, said that the Allies were fighting to give certain freedoms to all people of the world. These freedoms included freedom from want and freedom from fear.

The "Big Three" Leaders Meet

The Atlantic Charter was signed by twenty-six nations. The decisions on how to fight the war and plan for the time after it were made by the leaders of the *Big Three nations*, however—the United States, Great Britain, and the Soviet Union. Their leaders, President Roosevelt, Winston Churchill, and Joseph Stalin, met several times during the war.

At a meeting in Casablanca (KAS-uh-BLANG-ka) in North Africa, in January of 1943, Roosevelt and Churchill decided that the Allies would demand that Germany surrender unconditionally. This meant it must give up completely. Later, Stalin agreed with this policy.

Plans for Peace

In 1944, the leaders of the United States, Great Britain, China, and the Soviet Union met to make plans to organize the *United Nations*. This new organization would try to keep peace in the world after the war ended. In April 1945, the

Think: Truman spoke at the 1945 United Nations conference. Respond: Why did more Americans support the United Nations in 1945 than had supported the League of Nations in 1920?

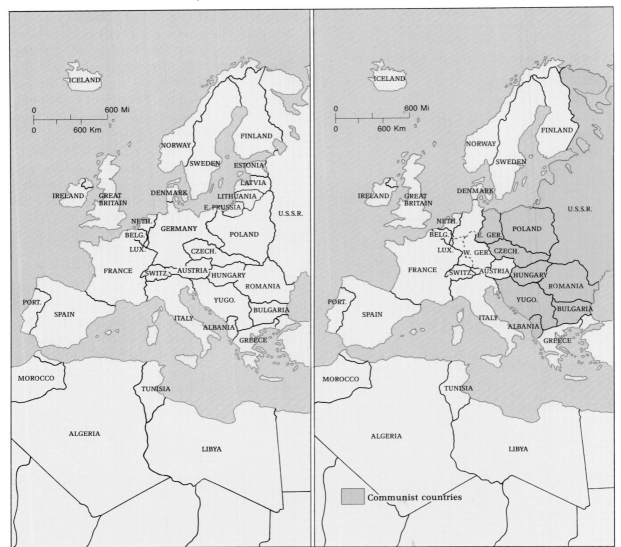

EUROPE BEFORE WORLD WAR II, 1938

ICELAND

0   600 Mi
0   600 Km

NORWAY
SWEDEN
FINLAND
ESTONIA
LATVIA
LITHUANIA
E. PRUSSIA
U.S.S.R.
IRELAND
GREAT BRITAIN
DENMARK
NETH.
BELG.
LUX.
GERMANY
POLAND
CZECH.
FRANCE
SWITZ.
AUSTRIA
HUNGARY
ROMANIA
YUGO.
ITALY
BULGARIA
ALBANIA
GREECE
PORT.
SPAIN
MOROCCO
TUNISIA
ALGERIA
LIBYA

EUROPE AFTER WORLD WAR II, 1945

ICELAND

0   600 Mi
0   600 Km

NORWAY
SWEDEN
FINLAND
IRELAND
GREAT BRITAIN
DENMARK
U.S.S.R.
NETH.
BELG.
LUX.
E. GER.
W. GER.
POLAND
CZECH.
FRANCE
SWITZ.
AUSTRIA
HUNGARY
ROMANIA
YUGO.
BULGARIA
ITALY
ALBANIA
GREECE
PORT.
SPAIN
MOROCCO
TUNISIA
ALGERIA
LIBYA

   Communist countries

leaders of fifty nations met in San Francisco, California, and drew up the Charter of the United Nations (U.N.).

The Charter was like a constitution. It said the United Nations would work something like the United States Congress. It would have two houses. Five important nations—the United States, Great Britain, the Soviet Union, France, and China—made up the regular members of the **Security Council**. Other nations would take turns at serving two-year terms on this council. All member nations served in the other house, the **General Assembly**.

The United Nations also had other agencies, or parts, that would try to improve health, education, and living conditions around the world. The United Nations also established the **International Court of Justice** to settle disputes as they occurred among nations.

Germany's Future Is Decided

Since the United States defeated Japan practically by itself, it could decide how to deal with Japan after it surrendered.

The situation with Germany was much more complicated. At a conference at Yalta in southern Russia early in 1945, Roosevelt, Churchill, and Stalin agreed that Germany would be occupied by the Allies. Germany and the city of Berlin would be divided into four separate areas. The United States, Great Britain, France, and the Soviet Union would each control one area. The Big Three also agreed to hold free elections in the nations of eastern Europe which were occupied by the Soviet Union.

In the summer of 1945, the Big Three leaders met again. Stalin was still head of the Soviet Union, but Harry S. Truman was now President of the United States, and Clement Attlee had replaced Churchill as Prime Minister of Great Britain.

The nations agreed to give part of eastern Germany to Poland and part of Poland to the Soviet Union. The Soviet Union also gained Estonia, Latvia, and Lithuania. They agreed that the leaders of the former Nazi government would all be

Think: The Big Three—Churchill, Roosevelt, and Stalin—met at Yalta in Russia to discuss how to solve the problems of the post-war world. They agreed to set up a world peace-keeping organization. They also agreed to help many countries rebuild their economies. Respond: Why is *Big Three* an appropriate name for these men?

The United Nations had its fortieth birthday in 1985. To find out more about the birthday celebration, you could read magazine articles written at that time. The *Readers' Guide to Periodical Literature* can help you find those articles. It is an index to more than one hundred magazines. You can find this guide in most large libraries.

On this page is part of a *Readers' Guide* entry for the subject "United Nations." You can see from the listing that an article called "The Big Birthday Bash" appears on page 21 of the magazine *Newsweek* in the November 4, 1985 edition. The abbreviation *il* means the article is illustrated with pictures. A librarian could help you find that magazine and get information on what happened at the United Nations' fortieth birthday party.

Use the *Readers' Guide* entry to answer the questions that follow it.

> **United Nations**
> The big birthday bash, il *Newsweek* 106:21 N 4 '85
> Flying flags and flowing words [security surrounding U.N.'s 40th anniversary commemoration] E. Thomas. il *Time* 126:15 O 7 '85
> A global family album [photographs of visiting heads of state] il *Time* 126:18-19 N 4 '85
> Parties and politics at the United Nations *Newsweek* 106:43 O 7 '85
> United Nations Children's Fund. *See* UNICEF
> **UNICEF**
> Harry Belafonte to get Chicago UNICEF's honor. *Jet* 69:36 S 30 '85
> Cicely Tyson tours famine areas in Africa as head of UNICEF projects. il pors *Jet* 69:60-2 O 28 '85

1 In what three magazines are the articles that are listed in this part of the *Readers' Guide*?

2 What is the name and date of the magazine with the article "Flying Flags and Flowing Words"? On what page is the article found?

3 What is the title of the *Time* article that has pictures of the leaders of several countries?

4 What does the abbreviation UNICEF stand for?

5 What two people are featured in articles about UNICEF? In what months of 1985 did the articles appear in magazines?

6 Do you think the magazine articles about the United Nations' birthday are primary sources? Why?

7 Listings in the *Readers' Guide* are alphabetical. Would magazine articles on the subject "United States" be listed before or after the articles shown on this page?

Think: **Surprisingly, shortly after the war ended, the British people voted to replace Churchill with Clement Atlee. Truman became president upon Roosevelt's death. Thus, Stalin was the only original Big Three leader to attend the final meetings at Potsdam.** Respond: **To what did the Big Three nations agree?**

removed from power. Many of them were later tried as war criminals for going far beyond even the normal violence of war.

The Soviet Union refused to go ahead with the planned elections for the eastern European nations, however. Instead, the Soviets installed hand-picked governments that would carry out their orders. The United States and the Soviet Union, reluctant allies during the war, began to move farther and farther apart.

The United States had responded magnificently to the challenge of World War II. The post-war world would bring many difficult problems, however. In the next chapters, you will see the United States struggling with its commitments in a world where victory would be much less clear-cut.

Section Review

1. What was the purpose of the Atlantic Charter?

2. What happened to Germany when the war ended?

3. What was the main purpose of the United Nations?

CHAPTER SUMMARY

As Japan expanded into Asia, the United States and Japan were unable to come to an agreement because Japan wanted a free hand in China. In December 1941, the Japanese attacked Pearl Harbor. The United States was soon at war with all the Axis nations.

The war put Americans back to work and provided opportunities for women and blacks.

When the United States entered World War II, both the Germans and Japanese were winning. The United States and its allies, Great Britain, France, and the Soviet Union, agreed to concentrate on stopping Germany first.

In Europe, the Allies won in Africa, Sicily, and eventually Italy. In 1944, the Allies invaded France with a huge army. Meanwhile, the Soviet Union stopped the Germans at Stalingrad and began to push the Germans back toward Germany. When Allied forces poured into Germany from both sides, Germany surrendered.

The United States turned the tide in the Pacific with a decisive victory at the Battle of Midway. Gradually, the Americans recaptured the territory the Japanese had taken and forced the Japanese to surrender with the aid of the atomic bomb.

Conferences among the allies during the war also led to the founding of the United Nations.

Key Words

Write a sentence to explain the meaning of each of these terms.

treaty of
  alliance
War Production
  Board
Executive Order
  8802

Battle of
  the Coral Sea
concentration
  camps
United
  Nations

Major Events

Choose the answer that best completes the statement.

1. Pearl Harbor was a surprise

   a) because Americans thought Japan was peaceful.
   b) because Americans thought Japan would attack in Asia first.
   c) because the Japanese had promised not to attack Hawaii.

2. World War II ended the depression

   a) as unemployed were drafted.
   b) because the government took over all businesses.
   c) because many workers were needed for war production.

3. The Battle of the Atlantic was fought between

   a) Allied and Axis ships.
   b) British and German planes.
   c) American and British convoys and German submarines.

4. The Americans won the Battle of Midway mainly because

   a) they were able to learn the Japanese battle plans.
   b) they had more aircraft carriers.
   c) they had better pilots.

Review

Important Facts

Answer each question with at least one complete sentence.

1. Why did Japan sign the 1940 treaty of alliance?

2. Why was the United States better prepared for World War II than it had been for World War I?

3. How did the war change life for women?

4. Why were black leaders able to put pressure on the government to end racial discrimination?

5. How did the government raise money to pay for the war?

6. How did the government reduce the amount of inflation during World War II?

7. Why did the United States and its allies decide to make their main war effort against Germany?

8. Why did the Germans and Russians fight the Battle of Stalingrad? What was the outcome of this battle?

9. What was the Holocaust? What made it especially terrible?

10. How did America's "island-hopping" strategy in the Pacific work?

11. Why did President Truman decide to use the atomic bomb against Japan?

12. What were the Big Three nations and their leaders?

13. How does the United Nations work?

Skill Review

Study this map, then answer the following questions.

1. How many American divisions landed in France? How many British? How many Canadian?

2. About how many miles is it from Omaha Beach to Caumont? How many days did it take to get there? Do you think the fighting was heavy? Why, or why not?

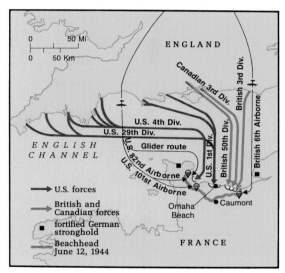

D-Day Invasion

Critical Thinking

Write a paragraph to answer each question.

1. Why do you think Japanese-Americans were put into detention camps, while most German-Americans and Italian-Americans were left alone?

2. Compare the effects and the outcomes of World War I and World War II.

Important People

Choose the answer that best completes the statement.

1. Sixty nations signed a peace agreement that was proposed in 1928 by

   a) Dawes and Young.
   b) Kellogg and Briand.
   c) Hitler and Mussolini.

2. The Good Neighbor Policy was proclaimed by

   a) Franklin Roosevelt.
   b) Herbert Hoover.
   c) Victoriano Huerta.

3. All of the following men were dictators *except*

   a) Adolf Hitler.
   b) Joseph Stalin.
   c) Winston Churchill.

4. Francisco Franco led

   a) the Spanish fascists.
   b) the Italian armies in Africa.
   c) the Spanish loyalists.

5. Neville Chamberlain

   a) led the defense of Britain against Hitler.
   b) wanted Britain to join the Axis Powers.
   c) wanted to make peace with Hitler by agreeing to his demands.

6. The American general who led the Allied forces against Germany in World War II was

   a) Harry S. Truman.
   b) Dwight D. Eisenhower.
   c) John J. Pershing.

Main Ideas

Choose the answer that best completes the statement.

1. All of the following led to World War II *except* that

   a) world leaders refused to sign peace agreements.
   b) the arms race wasn't really stopped.
   c) European leaders gave Hitler what he wanted instead of resisting him.

2. In the late 1930s, most Americans wanted the U.S. to

   a) help Britain fight Hitler.
   b) declare war against Germany.
   c) remain strictly neutral.

3. By 1941, the United States had begun to prepare for war by doing all of the following *except*

   a) establishing a draft.
   b) making war production plans.
   c) sending troops to China.

4. Talks between the United States and Japan broke down in late 1941 because

   a) the United States wanted Japan to give up its navy.
   b) the Japanese demanded the right to control China.
   c) the Japanese attacked Pearl Harbor.

5. The Allies made their first major counterattack against German forces in

   a) Africa.
   b) France.
   c) Sicily and Italy.

6. The Allies defeated the Axis forces in all of the following battles *except*

   a) Stalingrad.
   b) Dunkirk.
   c) Midway.

7. In 1940, Japan, Italy, and Germany signed

   a) a peace treaty.
   b) a treaty of alliance.
   c) an embargo agreement.

8. World War II ended the Great Depression because

   a) most workers were drafted.
   b) the government controlled wages and prices.
   c) many people were hired to produce war goods.

9. All of the following groups of Americans made some gains during World War II *except*

   a) blacks.
   b) women.
   c) Japanese-Americans.

10. The organization that the Allies founded to try to keep the peace after World War II was the

    a) United Nations.
    b) Atlantic Charter.
    c) League of Nations.

11. All of the following resulted from World War II *except*

    a) free elections were held in Eastern Europe.
    b) the United States and the Soviet Union were the two most powerful nations.
    c) Germany was divided and occupied by the Allies.

History Skills

Guam

Location: part of Mariana Islands in Pacific Ocean, 3,700 miles west of Hawaii

Area: 209 square miles (30 miles long, 4–8.5 miles wide)

Population: 119,540; 41.8% Chamorro (natives of Guam), 21.2% Filipino

Language: English, Chamorro

Climate: tropical, average temperature 70-90° F., average rainfall 70" per year

Economy: Manufacturing–petroleum products, foods, textiles; Agriculture–fruits, vegetables, cattle, hogs and pigs

Cities: Agana (capital), Apra Harbor (major port)

Choose the answer that best completes the statement.

1. Guam was important to the United States during World War II because it was part of

   a) D-Day.
   b) the country of Japan.
   c) the island-hopping strategy.

2. Soldiers fighting on Guam faced the problem of

   a) a hot, rainy climate.
   b) a vast area to conquer.
   c) no people who spoke English.

3. This type of information can be found in all of these reference books *except*

   a) an atlas.
   b) an almanac.
   c) the *Readers' Guide to Periodical Literature.*

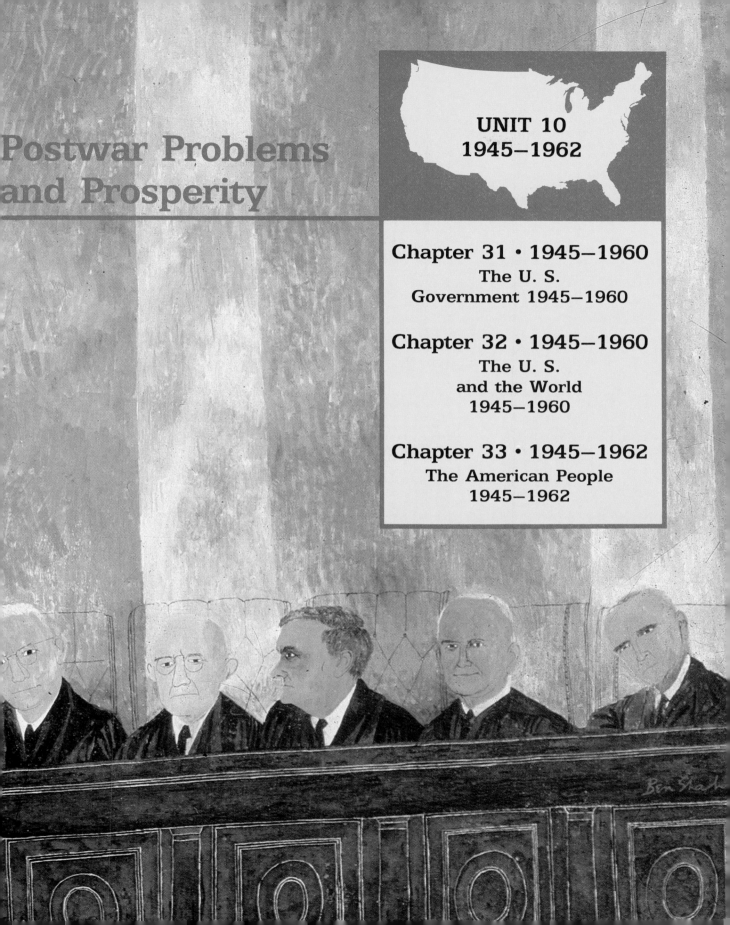

Postwar Problems and Prosperity

CHAPTER

31

The U.S. Government 1945–1960

Years 1945–1960

Roosevelt died
Harry S. Truman
became president

1945

Taft-Hartley Act passed
Department of Defense
set up

1947

Senator McCarthy
censured

1954

National Defense
Education Act passed

1958

Employment Act passed
Council of Economic
Advisers set up

1946

Dwight D. Eisenhower
elected president

1952

Sputnik I launched

1957

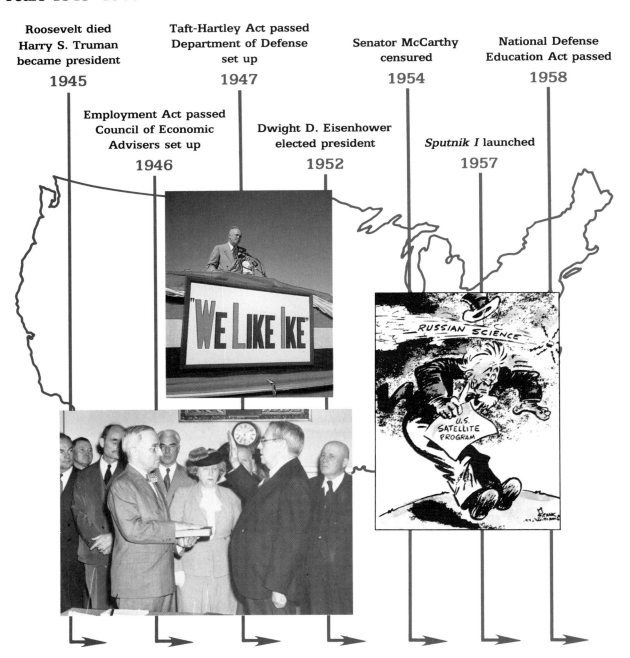

Harry S. Truman took the oath of office only hours after President Roosevelt's death on April 12, 1945. The following day he told the press that he felt like the moon, the stars, and all the planets had fallen on him. Franklin D. Roosevelt had been a popular and respected president. Following him would not be easy. Truman faced the responsibility of leading the nation into peace. Although Truman had been a strong decision-maker during the war, unknown problems lay ahead of him. You will see how well he dealt with these problems. You will also read about the roles Congress and Cabinet members played.

This chapter tells about America's return to peacetime. Think about what this meant to the country. The economy had to change. Many families had to start again. Soldiers had to readjust. As you read, consider the impact of these changes. How would American leaders fulfill the promise of peacetime America?

1. Winding Down from the War

Learn these important terms:

GI Bill of Rights
Council of Economic Advisers
Taft-Hartley Act
closed shop
Employment Act
National Security Act
Fair Deal
Atomic Energy Commission

Remember the main idea:

Winding down from World War II was no easy task. President Truman and Congress had to help millions of returning soldiers readjust to civilian life. They also had to deal with a prospering but changing peacetime economy.

Look for answers to these questions:

1. What law helped veterans adjust to peacetime conditions?

2. Why did so many workers go on strike after the war?

3. Why did so many Americans support Harry Truman in the election of 1948?

The men and women in the armed forces wanted to return quickly to peacetime living. These GIs, as they were called, numbered 12,500,000 at the war's end. Americans made it clear to Congress that they expected the GIs to return from Europe and Asia right away. So the

Think: The *USS Admiral Capps*, her decks packed with returning troops, arrived home on December 15, 1945. Respond: Why did Americans want the troops to return so quickly?

government directed the armed forces to release their troops as quickly as possible. By the end of 1946, the American armed forces were down to a little more than one million men and women.

But problems for the GIs did not end with their return. Most needed jobs, many needed medical attention, and large numbers wanted to be educated.

To help the GIs readjust, Congress passed a law known as the *GI Bill of Rights*. This law helped veterans to continue their educations. It also loaned them money to buy homes or businesses and gave them pensions and hospital care. Millions of veterans took advantage of this program.

Think: After returning from the war, many GIs wanted to go back to school. Many also bought homes. Respond: What did the government do to help the veterans? Why?

Business and Industry Adjust to Peace

The end of the war brought change to American business and industry. The government no longer needed to control what was being produced. As soon as the war ended, America's factories went back to making the peacetime goods that Americans needed and demanded.

At first, many American workers were afraid that they might lose their jobs. They feared competition from the millions of returning soldiers. They also worried that their workplaces would shut down as factories stopped making war materials. As it turned out, however, they had nothing to fear. The demand for goods was so great that few workers lost their jobs.

Why was the demand for goods so great? During the war, many goods were rationed or were in short supply. Since there was little for consumers to buy, most people put their money into banks. After the war, when most rationing ended, Americans began spending.

The increased demand for goods after the war drove prices up. During World War II, the prices of food, housing, and most products were controlled by the federal government. In 1946, however, Congress ended most price controls. After price controls were lifted, the prices of most products went up. This inflation was the main problem facing the economy during the early postwar years.

Although the economy grew rapidly after the war, Congress passed a law that assured jobs. The *Employment Act* of 1946 made it the government's duty to try to prevent unemployment. In addition, a *Council of Economic Advisers* was set up to help the president improve the American economy. By improving the economy, this council and the president provided more jobs.

The Unions Respond

The changing nature of the economy after the war led to many strikes by American workers. These strikes were protests against inflation and losses in pay. Many workers were earning less money because their working hours had been cut. They went from forty-eight hours per week during the war to forty hours after the war. Workers went on strike to demand higher wages. Strikes took place in the automobile, steel, coal, and railroad industries. These strikes brought wage increases to the workers.

Think: During the coal strike of 1946, many offices were lit by candlelight. Respond: After the coal strike, how and why did Congress control future strikes?

THE ELECTION OF 1948

The map and charts below show the results of one of the most dramatic presidential elections in history. The New York Republican Thomas E. Dewey was favored over the Democratic President Harry S. Truman. Third party candidates, Thurmond and Wallace, weakened Truman's chances. A majority of electoral votes is needed to win.

Look at the map, the map key, and the charts.

1. Who won the election of 1948, and by what percent? How do you know?

2. How many people voted in this election? How many voted for Dewey? How many voted for Truman? What percentage of the people voted for Truman? Does it make a difference whether these votes are in states with many electoral votes? Why?

3. How many electoral votes are needed to win the presidency? What is the fewest number of states that can reach this total? Name these states.

The four time zones across the country add drama to a close national election. By the time the votes are counted on the west coast, night has fallen in the East. In 1948, the *Chicago Daily Tribune* headlined Dewey as the winner, as Truman went to bed confident of victory. The map shows what happened.

4. Give two reasons why Dewey, sitting in New York, would feel happy about the early returns.

5. Why did Dewey's confidence fade with the sun in the Midwest?

6. As election day ended, how did each candidate and his supporters view California?

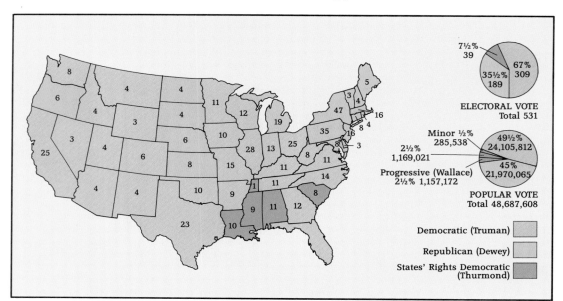

Think: Great debates took place over the Taft-Hartley Act. Respond: Would you have been for or against the act? Why?

could take place. The law also allowed the president to stop a strike that endangered the nation. A coal strike in 1946 had reduced the nation's coal supply to dangerously low levels. The Taft-Hartley Act would prevent this from ever happening again.

What angered union members the most about the Taft-Hartley Act was that it outlawed the **closed shop**. A closed shop occurs when a company agrees to hire only workers who belong to a union. Unions thought they would be weakened without closed shops.

Other War-Related Problems

The war left Congress with the responsibility of deciding what to do about atomic energy. Atomic energy is the powerful force that is set off when atoms are split. Atomic energy is used in atomic bombs. But it also has more peaceful uses as a source of electric power. In 1946, Congress decided to put the development of atomic energy in the hands of civilians, not the military. So the **Atomic Energy Commission** was created.

Congress also took a hard look at the way the country's armed forces were organized. In 1947, Congress decided to unite the armed forces under one Cabinet department. The **National Security Act** set up the Department of Defense headed by the secretary of defense.

The Twenty-second Amendment

Congress made another important decision when it responded to the issue of the number of terms a president could serve. For example, when President Roosevelt died, he was in his fourth term. Some thought this was too many. Congress suggested that a president be allowed to serve only two full terms in office. This plan later became the Twenty-second Amendment to the Constitution.

Because of these strikes, Congress began to feel that unions must be controlled. Therefore, in 1947, Congress passed the **Taft-Hartley Act** over President Truman's veto. This law required labor unions to give sixty days' notice before they started a strike. This gave business managers and workers time to settle their differences before a strike

Think: The victorious Truman happily holds up a newspaper that had reported Dewey as the winner.
Respond: Why had so many people believed that Dewey would win, not Truman?

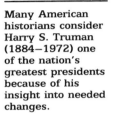

Many American historians consider Harry S. Truman (1884–1972) one of the nation's greatest presidents because of his insight into needed changes.

The Election of 1948

In the Congressional election of 1946, the Republican Party had won control of both houses of Congress. Therefore, in the 1948 presidential election, the Republicans were sure that their candidate would win. Their choice was Thomas E. Dewey, the governor of New York.

President Truman became the Democratic candidate, even though he lacked the support of two important groups in his party. One group was made up of Southerners who opposed the president's support of equal rights. The other group disagreed with Truman's postwar policy toward the Soviet Union. Truman's chances of winning looked slim.

But Truman had a program of change and reform that appealed to many Americans. He called this program the *Fair Deal.* The Fair Deal promised laws to enforce equal rights for all Americans. It also promised more public housing and federal aid to education. The Fair Deal called for the passage of a health insurance plan and the repeal of the Taft-Hartley Act. In a surprising upset, President Truman won the election of 1948. Many Democrats rode on his coattails to victory. The Democrats won back control of Congress. In the next section, you will find out about the problems and successes of the Truman presidency.

Section Review

1. How did the government help GIs returning to civilian life?
2. What caused inflation after World War II?
3. Why did union members oppose the Taft-Hartley Act?
4. Why did two groups of Democrats oppose President Truman's election in 1948?

2. Truman's Fair Deal

Learn these important terms:

social programs
National Housing Act of 1949
discrimination
communism
Internal Security Act

Remember the main idea:

President Truman's term in office was not always smooth or successful. He failed to get Congress to approve much of his Fair Deal program. He also had to deal with charges that government officials who were serving under him were dishonest and disloyal.

Look for answers to these questions:

1. Why did President Truman fail to win support for much of his Fair Deal program?
2. For which social programs was Truman able to win support?
3. What made the American people become concerned that communism was spreading inside the United States?

The Congress that President Truman had to work with was not a very cooperative one. Southern Democrats refused to support and vote for any part of the Fair Deal that involved equal rights issues. They were joined by the Republicans who opposed most parts of the Fair Deal. Republicans did not want to see the government grow bigger by involving itself in new and expensive *social programs*. Social programs aim to assist the poor, the sick, and the needy, improving the quality of their lives.

Efforts To Make the Nation Color Blind

As part of his Fair Deal program, President Truman asked Congress to pass laws to enforce equal rights for all Americans. He called for a federal law that would make lynching, or hanging someone without a trial, unlawful. He also wanted a law ending *discrimination* in hiring practices. Many employers would not consider some people for certain jobs simply because of their ethnic background. Truman wanted all jobs to be open equally to *every* qualified person.

Think: Life in the South was slow to change. This 1947 scene could have been from 1847. Respond: Why had it become necessary to pass a federal law ending discrimination in hiring?

Truman also proposed a law that would end segregation on all travel systems. Another proposed law would have stopped the use of the poll tax as a voting requirement. Congress did not pass any of these laws.

However, on his own, President Truman did much to bring about equal treatment for all Americans. He ended discrimination in hiring in the federal civil service system. Truman also ended segregation in the armed forces. Black and white Americans began to fight side by side in the army, navy, and air force.

Efforts To Help the Disadvantaged

President Truman was also defeated in his attempt to get federal aid for education. In addition, Congress turned down his plan for government health insurance. His proposal to repeal the Taft-Hartley law also fell through. It seemed as if the Fair Deal and Congress were constantly on a collision course.

But Congress was willing to expand and improve the Social Security system. The Social Security program grew to include over ten million more Americans. Moreover, the monthly payments to American workers over sixty-five were increased. Congress also agreed to raise the minimum wage for workers. It rose from forty cents an hour to seventy-five cents an hour. Over one million workers benefited from this increase.

Congress also passed the **National Housing Act of 1949**. This law made it possible to clear slums and to build low-cost public housing. The public housing projects built under this law helped to improve the living conditions of many poor Americans.

Efforts To Encourage Immigration

Between the 1920s and the 1940s, immigration to the United States had slowed to a trickle. Laws passed in the 1920s cut down the number of immigrants allowed to enter the country. During the Great Depression and World War II, immigration declined even further. However, after the war, many homeless

Think: The House Un-American Activities Committee was formed to investigate Communist activities in the United States. Above, Richard Nixon and other members hold a hearing investigating suspected Communists in the film industry. Many innocent people lost their jobs. Respond: Do you think these investigations were fair? Why, or why not?

Europeans wished to immigrate. But Congress wanted to move slowly. Large scale immigration could lead to problems of unemployment. As a solution, in 1948, Congress passed a law allowing limited immigration. Thus, about 200,000 carefully selected Europeans were permitted to enter the United States.

President Truman felt that this law did not go far enough. He thought that it

favored Europeans from western Europe. Meanwhile, homeless Europeans from southern and eastern Europe were largely excluded. In 1950, Congress agreed to change the law. The new law allowed 415,000 Europeans from all parts of Europe to enter the United States.

Spy Stories

In the years after the war, a fear of *communism* began to grip many Americans. Communism is a system of government that has only one party controlling all production of goods. A Communist government controls its people by telling them where to work and by limiting what

they can do. Many Americans feared a Communist takeover of America.

To some degree, this fear of communism was based on fact. Following the war, the Soviet Union gained control of the governments of a number of eastern European nations. But the United States did nothing to stop it. In addition, by the early 1950s, various spy rings had been uncovered in both the United States and Canada. These spy rings had stolen secret government documents and given the information to the Soviets. Americans assumed that there were many disloyal people in the government.

President Truman had to investigate the loyalty of government officials. In March 1947, he ordered a loyalty investigation of all government workers. Any employee found to be a member of a Communist organization was to be fired. By the time the investigation was completed in 1951, three million workers had been cleared. Only 212 had been fired. Those who were fired were not found guilty of spying. They merely belonged to what were thought to be suspicious organizations. Thus, the government considered them bad security risks. It seemed that Americans' fears of Communist spies in the government were exaggerated.

But Joseph McCarthy, a senator from Wisconsin, continued to make unfair charges against many Americans. He claimed to have a list of Communists who worked for the American government. These charges greatly increased the public's fear of communism.

As a result of these fears, Congress passed the *Internal Security Act* over President Truman's veto. This act required all Communist groups to file their membership lists with the government. Members were not allowed to work in defense factories, nor were they permitted to get passports. Even with this law, many Americans felt that the Truman

When you previewed the section you just read, you saw the heading "Efforts To Make the Nation Color Blind." You knew that this was the topic of the section, or what the section was mainly about. Then you read the main idea, which told you in a few sentences the most important thing the writer had to say about the topic. This information helped give you a purpose for reading.

A topic and main idea are also important parts of every paragraph of a section. To understand a paragraph, first ask yourself what the *topic* of the paragraph is. What person, place, or thing is the paragraph about? Then ask yourself what the *main idea* is. What is the most important thing the writer is saying about the topic? Finally, find the *topic sentence*, the sentence that expresses the main idea of the paragraph. Often it is the first sentence.

Look back at the heading "Spy Stories" on page 651, and read the first paragraph under that heading. The topic of the paragraph is communism in the United States. The main idea could be stated this way: People were afraid communism was spreading in the United States after the war. The writer has expressed the main idea in a topic sentence, which comes first in this paragraph.

Read the second, third, and fourth paragraphs below the heading. Then choose the best answers to the following questions.

1 What is the topic of the second paragraph?
a. the atomic bomb
b. World War II
c. fear of communism

2 What is the main idea of the second paragraph?
a. At that time, there was some communism in the United States.
b. The United States did not stop the spread of communism in east Europe.
c. Communism existed in the Soviet Union.

3 Which sentence is the topic sentence of the paragraph?
a. the second sentence
b. the first sentence
c. the third sentence

4 What is the topic of the third paragraph?
a. security risks
b. loyalty of U.S. government officials
c. firing of U.S. government workers

5 Which sentence is the topic sentence of the paragraph?
a. the first sentence
b. the second sentence
c. the third sentence

6 Write a sentence that expresses the main idea of the third paragraph.

"If There's Anything I Hate It's Sloppy Neighbors" — from The Herblock Book (Beacon Press, 1952)

Think: While Congress was pointing its finger at Truman's staff, it ignored the wrongdoings of its own members. To illustrate this, cartoonist Herbert Block presents Congress as a sloppy, cigar-smoking loudmouth shouting over the fence at an ultra-clean President Truman. Truman, looking upset, tries to clean his staff's dirty laundry. Respond: What does Block want his readers to think?

administration was not hard enough on Communists.

Dishonesty in High Offices

Between 1950 and 1952, a problem over the honesty of some important government officials developed. Investigations revealed that these officials had accepted gifts in return for doing special favors for their friends. President Truman acted swiftly to remove the guilty people from office. Although he was not involved in any of the dishonest deals, Truman's reputation suffered.

The presidential election of 1952 was approaching. Even though Truman could have run for another term, he chose not to. Instead, he gave his support to Adlai Stevenson, governor of Illinois. But the Republicans found a wildly popular war hero, General Dwight D. Eisenhower, to

head their ticket. In the rest of this chapter, you will read about Eisenhower's victory and his years as president.

Section Review

1. Which groups in Congress made it difficult for President Truman to get approval for his Fair Deal programs?

2. In what ways did Truman succeed in bringing about equal treatment for all Americans?

3. Who benefited from the social programs that were approved during Truman's terms?

4. How did the government deal with the claims that there were Communist spies in America?

3. The Middle-of-the-Road President

Learn these important terms:

landslide
balanced budget
censure
National Defense
  Education Act

Remember the main idea:

Dwight D. Eisenhower rode to victory in 1952 on his enormous popularity as a war hero. During his two terms in office, Eisenhower followed a moderate course. No new plans for reform and change were started, but many old laws were improved during his terms.

Look for answers to these questions:

1. How did President Eisenhower's style of leadership differ from that of Presidents Truman and Roosevelt?
2. What was Eisenhower's main concern during his presidency?
3. What event caused Americans to believe that American education needed to be improved?

Think: While campaigning, Eisenhower was friendly, while Stevenson came across as intellectual.
Respond: For whom would you have voted, the nice guy or the smart guy?

"I Like Ike," reflected the good feelings Americans had toward him.

The Democratic candidate, Adlai Stevenson, was a man of intelligence and wit. But he did not have Eisenhower's popular appeal.

Ike won the election by a *landslide*, receiving a vast majority of the votes cast.

Think: Politicians' personalities must fit their times. Consider, for example, Stevenson's unsuccessful campaign. Respond: Did his personality hurt him?

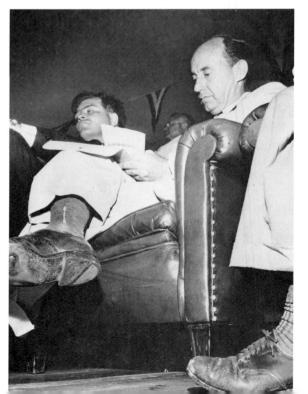

The personalities of the candidates seemed to be the big issue in the campaign of 1952. The Republicans chose General Dwight D. Eisenhower, the famous leader of the D-day invasion in World War II. Nicknamed Ike, Eisenhower was a respected and familiar figure to many Americans. His campaign slogan,

Energetic and sharp-witted, Dwight D. Eisenhower (1890–1969) excelled in the military. His popularity caused Republicans to push the reluctant Ike into the presidency.

He won the votes of all but eight states, winning even in Stevenson's home state of Illinois.

Eisenhower the President

President Eisenhower's background as a general shaped the way he acted as president. He chose not to try to handle all the nation's problems himself. Instead, he gave the members of his Cabinet the authority to make many decisions and plans for him. This left Eisenhower free to concern himself with the nation's most important problems. This plan often worked out well. But in some cases the president did not know enough about certain important issues. As a result, some people criticized him, claiming that he was losing touch.

Eisenhower and Congress

Unlike the two presidents who served before him, President Eisenhower did not try to influence Congress. He believed that it was up to Congress, not the president, to decide what laws should be passed. Eisenhower felt that Congress knew what the American people wanted. As a result, he did not try to force Congress to pass many laws.

President Eisenhower also had different ideas about the responsibilities of the federal government. He did not believe that it was the federal government's job to solve all of the nation's problems. He thought that state governments could handle many of them.

Following a Middle Course

Eisenhower once said, ''The path to America's future lies down the middle of the road. . . .'' The president chose not to undo the programs of the New Deal and the Fair Deal simply because they were Democratic plans. Nor did he intend to come up with a whole new program of his own. Instead he took a middle-of-the-road approach. He worked to improve the New Deal and the Fair Deal to further help the American people.

President Eisenhower asked Congress to raise the minimum wage to one dollar an hour. Congress also made the Social Security program larger, to include over ten million more Americans. In addition, monthly payments to those receiving Social Security were increased. The president set up the Department of Health, Education, and Welfare. This Cabinet

Think: Eisenhower cut program after program. Still he had to ask for more money than any president before him. **Respond:** What does this tell you about the country's budget?

A PRESIDENTIAL TOUCH

BROTHER— CAN YOU SPARE ABOUT 72 BILLION DOLLARS?

IKE

CONGRESS

Cy Hungerford for the Pittsburgh Post-Gazette 1/17/57

Think: In 1953, Oveta Culp Hobby took the oath of office as the federal security administrator. Soon after, she was made the first secretary of Health, Education, and Welfare. As such, she became a member of Eisenhower's Cabinet. **Respond:** Why was the Department of Health, Education, and Welfare begun?

department took charge of looking after the needs of the American people. To head this department, Eisenhower chose Oveta Culp Hobby. She was only the second woman to serve as a member of a president's Cabinet.

The president also asked Congress to raise money to build more public housing. By the time Eisenhower left office in 1960, many slums were cleared and many public housing projects were built. Laws were passed that made it easier to get loans to buy houses.

Eisenhower also took an interest in expanding the nation's highway system. He introduced the Highway Act of 1956, a shared federal and state program. Under this act, the nation's interstate highway system was built.

Eisenhower and the Balanced Budget

Eisenhower's main concern throughout his presidency was trying to create a *balanced budget*. This meant that the federal government would have to take in as much money as it spent. One way to do this was to reduce the amount of government spending.

But Eisenhower found that reducing government spending was difficult. Some parts of the budget were fixed, or unchangeable. For example, a certain amount of money was needed to pay the wages of the workers. In addition, money was spent for the nation's defense and for foreign aid. Most Americans felt that these two things were very important. They did not want the amount of money spent for them cut too much. Remarkably, Eisenhower was able to balance three of the government's budgets during his years as president.

More Hunting for Communists

Many Americans voted for Eisenhower in 1952 because they thought he would actively rid the government of Communists. As it turned out, Eisenhower did not have to conduct the hunt himself. Senator McCarthy was making it his mission to find every spy and Communist in Washington, D.C.

However, President Eisenhower and many members of Congress were against Senator McCarthy's unfair methods. The senator was accusing people of being Communists without having hard evidence. At first the president and Congress did nothing about it. But then, in 1954, McCarthy began an attack on the United States Army.

A series of hearings was held to look

HISTORY MAKERS

Hiram Fong

The Senator from Hawaii

Air raid sirens wailed. Boat whistles blew. Storekeepers closed their doors and joined the celebration in the streets. Students cheered as the voice of their high school principal came over the school intercom.

"I am delighted to announce that today, in Washington, D.C., the United States House of Representatives passed the statehood bill. This bill admits Hawaii to the United States and makes us the fiftieth state in the Union! All Hawaiians are invited to join in the celebrations, so school is dismissed for the next two days!"

Many Hawaiians worked hard to change Hawaii from a territory to a state. Territory laws could be vetoed by Congress. Furthermore, Hawaiians could not vote for president or have a voting representative in Congress. For these reasons, Hawaiians wanted to govern themselves as a state. Islanders wanted to participate in local and national government.

Hiram Fong was a leader in the Hawaiian movement for statehood. His parents came from China to work on the sugar plantations. There were eleven children in the Fong family, and very little money to spare. When he was four, Hiram Fong began working with his sisters and brothers, earning ten cents for every thirty pounds of beans they picked. As he grew older, Fong found other jobs. He shined shoes, sold newspapers, and worked as a delivery boy. He worked his way through college and law school. When Hiram Fong began practicing law, he had three partners: a Korean, a Japanese, and a Hawaiian. The firm mirrored the mix of backgrounds that made up Hawaiian society.

Hiram Fong served in the Hawaiian Territorial legislature for many years. He was vice president of the Hawaiian Constitutional Convention, and he campaigned long and hard for statehood. After Hawaii became a state, Hiram Fong was elected Hawaii's first U.S. Senator. Thus the man whose parents had been indentured servants on a sugar plantation became the first Asian-American senator in the United States.

into McCarthy's charges against the army. These hearings were shown on television. Americans saw for themselves that McCarthy was not able to prove his charges. Before long, Americans began to object to McCarthy's unfair methods.

In the end, the army was cleared of all charges. Finally in 1954, the Senate voted to *censure*, or officially criticize, Senator McCarthy. The American people realized that the hunt for spies had, for the most part, been a trick. McCarthy had political ambitions. For this reason, he had used the hunt for Communists to get the nation's attention. With his censure, the hunt for Communists ended.

A Second Term

President Eisenhower's first term was not filled with bold change or reform. Even still, he was very popular with the American people. In the presidential election of 1956, Eisenhower defeated Adlai Stevenson by an even larger margin than in 1952. However, the Republican Party lost seats in Congress in the elections of 1954, 1956, and 1958. As a result, the Democrats once again assumed control of Congress.

One of the biggest shocks of Eisenhower's second term came on October 4, 1957. On that day the Soviet Union put *Sputnik I*, the first man-made satellite, into orbit around the earth. Americans could barely believe the news. The United States had always believed it was way ahead of the Soviet Union in scientific achievement. No one had expected the Soviet Union to be the first to reach outer space.

Think: Joseph McCarthy had gone hunting for Communists from 1950 to 1954, during which time many innocent people were hurt by his accusations. Finally, when he tried to attack the United States Army, Congress censured him. Respond: What had McCarthy hoped to gain by his actions?

Reprinted with Permission from The Detroit Press.

Think: **As this 1957 cartoon shows,** *Sputnik I* **soared into space while the United States satellite program had yet to get off the ground.** Respond: **Why was it appropriate for Williams, the cartoonist, to draw Uncle Sam in the position shown?**

This one event convinced the nation that American education was weak in some important areas. It had to be made better. For this reason, Congress passed the **National Defense Education Act** in 1958. This law provided federal money to help improve the teaching of science, mathematics, and foreign languages. The law also provided loans to help needy college students pay for their education.

The launching of *Sputnik I* added to the growing rivalry between the United States and the Soviet Union. In the next chapter you will read about other postwar events that made these two great powers bitter enemies.

> **Section Review**
>
> 1. Why did Eisenhower win by a landslide in the elections of 1952 and 1956?
> 2. How did Eisenhower's background as a general influence the kind of president he became?
> 3. Why did Senator McCarthy unfairly accuse so many people of being Communists?
> 4. How did the United States respond to the Soviet launching of *Sputnik I*?

Chapter 31 **659**

CHAPTER SUMMARY

After 1945, the United States was again a nation at peace. But peace required almost as much planning and organizing as war. Millions of GIs had to be helped to adjust to civilian life. Problems of inflation, unemployment, and unrest among many of the nation's workers had to be dealt with. Americans showed their satisfaction with Truman's post-war leadership by electing him president.

Truman promised the American people a "Fair Deal." This was his program of change and reform. But many of his programs were rejected by Congress. Truman used his presidential powers to end discrimination in hiring in the federal government. He also ended the practice of segregation in the armed forces.

Throughout his term, Truman had to deal with charges that there were disloyal and dishonest workers in the government. He worked to restore the people's confidence in their government, but many felt he was not doing enough.

In 1952, a Republican, Dwight D. Eisenhower, was swept into office. Eisenhower supported social programs but felt it was important to keep a careful eye on government spending. He also saw to it that the United States would not fall behind the Soviet Union in the field of science. The federal government began to aid education for the first time.

Key Words

Write a sentence to explain the meaning of each of these terms.

GI Bill of
 Rights
social programs

communism
landslide
censure

Major Events

Choose the answer that best completes the statement.

1. The Taft-Hartley Act

   a) gave the unions more power.
   b) weakened the unions.
   c) allowed more industries to begin unionizing.

2. To improve living conditions, Congress passed the

   a) Twenty-second Amendment.
   b) Internal Security Act.
   c) National Housing Act.

3. President Truman convinced Congress that the nation should

   a) open its doors to more immigrants from Europe.
   b) open its doors to more immigrants from Asia.
   c) limit immigration.

4. Eisenhower's main concern throughout his presidency was

   a) expanding the highway system.
   b) clearing slums.
   c) balancing the budget.

5. The National Defense Education Act was passed as a result of

   a) the launching of *Sputnik I.*
   b) a national teachers' strike.
   c) McCarthy's hunt for spies.

Review

Important Facts

Answer each question with at least one complete sentence.

1. What kinds of problems did returning GIs face?

2. What caused inflation to occur after the war?

3. Why did so many workers go out on strike after the war?

4. What is a closed shop? Why was it outlawed?

5. What decision did Congress make regarding the development of atomic energy?

6. What was the Fair Deal?

7. Why did Republicans oppose the Fair Deal?

8. How did President Truman deal with the problem of disloyal government officials?

9. What role did Senator Joseph McCarthy play in the hunt for Communists in government?

10. How did Eisenhower's background as a general influence the kind of president he became?

11. Which social programs did President Eisenhower support?

12. Why was it difficult for President Eisenhower to achieve balanced budgets?

13. What ended the hunt for Communists in government?

14. What was *Sputnik I*? Why was the news of its launching such a shock to the American people?

Skill Review

Look at the map and graph, then answer the following questions.

1. How many Maryland districts voted Democrat? How many voted Republican?

2. What percentage of the popular vote went to Eisenhower? What percentage went to Stevenson?

3. How did Congressional results compare with presidential results? What does this mean?

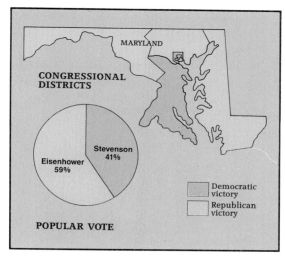

Maryland Presidential Election Results, 1956

Critical Thinking

Write a paragraph to answer each question.

1. Why do you think Truman called his program of change and reform the Fair Deal?

2. Why did Americans begin to fear that communism was spreading to the United States in the years after World War II?

CHAPTER 32
The U.S. and the World 1945–1960

Years 1945–1960

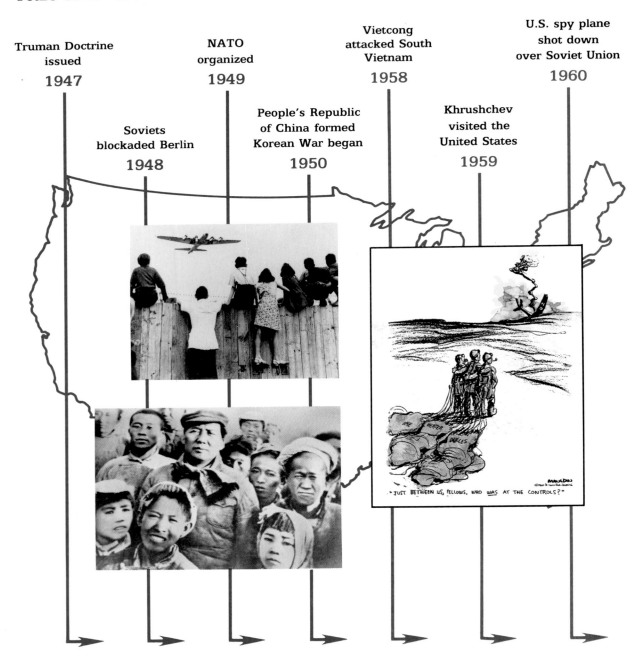

Truman Doctrine issued
1947

Soviets blockaded Berlin
1948

NATO organized
1949

People's Republic of China formed
Korean War began
1950

Vietcong attacked South Vietnam
1958

Khrushchev visited the United States
1959

U.S. spy plane shot down over Soviet Union
1960

"JUST BETWEEN US, FELLOWS, WHO WAS AT THE CONTROLS?"

1. The Cold War in Europe

Learn these important terms:

free market economy
Truman Doctrine
NATO
Berlin airlift
Cold War
Marshall Plan
Warsaw Pact
Berlin blockade

Remember the main idea:

After World War II, the Soviet Union tried to spread communism and gain control of other countries. The United States and other free nations worked to stop them.

Look for answers to these questions:

1. What caused the Cold War to break out between the United States and the Soviet Union?
2. What did the United States do to prevent communism from spreading in Europe after World War II?
3. Why did the Soviet Union's blockade of Berlin fail?

I magine hearing this news in 1946: "From Stettin in the Baltic to Trieste in the Adriatic, an iron curtain has descended across the Continent. . . . I do not believe that Soviet Russia desires war. What they desire is the fruits of war and the indefinite expansion of their power and doctrines." Winston Churchill, former prime minister of Great Britain, was describing the spread of communism across eastern Europe after World War II. Like others listening to this speech, you would probably worry how long peace would last.

In this chapter you will read about the threat that communism and the Soviet Union posed to the postwar world. Communism was spreading throughout Europe, Asia, and the Middle East. You will see what the United States did to stop it and to encourage the growth of democracy.

You will also read about how many nations joined together after the war. Nations with common beliefs thought unity would help their causes. This held true for Communists and for those who feared communism. Which alliances would prove to be strong enough to last?

World War II changed the world in many ways. Empires were destroyed, and Europe was in ruins. In this uncertain time, two countries emerged as the world's leaders—the United States and the Soviet Union.

Both nations were sworn to protect their people and their interests. Unfortunately, their interests could not have been more different. The United States was a democracy with a *free market economy.* In this type of economy, the government does not control production of goods, nor does it set prices. The United States wanted to see democracy restored to the nations of Europe. It also worked to see that democracy and free market economies grew in new nations.

The Soviet Union was a Communist nation with an economy that was strictly controlled by the government. It wanted to protect its borders as best it could from any future invasion. It was also determined to destroy the western way of life, which it saw as selfish and greedy.

Heading for Conflict

The two nations seemed to be headed for conflict. After the war ended, the conflict began to take shape. To protect its borders, the Soviet Union set up Communist governments in the nations of eastern Europe. In doing this, the Soviet Union broke its promise to the Allies to hold free elections in these nations. Soon East Germany, Poland, Hungary, Romania, Albania, and Bulgaria were under Communist control.

The United States was determined to stop the Soviet Union. As a result, a *Cold War* between the Soviet Union and the United States broke out. This Cold War was a new kind of war—a war without weapons. Instead, the two nations used military threats, economic pressure, and harsh words.

Containing Communism

After setting up Communist governments in eastern Europe, the Soviets in 1947 set their sights on Greece. They also wanted to control the water passage between the Black Sea and the Mediterranean Sea. This meant setting up a Communist government in Turkey as well.

But President Truman was determined to contain, or stop, the Soviet Union from spreading communism further. Therefore, in 1947, he asked Congress to provide $400 million to help Greece and Turkey defend themselves. He also promised to help any other European nation to protect itself against the Soviet Union. This plan of opposing the spread of communism was called the *Truman Doctrine.*

Congress approved Truman's request to aid Turkey and Greece. The Soviets were forced to back down soon after this. The Truman Doctrine had been successful in stopping the spread of communism this time.

Helping Europe Rebuild

The countries of western Europe were ripe targets for the Communists. The war had left their economies in ruins. Many of their people were homeless, and their governments were weak. In fact, Communists were elected to positions in several western European governments by promising the people food and better times. The only way to prevent the Communists from taking over completely was to help Europe recover from the war.

To do this, the United States developed the *Marshall Plan,* named after the secretary of state. The Marshall Plan sent money and goods to the western European

Think: Under the Marshall Plan, money and goods were sent to western Europe. Respond: Why was it necessary for the United States to send aid to western Europe, and did it help?

nations. This helped them rebuild their cities, farms, and factories. The aid amounted to more than seventeen billion dollars. Most Americans considered it money well spent. The nations of western Europe recovered and the strength of the Communist party in Europe declined.

A Divided Germany

In 1945, the Allies met at Yalta in the Soviet Union. They agreed to divide Germany and the city of Berlin into four zones, or parts. The United States, Great Britain, the Soviet Union, and France would each control one of the four zones. By dividing it up in this way, the Allies could keep Germany weak and unable to wage war again.

But after the war was over, the United States, France, and Great Britain changed their thinking. They wanted to rebuild Germany into a strong, free nation. The Soviet Union firmly opposed this idea. But in 1948, the United States, Great Britain, and France joined together their three zones of Germany. Their plan was to rebuild this western part of Germany and allow it to govern itself. This plan made the Soviet Union very angry.

The Berlin Blockade

As Germany was divided among the Allies, so was the city of Berlin. Berlin was located deep within the Soviet section of Germany. To get from western Germany to Berlin it was necessary to travel through the Soviet-controlled part of Germany.

In June 1948, the Soviet Union suddenly blockaded all roads leading to Berlin. All travel and all shipments of food and supplies between western Germany and Berlin were cut off. The United States, France, and Great Britain knew that they had to stop this *Berlin blockade.* Other-

Think: During the Berlin blockade the much-needed supplies were flown into the starving city. Respond: What message did the airlift convey to the Soviets?

wise, the people of Berlin would begin to starve, and the Soviet Union would take over their city.

The Americans, the French, and the British took action. American and British planes began flying in all the supplies that the city needed. This included everything from flour to coal. The planes landed at the Templehof Airport in Berlin at the rate of almost one every minute. The *Berlin airlift* brought almost three million tons of food and supplies to the city.

Almost one year later, in May 1949, the Soviet Union ended the blockade. The Soviets had been prevented from taking over Berlin. Several months later, two separate nations were created out of what had once been a single country. West Germany became the Federal Republic of Germany, while East Germany became the German Democratic Republic. Each nation formed its own government.

A Peacetime Alliance

The Berlin blockade was a warning to the United States and the free nations of Europe. It made them realize that western Europe needed protection against the risks of a Soviet attack. In April 1949, the United States, Canada, and ten European nations formed the **North Atlantic Treaty Organization (NATO).** The NATO nations agreed to build up their armed forces to protect themselves from attack by any enemy. Each NATO nation promised to help defend any other NATO nation if it were attacked. The command of NATO forces was given to General Dwight D. Eisenhower.

In response, the Soviet Union created an alliance of its own. The **Warsaw Pact** was an alliance similar in purpose to NATO. Making up the Warsaw Pact were the Soviet Union and its eastern European neighbors, all Communist nations.

Failing To Control Atomic Energy

One of the most serious problems facing the world after World War II was controlling the atomic bomb. Early in 1946, the United Nations set up an Atomic Energy Commission to resolve this problem. At that time, the United States was the only nation that had atomic weapons. The United States suggested that the United Nations be given complete control of atomic energy.

Think: **In their works, artists often express their opinions about important issues.** Respond: **What attitude toward atomic testing has Ben Shahn expressed in his print?**

The United States felt that the United Nations must be given the power to inspect atomic energy plants in every nation. Only then could all nations be assured that others were using atomic energy strictly for peaceful purposes. The Soviet Union refused to agree to this plan. Three years later, in 1949, the Soviet Union exploded its first atomic bomb. The Soviets' reason for refusing suddenly became clear.

In the years that followed, the arms race grew. Each side was building up its supply of weapons. At the same time, the Cold War spread to Asia. In the rest of this chapter, you will read about efforts to prevent communism from spreading to that part of the world.

Think: **When an atomic bomb explodes, a chain reaction releases a vast amount of energy.** Respond: **Why is it important to control atomic weapons and other uses of atomic energy?**

Section Review

1. What is a cold war?
2. How did the Truman Doctrine help to stop, for a time, the spread of communism?
3. What was the purpose of the Marshall Plan?
4. How are the Berlin blockade and the formation of NATO related?

MAP WORKSHOP STUDYING STRATEGIC POSITIONS

THE COLD WAR IN EUROPE, 1955

You can see on this map how the United States and its allies faced the Soviet Union and its satellites. This alignment soon created the Cold War.

Look at the map and the map key.

1. What strategic importance do the Warsaw Pact nations have for the Soviet Union? In other words, what military function could they perform?

2. What European nations not in the Warsaw Pact touch the Soviet Union?

3. Does any European NATO nation border on the Soviet Union? Does any other NATO nation on this map?

4. Strategically, how is Iran's position similar to Turkey's?

5. Make a list of the nonaligned nations that lie between the NATO nations and Warsaw Pact nations. Which of these seems to have the most strategic importance? Could the Soviets afford to have an unfriendly Albania? Why, or why not?

6. Look at the inset. In what way does East Berlin serve the Soviet Union strategically? How is it like a Warsaw Pact nation?

2. The Cold War in Asia

Learn these important terms:

Chinese Nationalists
38th parallel
Korean War
stalemate

Remember the main idea:

In the years after World War II, the United States tried to stop the spread of communism in Asia. However, many Asian nations did not trust the United States and its allies. Communist influence grew, and war broke out in Korea.

Look for answers to these questions:

1. Why did the United States occupy Japan after the war?
2. Why did the Chinese Nationalists lose control of China to the Communists by 1949?
3. What caused the Korean War?

At the end of World War II, the Japanese people were very frightened. Japanese leaders had told their people untrue stories about how the American army tortured its prisoners. Now the American army was coming to occupy Japan. Its purpose was to govern Japan until a democratic form of government could be adopted. But the Japanese were sure they would be tortured or killed.

The American occupation forces arrived in Japan in 1945. Their leader was General Douglas MacArthur. The Japanese watched as twenty-five of their former military and civilian leaders were put on trial for war crimes. When the trial was over, seven were executed. After the trial, the Japanese discovered that the Americans were there not to destroy Japan, but to help the Japanese rebuild their nation.

Democracy Comes to Japan

The United States Army ruled Japan from 1945 to 1947. During that time General MacArthur carried out a number of reforms that improved the Japanese economy. Large farms were divided and sold to small farmers and poor farm workers. The power of the few rich families who once controlled most of Japan's industry ended. The growth of labor unions was encouraged. In addition, Japan's system of education was expanded.

The United States also helped to set up a democratic government in Japan. In 1947, Japan adopted a constitution. Under this constitution, the Japanese emperor remained the head of the government. But he had very little power. The real

Think: **After World War II, Japan became a democracy. The new constitution gave women the right to vote.** Respond: **What do voting rights give to the people?**

power of the Japanese government was given to a two-house legislature. All Japanese citizens, including women, were given the right to vote. And a bill of rights was written to protect the freedoms of the Japanese people. With the adoption of this constitution, the American army no longer ruled Japan. However, American troops remained there until 1951.

Democracy in Other Parts of Asia

After World War II, many of Europe's colonial empires were broken up. Former colonies were given their independence. The United States led the way by giving the people of the Philippine Islands their independence in 1946. Great Britain also allowed its colonies in Asia to become independent nations. And it asked the United Nations to handle its territory of Palestine. The United Nations divided Palestine into an Arab state and a Jewish state, Israel. France and the Netherlands, however, were slower to free their colonies. The Dutch gave up their fight to hold Indonesia (in-duh-NEE-zhuh) in 1949. The French finally left Vietnam in 1954, after a long, hard war with the Vietnamese people.

Many of these newly independent nations started out with democratic governments. For some, democracy worked. For others, it did not, and other forms of government were tried in its place.

Those Asian colonies that had to fight for their independence strongly disliked their former European rulers. These European nations were now the allies of the United States. Therefore, many of the new Asian leaders did not trust the United States. This created problems for the United States when it looked for support in Asia to combat communism. Many of the new nations, such as India, Pakistan (PAH-kih-STAN), and Indonesia, preferred to stay out of the Cold War.

Think: **After World War II, Chiang Kai-shek met with Ambassador Stuart and General Marshall.** Respond: **Why did American leaders choose to support Chiang Kai-shek?**

A Communist Takeover in China

Communism spread in Asia during the Cold War, and China was its first target. When World War II ended, most of China was under the control of Chiang Kai-shek (CHY-AHNG KY-SHEK), the leader of the *Chinese Nationalists*. Many Chinese were unhappy with the Chinese Nationalist government, however, because it was quite corrupt.

Since 1927, another group had been battling the Nationalists for control of China. This group was the Chinese Communists, and their leader was Mao Zedong (MAOW zuh-DOONG). Mao's forces controlled only one section of China.

Think: **Mao Zedong put tight controls on the arts and education. He gave land to the poor.** Respond: **Who within China would have supported Mao, and who would have been against him? Why?**

But support for the Communists had been growing. Many Chinese liked Mao's policy of taking land from the wealthy and dividing it up among the poor. By 1945, the Chinese Communists were strong enough to start a revolt against the government of Chiang Kai-shek.

The United States tried to stop the war before it started, but American efforts failed. When war broke out, the United States started to send supplies and weapons to Chiang Kai-shek. However, by 1949, the Communists controlled nearly all of China. The Nationalists were forced to retreat to the island of Formosa (present-day Taiwan), off the mainland of China. In the end, Communist government was established in China. The new country became known as the People's Republic of China.

The United States still considered Chiang Kai-shek to be the ruler of all China. America refused to recognize, or deal with, the Communist government in China. The Soviet Union, however, immediately recognized the new Communist government. And in February 1950, the Soviet Union and the People's Republic of China formed an alliance.

The Korean Conflict

Japan had controlled the land of Korea since the early 1900s. When World War II ended, the Allies decided to break up the Japanese empire. Lands once ruled by Japan were to become free and independent. American and Soviet armies moved in and replaced the Japanese forces in Korea. The Americans occupied the part of Korea south of the **38th parallel**, or line of latitude. The Soviets occupied the northern part of the country. This occupation was temporary until free elections were held.

In 1948, free elections were held in the south under the supervision of the United

Think: **American soldiers moved across Korean mountains. American and South Korean troops tried to hold back the North Koreans.** Respond: **What were the causes of the war?**

Nations. However, the Soviets refused to allow an election in the north. Instead, the Soviets set up a Communist government. North Korea became the Democratic People's Republic of Korea. South Korea became the Republic of Korea, and its government was recognized by the United States. Each government thought it had a right to control the entire country.

Suddenly, in June of 1950, the North Korean army invaded South Korea. The United Nations asked the North Korean government to end its attack, but North Korea refused. The United Nations quickly formed an army and sent it to help South Korea. This army, led by General MacArthur, was mostly American.

THE KOREAN WAR, 1950-1953

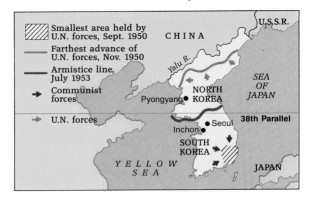

Think of a paragraph as being made up of different sizes of building blocks. Words are the smaller blocks, and sentences are the larger blocks. The way these building blocks are put together is the organization of the paragraph.

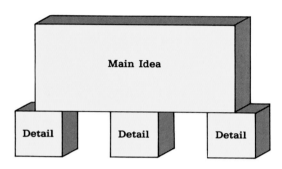

Every paragraph has a *main idea* that is stated in a sentence. The main idea might be the first sentence in a paragraph, but it can be any other sentence. Other sentences in a paragraph are *detail sentences* that support the main idea.

A paragraph can be organized in several ways. The detail sentences can *explain*, *describe*, or *give examples* of the main idea.

Notice how the following paragraph is organized.

General MacArthur returned home to a hero's welcome. The crowds that lined the streets of New York gathered under a cloud of ticker tape that showered down on MacArthur in 1951. The people of America remembered the heroism of his career in World War II more than his removal from the Korean War by President Truman.

The first sentence of the paragraph above is the main idea. Other sentences give details that *explain* the main idea. These detail sentences answer the questions *who*, *where*, *when*, and *why*.

Who: people of America
Where: New York
When: 1951
Why: MacArthur's reputation in World War II

Another way to organize a paragraph is with details that *describe* the main idea. Look at the first paragraph under the section heading "Democracy Comes to Japan." The main idea is stated in the second sentence. The sentences that follow the main idea are detail sentences. They describe the reforms that are stated in the main idea sentence.

1 What are the four reforms that are described?

A third way to organize a paragraph is with details that *give examples* of the main idea. Look at the first paragraph under the section heading "Democracy in Other Parts of Asia."

2 What is the main idea?

3 What examples are given to support the main idea?

Think: Hunching to avoid the force of their own gun, a United States mortar crew fired at North Koreans. Respond: Why were American soldiers involved in the Korean War?

A War Without a Winner

At first, the United Nations army was almost pushed off the Korean peninsula by the North Korean army. But by October 1950, the United Nations army began to push back. MacArthur's troops forced the North Koreans back across the 38th parallel. They fought their way deep into North Korea. General MacArthur was sure the **Korean War**, as the struggle was called, was almost over.

But the attack on North Korea frightened the Chinese Communists who shared a border with North Korea. They sent hundreds of thousands of soldiers to help North Korea fight the United Nations army. With the help of the Chinese, the North Korean army was able to succeed. The United Nations army was driven back across the 38th parallel into South Korea once again.

General MacArthur now felt that the only way to win the war was to attack Communist China. However, President Truman believed that an attack on China might bring the Soviet Union into the war. This could have led to a new world war. MacArthur disagreed with President Truman and spoke out against him. Truman warned MacArthur to stop. MacArthur ignored the warning, so President Truman removed him from command.

Peace talks were started in July 1951, but they made little progress. The war dragged on through 1951 and 1952. It had become a *stalemate*, with neither side able to win. In the rest of this chapter, you will read how the Korean War finally came to an end, only to be replaced by other conflicts around the world.

Think: In April 1951, Truman removed General MacArthur from command. Respond: According to this cartoon, how did the American people (John Q. Public) feel about Truman's decision?

Section Review

1. How did the United States help Japan to become a peaceful and free nation after World War II?

2. Why did some of the newly independent nations of Asia distrust the United States?

3. Why did the United States refuse to recognize the government of Mao Zedong?

4. Why is the word *stalemate* used to describe the Korean War?

3. The Cold War Continues

Think: The faces of these soldiers show how they felt when a truce was signed, ending the Korean War. Respond: Which side, if either, do you think won, and why?

Learn these important terms:

Vietminh
Eisenhower Doctrine
summit conference
Vietcong
17th parallel
SEATO
CENTO

Remember the main idea:

The end of the Korean War did not mark the end of the Cold War. In the 1950s, the United States found itself involved in cold-war conflicts in Asia and the Middle East.

Look for answers to these questions:

1. How did the Korean War come to an end?
2. Why and when did the United States get involved in the fighting in Vietnam?
3. What made the United States and the Soviet Union more willing to end the Cold War by the end of the 1950s?

Dwight Eisenhower promised that if elected president in 1952, he would go to Korea to try to end the war. Impatient with a war that seemed to be going nowhere, Americans gave their support to Eisenhower. President Eisenhower kept his promise. He left for Korea shortly after he was elected.

Eisenhower's visit was not enough to get both sides to lay down their arms. The two sides could not agree. One issue in particular was hotly debated. The Communists wanted the United Nations to return all prisoners of war. But some of the prisoners did not want to return to North Korea. The war dragged on.

An End to the Korean War

Finally, seven months after President Eisenhower's visit, an end to the fighting in Korea was arranged. Under an agreement reached in July 1953, Korea was still to be divided into two parts. A two-and-a-half-mile zone was set up between North Korea and South Korea. Neither side was to station any troops in this zone. The boundary that separated the two nations in 1953 was almost exactly where it had been before the war started.

Think: A ticker-tape parade welcomed home the soldiers who fought in the Korean War. Respond: Why is it important for soldiers to know that their country supported them?

After three years of fighting, the war was over, but there seemed to be little to celebrate. The war had cost the United States over fifteen billion dollars and the loss of over thirty thousand lives. Yet the United States had shown itself to be a world leader. In addition, the war had stopped communism from spreading in one part of Asia.

Trouble in Vietnam

Korea was not the only Asian trouble spot that concerned the United States in the 1950s. The situation in Vietnam seemed to be getting worse.

After World War II, a civil war tore Vietnam apart. On one side were Vietnamese Communists and other Vietnamese who supported independence from France. These people were called the **Vietminh**. On the other side were Vietnamese who wanted to maintain the ties with France.

Each side set up a government of its own, with the Vietminh in the north and the French in the south. In 1950, the People's Republic of China began to aid the Vietminh. The United States responded by giving military aid to the French.

In May 1954, the French forces were badly beaten at the battle of Dien Bien Phu (dee-enn bee-enn FOO). A peace conference was called at Geneva, Switzerland, to try to end the civil war. France, the United States, Great Britain, the Soviet Union, China, and four other nations made an agreement. This agreement would divide Vietnam into two zones until free elections could be held. The Vietminh were to move north of the **17th parallel**, while the French would stay south of that line. The elections, scheduled for July 1956, would allow the Vietnamese to choose the type of government they wanted. In this way, Vietnam would become one nation once again.

The government in the south kept putting off the elections. It feared that the Communists would win. In 1958, angry Communist rebels within South Vietnam began to attack government forces. These rebels were known as the **Vietcong**. In order to prevent the Communists from taking over South Vietnam, President Eisenhower sent money, war supplies, and American army advisors. He wanted America to help the government of South Vietnam fight the Vietcong.

Eisenhower's reason for defending the government of South Vietnam was made clear at a press conference. He said the nations of Southeast Asia were like a row of dominoes. If one country fell to the Communists, they would all fall. But in spite of American assistance, by 1961 the Communists controlled a large part of South Vietnam.

An Asian Alliance

The United States thought that a NATO-like alliance in Asia would help to stop the spread of communism. In 1954, the United States joined seven other nations in forming the **Southeast Asia Treaty Organization (SEATO)**.

Members of the alliance included Great Britain, France, Thailand, Australia, New Zealand, Pakistan, and the Philippines. However, India and other important Asian nations refused to join SEATO. Thus, SEATO was weaker than NATO.

Trouble in Formosa

You may recall that Chiang Kai-shek moved his government to the island of Formosa, now Taiwan. President Eisenhower, like President Truman before him, promised to protect this government from Communist attack. In 1958, an attack seemed likely. Keeping his promise, President Eisenhower sent a fleet of ships to defend the island. This stopped the Chinese Communists from attacking.

Think: **In the late fifties, American aid to South Vietnam came in many forms, such as this bulldozer.** Respond: **What other kinds of aid did the South Vietnamese receive from America?**

Think: **Although many strong nations were represented in SEATO conferences, some Asian nations refused to join in.** Respond: **What did the United States hope SEATO would prevent?**

Think: **During the battle of Dien Bien Phu, French and Vietminh soldiers clashed. French soldiers sought safety in trenches.** Respond: **What was the result of the French defeat?**

Think: **When a Communist attack on Formosa seemed likely, American ships were sent to protect the tiny island.** Respond: **What effect did the ships have on Communist China?**

ASIA IN 1954

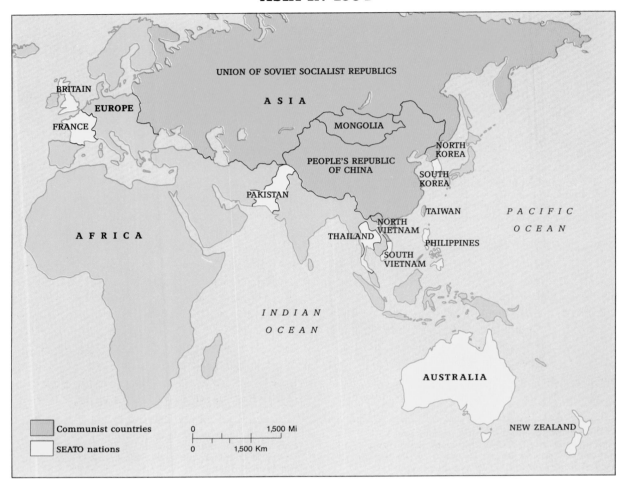

UNION OF SOVIET SOCIALIST REPUBLICS

BRITAIN

EUROPE

FRANCE

ASIA

MONGOLIA

PEOPLE'S REPUBLIC OF CHINA

NORTH KOREA

SOUTH KOREA

PAKISTAN

TAIWAN

NORTH VIETNAM

THAILAND

SOUTH VIETNAM

PHILIPPINES

AFRICA

PACIFIC OCEAN

INDIAN OCEAN

AUSTRALIA

NEW ZEALAND

Communist countries

SEATO nations

0   1,500 Mi

0   1,500 Km

Troubles in Other Parts of the World

In 1956 the Hungarian people tried to rise up against the Communist government that ruled them. But Soviet troops and tanks soon overpowered them. The United Nations called on the Soviet Union to withdraw. But the Soviets ignored the request. The United States could have helped the Hungarians, but only at the risk of starting another world war. The Soviet troops crushed the Hungarian revolt. As a result, the people of eastern Europe realized that Americans would not be the ones to free them. This was a sad defeat for the United States in the Cold War.

Think: When the Soviets drove tanks through the streets of Hungary, the United States chose to do nothing. Respond: Do you agree or disagree with this lack of action? Explain.

Think: **When Egypt seized the Suez Canal in 1956, Britain and France sent troops to retake the canal.** Respond: **How did the United States and the Soviet Union react?**

During the Hungarian revolt, a war broke out in the Middle East. This war started when President Gamal Abdel Nasser of Egypt seized control of the Suez Canal. The Suez Canal, though located on Egyptian territory, was owned by the British and the French. The nation that controlled the canal also controlled the amount of oil that could be shipped to western Europe. With Nasser in control of the canal, western Europe's oil supply could be cut off.

Why had Nasser seized the canal? The Americans and the British had promised to give Egypt money to help it build a huge dam on the Nile River. When the Americans discovered that Nasser was also asking the Soviets for aid, they withdrew their support. In anger, Nasser took control of the canal.

The British, the French, and the Israelis tried to negotiate a solution to the crisis with Nasser. But this proved unsuccessful. Instead, Egypt seemed to be building up its military strength. Finally in October 1956, the French and British sent troops into Egypt to try to retake the canal. The Israelis joined the invasion.

But within a few weeks, the United States and the United Nations forced these three nations to withdraw their troops. This led to bad feelings between the United States and its allies. Additionally, during the invasion, the Soviet Union had threatened to fight Britain, France, and Israel if they did not withdraw. As a result, the Soviet Union's image in the Middle East was strengthened.

The United States feared that the Soviet Union would become too strong in the Middle East. For this reason, President Eisenhower promised to send aid and to help defend any Middle Eastern nation against communism. This policy was called the *Eisenhower Doctrine*.

The Eisenhower Doctrine got its first test in 1958. The country of Lebanon asked for help against an Arab uprising thought to have Soviet support. Eisenhower sent American marines to help Lebanon fight these rebels. The United States also helped to form the *Central Treaty Organization* (*CENTO*) to defend the Middle East. But some Middle Eastern nations refused to join this group, and it was never very strong.

Think: **American marines helped the Lebanese government restore order when Arab nationalists rebelled in 1958.** Respond: **How effective do you think violence is in bringing about change?**

HISTORY MAKERS

Margaret Bourke-White

The Indestructible Photographer

The old lady stopped and stared at the young man running toward her across the rice paddies, then she rushed to meet him. "It's a dream," she said. "It can't be true. My son is dead. My son has been dead for two years. It's a dream."

As the old woman and her son hugged, the moment was recorded by photographer Margaret Bourke-White, documenting for the world the story of a family torn apart by war. Bourke-White was covering the Korean War for *Life* magazine, showing the effect of the war on the Koreans themselves.

Margaret Bourke-White began her photographic career in college. At first she concentrated on taking pictures of buildings and factories. But after a visit to the Dust Bowl in 1934, she became more and more concerned with human beings and their feelings. The first cover of *Life* was a Bourke-White picture of a new dam. Inside, the magazine featured her photo-essay of the people in the surrounding communities.

Bourke-White was the first woman war correspondent with the U.S. Army. She sailed with troops to North Africa during World War II.

When the ship she was on was torpedoed, she photographed the lifeboats and the rescue planes. This was not her only brush with danger and fear. When she flew with a pilot on a bombing raid, her plane was hit several times. And at the end of the war, her camera showed the horrors of the Nazi concentration camps to the world.

After World War II, Margaret Bourke-White did photo-essays in India and South Africa, always highlighting the human aspects of life. In 1952, she covered the Korean War. In Korea she began to have difficulty walking. She had developed Parkinson's disease, an illness that affects muscles and muscle coordination. Bourke-White had thought of herself as "Indestructible Maggie," survivor of wars and disasters. But now she faced an enemy she couldn't defeat.

Bourke-White fought against Parkinson's disease, and wrote about her illness in *Life*, so that others with Parkinson's could see the positive results of exercise and surgery. As in so many of her assignments, her personal courage and her insights into the human condition became an inspiration to many.

Trying To End the Cold War

Many events made it seem as if the world was on the verge of another global war. However, the United States, the NATO countries, and the Soviet Union tried to work out some of their differences during the 1950s.

New leaders came to power in the Soviet Union after the death of Joseph Stalin. These leaders saw no harm in meeting with western nations to work out differences. In addition, the growing arms race helped change attitudes. Both sides had the power to destroy each other many times over. With that kind of power, both sides recognized the need to avoid mistakes and to promote communication.

In this spirit of greater cooperation, a *summit conference* was held at Geneva, Switzerland in 1955. This was a meeting of the top leaders of the United States, the Soviet Union, Great Britain, and France. No problems were solved at this meeting. However, the free nations and the Communist nations showed that they might work together to live in peace.

The Cold War thawed further when the new Soviet ruler, Nikita Khrushchev (ne-KEE-ta KROOSH-choff), visited the United States in 1959. At that time, President Eisenhower and Premier Khrushchev agreed to hold another summit conference in May 1960 in Paris. Khrushchev's stated goal was "peaceful coexistence."

But just before the meeting was to take place, an American military plane flying over the Soviet Union was shot down. The pilot admitted that he had been taking photographs of Soviet military bases. Khrushchev was furious. He demanded that the United States end all spying missions and apologize for the incident. Eisenhower agreed to end the flights, but he refused to apologize. As a result, the Soviet leader walked out on the summit, and the Cold War continued.

Think: Things were looking up when Premier Khrushchev visited Washington in September 1959. Respond: What caused Khrushchev to walk out of the Paris summit in 1960?

The world was a very different place in 1960 than it had been in 1945. The same was true for the United States. In the next chapter, you will read about changes in American life during this time period.

Section Review

1. What did the United States gain from its involvement in the Korean War?

2. What caused a civil war to break out in Vietnam?

3. Which Cold War crisis represented a defeat for the United States? Why?

4. How did the United States and the Soviet Union try to work out their differences in the 1950s?

CHAPTER SUMMARY

After World War II, the United States and the Soviet Union emerged as the two most powerful nations in the world. But their different interests led them into a conflict that became known as the Cold War. This war was a war of words, military threats, and economic pressure. The two nations came into conflict in Greece, Turkey, and Berlin.

The United States tried to stop the spread of communism in Asia. It helped the Japanese rebuild their economy and create a constitutional government. It supported the Chinese Nationalists in their unsuccessful attempt to fight off a Communist takeover. The United States also joined the United Nations in preventing Communists from taking over South Korea.

The Cold War continued into the 1950s. The United States went to the aid of the South Vietnamese to keep the Vietnamese Communists from taking over. The United States also formed alliances with the free nations of Asia and the Middle East. The United States pledged itself to defend any Middle Eastern nation against communism. By the end of the 1950s, both the United States and the Soviet Union began to see the danger of letting the Cold War continue. Efforts were made to end the Cold War, but distrust and deception prevented these attempts from making any progress.

Key Words

Write a sentence to explain the meaning of each of these terms.

Cold War   Vietminh
Marshall Plan   summit
Korean War   conference
stalemate

Major Events

Choose the answer that best completes the statement.

1. The Truman Doctrine
   a) helped to stop the spread of communism.
   b) helped Europe rebuild.
   c) divided Germany among the Allies.

2. The alliance formed by the U.S., Canada, and Europe was
   a) the Warsaw Pact.
   b) SEATO.
   c) NATO.

3. The Cold War turned "hot" in
   a) Berlin.
   b) Korea.
   c) the Philippines.

4. As a result of the Korean War,
   a) the Communists gained land.
   b) the South Koreans profited.
   c) the boundary separating the two nations was unchanged.

5. To prevent more Communist takeovers in Southeast Asia, Eisenhower sent aid to
   a) Thailand.
   b) Taiwan.
   c) South Vietnam.

Review

Important Facts

Answer each question with at least one complete sentence.

1. Why did the Soviet Union blockade West Berlin?

2. How was the crisis in Berlin brought to an end?

3. How did the Soviet Union respond to the formation of NATO?

4. List the reforms carried out in post-war Japan by the American occupation forces.

5. Who were the Chinese Nationalists? Why did they lose the support of the Chinese people?

6. Why did President Truman remove General MacArthur from command in Korea?

7. Who were the Vietcong? How successful were they by 1961?

8. Explain why the United States did not help the Hungarians in 1956.

9. What was the outcome of the Suez crisis of 1956?

10. Where did the Eisenhower Doctrine get its first test?

11. Why did the Soviet Union become more willing to work out its differences with the United States during the last half of the 1950s?

12. What incident put an end to the Soviet Union's willingness to work out its differences with the United States?

Skill Review

Read the paragraph, then answer the following questions.

A chance for a peaceful control of nuclear weapons still existed in 1946. The Soviet Union may have begun the arms race by refusing to agree to a plan, proposed by the United States, for UN inspection of atomic production. One reason for the Soviet veto was that the USSR did not want to submit to inspections. Another reason was more frightening. At that time, the Soviets were close to developments that would give them nuclear weapons.

1. Which sentence is the main idea?

2. Which is the first detail sentence that helps to explain the main idea?

3. Which is the second detail sentence that helps to explain the main idea?

4. How do the other sentences in the paragraph function?

5. What other ways of organizing the paragraph might the author have chosen?

Critical Thinking

Write a paragraph to answer each question.

1. Why did a Cold War develop between the United States and the Soviet Union after World War II?

2. Compare the Truman Doctrine with the Eisenhower Doctrine.

33
The American People 1945-1962

Years 1945-1962

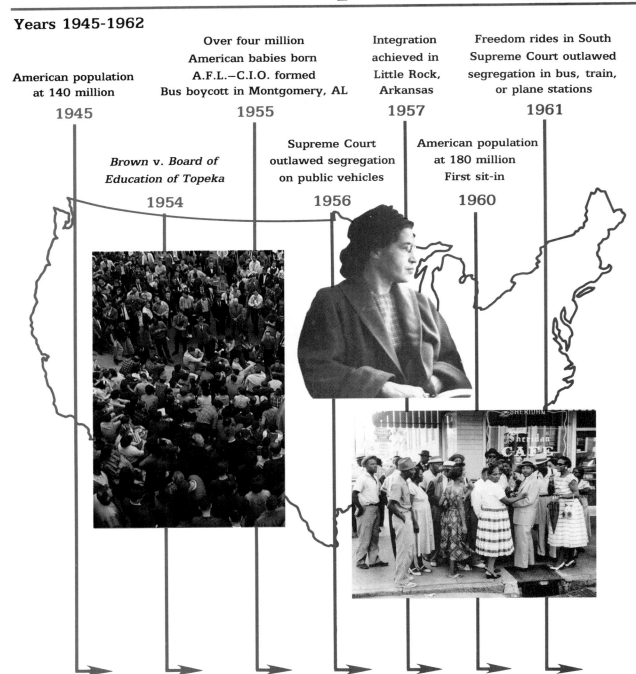

American population
at 140 million

1945

Over four million
American babies born
A.F.L.–C.I.O. formed
Bus boycott in Montgomery, AL

1955

Integration
achieved in
Little Rock,
Arkansas

1957

Freedom rides in South
Supreme Court outlawed
segregation in bus, train,
or plane stations

1961

*Brown v. Board of
Education of Topeka*

1954

Supreme Court
outlawed segregation
on public vehicles

1956

American population
at 180 million
First sit-in

1960

America was a very different place in the years after World War II. Patterns of work, play, and living changed. Most of these changes were caused by growth. America's population increased rapidly. More products of all kinds were needed. To make these products quickly enough, Americans discovered new ways of working. People's lives were changed.

Some Americans welcomed the changes, while others found the changes cause for concern. Critics warned that the American way of life was becoming mass-produced. Millions of Americans were wearing the same fashions and living in the same types of houses. Identical suburban communities sprang up.

But these similarities also meant that more Americans were enjoying a high standard of living. Americans bought more things than ever before. They owned cars, houses, televisions, and other items. Americans also enjoyed an easier time at work. They wanted paid vacations and other extras. And they got them. However, there were many Americans who did not receive what they wanted. These Americans did not enjoy the postwar prosperity. As you read this chapter, you will learn about these groups. You will read about their constant struggle for equality.

1. Changes in American Life

Learn these important terms:

"baby boom" generation
Sunbelt
abstract art
mass-produced culture

Remember the main idea:

After World War II, the population of the United States boomed, and many people moved to the suburbs. Newly built homes were soon filled with all sorts of consumer goods. With more spare time than ever before, Americans took an interest in many kinds of recreational and cultural activities.

Look for answers to these questions:

1. Why did America's population boom after World War II?
2. Why did many Americans move to the suburbs?
3. What new form of home entertainment captured the interest of Americans in the 1950s?

America's population grew rapidly after World War II. Between 1945 and 1960, the nation grew from 140 million to 180 million people. What sparked this growth? During World War II, many GIs had put off marriage. Now that they were home, millions of GIs were eager to get married and settle down.

This "wedding boom" sparked another boom as the number of babies born began

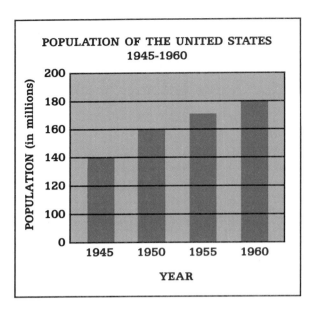

**POPULATION OF THE UNITED STATES
1945-1960**

to soar. Before the war, the number of babies born each year averaged about 2.5 million. By 1955, that number had grown to more than four million, and it continued to grow throughout the 1950s. The children born in the postwar years became known as the *"baby boom" generation.*

The Growth of the Suburbs

For many young families, the city did not seem to be a good place to raise children. Not only was city housing expen-

Think: **Levittown, Pennsylvania, was one of the first tract-housing developments.** Respond: **What changes did these rows of identical houses bring with them?**

sive, but it was also hard to find. The idea of living in a cramped apartment on a dirty, treeless street was not appealing.

Construction companies recognized the need for housing. After the war, they began buying up large pieces of farm land on the outskirts of the cities. There they built mass-produced homes that fit the budgets of families just starting out.

One of the pioneers in this type of homebuilding was William Levitt. He and his sons used the techniques of the assembly line in creating communities such as Levittown, New York, and Levittown, Pennsylvania. To build one of these suburbs, Levitt would hire armies of workers. First they leveled a huge piece of land. Then they installed water, gas, sewer, and electrical lines. Next, carpenters built row upon row of identical houses. Finally, roofers, plumbers, and decorators finished the job. When it was done, the new suburb had schools, playgrounds, and community centers, all ready to be immediately occupied.

Americans moved to the suburbs in large numbers. The new superhighways made it possible for them to commute to jobs in nearby cities. Thus, they had a double advantage. They lived in a clean, safe place, yet they were also close to work and the cultural activities of a city.

A Population on the Move

Most of the people who moved to the suburbs were young, white, and fairly well-off. But other groups of Americans were on the move, too. In fact, by the late 1950s, one-fifth of the population was changing its address each year.

One shift in the population occurred in rural America. Farm technology had improved so much after the war that fewer farmers were needed to feed the nation. By 1960, only three out of every ten Americans still lived on farms or in rural areas.

Think: One or two people working with farm machinery could do the work of ten people. Fewer farm hands were needed. Respond: How did this change affect all of America?

Think: Enjoying her retirement in Florida, this woman takes a leisurely ride in the sun. Respond: Why were so many retired people moving to the Sunbelt?

Americans also began to move from the northern and eastern parts of the country into the *Sunbelt.* This area consists of states in the southern and western parts of the country where the weather is warm and sunny most of the time. Retired Americans were attracted to the climate, while younger Americans were drawn to the growing job opportunities and the more casual lifestyle. The Pacific states saw their population increase by more than 40 percent between 1950 and 1960. Florida's growth rate was even larger, almost 79 percent.

Increased Leisure Time

Americans also had more leisure, or free, time than ever before. Part of the reason for this was the invention of new machines that made housework easier and faster. Steam irons, electric mixers, automatic dishwashers, electric clothes dryers, and other appliances reduced the amount of time needed for household chores. Frozen foods and freezers cut down on trips to the supermarket and shortened cooking time.

Leisure Time Activities

Finding things to do with all this free time was not hard. Many Americans made summer family vacations an annual event. More people bought motor boats, went out to dinner, visited the beauty parlor, and played golf than ever before.

At home, Americans were absorbed in watching the newest form of home entertainment, the television. The television itself was not a new invention, but World War II had interrupted work on its development. After the war, the television industry grew rapidly. By 1960, nine out of ten American families had a television set. More homes had television sets than had telephones, bathtubs, or even indoor

Think: Television brought entertainment into the home of nearly every American. Some questioned its value. Respond: What problems and benefits did TV bring with it?

toilets! And many Americans were watching television five hours a day.

Television had a powerful influence on American culture. Almost an entire nation could watch the same news program, variety show, or political debate. What was seen on television became a common topic of conversation. And advertisers could reach a nationwide audience.

Critics called television the "idiot box" and blamed it for popularizing what they called a *mass-produced culture.* They thought that culture was being created to fit the needs of broadcasters and the wants of viewers, rather than being created for its own sake. They feared that mass-produced culture would never be able to produce culture of quality.

Literature, Art and Music in the 1950s

The critics had little to worry about. Despite the fact that Americans were watching a great deal of television, they were also attending the theater, going to concerts, and visiting museums. Americans also were reading more books.

One reason that Americans were reading so much had to do with the great increase in the number of paperback books printed after 1945. Thousands of the world's finest books became available to Americans in a low-cost form.

In the world of art, many painters went their own ways and developed their own styles. Some became concerned with color, others with line, still others with texture. Their work became known as *abstract art*, or art that does not try to make what it shows look real.

Think: Not wanting to make his work look like that of a camera, Hans Hofmann made *The Gate* look far different from a real gate. Respond: How did the camera change art?

CITIES AND SUBURBS, 1947 AND 1957

Changes in the ways people live are as much a part of history as wars and politics. By comparing these two maps, you will see some of the important developments in the United States after World War II. These maps show the typical pattern of change in a *metropolitan area*. A metropolitan area includes a city and its surrounding suburbs.

Look at the map for 1947.

1. Where would you find large office buildings?

2. Where are the industrial sites?

3. What is a satellite city?

4. What are corporate city limits? What relationship do they have to the city's taxes?

5. How does Metro City compare in size with suburban areas?

Now look at the map for 1957.

6. Has the size of the central business district changed in Metro City? Has it changed in the satellite city?

7. What has happened to the industrial sites?

8. What improvements in transportation have been built?

9. Where are the new shopping centers located? Why?

10. What has happened to suburban sprawl? What factors do you think have contributed to this change?

11. What effects might suburban sprawl have on Metro City?

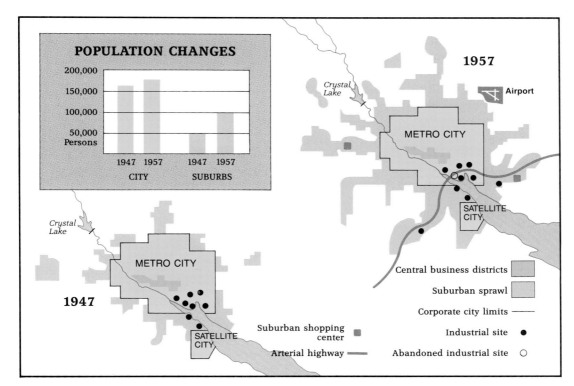

POPULATION CHANGES

	CITY		SUBURBS	
	1947	1957	1947	1957

Central business districts
Suburban sprawl
Corporate city limits
Industrial site ●
Abandoned industrial site ○
Suburban shopping center
Arterial highway

The voice of Elvis Presley (1935–1977) was quite famous. However, his movements on stage, the source of much controversy, contributed to his popularity.

Listening to records became a popular form of musical entertainment as the quality of record players and records improved. Many adults listened to jazz, while the younger generation made rock-and-roll its favorite popular music.

The American way of life had greatly changed by the end of the 1950s. In the next section, you will read about the changes that were also occurring in the American workplace and economy.

Section Review

1. How was a Levitt suburb built?
2. Why did many people move to the Sunbelt after the war?
3. What did Americans do with their leisure time in the 1950s?
4. Why were some Americans so critical of television?
5. How did art change in the 1950s?

---

2. Changes in the American Economy

Learn these important terms:

automation   A.F.L.–C.I.O.
fringe benefits   poverty

Remember the main idea:

The combination of the baby boom and the housing boom had a positive influence on the American economy. Jobs were plentiful, and wages were high. However, not everyone shared in the prosperity of the 1950s.

Look for answers to these questions:

1. What caused the American economy to boom in the 1950s?
2. How did automation affect American workers?
3. How did unions change during the 1950s?

The baby boom and the housing boom fueled the American economy during the 1950s. Families needed diapers, toys, and food for the young ones. They also needed furniture and appliances for their new homes. By 1956, 96 percent of American families had refrigerators, four out of five had a television set, and one in ten had air conditioning.

Americans also needed cars to get from their homes in the suburbs to their jobs in the cities. At the beginning of the 1950s, one out of every ten American families owned more than one car. By the end of the 1950s, one out of five American families owned more than one car.

The Boom Industries

A boom in one industry seemed to create a boom in others. More cars meant more gas stations, restaurants, drive-in movie theaters, and motels. Shopping centers, with their huge parking lots, became a common sight on the suburban landscape. These centers attracted suburban shoppers in droves as store owners began to issue credit cards. Americans were caught up in a ''buy now, pay later'' frame of mind.

The largest industry in America was still automobile manufacturing, but the chemical industry was close behind. The use of plastics, detergents, and new types of drugs helped the chemical industry grow. The electrical industry and the electronics industry, which made parts for televisions, radios, and computers, were also growing. As airplane travel became more affordable and convenient, airplane manufacturing became a major industry, too. All of these industries provided many new jobs for American workers.

Workers in the 1950s

Most American workers prospered during the 1950s. Although the prices of most items were high, wages were good and always rising. More people had jobs than ever before.

The reason workers were making good wages was **automation**. Automation is the use of automatic, or self-operating, machines to do many jobs. Automated equipment can quickly perform tasks that usually require many people and many hours. Automation enabled workers in the 1950s to produce more goods in a shorter amount of time than ever before. For example, an automobile that took 310 work hours to produce in 1945 took only 155 hours to produce in 1960. With this increase in production, the owners of businesses could raise the wages of workers without raising the prices of goods.

Increased production also meant a shorter work week for many American workers. In the 1940s, the average work week was forty-four hours. By 1960, it

Think: The first shopping centers look different from today's shopping malls. But the idea of grouping together a variety of services and retail stores near a large parking area began with these early centers. Respond: How did the car and suburb living influence the way many Americans shop?

had fallen to forty hours, and in some industries employees worked only thirty-five hours per week.

Vacation time was increased, too. Before World War II, paid vacations were practically unknown. In the 1940s, the average paid vacation was one week. By 1960, most employees received two weeks of paid vacation.

But automation was not welcomed by all workers. Unskilled workers found fewer jobs available as machines did their work for them. Although automation eliminated certain jobs, it did create others because workers were needed to service and operate the machines. Unskilled workers realized that they needed to learn a skill in order to get a job.

Think: Unions tried to get companies to train people or find jobs for those replaced by machines. To belong to a union, men like those below paid dues. Respond: Would you support unions? Explain.

More Powerful Unions

Unions continued to grow in size and to become stronger in the 1950s. In 1955, the two main labor unions, the American Federation of Labor (A.F. of L.) and the Congress of Industrial Organizations (C.I.O.), joined together and formed one union, the *A.F.L.–C.I.O.* Almost nine out of ten Union members belonged to this organization. Its size gave it power, which

Think: CIO president Walter Reuther and AFL president George Meany together begin the first convention of the AFL-CIO. Respond: Why did the two unions join together?

meant most problems among workers and employers could be settled by talks and meetings rather than by strikes.

The strikes that did occur were not over wages or hours. Sometimes labor unions held strikes to gain *fringe benefits* for American workers. Fringe benefits are special benefits, such as paid vacations, health insurance, and pension plans, given to workers by the companies they work for. More importantly, labor unions in the 1950s called strikes because of automation. Unions wanted companies to retrain their workers and find jobs for the people who were being replaced by machines.

Poverty amid Prosperity

Although most Americans lived well during the 1950s, some lived in *poverty*. They could not afford proper food, clothing, or housing. In the 1950s, 25 million American families lived on an income of less than $4,000 per year. This meant nearly one out of every five Americans lived in poverty.

Who were these people? Many below the poverty line lived in rural America. Many farm families, including Mexican-Americans who were traveling farmworkers, earned far less than $4,000 a year. Whether on farms or in cities, many Americans older than sixty-five also had barely enough money to live on.

By far the largest number of poor people lived in cities. Puerto Ricans who had left their island for a better life settled in the big cities of the Northeast. Growing numbers of black Americans also left their homes in the South for the cities of the Northeast and the Midwest. These groups were disappointed by what they found. A pattern seemed to be emerging by the end of the 1950s. Young, well-off white families were moving to the suburbs, while poorer black families were settling into the older housing in the cities. When higher income people moved out, property values dropped. Lower property values meant less income for cities from property taxes.

As a result, it became much more difficult for many cities to pay for the services they had to provide. Downtown sections began to decline. Old neighborhoods turned into slums. Schools became overcrowded, and the quality of education fell. Inner city poverty became an unofficial kind of segregation. It was a trap that was almost impossible to escape.

In the rest of this chapter, you will find out what black Americans did to end segregation, overcome poverty, and try to win their share of the American dream.

Think: Like many Americans, these Puerto Ricans lived in poverty in a big city. Respond: What caused the cities to change from areas of wealth to places of poverty?

Section Review

1. Give an example of how a boom in one industry created a boom in others.

2. What types of workers were affected in a negative way by the coming of automation?

3. What issues caused unions to go out on strike in the 1950s?

4. Which groups of Americans did not share in the prosperity of the 1950s?

In Section 1 of this chapter, you read these facts about television in the 1950s:

By the end of the 1950s, nine out of ten American families had a television set.

Many Americans were watching television five hours a day.

Advertisers could reach a nationwide audience through television.

From these facts, a *generalization* could be made. A generalization is a statement about several facts that have something in common. Which of the following statements is a generalization?

a. Many people in the 1950s thought that Americans watched too much television.
b. In the 1950s, people were more interested in television than in anything else in life.
c. Television had a great impact on American society in the 1950s.

Statement *a* is not a valid generalization. It states what some people thought, or gives an *opinion*.

Statement *b* is not a valid generalization either. There is nothing in the three facts about television that supports that statement.

Statement *c* is a valid generalization. It states what the facts about television have in common.

Almost every generalization has one or more *exceptions*. An exception is a fact that does not fit a generalization. One exception to the generalization about television is the fact that some people in the 1950s chose to have no televisions. Their homes were not as heavily influenced by television. However, the number of people not affected by television was small compared to the number of people who were involved with television. The generalization is still a valid one.

1 Read the following three facts about the American economy in the 1950s.
a. Wages for workers in the 1950s were high, and they kept rising.
b. In the mid-1950s, three out of four families owned at least one automobile.
c. Automation helped owners of businesses raise the wages of workers.

2 Now choose the statement below that is a valid generalization about the facts above.
a. Labor unions were not needed in the 1950s.
b. Most American workers were making a good living in the 1950s.
c. American workers made more money than workers in any other country in the 1950s.

3 Think of an exception to the generalization about American workers. Write the exception as a statement.

3. The Civil Rights Movement

Learn these important terms:

separate but equal
Brown v. Board of
  Education of Topeka
civil rights
bus boycott
sit-ins
freedom rides
nonviolent resistance

Remember the main idea:

During the 1950s, black Americans fought to end segregation in the public schools, on public transportation, and in public places. Their efforts to gain equality made up the civil rights movement.

Look for answers to these questions:

1. What was the civil rights movement?
2. What Supreme Court decision outlawed school segregation?
3. What methods did Americans use to end segregation in restaurants and bus stations?

Think: In 1947, Jackie Robinson became the first black baseball player allowed in the major leagues. Respond: What positive effects did the inclusion of blacks have on American sports?

Through such means, black Americans protested segregation in public places. The struggle was long and difficult, but black Americans did not give up.

The Beginning of the Civil Rights Movement

To most Americans, *civil rights* include such freedom as the right to vote, the right to a good education, and the right to any job for which a worker is qualified. Americans believe they have the right to buy or rent housing wherever they choose, the right to a fair trial, and the right to be admitted to all public places. Some of these rights are guaranteed by the Constitution and its amendments. Others are protected by acts passed into law by Congress.

However, some groups of Americans have at times been denied these civil rights. Among them are black Americans. In the 1950s, many black Americans joined in an effort to gain their civil rights. This effort became known as the civil rights movement.

In April 1962, five college students entered a restaurant in a small southern town. They sat down at the counter and waited to order. After half an hour, the five students were finally told that they would not be served. They refused to leave. Soon the police arrived and ordered them to leave. When the students refused, they were arrested.

Scenes such as this one began occurring throughout the South in the 1950s.

Attacking School Segregation

The nation's public schools became one of the first targets of the civil rights movement. Public schools had been legally segregated ever since the *Plessy* v. *Ferguson* decision of 1896. In that case, the Supreme Court ruled that **separate but equal** educational facilities were constitutional. But in actual practice, black schools and white schools were not equally good.

In 1954, the National Association for the Advancement of Colored People (NAACP) took a school segregation case to court. The case was **Brown v. Board of Education of Topeka.** In its ruling on the case, the Supreme Court decided that segregation in public schools was unlawful and must be ended. It also declared that all children—both black and white—had an equal right to a good education.

Since segregating children on the basis of race was hurting black children, segregated schools were not equal schools. The Court ordered the nation's schools to desegregate "with all deliberate speed."

White Resistance in the South

A few southern communities obeyed the Supreme Court's ruling. They began to allow black children and white children to attend the same schools. However, three years after the *Brown* decision, fewer than seven hundred out of three thousand school districts in the South had ended segregation. Most communities simply refused to obey the Supreme Court.

The federal government did little to force the schools of the South to integrate until September 1957. At that time, nine black students attempted to register at an

---

Think: **In 1954, the Supreme Court ruled that laws requiring separate schools for black and white students were unconstitutional.** *Integration, Supreme Court* by Ben Shahn recalls the historic decision. Respond: **Why is it important that all students be given an equal chance to educate themselves?**

Think: **In 1957, federal troops guarded nine black students as they registered to attend Little Rock Central High School. This small victory marked the beginning of desegregation in southern schools.** Respond: **Why was segregation in northern and western schools not as obvious as it was in southern schools?**

all-white high school in Little Rock, Arkansas. To prevent this integration, the governor of Arkansas called in the National Guard. Although the Guard was later removed, angry white citizens replaced them and prevented the students from registering. President Eisenhower was finally forced to call in federal troops so that the students could register and attend the school.

Despite the victory at Little Rock, the pace of school integration remained slow in all sections of the nation. Northern communities did not have laws requiring segregated schools, but most black Americans lived in all-black neighborhoods. This meant that most black students attended all-black schools because of where they lived.

Ending Segregation on Public Transportation

Pushing for an end to school segregation was just the beginning for members of the civil rights movement. Many also wanted to see segregation stopped on

public buses in the South. Most southern cities required blacks to sit in the back of the buses. If a bus became crowded, blacks were supposed to give up their seats to white passengers and stand.

This law was challenged on December 1, 1955, when Rosa Parks, a black woman, sat down in the front section of a bus in Montgomery, Alabama, and refused to move. She was arrested and put in jail for breaking the city's segregation law.

Mrs. Parks's arrest sparked the black citizens of Montgomery to boycott the city buses. They refused to ride the buses as long as they remained segregated. The leader of this *bus boycott* was a young minister from Georgia, Dr. Martin Luther King, Jr.

The bus boycott had the wide support of the large black community in Montgomery. The city's buses began to lose a great deal of money as black riders stayed away. Finally, the city of Montgomery agreed to end segregation on the buses. And in 1956, the Supreme Court ruled that segregation on buses, trains, planes, or other public vehicles was unlawful.

HISTORY MAKERS

──── Rosa Parks ────

The Mother of the Civil Rights Movement

"You'll have to get up and give the man a seat," the bus driver said. The tired woman didn't move.

"Get up, or I'll get the police."

"No," she said quietly. Everyone in the bus was very still.

"This is the last chance. Will you get up?"

"No," she said again, firmly.

The driver got off the bus. Soon he was back with two police officers. They walked down the aisle to the seated woman.

"You're under arrest," one of the police officers told her.

Quietly she stood up. Quietly she left the bus. The police officers took her to the station. There she was photographed, fingerprinted, and locked in a cell. Then she sat and waited in her usual patient way. Several hours later Rosa Parks was free on bail.

Rosa Parks was a quiet, gentle woman who had lived in Alabama all her life. Because she was black, she suffered the effects of segregation. That meant going to overcrowded schools with poor facilities. It meant sitting in segregated sections of movie theatres. Often Rosa Parks would walk rather than ride in the back of the bus, climb stairs rather than ride in segregated elevators, and go thirsty rather than drink out of segregated drinking fountains. On December 1, 1955, tired after a long day's work, she took the bus home. Told to give up her seat, she decided it was time to refuse. She was ready to face the consequences.

Montgomery's black leaders met with Mrs. Parks and decided to protest segregated buses. Dr. Martin Luther King, Jr., was elected president of The Montgomery Improvement Association, a group organized to plan a bus boycott. For nearly a year, people in Montgomery walked or carpooled, refusing to ride on segregated buses. Finally a federal court ruled that segregated buses were unconstitutional.

Rosa Parks's refusal to give up her seat on the bus was the beginning of a national civil rights movement. Her steadfast courage made her a symbol of nonviolent resistance to injustice.

Think: **Martin Luther King, Jr., and other young blacks held sit-ins to protest segregation in public places.** Respond: **Why do you think Dr. King favored nonviolent resistance?**

Sit-ins and Freedom Rides

The bus boycott was an effective method for bringing about change. It was just one example of the kind of *nonviolent resistance* supported by Dr. King. King urged black Americans to fight segregation peacefully. In this way he hoped to win the sympathy and support of more white Americans.

Sit-ins were another form of protest Dr. King favored. In February 1960, four black college students sat down at a lunch counter in Greensboro, North Carolina, to force an end to segregation in public eating places. When they were refused service, they remained seated and refused to leave. Soon, thousands of black citizens and white citizens were holding sit-ins at eating places all over the South. The sit-ins finally led to the end of segregation at lunch counters, hotels, and theaters in many southern cities.

In 1961, black citizens and white citizens began *freedom rides* in the South. The purpose of these rides was to end segregation in southern bus and train stations. By law, black passengers had to sit in separate waiting areas and use separate drinking fountains and toilet facilities. Freedom riders traveled to many cities on the buses and trains until they won their fight against these laws. In November 1961, the Supreme Court ruled that segregation was unlawful in bus, plane, or train stations.

By the time President Eisenhower left office in 1961, black Americans were beginning to see some progress in their efforts to gain equal rights. But much still remained to be done. In the next chapter you will read about the continuing fight for civil rights during the terms of John F. Kennedy and Lyndon B. Johnson.

Think: **In 1961, Gwendolyn Jenkins was arrested for using white facilities at Jackson Airport.** Respond: **What other methods did freedom riders use to desegregate public places?**

Section Review

1. What are civil rights?
2. Why did the Supreme Court outlaw segregated schools in 1954?
3. How was segregation on public buses brought to an end in Montgomery, Alabama?
4. What method for bringing about change was favored by Dr. Martin Luther King, Jr.?

CHAPTER SUMMARY

The years after World War II were times of growth and prosperity. The population of the United States soared as returning GIs married, settled down, and had families. Many of these families moved to the suburbs where housing was inexpensive and plentiful. Many Americans had more free time than ever before. They watched television, and they read books. They went to museums and listened to new musical forms.

All of this movement and growth fueled the American economy as Americans bought all kinds of consumer goods. Automation kept the prices of goods low and workers' wages high. In many industries, shorter hours and paid vacations became common. But not everyone shared in this prosperity. In the 1950s, one out of every five Americans was living in poverty.

"Freedom" became the rallying cry for black Americans in the 1950s, as they worked to end segregation in public life. Segregation in the nation's public schools was outlawed in 1954. Bus boycotts, sit-ins, and freedom rides brought an end to segregation in the nation's eating places, theaters, hotels, and transportation systems. By the end of Eisenhower's presidency, the civil rights movement was beginning to win its fight against segregation and discrimination in America.

Key Words

Write a sentence to explain the meaning of each of these terms.

"baby boom" generation *poverty*
civil rights *Sunbelt*
automation *sit-ins*

Major Events

Choose the answer that best completes the statement.

1. To create affordable homes, the builder William Levitt used
   a) non-union workers.
   b) imported materials.
   c) assembly line techniques.

2. Because of improvements in technology, the nation's rural population
   a) declined.
   b) increased.
   c) bought more farmland.

3. All of the following were "boom" industries of the 1950s *except*
   a) aerospace.
   b) chemicals.
   c) electronics.

4. The Supreme Court outlawed segregated schools in the case
   a) *Plessy v. Ferguson.*
   b) *Brown v. Board of Education.*
   c) *Eisenhower v. Little Rock.*

5. Civil rights supporters used all of the methods below to achieve integration *except*
   a) boycotts.
   b) hostage-taking.
   c) freedom rides.

Review

Important Facts

Answer each question with at least one complete sentence.

1. What caused a "baby boom" in the years after World War II?

2. Why did so many Americans move to the suburbs?

3. What was meant by the phrase "mass-produced culture"?

4. How was abstract art different from earlier styles of art?

5. Explain how the baby boom and the housing boom fueled the American economy during the 1950s.

6. What were the advantages of automation? What were the disadvantages?

7. What happened to the union movement during the 1950s?

8. Over which issues did the members of unions strike?

9. What is poverty? How serious a problem was poverty during the 1950s?

10. What happened in Little Rock, Arkansas, in 1957? How did it affect the pace of school integration elsewhere?

11. What caused the Montgomery bus boycott? What was the outcome of the boycott?

12. What did Dr. Martin Luther King, Jr., mean by the phrase "nonviolent resistance"? Why did he support this method?

13. What was the purpose behind freedom rides?

Skill Review

Read this paragraph, then answer the following questions.

The postwar baby boom also produced a boom in education. Between 1945 and 1960, more American children were in school than ever before. As a result, more teachers were needed, and many new schools were built. Almost every child finished elementary school. Nine out of ten students went to high school for at least a year. Thanks in part to the GI Bill, the number of college students doubled between 1945 and 1960.

1. *Less tax money was needed for education in 1960 than in 1945.* Is this a valid generalization? Explain.

2. *School enrollment at all levels soared in the 1950s.* Is this a valid generalization? Explain.

3. *Teaching was a secure profession during the 1950s.* Is this a valid generalization? Explain.

Critical Thinking

Write a paragraph to answer each question.

1. One economist described post-war America as "affluent." *Affluent* means rich. What facts support the economist's description?

2. Explain three factors that could affect the number of Americans living in poverty.

Important People

Choose the answer that best completes the statement.

1. The Fair Deal was a program of change and reform developed by

   a) Dwight D. Eisenhower.
   b) Harry S. Truman.
   c) Thomas E. Dewey.

2. The senator who hunted for Communists through the use of unfair methods was

   a) Adlai Stevenson.
   b) William Taft.
   c) Joseph McCarthy.

3. After World War II, George C. Marshall

   a) developed a plan to help Europe rebuild.
   b) directed the Berlin airlift.
   c) commanded NATO forces.

4. The Chinese Communist leader who controlled China after its civil war was

   a) Chiang Kai-shek.
   b) the Emperor Hirohito.
   c) Mao Zedong.

5. A pioneer builder of mass-produced homes was

   a) William Levitt.
   b) Frank Lloyd Wright.
   c) Henry Ford.

6. The Montgomery bus boycott was sparked by the arrest of

   a) Martin Luther King, Jr.
   b) nine black students who tried to board the bus.
   c) Rosa Parks.

Main Ideas

Choose the answer that best completes the statement.

1. To help returning soldiers after the war, Congress passed

   a) the GI Bill of Rights.
   b) the Taft-Hartley Act.
   c) the Twenty-second Amendment.

2. The main economic problem facing the United States after the war was

   a) high unemployment.
   b) inflation.
   c) labor union strikes.

3. During the postwar years, the nation was gripped by

   a) a depression.
   b) a fear that communism was spreading within the U.S.
   c) corruption in government.

4. The Soviet launch of *Sputnik I*

   a) convinced Americans to spend more money on defense.
   b) followed the successful launch of an American satellite.
   c) convinced Congress to spend more money on education.

5. After World War II, a Cold War broke out

   a) in Korea.
   b) in eastern Europe.
   c) between the United States and the Soviet Union.

6. The Soviet blockade of Berlin

   a) was a failure.
   b) forced the city to surrender to the Soviets.

Review

c) brought the world to the brink of war.

7. The Soviets responded to the formation of NATO by forming

   a) an alliance with China.
   b) the Warsaw Pact.
   c) SEATO.

8. As a result of the Korean War,

   a) Korea remained divided.
   b) Korea became a Communist nation.
   c) Korea became a democratic nation.

9. The Eisenhower and Truman Doctrines were designed to

   a) stop the spread of communism.
   b) promote peaceful negotiations with the Soviets.
   c) spread democracy to other nations.

10. The invention of new machines

    a) encouraged more Americans to become farmers.
    b) gave Americans more leisure time than ever before.
    c) was welcomed by all workers.

11. *Brown v. Board of Education*

    a) permitted separate but equal educational facilities.
    b) ended bus segregation.
    c) ended school segregation.

12. Sit-ins and freedom rides were

    a) examples of nonviolent resistance.
    b) methods for change supported by Martin Luther King, Jr.
    c) Both of the answers above are correct.

History Skills

Eastern Mediterranean Nations

Choose the answer that best completes the statement.

1. Greece is bordered by

   a) two Communist countries.
   b) three Communist countries.
   c) four Communist countries.

2. Turkey has strategic value to the Soviet Union because it

   a) offers a water route to the Mediterranean Sea.
   b) could block the spread of democracy.
   c) borders on two seas.

3. A valid generalization about this map would be to say that

   a) Greece and Turkey feared war with Bulgaria.
   b) eastern Mediterranean nations risked Communist takeovers.
   c) Cyprus was of little value to Turkey or Greece.

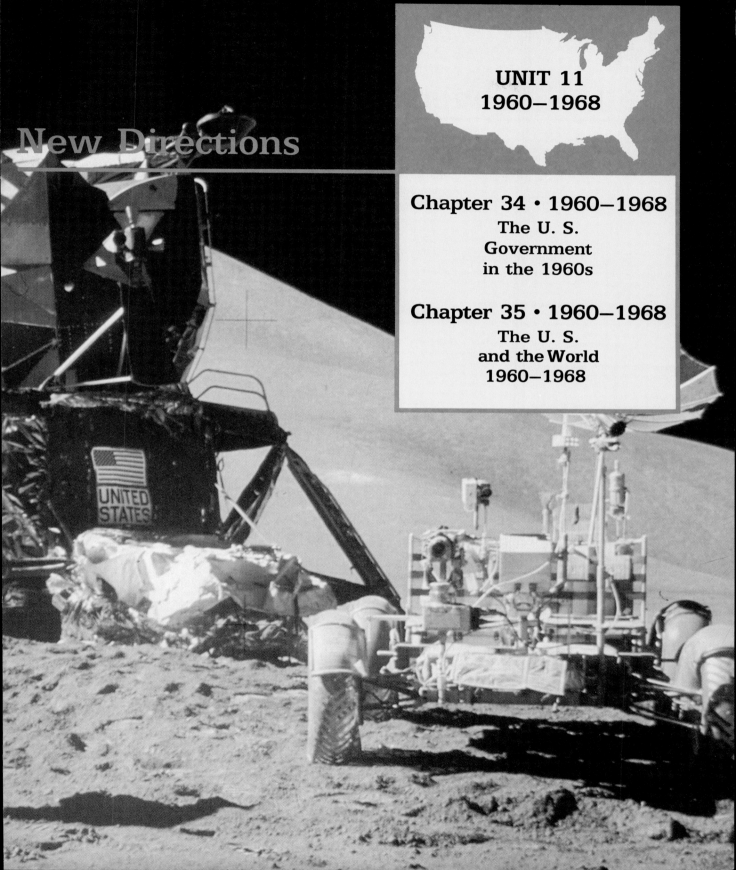

New Directions

34
The U.S. Government in the 1960s

Years 1960–1968

John F. Kennedy
elected president
1960

March on Washington
President Kennedy assassinated
Lyndon Johnson
became president
1963

Civil Rights
Act passed
Lyndon Johnson
elected president
1964

Voting Rights Act passed
Medicare passed
Immigration and
Nationality Act passed
1965

Rioting
in ghettos
1967

Dr. Martin Luther King, Jr.,
assassinated
Robert Kennedy assassinated
Richard Nixon elected president
1968

The night before the presidential election of 1960, John F. Kennedy spoke to a large crowd in Boston. He was tired from months of campaigning. But, as usual, he made a memorable speech. He told those who were there that he did not expect the presidency to be an easy job. He said, "I run for the Presidency of the United States because it is the center of action, and, in a free society, the chief responsibility of the President is to set before the American people the unfinished public business of our country."

Taking care of unfinished business was the primary concern of America's presidents in the 1960s. In this chapter you will read about these presidents. You will see how they worked with Congress to deal with the nation's unsolved social problems. You will read about the many new laws passed during the 1960s. You will learn about some exciting American accomplishments. However, you will also read about tragedies. Shootings and riots were part of the 1960s. So were more peaceful ways of bringing about change. And, as you will see, the 1960s in America meant a great deal of change.

1. John F. Kennedy and the New Frontier

Learn these important terms:

New Frontier
Warren Commission
polls
March on Washington

Remember the main idea:

President Kennedy called his plan to improve the American nation the New Frontier. However, problems with Congress prevented him from getting most of his plan approved as law.

Look for answers to these questions:

1. What role did television play in the election of 1960?
2. What was the New Frontier?
3. What did President Kennedy do to protect the civil rights of black Americans in the South?

In 1960, the Republican candidate for president was Richard M. Nixon. As Eisenhower's vice president, Nixon had traveled around the world. Many Americans considered him a wise and experienced statesman. The Democratic candidate was the smiling and youthful senator from Massachusetts, John F. Kennedy.

The Election of 1960

At the start of the campaign, the ***polls***, or public opinion surveys, showed that American voters preferred Nixon to Kennedy. They knew Nixon better, and they did not know how Kennedy's religion would influence his decisions. Kennedy was a Catholic, the only Catholic to run for president since Alfred E. Smith in 1928. Some people feared Kennedy's first loyalty would be to the Pope in Rome, rather than to the Constitution.

But Kennedy dealt with this issue head-on. He told the public in speech after speech that he would never violate his presidential oath. He promised to always support the Constitution, even if church

Think: During the 1960 campaign, Republicans tried to dismiss Kennedy as young and inexperienced. However, he appeared mature and knowledgeable. Respond: How do public appearances affect politicians?

John Fitzgerald Kennedy (1917–1963) devoted himself to fighting ". . . against the common enemies of man: tyranny, poverty, disease, and war itself."

authorities told him he must do otherwise. Kennedy had great personal charm, and he was a good public speaker. Americans were impressed by his youth and his energy.

Public appearances meant a great deal in the election of 1960. For example, television played an important part in the campaign. The two candidates met in four debates that were seen by television audiences estimated at sixty million. Neither candidate "won" the debates. However, Kennedy came across as the more relaxed, confident, and healthy-looking candidate. Viewers were impressed. The polls began to shift toward him.

Nevertheless, the election was one of the closest ever held. John F. Kennedy was elected president by only 118,000 votes. Lyndon B. Johnson of Texas became vice president.

Kennedy as President

John F. Kennedy was in office a little more than a thousand days when he was struck down by an assassin's bullet. But even though his term was brief, his presidency left a lasting impression on the American people. He is remembered not so much for what he did, but for what he hoped to do and for what he inspired others to do.

Kennedy came to office with a plan to help improve the American nation. He called his plan the *New Frontier*. The New Frontier promised stronger civil rights laws and offered health insurance for Americans over sixty-five. It called for federal aid to education, more public housing, and better conditions for farmers and workers.

However, President Kennedy had a hard time getting Congress to pass his programs into law. Although the Democrats controlled both houses of Congress, conservative southern Democrats often lined up with conservative Republicans. Together they watered down or defeated bills that the president supported.

New Frontier Successes

President Kennedy did get Congress to raise the minimum wage from $1.00 an hour to $1.25 an hour. Congress also agreed to raise the amount of Social Security payments to older Americans. And Congress voted to provide more than six billion dollars to clean up slums and build public housing for families with low incomes. A training program was started to help teach new job skills to unemployed workers. Also, money was loaned or given to areas of the country that were suffering from economic problems.

One New Frontier program that had the support of southern conservatives was the space program. President Kennedy called for a huge program that would put an American on the moon by 1970. Southern conservatives supported the space program largely because the space technology industry would be located in their states. Within a few years, thousands of companies and millions of people were

Think: **On August 28, 1963, thousands joined the March on Washington. President Kennedy met with the March's leaders, including Martin Luther King, Jr. That day King said turmoil in America would continue "until the Negro is granted his citizenship rights."** Respond: **What did the leaders hope to accomplish?**

Think: **On February 28, 1962, John Glenn became the first American to orbit the earth. He's seen here aboard** *Friendship 7.* Respond: **Why was the space program important to America?**

Despite Kennedy's efforts, resistance to integration was still strong in the South. The southern states refused to integrate their universities. For example, in 1962, a federal court had to order the University of Mississippi at Oxford, an all-white school, to admit a black transfer student. President Kennedy sent federal marshals to Mississippi to protect the student, James Meredith, and to make sure the law was obeyed.

Meredith's arrival on the campus led to rioting. It took fifteen hours to restore calm. The rioting left two men dead and many people injured, but Meredith was finally admitted to the university.

Nine months later, segregation was challenged again, this time at the University of Alabama. A court ordered the university to integrate, but Alabama's governor, George Wallace, refused to obey the order. He personally blocked the entrance

involved in space-related activities. By 1962, America's space program was on its way. John Glenn became the nation's first astronaut to orbit the earth.

Kennedy and Civil Rights

During his term in office, President Kennedy took great interest in expanding and protecting the civil rights of all Americans. One of his first acts as president was to appoint several black Americans as judges and ambassadors. Kennedy also ordered the government and all companies that did work for it to hire workers on the basis of their abilities, regardless of their race. And in 1962, he issued an order making segregation unlawful in housing built with federal money.

Think: **When Governor Wallace tried to stop black students from attending the University of Alabama, federal marshals were called in.** Respond: **What was the result?**

to the school when black students tried to enroll. Once again, Kennedy sent in federal marshals. Wallace was forced to step aside and allow the integration.

Growing Pressure to Act

Increasing violence against blacks and civil rights workers made the president realize that stronger action was necessary. On May 3, 1963, police in Birmingham, Alabama, used water hoses and police dogs against defenseless civil rights marchers. A week later, the protestors' office was bombed. On June 11, President Kennedy announced that he would ask Congress for new civil rights laws. The next day, Medgar Evers, field secretary of the NAACP in Mississippi, was shot to death. The time to act had arrived. Kennedy sent to Congress a major civil rights bill that outlawed segregation in employment, in any public facilities, and in schools.

In August 1963, black Americans showed their support for the bill by coming to Washington, D.C., for a demonstration. The **March on Washington** was a peaceful gathering of more than 200,000 Americans calling for an end to racial discrimination in America. This day-long event at the Lincoln Memorial was the largest civil rights demonstration in American history. Despite this show of support, Kennedy's civil rights bill remained stalled in Congress.

The Loss of a Leader

Several months later, in November 1963, the president and the vice president went to Texas to win support for their program. As the president's car made its way through the crowd-lined streets of Dallas, shots rang out. Suddenly, the president slumped forward. President Kennedy was rushed to the hospital, but it was too late.

Think: **America was shocked by the death of its young president. Many feared that Kennedy's dreams would die with him.** Respond: **What do you think was Kennedy's greatest goal?**

Think: **Bill Mauldin created this political cartoon to express his feelings about Kennedy's death.** Respond: **Why do you think he chose to show Lincoln grieving for Kennedy?**

HISTORY MAKERS

Dr. Martin Luther King, Jr.

The Voice of our Conscience

News stories appeared throughout the country the day after Martin and Coretta King's home was bombed. They told the story of a bomb being thrown onto the Kings' front porch. They told of the narrow escape of Mrs. King and her infant daughter. The stories also told about the angry crowd that gathered at the Kings' home. When Dr. King arrived, he told the crowd that his family was safe, and he urged them to remain peaceful. As usual, he stated that responding to violence with violence was not the answer. The crowd, impressed by Dr. King's commitment to nonviolence, broke up and went home.

Dr. King's nonviolent means of protest were often featured in news stories of his time. Beginning with his role in the Montgomery bus boycott, Dr. Martin Luther King, Jr., made his belief in nonviolent resistance the foundation of a great civil rights movement. Many followed his suggestions for peaceful protests.

Martin Luther King traveled all over the country to protest discrimination. He was the target of harassment and violence, but he always preached and practiced peaceful resistance to violence. As he often said, he was not an outside agitator trying to stir up trouble. He wrote, ''Injustice anywhere is a threat to justice everywhere.'' To people who said it wasn't a good time to demonstrate, King wrote, ''For years I have heard the word 'Wait'. . . . This 'Wait' has always meant 'Never.' '' Dr. King was done waiting.

In 1963, the hundredth anniversary of the Emancipation Proclamation, Martin Luther King led thousands of people on a march in Washington, D.C., in support of the civil rights bill in Congress. In 1964, King was awarded the Nobel Prize for Peace. In 1968, his life was ended by an assassin's bullet. The peaceful man was killed by act of violence.

Martin Luther King gave his life to the nonviolent movement for civil rights for all people. Today his spirit stands as a symbol of peaceful resistance to injustice of any kind, and Dr. King still has many followers.

Several hours later, the police arrested Lee Harvey Oswald as a suspect in the assassination. A check of Oswald's background showed that he had lived in the Soviet Union for a short time. He had also been involved with some extreme political groups. But whether Oswald was the only one involved in the killing would never be known. Two days after his arrest, Oswald was shot and killed as he was moved from one prison to another.

Unanswered questions about the assassination remained. One of Lyndon Johnson's first acts as president was to ask the Chief Justice of the Supreme Court, Earl Warren, to head a commission to investigate the assassination. Months later, the **Warren Commission** issued its findings. There was no evidence of a plot to kill the president. Oswald had acted alone.

Kennedy's New Frontier program was taken over by the new president, Lyndon Johnson. In the rest of this chapter you will read about President Johnson's success in getting Congress to approve the programs that Kennedy only had the time to plan for.

Section Review

1. What advantages did Kennedy have over Nixon in the election of 1960?
2. Why did Kennedy have a hard time getting Congress to support his New Frontier programs?
3. Which New Frontier program had the support of southern conservatives?
4. What was the 1963 March on Washington?
5. Why did Lyndon Johnson set up the Warren Commission?

2. Johnson's Great Society

Learn these important terms:

Civil Rights Act of 1964
Great Society
Office of Economic Opportunity
Job Corps
VISTA
Medicare
Voting Rights Act of 1965
Elementary and Secondary Education Act
Head Start
Appalachian Regional Development Act
Housing and Urban Development Act
Department of Housing and Urban Development
Medicaid

Remember the main idea:

President Johnson called his plans to improve the nation the Great Society. A skilled politician, Johnson persuaded Congress to enact into law his Great Society programs.

Look for answers to these questions:

1. In what ways was President Johnson different from President Kennedy?
2. What was the Great Society?
3. Why was it necessary to pass the Voting Rights Act of 1965?

Within hours of President Kennedy's assassination, Lyndon Johnson had taken

Think: **Johnson was sworn in as president before leaving Dallas on the day Kennedy died.** Respond: **Why is a swift and smooth change of command important to American security?**

the oath of office at Love Field in Texas and was on a plane headed for Washington, D.C. The new president was a very different man from Kennedy. Kennedy was a wealthy, Harvard-educated Bostonian. Johnson was a down-home Texas rancher who spoke with a distinct southern accent. But what Johnson may have lacked in "class," he made up for in political skill and experience.

From the time he graduated from Southwest State Teachers College, Lyndon Johnson's life became politics. He was first elected to the House of Representatives in 1937, and he served as a senator from Texas from 1948 until he became vice president in 1960. All of this time spent in Congress meant that he thoroughly knew the personalities, the rules, and the workings of the legislative branch. Johnson was an expert at getting legislation passed.

Carrying on the New Frontier

President Johnson shared Kennedy's concern for the poor, the elderly, and the less advantaged. He promised the American people to carry on the former presi-

dent's program. Because Johnson knew Congress so well, he was able to get Congress to pass most of the laws that President Kennedy had submitted to them.

In the first few months of 1964, Congress passed a wave of New Frontier legislation. More money was provided to aid education. Congress approved funds to help American cities solve their transportation problems. And money was also set aside to build more public housing.

But one of the most important laws of the New Frontier, the Civil Rights Act, was still facing strong opposition in Congress. President Johnson had to use all of his skill and know-how to get the bill passed into law. The *Civil Rights Act of 1964* forbade segregation in hotels, restaurants, and other public places. It required all states to allow qualified voters to register and vote. The law gave the government the power to ask the courts to force segregated schools to admit black children. It forbade employers, labor unions, or job agencies to treat anyone unfairly because of race, color, or religion. And the law allowed the government to take away federal money from any state program that treated citizens unfairly.

Think: **Martin Luther King, Jr., one of America's most gifted speakers, was arrested many times while peacefully attempting to bring about change.** Respond: **Why did some fear him?**

Think: **Educational programs for poor children were started throughout the nation to give these students a chance to succeed.** Respond: **Why is education so important?**

The Great Society

After President Johnson carried out much of Kennedy's New Frontier program, he developed his own plans to help improve the American nation. Johnson called this program the **Great Society**. Johnson wanted to see America become a land in which all people had enough food to eat, decent clothes to wear, and good housing. He wanted to see every worker employed. And he dreamed of a society in which a person's race, color, or religion would not interfere with opportunities for advancement.

One of the first steps in Johnson's "war on poverty" was to create a federal agency dedicated to helping low-income families. This agency became known as the **Office of Economic Opportunity**. This office helped children from low-income families keep pace in school through the

Head Start program. It also ran the *Job Corps*, which gave job training to young Americans who had left school but were unable to find work. And it started *VISTA*, Volunteers in Service to America. VISTA workers offered educational and social services to poor communities.

The Election of 1964

Within months of becoming president, Johnson had to begin campaigning for the election of 1964. He was the clear choice of the Democratic Party, having proved to the party that he was an able president. As his running mate, he chose Senator Hubert Humphrey of Minnesota. The Republican candidate for president was Senator Barry Goldwater, an extreme conservative from Arizona.

Both candidates campaigned in all parts of the nation. However, because of his extreme views on the issues, Senator Goldwater lost the support of many voters. Lyndon Johnson won the election by a landslide, with almost sixteen million votes more than Goldwater. The Democrats also won control of Congress.

Think: **During his campaign for president, Goldwater gave the impression that he would use extreme measures against communism.** Respond: **How did his position affect the outcome of the election?**

Lyndon Baines Johnson (1908–1973) admired Roosevelt and his New Deal. When he became president, Johnson concentrated in a similar way on domestic reform.

Stepping up the War on Poverty

After his enormous victory in 1964, President Johnson felt that it was time to put the war on poverty into high gear. He asked Congress to pass the *Appalachian Regional Development Act*. This law provided for a large sum of money to be spent fighting poverty in Appalachia. Appalachia was a large but poor region stretching from Pennsylvania all the way down to Alabama.

Congress also passed the *Housing and Urban Development Act* to help American cities solve their growing problems. Money was set aside to build more public housing as well as to help poor people pay their rent. The act also created a new Cabinet department, the *Department of Housing and Urban Development*, to deal

---

Think: Failing rural stores dotted the economically deprived Appalachia. Respond: Why did roads, tourist attractions, industry, and new schools improve this region?

specifically with the problems of the cities. Robert C. Weaver was appointed to head this department. He became the first black man ever to be a member of the president's Cabinet.

Congress next turned to President Johnson's request to provide health insurance for elderly Americans. The *Medicare* program they passed provided for free hospital care for people over sixty-five. It also helped older persons pay doctor bills. Congress also passed the *Medicaid* program, which provided medical care to poor Americans under sixty-five.

Aid to Education

Because President Johnson realized the importance of a good education for all Americans, he made aid to education an important part of his Great Society program. Federal aid went to colleges for the construction of new buildings. And more money was set aside for scholarships for needy students.

Yet, by far the most important education law proposed by the president was the *Elementary and Secondary Education Act* of 1965. This act allowed the federal government to provide large amounts of aid to the nation's public schools. Much of this money went to city schools to improve education for children from low-income families.

Dealing with Voting Rights

Even after the Civil Rights Act of 1964 was passed, many black Americans still had trouble voting in certain parts of the South. For example, officials in Selma, Alabama, refused to register black voters or allow them to vote.

Realizing that action had to be taken, Congress passed the *Voting Rights Act of 1965*. This law forbade the use of literacy, or reading, tests to prevent Americans from voting. It also granted the federal

APPALACHIA IN THE 1960s

Why did President Johnson begin his war on poverty with Appalachia? If you combine the information on these maps, you can find answers to this question. Appalachia is a region that stretches through the Appalachian Mountains from Alabama to New York.

Locate Appalachia on these maps. Then use the states of Pennsylvania and West Virginia to answer the following questions.

1. What mineral resources lie below each state? Which minerals does Pennsylvania have that West Virginia lacks?

2. What industries does each state have? What differences do you notice between the two states? What allows Pennsylvania to have industries not based on local resources?

3. How many cities are in each state? How do cities indicate the wealth of a state? What can you conclude about the wealth of West Virginia?

President Johnson's bill called for 2,850 miles of highway for Appalachia, flood control, vocational training, and improvements in coal mining and lumbering. In West Virginia, for example, the federal government spent $48 million for highways in 1964 and $115 million in 1965.

4. How would highways improve the economy of West Virginia?

5. What other industries might be improved in West Virginia?

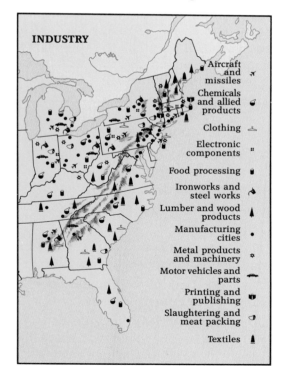

MINERAL RESOURCES

Coal ▢
Aluminum ○
Beryllium ◼
Chromium ☐
Copper ●
Lead and zinc ●
Manganese ▲
Oil and natural gas ⚒
Titanium ◼
Vanadium ▲

INDUSTRY

Aircraft and missiles ✈
Chemicals and allied products
Clothing
Electronic components
Food processing
Ironworks and steel works
Lumber and wood products ▲
Manufacturing cities ●
Metal products and machinery ✿
Motor vehicles and parts
Printing and publishing
Slaughtering and meat packing
Textiles ▲

Think: **The Voting Rights Act of 1965 gave the power of the vote to many blacks who had previously been barred from voting.** Respond: **Why had many blacks been denied this right?**

government the power to register black voters when local officials refused to do so. This law greatly increased the number of black voters in the South.

Despite Johnson's concern for civil rights issues, many black Americans were beginning to grow impatient with the pace of change. In the rest of this chapter you will read about the issues that began to tear American society apart in the last years of Johnson's term.

Section Review

1. Why was Lyndon Johnson considered an expert at getting legislation passed?

2. What did the Civil Rights Act of 1964 outlaw?

3. Why was Johnson so much more popular than Goldwater in 1964?

4. What did President Johnson do to help the cities?

5. For which political party do you think the newly registered black voters of 1965 would have voted? Why?

---

3. A Nation Divided

Learn these important terms:

Immigration and Nationality Act
black power
ghetto
white backlash

Remember the main idea:

America was a divided nation by the end of the 1960s. Many blacks were frustrated by the pace of change. Other Americans wanted to see an end to the war in Vietnam. Americans elected Richard Nixon president, hoping that he would bring the nation together again.

Look for answers to these questions:

1. What did "black power" mean?

2. Why were there riots in the nation's ghettos in the 1960s?

3. Why did Lyndon Johnson decide not to run for reelection in 1968?

Not all Americans welcomed the changes taking place in the country during the 1960s. Some whites responded violently to the gains blacks were making. Instances of violence became common. For example, after the Civil Rights Act of 1964 became law, three civil rights workers who were registering black voters in Mississippi were murdered. In March 1965, two civil rights workers were murdered in Alabama as they prepared for a protest march.

This violent resistance to black equality became known as *white backlash*. As the decade wore on, white backlash seemed to grow worse instead of better. And white backlash caused a reaction of its own among blacks.

Black Power

White backlash frightened many blacks and slowed down the pace of voter registration in many parts of the South. To "march against fear," James Meredith, the man who had integrated the University of Mississippi, began a one-man march across Mississippi in June 1966. On the second day of his walk, he was shot.

Civil rights leaders from all over the country took up Meredith's march where he left off. But they met with violence all along the way. A new leader emerged during the march. He was Stokely Carmichael. Carmichael urged the marchers to take up a new slogan, "black power."

Black power had different meanings for different people. Some thought that black power meant voting in large numbers. But others saw it as a statement that integration was impossible. These people felt that blacks should separate themselves from white society and organize a society of their own. In this society, everything would be owned, operated, and governed by blacks.

Riots in the Cities

The black power movement had a large following among blacks living in the cities of the North. Most of these blacks lived in *ghettos*, or sections of the city where members of one racial or ethnic group live. They had seen little improvement in their lives as a result of the civil rights movement. Most either could not find work or worked at menial jobs. Many lived in run-down housing. The schools in their neighborhoods were poor. Black

Think: **Consider the conditions in which this family lived in a Harlem ghetto.** Respond: **Without the chance to get a good job, how could this mother support her children?**

ghetto dwellers looked around and asked themselves who they should blame for their situation. Their answer was white landlords, white store owners, white employers, and white teachers.

Beginning in the summer of 1964, the ghettos of America's cities exploded in violent and destructive riots. From Harlem in New York to Watts in California,

Think: **Detroit firefighters battled a blaze started in a violent riot.** Respond: **Why were some blacks angry enough to explode in violence?**

black anger and frustration showed itself in violence. Property was destroyed, homes were burned, and ghetto residents were injured and killed. In 1967, there were riots in 164 cities. In that year alone, eighty-two people died in the riots, thirty-four hundred were injured, and more than eighteen thousand were arrested.

New Black Leaders

Backing this fighting mood were new black leaders who encouraged blacks to cut their ties to white society. Leaders such as Malcolm X, a Black Muslim, told blacks that they had a "right to resist" being treated unjustly by whites. They said blacks should resist "by any means necessary." Still other black leaders suggested that ghetto residents carry guns to resist being mistreated by local police.

These new leaders stood for violence. They thought violence would bring faster results than those gained by Martin Luther King's nonviolent methods.

The civil rights movement became divided, and both sides lost strength. Supporters of nonviolence suffered their biggest loss when Dr. King was shot and killed in Memphis, Tennessee, in April 1968. King had gone to Memphis to lend support to striking garbage collectors. He was shot by James Earl Ray as he stood outside his motel room. The nation's cities exploded in violence once again as the news of King's death spread.

Johnson's Successes

President Johnson still had many plans in mind for achieving the Great Society. Johnson got Congress to agree to set up the Department of Transportation as a Cabinet-level department. And he also convinced Congress to pass a gun control law. This act made it unlawful to purchase a handgun outside the buyer's home state.

Congress also passed a new immigration law called the *Immigration and*

Think: **King and his followers often ended their meetings by joining hands and singing "We Shall Overcome."**
Respond: **Why do you suppose they chose to sing this hymn?**

Nationality Act. This law ended the quota system that had been in effect since the 1920s. Although the new law limited the total number of immigrants allowed to enter the United States, it permitted in people from all over the world.

A Broad-minded Supreme Court

The Supreme Court took a fresh look at many issues in the 1960s. As a result, it made a number of decisions that expanded the rights of the individual. In a series of cases, the Court gave its support to the civil rights laws that Congress had passed. The Court also supported cases that were trying to speed up the end of segregation in schools. And the Court ruled that Bible reading and prayers in the public schools were unlawful.

In a series of cases relating to the rights of those accused of crimes, the Court made several new rulings. The Court said police had to inform accused parties of their rights upon arrest. Also, the accused had to have a lawyer present when questioned by the police. Finally, states had to provide a lawyer for anyone accused of a crime if that person could not afford to hire one.

Johnson's Decision

Most Americans expected President Johnson to run for a second term in 1968. But Johnson faced some stiff challenges in the primary elections.

In New Hampshire, Johnson was defeated by Senator Eugene McCarthy of Minnesota. McCarthy was strongly opposed to the war in Vietnam, and he made his position on the war the key issue in his campaign. McCarthy's victory encouraged Senator Robert F. Kennedy of New York to also try to become the Democratic candidate. Kennedy opposed the war, and he had strong support among blacks and workers.

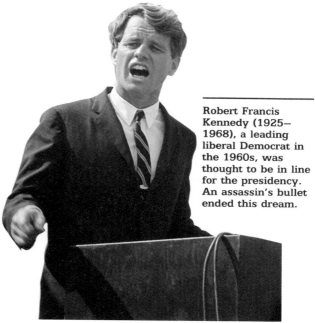

Robert Francis Kennedy (1925–1968), a leading liberal Democrat in the 1960s, was thought to be in line for the presidency. An assassin's bullet ended this dream.

President Johnson saw that the war in Vietnam was so unpopular with the people that he might not be able to win his party's nomination. On March 31, 1968, Johnson announced that he would not be a candidate for president.

Johnson's decision brought another challenger into the race, Vice President Hubert Humphrey. While McCarthy and Kennedy spoke against the president's policies, Humphrey defended them.

Think: Johnson's vice president, Hubert Humphrey, won the Democratic nomination, but lost the election by a narrow margin. **Respond:** What had weakened Humphrey's chance of winning?

The black power movement of the 1960s had different meanings for black leaders. Compare the views of three black leaders in these words taken from their speeches.

Martin Luther King, Jr.:

. . . We must not allow our creative protest to degenerate into physical violence . . . I have a dream that one day little black boys and black girls will be able to join hands with little white boys and white girls and walk together as sisters and brothers.

Malcolm X:

Our enemy is the white man! . . . The collective white man's history has left the non-white people no alternative but to draw closer to each other . . . no one will know who we are until we know who we are! And I don't mean all of this non-violent, begging-the-white-man kind of dying . . .

Stokely Carmichael:

For too many years, black Americans marched and had their heads broken and got shot . . . We cannot be expected any longer to march and have our heads broken in order to say to whites: come on, you're nice guys. For you are not nice guys. We have found you out . . .

1 Which black leader had the most hope for blacks and whites working together?

2 Which black leaders thought blacks and whites could not work together?

3 Which black leader talked about the blacks' fellowship with other non-white people?

4 Which black leader would you think would be likely to use only nonviolence in his protests?

5 Which black leader seemed to disagree most strongly with nonviolent protests?

6 Do you agree with any of these black leaders' views? Why, or why not?

On June 5, 1968, Robert Kennedy won the California primary election. That night, after he spoke to his campaign supporters, the senator was shot to death. Kennedy's followers split their support between McCarthy and Humphrey. Thus, when the Democrats met at their convention in Chicago, they were divided. Humphrey was eventually chosen as the Democratic candidate. But his selection caused a wave of protest among McCarthy's backers. They refused to support Humphrey. This severely weakened Humphrey's chances in the election.

The Election of 1968

The Republican Party chose Richard Nixon to be its candidate for president. Nixon took advantage of the split among Democrats by focusing his campaign on the war issue. Nixon told the voters that he had a plan to end the war. However, he would not reveal the details of his plan until he was elected. Nixon also promised to restore "law and order" to the nation by taking a firm stand against violent rioters and protestors.

There was a third party candidate in the election of 1968. He was Governor George C. Wallace of Alabama. Wallace

Richard Milhous Nixon (1913–   ) is remembered positively for his effective foreign policy. However, the Watergate scandal casts a shadow over all of Nixon's accomplishments.

was the candidate of the American Independent Party. He was still a strong defender of segregation.

Richard Nixon won the election of 1968 by a very slim margin. His victory marked the end of eight years of Democratic leadership. As a result, the country would follow a very different path.

A major problem that Nixon inherited from Kennedy and Johnson was the war in Vietnam. In the next chapter you will read about this war and about America's dealings with other nations during the uneasy 1960s.

Think: During his campaign for the presidency, George Wallace supported segregation. Respond: What previous actions by Wallace showed how strongly he would support segregation?

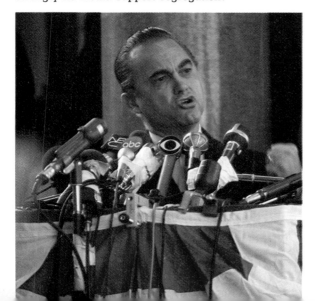

Section Review

1. What was white backlash?
2. How did the new black leaders differ from earlier leaders such as Martin Luther King?
3. Why was the Immigration and Nationality Act important?
4. In what ways did the Supreme Court expand the rights of a person accused of a crime?
5. Why did Richard Nixon win the election of 1968?

CHAPTER SUMMARY

John F. Kennedy brought to the presidency many ideas for solving America's social problems. Most were rejected by Congress. But the space program and a few New Frontier programs did get approved. Kennedy also sent a major civil rights bill to Congress. But before he could see the bill become law, Kennedy was shot and killed by an assassin.

Lyndon Johnson took over the reins of government smoothly. His style and background were quite different from Kennedy's, but Johnson was successful at getting bills through Congress. He saw to it that most of the bills Kennedy left behind were passed into law. Johnson then proposed his own program, which he called the Great Society. Congress gave its support to most of his programs, including Medicare, aid to education, and the Voting Rights Act.

Despite progress in the area of civil rights, many blacks were frustrated by the pace of change and by white resistance. New black leaders called on their followers to fight. Many of the nation's ghettos erupted in riots.

By 1968, Lyndon Johnson had lost the support of many Americans. He decided not to run for reelection. In a close race, Richard M. Nixon was elected to the presidency, and a new period of Republican leadership was about to begin.

Key Words

Write a sentence to explain the meaning of each of these terms.

New Frontier   *Medicare*
VISTA   *black power*
Great Society   *ghetto*

Major Events

Choose the answer that best completes the statement.

1. The election of 1960

   a) involved the nation's first Catholic candidate.
   b) was one of the closest held.
   c) was decided by the debates.

2. America's space program was on its way

   a) when Glenn orbited the earth.
   b) with the moon landing.
   c) when *Sputnik* was launched.

3. Black Americans showed their support for the Civil Rights Bill through

   a) the sit-in at the University of Alabama.
   b) the March in Birmingham.
   c) the March on Washington.

4. The Voting Rights Act of 1965

   a) outlawed segregated voting booths.
   b) forbade the use of literacy tests.
   c) lowered the voting age to 18.

5. The election of 1968

   a) saw the Democrats win again.
   b) was influenced by American involvement in Vietnam.
   c) was decided by black voters.

Review

Important Facts

Answer each question with at least one complete sentence.

1. What are polls? What did they show at the beginning of the election campaign in 1960?

2. Why did Kennedy have a hard time getting Congress to pass his programs into law?

3. How did Kennedy expand and protect the civil rights of black Americans?

4. What was the Warren Commission? What findings did it issue?

5. What made Lyndon Johnson such a skilled politician?

6. How did Johnson begin to wage the "war on poverty"?

7. Why did Johnson win by such a large margin in the election of 1964?

8. What did Johnson do to improve education for all Americans?

9. What was "white backlash"? What effect did it have on voter registration in the South?

10. Why did the black power movement gather a large following among blacks living in northern cities?

11. How did the Immigration and Nationality Act change the pattern of immigration to America?

12. In what ways did the Supreme Court of the 1960s expand the rights of the accused?

Skill Review

Compare the views of the presidential candidates of 1964, then answer the questions.

"A government that is big enough to give you all you want is big enough to take it all away."

—Barry Goldwater

"For the first time in our history it is possible to conquer poverty."

—Lyndon Johnson

"We shall return to proven ways—not because they are old, but because they are true."

—Barry Goldwater

"So I ask you tonight to join me and march along the road to the future, the road that leads to the Great Society."

—Lyndon Johnson

1. Which candidate wanted to do things in new ways? Which preferred old ways?

2. Which candidate thought that the growing size of government could be harmful to citizens?

3. Which candidate thought that the government could solve many of its peoples' problems?

Critical Thinking

Write a paragraph to answer each question.

1. Why did the civil rights movement lose strength?

2. Americans rejected Richard Nixon in 1960 but elected him in 1968. What events can account for this change?

The U.S. and the World 1960–1968

Years 1960–1968

Bay of Pigs invasion
Peace Corps started
Soviets began
building Berlin Wall

1961

Hot line set up
South Vietnamese
government
overthrown

1963

American troops sent to
the Dominican Republic
First American combat
troops sent to Vietnam

1965

Cuban
missile
crisis

1962

Leonid Brezhnev
named new Soviet leader
Tonkin Gulf
Resolution passed

1964

Soviets invaded
Czechoslovakia
Tet offensive
Vietnam peace talks began

1968

Learn these important terms:

Alliance for Progress
Third World
Peace Corps
Berlin Wall
Bay of Pigs invasion
hot line
test ban treaty

Remember the main idea:

During Kennedy's term in office, the United States tried to stop the spread of communism in Latin America, Africa, and Europe. By 1963, tensions between the United States and the Soviet Union had worsened, then eased.

Look for answers to these questions:

1. What did the United States do to stop the spread of communism in Latin America?
2. Why did the Soviets build the Berlin Wall?
3. What caused the Cuban missile crisis in 1962?

To many Americans the world situation looked grim in the summer of 1960. The Soviets appeared to have the lead in the space race. Economists were predicting that the Soviet economy would soon be outproducing America's. To add to this sense of weakening power, the Soviet leader, Nikita Khrushchev, proclaimed to America, "We will bury you!" Was the United States about to lose its power and influence in the world? Many Americans were worried that this might be so.

Throughout the 1960s, the American government faced stress in its dealings with other governments. Many questions had to be answered. How much involvement would the United States have in other governments? How strongly would the United States react to Communist threats? How much could the United States really help other countries?

As you read this chapter, you will see how the United States answered these questions. You will read about American foreign relations between 1960 and 1968. You will see why certain decisions were made. And you will learn about the stand-offs, hot spots, and wars that characterized the world during the 1960s.

Even before John F. Kennedy took office, the Communists seemed to be hard at work creating new trouble spots around the globe. In July 1960, the newly independent African nation of the Congo (present-day Zaire) was suddenly caught up in a civil war. The Soviet Union tried to set up a Communist government there. It did this by sending arms and technicians to the country.

The United Nations responded by sending a peace-keeping force to restore order. But it took the UN force a number of years to defeat the Communists. Although the Soviets were not successful in the Congo, concern over Soviet plans for other African nations remained.

Troubles with Cuba

Trouble had been brewing in Cuba ever since early 1959 when the government of dictator Fulgencio Batista (fuhl-HEN-see-oh bah-TEE-stah) was overthrown by Fidel Castro (fee-DEHL KASS-troh). At first, the United States supported Castro because he promised to build a democratic government in Cuba. But Castro soon demonstrated that he, too, was a dictator and that he supported communism.

Castro seized privately owned property, some of it owned by Americans, and divided it among many of Cuba's poor farmworkers. When the United States

Think: **Fidel Castro (seated on right) overthrew the corrupt dictator Batista.** Respond: **How did the United States react to Castro's plan to give American-held land to workers?**

CUBA, 1959-1962

responded by cutting off imports of Cuban sugar, Castro seized even more American property. He then turned to the Soviets for economic and military aid.

The United States now had an enemy nation only ninety miles from its shores. To protect the nation's security, President Eisenhower gave the Central Intelligence Agency (CIA) the authority to train and equip a group of anti-Castro Cubans. These Cubans were to invade Cuba and overthrow the Castro government.

On April 17, 1961, President Kennedy gave the anti-Castro Cubans the go-ahead. About a thousand Cubans landed at the Bay of Pigs on the southern coast of Cuba. But the Cuban people did not rise up to support the invaders. The anti-Castro Cubans were soon crushed by Castro's army. This ***Bay of Pigs invasion*** was an embarrassing defeat for the United States. Afterward, Castro turned even more strongly to the Soviet Union.

Strengthening Ties with Latin America

The failure of the Bay of Pigs invasion made the American government realize the importance of preventing communism from spreading any farther in Latin America. President Kennedy came up with a plan that would do for Latin America what the Marshall Plan had done for Europe after World War II.

Kennedy's program was the *Alliance for Progress*. It was a ten-year plan for improving life in Latin America. Kennedy proposed giving Latin American nations money to build homes, schools, and hospitals. Additional funds would be used to build up manufacturing and to improve farming. Congress approved the program in May 1961, but change in Latin America proved to be very slow.

Think: **President Kennedy's Alliance for Progress set up social and economic programs to aid Latin American countries.** Respond: **What were the specific goals of the alliance?**

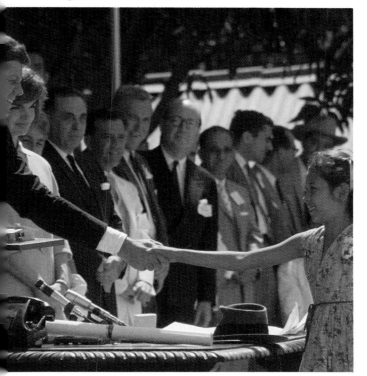

Four months later Congress gave permanent approval to another program proposed by Kennedy called the *Peace Corps*. The Peace Corps was made up of American volunteers who wanted to help the people of Third World nations. The *Third World* referred to nations that were newly independent or nations that were trying to become modernized and better developed economically.

Think: **From the beginning, Peace Corps volunteers have provided underdeveloped nations with valuable skills.** Respond: **Why has the Peace Corps been so successful?**

The Peace Corps was one of Kennedy's most successful programs. It is still in operation. Peace Corps volunteers have gone to more than fifty nations of Asia, Africa, and Latin America. There they work as teachers, nurses, farm laborers, scientists, and, above all, ambassadors of good will.

Protecting West Berlin

Within months of the Bay of Pigs invasion, Kennedy faced new threats. This time they centered on the security of West Berlin. West Berlin was a West German city, although it was located within Communist East German territory. In June 1961, Soviet Premier Khrushchev demanded that the United States and its allies leave West Berlin.

During the Cuban Missile Crisis, President Kennedy had to draw an important conclusion. He probably asked questions about the Soviet missiles in order to reach that conclusion. He may have asked if the missiles were within striking distance of the United States. The answer, of course, was *yes*. Then he may have asked what the Soviets might do with those missiles. Although he could not know for certain, the Soviets may have planned to attack the United States. When the president had answers like these, he was ready to draw a conclusion about how the missiles affected the United States. His conclusion was that the missile bases posed an unacceptable threat.

Drawing a conclusion is the last step of a reasoning process. The reasoning process may involve asking and answering several questions.

Read the paragraphs below. Then answer the questions to draw some conclusions about the Peace Corps.

When President Kennedy introduced the Peace Corps in 1961, it was an idea that captured the imagination of Americans. By 1966, the number of volunteers reached its peak of 15,550. In contrast, the number since 1981 has remained at about 5,500 per year.

Other changes have taken place in the Peace Corps. Well over half the volunteers in the early years were people who had broad educations but no special skills. Today, the majority have skills in such fields as agriculture and health.

Peace Corps volunteers have served in a total of ninety-two countries, but the number where they are serving at any time seems to change continually. In the African country of Guinea, for example, the Peace Corps entered in 1963 and left in 1966. A return in 1969 lasted only two years. Finally, Peace Corps volunteers returned to that country in 1985.

1 To draw a conclusion about the qualifications of Peace Corps volunteers, first answer these questions:
What kind of background did most of the early volunteers have? What kind of education did most of the later volunteers have? What conclusion can you draw about the educational background of people accepted by the Peace Corps today?

2 To draw a conclusion about the Peace Corps in Guinea, answer these questions:
How many times has the Peace Corps entered the area? How many times has it left the area? What conclusion can you draw about the Peace Corps' involvement in Guinea?

Think: During his well-received speech in West Berlin, Kennedy spoke these memorable words, "Ich bin ein Berliner." (I am a Berliner.) Respond: What do Kennedy's words imply?

The Soviet Union wanted to take over all of Berlin because hundreds of East Germans were escaping into West Berlin. The Soviets intended to halt this flow. To force the United States and its allies out, Khrushchev threatened to blockade, or close off, West Berlin.

President Kennedy refused to give up the city. He sent troops to West Berlin to prevent the Communists from setting up a blockade. When Khrushchev saw this, he backed down. But to make sure that no more East Germans escaped to West Berlin, the Russians built the **Berlin Wall**. The wall was little more than barbed wire when it was first begun on August 13, 1961. But over the years, concrete has been added, and the wall now extends along the entire length of the East German border.

The Cuban Missile Crisis

The greatest crisis of Kennedy's administration took place in October 1962. Photographs taken by American U-2 planes showed that the Soviet Union was building rocket-launching bases on Cuba. Because Cuba is so close to the United States, missiles from these bases could strike many American targets with ease.

Kennedy regarded the missile bases as a threat to America's security. On October 22, 1962, Kennedy warned the Soviet Union to remove the bases. He also ordered a naval blockade of Cuba. This would prevent any Soviet ship that was carrying missiles from reaching Cuba.

For a few days, it seemed as if the United States and the Soviet Union might go to war. But on Ocotober 26, Khrushchev finally agreed to remove the bases. In return, the United States promised not to attack Cuba. The Cuban missile crisis made the United States and the Soviet

Think: Soviets tightened their grip on East Berlin by building the Berlin Wall. They wanted to stop people from escaping the city. Respond: What does the Berlin Wall symbolize?

Union realize how easy it would be for the Cold War to turn hot. As a result, the two nations made an effort to avoid getting into direct conflicts with each other.

Curbing the Testing of Weapons

The Cuban missile crisis also made both sides more interested in curbing the nuclear weapons race. In August 1963, the Soviet Union and the United States agreed to set up a **hot line** between the capital cities of Moscow and Washington, D.C. This direct line of communication was designed to prevent an accident from causing a nuclear war.

That same month, the Americans and Soviets reached agreements on a **test ban treaty**. Under the terms of this treaty, nuclear weapons testing could no longer take place on the earth's surface, under water, or in outer space. Only underground nuclear testing was allowed to continue. The United States, the Soviet Union, and many other nations signed the test ban treaty.

Relations between the Soviet Union and the United States were better by the end of Kennedy's brief term in office. In the rest of this chapter you will read how other world trouble spots came to dominate the attention of Americans.

Section Review

1. What was the Bay of Pigs invasion? Why did it fail?
2. In what way was the Alliance for Progress like the Marshall Plan?
3. What did the United States do after discovering missile bases in Cuba in 1962?
4. What limits were placed on nuclear testing as a result of the test ban treaty of 1963?

---

2. Foreign Relations, 1963–1968

Learn these important terms:

liberal
purge
Brezhnev Doctrine

Remember the main idea:

President Johnson used both negotiation and military force in solving foreign problems. He also had to deal with a tough new Soviet leader, Leonid Brezhnev, who was a dedicated Communist.

Look for answers to these questions:

1. Why caused widespread rioting in Panama in 1964?
2. Why did the United States send military forces to the Dominican Republic in 1965?
3. What did the Brezhnev Doctrine state?

In a campaign speech in Los Angeles in October 1964, President Lyndon Johnson summarized his views on foreign relations. He said: ``. . . we cannot keep the peace by bluff and bluster and by threats and ultimatums. . . . we can only keep the peace by two methods: first, with a strong defense, . . . and second, . . . by reasoning together, by responsibility, by negotiation.'' Johnson wanted Americans to know that he intended to conduct foreign relations in a thoughtful manner. The president used negotiation whenever possible, but some crises in his administration called for military action.

Think: **Riots in Panama occurred after an American flag was flown over a school for American children.** Respond: **What problem was at the root of these riots?**

Trouble in Panama

In January 1964, bloody riots suddenly broke out in the Latin American nation of Panama. The people of Panama demanded that the United States turn over to them control of the Panama Canal Zone.

American control of the Canal dated back to a treaty that had been signed in 1903. This treaty gave the United States a permanent lease on a ten-mile strip of land that became the site of the Canal. In return, the United States agreed to pay Panama ten million dollars and a yearly rental fee of $250,000.

The Panamanians wanted to negotiate a new treaty with the United States. President Johnson agreed, and a new treaty was drafted that gave Panama control of the Canal Zone. However, the operation of the Canal itself became a joint American-Panamanian job. The United States felt the Canal was important to America's security—too important to turn over totally to Panama.

Trouble in the Dominican Republic

The Dominican Republic is an island nation located in the Caribbean Sea. For many years it had been ruled by a series of dictators. In 1961 the dictator, General Rafael Trujillo (troo-HEE-yoh), was assassinated. His government was overthrown, but the government that replaced it was just as unpopular as Trujillo's had been. The situation in the Dominican Republic came to a boil in 1965 when civil war broke out.

President Johnson was afraid that this civil war might make it possible for the Communists to take over the Dominican government. Therefore, he ordered more than twenty thousand American soldiers to the Dominican Republic. Their job was to restore peace.

Most Latin American nations strongly opposed President Johnson's action. They feared that this marked the start of a new American policy toward the nations of Latin America.

Think: **American marines searched cars and people in the Dominican capital, Santo Domingo.** Respond: **How did Latin America react to America's involvement in the Dominican Republic?**

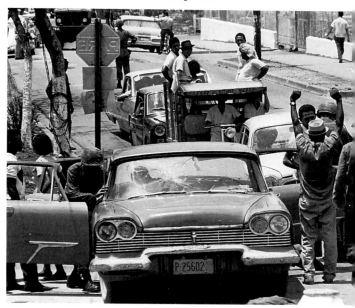

Think: President Johnson often sat in this chair while meeting with advisors. Study his expression; note his clenched fist. Respond: What issue might he be considering?

The United States seemed to be saying that it had a right to interfere in the affairs of Latin American nations in order to prevent the spread of communism. It looked as though the United States was breaking a promise it had made many years earlier. The Good Neighbor Policy of the 1930s contained a promise to Latin American nations that the United States would never interfere in their affairs unless asked to do so.

To calm the fears of Latin Americans, President Johnson agreed to remove American troops as soon as they could be replaced by peace-keeping forces from other Latin American nations. Four Latin American nations sent troops, and a peace-keeping army was formed. In 1966, free elections were held. Soon after that all the troops left the Dominican Republic. As an act of good faith, Johnson continued the Alliance for Progress program to help the nations of Latin America.

A Shake-up in the Soviet Union

The Cuban missile crisis was a source of embarrassment to Nikita Khrushchev and the Soviet Union. The Communist Party decided that a change of leadership was needed in 1964, and it removed Khrushchev from office.

The new Soviet leader was Leonid I. Brezhnev (LEE-oh-nid BREZH-nef). Brezhnev believed that Khrushchev had been too *liberal*, or open to granting the people more rights. As a result, Brezhnev saw to it that the press and free speech were controlled more tightly. He also tightened the Soviet Union's grip on the nations of eastern Europe.

Brezhnev's authority and leadership were tested in the spring of 1968. At that time, a new Communist leader came to power in Czechoslovakia. This new leader, Alexander Dubcek (DOOB-check), expanded freedom of speech and adopted some economic reforms. Dubcek promised the Soviets that Czechoslovakia would remain an ally.

The Soviets Invade Czechoslovakia

Dubcek's independent spirit was too much for Brezhnev. In August 1968, the Soviet Union and its Warsaw Pact allies invaded Czechoslovakia. The invasion was so sudden that the Czechs had no chance to resist. Dubcek was removed from power, and a new leader, hand-picked by the Soviets, took his place. The Soviets also *purged*, or got rid of, all of Dubcek's supporters.

To the rest of the world, Brezhnev described the invasion as necessary in order to uphold what became known as the **Brezhnev Doctrine**. This doctrine said that the Soviets had the right to interfere in the affairs of any eastern European nation if its Communist system of government was being threatened.

MAP WORKSHOP USING MAPS WITH THE TEXT

TROUBLE SPOTS AROUND THE WORLD, 1963–1968

In Section 2 of this chapter, you read about certain trouble spots around the world. When you locate these trouble spots on a map, you can see why the United States took the action described in the text.

Find Panama on the map and answer these questions.

1. What nations and bodies of water border on Panama?

2. If the United States lost control over the Panama Canal, how would the navy suffer?

Find the island nation called the Dominican Republic on the map.

3. How far is it from the Dominican Republic to Miami? How far is it to Venezuela from the Dominican Republic?

4. If the Dominican Republic fell into Communist hands, what nearby nations would be threatened?

Find Czechoslovakia on the map.

5. What nations border on this nation?

6. Reread the Map Workshop for Chapter 32 (page 667). Then explain Czechoslovakia's strategic importance.

The following quotations are from Section 2 of this chapter. Use the map to explain each one.

7. ''The United States felt the Canal was important to America's security—too important to turn over totally to Panama.''

8. ''President Johnson was afraid that this civil war might make it possible for the Communists to take over the Dominican government.''

9. ''Dubcek's independent spirit was too much for Brezhnev. In August 1968, the Soviet Union and its Warsaw Pact allies invaded Czechoslovakia.''

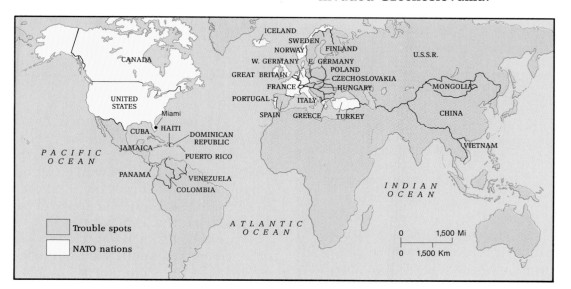

Think: **In 1968, Communist troops invaded Czechoslovakia, putting down a rebellion.** Respond: **What did the actions of the Soviet Union and the United States tell the world?**

With the Soviet Union gaining power in eastern Europe, the NATO nations decided that they should strengthen their defenses. The United States itself did little in response to the invasion.

Why was the United States so silent? American attention was focused on events that were occurring in a different part of the world. The war in Vietnam was widening, and so was America's role in it. In the rest of this chapter you will read about this war and America's involvement in it during the 1960s.

Section Review

1. How did the United States solve the Panama Canal conflict?

2. Why were Latin American nations disturbed by the American interference in the Dominican Republic?

3. How did Leonid Brezhnev come to power in the Soviet Union?

4. Why did the Soviet Union invade Czechoslovakia in 1968?

---

3. The Vietnam War, 1960–1968

Learn these important terms:

guerilla warfare
Tonkin Gulf Resolution
Green Berets
relocation
Tet offensive
escalate

Remember the main idea:

In the 1960s, America's involvement in the war in Vietnam grew. As the war continued, the number of Americans who opposed it increased. Pressure grew to withdraw the American forces and to negotiate peace.

Look for answers to these questions:

1. What was President Kennedy's position on Vietnam?

2. What was the Tonkin Gulf Resolution? When was it passed?

3. Why was it so difficult for the United States and South Vietnam to win the war?

In February 1954, President Dwight D. Eisenhower said, "I cannot conceive of a greater tragedy for America than to get heavily involved now in an all-out war in any of those [Southeast Asia] regions." The tragedy Eisenhower spoke of came to pass during the 1960s.

President Eisenhower tried to help the government of South Vietnam defeat the Vietcong, or Communist rebels from within South Vietnam. He sent military advisors to help train the army of South

Vietnam, and provided money to keep them well-supplied. However, the Vietcong controlled large areas of the country by the time Eisenhower left office.

Involvement Grows

By the time John F. Kennedy became president, there were about 650 American military advisors in Vietnam. President Kennedy's position on Vietnam was stronger than Eisenhower's. He believed that Vietnam was a sort of testing ground for the Soviets. If the Communists could topple the government of South Vietnam, they would try to do the same elsewhere in Southeast Asia.

To prevent this from happening, Kennedy sent a few thousand **Green Berets** to South Vietnam to train the South Vietnamese army. The Green Berets were a new type of American fighting unit. The members of the Green Berets were specially trained for **guerilla warfare**. This kind of warfare involves small bands of fighters who engage in "hit-and-run" attacks to keep an enemy off balance. The Green Berets trained the South Vietnamese army in guerilla fighting methods. For a while the South Vietnamese army held off the Vietcong.

Think: **American military advisors trained South Vietnamese soldiers in the early 1960s.** Respond: **Why did American leaders involve the United States in Vietnam's problems?**

The South Vietnamese Government Falls

But the war took a turn for the worse in 1963. The Vietcong defeated the South Vietnamese army in battle after battle. The people grew more dissatisfied with the South Vietnamese government. Finally, in early November of 1963, the South Vietnamese government was overthrown by leaders of the South Vietnamese military. The United States government secretly approved of these events. A series of military leaders ruled the country after the overthrow.

At the time of Kennedy's death, there were sixteen thousand American advisors in Vietnam. And Kennedy had been thinking about increasing America's role in the war.

The Incident in the Gulf of Tonkin

The war continued to go badly for the South Vietnamese. In early 1964, large numbers of soldiers from North Vietnam began to enter South Vietnam. Communist troops from the north were now helping the Vietcong in their battle to take over South Vietnam.

Then in August 1964, President Johnson informed the nation that a North Vietnamese gunboat had attacked an American warship in the Gulf of Tonkin, about thirty miles off the coast of North Vietnam. He asked Congress for the authority to "take all necessary measures" to protect American armed forces in Vietnam and to protect South Vietnam against invading armies. The aptly named **Tonkin Gulf Resolution** was passed almost unanimously by Congress. It gave the president wide powers to do whatever he felt necessary in Southeast Asia.

The president began to use those powers in February 1965. Johnson ordered the American air force to begin bombing certain targets in North Vietnam. Johnson

Think: As the years passed, America sent more and more troops and money to South Vietnam. Respond: What were the results of the increased United States involvement in Vietnam?

the United States tried *relocation*. This involved moving whole villages of people out of an area when Communists were found nearby. The village and the area around it would then be destroyed by bombs, bulldozers, and chemicals. But relocation failed also. The Communists responded to relocation by moving their forces to other areas.

The United States was caught in a dilemma, or a situation in which all the available choices have drawbacks. The United States could expand its involvement in the war with more bombing and more troops. This might bring the Soviet Union or China into the war. Or the United States could reduce its involvement by letting the South Vietnamese handle all the fighting. This meant sure defeat for South Vietnam.

escalated, or expanded, the war further in March 1965 by sending the first American combat soldiers into battle. In April, there were 33,500 American troops in Vietnam. By the end of the year, there were more than 125,000.

A Hard War To Win

Winning the war in Vietnam proved to be difficult. Many people in the South Vietnamese countryside supported the Vietcong and provided them with food, shelter, and information. Guerilla warfare made it hard to maintain control of large areas of land. For example, American forces might win control of a village, but as soon as the Americans left the town, the Vietcong would return.

To solve these problems, the United States at first tried to win the support of the Vietnamese people through a propaganda campaign and large amounts of economic assistance. When this failed,

Think: When many South Vietnamese began helping the Communists, entire villages were moved to avoid contact with the Vietcong. Respond: What problems did this create?

The Debate at Home

The war in Vietnam deeply divided the nation. There were those who supported America's involvement in the war because they saw it as a war against communism. They believed the United States must support its allies and maintain its reputation as a defender of freedom. Others saw the war as a civil war among Vietnamese. These people saw no need for American involvement. They wanted to end the destruction of lives and property in Vietnam. Still other people opposed the Vietnam War because they believed it was unwinnable.

As the war dragged on, the number of people opposed to the war grew. The antiwar movement was centered at first on college campuses. Student demonstrations became common by 1967. Then many newspapers and magazines became critical of the war, as did some members of Congress. Television news reports brought scenes of the war into millions of American homes every evening. People began to question the government's policies on Vietnam.

The Tet Offensive

In January of 1968, the Vietcong launched a surprise attack on almost every city, including many American air force bases in South Vietnam. This attack took place during the Vietnamese New Year, called Tet. The *Tet offensive* showed that the Vietcong were not prepared to give up their fight despite American aid to South Vietnam. It also proved that many South Vietnamese were aiding the Communists. The offensive would not have been so widespread or so forceful without the help of local people.

Think: In the late 1960s and early 1970s, antiwar demonstrations were held on numerous college campuses, on streets in countless cities, and at the Democratic Convention in Chicago. Read the slogans on the signs carried by protestors. Respond: Why were feelings about the Vietnam War so strong?

HISTORY MAKERS

Al Santoli

Voice of the Vietnam Veterans

They turned off the tape recorder. It had been an exhausting evening. The two men had been talking for hours, recalling the past. They compared experiences, remembering places and friends. Not all of their memories were happy. Both men relived the agony of friends dying, the anger and frustration of a lost cause, and the pain of old wounds.

"Thanks, Al, for interviewing me. I haven't been able to talk about this before. And it still bothers me, you know. Sometimes I wake up at night and I'm back there, listening for some sound that will give me their position. I'm waiting to fire, and wondering if I'll ever get home alive. Finally I realize I'm home. I'm alive and well. But 'Nam will be with me for the rest of my life."

Al Santoli was nineteen years old when he fought in Vietnam. He was wounded three times, but he came back to the war after each injury. He couldn't leave his friends, and he felt that the war could be ended. The last time Santoli went into the field, it was with a platoon of Vietnamese and American soldiers who lived with Vietnamese villagers in the jungle. As Santoli got to know the villagers, he discovered that Americans didn't understand Vietnamese culture. He became convinced that the war could only be won after the Americans learned to respect their Vietnamese allies.

Santoli returned from Vietnam in 1969. He was proud to have fought, but angry that the war was dragging on. He felt hurt by the attitudes Americans had toward veterans. Worst of all, he was unable to talk about his experiences. After ten years, he finally began to heal. As he said, ". . . as if coming out of a shock-induced trance, I stopped running from my experiences there. I began interviewing and soul-searching with fellow veterans for an oral history of the war . . ."

From these interviews, Santoli wrote a book, *Everything We Had*. It presents a range of feelings and attitudes about the Vietnam War by Americans who were part of it. Through the voices of soldiers and medical workers, Santoli gives us some understanding of the chaos that war creates. The Vietnam War created chaos both within countries and within human beings.

Think: **Scenes such as the one above flashed into living rooms across America. The horrors of war could not be ignored. Despite feelings against it, the war dragged on. It was to become the longest war in American history.**
Respond: **Why was it so difficult for the United States to remove itself from the war?**

The South Vietnamese and American troops were able to recapture every city taken by the Vietcong. Even so the Tet offensive added to the discouragement that Americans were feeling about the war. More than 540,000 American soldiers were in South Vietnam. About 30,000 had been killed, and more than 100,000 had been wounded. The war was costing the United States over twenty-five billion dollars a year.

President Johnson recognized how unpopular the war had become. He tried to make peace in March 1968. He limited the bombing of North Vietnam. Soon after, North Vietnam agreed to start peace talks in Paris. But the talks, which began in May 1968, made little progress. The Vietcong demanded a role in the government of South Vietnam, and the military leaders of South Vietnam refused to agree to this.

In an attempt to help Hubert Humphrey win the election of 1968, Johnson ordered a halt to all bombing in Vietnam. But the order did little to help Humphrey or the peace process. Richard Nixon won the election and inherited the war. You will read about his presidency next.

Section Review

1. Who were the Green Berets?
2. How was Lyndon Johnson able to escalate the war in Vietnam?
3. What dilemma did the United States face in Vietnam?
4. What did the Tet offensive demonstrate to the United States?
5. Why was a peace agreement difficult to achieve in Vietnam?

CHAPTER SUMMARY

Within months of becoming president, John Kennedy authorized an invasion of Cuba in an attempt to overthrow the island's Communist leader. But the invasion failed. Kennedy tried other ways of preventing the spread of communism. He gave aid to Latin American nations and organized the Peace Corps. Kennedy also stood firm against Soviet attempts to take over West Berlin and to build missile bases in Cuba.

Lyndon Johnson had to deal with crises in Panama and the Dominican Republic. The crisis in Panama was resolved through negotiation, but the Dominican crisis required the intervention of American marines. In the Soviet Union, a staunch Communist, Leonid Brezhnev, came to power.

The war in Vietnam dragged on throughout the 1960s, and America's involvement in it grew. After an American warship was attacked by the North Vietnamese in 1964, Congress gave President Johnson wide powers to do what was necessary to prevent Communist aggression in Southeast Asia. As the war escalated, so did the number of Americans who opposed it. By 1968, Johnson had halted the bombing of North Vietnam in an attempt to get the peace process started. Peace talks began, but little progress was made. Ending the war was left to a new president, Richard M. Nixon.

Key Words

Write a sentence to explain the meaning of each of these terms.

Third World
Peace Corps
purge
escalate

Brezhnev
Doctrine
guerilla
warfare

Major Events

Choose the answer that best completes the statement.

1. The 1961 attempt to overthrow the Castro government was the

   a) Cuban Missile Crisis.
   b) Battle of Batista.
   c) Bay of Pigs invasion.

2. To prevent East Germans from escaping to West Berlin, the Russians

   a) built missile bases.
   b) built the Berlin Wall.
   c) blockaded West Berlin.

3. In 1963, the United States and the Soviet Union

   a) agreed on a test ban treaty.
   b) almost came to war in Cuba.
   c) sent troops to Czechoslovakia.

4. Congress gave the president wide powers to do what was necessary in Vietnam by passing

   a) the Vietcong Treaty.
   b) the Tet Resolution.
   c) the Tonkin Gulf Resolution.

5. Support for the Vietnam War

   a) declined as the war went on.
   b) increased as it continued.
   c) was always strong.

Review

Important Facts

Answer each question with at least one complete sentence.

1. Who was Fidel Castro? Why did the United States regard him as an enemy?

2. What was the Alliance for Progress? How successful was it?

3. Why did Kennedy regard the construction of missile bases in Cuba to be a threat to America's security? How was the crisis resolved?

4. What caused bloody riots to break out in Panama in 1964?

5. Why did Johnson send American soldiers to the Dominican Republic in 1965?

6. What brought Leonid Brezhnev to power in the Soviet Union? How did he differ from Khrushchev?

7. Why did the Soviet Union invade Czechoslovakia?

8. Why did Kennedy send the Green Berets to South Vietnam?

9. Why was it so difficult to win the war in Vietnam?

10. What was "relocation"? How successful was it?

11. What dilemma did the United States face as a result of the war in Vietnam?

12. What was the Tet offensive?

13. Why did Johnson try to make peace in March 1968? Why did the peace talks make little progress?

Skill Review

Study this map, then answer the following questions.

1. How many African nations became independent in 1960?

2. What conclusion can you draw about colonialism in Africa?

3. Which country has a Communist government?

4. What conclusion can you draw about Soviet interest in Zaire?

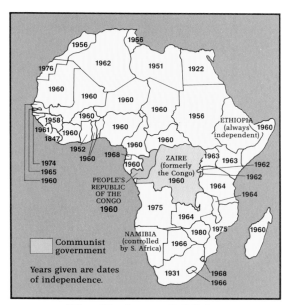

The Nations of Africa

Critical Thinking

Write a paragraph to answer each question.

1. The war in Vietnam was the first to be covered by television. What effect do you think this had on the public's opinion of the war? Why?

2. Why was the anti-war movement centered on college campuses?

Important People

Choose the answer that best completes the statement.

1. President Kennedy

   a) opposed integrated housing.
   b) was favored to win in 1960.
   c) was able to win support for America's space program.

2. President Johnson

   a) was a master at getting legislation passed.
   b) was concerned with balancing the budget.
   c) was a wealthy Bostonian.

3. One leader of the black power movement was

   a) James Meredith.
   b) James Earl Ray.
   c) Stokely Carmichael.

4. The Bay of Pigs invasion showed that Cubans

   a) supported Fidel Castro.
   b) wanted to overthrow Batista.
   c) were building missile bases.

5. Nikita Khrushchev was removed from power in Russia because

   a) he failed to crush an uprising in Czechoslovakia.
   b) the economy began to weaken.
   c) he was too liberal.

6. The Green Berets were

   a) Communist rebels from within South Vietnam.
   b) American soldiers trained for guerilla warfare.
   c) in charge of rebuilding Vietnamese villages.

Main Ideas

Choose the answer that best completes the statement.

1. The election of 1960

   a) was one of the closest ever held in America.
   b) focused on the issue of Kennedy's religion.
   c) left the Republicans in control of the White House.

2. The 1963 March on Washington

   a) was the largest anti-war demonstration in American history.
   b) called for an end to racial discrimination.
   c) ended in violence.

3. Johnson's program to improve the American nation was called

   a) the New Frontier.
   b) the attack on poverty.
   c) the Great Society.

4. The Civil Rights Act of 1964

   a) forbade literacy tests as a voting requirement.
   b) required employers to hire a certain percentage of minority workers.
   c) forbade segregation in public places.

5. Because many whites violently resisted black attempts to gain equality,

   a) the civil rights movement was abandoned.
   b) the black power movement gained strength.
   c) the government repealed many civil rights laws.

R e v i e w

6. Johnson did not run for a second term because

   a) people blamed him for the riots in the ghettos.

   b) people blamed him for the nation's economic problems.

   c) people blamed him for the war in Vietnam.

7. The greatest military crisis of Kennedy's administration took place in

   a) Cuba.

   b) Vietnam.

   c) Berlin.

8. Johnson aroused the anger of Latin American nations when he sent American soldiers to the country of

   a) Panama.

   b) Cuba.

   c) the Dominican Republic.

9. American involvement in Vietnam began to escalate

   a) with the passage of the Tonkin Gulf Resolution.

   b) when bombing of North Vietnam began.

   c) when relocation of whole villages of people occurred.

10. The Tet offensive

   a) was America's first clear-cut victory in the war in Vietnam.

   b) was evidence that the Vietcong were not giving up the fight.

   c) prompted anti-war demonstrations to be held by Americans throughout the country.

History Skills

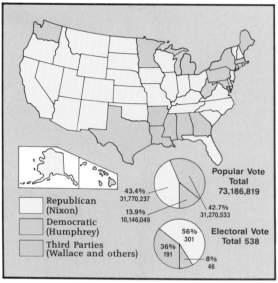

1968 Presidential Election

Choose the answer that best completes the statement.

1. From this map, you can conclude that Americans were

   a) dissatisfied with the Democrats.

   b) supporting segregation.

   c) voting for the man in office.

2. The candidate who supported Johnson's views on the war in Vietnam was

   a) Richard Nixon.

   b) Hubert Humphrey.

   c) George Wallace.

3. If independent voters had joined with Democrats,

   a) Humphrey would have won the electoral vote.

   b) the Democrats would still not have won the popular vote.

   c) the Republicans would still have won the electoral vote.

Crises and Challenges

36
America 1968–1980

Years 1968–1980

Environmental Protection
Agency created

1970

Vice President Spiro
Agnew resigned
Oil embargo began

1973

Jimmy Carter elected
president

1976

Inflation topped 12
percent

1980

Watergate break-in
Equal Employment
Opportunity Act passed

1972

President Nixon
resigned
Oil embargo was lifted

1974

Nuclear power incident
at Three Mile Island

1979

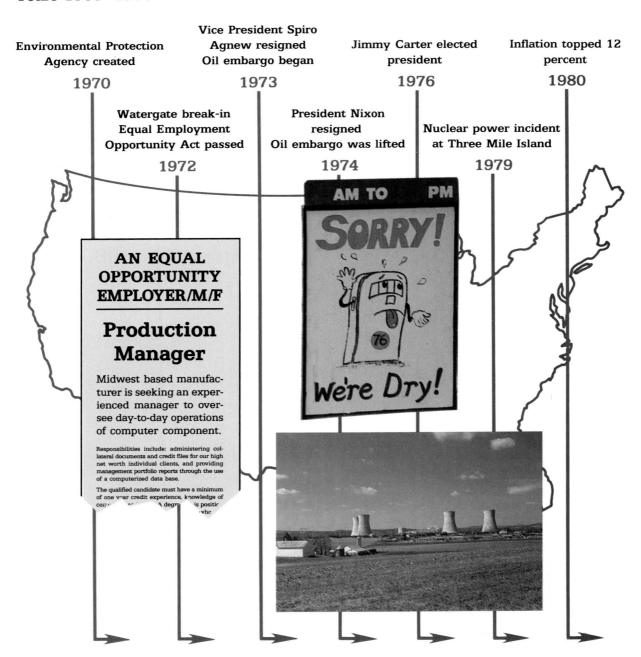

**AN EQUAL
OPPORTUNITY
EMPLOYER/M/F**

Production Manager

Midwest based manufacturer is seeking an experienced manager to oversee day-to-day operations of computer component.

Responsibilities include: administering collateral documents and credit files for our high net worth individual clients, and providing management portfolio reports through the use of a computerized data base.

The qualified candidate must have a minimum of one year credit experience, knowledge of com... degr... is positic ...whe

AM TO   PM

SORRY!

We're Dry!

1. Nixon and Watergate

Learn these important terms:

wage and price controls
Cost of Living Council
Watergate scandal
kickbacks

Remember the main idea:

Richard Nixon was forced to resign the presidency because of his involvement in the cover-up of the Watergate scandal.

Look for answers to these questions:

1. What accomplishments did Richard Nixon achieve during his first term?
2. How did the Watergate scandal begin? Why did it spread?
3. Why did Richard Nixon resign from office?

We like to think that our government is stable. It is, after all, one of the oldest governments in the world. But during the early 1970s, Americans' confidence in their government was badly shaken. A major scandal, known as Watergate, forced Americans to take a long, hard look at their political leaders.

In addition to political problems, America during the 1970s faced economic and social concerns. Americans spent more money and received fewer goods. Many had no jobs. Gasoline was scarce. Americans felt caught up in worsening economic conditions.

At the same time, women and minorities made their unhappiness known. They demanded equal rights, and the government responded. Still, years of inequality could not be forgotten quickly.

In this chapter you will read about many problems. But you will also read about solutions. You will see how the United States dealt with its problems and looked toward the future. You will also begin to see some long-term consequences for American actions of the 1960s and 1970s.

Richard Nixon became president at a difficult time in our nation's history. In 1968, the country was badly divided over the Vietnam War. Civil rights were a burning issue. The level of violence in America was high. News on the economic front was not encouraging. Inflation, or a general rise in the level of prices, was becoming a major problem.

During his campaign, Nixon had promised to put an end to America's woes. That, however, was not an easy promise to keep. Throughout his first term, Nixon

Think: **Anti-war senator George McGovern took a strong stance against American involvement in Vietnam. Although McGovern received their support, many young people did not even take the time to vote.** Respond: **Why is it important for people to exercise their voting rights?**

struggled to deal with the Vietnam War. He also worked hard to bring law and order to the streets of America.

Supreme Court Appointments

Nixon was given a big chance to influence the future of the American justice system. In 1969, the Supreme Court's liberal Chief Justice Earl Warren retired. Nixon named the conservative Warren E. Burger to replace him. Two of Nixon's later appointments were rejected by the Senate. Still, Nixon was able to name four new members to the Court. In doing so, he created a much more conservative Supreme Court.

The Economy

One of Nixon's biggest challenges was the economy. To battle inflation, he made *wage and price controls.* For ninety days, no one could raise wages or prices. For ninety days after that, wages and prices could go up only in certain circumstances. A *Cost of Living Council* was set up to review all proposed increases. Many peo-

ple grumbled about these tactics. But Nixon's plan worked. The rate of inflation slowed down. However, the rate of unemployment began to rise.

The 1972 Presidential Election

Richard Nixon was obviously set to win reelection in 1972. The polls showed that he was far ahead of any Democratic rival. But some Nixon supporters did not want to leave anything to chance. They wanted to be absolutely certain of victory. So they went beyond the law. They engaged in so-called "dirty tricks" like forging letters and disrupting campaign schedules in order to discredit the Democrats.

Meanwhile, the Democratic Party was divided. Several candidates fought for the nomination. One by one, they dropped out of the race. In the end, the Democrats nominated Senator George McGovern of South Dakota. His ideas on ending the Vietnam War were too extreme for most Americans, however. Nixon defeated McGovern soundly in the election, winning forty-nine out of the fifty states.

The Watergate Break-in

Early in the morning of June 17, 1972, the police arrested five men at a complex of apartments and offices called the Watergate. The men were trying to break into the headquarters of the Democratic National Committee. They carried cameras and electronic listening devices. They wanted to find sensitive information that could be used against the Democratic Party.

At first, no one paid much attention to the break-in or the arrests. A White House spokesperson called it a ''third-rate burglary.'' Nixon ordered a special White House investigation headed by John Dean. Dean's report declared that no one in the White House was involved in the **Watergate scandal.**

The Democrats thought otherwise. They tried to turn the Watergate scandal into a campaign issue. The attempt failed miserably. Most Americans were not interested. The Democrats' cries of scandal sounded to many like a desperate campaign tactic. Nixon's easy victory, however, did not put the issue to rest. For the next two years, the story of Watergate continued to grow.

The Scandal Spreads

Robert Woodward and Carl Bernstein, reporters for the *Washington Post*, would not let the story die. They kept digging for clues of a wider scandal. Eventually, their efforts paid off. They uncovered evidence that led directly to the White House. John Mitchell was the first major official to be singled out. He had been Nixon's Attorney General. He had resigned that post to head Nixon's reelection campaign. Woodward and Bernstein showed that Mitchell had known about the plans for the break-in. They also showed that he had tried to cover up the crime. This news aroused the public's interest.

Think: This peaceful view of the Watergate Building contradicts the storm that rocked the White House when the scandal was revealed. Although Nixon did not know about the break-in until after it happened, he tried to cover it up when he learned about it. Respond: **What might have been some of his reasons for doing so?**

In 1973, the United States Senate began its own investigation. It set up a special committee headed by Senator Sam Ervin, a Democrat from North Carolina. Slowly, evidence began to mount against Nixon. People involved in the cover-up, like John Dean, began to talk. Still, the president denied any knowledge of the break-in or the efforts to cover it up.

Agnew Resigns

As Nixon became more linked to Watergate, another scandal rocked the White House. Vice President Spiro Agnew was charged with taking bribes while he was governor of Maryland. He was accused of receiving *kickbacks*, or illegal payoffs, from building contractors. Agnew was also charged with filing false tax returns. At first, he denied everything. When all the evidence was laid before him, however, the vice president saw that he could not prove his innocence. In October 1973, he agreed to resign his office if all the major charges against him were dropped. This arrangement was accepted. Most people did not want to see Agnew put on trial while a cloud of suspicion still hung over the president. Under the Twenty-Fifth Amendment, Nixon nominated Gerald Ford to replace Agnew.

Think: Problems for the White House were made worse by the forced resignation of Spiro Agnew in October 1973. Respond: Why was Agnew allowed to bargain for lesser charges?

The Investigation Continues

The Agnew scandal did not slow down the Watergate investigation. By this time, the Watergate affair was being talked about everywhere. One presidential advisor after another was linked to either the break-in or the cover-up. It seemed clear that Nixon knew more than he was telling. Still, investigators needed proof that the president was directly involved in the cover-up.

A means of finding proof was finally discovered during the Senate hearings. An aide just happened to mention that all of Nixon's White House conversations were tape-recorded. The tapes would prove once and for all what Nixon knew. Both the Ervin Committee and the Special Prosecutor, Archibald Cox, wanted to play the tapes. Nixon refused to hand them over. He insisted that they were private. The matter was finally brought to court, and Nixon lost.

The President Resigns

Nixon tried to please Cox by giving written summaries of the tapes. Cox insisted on hearing the actual tapes. Nixon then had Cox fired. However, the pressure on Nixon was too great. At last, he was forced to give the tapes to the court.

The tapes proved that Nixon had been involved in the Watergate affair. He had known about the cover-up from the beginning. He had not been truthful with the American public. Even his closest supporters could no longer back the president. It seemed certain that Nixon would be impeached, or charged with a high crime. To avoid impeachment, Nixon resigned from office on August 9, 1974. He was the first president to do so.

Think: **Read the headlines from the August 9 edition of the** *Washington Post.* Respond: **What do you think Americans were thinking and feeling when they read the news?**

Think: **On August 9, 1974, Richard Nixon became the first president of the United States to resign from office.** Respond: **What do you think he was thinking as he left Washington?**

Effects of the Watergate Scandal

The Watergate scandal left Americans disappointed by their leaders. The president had betrayed the people's trust. He had broken the law and falsely represented himself. Many people felt that if the president himself could not be trusted, then no politician could be. As a result, Americans in general became very suspicious of all political figures. Fortunately, they kept their faith in the structure of American government. They began looking for new leaders. The American system of government had withstood a difficult crisis.

Section Review

1. Why did Nixon win the 1972 presidential election so easily?
2. Why did five men break into the headquarters of the Democratic National Committee in 1972?
3. What role did Woodward and Bernstein play in uncovering the Watergate scandal?
4. Why did Vice President Spiro Agnew resign?
5. Why were the Nixon White House tapes so important?

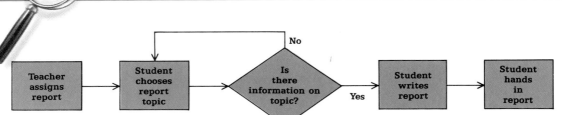

A flow chart is a way of showing information. The flow chart above shows the steps that might be involved in writing a report for a class. The squares stand for steps in the job, and the diamond stands for a point at which a decision about the job must be made.

The arrows show that the steps in this job go from left to right. First the teacher assigns a report, and then the student chooses a topic for the report. A decision point is reached when the student looks for information on the chosen topic. At that point the flow of the job can go two ways. If the student decides, "Yes,

there is enough information on the chosen topic," he or she goes ahead on the line that says "yes." If the student decides, "No, there isn't enough information," he or she follows the "no" arrow and goes back to the step of choosing a topic. This time, if the answer at the decision point is "yes," the student goes ahead to the next step, writing the report, and to the final step, handing in the report.

The flow chart below shows the steps and decision points in the process of impeaching a government official. Impeachment is a formal charge accusing of wrongdoing.

The Impeachment Process

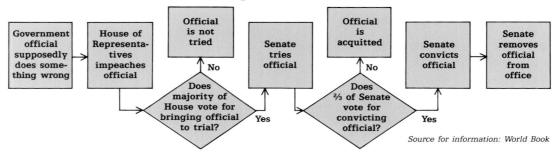

Source for information: World Book

Study the flow chart, then answer the questions that follow it.

1 What group can impeach a government official?

2 What are the decision points on this flow chart?

3 What happens at each decision point if the answer is "no"?

4 What happens at each decision point if the answer is "yes"?

5 What is the next step after the Senate convicts an official?

2. Ford and Carter

Learn these important terms:

stagflation
voluntary wage and price controls
pardon
amnesty
recession
embargo

Remember the main idea:

Both Gerald Ford and Jimmy Carter struggled with domestic tensions and a troubled economy during their years as president.

Look for answers to these questions:

1. How did President Ford try to heal the wounds of past government problems?
2. What economic problems did Ford and Carter face?
3. What were the causes and effects of the energy crisis?

Gerald R. Ford (1913-) came to office during very troubled times. Painfully aware of having been appointed rather than elected, Ford was called overly cautious by some, honest and decent by others.

On August 9, 1974, Gerald Ford was sworn in as president. Americans saw Ford as an honest man who had nothing to hide. He was also modest. As he once said, "I'm a Ford, not a Lincoln." President Ford chose Nelson A. Rockefeller, former governor of New York, as his vice president.

Ford Pardons Nixon

Ford was a well-liked president at first. Most people trusted this former representative from Michigan. Then he made an unpopular decision. On September 8, 1974, he granted Richard Nixon a full *pardon*. That meant that Nixon could not be charged for any crimes he had committed while president.

This decision shocked many Americans. Why, these people thought, should Nixon get off without even a trial? It did not seem fair. Nonetheless, Ford defended his decision, saying he wanted Americans to put Watergate behind them.

Amnesty for War Protestors

Ford then made another unpopular decision. Again, his decision was meant to help Americans bury the past. He granted limited *amnesty* to certain Vietnam war protestors. This meant that those who had evaded the draft or deserted the army would not be punished. They would, however, have to take the oath of allegiance to the United States. They would also have to give two years of service to the government. Some people attacked the amnesty program as too generous. Others attacked it as not generous enough. In the end, President Ford's attempt to heal the wounds created by the Vietnam War failed.

Stagflation

During Ford's presidency, inflation was a big problem. In 1974, the rate of inflation was about 12 percent. That was much too high. To make matters worse, the economy itself was doing poorly. Production was down, and many people were out of work. This economic slump, called a *recession*, was the worst since World War II.

Economists were surprised by this situation. Usually inflation occurs only when an economy is booming. Little or no inflation usually happens when there is a recession. Clearly, this combination of inflation and recession was something new. Economists created a new term—*stagflation*—to describe this unusual condition. The economy was *stag*nant, and there was high in*flation*.

Ford tried to fight stagflation with his **voluntary wage and price controls**. He urged workers not to ask for higher wages, and he asked businesses to keep their prices low. These voluntary measures did not work. Costs kept rising.

The Energy Crisis

America's economic woes were made worse by the shortage of oil. For years Americans had been burning more and more imported oil. Then, in 1973, the Arab nations stopped shipping oil to the United States. They intended this as punishment for American support of Israel. This oil *embargo* sent the price of available oil skyrocketing. People had to wait in long lines to get expensive gasoline for their cars. Sometimes there was no gas.

High fuel prices drove up other prices, too. Higher costs for shipping goods meant higher prices for the consumer. Higher costs for producing electricity pushed up the costs of manufacturing. These costs were passed along to the consumer. Prices rose to cover expenses.

In March 1974, the Arab nations lifted their embargo, but the price of oil kept going up anyway. At the start of 1973, oil was three dollars a barrel. Two years later

Think: The nation was often paralyzed by rising prices and the oil embargo. Motorists often waited hours to get gas. Respond: Why was "They've got us over a barrel" an appropriate saying?

it was twenty dollars a barrel. When Ford became president, the energy crisis continued. It was one of the causes of stagflation in the mid-1970s.

The Election of 1976

By the end of President Ford's term of office, stagflation began to ease. Oil prices stabilized. Tax cuts and increased government spending helped to improve the economy. In 1976, Ford ran for reelection. His challenger was Jimmy Carter, a former governor of Georgia.

HISTORY MAKERS

─────Cesar Chavez─────

Leader of Farmworkers

He was hot and tired, and his back was killing him. The California air was dusty and hard to breathe. He bent over and cut another bunch of grapes. Slowly he moved down the row of vines, bending and cutting. Every time he stooped over, the ache in his back grew more painful. In the distance he heard the faint drone of an airplane. The sound grew louder as the crop duster approached. Suddenly the air was full of mist. He began to cough, and his eyes began to water. Other workers struggled for breath. The fog of DDT settled on the grapes and vines and invaded the fieldworkers' lungs. He continued working, stooping and cutting the grapes. By the end of the day he could hardly stand up straight. By the end of the day he had earned less than ten dollars. For his backbreaking fieldwork, Cesar Chavez was paid very little.

Cesar Chavez began fieldwork when his family lost their farm during the depression. Pay was poor, housing was worse, and the Chavez family often lived in their car. As Mexican-Americans, they suffered much discrimination.

Cesar Chavez wanted to make life better for fieldworkers. Their living and working conditions convinced him that they needed the strength and protection of a labor union. He began to organize the workers into the United Farmworkers. Farmers and growers refused to bargain with the new union, so Chavez led a strike.

California growers were not interested in workers' problems. They threatened the strikers with violence. Like Martin Luther King, Cesar Chavez believed in nonviolence. He organized fasts, marches, and finally a national boycott of grapes and lettuce. The boycott was successful, and the growers signed contracts with the United Farmworkers. In 1975, California passed a law giving farmworkers the right to hold union elections and to bargain collectively with growers.

Under Cesar Chavez's leadership, the National Farmworkers Union has improved wages and living conditions of farmworkers. It has given them back their dignity, as people recognize the importance and worth of those who harvest food.

James Earl Carter, Jr. (1924-   ) rose to the nation's highest office more quickly than any president before him. His campaign was based on human rights and honesty in government.

Carter was new to national politics. He had nothing to do with Watergate or the pardoning of Nixon. People found his inexperience refreshing. They hoped he would clean up government and restore integrity to the presidency. The race between Ford and Carter was a close one, but Carter eked out a victory.

Carter's Troubles Begin

Once in the White House, Carter's inexperience was no longer an asset. He was an outsider in Washington with no close friends in Congress. His staff was made up mostly of friends from Georgia. When Carter tried to push through legislation, he ran into trouble.

Carter also suffered from many of the problems that had bothered Ford. By 1976, inflation was down to about 5½ percent. But during Carter's term it rose again. In 1979, it stood at 10 percent. And in 1980, it had climbed to more than 12 percent. At the same time, unemployment remained high. Again, the economy was suffering from stagflation.

Battling Stagflation

Like Ford, Carter tried voluntary wage and price controls to stop inflation. Once again, these measures had little effect. Carter also tried to help the economy by attacking the energy crisis. He encouraged people to cut down on their use of

Think: A variety of solutions to the energy crisis surfaced in the 1970s. One solution, nuclear power, was undesirable to many because of the poisonous waste. Solar energy became a new possibility. Solar-powered houses became popular.
Respond: Why is it necessary for people to find new sources of energy?

gas and oil. He also called for more research into new energy sources.

This research was at least one valuable thing that came out of the energy crisis. People learned to use less energy. They built more efficient cars and oil burners. And scientists began to look for alternative sources of energy. Solar energy, for example, became popular for heating homes. Wind power and nuclear energy also looked promising. Despite this progress, however, the economy remained in bad shape.

The End of Carter's Term

By 1980, Carter had lost most of his popularity. The United States was suffering from double-digit inflation at home and a painful loss of respect abroad. Americans viewed Carter as weak and ineffective because he had failed to solve the nation's problems. Americans began searching for yet another new face. They looked for a president who would make them feel good about America again. They wanted a strong, positive leader. Jimmy Carter, it seemed, was no longer the right man for the job.

Section Review

1. Why was Ford's decision to pardon Nixon so unpopular? How did Ford defend his decision?
2. What were the two conditions of Ford's amnesty program?
3. What is stagflation?
4. Was Carter's inexperience with national politics an advantage or a disadvantage to him?
5. What measures did both Ford and Carter take to try to help the economy?

3. The American People, 1968–1980

Learn these important terms:

women's rights
Equal Rights Amendment
Hispanics
Equal Employment Opportunity Act
Environmental Protection Agency
American Indian Movement
Gray Panthers
ecology
toxic waste
League of United Latin American Citizens

Remember the main idea:

During the 1970s, Americans increasingly turned their attention to the problems of women's rights, minority rights, and pollution.

Look for answers to these questions:

1. How did the role of women change in the 1970s?
2. What progress did minority groups make during this decade?
3. What were the goals of the ecology movement?

The dawn of the 1970s did not wash away the problems of the 1960s. The war in Vietnam still raged. Blacks still struggled for racial equality. And poverty still had not vanished from the land. During the 1970s, Americans faced yet another set of social issues.

Think: Gloria Steinem and other women marched to gain support for the Equal Rights Amendment. The ERA was meant to end all laws that discriminated against women. Respond: What were the successes and failures of the women's movement?

Women's Rights

One of the hottest issues in the 1970s was that of **women's rights**. Women made up more than 50 percent of the population. Despite being the majority, they did not enjoy the same rights as men. Most women working outside the home found themselves in low-paying, low-level jobs. Only a small number were hired as doctors, lawyers, or executives. Other jobs, such as truck driving and carpentry, were not considered appropriate for women at all. Even when women performed the same jobs as men, they often received less money.

Since the 1960s, many women like Betty Friedan and Gloria Steinem had been working for women's rights. In the 1970s, the women's rights movement gained strength. People realized that men and women should be treated equally.

The government began passing laws to ensure equality. The **Equal Employment Opportunity Act** of 1972 required equal pay for equal work. And that same year, Congress approved an **Equal Rights Amendment** (ERA) to the Constitution. It was designed to guarantee women equal rights under the law. This amendment failed to become law because not enough states ratified it. Thirty-eight states needed to vote for it; only thirty-five did so. Still, the campaign for the ERA helped make Americans aware of the women's rights movement.

As attitudes changed, new career paths opened up to women. More women began working outside the home. Some took jobs because they or their families needed the money. Others worked because they enjoyed the challenge. By 1980, there were significant numbers of women in almost every occupation. New choices brought new problems, however. Women struggled to balance their careers with their roles as wives and mothers.

Hispanics Seek Equal Rights

Many **Hispanics**, or Spanish-speaking peoples, also began demanding better treatment. Some Hispanics had just arrived in America. Others had lived here for generations. No matter how long they had been in America, though, Hispanics often had trouble entering the mainstream of society. Their language, skin color, and culture set them apart from other Americans. This made them easy victims of discrimination.

In the 1960s and 1970s, Hispanic leaders worked to improve the status of their people. They began the *League of United Latin American Citizens* to fight for equal rights. They formed similar groups on college campuses. At election times, Hispanics supported Hispanic candidates for public office.

Native Americans Unite

Native Americans also called for an end to the discrimination they had suffered for so long. Some worked toward this goal through the Bureau of Indian Affairs. Others formed a more radical group called the *American Indian Movement* (AIM). In 1973, two hundred AIM members gathered at the village of Wounded Knee in South Dakota. This had been the site of an Indian slaughter in 1890. For two months, the AIM members occupied the town. They burned buildings and brandished guns. Such violence was unusual, though. Most Native Americans used peaceful methods to advance their cause. By the late 1970s, they had won a series of court rulings giving them more power.

Think: Native Americans worked to improve their housing, medical care, education, and employment opportunities. Respond: Why do you think a Native American group placed this tepee near the White House?

Think: The Gray Panthers helped change attitudes about older people. This awareness led to lower prices for senior citizens. Respond: What special needs do older people have?

New Minority Groups Form

Encouraged, perhaps, by the success of others, new minority groups popped up. Older people formed an organization called the *Gray Panthers* to fight for equal rights for senior citizens. People with all types of physical handicaps formed similar groups. Consumers, too, organized special groups. They wanted more government protection of their rights.

The Ecology Movement

Americans became aware of their environment in the late 1960s. They suddenly became concerned about *ecology*. Ecology is the way living creatures relate to the environment. People realized how dangerous it was to dump pollutants into the air, water, and land. They questioned the wisdom of spraying chemicals on crops. They cringed at the litter along America's

OIL FROM THE MIDDLE EAST

You can combine your map and reading skills for a better understanding of an issue. When you read the paragraph below, you will learn certain facts about oil in the Middle East. When you study the map, you will see the problem of oil supply more clearly.

Read the following paragraphs.

At the time of the Arab oil embargo of 1973, more than 15 percent of America's imported oil, or about one million barrels per day, came from the Middle East. That figure was increasing daily.

Since the Middle East holds about two-thirds of the world's oil reserves, American companies wanted to help develop Mideast oil supplies. They built oil wells, pipelines, and shipping ports.

These investments in Mideast oil operations were highly profitable. They were also very risky because the governments of the oil-producing countries controlled the flow of oil to the United States. Most of these were Arab countries that opposed the United States' aid to Israel.

Now look at the map.

1. Why are oil pipelines important? Which countries pipe their oil to the Mediterranean Sea?

2. Which countries took part in the oil embargo? Which of these used Mediterranean ports?

3. From which other countries could the United States get oil? What problems might it face in doing so?

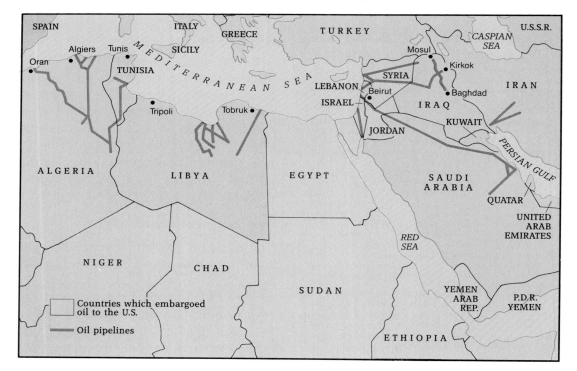

Countries which embargoed oil to the U.S.

Oil pipelines

Think: **People were becoming more aware of hazardous wastes. Closely examine this contaminated truck and the man who is spraying it down.**
Respond: **Where will the waste go?**

highways. And they protested the dirty fumes spewed out by automobiles.

The government responded to these concerns by passing stricter pollution laws. And in 1970, Congress created the **Environmental Protection Agency**. This agency was set up to coordinate pollution control programs. It was also designed to set tough environmental standards.

Energy Versus the Environment

Still, the problems of pollution did not go away. Certain lakes, for example, had already been damaged beyond repair. Also, some anti-pollution measures conflicted with America's need for energy. Modern lifestyles required the use of coal, gas, oil, and other fuels. But mining and burning these fuels polluted the environment. Nuclear energy, too, came under attack. When nuclear energy is produced, a toxic, or poisonous, waste is created. There is no quick or easy way to get rid of this **toxic waste**. It remains deadly for thousands of years.

In 1979, another danger of nuclear energy became clear. At the Three Mile Island electric power plant in Middletown, Pennsylvania, a small pump broke down. It threatened to unleash 600,000 gallons of deadly radioactive gas. Luckily,

disaster was prevented, but nuclear energy suddenly seemed riskier than ever. Certainly nuclear energy threatened the environment, but to stop using it would cut down the country's energy supply. Were people willing to lose a major source of energy for the sake of the environment? Some were, and some were not. And so the debate about nuclear energy, and other forms of pollution-producing energy, continued.

The End of the 1970s

Americans saw great changes at home during the 1970s. Public confidence in national leaders was badly shaken by the Watergate scandal. The economy was in bad shape. Inequality still hurt many Americans. Yet, the nation managed to survive. Ford and Carter worked hard to restore the people's faith in their government. They tried, although unsuccessfully, to solve the country's economic problems. And they addressed the demands made by women and minorities for greater rights.

As Americans headed into the 1980s, these and other issues at home continued to pose great challenges. As you read the next chapter, you will learn about the challenges the United States faced abroad during the 1970s.

Section Review

1. What was the Equal Rights Amendment? Why didn't it become law?
2. What happened at Wounded Knee in 1973?
3. What dangers does nuclear energy pose to the environment?
4. Why haven't pollution-producing energy sources been abandoned?

CHAPTER SUMMARY

During his first term, President Richard Nixon attacked America's problems. These problems included the Vietnam War, domestic violence, and inflation. In 1972, Nixon was reelected by a landslide. During the campaign, though, his workers were caught breaking into Democratic headquarters. Later it was learned that Nixon's advisors had known about the break-in and resulting cover-up. Then it was discovered that Nixon himself had been in on the cover-up. An angry House prepared to impeach Nixon. Before it had the chance, however, he resigned.

People lost much of their faith in politicians. Gerald Ford, who finished Nixon's term, could not totally restore that faith. His pardon of Nixon displeased many people. His limited amnesty program also drew sharp criticism. In addition, during Ford's term, America was hit by stagflation and the energy crisis. Jimmy Carter, elected in 1976, appealed to people as an honest politician. But he, too, proved largely powerless against the troubled economy.

Meanwhile, other changes were occurring in America. Women and other minority groups were demanding equal rights. The ecology movement alerted people to the dangers of pollution. That, in turn, led to a closer look at nuclear energy and other pollution-producing forms of energy.

Key Words

Write a sentence to explain the meaning of each of these terms.

Watergate scandal   amnesty
pardon   embargo
stagflation   ecology

Major Events

Choose the answer that best completes the statement.

1. Before Congress could impeach Nixon, he

   a) resigned from office.
   b) was pardoned.
   c) had his advisors arrested.

2. In an effort to help the economy, both Ford and Carter turned to

   a) the Cost of Living Council.
   b) embargos.
   c) voluntary wage and price controls.

3. Ford lost popularity when he

   a) granted limited amnesty to Vietnam war protestors.
   b) declared, "I'm a Ford, not a Lincoln."
   c) made tax cuts.

4. Betty Friedan and Gloria Steinem helped launch the

   a) AIM movement.
   b) fight for women's rights.
   c) anti-nuclear campaign.

5. The 1979 accident at Three Mile Island heated up the debate over

   a) nuclear energy.
   b) stagflation.
   c) minority rights.

Review

Important Facts

Answer each question with at least one complete sentence.

1. How was Richard Nixon able to influence the future of the American justice system?

2. How did Democrat George McGovern fare in the 1972 presidential election?

3. Why did Nixon supporters break into Democratic Party Headquarters?

4. What role did Robert Woodward and Carl Bernstein play in the Watergate scandal?

5. What crime was Spiro Agnew accused of committing?

6. What conditions did Ford impose on his offer of amnesty?

7. Why did Arab nations impose an oil embargo on the United States?

8. What political experience did Jimmy Carter have before becoming president? Did it help or hurt him?

9. Name two ways that women's lives changed as a result of women's fight for equal rights.

10. What was the purpose of the League of United Latin American Citizens?

11. Other than women and Hispanics, name two groups that began fighting for equal rights in the 1970s.

12. What is toxic waste? What danger does it pose to the environment?

Skill Review

Study this diagram, then answer the following questions.

1. Which process does this flow chart show? When did it occur?

2. According to this diagram, why do people demand higher wages?

3. What are the results of the demand for higher wages?

4. What happens when this process occurs during a recession?

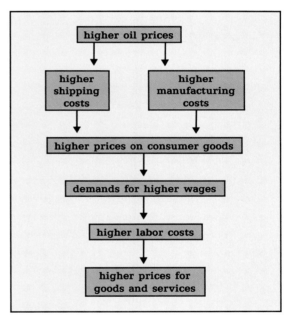

Critical Thinking

Write a paragraph to answer each question.

1. What impact did the Watergate scandal have on politics in the 1970s?

2. Why do you think the economy was so hard to control in the 1970s?

37

The U.S. and the World 1968–1980

Years 1968–1980

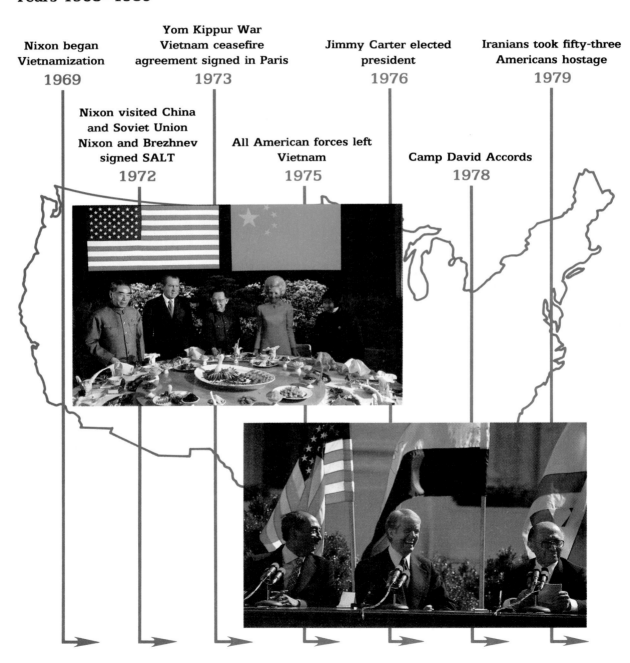

Nixon began
Vietnamization
1969

Yom Kippur War
Vietnam ceasefire
agreement signed in Paris
1973

Jimmy Carter elected
president
1976

Iranians took fifty-three
Americans hostage
1979

Nixon visited China
and Soviet Union
Nixon and Brezhnev
signed SALT
1972

All American forces left
Vietnam
1975

Camp David Accords
1978

Learn these important terms:

Vietnamization
ceasefire
POWs

Remember the main idea:

After nearly a decade of fighting in Vietnam, the United States finally left. South Vietnam then fell to the Communists.

Look for answers to these questions:

1. What was Nixon's plan to end the war in Vietnam?
2. In what ways did Nixon widen the war?
3. Why did the North Vietnamese win the war?

If you had fallen asleep in 1968 and awakened in 1980, you would have discovered that the world was quite a different place. China, a former enemy, had become almost a friend. Old allies, like Iran and Nicaragua, had become enemies. But the biggest news for Americans was that the war in Vietnam was over. After a long struggle, the United States had pulled out. North and South Vietnam were finally united again. But this time it was under Communist rule.

In this chapter you will read about the role the United States played in several world trouble spots. You will see how American leaders worked for peace in the Middle East. You will also see why such efforts did not please everyone. Different groups of people began blaming the United States for their troubles. As a result, the United States and its citizens became prime targets for attacks by terrorists throughout the world.

Americans watched the Vietnam War on the nightly news for nearly a decade. Camera crews brought home images of the war. The American public saw war as it had never seen war before.

But many Americans had a hard time believing what they saw on April 30, 1975. One lonely helicopter was perched on the roof of the American embassy in Saigon. The end was at hand. The last Americans were leaving the country. And the Communists were in control. How did it happen? Why did the United States lose a war for the first time in its history?

Nixon Takes Over

During the 1968 presidential campaign, Richard Nixon promised to end the

Think: **In 1969, 25,000 American troops returned home from Vietnam. Americans wanted out of the war.** Respond: **What was Nixon's plan to get the United States out of the war?**

war in Vietnam. But that was not an easy thing to do. Nixon did not want simply to pull out, for that would be seen as an American defeat. Nixon wanted a settlement that would look something like an American victory.

Nixon based his plan on turning the war back over to the South Vietnamese. Since 1965, Americans had carried the main burden of the war. By 1968, more than 500,000 American soldiers were in Vietnam. Nixon believed it was South Vietnam's turn to do the fighting.

This new policy became known as **Vietnamization**. In June 1969, Nixon announced that twenty-five thousand American troops were coming home. More, he said, would follow. He planned to have the last soldier home by March 1973. The United States would still support South Vietnam with air and naval power. But the actual fighting would be left up to the South Vietnamese.

There was, however, one problem with Vietnamization. South Vietnam, fighting alone, was no match for North Vietnam. The army of the North was much stronger than that of the South. Even with American help, the South Vietnamese continued to lose the war. There was really no reason for the North Vietnamese to negotiate a settlement.

The War Widens

Nixon wanted to force the North Vietnamese to negotiate. He tried to weaken them by secretly bombing targets in Cambodia. Cambodia was a neutral country, which meant it had not taken sides in the war. Because Cambodia shared a long border with Vietnam, though, it was often used by North Vietnam to stage raids against the South. Despite the bombings, North Vietnam refused to bargain.

Then, in April 1970, Nixon ordered an invasion of Cambodia. The goal was to destroy North Vietnamese camps. The invasion was a complete failure. Americans captured some supplies but destroyed no major enemy camps.

Think: **In the spring of 1970, Nixon went on television to explain why the United States invaded Cambodia.** Respond: **What reasons did Nixon give for raiding Cambodia?**

Think: This aerial view shows a rubber plantation that was bombed during the invasion of Cambodia. Respond: What were the results of the American raids?

Protests at Home

The Cambodian invasion set off a storm of protest across the United States. People had hoped the war would come to an end soon. Now Nixon was widening the war. Americans from all walks of life took to the streets denouncing the invasion. At Kent State University in Ohio, violence broke out. The governor called in the National Guard. The inexperienced and nervous soldiers opened fire. Four students were killed.

Think: America became a nation divided. Demonstrations against the war, such as the May Day Protest, were common. Respond: Why were feelings about the war so strong?

Think: TV brought scenes from the war into American homes. The harsh reality of war could not be romanticized. Respond: How did TV influence people's opinions about the war?

Despite strong opposition at home, Nixon stayed with his plan. In February 1971, Vietnam's neighbor Laos was invaded by South Vietnam. Even with American backing, the invasion failed to weaken the North Vietnamese. North Vietnamese soldiers continued to use Cambodia and Laos to enter South Vietnam. As the North's strength increased, Nixon ordered massive bombing raids of all enemy bases. In December 1972, he ordered air attacks on the cities of Hanoi and Haiphong in North Vietnam.

Peace Talks

Finally, the North Vietnamese agreed to serious talks with President Nixon's assistant for national security affairs, Henry Kissinger. In January 1973, a *ceasefire* agreement was signed in Paris, France. It called for all American combat troops to leave Vietnam. All the fighting was to end. In addition, all the American *prisoners of war (POWs)* were to be quickly released.

The peace was a shaky one at best. The United States had withdrawn its forces, but the North Vietnamese had not. Under the ceasefire agreement, they were allowed to keep 145,000 soldiers in South Vietnam. Nixon had wanted an agreement that would look like a victory for the United States. This agreement was not it. It was a victory for North Vietnam.

As many people predicted, the ceasefire did not last. Fighting again broke out between North and South Vietnam. The much stronger Communists began to advance on all fronts. After President Nixon resigned, President Ford asked Congress to increase military aid to South Vietnam. Congress turned him down. Americans no longer wanted any part of the war. Without more American aid, the

Think: **Children are perhaps the worst victims of war. Here, Americans help a youth.** Respond: **What was the fate of this boy's nation after United States troops withdrew?**

Think: **Anxious moments were spent waiting in line outside the U. S. embassy in Saigon. These refugees hoped to get visas allowing them to enter America.** Respond: **Why did they need to leave their homes?**

GEOGRAPHY AND THE VIETNAM WAR

Between 1954 and 1973, the United States spent $139 billion to stop the spread of communism in Vietnam. The United States supported the government of South Vietnam against the Viet Cong—Communist guerrillas from both North and South Vietnam. But the effort failed. From this map, you will learn about the geography of Vietnam. This information will help you understand some of the difficulties that American troops faced in Vietnam.

Study the map, scale, and key.

1. How long is Vietnam from north to south? How wide is it at its narrowest point from west to east?

2. What countries border on North Vietnam? Which border on South Vietnam?

3. What bodies of water are named on the map?

4. What kinds of information are given in this key?

5. Where did the Ho Chi Minh trail start? Through what type of landscape did it pass? Who used it? Why? Where did the trail end? How many miles long was it?

Study the symbols showing plant life and landforms.

6. Which regions are flat? Which are mountainous?

7. Where would you expect to find farming? Where would you expect to find cities?

8. Where would you expect to find the most people?

9. What generalizations can you make about Vietnam's climate?

Draw inferences from the map.

10. What disadvantages would American troops have in fighting in Vietnam?

11. What advantages would native guerrillas have over American troops?

12. Why was the Ho Chi Minh Trail so important to the Communists? Why was it so hard for the American troops to shut down the activity along the trail?

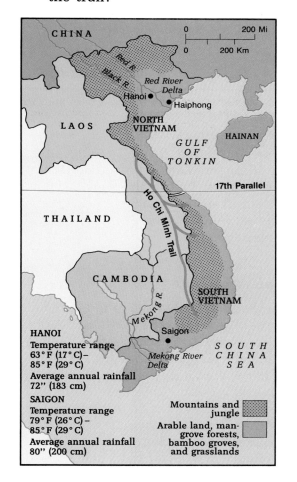

HANOI
Temperature range
63°F (17°C)–
85°F (29°C)
Average annual rainfall
72" (183 cm)

SAIGON
Temperature range
79°F (26°C)–
85°F (29°C)
Average annual rainfall
80" (200 cm)

Mountains and jungle

Arable land, mangrove forests, bamboo groves, and grasslands

Think: **When American troops withdrew from Vietnam, people who supported the Americans were in danger. Some were airlifted by helicopter.** Respond: **Why did Americans help many of these refugees escape?**

way was prepared for the swift fall of South Vietnam. Lacking American support, the South Vietnamese army totally collapsed. The few remaining American citizens in South Vietnam had to be rescued by helicopter.

A Summary View

The Vietnam War was a long and painful experience for the United States. America went into South Vietnam to help an ally and to stop the spread of communism. In the end, it did neither. More than fifty-five thousand American men and women died in Vietnam. At home, the war turned American against American. In addition, the conflict cost more than $140 billion. These war costs contributed to America's economic troubles during the 1970s.

One of the saddest results of the war was the poor treatment veterans received. Many fellow Americans shunned them. By the mid-1980s, however, things began to change. Americans began to see and understand the sacrifices which Vietnam veterans had made in service to their country.

Section Review

1. What was the goal of Nixon's Vietnamization?
2. Why did Nixon first bomb and then invade Cambodia?
3. How did Americans react to the invasion of Cambodia?
4. What was the major flaw in the Paris ceasefire agreement?

2. America's Relations with the Communist World

Learn these important terms:

detente
SALT
Sandinistas
human rights
dissidents

Remember the main idea:

During the 1970s, relations with Communist China, the Soviet Union, and Cuba were uneasy. In the early 1970s, relations improved. But a change in American foreign policy and continued Communist aggression made relations difficult.

Look for answers to these questions:

1. Why did United States relations with the Soviet Union change during the early 1970s?

2. Why did Nixon seek better relations with Communist China?

3. What problems existed between Cuba and the United States?

During the first half of the 1970s, Americans focused their attention on Vietnam. But Vietnam is a small country halfway around the globe. Once direct involvement in Vietnam ended, Americans shifted their attention. They became more aware of the Soviet Union and Communist China. These two Communist countries are giants. The Soviet Union is easily the largest nation in the world. And China, with more than one billion people today, is easily the most populated nation. These two Communist countries are much too big to ignore.

Detente

President Nixon was a strong anti-Communist. But he did not want to risk nuclear war over his beliefs. So Nixon gradually tried to relax tensions with the Soviet Union. Henry Kissinger, secretary of state for both Nixon and Ford, used the term **detente** [day-TAHNT] to describe this policy. Detente is a French word which means a relaxing of tensions.

In May 1972, Nixon visited the Soviet Union to meet with Communist leader Leonid Brezhnev. The two men reached agreements on several issues. The most important agreement dealt with nuclear weapons. Nixon and Brezhnev agreed not to build any new missiles for five years. This agreement was the *Strategic Arms Limitation Treaty (SALT)*. It appeared that detente was working.

Think: In 1973, Brezhnev met with Nixon in the United States. They discussed weapons control, the environment, and space. **Respond:** What did the two men accomplish?

Chapter 37 **771**

China Policy

Nixon also wanted to change the United States's policy toward China. In 1949, the Communists had taken over China. Their opponents, called the Nationalists, were left with only the small island of Taiwan. The United States, however, refused to recognize the Communist government. America regarded the Nationalist government as the "real" government of China. But this policy proved to be unrealistic. The Communists controlled the mainland of China. By the 1970s, Communist China had 800 million people. It was not wise for the United States to ignore a country of this size.

President Nixon was a realist. For years he had condemned the Chinese Communists. But, as president, he began to change his attitude. The Chinese and the Russians had become bitter enemies. If the United States developed better relations with the Chinese, it could take advantage of this split.

In 1971, Nixon allowed a group of American table tennis players to play a few matches in China. Then, in February 1972, Nixon himself visited China. This was a dramatic diplomatic breakthrough. Communist China was at last recognized by the United States. Before long, the Chinese began drinking American colas and wearing blue jeans.

Think: **A new era of cooperation began when President Nixon made his historic visit to China. After years of tension, the Chinese and Americans set up a program of scientific, technological, and cultural exchanges.**
Respond: **How did Nixon use the visit to China to improve American relations with the Soviet Union?**

Think: **President Carter was dedicated to human rights around the world. He spoke out strongly against the Soviet Union's refusal to allow mistreated Jews to leave the country. Above, Israelis are shown demonstrating against Soviet treatment of Jews.** Respond: **What were the good and bad points of Carter's goals?**

Foreign Policy Under Carter and Ford

When Gerald Ford took over as president on August 9, 1974, he did not alter Nixon's foreign policy. Instead, he picked up where Nixon left off. Ford continued the policy of detente. He also pursued closer ties with Communist China.

U.S. policies did change, however, when Jimmy Carter took office in 1977. Carter had his own ideas about foreign policy. He strongly believed in *human rights*. That is, he thought all people should be free to speak and live as they pleased. They should not have to fear bad treatment by their own government.

U.S.—Soviet Relations Turn Sour

Carter's ideas led to increased tensions with the Soviet Union. In the Soviet Union, people were not allowed to criticize the government. Those who did were called *dissidents* and were promptly silenced. Some were sent to labor camps. Others were sent to Siberia, a cold and remote corner of the Soviet Union.

Carter condemned the Soviets for their actions. He also condemned them for their discrimination against Jews. Soviet Jews, for example, were not allowed to travel freely. Carter's position angered the Soviets. They accused him of poisoning relations between the two countries.

In 1979, the Soviet Union invaded its neighbor, Afghanistan. Carter felt the Soviet invasion was a violation of the rights of the people of Afghanistan. In protest, Carter ordered American athletes to boycott the 1980 Olympics in Moscow. The spirit of detente was dead.

RELATIONS WITH THE COMMUNIST WORLD, 1970s

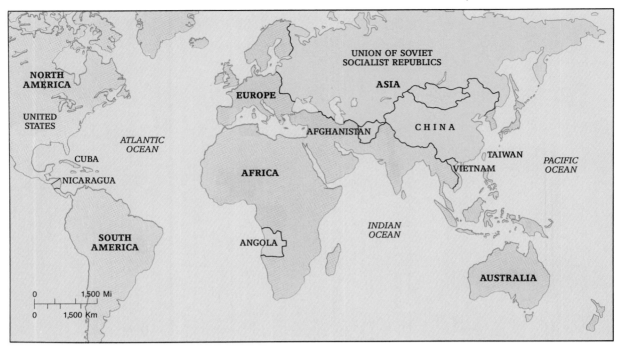

The Cuban Problem

Relations with Communist Cuba did not fare well, either. In 1977, Cuba and the United States agreed to exchange diplomats. In addition, they agreed to regulate offshore fishing. But such goodwill gestures did not end Cuba's aggressive foreign policy. Between 1975 and 1978, Cuba sent twenty thousand troops to fight in the African country of Angola. Cuban soldiers also went to several other African countries. Such meddling worsened U.S.–Cuban relations.

Cuba also tried to promote revolution in Central America. In 1979, Cuban aid helped to overthrow a repressive government in Nicaragua. The victorious rebels, who were called *Sandinistas*, set up a new government. After they gained control, they sought help from Cuba and the Soviet Union. This meant there were two pro-Communist governments in Latin America. American leaders viewed this development with great alarm.

Problems Remain

At the end of the 1970s, U.S. relations with Communist countries remained shaky. Some progress had been made, particularly with China. But it was clear that most Communist countries did not share America's values. For this reason, it was difficult to maintain good relations with these countries.

Section Review

1. What was the policy of detente?
2. What were the terms of the SALT agreement?
3. Why did Nixon visit China?
4. Why did relations between the United States and the Soviet Union sour during Carter's term?
5. What did Cuba do to worsen relations with the United States?

HISTORY MAKERS

Henry Kissinger

Secretary of State

The interview was almost over.

"One last question, sir," asked a television reporter. "Could you tell us what you hope to accomplish as secretary of state?"

The secretary paused and thought for a moment before he spoke. "It is my hope," he said slowly, "to leave behind a world that seems more peaceful than the one we entered."

"Thank you, Mr. Kissinger."

Henry Kissinger was not a newcomer to affairs of state. In 1938, his family escaped from Nazi Germany to the United States. During World War II, Kissinger served in the U.S. Army and became an American citizen. After the war, he studied and taught international relations at Harvard University.

Henry Kissinger was a foreign policy advisor to Presidents Eisenhower, Kennedy, and Johnson. He served as assistant to Presidents Nixon and Ford for national security affairs. In 1973, he became the first naturalized American citizen to be appointed secretary of state.

During the Nixon and Ford administrations, Kissinger planned and carried out the United States' foreign policy. He had to deal with the war in Vietnam, tension in the Middle East, newly developing nations, and, most important to Kissinger, the United States' relations with the U.S.S.R.

Kissinger encouraged detente with the U.S.S.R. The SALT Talks (Strategic Arms Limitation Talks) resulted in a 1972 weapons treaty limiting strategic missiles.

As secretary of state, Kissinger practiced shuttle diplomacy, flying back and forth between countries to settle disputes. By 1972, he had negotiated a settlement in Vietnam. After the 1973 October War in the Middle East, Kissinger flew back and forth between Egypt and Israel, arranging for peace.

One of Kissinger's most important diplomatic accomplishments was arranging President Nixon's 1972 trip to China. This trip began the thaw in American relations with China.

Was United States foreign policy successful under Henry Kissinger? Did it leave the world a more peaceful place, as he hoped? As with all people who shape history, only time will make the final judgment about Kissinger's accomplishments.

3. Other Problem Areas

Learn these important terms:

Yom Kippur War
Savak
Camp David Accords

Remember the main idea:

In the 1970s, the United States had to deal with trouble spots in many parts of the world.

Look for answers to these questions:

1. How did the situation in the Middle East change in the 1970s?

2. What policy did Carter follow regarding the Panama Canal?

3. What were some of the causes of the revolution in Iran? What were some of its effects?

Suppose the threat of communism was America's only problem. The world would still be a dangerous place. But it would also be a much simpler place to understand. Unfortunately, the world is complex. Americans have much more to worry about than communism. During the 1970s, problems other than communism faced the United States. Hot spots developed in parts of the world not threatened by the Russians, Chinese, or Cubans.

The Camp David Accords

The tiny nation of Israel was founded in 1948. By 1970, it had already fought three wars against its Arab neighbors. Throughout the 1970s, the situation in the Middle East remained explosive. On October 6, 1973, war broke out. Egypt and Syria launched a surprise attack on Israel. The attack came on Yom Kippur (yom ki-POOR), the holiest day of the Jewish year. With American aid, Israel

Think: In September 1978, Anwar Sadat, Jimmy Carter, and Menachem Begin met at Camp David, the presidential retreat in Maryland. Israel agreed to return the Sinai, and Egypt formally recognized Israel. The two foreign leaders were later awarded the Nobel Peace Prize. **Respond:** Why were the Camp David Accords important?

MIDDLE EAST HOT SPOTS

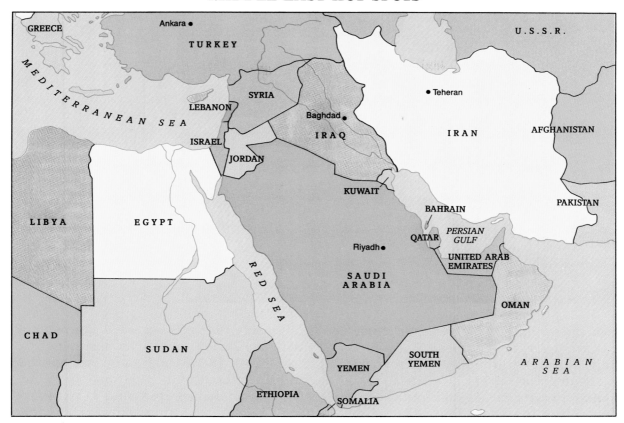

was able to beat back the Arabs. A cease-fire ended the fighting after eighteen days. The *Yom Kippur War* was the fourth war between the Israelis and the Arabs since 1948. After the last war, some Arab nations punished western nations for their support of Israel. They refused to send oil to the West for several months.

There was, however, a bright spot in this struggle between Israel and its Arab neighbors. Henry Kissinger began to talk with Egyptian President Anwar Sadat (AN-wahr suh-DAHT). Their discussions paved the way for Carter's biggest triumph as president.

In 1978, Carter invited Prime Minister Menachem Begin (men-AH-kum BAY-gin) of Israel to meet with Sadat at Camp David in Maryland. It was an historic event. The three men discussed the prob-lems of the Middle East. Sadat and Begin discussed their conflicting demands. With Carter's help, they reached a number of agreements known as the *Camp David Accords*. These agreements ended more than thirty years of war between Israel and Egypt.

Giving up the Panama Canal

Another issue facing the United States was the fate of the Panama Canal. Since its creation in the early 1900s, the canal had been controlled by the United States. President Carter believed it was time to turn the Panama Canal over to the Republic of Panama. For years, many Panamanians had been clamoring for control of the canal. After all, the canal splits the country in two. Foreign control of this canal zone angered many Panamanians.

Think: **Many Americans were angered by Carter's decision to give control of the Panama Canal to the Republic of Panama. But people throughout the free world supported Carter's decision. Respond: What were the reasons for the differing opinions?**

In any event, the canal was no longer as important as it once was. Many newer ships did not fit through the narrow locks. In September 1977, President Carter signed a treaty turning the canal over to Panama by the year 2000. After a long and bitter debate, the Senate finally approved the treaty.

People throughout the free world applauded Carter's action. But at home, many Americans disapproved of the move. After all, they argued, the United States had built and paid for the canal. They called the canal treaty a "giveaway." They also saw it as another sign of America's declining world power. Carter, these Americans stated, was too weak of a president.

Revolution in Iran

For many years Iran had been a close ally of the United States. It had the oil Americans needed. In addition, Iran shares a long border with the Soviet Union. A friendly Iran could block Russian moves toward the oil-rich Persian Gulf. Unfortunately, the Shah of Iran was a bru-

tal ruler who allowed no disagreement with his government. His secret police, the *Savak* [SAH-vahk], imprisoned and tortured thousands of Iranians. Many feared and disliked the Shah's iron rule.

The Shah was unpopular among his people for another reason, too. For years he tried to push Iran into the twentieth century by bringing in Western-style industry. He favored Western culture over his own Iranian culture. He even encouraged Iranian women to dress and act like American women. The Shah's Western tastes offended his people, who wanted to preserve their own way of life.

In 1978, a revolt broke out in Iran. In January 1979, the Shah was overthrown. His replacement, the Ayatollah Khomeini [eye-uh-TOH-lah koh-MAY-nee], was very different from the Shah. He hated everything about the West. Khomeini was determined to return Iran to its old Moslem ways. He insisted, for example, that women wear veils to cover their faces. He punished anyone who opposed his policies. His government was just as brutal as the Shah's had been.

Think: Demonstrators in Teheran, Iran, burned a picture of the former Shah of Iran to show their feelings against him. Respond: How did these strong feelings against the Shah affect Iran's relationship with the United States?

The Hostage Crisis

Khomeini encouraged street demonstrations against the United States. He was angered by American support of the Shah. Then President Carter allowed the sick Shah to visit the United States for medical treatment. This triggered outrage in the streets of Teheran, the capital of Iran. In October 1979, Iranian students stormed the American embassy and seized fifty-three hostages.

This act clearly broke international law. But the Ayatollah's supporters were not interested in legal issues. President Carter tried every means to free the hostages. Each one failed. Khomeini wanted to humiliate the United States. President Carter had few options. He did not want to see the hostages killed, and he did not want to start a war that might spread throughout the Middle East.

But even Carter's patience finally wore out. In April 1980, he took a bold step. He ordered a specially trained group of soldiers to free the hostages by force. Tragically, two of the helicopters crashed in the

Think: When the former Shah of Iran was allowed to enter the United States for medical treatment, Iranian students stormed the American embassy in Teheran. They took fifty-three Americans hostage. Respond: How did the Ayatollah use the hostages to gain more power?

The history of an event does not exist only between the covers of books. It also exists in the minds of people. Everyone who experiences an event has his or her own version of that event. An event that touches a person's life becomes a part of that person's own personal history. When he or she shares that personal history in speaking, it becomes what is called *oral history*.

Sources for oral history can be parents, other relatives, teachers, friends, or even one's self. Everyone who lives through an event has his or her own way of remembering it.

Your parents probably remember the gasoline shortage of 1973. It happened when some of the Arab nations would not send their oil to the United States for several months. This shortage affected millions of people, each in a different way. To learn about the history of this event, you might prepare some questions and gather the oral history of people you know.

Before you start your interviews, you should get some background on the event. You have learned from your book what happened, when it happened, and why it happened. Since you already have those answers, you can concentrate on asking about how the shortage affected people in their own daily lives. Here are some questions you might ask:

1. What difficulties did you have during the gasoline shortage?

2. How did the shortage affect your daily life in getting to work and doing errands?

3. What did you do when you couldn't get gas for your car?

Notice that none of the questions ask for a short answer or a yes-or-no answer. Instead, the questions aim at getting more complete information about people's attitudes and actions.

Another crisis involving the United States and an oil-producing country began in 1979. In that year Iran took fifty-three American citizens as hostages. Most Americans had strong opinions about this event. Their oral histories could give you different information than you could find in printed sources.

Read the questions below. Some of them are the kinds of questions that would be useful in getting an oral history of the hostage crisis. Decide which questions would be good ones to use.

1 When did the hostage crisis begin?

2 What did you think should have been done to gain the release of the hostages?

3 Did you know about the hostage crisis and follow it?

4 What did you think of the president's attempts to free the hostages?

Think: On January 20, 1981, the Americans held hostage in Iran were released. The crisis, which had united the American people against a common enemy, was finally over. The hostages were honored in parades and celebrations across America. Respond: How did the hostage crisis affect the election of 1980?

Iranian desert. The rescue effort was an embarrassing flop. All hopes for a negotiated end to the crisis seemed doomed.

After several more months, both sides started talking again. At last a settlement was reached. But it was not until January 20, 1981—the day that Carter left office—that the hostages were released. They had been held by the Iranians for 444 days.

A Complex World Scene

By 1980, the United States found itself in a difficult position. American relations with many foreign countries had been strained. Many serious issues remained unresolved. It seemed the world scene was becoming more and more complex every day. Keeping peace and stability in such a world would not be easy. It would, in fact, be the major foreign policy challenge of the future.

Section Review

1. Why did some Arab nations stop shipping oil to Western nations?

2. What took place at Camp David in 1978?

3. Why did some Americans disapprove of Carter's Panama Canal treaty?

4. How did the Shah make the Iranian people unhappy? How did Khomeini differ from the Shah?

CHAPTER SUMMARY

Richard Nixon tried to end the Vietnam War with his policy of Vietnamization. Actually, he widened the war by bombing and then invading Cambodia. Eventually the United States did pull out of Vietnam. But that enabled North Vietnam to take over South Vietnam. The war cost the United States a great deal. More than 55,000 Americans lost their lives. Vietnam veterans were left feeling shunned and misunderstood.

Meanwhile, the United States was charting new courses with Communist countries. Nixon brought America closer to those countries. He established a policy of detente with the Soviet Union. He also established diplomatic contact with Communist China. Under Jimmy Carter, however, things changed again. The policy of detente crumbled when Carter condemned the Soviets for human rights violations. Efforts to improve relations with Communist Cuba also failed. Cuba's aggressive actions in Africa and Central America angered Americans.

The United States faced other challenges, as well. Jimmy Carter worked hard to help Israel and Egypt end their feud in the Middle East. Carter also signed a treaty to turn the Panama Canal over to the Panamanians. Carter proved helpless against hostile Iranians, however. American hostages were kept in Iran for 444 days.

Key Words

Write a sentence to explain the meaning of each of these terms.

Vietnamization   *human rights*
detente   *Camp David*
SALT   *Accords*

Major Events

Choose the answer that best completes the statement.

1. In April 1970, Nixon tried to end the war by

    a) bombing Hanoi and Haiphong.
    b) ceasing all bombings.
    c) invading Cambodia.

2. After Americans pulled out of Vietnam, South Vietnam

    a) fell to the North Vietnamese.
    b) won the war.
    c) signed a ceasefire agreement with North Vietnam.

3. Nixon was the first American president to

    a) call for human rights.
    b) establish diplomatic contact with Communist China.
    c) support the Sandinistas.

4. Carter agreed to give the Panama canal to Panamanians

    a) by September 1977.
    b) in 1990.
    c) by the year 2000.

5. As a result of the 1978—79 revolt in Iran,

    a) the Shah was overthrown.
    b) the Ayatollah Khomeini was overthrown.
    c) the Savak seized power.

Review

Important Facts

Answer each question with at least one complete sentence.

1. What happened at Kent State University?

2. What purpose did Laos serve in the Vietnam War?

3. What were the terms of the ceasefire agreement signed in January 1973, in Paris, France?

4. After the 1949 revolution, what part of China did the Nationalists control?

5. What foreign policy did Gerald Ford follow during his years in the White House?

6. What stance did the Soviet Union take toward Soviet dissidents?

7. Why did the United States boycott the 1980 Moscow Olympics?

8. Name two ways that Cuba angered United States leaders in the 1970s.

9. How did the Yom Kippur War begin? How did it end?

10. Who was Henry Kissinger? How did he pave the way for the Camp David Accords?

11. What were the arguments for and against turning the Panama Canal over to the Panamanians?

12. Why did Iranians dislike the Shah of Iran?

13. What action by Jimmy Carter triggered the Iranian hostage crisis?

Skill Review

Read this oral history, given by Vietnam war correspondent Peter Braestrup concerning the Ho Chi Minh Trail and the ''frontiers'' of Laos and Cambodia. Then answer the following questions.

> . . . With that six-hundred-mile frontier . . . the Communists had a free shot at South Vietnam, a safe place to retreat to, and a secure supply line . . . And of course, Lyndon Johnson and Richard Nixon preferred to make us all think about the war as if South Vietnam was an island.
> —from *To Bear Any Burden,*
> by Al Santoli

1. How many miles of safe border did the Communists have?

2. How did the Ho Chi Minh Trail help the Communists?

3. How did sanctuaries in Laos and Cambodia help the Communists?

4. What attitude does the reporter have toward Presidents Johnson and Nixon? Why?

5. What is an oral history?

Critical Thinking

Write a paragraph to answer each question.

1. How did the Vietnam War affect America?

2. Compare the foreign policy of Richard Nixon with that of Jimmy Carter.

38
The Challenge of the Future

Years 1980–?

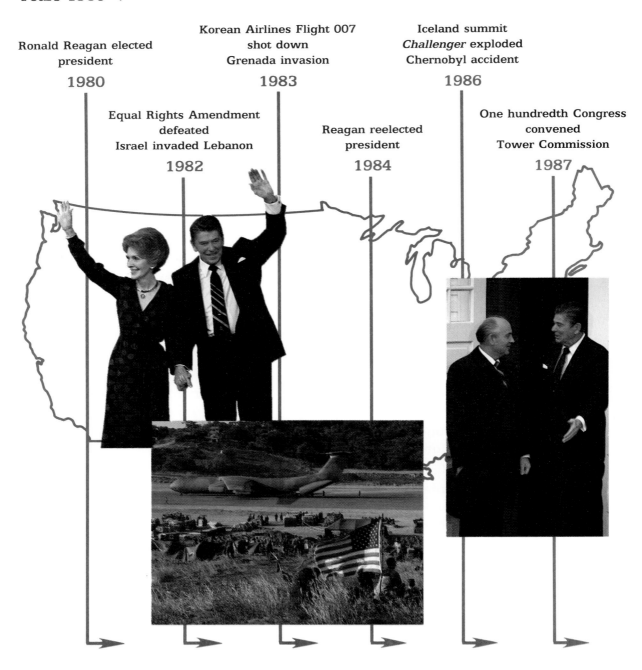

Ronald Reagan elected
president
1980

Korean Airlines Flight 007
shot down
Grenada invasion
1983

Iceland summit
Challenger exploded
Chernobyl accident
1986

Equal Rights Amendment
defeated
Israel invaded Lebanon
1982

Reagan reelected
president
1984

One hundredth Congress
convened
Tower Commission
1987

1. The Reagan Years—Domestic Issues and Events

Learn these important terms:

supply-side economics
budget deficits
Gramm-Rudman Bill
trade deficit

Remember the main idea:

Although Ronald Reagan faced his share of problems, he proved to be a very popular president. America's economic issues received a great deal of his attention.

Look for answers to these questions:

1. What made Ronald Reagan such a popular president?
2. How did growing budget deficits affect the nation?
3. What issues became problems for President Reagan during his second term?

Now you are ready to cover some history that you might remember from your own lifetime. That, however, may not make it easier to understand. Things are happening very fast. Sometimes it seems there is no time to stop and sort out what has just happened before the next wave of events arrives. For example, you probably have not had time to consider what effect the 1980s will have on the future. Before you can think about that question, you will need to take a closer look at exactly what happened during those years.

In this chapter you will read about President Ronald Reagan's economic policies and how they affected inflation and federal deficits. You will see how Reagan tried to control communism and how he dealt with the threat of nuclear war. You will also read about challenges brought on by immigration, technology, energy needs, and the environment. These challenges are certain to have a powerful impact on your life.

In 1980, the American voters chose not to reelect Jimmy Carter. The Carter years had been marred by problems both in the economy and in foreign relations. Carter's honest, down-to-earth image no longer seemed that appealing. People wanted a president who would inspire confidence. They were finally ready to put the defeat in Vietnam and the shame of Watergate behind them. They wanted someone who would make them feel good about their country again. The man they chose was Ronald Reagan.

A Different Kind of President

Reagan, who was swept into office by a landslide, was very different from Carter. Carter was a Southerner with a small-town background. Reagan was a Californian who had been a Hollywood actor in his early years. Carter was a modest man. Reagan was charming and inspiring. Carter had not been a very popular president. Reagan proved to be one of the most popular presidents in recent years. The Carter years had left Americans feeling unsure of themselves and their country. Reagan managed to restore Americans' pride in their country.

Supply-Side Economics

When Reagan became president, he promised to do what Ford and Carter had

Think: President-elect Reagan and his supportive wife Nancy wave victoriously. Respond: What changes occurred in Reagan and in the country during his presidency?

Think: Reagan gathered support for his reforms by speaking to a variety of groups across America. He rallied for cutting taxes to encourage economic growth and for reducing the federal budget deficit. Respond: What were the successes and failures of Reagan's plan for economic reform?

failed to do—fix the economy. His plan was to encourage economic growth by cutting taxes. He believed lower taxes would leave people with more money to spend on consumer goods. The extra spending would lead to economic growth. This approach was called *supply-side economics*.

Reagan also promised to reduce federal *budget deficits*. A deficit occurs when the government spends more money than it collects in taxes. When a deficit occurs, the government borrows money to make up the difference. For years, the annual deficits had been growing larger and larger. Reagan planned to put an end to deficit spending by cutting back on government programs. He did not want to cut Social Security. He also did not want to cut military spending. He made most of the cuts in domestic spending. Reagan did not agree with the Democrats' tradition of spending federal money to solve social problems. Reagan believed the country would run more smoothly if the government were less involved in social welfare programs. He believed that private enterprise could solve the country's economic problems. He also believed that private charities and self-help programs should play a much larger role in solving the nation's social problems.

Supply-side economics did have some success. By 1983, the economy was showing signs of improvement. Unemployment and inflation were dropping. But other problems remained. The budget deficits continued to rise. Foreign trade deficits also became worrisome. A *trade deficit* occurs when a nation buys more from other countries than it sells abroad.

The 1984 Election

Mounting deficits did not affect Reagan's popularity, however. Most Americans thought he was doing a fine job. As

Think: **Walter Mondale chose Geraldine Ferraro as his running mate in the 1984 elections.** Respond: **How were the role and image of women beginning to change?**

the 1984 election race began, polls showed Reagan to be the overwhelming favorite of the voters.

The Democrats chose Walter Mondale as their nominee. Mondale had served as vice president under Jimmy Carter. But that association was no help. It simply linked him to Carter's failed policies. Mondale tried to stir up enthusiasm for his campaign by choosing Geraldine Ferraro as his running mate. Ferraro was the first female candidate for vice president. She did not, however, give Mondale the boost he needed. Reagan won the election by one of the largest margins ever.

Reagan's Second Term

Heading into his second term, Reagan faced several challenges. He had to address the problem of budget deficits. By 1986, these deficits were threatening to choke off the economy because the federal government had to borrow so much money to pay for its debt. Federal borrowing used up so much of the nation's supply of money that there was not enough left for a healthy level of private investment to occur.

When actor Ronald Reagan (1911–   ) joined the Republicans in 1962, they were delighted. He had the image they needed. His popularity eased him into the presidency in 1982.

To end the deficits, Congress passed the *Gramm-Rudman Bill* in 1986. It called for a balanced budget in five years. It also ordered the government to meet targets for deficit reduction each year until the year 1991.

Reagan also had to cope with the economic collapse of thousands of America's farms. American farmers were having trouble selling their crops to other countries. This was due, in large part, to the fact that other countries were producing more of their own grain than ever before. American farmers were also hurt by falling land values and depressed prices. Finally, many farmers were hurt by a drought that struck the Southeast in the summer of 1986.

In the wake of these troubles, some Americans thought the government should increase its aid to farmers. Others thought the government was already doing too much. Finding an effective farm policy remained one of the most difficult problems facing American leaders.

Think: Five years before he retired, Chief Justice Burger welcomed Sandra Day O'Connor to the Supreme Court. Respond: What other new opportunities became available to women?

Think: Protesting in Washington, D.C., farmers wanted the government to support them by maintaining farm prices. Respond: What problems caused farm prices to drop?

Women and Minorities

By the mid-1980s, more and more women and minorities were gaining positions of power. In 1981, for example, Sandra Day O'Connor became the first female Supreme Court justice. In 1983, Sally Ride became the first American woman in space. And in 1984, Jesse Jackson, a black minister, ran for president. Still, equality was a long way off. The Equal Rights Amendment was defeated in 1982. Women continued to earn much less than men who performed similar

In 1971, Jesse Louis Jackson (1941–   ) founded Operation PUSH to promote blacks in business. Twelve years later, he announced his candidacy for the nation's highest office.

named to the Supreme Court. With these two appointments, Reagan ensured that the nation's highest court would maintain the conservative outlook it had developed under Burger.

Changes in Congress

On the other hand, Congress took on a different look with the elections of 1986. The Democrats took control of the Senate. That victory gave them a majority in both houses of Congress. When the new Congress convened in January 1987, it was the one hundredth Congress since the founding of the Republic. This Democratic Congress posed challenges to President Reagan, both on domestic legislation and on the conduct of foreign policy.

jobs. Unemployment rates remained higher among minorities than among whites. And cuts in social welfare programs made life much harder for many minorities and single mothers.

Changes on the Supreme Court

In the summer of 1986, Chief Justice Warren Burger announced his retirement. Reagan named Justice William Rehnquist as the new Chief Justice of the Supreme Court. He then named Antonin Scalia to fill Rehnquist's old spot on the bench. Scalia was the first Italian-American to be

Section Review

1. How did Reagan's approach to domestic problems differ from the Democrats' approach?

2. What was Reagan's supply-side economics?

3. How did Mondale try to attract voters in the 1984 election? Did his attempt work?

4. What problems did Reagan face during his second term?

Think: The Burger Court emphasized the rights of society over those of the individual. Upon Burger's retirement, Reagan appointed Rehnquist as Chief Justice. Reagan wanted the Rehnquist Court (pictured below) to continue making conservative rulings. Respond: Which do you think are more important, the rights of society or the rights of the individual? Why?

HISTORY MAKERS

—Sally Ride—

America's First Woman in Space

It was June 18, 1983. The crew was awakened at 3:15 in the morning. They ate breakfast, drove to the launch pad, put on their flight suits, and entered the space shuttle. The mission commander and the pilot strapped themselves into the front seats on the flight deck. The two mission specialists sat behind them. The fifth crewmember, a doctor, sat on the lower deck. Launch control ran the last instrument check. All systems were go. The final countdown began. An astronaut radioed a message to his wife.

"Sally," he said, "have a ball!"

The main engines fired, igniting the solid rockets. As the solid rockets began to fire, the shuttle trembled, lifted off the launch pad, and headed into space while the watching crowd cheered. The seventh flight of the space shuttle was making history. Crewmember Sally Ride was the first American woman in space.

Sally Ride grew up in southern California. She loved sports and reading. In high school Sally Ride was fascinated by her science classes. In college she majored in physics and English, and she also received a graduate degree in astrophysics.

When she finished school, Sally Ride applied for a new job: mission specialist in the space shuttle program. Mission specialists are astronauts who handle shuttle cargo and conduct on-board experiments. Ride was one of the original six women and fourteen men chosen to be trained for the job.

Mission specialist Ride learned how the shuttle worked, how to launch satellites, and how to manage weightlessness in the shuttle. In April 1982, NASA announced the seventh shuttle flight. Sally Ride was one of the crew. Her husband, astronaut Steve Hawley, sent Ride the message from ground control before the shuttle lifted off.

The flight was a success. Afterward Sally Ride said, "I'm sure that it was the most fun that I'll ever have in my life." Sally Ride opened the door to space-age opportunities for all American women.

2. The Reagan Years—Foreign Policy and Problems

Learn these important terms:

PLO
Grenada
Tower Commission
Contras
arms race
Star Wars
START

Remember the main idea:

President Reagan followed an anti-communist policy in foreign affairs. A scandal over trading arms for hostages tarnished his popularity.

Look for answers to these questions:

1. What policy did Reagan follow in the Middle East?
2. Why did Americans invade the Caribbean island of Grenada?
3. How did Reagan deal with the threat of nuclear war?

Ronald Reagan was a firm anticommunist. He did not trust Communist leaders. This distrust showed in the way he handled foreign affairs.

Dealing with the Soviet Union

Reagan took a firm stand with the Soviet Union. He had never liked the policy of détente, and he had a low opinion of the Soviet Union. Once he even referred to it as "the evil empire." He believed that the only thing the Soviets respected was military strength.

Reagan therefore pushed for a large military build-up. Congress agreed. It set money aside for many new bombers and other military equipment.

Reagan's distrust of the Soviet Union grew stronger on September 1, 1983. On that day, Soviet fighter planes shot down Korean Airlines Flight 007, a commercial airplane. Everyone on board was killed. People around the world were shocked. President Reagan termed the incident a massacre. The Soviets never apologized for their actions. Instead, they accused the passenger plane of being on a spy mission. Relations between the United States and the Soviet Union reached a new low.

The Middle East

Reagan's anticommunist policy colored his approach to the Middle East as well. He wanted to be sure the Communist influence there did not spread. As things stood, Israel was battling the *Palestinian Liberation Organization (PLO)* for possession of land. The PLO wanted to create a homeland for Arab Palestinians out of land held by the Jewish state of Israel. The PLO was backed by the Arab country of Syria and by the Soviet Union. Israel was backed by the United States. Reagan vowed to continue support of Israel.

Reagan also tried to keep peace in the country of Lebanon. It had been involved in a civil war between Christian and Moslem groups since 1975. The PLO staged attacks against Israel from Lebanon. Then, in 1982, Israel invaded Lebanon. The PLO was forced out, but the civil war did not end.

Americans in Lebanon

Early in 1983, Reagan sent eighteen hundred Marines to Beirut, the capital of Lebanon. Their goal was to maintain peace. But peace was easier to talk about than to achieve. The Marines could only shoot in self-defense. There were too few

Think: **Americans in Lebanon on a peace-keeping mission rescued fellow Marines after a terrorist attack on their headquarters.** Respond: **Why were the Marines attacked?**

Grenada

The problems in Lebanon did not weaken Reagan's resolve to fight terrorism or communism. He stated that the United States refused to negotiate with terrorists for the hostages. And two days after the suicide bombing in Beirut, Reagan took a bold stand against communism. This time the confrontation took place in the Caribbean. A new leader came to power in the nation of **Grenada**, a small island. He and his followers had the support of Fidel Castro, the Communist leader of Cuba. Reagan did not want to see communism spread in this hemisphere. When civil war broke out in Grenada, Reagan acted quickly. He claimed the war threatened American students on the island. On October 25, 1983, Reagan ordered American troops to invade Grenada. Heavy fighting raged for several days. In the end, however, the Grenadian Communists and their Cuban allies surrendered. The threat of a Communist-controlled Grenada was over. In general, Americans applauded Reagan's quick action.

Marines to control the situation. And, to some Arabs, the Marines appeared to be allies of Israel. In an effort to support the Marines' position, Reagan sent an extra two thousand Marines to Lebanon.

The strategy did not work. On October 23, 1983, terrorists went on a suicide mission. They filled a truck with explosives and drove it straight into Marine headquarters. Two hundred forty-one Marines were killed. The United States believed Syria was responsible for the bombing.

President Reagan withdrew the Marines from Beirut. But other Americans became the victims of Moslem extremists. During the next few years, a number of American citizens were taken hostage by terrorist groups. The kidnappers were in communication with Iranian rulers.

Think: **Victorious American troops stopped a Communist takeover of Grenada.** Respond: **How did Reagan use the victory in Grenada to counter the removal of troops in Lebanon?**

Central America

Reagan was also distressed to see Communists making inroads in Central America. Cuba was supporting Communist rebels in El Salvador. Cuba was also helping the Sandinista government in Nicaragua. Reagan firmly believed the United States should fight this development. He offered support to El Salvador's government. He also pushed for United States aid to the *Contras*, anticommunist rebels in Nicaragua. Reagan's policy worried some Americans. They feared Central America would turn into another Vietnam. Still, in 1986, Congress decided to follow Reagan's wishes. It voted $100 million in aid to the Contras.

The Iran–Nicaragua Connection

Popular support for the Contras and for Reagan's foreign policy dropped dramatically, however, in November 1986. It became known that an aide to Reagan's national security advisor had secretly arranged for the sale of arms to Iran. Profits from this sale were then used to help the Contras in Nicaragua. This secret arrangement took place during a period in which Congress had banned military aid to the Contras.

President Reagan at first claimed to know nothing of this deal. But it became a scandal nonetheless. It appeared that the Reagan administration was trading arms with Iran in hopes of obtaining the release of American hostages held in Lebanon by Moslem extremists. This action contradicted Reagan's stated policy of not negotiating with terrorists. It also appeared that a White House aide could defy Congress in matters of foreign policy. And the action failed to win the hostages' release.

Early in 1987, President Reagan appointed a commission, headed by former Senator John Tower, to investigate. The *Tower Commission* reported that the

Think: Lt. Col. Oliver North, once an aide to the national security advisors, was questioned by the Foreign Relations Committee about his role in the Iran-Nicaragua scandal. Respond: Why was the affair so scrutinized?

president had relied too much on his staff and had not used proper judgment. As a result, Reagan replaced several members of his staff. But the damage to his credibility was severe. Six years earlier, the return of hostages from Iran had swept Reagan into office on a wave of popularity. In a strange twist of fate, his popularity suffered its most serious blow from the issue of hostages and relations with Iran.

The Threat of Nuclear War

Many Americans agreed with Reagan's tough stance against communism. But they worried about the threat of nuclear war. By the 1980s, the threat of such a war loomed large. Both the Soviet Union and the United States had enough nuclear weapons to destroy all human life several times over. Still, both countries continued to build even more nuclear arms. This build-up was called the *arms race*.

Think: **Awareness of the dangers of nuclear war grew during the 1980s. People began to realize that even a small nuclear war might not be survivable. Peaceful protestors made their voices heard. People throughout the world united on this issue.** Respond: **How did world leaders react to the public outcry?**

As Ronald Reagan completed his first term, Americans urged him to address the problem. They wanted an end to the arms race. The original SALT treaty had expired. A second treaty, called SALT II, had been hammered out. But it had never been approved by the Senate. Although Reagan had honored the treaty, he had never liked it. Moreover, it, too, had expired. Reagan had suggested a new series of talks with the Soviets. These *Strategic Arms Reduction Talks*, known as *START*, began in Geneva, Switzerland, in 1982, but they did not result in any new agreements.

Meanwhile, Reagan announced plans for a new kind of defense system. It would be a defensive shield set up in space to destroy incoming missiles. Scientists were not sure such a system was practical. But Reagan resolved to begin research on it right away. He called his idea the Strategic Defense Initiative. The media dubbed the plan *Star Wars*.

Reagan argued that Star Wars was America's best hope of preventing nuclear war. A shield against Soviet missiles would prevent any attack. The Soviets, for their part, did not like Star Wars. In October 1986, Reagan met with Soviet leader Gorbachev in Iceland. Gorbachev made some startling new offers to cut down the arms race. The two leaders seemed close to a historic breakthrough. The meeting

LEGAL IMMIGRATION FROM LATIN AMERICA, 1981–1985

For hundreds of years, most immigrants to America came from Europe. Recently, that trend changed a great deal. Combining information from the circle graph and map will give you a better understanding of how many new immigrants came from Latin America. (''Latin America'' means countries in the western hemisphere where people speak Spanish or Portuguese.)

Look at the circle graph.

1. For which years does it present information?

2. Which part of the world sent the most immigrants? What percentage of the total was this figure?

3. Which two parts of the circle show Latin American countries? What is their combined percentage? How does this figure compare with the largest percentage of immigrants?

Now look at the map. The figures in parentheses show the number of immigrants to the United States from 1981 to 1985 for each country.

4. On a separate piece of paper, list the countries in order of the number of people who emigrated to the United States during this time. From which country did the largest number come? From which country did the smallest number come?

5. Which countries are in the Caribbean Sea? What is the total of immigrants from these countries? Why do you think this figure is so high?

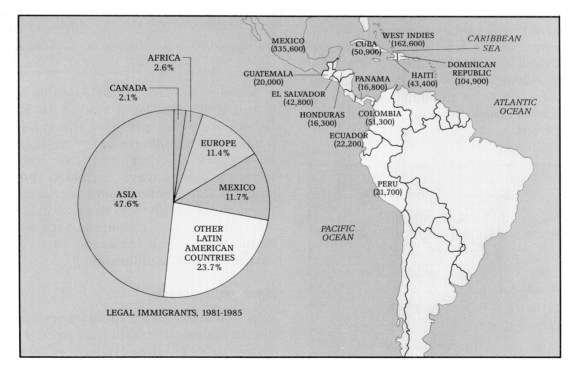

LEGAL IMMIGRANTS, 1981-1985

fell apart, however, when Gorbachev insisted the United States stop work on Star Wars. Several months later, in February 1987, Gorbachev made new offers on limiting intermediate range missiles. Both sides continued to wrestle with the issue of arms control.

An Overview

Although American prestige was compromised by the Iran–Nicaragua scandal, Reagan's anticommunist policy seemed to work. He could say that during his years in the White House he had prevented the spread of communism on many fronts. He believed that his tough attitude toward the Soviets would make the world a safer place. However, not everyone agreed with him. How to prevent nuclear war remained a crucial issue of American foreign policy.

Section Review

1. How did the shooting down of Korean Airlines Flight 007 affect U.S.–Soviet relations?
2. Why did Reagan send Marines to Lebanon?
3. What was the Iran–Nicaragua connection?
4. What was the purpose of the Star Wars plan?

3. Looking Ahead

Learn these important terms:

acid rain
Chernobyl

Remember the main idea:

The 1980s brought many challenges in the areas of technology and international relations. These challenges continue into the future.

Look for answers to these questions:

1. What challenges did immigration pose for America in the 1980s?
2. What improvements in daily life did technology make? What problems did it bring?
3. How do the problems of one country affect other countries?

Some of the challenges America faced in the 1980s had been around for years. Others were the result of the changing times. One challenge was the flood of newcomers pouring into the country. America has always attracted people longing for freedom and opportunity. Throughout its history, America has taken in immigrants from around the world. In the 1980s, the challenge came from absorbing new immigrants.

New Americans

In the past, most immigrants to the United States came from Europe. The new immigrants of the 1980s came from Southeast Asia and Latin America. After the Vietnam War, many refugees from

South Vietnam, Cambodia, and Laos came to this country to escape the Communists. Once here, they had to begin a whole new way of life. They had to adjust to a totally new set of customs and learn a new language. The presence of these people forced other Americans to look at their prejudices toward Asians. It also proved a painful reminder of America's failure in the Vietnam War.

Other new immigrants came from Mexico and the countries of Central America. Some came to escape from poverty. Some came to escape from harsh governments. Most were willing to do any job and to work for very low wages. To them, anything looked better than returning home.

Think: **Immigrant workers from Mexico and Central America were willing to do any job for low pay.** Respond: **What groups in the past were forced to work in the fields for low pay?**

Some of these people were so desperate that they came to America illegally. By 1985, there were an estimated seven million illegal immigrants living in the United States. Each year about half a million more entered the country.

Like the Southeast Asian immigrants, Hispanic immigrants had to learn to get along in a new culture with a new language. But the problems they faced were matched by problems they caused for the United States. It was impossible to have open borders. Yet it also seemed impossible to stem the tide of newcomers. The large number of illegal immigrants willing to work for low pay was driving down the level of wages in parts of America. Millions of people who did not speak English created a language problem. And slow acceptance of the newcomers by the native born led to tensions within communities.

In October 1986, Congress passed a new immigration law. It allowed certain illegal immigrants to become United States citizens. Those who came to America before January 1, 1982, could apply for citizenship. The law also punished employers who knowingly hired illegal immigrants. It did not appear, however, that this new law would end the problem of future illegal immigrants.

The Age of the Computer

The 1980s brought amazing new advances in the field of technology. Computers had existed for years, but it was during the 1980s that "the Age of the Computer" really arrived. Computers were installed in banks, offices, schools, airports, libraries, and private homes. Computers changed the ways people worked, shopped, studied, and played. They also made possible many advances in science and medicine. So powerful was the impact of the computer that, in 1982,

Think: Computers made work much easier in almost every field. Here, geographers create a map.
Respond: What changes have computers brought with them?

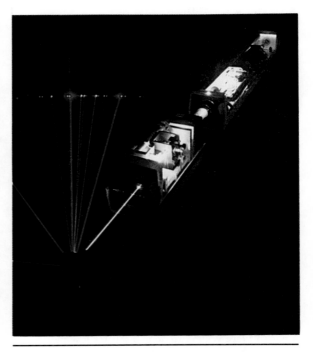

Think: Lasers are strong enough to cut holes in metal, yet delicate enough to aid in eye surgery. Here, a laser creates the beauty of the color spectrum. Respond: What other modern breakthroughs have many uses?

Time magazine named the computer its "Man of the Year."

Other Breakthroughs in Technology

Computers were not the only technological wonders of the 1980s. Robots became more and more commonplace. These mechanical creatures were programmed to do all kinds of tasks. Some began doing assembly work in factories. Others performed more spectacular feats. In July 1986, the robot "Jason Jr." explored every inch of the *Titanic,* a sunken luxury liner. The ship had gone down in the North Atlantic, in water too deep for humans to reach. Without the aid of the robot, the mysteries of the *Titanic* could not have been uncovered.

In medicine, too, some amazing things were happening. Doctors learned to operate using lasers instead of knives. Lasers are bright beams of light that can make extremely accurate cuts. Another advance came with the creation of artificial hearts. These helped prolong life for months or even years. These breakthroughs held great promise for the future.

Foreign Competition in Industry

As you have seen, Americans enjoyed some great successes in the field of technology. But other countries also developed advanced technologies. By the mid-1980s, America was no longer the world leader in technology. Japan had taken over that role. And the Japanese were using their technology to rival the United States as an industrial giant. The Japanese had a new and different approach to management, which seemed to be one reason their workers were so productive. And their educational system promoted specialized skills. Japanese imports began to flood the American market.

American companies were alarmed by the Japanese advances. Many began making an effort to regain the ground they had lost. Some sent American managers to Japan for training. Some introduced Japanese methods into their businesses. A few companies even began joint ventures with the Japanese. In Fremont, California, for example, General Motors joined with Toyota to produce cars.

The Space Shuttle Disaster

America faced other problems in technology, as well. On January 28, 1986, the space shuttle *Challenger* exploded shortly after launching. Six professional astronauts and a schoolteacher named Christa McAuliffe were killed. It was later learned that the tragedy had been caused by faulty equipment. Clearly, scientists still had a lot to learn about the technology of space travel. In the wake of this disaster, the future of America's space program seemed uncertain.

Energy and Environment

Meanwhile, the environment remained a big concern. The problem of *acid rain* was particularly frightening. Acid rain is one of the negative results of modern industry. It is caused by factories which burn oil, coal, and similar fuels. Particles from the burning fuel float up into the air. They later come back to earth in the form of highly acidic rain.

This acid rain stunts the growth of trees and kills the fish in lakes and streams. It poses a threat to wildlife not just in America, but in other countries as well. The acidic particles do not stop at America's borders. They float freely into Canada. In the 1980s, acid rain quickly became a worldwide problem, as factories in Europe and other regions also polluted the air. Coping with this problem is a major test for the nations of the world.

Chernobyl

On April 26, 1986, an explosion rocked the town of **Chernobyl** [chur-NOH-buhl] in the Soviet Union. An accident at a nuclear power plant there sent massive amounts of radioactive gases into the air. It was the world's worst nuclear disaster. Within three months, thirty people had died. More than 100,000 others had been exposed to the poisonous gases. Damage was not limited to the Soviet Union. People in Poland, Sweden, and Norway also saw signs of radioactivity. The long-term effects will only be known over time.

The Chernobyl accident made people everywhere much more nervous about nuclear energy. To many people the accident was proof that nuclear power was unsafe. The Chernobyl explosion killed any lingering hopes that nuclear power could solve all future energy needs.

Think: **Plant 4 of the Chernobyl facility was entombed to prevent further damage to people or the environment.** Respond: **What important lessons were learned from the accident?**

Predicting the future of the economy is important for business planning, but it is hard to do. *Economic forecasters* look at past trends and present conditions. Then they make an educated guess about what will happen in the future.

One major area of concern is foreign trade in manufactured goods. Every country tries to export, or sell, more goods than it imports, or buys. Sometimes a country meets its goals, but other times it does not.

American industry has seen many changes since 1960. In that year, the United States led world production in steel, cars, and TVs. Currently, however, Japan is the major supplier of all these products. Industry leaders in the United States have watched these changes over a number of years. They probably predicted that United States exports would fall behind Japan's. What they might not have predicted is how much American exports would decline or how quickly.

Experts have been trying to find ways in which the United States can more successfully compete with Japan in selling products. The chart below shows what one group of experts thought about each country's strong points in the production of goods related to computers, one very important market.

Comparison of U.S. and Japanese Strengths in the Computer Marketplace

Japanese Strengths	U.S. Strengths
Applied research and development	Basic research
Improvements in existing products	Breakthroughs and inventions
Business applications	Military applications
Parts of systems	Whole systems
Computer hardware	Computer software
Standardized systems	Customized systems
Miniaturized systems	Designs for new systems

Source: The Economist, 23 August 1986

Use the chart above to make some predictions about the future success of each country in selling its products. Tell which country seems likely to sell more of each of the following products.

1 Computer hardware

2 Programs for computers

3 Smaller computers

4 Weapons

5 Systems that fit a particular user

6 New inventions

7 Office systems

Think: The America's Cup races of the 1980s showed that Americans can face defeat and glory with dignity. In 1984, Dennis Conner lost the Cup to the Australians, who had a technologically advanced boat. Then, in 1987, Conner and the crew of the *Stars and Stripes* made a remarkable comeback, beating the Australians 4–0. **Respond:** What lessons can be learned from the American loss and victory in this event?

Toward the Future

Increasingly, the problems of one country affect other nations. Immigration is changing the distribution of the world's population. Progress in technology is requiring cooperation among countries. Energy and environmental issues are affecting everyone, as shown by acid rain and the Chernobyl accident. Countries need to work together to share information and solve problems. And everyone has to work together to prevent nuclear war. Achieving a level of cooperation remains the biggest challenge of the future.

Section Review

1. How did computers change people's lives?
2. How have American businesses dealt with competition from the Japanese?
3. What happened at Chernobyl?
4. In what ways do modern problems in one country affect other nations?

CHAPTER SUMMARY

President Ronald Reagan helped generate new pride in America. His belief in America helped make him one of the most popular presidents in modern times. Reagan tried to improve the economy with his supply-side economics. This approach had some success. It did not, however, end the problem of huge federal deficits. During his second term, Reagan searched for new ways to attack this problem. He faced a Democratic Congress, however.

In foreign affairs, Reagan took a hard line again communism. His actions in the Middle East, Grenada, and Central America did help prevent the spread of communism. However, his involvement in the Iran-Nicaragua connection adversely affected his presidency. Arms control was another problematic area in foreign policy.

As the decade progressed, Americans faced many new challenges. They had to cope with a wave of immigrants. They witnessed many exciting developments in the fields of science and technology. Technology also brought new problems, however. Acid rain, the space shuttle tragedy, and the Chernobyl accident showed technology's darker side.

Problems like acid rain and the threat of nuclear war also pointed to another challenge. The need for worldwide cooperation was an important concern of the future.

Key Words

Write a sentence to explain the meaning of each of these terms.

supply-side economics *arms race*
budget deficits *acid rain*
Contras *Chernobyl*

Major Events

Choose the answer that best completes the statement.

1. American farmers suffered from
   a) a worldwide grain shortage.
   b) falling land values and depressed prices.
   b) lack of competition.

2. The United States invaded Grenada to
   a) prevent Communists from taking over.
   b) keep the peace.
   c) show support for the Cubans.

3. At the 1986 Iceland Summit, Reagan and Gorbachev
   a. signed an historic treaty.
   b. ended the SALT II treaty.
   c. could not reach an agreement.

4. The explosion of the space shuttle *Challenger* was caused by
   a. a bomb.
   b. faulty equipment.
   c. a computer.

5. The 1986 explosion in Chernobyl caused people to
   a. question using nuclear power.
   b. leave Russia.
   c. close all nuclear plants.

Review

Important Facts

Answer each question with at least one complete sentence.

1. From what part of the federal budget did Reagan make most of his budget cuts?

2. What was the 1986 Gramm-Rudman Bill designed to do?

3. In what ways did women and minorities continue to suffer from inequality?

4. What appointments did Reagan make to the Supreme Court?

5. What happened to Korean Airlines Flight 007 that shocked the entire world?

6. What role did Syria play in the Middle East?

7. What policy did Reagan follow regarding El Salvador?

8. What did the Tower Commission report?

9. What was Star Wars? Why did Reagan believe it was important?

10. Where did most illegal immigrants come from?

11. Why were the 1980s called "the Age of the Computer"?

12. What was "Jason Jr."? How did it contribute to the investigation of the *Titanic?*

13. How did American companies try to recover the ground they had lost to Japan in the field of technology?

14. How many people were affected by the Chernobyl accident?

Skill Review

Study this graph, then answer the following questions.

1. From which area did the smallest number of immigrants come? What prediction can you make for future immigration from this area?

2. In 1982, what happened to immigration from Asia?

3. From which area would you predict an increasing number of future immigrants? Why?

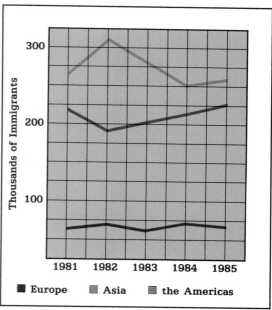

Immigration to the U.S., 1981-1985

Critical Thinking

Write a paragraph to answer each question.

1. Why did Walter Mondale lose the 1984 presidential election?

2. What did Reagan's anticommunist policies accomplish?

Important People

Choose the answer that best completes the statement.

1. McGovern was defeated in the 1972 presidential election by

   a) Gerald Ford.
   b) Richard Nixon.
   c) Jimmy Carter.

2. Nixon was granted a pardon by

   a) Jimmy Carter.
   b) Warren Burger.
   c) Gerald Ford.

3. The policy of detente was developed by

   a) Leonid Brezhnev.
   b) Henry Kissinger.
   c) Jimmy Carter.

4. The Egyptian leader at Camp David was

   a) Menachem Begin.
   b) the Shah.
   c) Anwar Sadat.

5. The first president to adopt supply-side economics was

   a) Richard Nixon.
   b) Jimmy Carter.
   c) Ronald Reagan.

6. Sandra Day O'Connor was the first woman

   a) Supreme Court justice.
   b) astronaut.
   c) senator.

7. Christa McAuliffe, who died in a space shuttle, was a

   a) professional pilot.
   b) political leader.
   c) schoolteacher.

Main Ideas

Choose the answer that best completes the statement.

1. Nixon's nominations to the Supreme Court made the Court

   a) more liberal.
   b) more active.
   c) more conservative.

2. Nixon resigned the presidency because of

   a) the Vietnam War.
   b) Watergate.
   c) the Agnew scandal.

3. In 1973, the price of oil went up because of

   a) an Arab oil embargo.
   b) an economic recession.
   c) the resignation of Richard Nixon.

4. The Equal Rights Amendment

   a) failed to win approval.
   b) was easily ratified.
   c) gave civil rights to blacks.

5. Ecology is concerned with

   a) minority rights.
   b) environmental protection.
   c) stagflation.

6. Nixon widened the war in Vietnam by

   a) secretly bombing Cambodia.
   b) Vietnamization.
   c) evacuating Saigon.

7. The 1973 Paris ceasefire agreement was a victory for

   a) South Vietnam.
   b) North Vietnam.
   c) the United States.

Review

8. The Camp David Accords, held during Carter's administration, were a step toward peace in

   a) the Middle East.
   b) Asia.
   c) Latin America.

9. The Ayatollah Khomeini hated everything about

   a) Iran.
   b) the West.
   c) the Middle East.

10. Carter's attempt to free the American hostages in Iran by force was a

    a) total success.
    b) partial success.
    c) complete failure.

11. Reagan's economic policy was based on

    a) cutting taxes.
    b) increasing taxes.
    c) increasing government spending.

12. Reagan worked hard to build up the nation's

    a) defense.
    b) highways.
    c) youth programs.

13. On October 25, 1983, American troops

    a) invaded Grenada.
    b) occupied Nicaragua.
    c) withdrew from Europe.

14. During the 1980s, America's lead in technology

    a) increased significantly.
    b) remained about the same.
    c) was challenged by Japan.

History Skills

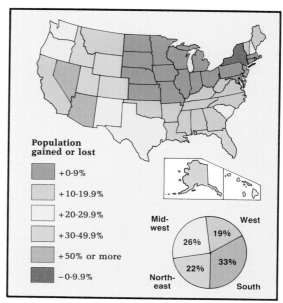

Population Changes, 1970-1980

Choose the answer that best completes the statement.

1. The regions which gained the most population during this decade were the

   a) Northeast and Northwest.
   b) South and West.
   c) Plains and Great Lakes.

2. You can infer that some people moved because of the

   a) energy crisis.
   b) hostage crisis.
   c) use of robots.

3. From this map, you can predict

   a) the Southwest will lose population in the future.
   b) the Great Lakes region will regain population.
   c) the South and West will continue to grow.

ATLAS AND REFERENCE SECTION

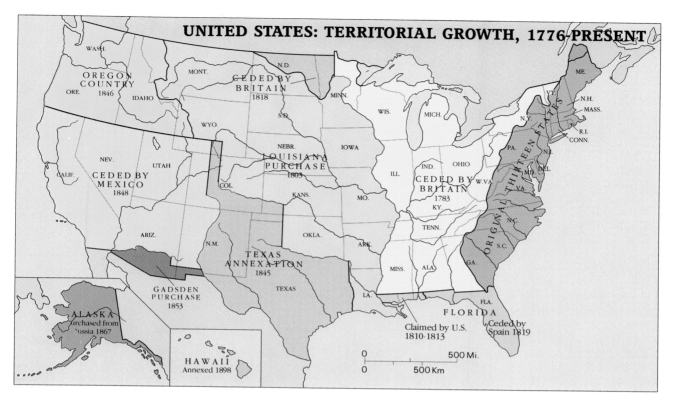

UNITED STATES: TERRITORIAL GROWTH, 1776-PRESENT

WASH.

OREGON COUNTRY 1846

ORE.

IDAHO

MONT.

CEDED BY BRITAIN 1818

N.D.

MINN.

S.D.

WIS.

MICH.

NEV.

UTAH

WYO.

NEBR.

IOWA

LOUISIANA PURCHASE 1803

CALIF.

CEDED BY MEXICO 1848

COL.

KANS.

MO.

ILL.

IND.

OHIO

CEDED BY BRITAIN 1783

KY.

ARIZ.

N.M.

TEXAS ANNEXATION 1845

OKLA.

ARK.

TENN.

GADSDEN PURCHASE 1853

TEXAS

MISS.

ALA.

GA.

N.C.

S.C.

ORIGINAL THIRTEEN STATES

ME.

VT.

N.H.

MASS.

N.Y.

R.I.

CONN.

PA.

N.J.

DEL.

MD.

W.VA.

VA.

LA.

FLA.

ALASKA Purchased from Russia 1867

FLORIDA Claimed by U.S. 1810-1813 Ceded by Spain 1819

HAWAII Annexed 1898

0   500 Mi.

0   500 Km

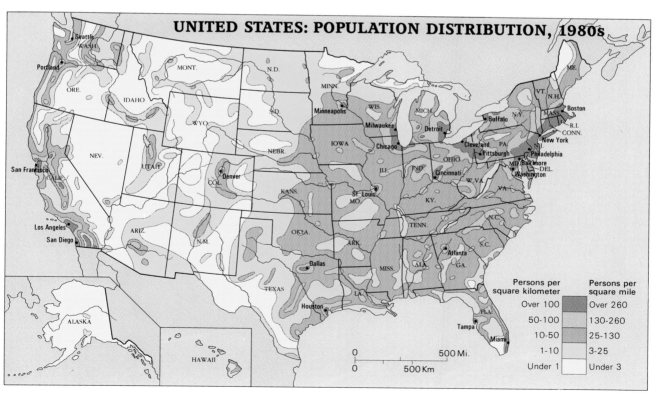

UNITED STATES: POPULATION DISTRIBUTION, 1980s

Seattle

WASH.

Portland

ORE.

IDAHO

MONT.

N.D.

MINN.

Minneapolis

S.D.

WYO.

NEBR.

IOWA

Milwaukee

WIS.

MICH.

Detroit

Buffalo

VT.

N.H.

ME.

Boston

MASS.

N.Y.

R.I.

CONN.

San Francisco

NEV.

UTAH

Denver

COL.

KANS.

Chicago

ILL.

IND.

OHIO

Cleveland

Pittsburgh

PA.

Cincinnati

W.VA.

New York

Philadelphia

N.J.

Baltimore

MD.

DEL.

Washington

VA.

Los Angeles

San Diego

CALIF.

ARIZ.

N.M.

St. Louis

MO.

KY.

TENN.

N.C.

S.C.

OKLA.

ARK.

Dallas

TEXAS

MISS.

ALA.

GA.

Atlanta

LA.

Houston

FLA.

Tampa

Miami

ALASKA

HAWAII

Persons per square kilometer	Persons per square mile
Over 100	Over 260
50-100	130-260
10-50	25-130
1-10	3-25
Under 1	Under 3

0   500 Mi.

0   500 Km

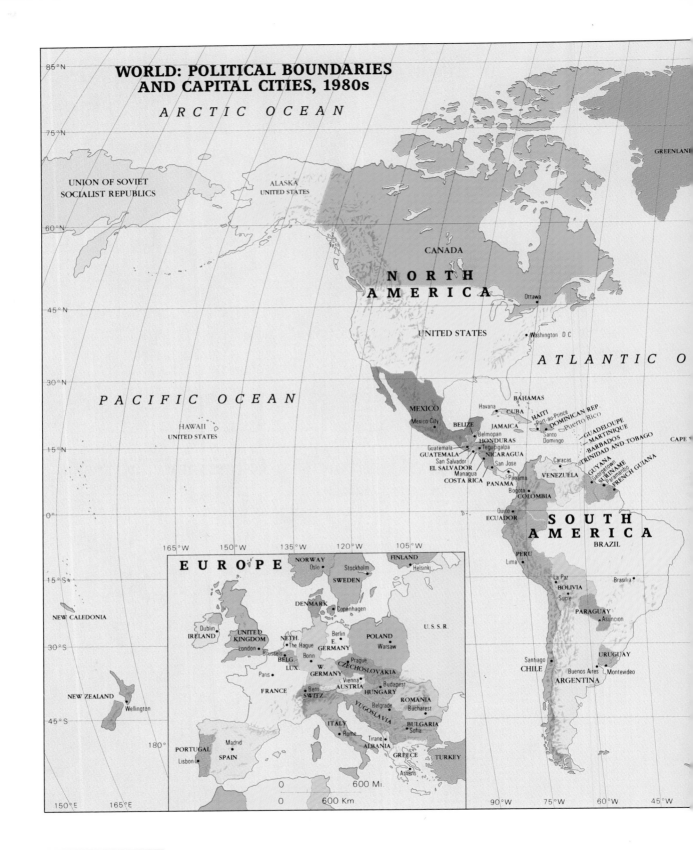

WORLD: POLITICAL BOUNDARIES AND CAPITAL CITIES, 1980s

ARCTIC OCEAN

UNION OF SOVIET
SOCIALIST REPUBLICS

ALASKA
UNITED STATES

GREENLAND

CANADA

**NORTH
AMERICA**

• Ottawa

UNITED STATES

• Washington D C

ATLANTIC O

PACIFIC OCEAN

BAHAMAS

HAWAII
UNITED STATES

MEXICO
Mexico City •

Havana
CUBA

HAITI
Port-au-Prince
DOMINICAN REP
Santo • Puerto Rico
Domingo

GUADELOUPE
MARTINIQUE
BARBADOS
TRINIDAD AND TOBAGO

CAPE

BELIZE
Belmopan
HONDURAS
Guatemala • Tegucigalpa
GUATEMALA •
San Salvador • NICARAGUA
EL SALVADOR • San Jose
Managua
COSTA RICA
PANAMA

JAMAICA

Caracas •
VENEZUELA

GUYANA
Georgetown
SURINAME
Paramaribo
FRENCH GUIANA

Panama •
Bogota •
COLOMBIA

Quito •
ECUADOR

**SOUTH
AMERICA**

BRAZIL

Lima •
PERU

La Paz •
BOLIVIA
Sucre •

Brasilia •

PARAGUAY
Asuncion •

NEW CALEDONIA

EUROPE

NORWAY
Oslo •
Stockholm •
SWEDEN

FINLAND
Helsinki •

DENMARK
• Copenhagen

U.S.S.R.

Dublin •
IRELAND

UNITED
KINGDOM
London •

NETH.
• The Hague
Brussels •
BELG.
LUX.

Berlin
E. •
GERMANY
Bonn •
W.
GERMANY

POLAND
Warsaw •

Prague •
CZECHOSLOVAKIA
Vienna •
AUSTRIA
Bern • SWITZ.

Budapest •
HUNGARY

ROMANIA
Bucharest •

Paris •
FRANCE

Belgrade •
YUGOSLAVIA

ITALY
• Rome

BULGARIA
• Sofia

NEW ZEALAND
Wellington •

Tirane •
ALBANIA

PORTUGAL
Lisbon •

Madrid •
SPAIN

GREECE

TURKEY

Athens •

Santiago •
CHILE

URUGUAY
Buenos Aires • Montevideo
ARGENTINA

0 _____ 600 Mi.

0 _____ 600 Km.

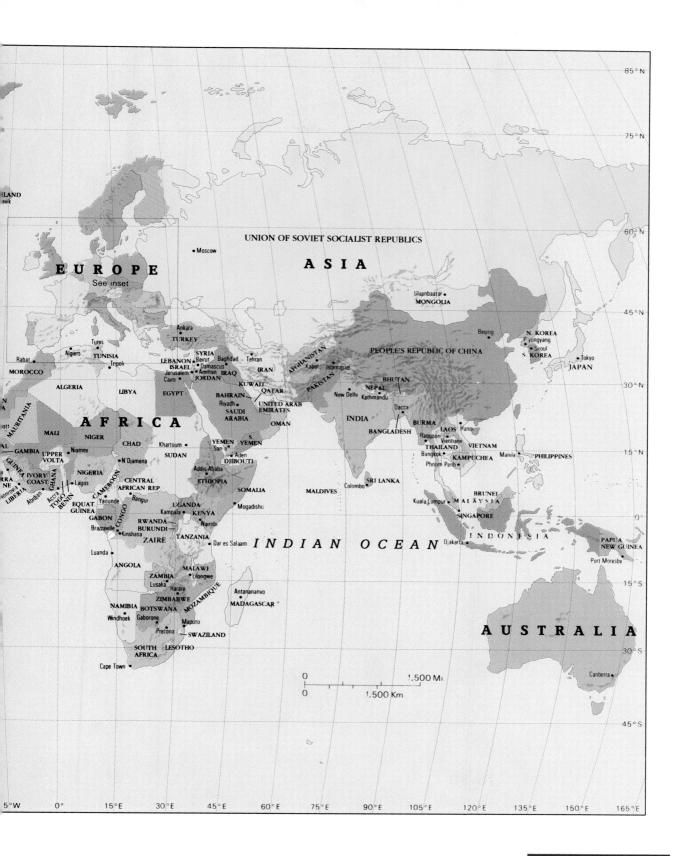

85° N

75° N

ELAND
avik

60° N

UNION OF SOVIET SOCIALIST REPUBLICS

• Moscow

EUROPE
See inset

ASIA

45° N

Ulaanbaatar •
MONGOLIA

Beijing •

N. KOREA
P'yongyang •
• Seoul
S. KOREA

• Tokyo

JAPAN

Ankara •
TURKEY

Tunis •

Algiers •

TUNISIA

Rabat •

MOROCCO

ALGERIA

LIBYA

SYRIA
LEBANON • Beirut
ISRAEL • Damascus
Jerusalem • Amman
Caıro • JORDAN

Baghdad • Tehran

IRAQ

Tripoli •

EGYPT

KUWAIT

BAHRAIN
Riyadh • QATAR
SAUDI UNITED ARAB
ARABIA EMIRATES

IRAN

AFGHANISTAN
Kabul •
• Islamabad

OMAN

PAKISTAN

New Delhi •

PEOPLE'S REPUBLIC OF CHINA

30° N

BHUTAN
NEPAL
Kathmandu

Dacca •

INDIA

BANGLADESH

BURMA
Ranggon •
LAOS
Vientiane

Hanoi •

MAURITANIA

MALI

NIGER

CHAD

Khartoum •

YEMEN
San'a •

S
YEMEN

DJIBOUTI

AFRICA

NIGERIA

Niamey •
N'Djamena •

SUDAN

• Aden

ETHIOPIA

THAILAND
Bangkok •
Phnom Penh

KAMPUCHEA

VIETNAM

15° N

Manila •

PHILIPPINES

Addis Ababa •

GAMBIA UPPER
VOLTA
GUINEA
IVORY
NE COAST GHANA
Monrovia • Lagos
LIBERIA Abidjan

CENTRAL
AFRICAN REP
CAMEROON

Bangui •

SOMALIA

MALDIVES

SRI LANKA
Colombo •

BRUNEI

Mogadishu •

Kuala Lumpur • MALAYSIA

EQUAT.
GUINEA

Yaounde •

SINGAPORE

TOGO BENIN
Accra

GABON
Brazzaville •
Kinshasa •

CONGO

UGANDA
Kampala • • KENYA
RWANDA Nairobi •
BURUNDI
ZAIRE TANZANIA

INDONESIA

0°

Luanda •

Dar es Salaam •

INDIAN OCEAN

Djakarta •

PAPUA
NEW GUINEA

Port Moresby •

ANGOLA

MALAWI
ZAMBIA Lilongwe
Lusaka •
Harare •

NAMIBIA BOTSWANA
Windhoek • Gaborone •
Pretoria •

ZIMBABWE

Antananarivo •
MADAGASCAR

15° S

MOZAMBIQUE

Maputo •
SWAZILAND

AUSTRALIA

SOUTH LESOTHO
AFRICA

Cape Town •

0
0

1,500 Mi

1,500 Km

30° S

Canberra •

45° S

5° W   0°   15° E   30° E   45° E   60° E   75° E   90° E   105° E   120° E   135° E   150° E   165° E

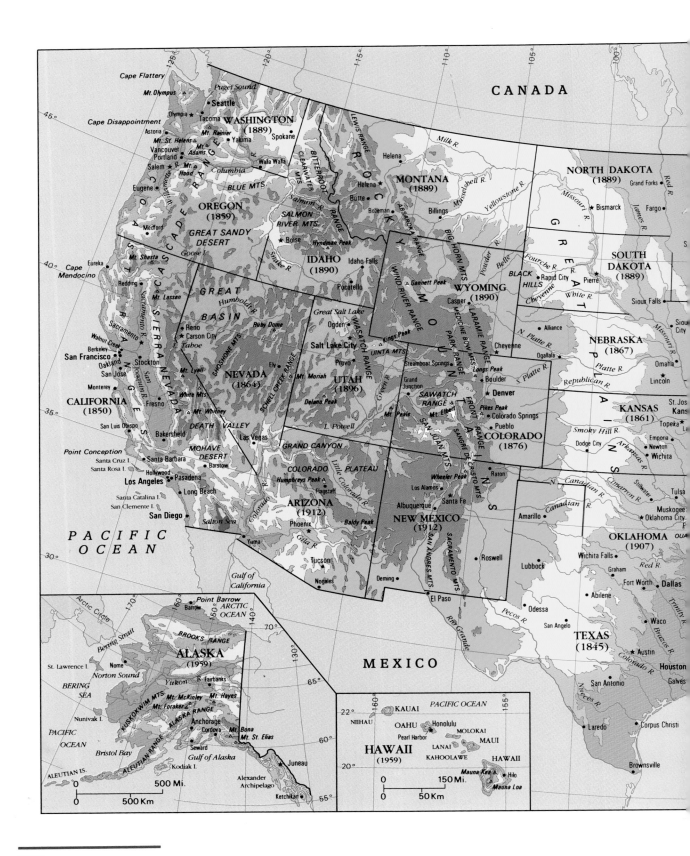

CANADA

WASHINGTON (1889)

Cape Flattery
Mt. Olympus
Puget Sound
Seattle
Cape Disappointment
Olympia ★
Tacoma
Astoria
Mt. St. Helens △
Mt. Adams △
Vancouver
Portland
Salem ★
Mt. Hood △
Eugene
Columbia R.
Walla Walla
Yakima
Spokane
BLUE MTS.
Medford
OREGON (1859)
GREAT SANDY DESERT
Goose L.
Cape Mendocino
Eureka
Mt. Shasta △
Redding
Mt. Lassen △

BITTERROOT MTS.
CLEARWATER MTS.
Salmon R.
SALMON RIVER MTS.
Boise
Hyndman Peak △
IDAHO (1890)
Idaho Falls
Pocatello
Snake R.

LEWIS RANGE
Helena
Butte
Bozeman
MONTANA (1889)
Billings
Helena ★
Musselshell R.
Yellowstone R.
ABSAROKA RANGE

Milk R.

NORTH DAKOTA (1889)
Grand Forks
Red R.
Fargo
★ Bismarck
James R.
Missouri R.

SOUTH DAKOTA (1889)
Rapid City
BLACK HILLS
Pierre ★
White R.
Sioux Falls

GREAT

BIG HORN MTS.
Powder R.
Belle
Fourche R.
Cheyenne R.

WYOMING (1890)
Gannett Peak △
WIND RIVER RANGE
Casper
MEDICINE BOW RANGE
LARAMIE RANGE
Cheyenne ★
N. Platte R.
Ogallala

NEBRASKA (1867)
Alliance
Platte R.
Omaha
Lincoln ★

GREAT
BASIN
Humboldt R.
Reno
Carson City
L. Tahoe
Ruby Dome
Great Salt Lake
Ogden
Salt Lake City
WASATCH RANGE
Provo
UINTA MTS.
Kings Peak △
Steamboat Springs
PARK RANGE
Longs Peak △
Boulder
S. Platte R.
Denver ●
Republican R.

KANSAS (1861)
St. Jos.
Kans
Topeka ★
Smoky Hill R.
Dodge City
Arkansas R.
Empo
Newton
Wichita

Walnut Creek
Berkeley
San Francisco
Oakland
San Jose
Stockton
Monterey
Mt. Lyell △
White Mts.
Fresno
SHOSHONE MTS.
SCHELL CREEK RANGE
Ely
NEVADA (1864)
Mt. Moriah △
Delano Peak △
UTAH (1896)
Green R.
L. Powell
Grand Junction
SAWATCH RANGE
Mt. Peale △
SAN JUAN MTS.
Pikes Peak △
Mt. Elbert △
FRONT RANGE
Colorado Springs
Pueblo
COLORADO (1876)

CALIFORNIA (1850)
San Luis Obispo
Point Conception
Santa Cruz I.
Santa Rosa I.
Bakersfield
DEATH VALLEY
Las Vegas
MOHAVE DESERT
Barstow
Santa Barbara
Hollywood
Pasadena
Los Angeles
Long Beach
Santa Catalina I.
San Clemente I.
San Diego
Salton Sea
Mt. Whitney △
SIERRA NEVADA
San Joaquin R.
Sacramento R.

GRAND CANYON
COLORADO PLATEAU
Little Colorado R.
Humphreys Peak △
Flagstaff
ARIZONA (1912)
Phoenix ★
Baldy Peak △
Gila R.
Tucson
Nogales
Colorado R.

Los Alamos
Albuquerque ●
Santa Fe ★
NEW MEXICO (1912)
SAN ANDRES MTS.
Wheeler Peak △
Raton
SANGRE DE CRISTO MTS.
Roswell
SACRAMENTO MTS.
Deming
El Paso
Rio Grande

Amarillo
Canadian R.
N. Canadian R.
Stillwater
Tulsa
Muskogee
★ Oklahoma City
OKLAHOMA (1907)
OUA
Wichita Falls
Lubbock
Graham
Red R.
Fort Worth
Dallas
Abilene
Waco
Brazos R.
Odessa
Pecos R.
San Angelo
TEXAS (1845)
Austin ★
Colorado R.
Houston
Galves
San Antonio
Nueces R.
Laredo
Brownsville
Corpus Christi

PACIFIC OCEAN
Gulf of California

MEXICO

Arctic Circle
Point Barrow
Barrow
ARCTIC OCEAN
BROOKS RANGE
Bering Strait
Nome
St. Lawrence I.
Norton Sound
ALASKA (1959)
KUSKOKWIM MTS.
Yukon R.
Fairbanks
Mt. McKinley △
Mt. Hayes △
Mt. Foraker △
ALASKA RANGE
Nunivak I.
Anchorage
Cordova
Mt. Bona △
Mt. St. Elias △
BERING SEA
PACIFIC OCEAN
Bristol Bay
Seward
Gulf of Alaska
ALEUTIAN RANGE
ALEUTIAN IS.
Kodiak I.
Alexander Archipelago
Juneau ★
Ketchikan

0   500 Mi.
0   500 Km

PACIFIC OCEAN
KAUAI
NIIHAU
OAHU
Honolulu
MOLOKAI
Pearl Harbor
LANAI
MAUI
HAWAII (1959)
KAHOOLAWE
HAWAII
Mauna Kea △
Hilo
Mauna Loa △

0   150 Mi.
0   50 Km

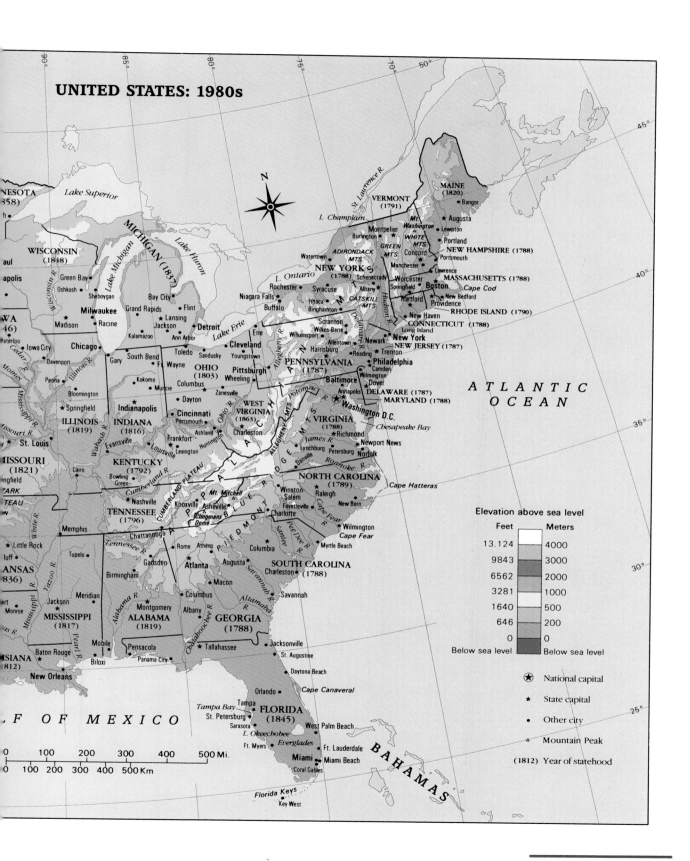

UNITED STATES: 1980s

N

MINNESOTA
(1858)

Lake Superior

WISCONSIN
(1848)

MICHIGAN (1837)

Lake Michigan

Lake Huron

St. Lawrence R.

L. Champlain

VERMONT
(1791)

MAINE
(1820)

• Bangor

• Augusta

Mt. Washington

WHITE MTS.

GREEN MTS.

NEW HAMPSHIRE (1788)

• Portland

• Lewiston

IOWA
(846)

• Paul

• apolis

Green Bay

Oshkosh

Sheboygan

Bay City

Grand Rapids

Flint

Madison

Milwaukee

Racine

Kalamazoo

Ann Arbor

Lansing

Jackson

Detroit

Montpelier

Burlington

Watertown

ADIRONDACK MTS.

Concord

Manchester

Portsmouth

Lawrence

MASSACHUSETTS (1788)

Boston

Cape Cod

Worcester

Springfield

New Bedford

Providence

RHODE ISLAND (1790)

NEW YORK
(1788)

Schenectady

Albany

Hartford

New Haven

CONNECTICUT (1788)

Long Island

CATSKILL MTS.

Hudson R.

Rochester

Syracuse

Ithaca

Binghamton

Niagara Falls

Buffalo

Williamsport

Scranton

Wilkes-Barre

Newark

New York

NEW JERSEY (1787)

Waterloo

Iowa City

Davenport

Chicago

South Bend

Ft. Wayne

Gary

Toledo

Sandusky

Erie

Cleveland

Youngstown

Harrisburg

Allentown

Reading

Trenton

Philadelphia

Peoria

Bloomington

Kokomo

Muncie

OHIO
(1803)

Columbus

Dayton

Pittsburgh

Wheeling

Zanesville

PENNSYLVANIA
(1787)

Baltimore

Wilmington

Camden

Dover

Annapolis

DELAWARE (1787)

Washington D.C.

MARYLAND (1788)

Springfield

Indianapolis

Cincinnati

Portsmouth

Ashland

Charleston

WEST VIRGINIA
(1863)

Ohio R.

Potomac R.

ILLINOIS
(1819)

INDIANA
(1816)

Frankfort

Lexington

Huntington

VIRGINIA
(1788)

Richmond

Chesapeake Bay

• St. Louis

MISSOURI
(1821)

Louisville

Evansville

KENTUCKY
(1792)

James R.

Lynchburg

Petersburg

Danville

Newport News

Norfolk

ngfield

Cairo

Bowling Green

CUMBERLAND PLATEAU

Cumberland R.

Roanoke R.

ZARK

TEAU

White R.

Mt. Mitchell

Winston-Salem

Raleigh

New Bern

NORTH CAROLINA
(1789)

Cape Hatteras

Memphis

Nashville

Knoxville

Asheville

Clingmans Dome

Fayetteville

Charlotte

TENNESSEE
(1796)

Chattanooga

Tennessee R.

Cape Fear R.

Wilmington

Cape Fear

Myrtle Beach

• Little Rock

luff

Tupelo

Rome

Athens

PIEDMONT

Columbia

Santee R.

Pee Dee R.

ANSAS
(836)

Gadsden

Atlanta

Augusta

SOUTH CAROLINA
(1788)

Birmingham

Macon

Charleston

rt

Monroe

Jackson

Meridian

Columbus

Savannah R.

Savannah

es R.

MISSISSIPPI
(1817)

ALABAMA
(1819)

Montgomery

Albany

GEORGIA
(1788)

Altamaha R.

Chattahoochee R.

SIANA
812)

Baton Rouge

Mobile

Pensacola

Tallahassee

Jacksonville

New Orleans

Biloxi

Panama City

St. Augustine

Daytona Beach

Orlando

Cape Canaveral

Tampa Bay

Tampa

FLORIDA
(1845)

St. Petersburg

Sarasota

L. Okeechobee

West Palm Beach

GULF OF MEXICO

Ft. Myers

Everglades

Ft. Lauderdale

Miami

Miami Beach

Coral Gables

Florida Keys

Key West

BAHAMAS

ATLANTIC OCEAN

Elevation above sea level

Feet	Meters
13,124	4000
9843	3000
6562	2000
3281	1000
1640	500
646	200
0	0
Below sea level	Below sea level

✪ National capital

★ State capital

• Other city

△ Mountain Peak

(1812) Year of statehood

0	100	200	300	400	500 Mi.
0	100	200	300	400	500 Km

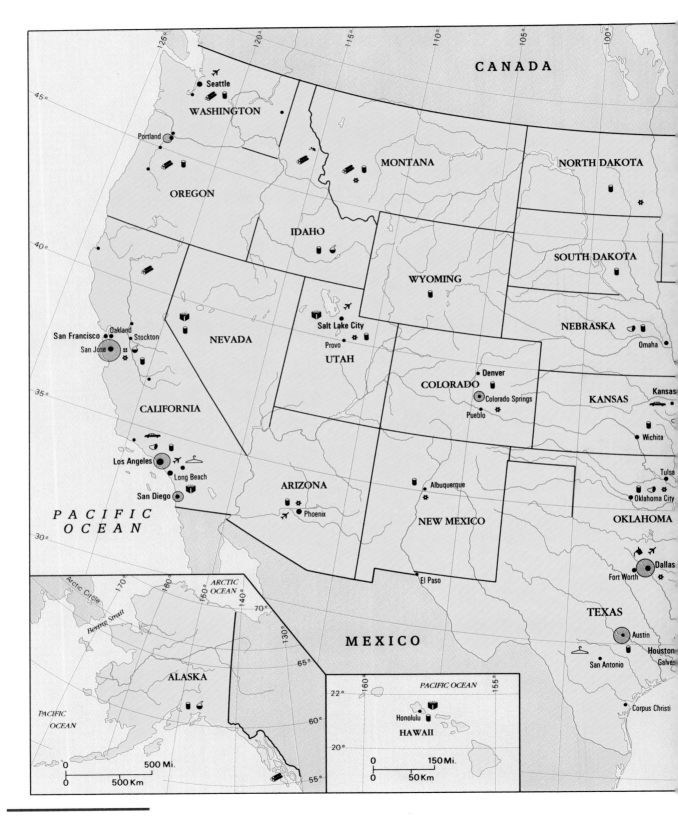

CANADA

WASHINGTON
Seattle

Portland
OREGON

MONTANA

NORTH DAKOTA

IDAHO

SOUTH DAKOTA

WYOMING

NEBRASKA
Omaha

San Francisco
Oakland
Stockton
San Jose

NEVADA

Salt Lake City
Provo
UTAH

Denver
COLORADO
Colorado Springs
Pueblo

KANSAS
Kansas

Wichita

CALIFORNIA

Tulsa

Los Angeles
Long Beach

San Diego

ARIZONA

Albuquerque

Oklahoma City

Phoenix

NEW MEXICO

OKLAHOMA

PACIFIC
OCEAN

El Paso

TEXAS
Dallas
Fort Worth

Austin
Houston
Galves

Arctic Circle
ARCTIC
OCEAN

Bering Strait

MEXICO

San Antonio

Corpus Christi

PACIFIC
OCEAN

ALASKA

PACIFIC OCEAN

Honolulu

HAWAII

0   500 Mi.

0   500 Km

0   150 Mi.

0   50 Km

812

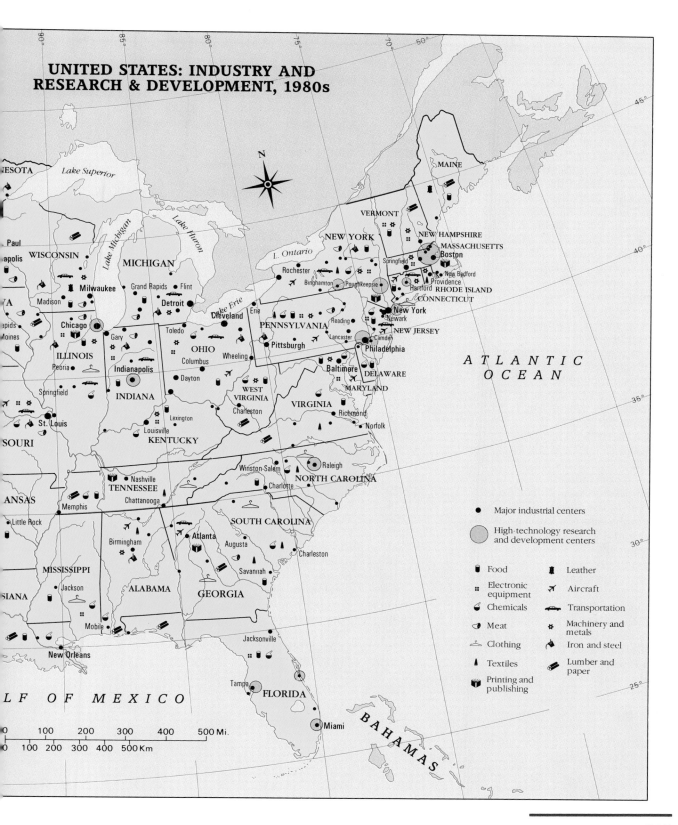

UNITED STATES: INDUSTRY AND
RESEARCH & DEVELOPMENT, 1980s

MAINE

Lake Superior

VERMONT

NEW HAMPSHIRE

NESOTA

WISCONSIN

MICHIGAN

NEW YORK

MASSACHUSETTS
Boston

Paul

L. Ontario

Springfield

apolis

Lake Michigan

Lake Huron

Rochester

New Bedford

Madison

Milwaukee

Grand Rapids

Flint

Binghamton

Poughkeepsie

Providence

RHODE ISLAND

IA

Detroit

Lake Erie

Hartford

CONNECTICUT

rapids

Chicago

Erie

New York

Moines

Gary

Toledo

Cleveland

PENNSYLVANIA

Reading

Newark

NEW JERSEY

ILLINOIS

Peoria

OHIO

Columbus

Pittsburgh

Lancaster

Camden

Philadelphia

ATLANTIC
OCEAN

Springfield

Indianapolis

Dayton

Wheeling

Baltimore

DELAWARE

INDIANA

WEST
VIRGINIA

MARYLAND

SOURI

St. Louis

Lexington

Charleston

VIRGINIA

Louisville

KENTUCKY

Richmond

ANSAS

Nashville

TENNESSEE

Norfolk

Winston-Salem

Raleigh

Memphis

Chattanooga

Charlotte

NORTH CAROLINA

Little Rock

SOUTH CAROLINA

Birmingham

Atlanta

Augusta

SIANA

MISSISSIPPI

Jackson

ALABAMA

GEORGIA

Savannah

Charleston

Mobile

Jacksonville

New Orleans

Tampa

FLORIDA

LF   OF   MEXICO

Miami

BAHAMAS

● Major industrial centers

High-technology research
and development centers

Food   Leather

Electronic   Aircraft
equipment

Chemicals   Transportation

Meat   Machinery and
                    metals

Clothing   Iron and steel

Textiles   Lumber and
                    paper

Printing and
publishing

0   100   200   300   400   500 Mi.

0 100 200 300 400 500 Km

Maps Index

Tables, Graphs, and Charts Index

Glossary

A

abolition movement The campaign by Americans to end slavery.

Abraham Lincoln Brigade American volunteers who participated in the Spanish civil war, fighting on the side of the loyalists.

abstract art Art that does not try to make what it shows look real.

academies The earliest high schools.

acid rain Factories which burn oil, coal, and similar fuels, producing particles that float up into the air and come back to earth in the form of highly acidic rain.

Adamson Act Passed in 1915, this law gave workers on interstate railroads an eight-hour workday.

admiralty courts British courts used to try the colonists accused of breaking the Navigation Acts and smuggling goods into the colonies without paying tax. These courts had no juries.

A.F.L.-C.I.O. The union formed in 1955 from two main labor unions in America.

Agricultural Adjustment Act A law passed by Congress in 1933 to pay farmers who agreed to grow smaller amounts of crops. This action was aimed at improving the price of farm products.

Albany Congress A meeting called in Albany, New York, by the British government to organize the colonies to help fight the French and Indian War. The British also sought to gain the help of the Iroquois Indians.

Albany Plan of Union The name of the plan the British proposed at the Albany Congress. The plan was unpopular with the colonists because they did not want to surrender local power to the British nor pay taxes for joint defense.

Alien Acts The 1789 acts of Congress which made it harder to become an American citizen, gave the president power to order dangerous aliens to leave the country, and allowed the president to imprison aliens during wartime.

aliens Persons who have moved from foreign lands to America and are not yet citizens.

alliance 1. A group such as those formed in the 1880s by farmers. The alliances formed cooperatives and worked for laws to help farmers. 2. A treaty among nations promising to protect one another in case of attack.

Alliance for Progress President Kennedy's 10-year plan for improving life in Latin American countries. It was approved by Congress in May 1961.

Allied Powers During World War I, the alliance of Britain, France, and Russia.

almanacs Books containing helpful ideas for farmers, as well as calendars, weather predictions, stories, and jokes.

amendments Changes to the Constitution.

American Federation of Labor A labor organization formed by Samuel Gompers in 1886 which joined together several separate unions of skilled workers.

American Indian Movement A radical group of American Indians who occupied Wounded Knee, South Dakota, for two months in 1973.

American System A plan proposed by Henry Clay to help the different sections of the United States work together. Clay's American System dealt with roads, banking, and high tariffs to protect American manufacturing.

amnesty To grant freedom from punishment for an action that ordinarily would be against the law.

Amnesty Act An act of Congress passed in 1872 that gave the right to vote and the right to hold office to most Southerners who had supported the Confederacy.

anarchists Revolutionaries who do not believe in having any type of government at all. Sacco and Vanzetti were anarchists.

annex To take over a territory and make it an official part of a nation.

Anti-Federalists Persons who did not favor adopting the Constitution as drafted at the Constitutional Convention. They felt the Constitution did not adequately protect the rights of the individual and/or gave the president too much power.

Appalachian Mountains A mountain range some 200 miles inland that formed the American frontier in 1775.

Appalachian Regional Development Act A law passed as part of Lyndon Johnson's Great Society legislation to provide a large sum of money for fighting poverty in Appalachia.

appeasement The policy of giving in to demands in exchange for peace. For example, European leaders practiced appeasement in dealing with Hitler.

arbiters A group of people who have the power to settle a strike between workers and owners.

armistice An agreement to end fighting when a war is over.

arms race The build-up of nuclear weapons between the Soviet Union and the United States.

Articles of Confederation A written document which created the first union among the states. The Articles gave the Continental Congress the right to wage war and make peace. The Congress also had the right to borrow money from foreign governments.

artifacts Articles made by humans, often for use in daily life.

artisans Persons who make goods by hand.

assembly The lower house of the legislature in colonial government. The assembly in colonial government was the counterpart to the House of Commons in the English Parliament.

assembly line A method of using labor very efficiently. The assembly line moves parts from worker to worker, so that each worker simply does one job over and over again.

astrolabe A navigational tool which helps guide sailors by measuring the ship's distance from the equator.

Atlantic Charter A statement formulated by President Roosevelt and Winston Churchill explaining their war aims, including freedom from want and fear.

Atomic Energy Commission A commission created by Congress in 1946 to put the development of atomic energy under civilian rather than military direction.

attorney general The person who advises the president on the nation's legal affairs.

automation The use of automatic, or self-operating machines, to do many jobs, especially repetitive and tedious ones.

Axis Powers An agreement between Hitler and Mussolini calling themselves the Axis Powers and claiming that Europe would revolve around an axis, or line, between Berlin and Rome.

Aztec Indians A tribe of Indian people who lived where Mexico City now stands. The Aztecs occupied this city from before 1300 to the arrival and conquest of Cortés shortly after 1500.

B

"baby boom" generation Children born during the years after World War II. The population increased dramatically, by 40 million people, between 1945 and 1960.

Bacon's Rebellion A 1676 frontier revolt led by Nathanial Bacon to protest the insensitivity of the colonial government of Virginia.

balance of trade The difference between what one nation buys from all the world as compared to what all nations buy from that one.

balanced budget The situation in which the federal government spends only as much money as it takes in.

barter To exchange one kind of goods for another.

Battle of the Bulge In December 1944, Germany's attempt to slow the Allied advance in the west. It was the last big battle of German resistance.

Battle of Bunker Hill A June 1775 fight between the British and the colonists on the outskirts of Boston. The British did not win until their third attack on the hill, when the colonists had run out of ammunition. (The battle actually took place on Breed's Hill.)

Battle of Coral Sea In May 1942, the navies of Japan and the U.S. fought without coming into gun range of each other. Each side's aircraft carriers sent airplanes to find and bomb the enemy. The Japanese were forced to turn back rather than proceed to New Guinea, their destination.

Battle of Gettysburg A three-day battle that many historians consider the turning point of the Civil War. The Confederate army lost and had to retreat into Virginia. This battle was the last time the Confederate troops penetrated Northern territory.

Battle of Midway In June 1942, the decisive naval battle between the U.S. and Japan which took place at Midway Island. The Americans surprised the Japanese and sank their four largest carriers, a loss from which the Japanese never recovered.

Battle of Saratoga The turning point of the Revolutionary War (October 1777, Saratoga, New York). British General John Burgoyne was forced to surrender his entire army to the Americans.

Bay of Pigs invasion An invasion on April 17, 1961, of 1,000 anti-Castro Cubans supported by the U.S. The Cuban people did not rise to support the invaders as expected, and the defeat was an embarrassment for the U.S.

Bear Flag Revolt In 1847, Americans and some Mexicans living in what is now California declared themselves an independent republic, free from Mexican rule. Their declaration is known as the Bear Flag Revolt.

benefit societies Organizations formed before 1800 by free blacks living in the Northeast to help their members get good educations and better jobs.

Berlin airlift From June 1948 to May 1949, during the blockade, when everything Berlin needed had to be brought in by air.

Berlin blockade In June 1948, the Soviet Union blocked all roads leading to Berlin in an attempt to take over Berlin completely. This attempt was defeated by the Berlin airlift.

Berlin Wall A wall between East and West Berlin, first built on August 13, 1961, to prevent East Germans from escaping into West Berlin.

Bessemer process An important process invented in 1856 for the inexpensive manufacturing of steel. The process is named after one of its inventors, an Englishman, Henry Bessemer; the other was an American, William Kelly.

Big Three nations Allied powers during World War II—the United States, Great Britain, and the Soviet Union.

bill of rights A list of individual freedoms which is attached to a constitution.

Bill of Rights The first 10 amendments to the Constitution. The Bill of Rights guarantee individual freedom of worship, free speech, and the right to a fair trial.

Black Cabinet Black citizens appointed to Franklin Roosevelt's Cabinet during his New Deal.

black codes Laws passed by state legislatures regulating the lives of blacks in southern states after the Civil War.

black conventions During the 1830s and 1840s, groups of black leaders who met to ask Congress to end slavery and give blacks equal rights.

black power The political and economic power of blacks. In the late 1960s, black leaders differed on the use of black power. Some wished to exercise their power within American society while others wished to set up a separate society for blacks only.

blitzkrieg In German, "lightning war." It describes the swift strike of Germany's tank divisions on the Netherlands, Belgium, and Luxembourg at the beginning of World War II.

blockade A naval manuever that blocks the ports of an enemy.

blue laws Laws passed by the colonies before 1700 to regulate Sunday activities.

Board of Trade A group of men from the Privy Council appointed by the king to help him rule the colonies.

boom towns Towns that seemed to grow up overnight as miners rushed to newly discovered gold and silver strikes in the West.

bootlegging Illegally producing whiskey. During Prohibition, bootlegging became big business. It made some people rich and powerful and led to much corruption in local government.

border states The southern states which did not secede from the Union.

Boston Massacre A conflict on March 5, 1770, between Boston colonists and British troops.

Boston Tea Party Colonists, dressed as Indians, boarded the British East India Company's ship after dark on December 16, 1776, and threw its entire cargo of tea into Boston harbor. They were protesting the tea tax.

Boxers A group of native Chinese who wanted all foreigners to leave China. Their 1900 uprising is known as the Boxer Rebellion.

boycott To refuse to buy or refuse to use.

breadbasket colonies The middle colonies which produced so much wheat that they were able to feed the other colonies.

Brezhnev Doctrine Proclaimed in 1968, this doctrine states that the Soviets have the right to interfere in the affairs of any eastern European nation if its Communist system of government is being threatened.

Brown v. Board of Education of Topeka A 1954 Supreme Court case in which the court ruled that segregation in public schools was unlawful and must be ended.

budget deficits When the government spends more money than it collects.

Bull Moose Party The Progressives, led by Theodore Roosevelt, who split away from the Republican Party in 1912 and formed a new political party.

bus boycott A protest movement that started in Montgomery, Alabama, on December 1, 1955. Black citizens refused to ride the city buses because of Montgomery's segregation laws.

C

Cabinet All of the secretaries who advise the president.

Camp David Accords A 1978 agreement between Prime Minister Menachem Begin of Israel and Anwar Sadat of Egypt ending more than thirty years of war between the two countries. The agreements (Accords) were worked out at Camp David, Maryland, with the help of President Carter.

canal A manmade waterway used to move goods and people on water.

Canal Zone The strip of land across Panama through which the Panama Canal was built.

capital Large amounts of money needed to finance a business.

caravel An improved sailing ship for transporting goods from one country to another. When the caravel was invented, it could carry larger loads than previous vessels and it could sail into the wind faster than earlier sailing ships.

carpetbaggers Northerners who moved to the South after the Civil War. Government positions were often filled by these Northerners, whom the Southerners greatly resented.

cash crop A crop that can be sold for money.

cattle kingdom From 1865 to 1885, the Great Plains were occupied by large ranches collectively known as the cattle kingdom.

ceasefire An agreement to end a war. A ceasefire between the Americans and the North Vietnamese was signed in Paris in January 1973.

censure To officially criticize.

Central Powers During World War I the alliance between Germany, Austria-Hungry, Turkey, and Bulgaria.

Central Treaty Organization (CENTO) An agreement between the United States and several Middle Eastern nations aimed at stopping the influence of communism in the Middle East.

chain stores When one company owns many stores, often in different parts of the country.

charter A list of rights given to a colony from the English king.

cheap money Money in circulation that is not backed by gold.

Chernobyl A town in the Soviet Union where the world's worst nuclear disaster occurred in 1986.

child labor laws Laws passed in the early 1900s to protect children working in factories.

Chinese Exclusion Act Passed by Congress in 1882, this law stopped Chinese immigration.

Chinese Nationalists The Chinese who controlled the mainland at the end of World War II. They were led by Chiang Kai-shek and represented the old China where most of the land was held by a wealthy few.

Chisholm Trail A long route over which cattle were herded from Texas to the railroad towns in Kansas to be shipped to Chicago by rail.

Church of England Formed by Henry VIII in 1534 to oppose the Catholic Church in England.

civil rights The basic rights enjoyed by all Americans—the right to vote, the right to a good education, the right to any job for which a worker is qualified, the right to buy or rent housing wherever one might choose to live.

Civil Rights Act of 1964 The law which forbids segregation in hotels, restaurants, and other public places.

civil service A government job.

Civil War The American war between the North and the South. It began in 1861, lasted four years, and proved to be one of the bloodiest wars in history.

Civilian Conservation Corps An organization begun in 1933 to give jobs to young people between the ages of 18 and 25. The Corps lived in camps. They planted trees, built roads, and improved the national parks.

Clayton Anti-Trust Act The 1914 law aimed at overseeing the activities of large trusts. The law clearly listed things big companies were not allowed to do.

closed shop When a company agrees to hire only those workers who already belong to a certain union.

coastal plain A small, level land area along the Atlantic coast.

Cold War A conflict that broke out between Russia and America after World War II. The Cold War was a war without weapons, but was fought with military threats, economic pressure, and harsh words between the opposing parties.

colonies Settlements controlled by the mother country.

commercial farming When the products produced by a farm are for cash sale.

commercial industry Goods manufactured for sale.

Committees of Correspondence Groups of citizens formed first in Massachusetts and later throughout the colonies to exchange letters telling what was happening in the colonies and in England.

Common Sense A book written by Thomas Paine in January 1776 which argued forcefully that Americans had everything to gain by becoming independent.

communism A system of government in which only one party controls all production of goods; it controls its people by telling them where to work and by limiting what individuals can do.

Communists Members of the political party which proposes that the government run all business and divide the profits among all the workers.

Compromise of 1850 A compromise worked out by Henry Clay to admit California to the Union as a free state and still keep the southern states from seceding.

Comstock Lode The biggest gold and silver deposit ever found in Nevada. The Comstock Lode produced 300 million dollars worth of gold and silver over a twenty-year period.

concentration camps Camps set up by Hitler to destroy the Jewish people and other people Hitler hated. People in the camps were victims of forced labor, starvation, torture, and murder.

Confederacy The Confederate States of America (the states which seceded from the Union).

Confederate States of America Seven southern states which seceded from the United States to form their own country. The states were South Carolina, Georgia, Florida, Alabama, Mississippi, Louisiana, and Texas.

Congress of Industrial Organizations A union organization headed by John L. Lewis. It aimed to help unskilled and semi-skilled workers, who until the mid-1930s had not been asked to join any labor unions.

conquistadors Spanish word for conquerors.

conservation The protection of natural resources for future generations.

constitution A plan of government.

Constitutional Convention In May 1787, in Philadelphia, Pennsylvania, fifty-five American leaders met to rewrite and strengthen the Articles of Confederation. Their discussions soon brought to light the need for a whole new constitution and their meeting became known as the Constitutional Convention.

Constitutional Union Party A new political party formed in 1860 when the Democratic Party was not able to agree on a candidate. The new party's candidate was John Bell of Tennessee.

consumer goods Products manufactured to be sold directly to the public.

Contras Anticommunist rebels in Nicaragua, supported by the Reagan administration against the Cuban-backed Sandinista government of Nicaragua.

convoy A ship formation in which ships carrying soldiers and supplies are surrounded and escorted by navy vessels which guard them from enemy attack.

cooperatives During the 1880s, groups of farmers who sold their farm products and bought farm machinery together.

Copperheads During the Civil War, Northerners who were sympathetic to the Southern side of the conflict and tried to help the Southerners win the war.

corporation A company owned by many individuals. Persons called stockholders each own part of the company.

Cost of Living Council Under President Nixon this council was set up to review all wage and price increases during a ninety-day freeze followed by ninety days when prices could only increase in certain circumstances.

cotton gin Invented by Eli Whitney, this machine could remove seeds from cotton fifty times faster than the previous hand method.

Council of Economic Advisers A group of economic leaders created in 1946 to advise the president, especially on how to prevent unemployment.

cowboy The workers who herded the cattle on large Texas ranches.

credit plans For a small amount of money a customer can take home a purchase right away and pay the balance of the purchase price in monthly payments.

Crittenden Compromise A proposal by Senator John Crittenden intended to solve the differences between the North and South and avoid the Civil War. Crittenden proposed that slavery be protected in the South and that the line agreed to in the Missouri Compromise be extended to California. The plan was never approved by Congress.

Crusades Holy wars which began in 1096 and lasted for the next 2,000 years. The Crusades were an attempt by European Christians to recapture Palestine (where Israel is today), the home of Christianity, from the Turkish Muslims.

D

Dawes Act The 1887 act which gave Indians on reservations title to their own part of the land. Instead of the reservation land belonging to the whole tribe, each family was given 160 acres of its own. The government hoped the Indians would then become farmers.

Dawes Plan An agreement in 1924 whereby the U.S. loaned Germany money to make its reparation payments from World War I to the rest of Europe.

Declaration of Independence A document written during the Second Continental Congress which explained in writing to the world why the American colonies were forming a new nation.

Declaratory Act A law passed by Parliament that gave Parliament the right to pass any law it wished to make for the colonies.

Democratic Party Founded by Andrew Jackson, the party developed into a national political party between 1824 and 1828. In 1828, Jackson was elected the seventh president of the United States.

Department of Housing and Urban Development A Cabinet-level department formed during the 1960s to deal specifically with the problems of American cities.

depression A period of economic hard times.

détente A policy to gradually relax tensions between the Soviet Union and the United States. It was begun under Nixon and continued under Ford.

dictatorship A form of government in which all power is in the hands of one person or a small group of people.

direct primary elections Primary elections in which the voters decide from a group of candidates which one candidate will be the one to run for office.

disallow To overturn. The King of England had the power to disallow, or overturn, laws passed by the colonial legislatures.

discrimination To mistreat a person simply because of his or her skin color, religion, beliefs, or political party.

dissidents Persons in the Soviet Union who criticize their government. The activity is illegal in Russia.

dividends A portion of a company's profit which is divided among the company's stockholders.

dollar diplomacy The use of investments to influence foreign governments.

domestic industry Products made in the home for sale to others.

draft law Passed in 1940, this law required all men between 21 and 35 to serve in the army.

Dred Scott Decision A decision by the Supreme Court in 1857 which made slavery legal anywhere in the United States.

drought A long period of time with little or no rainfall.

dry farming A method of farming which uses as little water as possible. The soil is broken into small pieces using steel-tipped plows that dig deep into the soil. This provides for maximum absorption and minimum evaporation.

Dust Bowl The midwestern part of the country, especially Kansas and Oklahoma, which experienced a long drought between 1932 and 1939. Crops could not hold the topsoil the way prairie grasses had. When the winds came, the soil simply blew away, creating gigantic dust storms and ruining many farmers.

duty A tax paid by the final buyer on imported goods.

E

Eastern Woodland Indians A tribe of Indians who built houses of wooden poles and wood bark.

ecology The science of how living things relate to their environment.

Eighteenth Amendment The "Prohibition Amendment" of 1919 which made it unlawful to buy or sell alcoholic drinks.

Eisenhower Doctrine President Eisenhower's promise to send aid and help defend any Middle-Eastern nation against communism.

Elementary and Secondary Education Act Passed in 1965, this law allowed the federal government to provide large amounts of aid to the nation's public schools.

Elkins Act A law passed by Congress in 1903 making it unlawful for the railroads to give rebates to favored customers.

Emancipation Proclamation A proclamation written by President Lincoln in September of 1862 which stated that all slaves in the Confederate states would be set free on January 1, 1863, unless the South surrendered before then. Lincoln's main purpose was to get the South to return to the Union, but that part of the plan failed.

embargo To refuse to trade with another

country, or to withhold exported goods from another country. The Arabs imposed an oil embargo on the United States to express their anger over American support for Israel.

Embargo Act An 1807 act of Congress which stopped foreign ships from carrying goods to or from the United States.

Emergency Banking Act Passed in March 1933, this law provided a four-day bank holiday. Federal inspectors examined the banks and determined which ones could be reopened with federal guarantees of the money deposited in them.

Employment Act This 1946 act of Congress made it the government's duty to try to prevent unemployment.

Environmental Protection Agency Created by Congress in 1970, this agency is responsible for coordinating pollution control programs and designing tough environmental standards.

Equal Employment Opportunity Act A law passed in 1972 which guarantees equal pay for equal work for all persons.

Equal Rights Amendment An amendment passed by Congress in 1972 to guarantee women equal rights under the law. The amendment was not ratified by enough states to become a law.

Erie Canal A canal 364 miles long across upstate New York. The Erie Canal connects the Great Lakes to the Hudson River.

escalate To expand, as when Johnson's administration increased American involvement in Vietnam.

executive branch That branch of American government headed by the president. Its duty is to see that laws passed by Congress are carried out. The executive branch also has the responsibility of communication with foreign governments.

Executive Order 8802 Issued by Franklin Roosevelt, this order made it unlawful for any factory producing war supplies to refuse to hire workers because of their race, color, or religion.

expedition A journey, usually to explore little known territory.

F

Fair Deal Truman's 1948 presidential campaign platform. The Fair Deal was his program of change and reform. It promised equal rights for all Americans, more public housing and more federal aid to education, a health insurance plan, and the repeal of the Taft-Hartley Act.

Fair Employment Practices Commission Formed to make sure that President Roosevelt's Executive Order 8802 was being carried out and that workers were not being discriminated against because of race, color, or religion during the war manufacturing effort.

Farewell Address George Washington's famous speech, given at the end of his second term as president.

Federalist Party One of the first political parties in the United States, it favored strong central government and a strong president. Its first leader was Alexander Hamilton.

Federalists The persons who favored adopting the Constitution that the Constitutional Convention had produced.

Federal Farm Loan Act A law passed under President Wilson which set up special banks to provide easy loans to farmers.

Federal Reserve Act The 1913 law which created the Federal Reserve System, the basic banking system by which the United States still operates today.

Federal Reserve System Created by the Federal Reserve Act of 1913, this is a system of twelve Federal Reserve Banks located throughout the country. The Federal Reserve System is responsible for the flow of money. It issues paper money and handles all the federal government's money. It also sets the interest rate at which smaller banks can borrow money from the twelve Federal Reserve Banks.

Federal Trade Commission A five-member board set up by the Clayton Anti-Trust Act to oversee the enforcement of the act.

feudal system A way of life, predominant in Europe around 1,000 A.D., in which all lives revolved around a lord who lived in and maintained a castle. There were social levels within the feudal system, mainly vassals and serfs, but all levels recognized their first allegiance was to the lord of the castle.

field hands Those slaves who did the farm work on the plantations. Their lives were the hardest of all slaves.

fireside chats Radio addresses by President Franklin Roosevelt directly to the American people during the difficult days of the Great Depression.

First Continental Congress A meeting in

Philadelphia in September 1774 attended by citizens and leaders from all the colonies except Georgia to discuss their problems with England.

fishing banks Areas in the sea where unusually large concentrations of fish can be found.

flapper A modern woman of the 1920s. The "uniform" of the flapper was a short skirt, a boyish bob haircut, and lots of lipstick and rouge.

flatboat Large rafts which floated down the Mississippi River. They carried goods from the western states for shipment by boat around Florida to be sold in the eastern cities.

Forty-Niners People who went to California to look for gold when it was discovered there in 1849.

Fourteen Points President Wilson's peace plan at the end of World War I.

free market economy an economy in which goods and services are regulated only by the demands of the market. The government stays completely out of the production and pricing of goods.

Freedmen's Bureau A bureau created by Congress during the Civil War to help blacks get food, clothing, education, and medical treatment.

freedom rides A form of nonviolent resistance in the early 1960s. People protesting segregation rode on buses and trains throughout the South.

Free-Soilers A political party formed in 1848 by Democrats who were strongly against the spread of slavery to new American territories.

fringe benefits Special benefits given to workers, such as paid vacations, health insurance, and pension plans.

frontier New land which has no settlers on it.

Fugitive Slave Act A strong law passed by Congress as part of the Compromise of 1850. The act required northern states to return runaway slaves to their owners.

G

Gadsden Purchase The purchase by the United States from Mexico of a small strip of land in southern New Mexico territory. The United States needed this land to build a railroad from New Orleans to California.

General Assembly One house of the governing body of the United Nations. All member nations of the body serve in the General Assembly.

ghetto A section of a city where members of one racial or ethnic group live.

GI Bill of Rights A law passed by Congress at the end of World War II which gave returning GIs educational help, loaned them money for homes or businesses, paid them pensions, and continued hospital care for those who had been wounded.

girdling An Indian method for felling trees in which the bark was stripped from around the tree in a ring so that the tree died from lack of nutrients.

Good Neighbor Policy Franklin Roosevelt's plan for American dealings with Latin American countries. The plan promised to respect the rights of these countries and to work peacefully with them to settle differences.

governor's council A small group of men appointed to help the governor rule a colony. The members were usually the richest and most important people in the colony.

gradual abolition A plan to end slavery gradually. The owners would be paid for the slaves set free under this plan.

graduated income tax Wealthy citizens pay a higher rate of income tax than people with low incomes.

Gramm-Rudman Bill Passed in 1986, this law called for a balanced budget within five years and required target deficit reductions each year until the 1991 deadline.

Grange The farmers' support group organized in the 1870s. It worked to get states to pass laws to regulate the railroads so farmers could get their products to market more cheaply.

Gray Panthers An organization formed in the 1970s to fight for equal rights for senior citizens.

Great Awakening A renewal of interest in religion marked by greater church attendance and an attitude of greater religious freedom in the 1730s and 1740s.

Great Compromise An agreement between the large and small states during the Constitutional Convention regarding representation in the Congress. Each state would elect the same number of senators, but the number of representatives would be based on population. Thus, the interests of both the large and small states were represented.

Great Society President Lyndon Johnson's plan

to improve the quality of life for all people throughout America.

Green Berets A special type of American fighting unit specializing in guerilla warfare.

Green Mountain Boys A band of patriots in northern New York led by Ethan Allen. The Green Mountain Boys attacked and captured the British Fort Ticonderoga the very day the Second Continental Congress began meeting in Philadelphia.

Grenada A small island in the Caribbean. Ronald Reagan ordered American troops to invade Grenada in 1983 when a civil war broke out against the Cuban-backed government.

guerilla warfare A special kind of war tactic in which small bands of fighters engage in "hit-and-run" attacks to keep the enemy off balance.

H

hard money Money backed by gold.

Harlem Renaissance A black cultural movement during the 1920s centered in New York City's Harlem.

Haymarket Riot A peaceful labor union meeting in Haymarket Square, Chicago, turned sour in 1887 when a bomb went off, killing several police officers.

headright system An early plan devised by the London Company to encourage settlement in the Virginia colony. Any person who paid his or her own passage to Virginia was given fifty acres of land. In addition, if the person brought other family members or servants, each received fifty acres.

Head Start A government program organized during the 1960s to help children from low-income families keep pace in school.

heavy industry Factories which make machinery, engines, iron rails, and other heavy-duty end-products.

Hepburn Act A law passed by Congress in 1906 which gave the Interstate Commerce Commission the right to regulate the rates railroads were allowed to charge.

Hispanics Spanish-speaking peoples.

Holocaust The system of German concentration camps in which six million Jews and other enemies of the Nazis died during World War II.

Home Owners Loan Corporation An organization formed in 1933 to lend homeowners money to pay off bank loans against their homes. This prevented banks from foreclosing on homeowners who could not repay their loans during the depression.

Homestead Act Passed by Congress in 1862, this act gave free land on the Great Plains to anyone willing to settle on the land and farm it for five years.

hotline A direct line of communication between Washinton, D.C., and Moscow intended to prevent an accident from triggering a nuclear war.

House of Burgesses The legislature, or law-making body, of the Virginia Colony.

House of Commons The lower, more powerful house of Parliament. Its members are elected by a vote of landowners.

House of Lords The upper house of Parliament. Its members are nobles who inherit their positions.

House of Representatives One of the two houses of Congress. Based on its population, each state elects legislators to the House of Representatives to serve two-year terms.

house servants Those slaves who worked in the master's house, usually as cooks, maids, and coachmen.

Housing and Urban Development Act A law passed by Congress in the 1960s to provide cities with help to solve their problems.

Huguenots French Protestants, persecuted in France for their non-Catholic beliefs, who moved to the English colonies along the Atlantic coast.

Hull House A famous settlement house in Chicago founded by Jane Addams in 1889.

human rights The belief that all people should be free to speak and live as they pleased. This policy, upheld by Jimmy Carter, led to increased tension between the United States and the Soviet Union.

I

Ice Age The last global change. Dramatically lower temperatures caused the polar ice caps to grow until they covered much of the globe. The Ice Age lasted from 50,000 years ago to 10,000 years ago.

immediate abolition A plan to end slavery immediately, without paying the owners for the slaves that would be set free.

immigrants People who come to live in a country other than the country in which they were born. Many immigrants come to America looking for a better way of life.

Immigration and Nationality Act A law passed in the 1960s that ended the quota system for the number of immigrants who could legally come to America from other countries. The law limited the number of persons who could legally immigrate each year, but it permits people from all over the world.

impeach The process by which a government official is charged with breaking the rules of his or her office and must stand trial. The Senate acts as the jury. If the accused is found guilty, he or she is removed from office.

imperialism The idea that a nation needs many colonies and territories to be rich and powerful.

impress To force a citizen of one country into the service of another country.

Inca Indians A tribe of South American Indians who built an extensive civilization high in the Andes mountains. It is believed the Incas were the first people in the Americas to practice agriculture.

indentured servants Persons who exchanged their labor for passage to the New World. Usually the indenture contract was binding for seven years.

Indian Reorganization Act Passed in 1934, this act stopped the government policy of dividing Indian reservations into small parcels of farm land.

Indies The name Columbus gave the island in the Caribbean where he first landed. He thought he had reached Asia, or the Indies, as the Europeans called it.

indigo A plant used to make a rich blue dye. Indigo was a cash crop for the colony of South Carolina.

Industrial Revolution A change from artisan, or handmade, goods to production by machines in factories. The change occurred in the 18th century.

inflation When the prices charged for goods increase faster than other segments of the economy, such as wages and interest rates.

injunction A court order forbidding a certain action.

interchangeable parts When parts from one item can be substituted for parts from another. Eli Whitney first invented this idea.

integrated industry an industry that controls everything from the raw material to the finished product.

interest The fee charged by banks for lending money.

International Court of Justice A court established by the United Nations to settle disputes as they occur among nations.

Internal Security Act A 1947 law passed by Congress requiring all Communist groups to file their membership lists with the government.

initiative The law which gives voters the right to suggest new laws to the state legislature. When a citizen gathers enough signatures for a proposed new law to appear on the ballot, the citizen has exercised the right of initiative.

Intolerable Acts Laws passed by Parliament in May 1774 to punish the colonists in Massachusetts after the Boston Tea Party. The colonial legislature was made powerless and General Gage, the leader of the British army in North America, was appointed governor of Massachusetts. The port of Boston was closed until the colonists agreed to pay for the tea that had been destroyed in the Boston Tea Party.

Isthmus of Panama A narrow strip of land in Panama which connects North and South America, through which the Panama Canal was built.

J

Jackson, Helen Hunt An American writer whose books helped make people aware of injustices to the Indians.

Jacksonian Democracy The ideas of Andrew Jackson expressed in changes in government while he was president. Some of the actions of Jacksonian Democracy included: all white men gained the vote, free public schools were established throughout America, state governors were elected by public vote rather than by state legislatures, judges and state officials were elected by public vote.

Job Corps A government organization responsible for job training for young Americans who have left school but are unable to find work.

judicial branch The branch of American government made up of the federal courts. The duty of the judicial branch is to make sure the government does not act unjustly to the citizens and that Congress does not pass laws that are in conflict with the Constitution.

judicial review The Supreme Court's authority to decide whether laws passed by Congress or the states are constitutional or unconstitutional.

Judiciary Act This 1789 law created the three-level system of federal courts: the district courts (one for each state), the circuit courts (to hear appeals of district court decisions), and the Supreme Court (the highest court in the land).

K

Kansas-Nebraska Act Passed by Congress in 1854, this act repealed the Missouri Compromise. It stated that Kansas and Nebraska could each decide whether slavery would be legal in its territory.

Keating-Owen Act A 1916 law strictly regulating child labor. Later, the Supreme Court declared this law unconstitutional.

Kellogg-Briand Pact A 1928 agreement among sixty nations to settle all their problems peacefully. Aimed at avoiding further war, the pact had no enforcement mechanism.

kickbacks Illegal payoffs, usually to an official who has been instrumental in the awarding of a contract.

Knights of Labor Established in Philadelphia in 1869, it was one of the earliest national labor organizations. It included skilled and unskilled workers, women, and blacks from all over the nation. The Knights advocated the end of child labor and wanted an eight-hour work day.

Know-Nothings A group of Americans opposed to immigrants coming into the country. Since they wanted their meetings and members to be a secret, when anyone asked a member about the group, the member would answer, "I know nothing."

Korean War The 1950–1953 conflict in Korea between the United Nations army and the Communist North Korean army. The war ended in a stalemate.

Ku Klux Klan A secret group formed to try to stop Reconstruction. The group's goal was to keep blacks, carpetbaggers, and scalawags from running the South. Their tactics were fear and intimidation.

L

lame duck 1. The period between an election and the winner's inauguration. 2. The officeholder who is virtually powerless during the period described above.

landslide When an election is won by a vast majority.

League of Nations An organization, proposed by President Wilson at the end of World War I, of all the countries of the world. The purpose of the League was to settle disputes by discussion rather than war.

League of United Latin American Citizens An organization created in the 1960s to fight for equal rights, especially for Hispanics in America.

legislative branch One of the three branches of American government. Made up of the Senate and the House of Representatives, this branch functions to make laws.

legislature Any law-making group.

Lend-Lease Act Passed by Congress in 1941, this law allowed the United States to lend, rather than sell, war supplies to Britain, and later, to other countries fighting against Germany.

liberal A political philosophy that encourages granting individuals more rights and open expression.

literacy The ability to read.

literacy test A test that required a voter to be able to read before he or she could vote. It was one of many ways blacks were blocked from voting after the Civil War.

lockout A labor tactic by which a company stops workers from working until the workers agree to the company's terms. The workers are simply locked out of the company's property.

Lone Star Republic The name for Texas after it won its independence from Mexico in 1836 and before it became a part of the United States.

long drive In the latter half of the 1800s, the trip cowboys made to drive cattle from Texas to the railroad towns of Abilene and Dodge City, Kansas. From there, the cattle were shipped by rail to Chicago.

longhorns A kind of cattle raised in Texas and characterized by sets of long horns.

Louisiana Purchase Land purchased from France during Jefferson's first term as president. The purchase stretched from the Mississippi River to the Rocky Mountains, and from the

Gulf of Mexico to Canada. The land, purchased in 1803 for $15 million, doubled the size of America.

Loyalists Colonists who wanted America to remain a part of England.

M

Mann-Elkins Act A law passed under Taft which gave the Interstate Commerce Commission the power to regulate the telephone and telegraph companies, as well as the power to regulate the rates railroads charged their customers.

manufacturing The making of finished products.

March on Washington A peaceful gathering in August 1963 of more than 200,000 persons who called for an end to racial discrimination in America.

margin To buy a stock by only making a down payment on it and then borrowing the remainder of the money needed to buy the stock.

market A place for manufactured goods to be sold.

Marshall Plan A plan for rebuilding European nations after World War II. The plan, named after the American secretary of state, provided money and goods to the nations of western Europe to rebuild cities, farms, and factories.

mass produce To manufacture in large quantities.

mass-produced culture Culture created to fit the needs of broadcasters and the wants of viewers, rather than being a culture of quality, produced for its own sake. The coming of television, with its ability to reach a nationwide audience, at one time brought the cry from critics that culture was now being mass-produced.

mass production A manufacturing system by which a factory makes large amounts of one product through the use of standardized parts and assembly lines.

Maya Indians A tribe of Indians who built an extensive civilization in what is now Guatemala and southern Mexico. The Mayans had the first system of writing in the Americas, and they built cities and huge pyramids on land they had cleared from dense jungle.

Mayflower Compact An agreement drawn up by the Pilgrims in 1620 to make fair laws and to obey them. The Mayflower Compact stated for the first time the colonists' right to form their own government.

McCulloch v. Maryland This 1819 case established the constitutionality of the Bank of the United States and made it unlawful for states to charge the Bank a tax for doing business within the states.

McNary-Haugen Bill A 1924 bill which ordered the government to buy any crops the farmers could not sell, and then to sell the crops to foreign countries. Congress passed the bill twice, but President Coolidge vetoed the bill both times.

Meat Inspection Act This 1906 law required federal inspectors to check all meat, fresh and canned, to make sure it was safe to eat.

Medicaid The government program, begun in 1965, to provide medical care for poor Americans under the age of sixty-five.

Medicare The government program, begun in 1965, offering free hospital care for Americans over the age of sixty-five.

melodrama A form of dramatic play popular in the late 1800s. The play always had a poor, honest hero; a mean rich villain; and a beautiful, brave heroine over whom the hero and villain fought.

merit system A system for choosing applicants for government jobs on the basis of test scores. The merit system replaced the spoils system, in which friends of politicians were given government jobs, often regardless of their abilities or qualifications.

Mexican Cession Lands won from Mexico in 1848 when the United States defeated Santa Anna in the Mexican War.

Mexican War Begun on May 13, 1846, when Congress declared war on Mexico. The Mexican army had crossed the Rio Grande and fired on Americans there. The war ended in victory for the Americans in 1848.

middle passage The middle portion of the slaves' journey from Africa. Slaves were chained closely together aboard a ship, with no room to even stand or stretch, from Africa to the New World.

Minutemen Colonists trained and willing to fight the British "at a minute's notice."

missionaries Religious workers who go into an area to convert persons living there to their religion.

missions Religious centers set up by the Catholic Church in the New World.

Missouri Compromise Henry Clay's 1820

proposal wherein Missouri could be admitted to the Union as a slave state if Maine could be admitted as a free state. Thus, equal numbers of free and slave states were preserved within the Union.

monopoly When one company becomes so strong it controls an entire industry.

Monroe Doctrine In a speech given in 1823, President James Monroe told the nations of Europe to stay out of the affairs of the United States and South America. In return, the United States would stay out of the affairs of Europe. The Doctrine was enforced until the 1860s.

Mormons A religious group begun in the 1820s which was forced in 1846 to leave Illinois. The Mormons then traveled west to settle near the Great Salt Lake in Utah.

Mormon Trail The route the Mormons traveled to get to Utah from Illinois in 1846.

Mound Builders A tribe of Indians who settled along the Ohio and Mississippi River valleys. Their cities, in which thousands of people lived, contained huge earth mounds, often in the shape of animals and sometimes hundreds of feet long.

muckrakers Writers in American society in the early 1900s who pointed out and exposed problems in American life.

murals Large wall paintings, often done by WPA artists to decorate public buildings.

musicals Extravagant movies, especially popular during the 1930s, which feature singing and dancing.

N

National Association for the Advancement of Colored People (NAACP) An organization formed in 1909 when white Progressives joined W.E.B. Dubois and his Niagara Movement to fight together through legal action to win equal rights for black citizens.

National Defense Education Act The act passed in 1958 to provide increased federal money for teaching science, mathematics, and foreign languages and also to provide loans for needy college students. The act was spurred by the 1957 launching of *Sputnik I.*

National Housing Act of 1949 The federal legislation making it possible to clear slums and build low-cost public housing.

National Labor Relations Act Passed by Congress in 1935, this act provided for elections where workers could vote to form a union. If the union won, the company had to recognize it.

National Recovery Administration (NRA) An organization established by Congress in 1933 to set up codes, or rules, to help each industry recover from the depression. The NRA codes cut down working hours, raised wages and prices, and limited the amount of goods that could be produced.

National Road A road funded by the federal government and begun in 1811 to connect the country east to west. When finished, the National Road ran from Cumberland, Maryland, to southern Illinois.

National Security Act After World War II Congress wanted to unite all branches of the armed services under one Cabinet department. This 1947 act therefore created the Department of Defense headed by the secretary of defense.

National Urban League An organization formed in 1911 to help black Americans in northern cities find jobs.

NATO The North Atlantic Treaty Organization formed in April 1949 by the United States, Canada, and ten European allies. Each nation agreed to help defend any other nation if it were attacked. The NATO nations also agreed to build up their defenses together to protect themselves from attack.

Navigation Acts A series of laws passed by England in 1660 to control the colonies' trade.

naval stores Supplies used on ships, such as tar, pitch, resin, and turpentine.

navigator The officer on a ship who sets its course and determines its position as the ship sails toward its destination.

Nazi Adolf Hitler's political party. Also known as the National Socialist party.

neutral When a country refuses to take sides in a conflict.

Neutrality Act of 1935 An isolationist measure that stated American factories could not sell weapons to any nation at war, American ships could not carry weapons to any nation at war, and American citizens could not travel on ships belonging to a nation at war.

New Deal Franklin Roosevelt's 1932 plan to lead the country out of the Great Depression.

New France French settlements in the New World, principally in Nova Scotia, Canada, and along the Saint Lawrence River.

New Freedom Woodrow Wilson's objectives for

government when he became president in 1912. New Freedom stood for lowering the tariff, reforming the nation's banks, and breaking up the monopolies.

New Frontier President Kennedy's plan to improve life in America.

new immigrants Starting in 1880, the immigrants who began to arrive in America from southern and eastern European countries—Italy, Hungary, Poland, Russia.

Newlands Reclamation Act A 1902 law which allows funds from the sale of federal lands to be used for irrigation or reclamation of damaged land.

New South What rebuilders of the South after the Civil war hoped for—an economic base of manufacturing and trade.

Niagara Movement Founded in 1905 by W.E.B. Dubois and other black leaders to state the goals of black Americans. The group fought for the right to vote, the right to be educated, and the right to be admitted to all public places.

nickelodeon The early movie theaters; the price of admission was a nickel.

Nisei Japanese-American citizens. More than 100,000 of them were rounded up and put into special camps after Pearl Harbor was bombed by the Japanese.

nonviolent resistance Peaceful protest of an injustice in the law. During the 1960s, black Americans and their sympathizers used nonviolent resistence in the form of sit-ins, freedom rides, and other such techniques to protest segregation throughout the South.

Norse A sailing people of northwestern Europe. It is believed they sailed the Atlantic and reached North America about A.D. 1000, 500 years before Columbus. (Also called Vikings.)

Northwestern Indians North American Indians living in the present northwestern states. These Indians were wealthy and lived in log houses. They possessed advanced woodworking skills which they used to carve colorful totem poles.

Northwest Ordinance A law passed by the Continental Congress which set up a plan for settling the territory north of the Ohio River. The Ordinance stated that when sixty thousand settlers lived in an area their territory could become a new state.

Northwest Passage A mythical sea route to Asia from Europe sought by early New World explorers.

nullify To refuse to obey. Before the Civil War, the South believed that a state had the right to refuse to obey, or to nullify, a federal law that it found unconstitutional.

O

Office of Economic Opportunity The federal agency created by President Lyndon Johnson to help low-income families. This agency was set up to administer Head Start, the Job Corps, and VISTA.

Office of Price Administration An office set up during World War II to set prices, wages, and rents.

Office of Production Management This office, created in 1941, set up plans for helping industry change from peacetime to wartime production.

old immigrants The original immigrants to America who came from the northern and western European countries—England, France, Germany, Norway, Sweden, Denmark.

Old South States in the South which had been part of the colonies. These included Maryland, Virginia, Georgia, North and South Carolina.

Old Southwest States located south of the Ohio River: Kentucky, Tennessee, Alabama, and Mississippi.

Open-Door Policy The American policy toward China begun in 1899 as proposed by Secretary of State John Hay. He asked all European nations to agree with America on equal trading in China. He also asked for an agreement among the nations that none would seize land and lay claim to it.

Oregon Trail The trail by which Americans traveled to settle in the Oregon region.

P

Palestinian Liberation Organization (PLO) An organization of Arab Palestinians who want to create a homeland for themselves out of land held by Israel.

pardon To completely forgive an offender for breaking the law.

Parliament The English lawmaking body, it is formed of two houses, the House of Lords and the House of Commons. Parliament has the right to pass laws, set taxes, and control the military forces. The king cannot veto the laws it passes.

party boss A strong party leader. The individual who ran a political machine was called a party boss.

Patriots American colonists who favored independence from England.

Paxton Boys A group of western Pennsylvania farmers who marched on Philadelphia to demand greater representation in the colonial legislature.

Peace Corps Begun by President Kennedy in 1962, this organization of American volunteers helps Third World nations.

peace treaty An agreement ending the disputes among nations which are at war.

Pendleton Civil Service Act The law passed by Congress in 1883 which began the merit system as the method by which applicants for government jobs were selected.

Pennsylvania Dutch Descendants of German settlers now living in Pennsylvania.

personal liberty laws Laws passed by northern states to protect blacks living there. These laws protected blacks from being arrested as runaway slaves and guaranteed free black people the right of a jury trial.

picket line A line formed by workers on strike from a business to prevent other workers from going to work in the business.

Pilgrims An English religious group that differed from both the Catholics and the Church of England. When a chance for religious freedom came in an English colony, they were among the first to move to the New World.

pioneers Those persons who left the cities and towns of the East to settle the American frontier.

Plains Indians North American Indian tribes who lived in the center of the country on the Great Plains. They built houses of wooden poles and buffalo hides called tepees. These houses could be torn down and easily moved as the Plains Indians followed the movement of great buffalo herds through the center of the country.

plantations Large farms.

Platt Amendment An amendment passed in 1901 prior to Cuban independence in 1902. The amendment put certain conditions on Cuba's freedom, the most important of which was the United States' right to intervene whenever political troubles threatened Cuba's independence.

Plessy v. *Ferguson* The Supreme Court ruling in 1896 which made "separate but equal" segregation legal in America.

political machine A political organization, common in the 1800s, which could guarantee a winning number of votes to politicians who cooperated with it. The political machine guaranteed to vote a politician into a certain office, the politician guaranteed to reward the machine by awarding contracts for city purchases to members of the machine.

political parties Groups of people who share certain ideas about government. They pool their resources and often sponsor candidates for office.

polls Public opinion surveys, usually closely watched by politicians to indicate public attitude on issues.

poll tax A voting tax charged by some states before a person was allowed to vote. Many poor blacks could not afford this tax and therefore were denied the vote.

popular votes The votes of the people.

Populist Party Party formed in the late 1800s by farmers and other workers who felt big business had become too powerful and often controlled the persons elected to office. The Populists' ideas eventually came to be accepted by both the Democratic and Republican parties. (Also known as the People's Party.)

potash Wood ashes produced in the colonies for use in England in the wool industry.

poverty A yearly income below a nationally established minimum amount for basic human necessities.

Prisoners of war (POWs) A term which came into current usage when the U.S. was fighting in Vietnam.

Proclamation of 1763 A law passed by the British Government which made it unlawful for the colonists to settle west of the Appalachian Mountains.

progressive education The theory of education which states that a student's education should match the student's needs, abilities, and interests. The theory was put forward by John Dewey in the 1920s.

Progressives Reformers in America around 1900 who believed in making progress toward the ideals of a democratic society. Specifically, Progressives believed that government could and should solve the country's problems. The targets of their actions were slums, poor factory working conditions, the plight of the poor, government control of big business, and corruption in government at all levels.

Prohibition The outlawing of alcohol. The Eighteenth Amendment passed in 1919 made it unlawful to buy or sell alcoholic drinks in America.

proprietary colony A colony owned and ruled by one or more people instead of by the English king.

proprietor An owner.

protective tariff An unusually high tax placed on foreign goods to make them more expensive than local goods.

privateers American merchant seamen, not part of the navy, who built a strong private force against British shipping during the War of 1812.

Public Works Administration (PWA) An agency created by Congress to give work to thousands of people during the depression. The PWA built buildings, bridges, and dams.

Pueblo Indians North American Indians who lived in the southwestern part of the country. They and the Mound Builders were the only North American Indians to practice agriculture which enabled them to build permanent cities.

Pure Food and Drug Act This 1906 law set standards for processed foods and medicines to protect the public from unsanitary packing conditions or the use of ingredients that might be harmful to the user.

purge To get rid of, to cleanse.

Puritans An English religious group who came to America seeking freedom from punishment for their beliefs. They were richer than the Pilgrims and with their own money were able to form the Massachusetts Bay Colony.

Q

Quakers A religious group that believes all people are equal.

quota system A law which limited the number of immigrants legally entering America each year. The original bill passed in 1921, but was made even more restrictive in 1924.

R

racism The belief that one race, or group of people, is better than all others.

Radical Republicans Post-Civil War Congressional leaders who wanted Congress, not the president, to make Reconstruction plans for the South.

ragtime A new style of music invented in the 1880s by black Americans in New Orleans.

rationing system A system for the fair distribution of scarce goods, such as shoes, tires, sugar, gasoline, coffee, and meat, especially during wartime.

raw materials Products from nature which can be used in industry.

realistic novel A book that describes people, places, and events as they are in real life.

reaper A machine invented in 1850 by Cyrus McCormick to help the farmer harvest crops more quickly.

rebates Refunds to good customers for using a service more than the ordinary customer.

recall The voters' right to remove dishonest officials from government.

recession An economic slump less severe than a depression.

reciprocal trade agreements Agreements among nations to mutually lower their tariffs for goods traded among them.

Reconstruction President Lincoln's plan for the return of the Southern states to the Union after the Civil War.

Reconstruction Act of 1867 A plan under which the South was divided into five districts, each governed by a Northern general and Northern troops. The Southern states were each to write new constitutions. Each Southern state also had to approve the Fourteenth Amendment and give blacks the right to vote.

Reconstruction Finance Corporation An organization set up by President Hoover in 1932 to lend money to railroads, banks, and other businesses. The purpose was to counteract the effects of the depression. However, the plan was too small in scope to deal with the national situation, and most people called it a failure.

referendum The direct voting mechanism whereby voters can accept or reject laws passed by a city council or state legislature.

reform To make something better.

regulate To control.

Regulators Frontier settlers in North Carolina who revolted against the colonial legislature.

relocation An American tactic during the war in Vietnam. A whole village was moved to another area when Communist troops were found in the area of that village. Once the village was moved, the area could be bombed and bulldozed, removing the Communist threat.

Removal Act A law passed by Congress in 1830 which said that Indians had to move to lands west of the Mississippi River.

reparations Money paid to the victors by the losers at the end of a war.

repeal To end a law.

Republican Party 1. An early political party led by Thomas Jefferson and James Madison. It favored small farmers and workers in the cities, and pushed for states' rights over a strong central government. 2. The party formed in 1854 by Whigs from the North and West and also Free-Soilers. They believed that slavery should not spread into the western territories.

reservation Lands set aside by the government for the exclusive use of Indians.

revival meetings Religious meetings held in the western states in the 1850s. Churches were scarce, so once a year people traveled from miles around to attend the revivals.

Revolutionary War The war between Great Britain and the colonies. By winning the war, America won its independence from England.

Rhineland The territory along the Rhine River in western Germany which Germany invaded in 1936.

Rio Grande A 1,885-mile river that forms the border between Mexico and the United States.

Roosevelt Corollary Roosevelt's 1904 provision to the Monroe Doctrine. The Corollary allowed the United States to take over the affairs of Latin American nations to prevent European invasions.

Rough Riders A group of volunteers who fought in Cuba during the Spanish-American War. The unit, led by Theodore Roosevelt, was an important part of the victory in the Battle of San Juan Hill.

royal colony A colony ruled directly by the English king.

Rural Electrification Administration An organization set up during the depression to make loans to farm cooperatives so that inexpensive electric power could be brought to farms.

S

Sandinistas A Cuban-backed rebel group that overthrew a repressive government in Nicaragua in 1979. The Sandinistas then became the recognized government of the country.

sanitation Clean and healthful living conditions.

Savak The secret police of the Shah of Iran.

scalawags Leaders of the South during Reconstruction. Previous Southern leaders were barred from office, and they felt this new group was against the best interests of the South.

Scotch-Irish People descended from Scots who had moved to northern Ireland in 1600. Continued persecution by the English authorities forced many to immigrate to America in the 1700s.

SEATO Southeast Asia Treaty Organization. A defense organization in Southeast Asia similar to NATO. Eight nations joined SEATO in 1954, including Great Britain, France, Thailand, Australia, New Zealand, Pakistan, the Philippines, and the United States.

secede To withdraw from an organization, as the Southern states withdrew from the Union.

Second Continental Congress A meeting of representatives from all the colonies in May 1885. To prepare for war, the representatives voted to raise money and train men for an army and a navy.

secretary of state The Cabinet member whose primary responsibility is to advise the president on dealings with foreign nations.

secretary of the treasury The Cabinet member responsible for helping the president control the nation's economy.

secretary of war The Cabinet member with the primary responsibility of advising the president on the nation's defense.

Securities Exchange Act Passed in 1934, this act set up a commission to regulate the way stocks were bought and sold.

Security Council One of the two governing houses of the United Nations. The Council has five regular members—the United States, Great Britain, the Soviet Union, France, and China. Other member nations take turns serving two-year terms on this council.

Sedition Act The 1798 act of Congress which made it a crime to write or say anything against the government or the president.

segregated To be separated. Blacks in America have often suffered from segregation.

Selective Service Act Passed by Congress in May 1917, this law required all men between the ages of 21 and 30 to register for service in the nation's armed forces.

Senate One of the two houses of Congress. Each state elects two senators to serve in the

Senate for a term of six years.

sensationalism The technique of appealing to people's emotions rather than their intellect in order to sell newspapers.

separate but equal The 1896 Supreme Court ruling that allowed segregated schools as long as the educational facilities for both blacks and whites were equally good.

separation of powers A division of governmental powers among different branches of the government so that no one branch can control the whole government.

serfs Under the feudal system, farmers who worked the land of the lord and were completely subject to his rule.

settlement house Community service houses found in poor neighborhoods during the 1800s. Settlement houses provided day care services so people could work. The settlement houses also taught job skills, gave English classes, and provided medical care for the poor.

17th parallel The line dividing Vietnam into two zones in 1954. A 1956 election, which was never held, was to determine whether the Vietminh or the French would control the government.

Seventeenth Amendment The 1913 law which gave American voters direct power to elect senators.

sharecroppers Poor tenant farmers who paid their rent in the form of the crops they grew.

Shays's Rebellion A 1786 revolt by farmers in western Massachusetts, led by Daniel Shays, who were revolting against high taxes.

Sherman Anti-Trust Act The 1890 law which made it illegal to organize a trust to gain a monopoly in an industry.

Sixteenth Amendment The 1913 law which gave the federal government the right to pass an income tax law.

sit-ins A form of nonviolent protest common in the 1960s. The protestors would simply fill a segregated lunch counter with black and white customers and refuse to leave until all of them had been served.

skilled workers Workers who have learned trades requiring training and skill.

slave codes Laws passed by southern states before the Civil War to control the lives of slaves.

slave revolt An uprising of slaves against their owners.

slavers The ships used to transport slaves from Africa to the colonies.

smuggling Unlawful trade, as when the colonists imported goods in defiance of England's Navigation Acts.

social class A person's position in society.

social programs Programs sponsored by the federal government aimed at assisting the poor, the sick, and the needy to improve the quality of their lives.

Social Securities Act Passed in 1935, this act provided for both businesses and workers to make regular payments to the government so that when workers reached the age of sixty-five they would receive regular pension payments.

sod houses Houses built by the settlers on the Great Plains out of bricklike chunks of earth and grass roots.

Sons of Liberty A group of people against the Stamp Act. They often used force to make sure no tax stamps were sold.

Spanish-American War The 1898 war between Spain and America over independence for the Spanish colonies of Cuba and the Phillipines.

Spanish Armada A huge Spanish military sailing fleet, the world's most powerful in 1588.

speculators Persons who buy land to resell it at a profit.

spectator sports Games watched by large groups of people.

speculation Putting money into stock with the idea of later selling the stock at a higher price.

spoils system When government jobs are given to members of a political party to reward them for helping the party.

squatters People who settled on government land in the early 1800s without first paying for it.

stagflation The unusual combination of inflation during an economic recession.

stalemate When neither side in a conflict can win.

state banks Banks established by state legislatures rather than by the Bank of the United States.

Stamp Act A law passed by the British Parliament in 1765 to place a tax on many items. The items had to be "stamped" before they could be sold.

Stamp Act Congress An October 1765 meeting in New York of leaders from nine of the colonies. The Congress asked Britain to end the Stamp Act. To put pressure on Britain, Congress also asked the colonists not to buy British goods as long as the Stamp Act was in force.

stampede Cattle running wildly and dangerously in all directions.

standard parts One part fits into any machine of the same model.

Star Wars Ronald Reagan's Strategic Defense Initiative, a plan to create a defensive shield in space to destroy incoming missiles.

steamboat A boat powered by steam.

stockholders Persons who share in the ownership of a corporation by owning its stock.

stock market The marketplace where people buy shares of stock in businesses.

Strategic Arms Limitation Treaty (SALT) The 1972 agreement between the Soviet Union and the United States not to build any new missiles for five years.

Strategic Arms Reduction Talks (START) Ongoing arms negotiations between the Soviet Union and the United States, begun in Geneva, Switzerland, in 1982.

strike When union members disagree with the policies of an employer and therefore order their union members to stop working until their demands are met.

strike breakers People who work for a company in place of workers on strike.

submarine A ship capable of traveling and attacking another ship from underwater.

subsistence farming When the products of a farm simply cover the needs of the farmer and his family. There are no excess crops or livestock produced for selling or barter.

suburbs A small town at the edge of a city.

Sudetenland A rich, industrial part of Czechoslovakia where many Germans lived and which Germany annexed in 1938.

Sugar Act A law passed by the British Parliament in 1764 that put a tax on sugar, molasses, and other products brought into the colonies from foreign countries. The money was used to pay for the British army stationed in the colonies.

summit conference A meeting between the heads of the major governments of the world.

Sunbelt States in the southern and western parts of America where the weather is warm and sunny most of the year.

supply-side economics A plan to stimulate the economy by lowering taxes to leave people with more money to spend on consumer goods.

surplus Crops and livestock grown by farm families beyond their own needs in order to be sold.

swing music A big band sound, popular in the 1920s, which was easy to dance to.

T

Taft-Hartley Act A 1947 law passed by Congress to deal with labor disputes between business managers and unions. The act required unions to give sixty days' notice before striking, empowered the president to stop a strike that endangered the nation, and made the closed shop illegal.

tariffs Taxes on goods coming into one nation from another.

Tariff Act of 1816 A tax imposed on foreign manufactured goods to make them more expensive than goods manufactured in America. The Act's purpose was to protect newly established American factories and give them a chance to grow.

Tariff of 1828 The highest protective tariff passed by Congress up to that time, it protected northeastern manufacturing but greatly angered Southerners.

Tea Act A law passed by Parliament in 1773 which made it lawful for the British East India Tea Company to sell its tea directly to the colonists without paying a tax to the British government. This gave British tea an unfair advantage over Dutch tea, which still was taxed and therefore sold at a higher price.

Teapot Dome A large deposit of oil in Wyoming that belonged to the government and was the subject of a government scandal in the early 1920s.

temperance movement A reform movement against the use of alcoholic drinks.

tenant farmers Poor farmers who rent the land they farm.

tenements Large, often poorly built buildings which house large numbers of people at low rents.

Tennessee Valley Authority A public works project set up in 1933 to build dams and generate cheap electrical power along the Tennessee River.

terraces Stairways of flat land up the sides of steep mountains. On the narrow stairways, or terraces, crops can be planted, as discovered by the Inca Indians.

test ban treaty A 1963 treaty between America and the Soviet Union banning nuclear weapons testing on the earth's surface, under water, or in outer space.

Tet offensive A surprise attack on South Vietnam by North Vietnam forces in January of 1968.

textile mills Factories which produce cloth.

Third World Nations that are newly independent or nations that are trying to become modernized and better developed economically.

38th parallel The line which divided Korea after World War II. The USSR controlled the territory north of the 38th parallel, and the United States occupied the territory south of the line. This division was supposed to be temporary until free elections could be held.

Three-Fifths Compromise The agreement at the Constitutional Convention which stated that every five slaves would count as three for purposes of taxation and representation.

Toleration Act Passed in Maryland in 1649, this act guaranteed religious freedom in Maryland and was an important step toward religious freedom in all the English colonies.

Tonkin Gulf Resolution The resolution passed by Congress in August 1964 which gave the president authority to involve America in the war in Vietnam.

Tower Commission A commission appointed by Reagan in 1987 to investigate the Iranian arms sale and the subsequent aid to the Contras. The commission, headed by former Senator John Tower, found that the president had relied too much on his staff and had not used proper judgment.

town meetings A method of government that began in the Massachusetts Bay Colony. The governor of the colony and the Puritan men met and made decisions about running the colony. They elected town officials and decided local matters.

Townshend Acts Laws passed in 1767 by Parliament which put taxes on all glass, lead, paper, paint, and tea brought into the colonies. The Townshend Acts also required the colonists to lodge British soldiers in their homes.

toxic waste Poisonous waste, often the by-product of nuclear energy.

trade association A group of businesses that join together to make decisions about how their industry will be run from year to year.

trade deficit When a country buys more from other countries than it sells abroad.

trade routes Paths followed by early merchants to carry goods back and forth between Europe and Asia.

trading company A company made up of merchants wanting to do business between the colonies and the mother country.

traditionalists People who dislike change and so cling to old ways of doing things.

Trail of Tears The forced march of the Cherokee Indians from their lands in Georgia to reservation lands in Oklahoma.

transcontinental railroad The railroad built between 1862 and 1869 which stretched from the east coast to the west coast.

treasuries Where the government's money is stored.

treaty of alliance The 1940 treaty which joined Japan with Germany and Italy as one of the Axis Powers.

Treaty of Ghent The 1814 treaty between the United States and England which ended the War of 1812.

Treaty of Guadalupe Hidalgo The 1848 treaty which ended the Mexican War between the United States and Mexico. The treaty made the territories of New Mexico and California part of the United States and made the Rio Grande River the southern border of Texas. Mexico received 15 million dollars in compensation.

Treaty of Paris The 1783 agreement between Britain and America ending the Revolutionary War. By the terms of the treaty, America became an independent nation whose western border was the Mississippi River.

Treaty of Versailles The treaty which ended World War I. The treaty's terms included reparations to be paid by Germany, the establishment of new borders and new nations, and the formation of a League of Nations.

triangular trade The three trade routes marking the pattern of trade among England, Africa, and the colonies. Manufactured goods from England and slaves from Africa were traded in the colonies for money and raw materials.

Truman Doctrine President Truman's plan to provide funds for European nations threatened by the spread of communism. In 1947, Congress voted $400 million toward the defense of such nations.

trust A large company that controls many smaller companies in the same industry.

turnpikes Roads that charge travelers a fee for use. In the early 1800s, turnpikes were privately built. Passage on the roads was blocked by a pole, or pike, until the traveler paid the required fee.

tutors Private teachers who teach students in their homes.

U

Underground Railroad A group of people organized to help slaves escape. The Underground Railroad was made up of "conductors" who led slaves out of the South to freedom in the North, often stopping at safe houses, or "stations," along the way.

Underwood Tariff The 1913 law which lowered the tariff for the first time since the Civil War. The purpose was to increase competition and break up the hold of monopolies on American business.

Union All the states of the United States. During the Civil War, the Union was those states which did not secede.

unions Groups of workers who join together in an attempt to improve working conditions.

United Nations An organization of member nations formed after World War II to try to keep peace in the world.

Universal Negro Improvement Association (U.N.I.A.) An organization for blacks formed in the 1920s and led by Marcus Garvey, a Jamaican immigrant. The U.N.I.A. believed that blacks would never be treated as equal citizens in America, and the group wanted blacks to return to Africa to build a new country there.

unskilled workers Persons entering the job market without any specific training or skills. Historically, unskilled workers have been paid little and fired first.

upward mobility The movement from a lower social class to a higher one.

utopian community In the 1800s, a community made up of people who wanted to live according to the ideals they shared.

V

vaquero Mexican cowboys.

vassals In the feudal system, men who held small parts of the lord's estate. They swore allegiance to the lord and helped to protect or extend the estate, as the lord wished.

Veteran's Bureau An organization set up by Congress to help returning veterans after World War I.

veto To overrule or turn down a law.

Vietcong Vietnamese Communist rebels operating south of the 17th parallel during the Vietnam War. They attacked government forces in guerilla raids. Their attempts to bring about a Communist takeover were ultimately successful.

Vietminh Communists and Vietnamese who ruled north of the 17th parallel and eventually took over the whole country of Vietnam.

Vietnamization President Nixon's plan in 1969 to turn the war in Vietnam back over to the South Vietnamese. However, when it looked as though the withdrawal of American troops would end in defeat for South Vietnam, Nixon widened the war again.

vigilantes Members of the committees formed in mining camps to restore law and order.

Vikings A sailing people of northwestern Europe who first settled in the British Isles, then in Iceland, and finally in Greenland. One of the Vikings, Leif Ericson, is known as the first European to set foot in North America.

voluntary wage and price controls A request by the government for workers to refrain from wage increases and for businesses to keep costs low.

Volunteers in Service to America (VISTA) A program, part of Johnson's Great Society, which offered educational and social services to poor communities.

Voting Rights Act of 1965 This law prohibits the use of literacy, or reading, tests as a requirement for voting. The law also gives the federal government the right to register local voters when local officials refuse to do so.

W

wage and price controls A 90-day freeze put into effect by Nixon as a means of bringing inflation under control.

Wages and Hours Law Passed in 1938, this law set a minimum hourly wage for most jobs at 25 cents an hour, limited the work week to 44 hours, and required overtime pay.

War Hawks Westerners in Congress who wanted the country to declare war against Britain in 1812.

War Industries Board A board formed in July 1917 to direct factory production during World War I. The purpose was to maximize output for the war effort.

War Production Board Created in 1942 to oversee the change to war production in American factories.

Warren Commission A commission appointed by

Lyndon Johnson to investigate President Kennedy's assassination. The commission, headed by Chief Justice Earl Warren, found that Oswald had acted alone.

Warsaw Pact A mutual defense pact formed in 1949 between the Soviet Union and its eastern European neighbors. Creating the Warsaw Pact was the Soviet Union's answer to the formation of NATO by the western powers.

Washington Naval Conference A conference in 1921 in Washington, D.C., at which nine major nations agreed to limit the size and number of large warships.

Watergate scandal The 1972 break-in at the headquarters of the Democratic National Committee. The Republicans, including President Nixon, denied involvement with the crime, but it turned into a scandal that resulted in Nixon's resignation from office.

Whigs A third political party formed prior to the 1836 presidential election by persons who were Democrats but disliked Jackson and his ideas.

Whiskey Rebellion A 1794 uprising in western Pennsylvania by farmers who refused to pay a tax the federal government had put on whiskey. Washington led 15,000 troops into the area and put down the rebellion without bloodshed. The event showed the strength of the federal government in enforcing the laws it had passed.

white backlash Violent resistance by whites to the advances made in equal rights for blacks during the 1960s.

Wilmot Proviso A rule passed in 1847 by the House of Representatives which said that slavery would not be allowed in any new territory won as a result of the Mexican War.

Winnemucca, Sarah Daughter of a Paiute chief, she spoke out and wrote in defense of Indian rights.

women's rights The right of women to participate equally and fairly in all aspects of American life. The women's rights movement became especially prominent in the 1970s.

work ethic A strong emphasis on the value and benefit of labor to ''better'' oneself in society.

Works Progress Administration An expansion of Franklin Roosevelt's Public Works Administration. In addition to undertaking large construction projects, the WPA hired writers, artists, and musicians to encourage the creative expression of American culture.

writs of assistance Search warrants issued by the British government before the Revolutionary War. The writs gave British officials the right to search houses, ships, and warehouses.

Y

yellow dog contract A contract between an employer and an employee in which the employee agrees not to join a union.

Yom Kippur War The 1973 war between Israel and its Arab neighbors. The war began when Egypt and Syria launched a surprise attack on Yom Kippur, the holiest day of the Jewish year. The Israelis were able to beat back the Arabs and a ceasefire was signed in 18 days.

Young Plan An adjustment to the post-World War I reparations plan to make it easier for Germany to make the payments.

Index

A

Abilene (Kans.), 371
Abolition movement/abolitionists, 111, 280, 282, 283, 284, 287–9, 312, 319–21, 325, 336
Abraham Lincoln Brigade, 604
Acid rain, 799, 801
Adams, Abigail, 151, 215
Adams, John (President), 152, 165, 179, 210, 214–16, 233
Adams, John Quincy (President), 250, 255–7
Adams, Samuel, 142, 145, 147, 174, 178
Adamson Act, 485
Addams, Jane, 393, 410
Admiralty courts, 134
Advertising, 451, 524, 553, 572
Afghanistan, 764, 773
AFL-CIO, 682, 690
Africa, 15, 25, 27, 69, 90, 91, 238, 443, 538, 599, 725–7, 774; in triangular trade, 72, 73; in WWII, 612. *See also* North Africa; Slave trade; South Africa.
Age of Exploration, 17
Agnew, Spiro (Vice President), 746, 750
Agricultural Adjustment Act (AAA), 552, 560, 567, 576
Agriculture. *See* Farming.
Aguinaldo, Emilio, 450
Airplanes, 522, 689; in WWII, 594, 604, 609, 613, 616, 622. *See also* Lindbergh, Charles.
Alabama, 238, 326, 696, 714, 716
Alamo, Battle of the, 296, 298, 299
Alaska, 440, 442–3
Albania, 664
Albany Congress, 129
Albany Plan of Union, 129
Alcohol, 55, 279, 529. *See also* Prohibition; Rum; Temperance movements.
Alien and Sedition Acts, 210, 216, 217
Allen, Ethan, 149
Allen, Fred, 582
Alliance for Progress, 724, 727, 732
Alliances, farmers, 430
Allied Powers (Allies): WWI, 491–4, 496–8, 500, 502, 534; WWII, 600, 612, 622, 624–6, 631, 633, 635, 664, 665, 670
Almanacs, 109, 110, 557
Amendments. *See* Bill of Rights; Constitutional Amendments.

American Federation of Labor (AFL), 418, 423, 426, 564–5, 690
American Independent Party, 721
American Indian Movement (AIM), 746, 759
American Indians, 5, 6, 8, 11, 17, 23, 24, 26, 41, 43, 46–8, 51, 52, 65, 66, 129, 183, 212, 218, 219, 259, 261, 301, 365, 376–8, 380; and colonists, 25, 27–9, 42, 43, 46–8, 51, 52, 64; discrimination against, 759; during the Great Depression, 580; first Americans, 4, 5, 11; in the French and Indian Wars, 129; on the frontier, 112, 113, 115, 131, 133, 134, 173, 221, 370, 376–8, 380, 381; removals of, 250, 259–61, 301, 380; in the Revolutionary War, 160, 163; rights of, 127, 347; as slaves, 97. *See also* Reservations.
American System, 252–4
American Tobacco Co., 474, 481
Amnesty (Vietnam War), 753
Amnesty Act (Civil War), 342, 351
Anarchists, 535
Anderson, Marian, 549
Andes Mountains, 5
Angola, 774
Annapolis (Md.), 174
Annexation, 303, 440, 444
Anthony, Susan B., 280
Antietam, Battle of, 328, 335, 336
Anti-Federalists, 179
Appalachian Mountains, 100, 112, 129, 133, 217, 242, 404
Appalachian Regional Development Act, 714
Appeasement, 605
Appomattox Court House (Va.), 339
Arab nations, 754, 776–7, 780, 791
Arizona, 494
Arkansas, 231, 238, 239, 327, 337
Arms control, 594, 764, 771, 775, 794, 796
Arms race, 594, 603, 666, 679, 793, 794
Armstrong, Louis, 546
Art, 110, 547, 585, 686
Arthur, Chester (President), 328, 418, 421
Articles of Confederation, 168, 171, 174
Artificial heart, 798
Artisans, 232
Asia, 385, 443, 727, 796–7; Cold War in, 666, 669; communism in, 669–70, 673, 674, 797; first Americans from 2, 4; sea routes to, 14–17, 22, 23, 28, 32, 42; trade with, 13–15
Assembly, right to, 170

Assembly line, 521, 523
Astrolabe, 15
Atlanta (Ga.), 343; Battle of 337
Atlantic, Battle of the, 622
Atlantic Charter, 612, 631
Atlantic Ocean, 17, 22, 27, 31, 32; territorial expansion in, 449, 450, 453
Atomic bomb, 603, 613, 628, 630, 647, 666. *See also* Nuclear weapons.
Atomic Energy Commission, 642, 647, 666
Attlee, Clement (Prime Minister), 633
Attucks, Crispus, 142
Austin, Moses, 297
Austin, Stephen, 296–8
Australia, 621, 626, 674
Austria, during WWII, 592, 604, 625; -Hungary, 491, 492
Automation, 689, 690
Automobiles, 514, 520, 521, 523, 539, 540, 571, 645, 682, 688, 689, 761, 799
Axis Powers (WWII), 601, 608, 612, 613, 621, 622
Aztecs, 6, 23, 26

B

"Baby boom," 682, 684, 688
Bacon's Rebellion, 100, 115
Balboa, Vasco de, 20, 22, 30
Ballinger, Richard, 480–1
Baltimore (Md.), 223, 288, 545
Baltimore, Lord, 51, 52
Bank of the United States, 267; First, 168, 182, 183, 252; Second, 250, 252, 253, 263
Banks/banking, 214, 231, 232, 235, 240, 262, 264, 343, 355, 419, 429, 466, 484, 485, 555, 556, 559, 601. *See also* Bank of the United States; Federal Reserve; State banks.
Barter, 12
Barton, Clara, 328
Baseball, 402, 412, 543, 545
Batista, Fulgencio, 726
Bay of Pigs invasion, 724, 726, 727
Bear Flag Revolt, 306
Begin, Menachem, 777
Beiderbecke, Bix, 546
Beirut (Lebanon), 791, 792
Belgium, 496, 497, 606
Bell, Alexander Graham, 388
Bell, John, 325
Belleau Wood, Battle of, 500
Benefit societies, 289
Benet, Stephen Vincent, 585
Benny, Jack, 582

Benton, Thomas Hart, 585
Bergen, Edgar, 582
Bering Strait, 4
Berkeley, John, 53
Berlin, 633, 665, 727, 729; airlift, 665; blockade, 662, 665; Wall, 724, 729
Bernstein, Carl, 749
Bessemer process, 384, 387–8, 390
Bethune, Mary McLeod, 580
Bicycling, 412
"Big Four" (WWI), 502
"Big Three" (WWII), 631, 633
Bill of Rights, English, 62, 63; U.S., 168, 170, 179, 180
Birmingham (Ala.), 354, 709
Black Beard (pirate), 126
"Black Cabinet," 580
Black codes, 345
Black Hawk (Indian chief), 259
Black power, 717, 720
Blacks, 44, 387, 412, 554, 691, 757; in the Civil War, 288, 329, 336; discrimination against, 342, 351, 536, 538, 544, 618, 619; during the Great Depression, 576, 578, 580; during Reconstruction, 343, 345–51, 353, 357; education of, 215, 270, 289, 342, 357, 399; free blacks, 95, 102, 127, 240, 284, 287, 289, 319, 320; in government, 347, 349–51, 708, 714; in the labor force, 398, 399, 424, 526, 536, 618–19; in music, 546, 547; organizations, 398, 430, 458, 463, 536–8, 694, 709; rights of, 271, 289, 345, 399, 462–3, 533, 536, 540; in the Spanish-American War, 448; in sports, 543; in the War of 1812, 224; in the West, 373; in WWI, 536; in WWII, 618. *See also* Abolition movement; Civil rights movement; Harlem Renaissance; Segregation; Slavery; Slave trade; Voting.
Black Sea, 664
"Black Thursday," 554. *See also* Stock market crash; Depression.
Blackwell, Elizabeth, 280
"Bleeding Kansas," 321
Blitzkrieg, 606
Blockades, 334, 335, 662, 665, 729
Blue laws, 110
Board of Trade, 128
Bonus Army, 552, 556
Boom towns, 367, 368
Booth, John Wilkes, 344
Bootlegging, 529
Bosnia (Austria-Hungary), 492
Boston (Mass.), 79, 142, 144, 145, 147, 149, 150, 161, 289, 712

F

Factories, 232, 235, 237, 240, 244, 252, 258, 262, 264, 272, 329, 343, 354, 356, 385, 387, 390, 396, 397, 399, 404, 405, 410, 430, 443, 460, 467–8, 499, 515, 516, 521, 525, 526, 553, 554, 602, 618, 621, 644, 799

Fairbanks, Douglas, 541

Fair Deal, 648–50, 655

Fair Employment Practices Commission, 619

Fall, Albert, 516

Fallen Timbers, Battle of, 168, 183

Families, colonial, 87, 103; in the 1920s, 540; during the Great Depression, 572–4; during the '50s and '60s, 684, 685, 688

Farm Board, 556

Farming, 33, 231, 264, 267, 271, 343, 349, 350, 353, 355, 357, 375, 385, 387, 403, 404, 408, 419, 461, 485, 498, 515, 517, 518, 527, 529, 544, 556, 684; in the colonies, 31, 33, 46, 52, 55, 63–9, 73, 84, 102, 103; and debt, 429, 527, 560, 618, 788; frontier/pioneer, 112, 173, 213, 214, 242, 244, 252, 259, 302, 365, 366, 373–5, 429; feudal system, 11, 12; and government support, 529, 707; and the Great Depression, 553–5, 559, 560, 563, 576–7, 580; and immigrants, 314, 396; of Indians, 5, 6, 8, 381; and industry, 528; machines, 272, 374, 429, 430, 484, 527, 618; organizations, 430, 556, 585; production increase, 429, 618; and tariffs, 421; and technology, 684. *See also* Cash crops; Homestead Act; Plantations.

Farm Security Administration, 577, 585

Farragut, David (Admiral), 336

Faulkner, William, 585

Federal Art Project, 585

Federal Farm Loan Act, 485

Federalist Party, 214, 216, 217, 220, 252, 256

Federalists, 179

Federal Music Project, 585

Federal Reserve System, 474, 485

Federal Theater Project, 585

Federal Town, 182. *See also* Washington, D.C.

Federal Trade Commission Act, 474, 485, 518

Ferdinand, Franz (Archduke), 490, 492

Ferraro, Geraldine, 787

Feudal system, 2, 12, 13

Field, Cyrus W., 388

Fillmore, Millard (President), 312

Fire departments, 408, 409

First Continental Congress, 140, 145

Fish/fishing, 72, 76, 129, 165, 443, 774

Fitzgerald, F. Scott, 547

"Flappers," 539

Flatboats, 245

Florida, 20, 22, 24, 30, 131, 165, 210, 216, 227, 245, 259, 326, 351, 353, 685

Flour mills, 392

Foch, Marshall, 600

Fong, Hiram (Senator), 657

Food: collections (WWI), 498, 515, 517; colonial, 27, 42, 67, 87, 104; cost of, 429, 572; preservation, 272, 412, 466; of slaves, 97. *See also* Farming; Meat-packing industry.

Football, 412, 543

Ford, Gerald (President), 746, 750, 753, 754, 756, 761, 768, 771, 773, 775, 786

Ford, Henry, 521, 523

Ford's Theater, 344

Formosa. *See* Taiwan.

Forten, James, 289

Fort McHenry (Md.), 223

Fort Sumter (S.C.), 327

Fort Ticonderoga (N.Y.), 149

Forty-Niners, 310. *See also* Gold strikes.

Founding Fathers, 169, 174, 176–8, 211

Fountain of Youth, 22

Fourteen Points, 502

Fox Indians, 259

Frame of Government, 53

France, 14, 15, 39, 111, 123, 128, 129, 131, 181, 217, 219, 304, 306, 441, 452, 453, 633, 674, 677, 679; colonies, 28–30, 126, 128, 129, 131, 669, 674; in the Revolutionary War, 161–3, 182; Revolution in, 212; in the United Nations, 632; U.S. conflicts with, 216, 221, 227, 440; war with Great Britain, 210, 214, 219; war with Mexico, 441–2; in WWI, 491, 492, 496, 497, 499, 500, 502, 527, 595, 600; in WWII, 601, 604–6, 612, 665

Franco, Francisco, 602, 604

Franklin, Benjamin, 110, 111, 115, 152, 165, 174

Fredericksburg, Battle of, 335

Freedmen's Bureau, 345

Freedom rides, 697

Free market economy, 664

Free silver issue, 460. *See also* Coinage; Silver.

Free-Soilers, 309, 321, 322

Fremont, John C., 306, 322

French and Indian War, 122, 128–31, 133, 134, 171

French immigrants, 86

Friedan, Betty, 758

Fringe benefits, 690

Frontier, Indian problems on, 112, 113, 115, 129, 131, 133, 134; settlement on, 84, 85, 100, 112–5, 163, 173, 221, 227, 277; theory, 48

Munich Conference, 592
Murrow, Edward R., 609
Music, 412, 533, 542–4, 570, 582, 688; blues, 546; folk, 579; jazz, 533, 543, 546, 582, 583, 688; ragtime, 412; rock-and-roll, 688; swing, 582–3
Muslims, 12, 13
Mussolini, Benito, 599, 601, 602, 619, 624

N

Nagasaki (Japan), 630
Napoleon Bonaparte, 217, 222, 223
Nasser, Gamal Abdel, 677
National Aeronautics and Space Administration (NASA), 790
National Association for the Advancement of Colored People (NAACP), 398, 458, 463, 536, 694, 709
National Cemetary, 328
National debt, 173, 182, 347
National Defense Education Act, 642, 659
National Guard, 695, 767
National Housing Act, 642, 650
Nationalists, Chinese, 772. See also China; Taiwan.
National Labor Relations Act, 552, 564
National parks and forests, 478–9
National Recovery Administration (NRA), 552, 560, 567
National Road, 230, 244, 252, 253
National Security Act, 647
National Urban League, 458, 463
Natural resources, 386–7, 404, 475, 478–80. See also Coal; Gold; Iron ore; Lumber; Oil; Silver.
Naval stores, 73, 77
Navigation Act, 63, 70, 75, 133, 134
Nazi (National Socialist) Party, 600, 603, 605, 613, 633
Nebraska, 320, 321, 579
Netherlands, 30, 31, 39, 44–5, 443, 606, 614, 669
Neutrality, 1790s policy of, 212; Acts (WWII), 592, 602, 606
Nevada, 366, 367, 368
New Amsterdam, 31
New Deal program, 553, 558–67, 578, 580, 655
New England, 51, 63, 94, 214, 223, 231, 275; cities in, 79; education, 108–9; farming, 65, 68; industry, 72, 77; manufacturing in, 227, 235; religion in, 109–10; in the Revolutionary War, 161; slavery in, 97; trade, 70, 72, 73, 134

Newfoundland, 10, 165
New France, 20, 28, 51
New Freedom program, 484, 486, 487
New Frontier program, 707, 712
New Guinea, 626, 627
New Hampshire, 38, 51, 719
New Jersey, 38, 53, 97, 231
Newlands Reclamation Act, 474, 478
New Mexico, 304, 306, 307, 311, 312, 314, 494
New Netherland, 31, 53
New Orleans, 28, 131, 217, 223, 224, 239, 245, 314, 320, 336; Battle of, 210, 224–5, 227, 254
Newport (R.I.), 79
"New South," 353, 354, 357
New Spain, 27, 28
Newspapers, 79, 100, 109, 216, 266, 283, 288, 428, 445–6, 451, 467, 582, 737, 749
"New World," origin of term, 21
New York, 31, 38, 53, 73, 83, 94, 149, 162, 163, 214, 223, 231, 245, 279, 328, 423, 446, 458, 467, 517, 566
New York City, 79, 135, 161, 179, 403, 404, 455, 467, 517, 543, 547, 566
New Zealand, 674
Nez Perce Indians, 380
Niagara Movement, 458, 463
Nicaragua, 596, 764, 765, 774, 793
Nickelodeons, 541
Nile River, 677
Nisei, 619. See also Japanese immigrants.
Nixon, Richard M. (President), 704, 705, 721, 724, 739, 746–50, 753, 756, 764–8, 771–3, 775
Nobel Prize, 393, 603, 710
Nonviolent resistance, 696, 697, 710, 718, 755. See also King, Dr. Martin Luther, Jr.
Normandy (France), 624
Norsemen. See Vikings.
North Africa, 622, 631, 678
North Atlantic Treaty Organization (NATO), 662, 666, 674, 679, 734
North Carolina, 38, 40, 41, 52, 68, 69, 86, 97, 115, 163, 238, 327, 358
North Dakota, 579
Northeastern states, 231, 241, 242, 247, 256, 263, 300, 323, 419; industry in, 232, 237, 238, 240, 244, 251, 253, 258, 271; and politics, 254, 258, 262; railroads in, 247; religion in, 275; schools in, 273
Northern Securities Company, 476–7
North Sea, 499
Norway, 799
Northwestern Indians, 8, 183, 212
Northwest Ordinance, 168, 171

Northwest Passage, 28, 30
Northwest Territory, 171, 183, 212
Norway, 10, 606
Norwegian immigrants, 314
Nova Scotia, 28, 129
Nuclear: power, 746, 757, 761, 799; race, 730; treaties, 724, 730; war, 785, 793, 794, 796, 801; weapons, 603, 771, 793. *See also* Atomic bomb; Détente; Strategic Arms Limitation Treaty.
Nueces River, 304
Nullification, 259
Nye, Gerald P. (Senator), 601

O

O'Connor, Sandra Day (Justice), 788
Odets, Clifford, 585
Office of Economic Opportunity, 713
Office of Price Administration (O.P.A.), 621
Office of Production Management, 617
Oglethorpe, James (General), 55
Ohio, 171, 183, 387; River, 6, 129, 131, 133, 150, 163, 171, 227
Oil, 354, 386, 387, 391, 392, 443, 516, 520, 596, 599, 614, 677, 754, 757, 761, 777, 778, 780, 799; Embargo, 746, 754
"Okies," 576
Okinawa, 628
Oklahoma, 261, 380, 576
"Old Ironsides" (ship), 222
Old South, 238, 357
Old Southwest, 238
Olympics, 764, 773
Omaha (Nebr.), 368
Oneida community, 278
O'Neill, Eugene, 547
Open-Door Policy, 440, 452, 615
Oregon, 297, 300, 303, 365, 458, 471, 486
Oregon Trail, 300, 308
O'Reilly, Pete, 366
Orlando, Vittorio, 502
Oswald, Lee Harvey, 711

P

Pacific Ocean, 20, 22; territorial expansion in, 443, 445, 449, 450, 453
Paine, Thomas, 146, 150
Paiute Indians, 378
Pakistan, 669, 674
Palestine, 12, 13, 669
Palestinian Liberation Organization (PLO), 791

Palmer, A. Mitchell (Attorney General), 535
Panama Canal, 440, 453, 455, 491, 731, 777; treaties, 724, 731, 764, 777–8
Paris (France), 500, 543, 624, 679, 739, 764, 768
Parks, Rosa, 695, 696
Parliament, 47, 63, 123–5, 127, 130, 135–7, 140, 142, 144, 145, 150, 174
Patriots, 148, 149
Patuxet Indians, 66
Paxton Boys, 115
Peace Corps, 724, 727, 728
Pearl Harbor (Hawaii), 443, 612, 615–17, 619, 620
Pendleton Civil Service Act, 418, 420
Penn, William, 53, 55, 84
Pennsylvania, 29, 38, 53, 84, 85, 115, 124, 212–14, 231, 336, 386, 387, 423, 477, 714, 761
Pennsylvania Dutch, 84
Pennsylvania Railroad, 390
Pensions, 559
Perkins, Frances, 566, 578
Perry, Oliver Hazard (Colonel), 222
Persian Gulf, 778
Pershing, John J. (General), 455, 500
Personal liberty laws, 320
Philadelphia (Pa.), 73, 79, 115, 145, 149, 161, 162, 171, 174, 403, 424
Philippines, 440, 446, 448–50, 491, 596, 669, 674; in WWII, 615, 621
Pickett, Bill, 373
Pickford, Mary, 541
Pierce, Franklin (President), 296, 314
Pilgrims, 44–6, 50, 66
Pinchot, Gifford, 481
Pine Tree Shilling, 74
Pioneers, 112, 365
Pitt, William, 130
Pittsburgh (Pa.), 390, 404, 532, 542
Pizarro, Francisco, 23–4, 30
Plains Indians, 8, 365, 376–8
Plantations, 44, 79, 89, 109, 238–40, 343, 355, 357, 445, 455; and slavery, 88, 90, 93–5, 97, 170, 239, 286, 289
Platt Amendment, 440, 450
Plymouth colony, 38, 46, 50, 51, 66, 151
Pocahontas, 42
Poe, Edgar Allen, 275
Poland, 181, 505, 633, 664, 799; during WWII, 592, 605–6, 624, 625
Polish immigrants, 397, 405
Political cartoons, 266
Political machines, 409–10, 462, 469, 471
Political parties, 211, 214, 257, 258, 419, 430,

Ray, James Earl, 718
Reagan, Ronald (President), 784–9, 791–4, 796
Recall, 458, 471
Recession, 754
Reciprocal trade agreements, 598
Reconstruction Finance Corporation, 556
Reconstruction period, 342–51, 353–7
Redcoats, 147
Red Cross, 328, 499
"Red Scare:" of 1920s, 535; of 1950s, 651, 656, 658
Reed, Walter, 450
Referendum, 458, 471
Reform movements, 278–80, 282–3, 410, 433, 445, 459–71, 475, 485, 529. *See also* Progressive Movement; Prohibition; Temperance Movement.
Regulators, 115
Rehnquist, William (Chief Justice), 789
Religion, 271, 277, 719; colonial, 33, 44, 46–8, 51–3, 109–13; and discrimination, 518, 619, 706; freedom of, 33, 45–7, 52, 53, 84, 86, 170, 180; Mayan, 6; movements, 110, 275, 277, 278; separation of church and state, 47, 719. *See also* Church of England; Mormons; Presbyterian Church; Pilgrims; Protestants; Puritans; Quakers; Shakers; Roman Catholic Church; Unitarians; Universalists.
Relocation, Vietnam War, 736; camps in WWII, 619, 620
Removal Act, 250, 259, 260
Reparations, 502
Representative government, 63, 113, 115, 127, 135
Republican Party, 214, 216, 220, 253, 322, 324, 325, 347–9, 351, 419–22, 433, 475, 480, 483, 485, 494, 505, 515–18, 558, 565, 648, 649, 653, 654, 658, 705, 707, 721
Reservations, Indian, 377, 378, 380, 381
Revels, Hiram, 350
Revere, Paul, 147
Revival meetings, 277
Revolutionary War, 111, 140, 147–53, 156–65, 169–71, 173, 174, 177, 178, 181–3, 212, 231, 238, 242, 273
Rhineland, 592, 601; Rhine River, 625
Rhode Island, 38, 47, 50, 109, 124, 170, 174, 233
Rice, 52, 68, 69, 70, 90, 238
Richmond (Va.), 286, 334, 339, 343
Ride, Sally, 788, 790
Rights, of English colonists, 123, 127, 128; of ownership, 39. *See also* Blacks; Civil rights; Slaves; Women.
Riis, Jacob, 467, 470

Rio Grande River, 304, 307
Rioting, 704, 705, 708, 718; in Latin America, 731; race, 536
Rivera, Diego, 574
Roads, 258, 259, 520, 556; to frontier lands, 113, 243, 244, 247; highway system, 656, 684; Inca, 5; paved, in cities, 409
Roanoke, 38–42
"Roaring Twenties," 539, 545
Robeson, Paul, 549
Robots, 798
Rockefeller, John D., 384, 391–2, 465
Rockefeller, Nelson A. (Vice President), 752
Rocky Mountains, 217, 297, 365
Rolfe, John, 43
Roman Catholic Church, 24, 25, 28, 33, 44, 52, 127, 518, 538, 706; anti-Catholicism, 518, 706
Romania, 664
Roosevelt, Eleanor, 578
Roosevelt, Franklin D. (President), 552, 553, 558–67, 578, 580, 596, 603, 605, 606, 613, 618, 620, 626, 631, 633, 642, 643, 647
Roosevelt, Theodore (President), 423, 440, 448, 453, 455, 466, 474–8, 480, 481, 483–5
Roosevelt Corollary, 440, 455
"Rosie the Riveter," 618
Roth, Henry, 585
Rough Riders, 448, 475
Royal colonies, 51, 52, 55, 124, 136
Rum, 72, 104
Rumania, 625
Rural Electrification Administration (REA), 577
Russia, 440, 442, 452, 491, 492, 497, 498; revolution in, 490, 497, 499, 502, 535, 596, *See also* Soviet Union.
Russian immigrants, 397
Ruth, George Herman "Babe," 543–5

S

Sacajawea, 218
Sacco-Vanzetti Case, 532, 535
Sacramento (Calif.), 368
Sadat, Anwar, 777
Saigon, 765
Saipan, 628
Saint Lawrence River, 28, 130
St. Louis (Mo.), 219, 245, 320, 403
San Antonio (Tex.), 27, 298
Sandburg, Carl, 547, 585
Sandinistas, 764, 774, 793. *See also* Nicaragua.
San Francisco (Calif.), 302, 310, 311, 397, 455, 632

T

Acknowledgments

Graphics research was done through Linda L Rill/Art and Photo Research Services, San Diego. With great appreciation we thank the following for special assistance with the project: Audrey Zook and Georgia Bumgardner/American Antiquarian Society, James Long/American Heritage, Linda Ziemer/Chicago Historical Society, Harriet Culver/Culver Pictures, Inc., Carolyn Park/Historical Society of Pennsylvania, John Hensel/Newberry Library, Chicago, Cammie Naylor/The New York Historical Society.

Maps: All cartographic material is by Book Production Systems, Inc., with the exception of the map on page 687 which was drawn after one on page U-54, U-55, of *Hammond United States History Atlas*, 1984.

WHHA: All presidential portraits, with the exception of George Washington, are Copyrighted © by the White House Historical Association, Photographed by The National Geographic Society—pages: 214, 217, 220, 252, 256, 257, 264, 265, 303, 309, 312, 314, 322, 325, 344, 348, 353, 420, 422, 433, 477, 481, 484, 516, 518, 559, 648, 655, 706, 714, 721, 753, 756, 788.

Table of Contents illustrations: vi, L—(see 23T)—#40, R—(see 107)—#339; vii, L—(see 162–63T)—#409, R—(see 236–7B)—#170; ix, L—(see 339)—#391; x, L—(see 612L)—#542, R—(see 684B)—#597; xi, L—(see 707)—#656.

PHOTO CREDITS

The letter(s) to the immediate right of the page reference (bold type) indicate position on page: L-left, R-right, C-center, B-bottom, T-top. The numbers to the extreme right of *each* reference and preceded by a dash and the # symbol are the publisher's internal code. Pages are separated by semi-colons.

UNIT 1

xiv, 1, Opener: 16th century Caravels. National Maritime Museum, London—#10; **2,** Time line: L—Ohio Historical Society—#584, C—Josephus, *The War of the Jews*, Chantilly. Giraudon/Art Resource, NY (Musée Conde)—#18, R—Sebastino del Piombo, *Christopher Columbus*, oil on canvas, 42×34¾″. The Metropolitan Museum of Art, Gift of J. Pierpont Morgan, 1900. (00.18.2)—#12; **5,** Photophile/Paul Ganster—#2; **6,** T—Photo Researchers/George Holton—#3, B—Ohio Historical Society—#4; **8,** Photo Researchers/George Dineer—#16; **9,** Photo Researchers/G. Whitney—#5; **10,** The Bettmann Archive—#770; **11,** L & R—University Museum of National Antiquities, Oslo, Norway—#6 & 7; **12,** LT—*Brevario Grimani: September*. SCALA/Art Resource, NY (Biblioteca Marciano, Venice)—#17, LB—Bibliotheque Nationale, Paris—#36, R—(see 2C)—#18; **13,** *Catalan atlas, Charles V*. Giraudon/Art Resource, NY (Bibliotheque Nationale, Paris)—#8; **15,** T—*Nurenberg Chronicles*—#9, B—*Prince Henry the Navigator*. Giraudon/Art Resource, NY (Museu Nacional de Arte Antiga, Lisboa)—#11; **17,** T—(see 2R)—#12; **20,** Time line: L—*Amerigo Vespucci*. SCALA/Art Resource, NY (Uffizi, Florence)—#38, C—Dumbarton Oaks Research Library and Collection—#39, R—*Nova Britannia*—#52; **22,** Courtesy John Carter Brown Library at Brown University—#41; **23,** T—Rare Book Division, New York Public Library, Astor, Lenox and Tilden Foundation—#40, C—Maestro Saldana, *Hernando Cortés*. Giraudon/Art Resource, NY (National Museum of History, Mexico City)—#43, B—A.y. R. MAS (Arxiu Mas) Barcelona—#42; **24,** The Hispanic Society of America—#44; **26,** Biblioteca Nacional, Madrid—#37; **28–9,** B—Courtesy The Huntington Library, San Marino—#46; **29,** T—*Orbis Habitabilis*. Rare Book Division, New York Public Library, Astor, Lenox and Tilden Foundation—#47; **32,** T—By Kind Permission of the Marquess of Tauistock and the Trustees of the Bedford Estates—#49, B—National Maritime Museum, London—#51; **33,** The Mansell Collection, London—#53; **35,** Trustees of the British Museum—#54; **38,** Time line: Courtesy of Pilgrim Hall Museum, Plymouth, MA—#100; **40,** T—William Clements Library—#93; B—De Bry, *America, Part I, 1590*. Rare Book Division, New York Public Library, Astor, Lenox and Tilden Foundation—#94; **41,** Maria Louisa Lander, *Virginia Dare*. The Elizabethan Gardens of the Garden Club of North Carolina, Inc.—#698; **42,** T—Smith, *Generall Historie of Virginia*, London, 1624. Rare Book Division, New York Public Library, Astor, Lenox and Tilden Foundation—#95, B—*Pocahontas* (detail). The National Portrait Gallery, Smithsonian Institution NPG#65.61, photo by Eugene L. Mante—#96; **43,** TR—Jamestown-Yorktown Foundation—#98, C—Courtesy of the Edward E. Ayer Collection, Newberry Library, Chicago, (Ayer 150 G6 1829)—#303; **44,** Fairholt, *A Tobacco Plantation, vol. I, pg. 136*. Rare Book Division, Arents Collection, New York Public Library—#99; **45,** (see 38)—#100; **46,** B—Courtesy American Antiquarian Society—#102; **47,** Historical Society of Penn-

sylvania—#103; **48–9,** Frederick E. Church, *Thomas Hooker's Party Coming to Hartford*. Wadsworth Atheneum, Hartford—#104; **52–3,** Bishop Roberts, *Charleston, South Carolina*, c. 1737, watercolor. Colonial Williamsburg Foundation—#105; **55,** Martyn, *Reasons for Establishing the Colony of Georgia, 1733*. Rare Book Division, New York Public Library, Astor, Lenox and Tilden Foundation—#108;

UNIT 2

60–61, Opener: *New Amsterdam*, 1650. J. Clarence Davies Collection, Museum of the City of New York—#106; **62,** Time line: All-American Antiquarian Society—#129 & 127; **64–5,** B—New York State Historical Association, Cooperstown—#112; **65,** T—W.J. Benett, *Burning Fallen Trees in a Girdled Clearing, Western Scene*, engraving. Yale University Art Gallery, The Mabel Brady Garvan Collection—#111; **66,** Culver Pictures, Inc.—#823; **67,** LC—The Historical Society of Pennsylvania—#113, LB—Trustees of the British Museum—#114; R—*Moravian Settlement* (detail). Print Division, New York Public Library, Astor, Lenox and Tilden Foundation—#115; **68,** T—*L'Obel, Plantarum ser Stripirmin*—#116, B—The Granger Collection—#118; **70,** James Frothingham, *Elias Hasket Derby*, oil, 41½×32¼″. Peabody Museum of Salem, photo by Mark Sexton—#121; **72–3,** T—The Library Company of Philadelphia—#125; **72,** C—*Traite Genereale des Pesches, 1769–1777*, Courtesy of the Newberry Library, Chicago (+R 72.245)—#309; **73,** C—American Antiquarian Society—#124; **74,** Courtesy The New York Historical Society—#126; **76,** Charles Taber & Company, *Sperm Whaling #2, "The Conflict"*. Courtesy New Bedford Museum, Shelburne, VT—#130; **77,** (see 62)—#129; **79,** William Britton, *Market Square, Germantown*, oil on canvas, 19⅞″×12¼″. Philadelphia Museum of Art: Collection of Edgar William and Bernice Chrysler Garbisch—#131; **82,** Time line: L—Lee Boltin Picture Library—#510, C—Musée des Beaux Arts, Nantes. Photograph courtesy of American Heritage—#511, R—Portrait attrib. to Henry Kinney, *Moses Brown*. Courtesy, The Rhode Island Historical Society—#328; **84,** L—The State Museum of Pennsylvania/Pennsylvania Historical and Museum Commission—#315, R—Ephrata Cloister/Pennsylvania Historical and Museum Commission—#318; **85,** The Mansell Collection, London—#319; **86,** T—*David and Phila Franks*. Courtesy American Jewish Historical Society, Waltham, MA—#320, B—Courtesy New York Historical Society—#426; **88–9,** *Albatross*, watercolor. The National Maritime Museum, London—#321; **90,** T—National Maritime Museum, London—#322, B—Lee Boltin Picture Library—#779, 510; **91,** From *The Interesting Narrative of the Life of Olaudah Equiano or Gustavus Vassa*. **92,** Library of Congress, neg. #262-33994—#324; **93,** Courtesy American Antiquarian Society—#325; **94,** Benjamin Henry Latrobe, *Overseer and Slaves*, watercolor. Maryland Historical Society—#327; **95,** Payne Limner, *Alexander Spotswood Payne and his Brother, John Robert Dandridge Payne, and their Nurse*. Virginia Museum of Fine Arts, Richmond, Gift of Dorothy Payne—#326; **97,** (see 82R)—#328; **100,** Time line: L—Culver Pictures, Inc.—#338, TR—*Almanac, 1792*, published by Johann Albrecht and Company. Courtesy The Henry Francis du Pont Winterthur Museum—#344, BR—Thomas Cole, *Oxbow on the Connecticut River*, oil on canvas. The Metropolitan Museum of Art, Gift of Mrs. Russell Sage, 1908—#789; **102,** Maryland Historical Society—#330; **103,** T—Courtesy American Antiquarian Society—#331, B—Benj. Henry LaTrobe, *Nondescripts attracted by a neighboring barbeque*. Maryland Historical Society—#332; **104,** L—Lewis Miller, *the York Hotels 1800*. Courtesy The Historical Society of York County—#333, R—Museum of American Textile History—#334, **105,** (ibid.)—#780; **106,** T—Library of Congress, neg. #USZ62 1470G—#336, B—Overmantle decorator in Martin van Bergen farmhouse, 1729, Leeds, NJ (detail). The Metropolitan Museum of Art, Gift of Mr. & Mrs. Samuel Schwartz, 1979—#335; **107,** The Connecticut Historical Society—#339; **108,** T—Lewis Miller, *Ludwig Miller, Teacher*, watercolor. Courtesy The Historical Society of York County—#337, B—(see 100L)—#338; **109,** Courtesy The New York Historical Society, neg. #41531—#340; **110,** From the Collections of Henry Ford Museum & Greenwich Village, #24-A-16—#341; **111,** The Library Company of Philadelphia—#346; **113,** TL—Clock 54,85.1 a,b: Philadelphia Museum of Art, Titus C. Geesy Collection—#343, TC—Dish 'oo.21: Philadelphia Museum of Art: Gift of John T. Morris—#342, TR—(see 100TR)—#344, B—Library of Congress, neg. #USZ62 7741G—#345; **115,** The Bettmann Archive—#425; **117,** (see 103T)—#331;

UNIT 3

120–21, Unit Three Opener: Attrib. to George Cook, *Patrick Henry Arguing the Parson's Cause*. Virginia Historical Society Collection—#142; **122,** Time line: L—Culver Pictures, Inc.—#829; R—Courtesy of the Essex Institute, Salem, MA, Photo by Mark Sexton—#146; **124,** Metropolitan Museum of Art, Rogers Fund, 1921,

#21.36.164.2—#134; **125**, (ibid., #21.36.164.1)—#135; **126**, (detail) Colonial Williamsburg Foundation—#767; **127**, Courtesy of the Henry R. Huntington Library and Art Gallery—#136; **129**, Courtesy The New York Historical Society—#138; **130–31**, Painting by Edward Willard Deming. State Historical Society of Wisconsin—#139; **131**, T—Courtesy of the Royal Ontario Museum, Toronto, Canada—#140; **134**, Courtesy of the Massachusetts State Art Commission, Photo by John Woolf—#141; **135**, T—(see 120–21)—#142, CL—American Antiquarian Society—#143, CR—(see 122R)—#146, BL—Culver Pictures, Inc.—#144; **137**, Library Company of Philadelphia—#145; **140**, Time line: L—Culver Pictures, Inc.—#840, TR—(ibid.)—#828, BR—Benjamin West, *Preliminary Peace Negotiations with Great Britain.* Courtesy The Henry Francis du Pont Winterthur Museum—#414; **142**, John Singleton Copley, *Samuel Adams,* c. 1772, oil on canvas, 50×40¼″. Deposited by the City of Boston, 1876, Museum of Fine Arts, Boston, #30.76C—#397; **143**, Paul Revere, *Boston Massacre,* mezzotint. Metropolitan Museum of Art, Gift of Mrs. Russell Sage, 1909—#395; **144**, The Granger Collection—#398; **145**, T—Ramsey, *George III.* Colonial Williamsburg Foundation, #G1963.375 #T75-1052—#399; **147**, Amos Doolittle, *A View of the South Part of Lexington,* Plate IV. Courtesy Chicago Historical Society—#401; **148–49**, John Trumbull, *Battle of Bunker's Hill,* oil on canvas, 24×36″. © Yale University Art Gallery—#400; **150**, Library of Congress, neg. #USZ62 50794—#402; **151**, John Singleton Copley, *Mrs. James Warren (Mercy Otis),* (detail) c. 1763, oil on canvas, 51¼×41″. Museum of Fine Arts, Boston—#415; **152**, John Trumbull, *The Declaration of Independence.* © Yale University Art Gallery—#404; **153**, Bernard, *The Manner in Which The American Colonies Declared Themselves Independent of the King of England.* Courtesy of the Fort Ticonderoga Museum—#407; **154**, Edward Savage, stipple engraving. Courtesy American Antiquarian Society—#406; **155**, *Warm'd by One Heart, United in One Band.* Courtesy The Henry Francis du Pont Winterthur Museum—#405; **156**, William Elliot, *The Action Between His Majesty's Ship Serapis Commanded by Capt. Pearson and the Bonhomme Richard Commanded by Paul Jones,* 9/23/1779, oil on canvas, 44×67″. From the Collection of U.S. Naval Academy Museum, Annapolis, MD—#412; **157**, John Trumbull, *Surrender of General Burgoyne at Saratoga,* oil on canvas. © Yale University Art Gallery—#410; **158–59**, T—Xavier della Gatta, *Battle at Germantown.* Courtesy of the Valley Forge Historical Society—#581, B—William Mercer, *Battle at Princeton.* The Historical Society of Pennsylvania—#582; **160**, T—J.H. Carl, *Hochfurst, Hessiches Corpse,* Uniform of a German Mercenary. Anne S.K. Brown Military Collection, Brown University Library—#421, TC—*Uniforms Militaires des Troupes Francoises et Etrangeres...,* French Uniform. The Anne S.K. Brown Military Collection, Brown University Library—#422, TR—Detail from *The Invitation, or Camp Politeness.* British Officer's Uniform. The Anne S.K. Brown Military Collection, Brown University Library—#423; B—Lloyd Branson, *Gathering of the Overmountain Men at Sycamore Shoals* (#1.893). Courtesy of the Tennessee State Museum—#793; **161**, After Johann Martin Will, hand-colored copper engraving, American rifleman. The Anne S.K. Brown Military Collection, Brown University Library—#424; **162–63**, T—William T. Trego, *The March to Valley Forge, December 9, 1777.* Courtesy The Valley Forge Historical Society—#409; **163**, B—George Rogers Clark National Historical Park, Photo by Dennis Latta—#411; **165**, (see 140BR)—#414; **168**, Time line: Courtesy The New York Historical Society—#25; **170**, Courtesy John Carter Brown Library at Brown University—#19; **173**, L—Courtesy The New York Historical Society—#23, R—(ibid.)—#22; **175**, W.L. Breton after C.W. Peale (detail). The Historical Society of Pennsylvania—#21; **177**, Courtesy American Antiquarian Society—#33; **179**, T—Kemmelmeyer: *The American Star.* The Metropolitan Museum of Art, Gift of Edgar William and Bernice Chrysler Garbisch, #62.256.7—#26, B—Independence National Historic Park Collection—#24; **180**, T—Library of Congress, neg. #USZ62 1306G—#27, B—(ibid.) neg. #USZ62 1686G—#28; **181**, Reproduced by permission from *Send For Haym Salomon* by Vick Knight, Jr., illustrated by Joseph Henninger. Published by Borden Publishing Company, Anaheim, CA—#34; **182**, Courtesy John Carter Brown Library at Brown University—#30, (inset)—John Trumbull, *Alexander Hamilton* (detail), oil on canvas, 30½×24½″. Courtesy Museum of Fine Arts, Boston, Bequest of Robert C. Winthrop, #94-167—#29; **183**, Probably F. Kemmelmeyer, *General Wayne Obtains a Complete Victory Over the Miami Indians, Aug. 20, 1794.* Courtesy, The Henry Francis du Pont Winterthur Museum—#31; **184**, FPG, International/J. Zehrt—#841;

UNIT 4 208–09, Opener, John Lewis Krimmel, *Election Day 1815.* The Historical Society of Pennsylvania—#152; **210**, Time line: T—Thomas Birch, *Constitution and Guerriere.* Courtesy United States Naval Academy Museum—#159, B—Boqueto de Woiserie, *A View of New Orleans Taken from Plantation of Marigny,* #1932.18 (detail). Courtesy Chicago Historical Society—#154; **212**, Gilbert Stuart, *George Washington,* unfinished portrait, oil on canvas. Courtesy Museum of Fine Arts, Boston, MA (courtesy of the Boston Atheneum)—#148; **213**, T—The Bettmann Archive—#149, B—Kemmelmeyer, *Washington Reviewing the Western Army at Fort Cumberland, Maryland.* The Metropolitan Museum of Art, Gift of Edgar William and Bernice Chrysler Garbisch, 1963

#63.201.2—#150; **214**, (see WHHA)—#151; **215**, Mather Brown, *Abigail Adams.* New York State Historical Association, Cooperstown, NY—#305; **217**, T—(see WHHA)—#153; **218**, State Historical Society of North Dakota—#428; **219**, (see 210B: entire piece is shown here)—#154; **220**, L—Courtesy The New York Historical Society—#156, R—(see WHHA)—#157; **221**, Margaret Reynolds, *View of Amherstburg 1813* (detail). Environment Canada—Parks: Fort Malden National Historic Park—#158; **222**, (see 210T)—#159; **223**, Edward Percy Moran, *By Dawn's Early Light.* The Peale Museum, Baltimore, Courtesy The Star-Spangled Banner Flag House—#162; **224–25**, Yale University Art Gallery, The Mabel Brady Garvan Collection—#163; **227**, Sir Amedee Forestier, *Signing of the Treaty of Ghent.* National Museum of American Art (formerly National Collection of Fine Arts) Smithsonian Institution, neg. #1922.5.2, Gift of the Sulgrave Institution of the U.S. and Great Britain—#164; **230**, Time line: TL—Picture Collection, New York Public Library—#172, T—Courtesy The New York Historical Society—#312, B—Culver Pictures, Inc.—#831; **233**, T—From *Memoirs of Samuel Slater,* 1836. Smithsonian Institution, neg. #68735—#166, B—William Giles Munson, *The Eli Whitney Gun Factory.* Yale University Art Gallery, Mabel Brady Garvan Collection—#167; **234**, Courtesy Beverly Historical Society—#165; **235**, T—Museum of American Textile History—#168, B—(ibid.)—#169; **236**, T—(inset) W.J. Bennett after G. Cooke, *Richmond from the Hill above the Waterworks,* 1834. I.N. Phelps Stokes Collection, p.1833/E.58, New York Public Library—#171; **236–37**, B—After T. Hornor, *Broadway, New York, Shewing (sic) each Building from the Hygeian Depot Corner of Canal Street to beyond Niblo's Garden,* 1834. Print Division, New York Public Library, Astor, Lenox and Tilden Foundation—#170; **239**, T—(see 230TL)—#172, B—Valentine Museum, Richmond, VA—#310; **240**, Pavel Petrovich Svinin, *Free Blacks Sawing Wood to Heat the Bank,* watercolor, 1814. The Metropolitan Museum of Art, Rogers Fund, 1942, #42.95.16—#174; **241**, L—Culver Pictures, Inc.—#796, R—(ibid.)—#795; **242**, James Wilkins, *Leaving the Old Homestead.* Outside Mo. #147. Missouri Historical Society—#175; **243**, Karl Bodmer. Rare Book Division, *KF++1844, vig.4, New York Public Library, Astor, Lenox and Tilden Foundation—#176; **244**, T—Edward Lamson Henry, *Entering the Lock.* Collection: Albany Institute of History and Art—#177; **244–45**, B—Robert Havell, aquatint, 1839. I.N. Phelps Stokes Collection p. 1839/E.120, New York Public Library—#179; **245**, (inset) (see 230TR)—#312; **247**, Edward Lamson Henry, *First Railway Train on the Mohawk and Hudson, 1831.* Collection: Albany Institute of History and Art, Gift of Mrs. Abraham Lansing—#180; **250**, Time line: TL—J.H. Whitcomb, *Our President, Old Hickory,* watercolor, c. 1830. M. and M. Karolik Collection of American Watercolors and Drawings, 1800–1875, Museum of Fine Arts, Boston—#207, TR—Courtesy The New York Historical Society—#219, B—Jerome Tiger, *Endless Trail* (detail). Philbrook Art Center, Tulsa, OK—#212; **252**, T—(see WHHA)—#200; **254**, T—The Old Print Shop, Courtesy of American Heritage—#205; **255**, Rembrandt Peale, *Chief Justice John Marshall.* Collection of the Supreme Court of the United States—#203; **256**, (see WHHA)—#206; **257**, L—(see 250TL)—#207, R—(see WHHA)—#208; **258**, Library of Congress—#209; **259**, Rembrandt Peale, *John C. Calhoun* (detail). National Portrait Gallery, NPG 65.58—#211; **261**, (see 250B: entire piece is shown here)—#212; **262**, George Catlin, *The Virginia Constitutional Convention of 1829–30.* Virginia Historical Society Collections—#213; **263**, T—Courtesy American Antiquarian Society—#216, B—Library Company of Philadelphia—#214; **264**, L—James Henry Beard, *The Long Bill.* Cincinnati Art Museum, Gift of Mrs. T.E. Houston—#218, R—(see WHHA)—#217; **265**, (see 250TR)—#219, R—(see WHHA)—#220; **266**, L—Library of Congress, neg. #USZ62 29206—#470, R—Courtesy The New York Historical Society—#304; **267**, T—Anne S.K. Brown Military Collection, Brown University Library—#221, B—(see WHHA)—#222; **269**, The Bettmann Archive—#842; **270**, Time line: C—Courtesy American Antiquarian Society—#240, R—(detail) National Portrait Gallery, Smithsonian Institution, neg. #NPG 74.72—#237; **272**, T—Courtesy Chicago Historical Society—#224, B—State Historical Society of Wisconsin, McCormick Collection—#223; **273**, Winslow Homer, *New England Country School.* Addison Gallery of American Art, Phillips Academy, Andover, MA—#225; **274**, T—Courtesy of the Essex Institute, Salem, MA—#230, RC—Courtesy The New York Historical Society, neg. #7255—#226, LC—(detail) Harvard University Portrait Collection, By permission of the Houghton Library—#229, B—Smithsonian Institution, neg. #83-6104—#231; **275**, John Quidor, *The Return of Rip Van Winkle.* National Gallery of Art, Washington, Andrew W. Mellon Collection—#227; **277**, The Old Print Shop, Courtesy of American Heritage—#232; **278**, Courtesy of Harrisburg State Hospital, Harrisburg, PA. Photo by Ken Smith—#234; **279**, Oneida Community Historical Committee—#233; **280**, T—Library of Congress, neg. #262–37938—#238, BC—Sophia Smith Collection, neg. #WRSL2, Smith College—#236, BL—(see 270R)—#237, BR—Courtesy of Schlesinger Library, Radcliff College—#239; **282**, T—(see 270C)—#240, B—Courtesy American Antiquarian Society—#242; **283**, C—Print Collection, New York Public Library, Astor, Lenox and Tilden Foundation—#243; **284**, The Historic New Orleans Collection—#308; **285**, T—Taylor, *The American Slave Market,* Courtesy Chicago Historical Society—#246, C—Courtesy The New York Historical Society—#247; **286**, B—Courtesy American Antiquarian Society—#248; **287**, L—Library of Congress, neg. #USZ62 7816G—#249; R—The Granger Collection—#250; **288**, National Archives, neg. #121–BA–74, #55 American Image—#251;

UNIT 5 294–95, Unit Five Opener: Charles Christian Nahl (USA, 1818–1878), *Crossing the Plains*, oil on canvas, 11′4″ × 17′5″. Stanford University Museum of Art—#12082, Gift of Jan Lathrop Stanford—#825; **296**, Time line: L—Library of Congress, neg. #USZ62 7370G—#349, R—A.D.O. Browere, *Mines of Placerville* (detail). Courtesy of National Cowboy Hall of Fame—#357; **298**, Courtesy Texas Capitol, Austin. Photo by Bill Malone—#347; **299**, T—Friends of the Governor's Mansion, Austin—#348, B—(see 296L)—#349; **300**, Albert Bierstadt (1830–1902), *The Oregon Trail*. Butler Institute of American Art, Youngstown, OH—#350; **301**, International Museum of Photography at George Eastman House—#365; **303**, L—*Polk-Dallas Campaign Poster*, c. 1844, oil on canvas, 32⅜ × 30¼″. Abby Aldrich Rockefeller Folk Art Center, Williamsburg, VA, #T–58–100.52—#352, R (see WHHA)—#353; **305**, National Academy of Design, New York City—#354; **306**, After a painting by Carl Nebel, *General Scott's Entry into Mexico*. Courtesy Chicago Historical Society—#355; **309**, (see WHHA)—#356; **310**, T—The Bancroft Library—#359; **310–11**, (see 296R: entire piece is shown here)—#357; **312**, T—Library of Congress, neg. #USZ62 689G—#360, B—(see WHHA)—#361; **314**, L—(see WHHA)—#362, B—Samuel B. Waugh, watercolor. Courtesy Museum of the City of New York—#363; **315**, Maryland Historical Society, Baltimore—#364; **318**, Time line: L—Courtesy American Heritage—#375, C—National Archives, neg. #111–B–250 #15 American Image—#366, Francis Bicknell, *Emancipation Proclamation*. National Graphic Center, neg. #86–12269—#383; **320**, Anonymous, *Harriet Beecher Stowe*, gray wash and pencil on cream paper, 11⅞ × 8⁷⁄₁₆″. M. and M. Karolik Collection of American Watercolors and Drawings, #161.247, Museum of Fine Arts, Boston—#367; **321**, B—S.J. Reader, *Battle of Hickory Point*. Kansas State Historical Society—#369; **322**, L—(see WHHA)—#370, R—Louis Schultze, *Dred Scott*. Missouri Historical Society, neg. #S–8—#371; **324**, National Archives. #111–B–4208—#372; **325**, L—Courtesy of the Baltimore and Ohio Transportation Museum—#373, R—(see WHHA)—#374; **327**, L—National Archives, neg. #111–B–4146 #151 Civil War list—#376, R—(ibid.) neg. #121–BA–914A #87 Civil War list—#377; **328**, (ibid.) neg. #111–B–1857 #51 American Image—#392; **329**, L—Edward Caledon Bruce, *Robert E. Lee*. Virginia Historical Society Collection—#379, R—William Gail Brown, *Thomas Jonathan (Stonewall) Jackson*. (ibid.)—#378; **330**, *Admiral Porter's Fleet Running the Rebel Blockade of Mississippi at Vicksburg*, color lithograph, #51.7.706. The Beverley R. Robinson Collection, U.S. Naval Academy Museum—#778; **331**, L—Conrad Chapman, *The Hunley*. Museum of the Confederacy Collection—#783, B—The Edward W.C. Arnold Collection, The Metropolitan Museum of Art, Photo Courtesy Museum of the City of New York—#822; **332**, TL—Valentine Museum, Cook Collection, Richmond, VA—#381, TR—Winslow Homer, oil sketch of young Union soldier. Courtesy of the Cooper-Hewitt Museum, Smithsonian Institution/Art Resource, NY—#782; **332–33**, B—James Hope, *The Army of the Potomac*, oil on canvas, 17¾ × 41¾″. M. and M. Karolik Collection, Museum of Fine Arts, Boston—#784; **333**, (inset) Library of Congress, Photo Courtesy of American Heritage—#785; **334**, Library of Congress, neg. #USZ62 147—#382; **335**, William Heepsham Overend, *An August Morning with Farragut, The Battle of Mobile Bay August 5, 1864*, oil on canvas, 77½ × 120″. © Wadsworth Atheneum, Hartford, Gift of Citizens of Hartford by subscription—#384; **336**, James Walker, *Battle of Gettysburg*. New Hampshire Historical Society, neg. #1921.4.2—#387; **337**, L—National Archives, neg. #111–B–36 #32 Civil War list—#389, R—(ibid.) neg. #111–B–1769 #50 American Image—#388; **339**, National Park Service, Courtesy of American Heritage—#391; **342**, Time line: BL—Library of Congress, Courtesy American Heritage—#390, TL—National Archives, neg. #111-B-4279—#539, CR—*Harper's Weekly*, 4/24/1875—#835; **344**, T—Anne S.K. Brown Military Collection, Brown University Library at Brown University—#537, B—(see WHHA)—#557; **345**, The Granger Collection—#744; **346**, (see 342TL)—#539; **347**, The Bettmann Archive—#747; **348**, (see WHHA)—#558; **349**, T—Culver Pictures, Inc.—#538, L—*Harper's Weekly*, 11/16/1867; **350**, T—Library of Congress, neg. #USZ62 2814—#440, B—*The Broken Shackle*, 1874. Courtesy Chicago Historical Society—#498; **351**, The Bettmann Archive—#745; **353**, (see WHHA)—#559; **354**, Culver Pictures, Inc.—#746; **355**, Library of Congress, neg. #LC J713 1148—#499;

UNIT 6 362–63, Opener: Theodore Groll, *Washington Street, Indianapolis at Dusk*, ca/1892–1895, 76″×98¼″, oil on canvas. Indianapolis Museum of Art, Gift of a Couple of Hoosiers, © 1987, All rights reserved. **364**, Time line: L—From *Bill Pickett, Bulldogger* by Colonel Bailey C. Hanes. Copyright 1977 by the University of Oklahoma Press, Western History Collection—#87, C—Union Pacific Museum Collection—#61, R—Culver Pictures, Inc.—#393; **366**, Amon Carter Museum—#56; **367**, William Hahn, *Market Scene Sansome Street, San Francisco* (detail), c.1872. Courtesy Crocker Art Museum, Sacramento,

CA—#59; **368**, California State Library—#60; **370**, T—Bancroft Library, University of California, Berkeley—#62, (inset) (see 364C)—#61; **372–3**, B—Library of Congress, neg. #USZ62 17997—#64; **374**, Solomon D. Butcher Collection, Nebraska State Historical Society—#65; **376**, National Museum of American Art, Smithsonian Institution, Gift of Mrs. Joseph Harrison, Jr. #L.1965.1.410—#66; **377**, Transparency Courtesy of Yale University Library—#67; **378–9**, T—Smithsonian Institution, neg. #71–3048—#69; **379**, BL—(see 364 R)—#393, BR—National Archives—#306; **380**, Smithsonian Institution, neg. #43.201–A—#55; **381**, Library of Congress, neg. #LC USZ62 19725—#70; **384**, Time line: L—Courtesy of American Petroleum Institute Historical Photo Library, Drake Well Museum—#81, TR—Library of Congress—#73, BR—*PUCK*, 1/23/1889, Vol. 24, pp 362–3. Courtesy of the Newberry Library, Chicago—#83; **386**, (see 384TR)—#73; **387**, Library of Congress—#76; **388**, T—S.B. Shirley, *Bessemer Converter*. Bethlehem Steel Corp.—#77, C—Reproduced with permission of AT & T Corporate Archive—#89; **391**, T—The Bettmann Archive—#90, TC—Culver Pictures, Inc.—#86, B—Photoworld/FPG International—#82, B—*VERDICT*, 1/30/1889. Courtesy The New York Historical Society—#80; **392**, (see 384L)—#81; **394–5**, (see 384BR)—#83; **396**, International Museum of Photography at George Eastman House—#75; **397**, T—Photoworld/FPG International—#85, B—Library of Congress, neg. #USZ62 22399—#84; **398**, Culver Pictures, Inc.—#92; **399**, The Bettmann Archive—#74; **402**, Time line: L—North View, about Congress Street. Chicago Historical Society—#188, TC—Mark Twain. Culver Pictures, Inc.—#471, CR—Chicago Historical Society, neg. #CRC—136H—#193, BR—Jane Addams Memorial Collection, Special Collections, University Library, University of Illinois at Chicago—#191; **404**, *PUCK*, 4/28/1880. Courtesy The Newberry Library, Chicago—#183; **405**, Library of Congress, neg. #USZ62 42207G—#187; **407**, National Archives, neg. #196–GS–369—#185; **408**, (see 402L)—#188; **409**, T—Courtesy Oak Park Public Library, Oak Park, IL—#190, B—Courtesy Chicago Historical Society, neg. #ICHI-05394—#189; **410**, T—(see 402CR)—#193, (inset) (see 402BR)—#191; **411**, U.S. Department of the Interior, National Park Service, Edison National Historic Site—#198; **413**, T—National Baseball Library, Cooperstown, NY—#194, B—Courtesy, Cincinnati Historical Society—#195; **415**, L—(see 402TC)—#471, R—Photoworld/FPG, International—#197; **418**, Time line: L—*PUCK*, 8/17/1887. Courtesy The New York Historical Society—#314, TR—AFL-CIO, Washington, D.C.—#266, BR—Courtesy The New York Historical Society—#262; **420**, L—(see WHHA)—#255, C—(see WHHA)—#258, R—(see WHHA)—#259; **421**, (see 418L)—#314; **422**, T—*PUCK*, 12/7/1887. Courtesy The New York Historical Society—#260, C—(see WHHA)—#261; **423**, United Electrical Radio and Machine Workers of America—#272; **425**, T—Amalgamated Clothing Workers, Print Courtesy Cornell University—#263, B—*PUCK*, 6/21/1882. Courtesy The New York Historical Society—#264; **426–27**, B—*PUCK*, 4/7/1886. Courtesy The Newberry Library, Chicago—#265; **426**, T—(see 418TR)—#266, **427**, T—Library of Congress, neg. #USZ62 10546G—#267; **430**, National Archives, neg. #83—FB 5594—#268; **431**, Library of Congress—#269; **433**, (see WHHA)—#271;

UNIT 7 438–39, Opener: Henry Reuterdahl, *United States Fleet in the Straits of Magellan the Morning of February 8, 1908*. U.S. Naval Academy Museum—#677; **440**, Time line: L—Lee Boltin Picture Library—#838, R—(ibid.)—#839; **442**, Courtesy Alaska State Museum—#274; **443**, *PUCK*, Vol. 48, no. 1226. Courtesy The Newberry Library, Chicago—#273; **444**, Hawaii State Archives, Photo by George Bacon—#276; **446**, Culver Pictures, Inc.—#277; **447**, T—Courtesy Chicago Historical Society, B—James G. Tyler, *The Battle of Manila Bay*. Franklin D. Roosevelt Library—#281; **449**, Library of Congress, neg. #LC USZ62 135—#279; **450**, *PUCK*, Vol. 44, no. 1133. Courtesy The Newberry Library, Chicago—#282; **452**, Trustees of the British Library—#283; **453**, The Bettmann Archive—#769; **457**, The Granger Collection—#843; **458**, Time line: T—Brown Brothers—#460, B—(ibid.)—#820; **460**, L—Culver Pictures, Inc.—#442, R—The Bettmann Archive—#466; **462**, TL—Brown Brothers—#443, R—The Bettmann Archive—#447, BR—Brown Brothers—#444; **463**, L—(see 458T)—#460, R—National Archives, neg. #16–G–116–1–C 119092, #117 American Image—#450; **464**, Courtesy The New York Historical Society—#463; **465**, Brown Brothers—#631, L—The Bettmann Archive—#462, R—Culver Pictures, Inc.—#464; **466–67**, C—Brown Brothers—#465; **467**, B—International Museum of Photography at George Eastman House—#468; **468**, Lewis Hine, *Breaker boys working in Ewen Breaker Mine*, 1/10/11. National Archives, neg. #102–LH–1941, #93 American Image—#469; **469**, Cleveland Public Library—#427; **470**, L—Photography by Jacob A. Riis, Jacob A. Riis Collection, Museum of the City of New York—#775, TR—(ibid.)—#776, BR—(ibid.)—#777; **471**, Culver Pictures, Inc.—#630; **474**, Time line: L—*PUCK*, 8/1/06. Courtesy The New York Historical Society—#570, R—Culver Pictures, Inc.—#570; **476**, Courtesy The New York Historical Society, neg. #50758—#502; **477**, L—Culver Pictures, Inc.—#501, R—(see WHHA)—#285; **478**, L—Brown Brothers—#496, R—Culver Pictures, Inc.—#503; **481**, T—(see 474L)—#505, B—(see WHHA)—#286; **484**, T—(see WHHA)—#287, B—Culver Pictures, Inc.—#500;

486, Photoworld/FPG, International—#509; **487,** (see 474R)—#570; **490,** Time line: L—Culver Pictures, Inc.—#613, TC—Harvey Dunn, *Machine Gunner,* charcoal. Smithsonian Institution, neg. #76–16915—#773, BR—*New York American Herald.* New York Public Library—#616; **493,** (see 490L)—#613; **494,** T—Library of Congress, neg. #USZ62 25290—#615, B—The Bettmann Archive—#614; **496,** (see 490BR)—#616; **497,** T—Henry de Groux, *Lanceurs de grenades,* 1915. Musee des Deux Guerres Mondiales—BDIC (Universites de Paris) Photo by Hubert Josse—#618, B—W.J. Aylward, *Troops Waiting to Advance, Hattonchatel, St. Mihiel.* Smithsonian Institution, Division of Armed Forces, neg. #CT73–5593—#617; **498,** L—National Archives, neg. #165–WW–474 D–8—#619, R—Culver Pictures, Inc.—#621; **499,** T—Jonas Lie, *On the Job for Victory,* 1920, lithograph, 29 x 36". Collection, The Museum of Modern Art, NY, Gift of Abby Aldrich Rockefeller—#622, B—National Archives, neg. #US–SC–35757—#623; **500,** George Harding, *On the Monterail–Château Thierry Road.* Smithsonian Institution, Division of Armed Forces, neg. #46046—#624; **503,** T—Photoworld/FPG International—#625; **504,** Sir William Orpen, *Hall of Mirrors.* The Trustees of the Imperial War Museum—#626; **505,** UPI/Bettmann Newsphotos—#627; **506,** (ibid.)—#628; **507,** Library of Congress, neg. #USZ62 14447 G—#439; **511,** Smithsonian Institution, Division of Political History—#844;

UNIT 8 512–13, Opener: Thomas Hart Benton, *College & City Life, Leisure, Literature,* mural (detail). University of Indiana Auditorium—#826; **514,** Time line: L—Brown Brothers—#394, C—Culver Pictures, Inc.—#827, B—Library of Congress—#790; **516,** L—(see WHHA)—#290, R—From *Louisville Courier Journal*—#291; **517,** L—(see WHHA)—#292, R—Fitzpatrick in the *St. Louis Post-Dispatch*—#692; **518,** T—Culver Pictures, Inc.—#691, B—(see WHHA)—#293; **520,** T—From the Collection of Henry Ford Museum & Greenfield Village, neg. #833–24—#294, B—Courtesy of The Henry A. Clark, Jr. Collection—#295; **521,** T—From the Collection of Henry Ford Museum & Greenfield Village, neg. #0–646—#296, B—Motor Vehicle Manufacturers Association—#297; **523,** From the Collection of Henry Ford Museum & Greenfield Village, neg. #0–5282T—#288; **524,** The Smithsonian Institution, neg. #45130A—#298; **526,** The Archives of Labor and Urban Affairs, Wayne State University—#300; **527,** T—Fitzpatrick in the *St. Louis Post-Dispatch*—#301; **528,** (see 514L)—#394; **529,** UPI/Bettmann Newsphotos—#302; **532,** Time line: Thomas Hart Benton, *City Activities With Dance Hall.* Courtesy of The Equitable Life Assurance Society of the U.S.—#524; **534,** B—Library of Congress, neg. #USZ62 11202G—#435; **535,** Ben Shahn, *Bartolomeo Vanzetti and Nicola Sacco,* From Sacco-Vanzetti series of twenty-three paintings (1931–32), tempera on paper. Collection, The Museum of Modern Art, New York, Gift of Abby Aldrich Rockefeller—#514; **536,** The Phillips Collection, Washington, D.C.—#700; **538,** UPI/Bettmann Newsphotos—#436; **539,** John Held, Jr. *Life* cover, 2/18/26. Culver Pictures, Inc.—#513; **540,** T—Library of Congress—#438, R—John Held, Jr., *McClures.* Culver Pictures, Inc.—#517; **541,** Culver Pictures, Inc.—#519; **542,** (ibid.)—#525, B—General Electric, Schenectady, NY—#520; **543,** Culver Pictures, Inc.—#523, (see 532)—#524; **545,** Culver Pictures, Inc.—#522; **546,** UPI/Bettmann Newsphotos—#528; **547,** L—Culver Pictures, Inc.—#527, R—(ibid.)—#529; **549,** UPI/Bettmann Newsphotos—#530; **552,** Time line: TL—National Archives, neg. #9–X–1—#629, BL—UPI/Bettmann Newsphotos—#741, R—Joe Jones, *We Demand.* Butler Institute of American Art, Youngstown, OH—#736; **554,** Library of Congress, neg. #USZ62 43690G—#434; **555,** L—*Run on the Erie National Bank, 1931,* photograph. The Historical Society of Pennsylvania—#729, R—Photoworld/FPG International—#728; **556,** Culver Pictures, Inc.—#726; **558,** UPI/Bettmann Newsphotos—#730; **559,** T—(see WHHA)—#702, B—UPI/Bettmann Newsphotos—#731; **560,** T—(see 552TL)—#629, B—Brown Brothers—#732; **562,** AP/Wide World Photos, Courtesy Franklin D. Roosevelt Library—#723; **563,** Courtesy TVA—#733; **564,** C—UPI/Bettmann Newsphotos—#735; **565,** L—(see 552TL)—#736, R—UPI/Bettmann Newsphotos—#734; **566,** Culver Pictures, Inc.—#727; **567,** Copyright © I.H.T. Corporation, reprinted by permission. From the *New York Herald Tribune,* 7/18/37—#738; **570,** Time line: L—National Archives, neg. #83–G–44360 #145 American Image—#580, C—Culver Pictures, Inc.—#694, R—Billy Rose Theatre Collection, New York Public Library at Lincoln Center, Astor, Lenox and Tilden Foundation—#578; **572,** Franklin D. Roosevelt Library—#569; **573,** UPI/Bettmann Newphotos—#576; **574,** Diego Rivera, *Body Presses and Assembly of Chassis* (detail), fresco 33.10 N, "Detroit Industry 1932–33." © The Detroit Institute of Arts, Founders Society Purchase, Edsel B. Ford Fund and Gift of Edsel B. Ford—#748; **577,** T—Library of Congress, neg. #LCUSZ62 19225—#432, B—Culver Pictures, Inc.—#572; **578,** L—Culver Pictures, Inc.—#749, R—Library of Congress, neg. #USF34 17983—#431; **579,** Culver Pictures, Inc.—#824; **581,** UPI/Bettmann Newsphotos—#579; **582,** L—Culver Pictures, Inc.—#693, R—(ibid.)—#695; **583,** Edward Hopper, *Nighthawks,* 1942, oil on canvas, 76.2 x 144 cm. © 1987 The Art Institute of Chicago. All rights reserved. Friends of American Art Collection, 1942.51—#574;

UNIT 9 590–91, Opener: Ogden Pleissner, *On the Road to St. Lô.* Courtesy Civic Center Commission, Cobo Hall, Detroit—#554; **592,** Time line: L—FPG International—#587, C—Photoworld/FPG International—#818, R—PhotoSource Ltd., London—#819; **594,** Henry Reuterdahl, *United States Fleet in the Straits of Magellan.* U.S. Naval Academy Museum—#677; **595,** FPG International—#585, (inset) (ibid.)—#632; **596,** (ibid.)—#586; **599,** BL—(ibid.)—#587, R—(ibid.)—#589; **600,** (ibid.)—#590; **601,** (ibid.)—#531; **602,** (ibid.)—#591; **603,** UPI/Bettmann Newsphotos—#596; **604,** AP/Wide World Photos—#678; **605,** FPG International—#532; **606,** Photoworld/FPG International—#592; **607,** T—Charles Gunall, *The Withdrawal from Dunkirk, June 1940.* Trustees of the Imperial War Museum, neg. #LD305—#740; **608,** B—UPI/Bettmann Newsphotos—#593; **609,** L—PhotoSource Ltd., London—#594, R—Illingworth, *The Way of the Stork,* cartoon appearing in *Punch,* 1/29/41. By permission of *Punch*—#595; **612,** Time line: L—Library of Congress, neg. #USZ62 22049—#542, C—U.S. Office of Information, Courtesy American Heritage—#562, R—Franklin D. Roosevelt Library, Hyde Park, NY—#565; **615,** Captured Japanese film. U.S. Navy Photo, Courtesy American Heritage—#541; **616,** UPI/Bettmann Newsphotos—#543; **617,** Assembly line of Dauntless bombers at Douglas Aircraft plant. Photo Courtesy McDonnell-Douglas Corporation—#544; **618,** L—Baker Library, Harvard Business School, Photo Courtesy American Heritage—#545, R—Library of Congress, neg. #USZ62 50747—#429; **619,** National Archives, neg. #210–GA–7—#534; **620,** Photo by Deborah Storms, Courtesy of Yoshiko Uchida—#768; **621,** UPI/Bettmann Newsphotos—#547; **622,** West Point Museum Collections, United States Military Academy—#548; **624,** L—Photoworld/FPG International—#549, R—U.S. Army Photo, Courtesy American Heritage—#552; **625,** T—Library of Congress, neg. #USZ62 15187—#430, B—(see 590–91)—#554; **626,** T—UPI/Bettmann Newsphotos—#556, B—U.S. Army Photo, Courtesy American Heritage—#560; **627,** (see 612C)—#562; **628,** T—U.S. Marine Corps Photo, Courtesy American Heritage—#563, B—George Silk, *Life Magazine,* © 1971 Time, Inc.—#564; **630,** National Archives, neg. #80–G–700777—#533; **631,** UPI/Bettmann Newsphotos—#566; **633,** (see 612R)—#565; **634,** Magnum Photos/© Eli Reed—#801; **635,** UPI/Bettmann Newsphotos—#568;

UNIT 10 640–41, Opener: Ben Shahn, *Integration, Supreme Court.* Des Moines Art Center, James D. Edmundson Purchase Fund, and by kind permission of Mrs. Barnarda Shahn—#609; **642,** Time line: TL—UPI/Bettmann Newsphotos—#821, BL—AP/Wide World Photos—#555, R—Frank Williams, 1957. Reprinted with permission from The Detroit Free Press—#649; **644,** T—AP/Wide World Photos—#633, B—Culver Pictures, Inc.—#635; **645,** AP/Wide World Photos—#637; **647,** R—George Meany Memorial Archives—#651; **648,** L—(see WHHA)—#655, R—AP/Wide World Photos—#639; **649,** AP/Wide World Photos—#640; **650–51,** UPI/Bettmann Newsphotos—#642; **653,** Herbert Block, "If There's Anything I Hate It's Sloppy Neighbors," from *The Herblock Book* (Beacon Press, 1952)—#643; **654,** T—UPI/Bettmann Newsphotos—#644, B—AP/Wide World Photos—#645; **655,** T—(see WHHA)—#654, B—Cy Hungerford, "Brother—Can you spare about 72 billion dollars?" By permission of *The Pittsburgh Post-Gazette*—#646; **656,** AP/Wide World Photos—#647; **657,** UPI/Bettmann Newsphotos—#794; **658,** AP/Wide World Photos—#648; **659,** (see 642R)—#649; **662,** Time line: TL—AP/Wide World Photos—#473, BL—Magnum Photos/© Rene Burri—#477, R—By permission of Bill Malden and Wil-Jo Associates—#495; **664,** AP/Wide World Photos—#472; **665,** (see 662TR)—#473; **668,** L—U.S. Department of Energy—#474, R—Ben Shahn, *Stop H-Bomb Tests,* serigraph. New Jersey State Museum, Trenton; Purchase FA1970.64.15, and by kind permission of Mrs. Barnarda Shahn—#536; **669,** T—AP/Wide World Photos—#476; **669,** T—(ibid.)—#478, B—(see 662BL)—#477; **670,** T—Magnum Photos/© Rene Burri—#480; **672,** L—AP/Wide World Photos—#481, R—Leo Joseph Roche, *Firing of MacArthur,* cartoon appeared in the *Buffalo Courier-Express.* Courtesy of Buffalo and Erie County Historical Society and Leo Roche—#482; **673,** T—UPI/Bettmann Newsphotos—#483, B—AP/Wide World Photos—#484; **675,** TL—AP/Wide World Photos—#487, CL—(ibid.)—#488, R—(ibid.)—#486, B—U.S. Navy Photo, Courtesy AP/Wide World Photos—#491; **676,** B—AP/Wide World Photos—#490; **677,** L—AP/Wide World Photos—#492, R—Magnum Photos/© Burt Glinn—#493; **678,** UPI/Bettmann Newsphotos—#772; **679,** AP/Wide World Photos—#474, B—AP/Wide World Photos—#482; **682,** Time Line: L—FPG International/Brenneis—#834, TR-UPI/Bettmann Newsphotos—#612, BR—Black Star/Charles Moore—#611; **684,** B—Photo Researchers/Van Bucher—#597; **685,** T—Magnum Photos/Erich Hartmann—#600, R—(Magnum Photos/Henri-Cartier Bresson)—#598; **686,** L—Monkmeyer Press/Hayel Carew—#599, R—Hans Hoffmann, *The Gate,* oil on canvas, 75⅛ × 48½". The Solomon R. Guggenheim Museum, NY, Photo by Carmelo Guadagno—#602; **688,** UPI/Bettmann Newsphotos—#601; **689,** Magnum Photos/Cornell Capa—#603; **690,** L—Magnum Photos/Wayne Miller—#608, R—George Meany Memorial Archives—#604; **691,** Black Star/Stephen Shames—#605; **693,** UPI/Bettmann Newsphotos—#676; **694,** (see 640–41)—#609; **695,** Magnum Photos/Burt Glinn—#610; **696,** (see 682TR)—#612; **697,** T—(see 682BR)—#611, R—Wide World Photos, Inc.—#641;

UNIT 11 702-03, Opener: 1st Lunar Landing, 1969. NASA, Houston—#798; **704,** Time line: L—Magnum Photos/© Cornell Capa—#799, C—Black Star/© Werner Wolff—#800, R—UPI/Bettmann Newsphotos—#706; **706,** L—Magnum Photo/© Cornell Capa—#652, R—(see WHHA)—#653; **707,** AP/Wide World Photos—#656; **708,** L—NASA, neg. #S64-36911, Houston—#657, R—Black Star/© Steve Schapiro—#658; **709,** T—Black Star/© Fred Ward—#659, B—By permission of Bill Mauldin and Wil-Jo Associates, Inc.—#660; **710,** UPI/Bettmann Newsphotos—#673; **712,** L—AP/Wide World Photos—#661, R—Black Star/© Charles Moore—#662; **713,** L—AP/Wide World Photos—#663, R—Black Star/© Gene Daniels—#664; **714,** T—(see WHHA)—#665, B—Black Star/© Bill Strode—#666; **716,** (see 704R)—#706; **717,** T—Black Star/© John Launois—#667, B—(ibid.)/© Dennis Brack—#668; **718,** Reproduced by permission of University of South Carolina Press from *A Lasting Impression: A Collection of Photographs of Martin Luther King, Jr.* by John Tweedle, compiled and edited by Hermene Hartman—#669; **719,** T—Black Star/© Joe Flowers—#670, B—(ibid.)/© Fred Ward—#671; **720,** TL—(see 710)—#673, BL—UPI/Bettmann Newsphotos—#672, R—(see WHHA)—#674; **724,** Time line: L—Black Star/© Pedro Meyer—#681, B—AP/Wide World Photos—#687, R—UPI/Bettmann Newsphotos—#679; **727,** L—Black Star/© Arthur Rickerby—#680, R—(see 724L)—#681; **729,** T—Black Star/© Robert Lackenbach—#682, B—Magnum Photos/© Marc Riboud—#753; **731,** L—AP/Wide World Photos—#683, R—(ibid.)—#684; **732,** Black Star/© Fred Ward—#722; **734,** AP/Wide World Photos—#685; **735,** U.S. Army Photo, Courtesy of AP/Wide World Photos—#686; **736,** L—(see 724B)—#687, R—Black Star/© James Pickerell—#688; **737,** (ibid.)/© Ted Cowell—#689; **738,** Courtesy E.P. Dutton, from *To Bear Any Burden*—#720; **739,** Black Star/© Robert Ellison/Empirenews—#690;

UNIT 12 744–45, Opener: *Earth from Space.* NASA, Houston—#837; **746,** Time line: TR—Black Star/© Dennis Brack—#719, BR—FPG International/© 1981 Palumbo—#833; **748,** Black Star/© Dennis Brack—#708; **749,** (ibid.)—#716; **750,** AP/Wide World Photos—#709; **751,** L-Magnum Photos/© Alex Webb—#752, R—Black Star/© Dennis Brack—#710; **753,** (see WHHA)—#703; **754,** AP/Wide World Photos—#711; **755,** Black Star/© Bob Fitch—#718; **756,** T—(see WHHA)—#704, B—Black Star/© Harry Schaefer—#712; **758,** Black Star/© Arnold Zann—#713; **759,** L—Black Star/© Frank Johnson—#714, R—Black Star/© Tom Sobolik—#715; **761,** Black Star/© Fred Ward—#717; **764,** Time line: T—Magnum Photos, Inc.—#760, B—Black Star/© D. Wilson—#742, R—(ibid.)/© Dennis Brack—#725; **767,** TL—AP/Wide World Photos—#724, BL—Magnum Photos, Inc.—#757, R—Black Star/© Robert Ellison—#755; **768,** T—Photoworld/FPG International—#756, B—Magnum Photos/© Hiroji Kubota—#758; **770,** (ibid.)—#759; **771,** Black Star/© Dennis Brack—#763; **772,** (see 764T)—#760; **773,** AP/Wide World Photos—#761; **775,** Animagraphics/FPG International—#766; **776,** (see 764B)—#762; **778,** AP/Wide World Photos—#743; **779,** T—Magnum Photos/© ABBAS—#765, B—(ibid.)/© Gilles Peress—#764; **781,** FPG International/B. Byers—#754; **784,** Time line: TL—AP/Wide World Photos—#802, BL—Magnum Photos/© ABBAS—#809, R—Black Star/© Peter Turnley—#812; **786,** T—(see 784TL)—#802, B—Magnum Photos/© Sebastiao Salgado—#803; **787,** Black Star/© Dennis Brack—#804; **788,** TL—(see WHHA)—#705, BL—Black Star/© 1985 John Troho—#806, R—UPI/Bettmann Newsphotos—#771; **789,** T—Black Star/© 1984 Dennis Brack—#807, B—AP/Wide World Photos—#307; **790,** NASA, Houston—#707; **792,** L—Magnum Photos/© Eli Reed—#808, R—(see 784BL)—#809; **793,** Black Star/© Dennis Brack—#810; **794,** Magnum Photos/© Susan Meiseles—#811; **796,** (see 784R)—#812; **797,** Black Star/© Nik Wheeler—#813; **798,** L—Photophile/© Tom Tracy—#814, R—(ibid.)—#815; **799,** Tass/Sovoto—#816; **801,** © Duomo/Daniel Forster 1986—#817, (inset) (ibid: © 1987)—#832.